CHRISTIAN THEOLOGY

Volume III

by

H. Orton Wiley, S.T.D.

BEACON HILL PRESS OF KANSAS CITY

Kansas City, Mo.

FIRST PRINTING, 1943

ISBN: 978-0-8341-2518-6

PRINTED IN THE UNITED STATES OF AMERICA

CONTENTS

PART IV. THE DOCTRINE OF THE HOLY SPIRIT
(Continued)

PART IV. THE DOCTRINE OF THE HOLY SPIRIT
(Continued)

CHRISTIAN THEOLOGY

CHAPTER XXX

CHRISTIAN ETHICS OR THE LIFE OF HOLINESS

Having considered the question of holiness as a doctrine and as an experience, it is but natural that we should now pass to a consideration of the same subject in its practical or ethical aspects. We have seen that a holy heart is the fundamental condition for holy living. It is specifically stated that *we are his workmanship, created in Christ Jesus unto good works, which God hath before ordained that we should walk in them* (Eph. 2:10). When, however, we pass from a consideration of Christian experience to the life consequent upon it, we are turning in some sense from the field of dogmatics to that of ethics. Dogmatics gives attention to doctrines, and answers the inquiry, What ought we to believe? Ethics seeks to answer the question, What ought we to do? Arminian theology has always given much attention to the morals and institutions of Christianity, as an examination of the works of Wesley, Watson, Clarke, Pope, Raymond, Summers, Ralston, and Lee will show. Dr. Miley also gives attention to the necessity of moral government, but treats it in relation to his governmental theory of the atonement. Our purpose, however, is not to consider the field of general or philosophical ethics; nor even the field of Christian ethics considered as a science, but only to examine more immediately the life of holiness as related to the doctrine and experience of entire sanctification. After a brief consideration of the Relation of Theology to Ethics; Revelation as the Source of Christian Ethics, and the Scriptural Basis of Ethics, we shall give our attention to the following: (I) The Development of Ethical Theory in the Church; (II) The Principles of Christian Ethics; and (III) Practical Ethics.

This latter will be considered under the threefold division of (1) Theistic Ethics: or Duties We Owe to God; (2) Individual Ethics: or Duties We Owe to Ourselves; and (3) Social Ethics: or Duties We Owe to Others.

The Relation of Theology to Ethics. As theology is the science of God and the mutual relations of God and man, so ethics as the science of duty, has to do with the end, the principles and motives of obligatory conduct. When the material of the two sciences is drawn wholly from nature, we have Natural Theology, and Natural or Naturalistic Ethics; when it is drawn from Revelation, we have Revealed Theology, and Revealed or Theological Ethics. There is no disharmony, however, between the two sources of material, since the one must

It must be evident that the outward or ethical life of the Christian takes its character from the quality of the inner or spiritual life. The life of holiness is, therefore, simply the outreachings of a holy heart. What this holiness is, General Superintendent Nease describes as follows: "The term holiness, when employed as referring to the experience of the believer, of necessity implies the act, which is sanctification, and the Agent, which is the Holy Ghost. We therefore employ the term holiness in practical usage as the all-inclusive, denoting the completed act of divine grace. Holiness is cleansing. It is that will of the Father, that provision of the Son, that act of the Holy Ghost, whereby the believer's heart, that is, his motive, his affections, his will—his entire nature, is cleansed from the pollution and the tendency to sin. Holiness is harmony. Complete inner harmony is not realized in regeneration. The Bible and experience agree that the unsanctified heart is a divided heart—a double heart. Outward defeat is occasioned by inward disharmony. Sanctification rids the soul of the inner foe, and aligns the forces of the moral nature against the outer enemy. Holiness is abandonment. The fathers referred to the act of human co-operation in sanctification as 'crucifixion of self,' as 'deathbed consecration.' They meant a giving-over of the all-of-one's life to the plan and authority of Deity. The man who is sanctified is thus given over to God. Every tie, every influence, every reserve is severed that will deter from complete and unrestrained participation in the fellowship and service of Deity. Holiness is power. Power is in the spiritual realm—the realm immediately affected by sanctification. It is in essence, the embodiment of all that is essential in the combined realms of human experience. Sanctification affects all that one is. Such enduement of power—the ability to discriminate, to evaluate, to influence, to single one's devotion, to command one's will, can be realized only as 'power from on high' possesses the believer. It is the fulfillment of 'the promise of the Father.' It is 'Christ in you the hope of glory.' Holiness is perfection. A perfection in love—Christian perfection. The sanctified one is not beyond the ability, nor liability to sin, but he is cleansed from the desire and nature of sin. He is not beyond the possibility of fall, but he is within the provision of divine grace, so that he is preserved from willful transgression. Sanctification is not fixedness of character, but fixedness of attitude and desire, enabling the participant to 'grow in grace and in the knowledge of our Lord and Saviour Jesus Christ.'"—Dr. Orval J. Nease.

be in some sense supplementary to the other. In our discussion of General and Special Revelation (Volume I, Chapter VI), we pointed out that God discloses Himself to man, (1) through a primary revelation in nature, in the constitution of man, and in the progress of human history; (2) in addition to this general revelation manifested through His created works there is a special revelation made through the Spirit to the consciences and consciousness of men. So also in the field of ethics, God reveals Himself in two classes of law—natural and positive. (1) Natural law is that which God has written upon the heart of every man, or that which the light of reason teaches us is good or evil. Thus, the apostle says of the heathen in contradistinction to the Jews, that *these, having not the law, are a law unto themselves: which shew the work of the law written in their hearts, their conscience also bearing witness, and their thoughts the mean while accusing or else excusing one another* (Rom. 2:14, 15). They are a law unto themselves, because they know in themselves what is good and what is evil, through reason which is to them the herald of divine law. Both history and experience teach us that all nations have a measure of divine revelation. This we have shown in our study of Religion and Revelation, and hence need only to point out that all nations acknowledge likewise, certain common principles of morality. Education, which has varied from age to age, cannot be the source of these uniform principles; consequently, we must find the common source of these max-

In the evangelical scheme doctrine and ethics are closely connected: its revelations of truth are the foundation of its new life; its morals and its doctrine are everywhere interwoven; and, finally, the ethics of the Christian religion are the crown and consummation of its entire system.—Pope, *Compend. Chr. Th.*, III, p. 143.

The truth, as we see it, is here the same as in dogmatics: as there are fundamental doctrines of religion adequately sustained by rational evidence constituting a system of natural religion, so there are certain prominent duties to the common intelligence obviously obligatory, which constitute a system of what may be called philosophical ethics. And as there are doctrines known and authenticated solely by revelation, constituting a system of revealed religion, so there are duties known and enforced in the same way constituting what might be called a system of Christian ethics. Nature and revelation, properly interpreted, are never antagonistic; their utterances are words proceeding out of the mouth of God, from which man may learn all things needful for faith and practice.—Raymond, *Systematic Theology*, III, p. 10.

ims in natural reason, which is from the Light that lighteth all men coming into the world. (2) Positive law is that which depends upon God's free will, and, therefore, can be known only through revelation. It should be noted, however, that what in one respect is the subject of natural law, in another may exist as positive law. Thus natural law reveals the necessity of a certain period of rest each week as essential to man's greatest efficiency in service; but this is also declared by positive law in the institution of the Sabbath, which is the setting apart of one day in seven as holy unto the Lord. In close connection with this, reason makes known also the necessity of divine worship; but that the time should be a full day, and this on a set day of the week, is a revelation of positive law. Similarly the Decalogue with its "ten words," all of which is based on man's relation to God, to others and to himself, is likewise accessible to reason. However, because of man's conscience being dimmed by failure to walk in the truth, the Decalogue, as a transcript of the law written in men's hearts, was also given by positive decree. We may say, therefore, of the Decalogue, that its precepts as to their substance belong to natural law; but as to the manner of their manifestation, they are a part of positive or revealed law.

Revelation as the Source of Christian Ethics. We are now brought to the position that Christian ethics must draw its material immediately from the Christian revelation. While we may and do admit that the light of the natural conscience furnishes corroborative testimony insofar as its feebler light can penetrate, we must affirm also, that nature alone can no more furnish Christianity with its system of ethics or morals, than it can furnish it with its system of doctrines. If dogma treats of God and the truth by which salvation is accomplished, so also ethics of the standards by which the Christian life is ordered, and by means of which it is given proper expression. Thus the morals or ethics of Christianity complete the science of religion; for it is only through a combination of dogma and ethics that the plan of salvation can be revealed in its perfection. The fact, however, that there is a greater unanimity of thought respecting the standards of morality, than there is concerning dogma, may be attributed to the greater light which the moral life receives from natural reason. Dogma, on the other hand, is purely a matter of the interpretation of the Scriptures. The highest revelation of God to man is in Jesus Christ as the Word made flesh. Hence the positive element in Christian ethics is a course of life introduced into human conditions—a life actualized in human history by Jesus Christ as the God-man, and through the Spirit communicated to the community of believers. The life of Christ, therefore, whether in word, in deed, or in the spirit underlying these words and deeds; becomes the norm of all Christian conduct. His words furnish us with the knowledge of the divine will; His actions are the confirmation of truth, and His Spirit the power by which His words are embodied in deeds. With this statement as to the positive element in Christian ethics, we turn to the Scriptures as the recorded revelation of the incarnate Word, and in them we find our standards of Christian conduct, together with the promised power of the Spirit by which these standards are to be maintained.

The Scriptural Basis of Ethics. Here we shall refer only to those scriptures which furnish the ground for the general system of Christian ethics, reserving such passages as refer to specific Christian duties for later consideration. The first question which arises is, Are the sources of Christian ethics to be derived solely from the New Testament, or are the Old Testament writings considered as a part of the Christian revelation? This subject has been previously considered in another connection (Volume I, pp. 202-205), and it is sufficient to say here that the Old Testament insofar as it is applicable to

It should be observed that the scriptures are not devoted exclusively to a development of a system of moral government, nor do they teach it on the scientific plan of one of our modern writers on the subject of Moral Philosophy. But all the principles are taught in the inspired writings, and so plainly and forcibly asserted as to make the principles and facts much more readily comprehended by an unlettered and unsophisticated mind, than the best written modern volume on the subject of moral science.—LUTHER LEE, *Elements of Theology*, p. 332.

Christian life is still binding upon men. Certain portions of it, however, especially the types or shadows of better things to come, had their perfect fulfillment in the great Antitype; while others of a ceremonial or political nature were abrogated as belonging only to the Mosaic economy. But as to the moral law of Moses, the substance of which was embodied in the Decalogue, this was not superseded, but referred to by our Lord as of abiding authority without any special re-enactment. *Think not that I am come to destroy the law, or the prophets:* He said; *I am not come to destroy, but to fulfil. For verily I say unto you, Till heaven and earth pass, one jot or one tittle shall in no wise pass from the law, till all be fulfilled. Whosoever therefore shall break one of these least commandments, and shall teach men so, he shall be called the least in the kingdom of heaven: but whosoever shall do and teach them, the same shall be called great in the kingdom of heaven* (Matt. 5:17-19).

The ethical teachings of the Gospels center in the idea of the kingdom, entrance to which is solely on the ground of repentance and faith. The acceptance of the call of God involves the subordination of all other loyalties. *Therefore take no thought, saying, What shall we eat? or, What shall we drink? or, Wherewithal shall we be clothed?* .... *But seek ye first the kingdom of God, and his righteousness; and all these things shall be added unto you* (Matt. 6:31, 33). The sermon on the Mount has been called the Magna Charta of the kingdom. Here the true inwardness of its nature is set forth as an attitude of spirit—of thought, feeling and will which finds its highest expression in word and deed. The description which Jesus gives is not that of certain acts, but of a certain type of character. The true spring of obedience is found in divine love. When asked concerning the

For as much as God requires that we should love, not above, but with all our strength, it is evident that nothing exceeding our abilities is required at our hands.—LIMBORCH, *Theologia*, Bk. v, chapter 25.

That it is possible to love God with all the heart is folly to deny. For he that saith he cannot do a thing with all his strength, that is, that he cannot do what he can do, knows not what he saith; and yet to do this is the highest measure and sublimity of perfection, and of keeping the commandments.—BISHOP JEREMY TAYLOR.

greatest commandment of the law, Jesus replied, *Thou shalt love the Lord thy God with all thy heart, ... and with all thy mind. This is the first and great commandment. And the second is like unto it, Thou shalt love thy neighbour as thyself. On these two commandments hang all the law and the prophets* (Matt. 22:37-40). The children of the kingdom are to be as *wise as serpents, and harmless as doves* (Matt. 10:16); they are to *resist not evil* (Matt. 5:39): and to *Fear him, which after he hath killed hath power to cast into hell* (Luke 12:5). According to Jesus, the supreme test of love is this, *that a man lay down his life for his friends* (John 15:13): and in close connection with this is the practical application, *For whosoever will save his life shall lose it; but whosoever will lose his life for my sake, the same shall save it* (Luke 9:24).

THE DEVELOPMENT OF ETHICAL THEORY IN THE CHURCH

The periods which mark the development of ethical theory in the church, differ somewhat from those which are important in the history of dogmatics. For our purpose, the subject may be conveniently summed up in the following periods: (1) The Patristic Period, from the earlier fathers to the time of Constantine; (2) The Middle Ages, from the time of Constantine to the close of the Middle Ages; (3) The Renaissance and the Reformation; and (4) The Modern Period.

The Patristic Period. During the first century, the interests of the church were primarily concerned with practical conduct rather than rational reflection. Harnack says that for the first century and a half, the church ranked everything secondary to the supreme task of maintaining its morality. The dominant note of the early church was that of divine love manifesting itself in the care of the poor, hospitality to strangers, avoidance of the sensuous luxury and vices of the pagans, and devotion to the purity of life set by Christ and the apostles. Not until the latter part of the second century was there serious reflection on ethical problems. In the progress

of Christianity in conflict with paganism, the more rigid
view of Montanism came to occupy a place in apologetics
alongside the milder tendency of previous times. Equally
dangerous but in another direction, were the mistaken
views of Christian liberty on the part of the Gnostics,
which led to the dangerous errors of the Carpocratians
and the later pantheistical sects. It thus became the task
of Christianity to more exactly determine its principles
and applications of morality. Some preliminary work
had been done in the Epistles of Clement, the Shepherd
of Hermas and the Epistle to Diognetus, but it remained
for the later fathers to formulate the ethical principles
of the church. In ethics as in dogmatics there is a difference of approach in the East and in the West. The former
regarded Christian ethics as in some sense supplementary to the ancient Greek philosophy, which in itself was
inadequate to a knowledge of God and immortality.
Christianity, therefore, brought to completion the Greek
ethical principles which were assumed to be grounded
in universal reason. This is the position of Justin Mar-

Clement of Rome in his First Epistle to the Corinthians states
that the motive of Christian conduct is derived from "fear" or "reverence" of God. "Let us see how near He is," he says, "and how that
nothing escapeth Him of our thoughts or our devices which we make.
It is right, therefore, that we should not be deserters from His will."
Ignatius insisted upon right beliefs as the basis for right moral practices.
False theology, he maintained, led to wrong attitudes and bad conduct.
"Faith is the beginning and love the end" of the Christian life. Among
the more important of his maxims are "Let there be one prayer in
common; one supplication; one mind; one hope, in love and in joy un-
blameable." "Shun divisions as the beginning of all evils." "Let all
things be done to the honor of God." Polycarp in his "Epistle to the
Philippians" appeals to the words of Jesus as sanctions. Faith, hope and
love are the essentials of the Christian life. Heresy was regarded as
a desire to live otherwise than according to the true faith. He warned
especially against covetousness, "the love of money is the beginning of
all trouble." The Didache and the Epistle of Barnabas have some
similarities. Christianity is regarded as a new covenant which brings
God and man into religious fellowship. The Shepherd of Hermas emphasizes the struggle necessary to maintain the Christian standards, and
hence the need for reliance upon divine mercy and grace. Cheerfulness, however, is given special emphasis. "Put away sorrow from
thyself"; "Clothe thyself with cheerfulness, which hath favor with
God always, and is acceptable to Him, and rejoice in it." "For every
cheerful man worketh good, and thinketh good and despiseth sadness;
but the sad man is always continuing in sin." The Epistle to Diognetus
emphasizes the spiritual principle which animates Christians and keeps
them from being absorbed in the things of the world. God is the
source of the Christian ideal, "Loving Him thou wilt be an imitator of
His goodness."

tyr who made the Logos doctrine the foundation of his exposition. The latter, or Western fathers, maintained that ethically, Christianity was something entirely new, and, therefore, was in no wise related to the ethics of paganism. Here Tertullian is the representative apologist. To him, Christianity was a spiritual power given to the church to preserve it from paganism, organize its children into a compact army to attack paganism, conquer it and judge it. Clement of Alexandria regarded philosophy as a propaedeutic to faith, and his work is a blending of contributions from Greek thought and Judaism. A number of striking ethical ideas are developed in his *Paedagogus, Stromata* and *Exhortations.* With Cyprian, one of the Latin fathers, the church came into prominence as the center of a whole field of ethics. This grew out of the controversy with the Montanists and the Novatians, and as a consequence, the relation of the individual to the church became the most prominent ethical relation of his life.

The Middle Ages. The conversion of Constantine in the fourth century brought about marked changes in the church. Freed from persecution by the State, prestige and power were soon achieved. An ecclesiasticism developed, which in turn began the persecution of pagans and heretics. Worldliness increased, and many Christians seeking for a way of sacrifice withdrew to monastic life. This gave rise to a different and distinct type of ethics.

Ambrose (340-397) in his work entitled *De Officiis Ministrorum,* gave to the church what is generally regarded as the first manual of Christian ethics. It was modelled after a Stoic work by Cicero, and the idea of natural law which it sets forth had a definite influence upon later scholastic ethics. This law of nature is the

Dr. I. A. Dorner points out that the Montanists accepted the sudden outbursts of individual enthusiasm as the true medium through which the Holy Spirit communicates with the congregation, and consequently demanded absolute obedience to the dictates of this ecstatic prophecy as a condition of communion between the Spirit and the individual. The Novatians on the other hand, found the true vehicle of spiritual communion in the church itself considered as a totality, as an organization of the universal priesthood under presbyterial forms, and, therefore, were rigorous with respect to admission of members.

law of things as God created them, and from it there is something to be learned concerning the requirements of morality. Higher than this, there is within man a knowledge of the moral through reason and conscience; but highest of all is the will of God as expressed in the Scriptures, culminating in the teaching and example of Christ. The beginnings of asceticism, however, are very noticeable in that Ambrose recognized two levels of morality—one obligatory upon all, the other as including works done beyond the requirements in order to a higher degree of perfection. He also definitely adopted the four cardinal Greek virtues—Prudence, Justice, Courage and Temperance. Prudence, however, was with him, not so much reason or wisdom, as it was the personal knowledge of God manifesting itself in human conduct. Justice must be exercised, "first towards God, secondly towards our country, thirdly towards our parents, and lastly towards all." Courage he interpreted as fortitude in the trials of ordinary life, and temperance as self-respect, modesty in all forms, and a due appreciation of others. The work of Ambrose was transitional, and led directly to Augustine's more distinctly Christian system of ethics.

Augustine (354-430) systematized the ethics of the Western church, and the principles which he advanced, were regarded as authoritative during the greater part of the Middle Ages. Here the central and dominating idea of the Christian life is union with God, an experience of perfect peace and blessedness which can be achieved only in the life to come. Hence in his *City of God*, he distinguishes between the earthly city which is temporal, and the city of God which is eternal. With Augustine, the moral life has its basis in God, and is in accord with the world He has created. He, therefore, opposes the theory that morality is based on social custom, a position which is commonly defined as "custom operating in consciousness." He also considered the Christian view of ethics as opposed to the Stoic apathy as regards the emotional life. He placed the greater emphasis, however, upon the will. Man must surrender his will in love. Two tendencies emphasized by Augustine led to ill effects in later history. (1) He conformed to the distinction that had become current, as to what was commanded for all, and what was counseled as going farther, and thus making for perfection. This led to an emphasis upon the works of supererogation, and the accumulation of merit, which in turn contributed to ascetic practices. (2) His idea of self-surrender, also, was no small incentive to the ecclesiastical suppression of individual liberty. He held that the church as a continuous organization had the truth and the authority to teach it. This required individual submission. Since it was of divine appointment that men should come into the church, they should do so willingly, but if not they were to be compelled to do so. It was, therefore, the sacred duty of the church to see that men came into the church, and if it lacked the power of compulsion, it was the sacred duty of the state to come to its rescue, and compel them to come, that the church might be filled. From these two tendencies, both ecclesiasticism and monasticism were given added impulse during the Middle Ages.

Monasticism became the characteristic feature of mediaeval Christianity, and provided its conception of Christian ethics. Asceticism had become established among Christians even in the time of Augustine, and much was made of those elements in the Gospels and Pauline writings which seemed to approve ascetic practices. Monasticism as a revolt against the growing worldliness in the state church, arose independently and frequently in opposition to the ecclesiastical organization. For this reason, even when allied with the church in later times, it retained much of its independence. The monastic ideal, however, soon came to be predominant, so that the vowed monks became "the religious" or regular clergy, while the nonmonastic priests became "the seculars." Basil (c. 329-379) was probably the first to inaugurate a definite movement toward community life among the ascetics. Benedict (480-543) introduced a new rule. Previous to this the monks had dwelt largely upon self-conquest, Benedict spoke of self-surrender. His monasteries were organized along communal lines with democratic rule. Perhaps no rule was less ascetic than that of Benedict. Bernard of Clairvaux (1094-1174) by his great saintliness and personal power was able to effect great reforms along spiritual lines. Francis of Assisi (1182-1226) and Dominic (1170-1221) brought about great changes in the conception of the ascetic life and its practices. They developed a human interest and love for mankind that drew them away from the cloister and sent them forth on an unhampered ministry of love. The ethical ideal of St. Francis was the imitation of Christ, specifically in spirit, but also largely in the details of conduct. The vows of poverty, chastity and obedience had as their purpose the full devotement of the individual to the welfare of others. Special emphasis was placed upon poverty. While the Franciscans were primarily evangelistic, the Dominicans established their houses near the universities and gave their attention largely to education. By this means they soon came to set the doctrinal standards of the church, and this through a period of several centuries. Among the later mystics, asceticism was of a higher type. John Scotus Erigena introduced Greek mysticism as found in Macarius the Egyptian, Dionysius and Maximus Confessor, and this became the starting point of mysticism in the Western church. The development took place in two forms—the Romanic, as in Hugo and Richard of St. Victor, Bernard of Clairvaux, Bonaventura, Gerson and Molinus; and the Germanic, as in Henry Suso, Ruysbroek, John Tauler and Meister Eckhart. So far as mysticism developed an ethics, however, it retained the false principle of asceticism as a contradiction between matter and spirit, God and the world. The chief reason assigned in the failure of the mystics to develop a true ethics is the lack of a proper conception of personality. That the created soul is capable of receiving the divine, and by this means achieving a perfect union between the finite and the infinite, is an idea which first came into prominence with Luther and his doctrine of justification by faith.

Thomas Aquinas (c. 1225-1274) treated ethics as an integral part of a general philosophical and theological system. In him, ethics reached its authoritative statement. The ultimate end for which man acts, or at least should act, he called "beatitude" or "true blessedness," which when attained is all-sufficient. Nothing can satisfy except the Infinite, or the eternal goodness of God himself. Thus he lays a firm foundation for ethical theory in Christian theism. The virtue, or proper excellence of a thing consists in its being well-disposed according to its kind. Man being constituted a rational soul, ethics must be according to reason. Virtues in man are therefore the habits of the soul in accordance with which it performs good acts. The virtues are classified as follows: (1) *Moral*—the four cardinal Greek virtues, Prudence, Justice, Temperance and Fortitude. (2) *Intellectual* — understanding, knowledge and wisdom; and (3) *Theological*—faith, hope and love. The first two may be known by reason, but the last only by revelation. The natural virtues lead to the development of character; the theological to spiritual happiness here and life in the world to come. Thomas treated the Greek cardinal virtues, however, after a Christian method. The passions in themselves he regarded as indifferent and, therefore, to be brought under the control of the will. Of the theological virtues, love or charity was the highest and included the others in itself. The influence of Augustine, however, is clearly seen, in that Thomas accepted the twofold attitude toward morality; and while he regarded the earthly and the heavenly as compatible, those who turned their attention to the heavenly received greater praise.

The Renaissance and the Reformation. As the dominant note of the Middle Ages was the subordination of the earthly life to that of the life to come, so it was followed by the reactionary development commonly known as Humanism. Here the emphasis was placed upon the individual life and the present world. But humanism produced no profound or widespread ethical theory. It was in fact, irreligious. The traditional views of sin and the atonement meant little or nothing, and no place was found for the contemplative type of experience. Humanism was in some true sense a return to the pagan ideals of Greece and Rome, but it did have the effect of broadening the horizons of men. The forerunners of the Reformation — Wycliffe, (c. 1324 or earlier - 1384) and Huss (1369 or 1373 - 1415) had pointed out the moral infirmities of the times, sought to awaken interest in classical studies, and also introduced a new feature into ethical teaching—that of exalting morality as a guide into the wisdom of Christianity for the government of affairs in practical life. This was developed by Petrarch (d. 1374), Marsilius Ficinus (d. 1499), Louis Vives (d. 1540) and Erasmus (d. 1536). Savonarola (1452-1498) especially opposed the moral corruption and worldliness of both the secular leaders of the Renaissance and the higher ecclesiastical officials. He made an effort to establish the ethical conception of the Mediaeval church, in which the thought of other worldliness should dominate both thought and conduct. "We live in this world, O my brothers," he said, "only to learn how to die."

The Protestant Reformation was, in some sense, a reaction from both Mediaevalism and the Renaissance. With the belief in other - worldliness inherited from Mediaevalism, and the insistence upon the present world as the contribution of the Renaissance, the ethical prob-

When the Reformation took its final stand upon Scripture, it not only escaped the great errors of the Middle Ages, but it also succeeded in establishing the true principles of Christian ethics. By the new doctrines of faith, and justification by faith, the fundamental ethical ideas of duty, virtue, and highest good, were, so to speak, melted down and recast. A new ethics appeared, bearing the characteristic marks of the double development of the Protestant or evangelical principle—the Lutheran Church with its talent for plastic representation, art, hymnology, science; and the Reformed Church, with its talent for practical action, discipline, missions, statesmanship. Though neither Luther nor Calvin has written on ethics, in the proper sense of the word, both have occasionally treated of various ethical subjects—especially in the form of expositions of the Decalogue in the Catechism. The Catechism is, indeed, the primitive form of evangelical ethics. Just as evangelical dogmatics arose from the *regula fidei* and the apostolical symbolum, so evangelical ethics grew out of the Decalogue.—I. A. DORNER, art. "Ethics," SCHAFF-HERZOG, *Encyclopedia of Religious Knowledge*.

lem of the Reformation period came to be, How to conceive of Christian ethics or morality, as including both the earthly and the transcendent. It insisted that life was not to be lived in a monastery but in active participation in human affairs. It opposed, however, the tendency of Humanism to make pleasure and intellectual culture the chief affairs of this life. Dr. Denny states the aim of the Reformation thus, "to expel things from religion and exhibit all its realities as persons and the relation of persons." Luther developed a form of ethical dualism in that he made morality the spontaneous manifestation of the inner life of the Spirit; and given this liberty of sonship, the Christian subjects himself to righteous service in a voluntary manner. "When we have taught faith in Christ," he says, "then do we teach also good works." Calvin was more systematic in his thinking, and grounded ethics in the nature of man as created by God. In his *Institutes* he includes ethics under regeneration, and expounds it in his study of the Christian Man, the Bearing of the Cross and similar subjects. He viewed the Decalogue as a statement of the fundamentals of the moral law engraved on the minds of men. To conform to the Decalogue is to obey God, and this is morality. Any tolerance of sin was a share in it. Hence in the Reformed churches, it became common practice to attach great value to the legal elements in the Old Testament, and to combine these into an ethical system in connection with the Decalogue.

Other writings of this period which contributed to Christian ethics were those of John Bunyan (1628-1688) who made redeeming grace the dominant characteristics of all his writings, but developed no distinct ethical theory; George Fox (1624 - 1690), who was singularly clear in his judgment on great moral issues; Jeremy Taylor (1613-1667) in his *Holy Living* regards the essential thing in morality as purity of intention; and William Law (1686-1761) gives an exposition of the Christian life according to ethical principles in his *Serious Call to a Devout and Holy Life*. This work has been compared to Thomas a Kempis' *Imitation of Christ*, in that underlying all is the principle of submission and the spirit of obedience which rules out all that is unholy. "All the wants which disturb human life, which makes us uneasy to ourselves, quarrelsome with others, and unthankful to God, which carry us from project to project, from place to place, in a poor pursuit of we know not what, are wants which neither God, nor nature, nor reason, hath subjected us to, but are solely infused into us by pride, envy, ambition and covetousness." (WILLIAM LAW, *Serious Call*). To these may be added the name of Joseph Butler (1692-1752) whose theory is similar to that of Thomas Aquinas, but was developed independently. Bishop Butler recognized two sources of ethical knowledge—nature and reason on the one hand and revelation on the other. To him, God is the source of the moral law in conscience, in the constitution of nature and in the Scriptures; and all Christian morality is included in the love of God, of others and of self. Thus Christian ethics is at once empirical and transcendent, anthropological and theological.

The first theologian in the Reformed Church to treat Christian ethics as distinct from Dogmatics, was Danaeus (d. 1536). His work entitled *Christian Ethics* was published in 1577. In the Lutheran Church, Calixtus followed the same method in his *Epitome of Moral Theology* (1634-1662). The Roman Catholic theologians sharply criticized this separation between Dogmatics and Ethics as tending toward humanism and minifying revelation. The Cartesian philosophy awakened a new interest in the study of ethics, especially in the Reformed Church; and the two movements of Pietism and Methodism likewise exerted a stimulating and purifying effect. Arminianism, especially, gave great promise to the ethical side of Christianity. As marking the close of the older order and the transition to a new period, we may mention Buddaeus, *Institutes of Moral Theology* (1711-1724), and Mosheim, *Ethics of the Holy Scriptures* (9 vols. 1735-1753). With Kant and his doctrine of the categorical imperative, a new period in the study of ethics began—one which freed the subject from many of the older restrictions, but which unhappily robbed it of its profound religious motive. For a time no principle of Christian ethics was adopted. Schwartz and Flatt adhered definitely to the Scriptures without attempting any principle of scientific classification. DeWette was probably the first in modern times to point out the necessity for such a principle, and from this time, Protestant works on ethics are characterized by an attempt to attain a more scientific character. It is to Schleiermacher, however, that we must turn as the founder of modern theological ethics. The subjectivism of Kant having reached its consequences in Fichte, philosophy again turned to objectivism. Schelling advanced the theory of the identity of the subject and object, and on this basis, Schleiermacher constructed his ethics. He returned to the old idea of the kingdom of heaven, which had entirely disappeared from the philosophy of Kant and Wolff. However, he did not with Buddaeus regard the kingdom as an indefinite realm beyond the grave; nor did he accept the position of the Roman Catholics in limiting it to the church on earth. Instead, he found the kingdom in every sphere of life, by the virtuous action of the individual. Following Schleiermacher, perhaps the most important work is Rothe's *Theological Ethics*. This has been praised as presenting an insight "into the innermost marrow of ethical speculation," and as demonstrating "that Christianity is the realization of the highest thought of God" (Bunsen). On the other hand, it is deserving of just criticism, in that it makes the state rather than the church, the highest good, and maintains that it should be the object of the church to resolve itself into the state. In this he follows Hegel who made the state the supreme good, in direct opposition to the ethics of both the Roman Catholic and the Protestant Church.

Among the more modern works on Christian ethics are the following: Martensen, *Christian Ethics* (3 vols. 1871); Luthardt, *History of Christian Ethics* (1889); Smyth, *Christian Ethics* (3rd Ed. 1894); Strong, *Christian Ethics* (1896); Robbins, *The Ethics of the Christian*

Life (1904); I. A. Dorner, *System of Christian Ethics* (1906); Stalker, *The Ethics of Jesus* (1909); Hall, *History of Ethics Within Organized Christianity* (1910); King, *The Ethics of Jesus* (1910); Alexander, *Christianity and Ethics* (1914); Scott, *New Testament Ethics* (1930); Niebuhr, *An Interpretation of Christian Ethics* (1935); and Widgery, *Christian Ethics in History and Modern Life* (1940).

THE PRINCIPLES OF CHRISTIAN ETHICS

We have shown the relation of Ethics to Dogmatics; have indicated the source of Christian Ethics as centering in Divine Revelation; traced briefly the development of ethical theory in the church; and must now consider the principles underlying Christian ethics and their application in daily life. In our examination of Christian Perfection as the norm of New Testament experience, we found that it was a purification of the heart from sin in order to a full devotement of the whole being to Jesus Christ. Grace must first express itself in Christian experience; and from the communication of this new life and love, new standards of daily living will be formed. Doctrine may not always issue in experience; but experience if it is to be maintained must always issue in Christian living. Every doctrine, therefore, not only has its experiential phase, but also its ethical expression. God is a Person, and man is a person, hence all their relationships must be ethical. The dominant note of Christian Perfection being that of full devotion to God, this devotement becomes a fundamental principle in Christian ethics. As such, it is exercised toward Christ in His divine-human nature as the mediatorial Person; and this both as Creator and Redeemer. As Creator, His law is written in the nature and constitution of man, and is commonly known as the law of conscience. As Redeemer, His whole life and history furnish a satisfaction to the Divine Will. There can be, therefore, no lack of harmony between the new law of Christ, and the old law of a fully redeemed and enlightened conscience. But the mediatorial cannot be properly understood unless it be seen that the Supreme Law-giver, and the perfect Example of His own presence are conjoined in the Deity and manhood of the Godman. In order that Christ might give His people a new commandment, and a perfect law of liberty through which that commandment could be fulfilled, He himself received a new commandment and learned obedience by the things which He suffered. And having learned obedience, He presented himself as at once the perfect law-giver, and the perfect Example of His own precepts. Here we find the unsearchable unity of His two natures in one personal Agent investing the subject of Christian ethics, as it does also, that of Christian dogmatics. His moral obligation, however, could not be shared, for the mystery of His suffering was twofold— for sin in us, and through temptation to impossible sin in Himself. For this reason St. Paul says that *he died unto sin once: but in that he liveth, he liveth unto God* (Rom. 6:10). In this death to sin, He secured for us forever, (1) the law of liberty by which we are delivered from the principle of sin; and (2) the law of love as a motive to righteousness. Here, then, is the fulfillment of *The oath which he sware to our father Abraham, that he would grant unto us, that we being delivered out of the hand of our enemies might serve him without fear, in holiness and righteousness before him, all the days of our life* (Luke 1:73-75).

The Law of Liberty. The new freedom provided by the death of Christ unto sin is called by St. James *the perfect law of liberty* (James 1:25); and again, *the royal law,* which according to the Scriptures is, *Thou shalt love thy neighbour as thyself* (James 2:8). St. Paul speaks of it as *the law of the Spirit of life in Christ Jesus,* which makes us free from *the law of sin and death* (Rom. 8:2). The external law ceases to be the law of sin and death, for the consciousness of sins is removed in justification; and the inner law of life by the Spirit furnishes the motive and the strength of obedi-

ON THE TRUE IDEA OF SPIRITUAL LIBERTY
On the above subject, Dr. Thomas C. Upham gives us the following excellent discussion in his work entitled *The Principles of the Interior*

Life. We present it in a greatly abbreviated form. He says, "It has probably come within the observation of many persons, that there is a form or modification of religious experience, which is denominated 'Liberty.' Hence, in common religious parlance, it is not unfrequently the case that we hear of persons being 'in the liberty,' or in the 'true liberty.' These expressions undoubtedly indicate an important religious truth, which has not altogether escaped the notice of writers on the religious life. The account as given by Francis de Sales of 'the liberty of spirit' is, that 'it consists in keeping the heart totally disengaged from every created thing, in order that it may follow the known will of God.' To this statement of De Sales, considered as a general and somewhat indefinite statement, we do not find it necessary to object. Certain it is that he who is in the 'true liberty' is 'disengaged,' and has escaped from the enslaving influence of the world. God has become to him an inward, operative principle, without whom he feels he can do nothing, and in connection with whose blessed assistance he has an inward consciousness that the world and its lusts have lost their inthralling power. Liberty—considered in this general sense of the term—is to be regarded as expressive of one of the highest and most excellent forms of Christian experience. And we may add, further, that none truly enjoy it in this high sense but those who are in a state of mind, which may with propriety be denominated a holy or sanctified state, none but those whom God has made 'free indeed.' We proceed now to mention some of the marks by which the condition or state of the spiritual liberty is characterized. Nor does there seem to be much difficulty in doing this, because liberty is the opposite of inthrallment; and because it is easy, as a general thing, to understand and to specify the things by which we are most apt to be inthralled.

"(1) The person who is in the enjoyment of true spiritual liberty is no longer inthralled to the lower or appetitive part of his nature. Whether he eats or drinks, or whatever other appetite may claim its appropriate exercise, he can say in truth that he does all to the glory of God.

"(2) The person who is in the enjoyment of true spiritual liberty is no longer inthralled by certain desires of a higher character than the appetites—such as the desire of society, the desire of knowledge, the desire of the world's esteem, and the like. These principles, which, in order to distinguish them from the appetites, may conveniently be designated as the propensities, or propensive principles, operate in the man of true inward liberty as they were designed to operate, but never with the power to enslave.

"(3) A man who is in the enjoyment of true religious liberty will not be inthralled by inordinate domestic or patriotic affections, however ennobling they may be thought to be—such as the love of parents and children, the love of friends and country. It is true that spiritual liberty does not exclude the exercise of these affections—which are, in many respects, generous and elevated—any more than it condemns and excludes the existence of the lower appetites and propensities.

"(4) When we are wrongly under the influence of disinclinations and aversions, we cannot be said to be in internal liberty. Sometimes, when God very obviously calls us to the discharge of duty, we are internally conscious of a great degree of backwardness. We do it, it is true; but we feel that we do not like to do it. There are certain duties which we owe to the poor and degraded, to the openly profane and impure, which are oftentimes repugnant to persons of certain refined mental habits; but if we find that these refined repugnances, which come in the way of duty, have great power over us, we are not in the true liberty. We have not that strength in God, which enables us to act vigorously and freely.

"(5) The person is not in the enjoyment of true liberty of spirit, who is wanting in the disposition of accommodation to others in the things which are not of especial importance. And this is the case when we needlessly insist upon having everything done in our own time and manner; when we are troubled about little things, which are in themselves indifferent, and think, perhaps, more of the position of a chair than the salvation of a soul; when we find a difficulty in making allowance for constitutional differences, in others, which it may not be easy or important for them to correct; when we find ourselves disgusted because another does not express himself in entire accordance with our principles of taste; or when we are displeased and dissatisfied with his religious, or other performances, although we know he does the best he can. We may properly add here, that the fault-finder—especially one who is in the confirmed habit of fault-finding—is not a man of a free spirit. Accordingly, those who are often complaining of their minister, of the brethren of the church, of the time and manner of the ordinances, and of many other persons and things, will find, on a careful examination, that they are too full of self, too strongly moved by their personal views and interests, to know the true and full import of that ennobling liberty which the Saviour gives to His truly sanctified ones.

"(6) The person who is disturbed and impatient when events fall out differently from what he expected and anticipated is not in the enjoyment of true spiritual freedom. In accordance with the great idea of God's perfect sovereignty, the man of a religiously free spirit regards all events which take place — sin only excepted — as an expression, under the existing circumstances, of the will of God. And such is his unity with the divine will, that there is an immediate acquiescence in the event, whatever may be its nature, and however afflicting in its personal bearings. His mind has acquired, as it were, a divine flexibility, in virtue of which it accommodates itself, with surprising ease and readiness, to all the developments of Providence, whether prosperous or adverse.

"(7) Those who are in the enjoyment of true liberty are patient under interior temptations, and all inward trials of mind. They can bless the hand that smites them internally as well as externally. Knowing that all good exercises are from the Holy Spirit, they have no disposition to prescribe to God what the particular nature of those exercises shall be. If God sees fit to try, and to strengthen, their spirit of submission and patience by bringing them into a state of great heaviness and sorrow, either by subjecting to severe temptations from the adversary of souls, or by laying upon them the burden of deep grief for an impenitent world, or in any other way, they feel it to be all right and well. They ask for their daily bread spiritually, as well as temporally; and they cheerfully receive what God sees fit to send them.

"(8) The person who enjoys true liberty of spirit is the most deliberate and cautious in doing what he is most desirous to do. This arises from the fact that he is very much afraid of being out of the line of God's will and order. He distrusts, and examines closely, all strong desires and strong feelings generally, especially if they agitate his mind and render it somewhat uncontrollable; not merely or chiefly because the feelings are strong; that is not the reason; but because there is reason to fear, from the very fact of their strength and agitating tendency, that some of nature's fire, which true sanctification quenches and destroys, has mingled in with the holy and peaceable flame of divine love.

"(9) He who is in true liberty of spirit is not easily excited by opposition. The power of grace gives him inward strength; and it is the nature of true strength to deliberate. Accordingly, when his views are controverted, he is not hasty to reply. He is not indifferent; but he

ence. This is the foundational fact of the New Covenant, *I will put my laws into their mind, and write them
in their hearts* (Heb. 8:10). While in Christianity, this
law is supernatural, it is in some true sense, the law of

replies calmly and thoughtfully. He has confidence in the truth, because
he has confidence in God.

"(10) The person of a truly liberated spirit, although he is ever
ready to do his duty, waits patiently till the proper time of action. He
has no choice of time but that which is indicated by the providence of
God. The Saviour himself could not act until his 'hour was come.' . . . .
An inthralled mind, although it is religiously disposed in part, will frequently adopt a precipitate and undeliberate course of action, which
is inconsistent with a humble love of the divine order. Such a person
thinks that freedom consists in having things his own way, whereas true
freedom consists in having things in the right way; and the right way
is God's way.

"(11) The possessor of true religious liberty, when he has sub-
missively and conscientiously done his duty, is not troubled by any undue
anxiety in relation to the result. It may be laid down as a maxim, that
he who asserts that he has left all things in the hands of God and at the
same time exhibits trouble and agitation of spirit in relation to the results of those very things (with the exception of those agitated movements which are purely instinctive), gives abundant evidence, in the
fact of this agitation of spirit, that he has not really made the entire
surrender which he professes to have made. The alleged facts are contradictory of each other, and both cannot exist at the same time.

"(12) Finally. In view of what has been said, and as a sort of
summary of the whole, we may remark that true liberty of spirit is
found in those, and in those only, who, in the language of De Sales,
'keep the heart totally disengaged from every created thing, in order
that they may follow the known will of God.' In other words, it is
found in those who can say with the Apostle Paul, that they are 'dead,
and their life is hid with Christ in God. The ruling motive in the breast
of the man of a religiously free spirit is, that he may, in all cases and
on all occasions, do the will of God. In that will his 'life is hid.' The
supremacy of the divine will—in other words, the reign of God in the
heart—necessarily has a direct and powerful operation upon the appetites, propensities, and affections; keeping them, each and all, in their
proper place. Another thing, which can be said affirmatively and
positively is, that those who are spiritually free are led by the spirit of
God. A man who is really guided by his appetites, his propensities, or
even by his affections, his love of country, or anything else than the
Spirit of God, cannot be said to be led by that divine spirit. The
Spirit of God, ruling in the heart will not bear the presence of any rival,
any competitor, that is to say, in all cases of voluntary action, he does
nothing under the impulse and guidance of natural pleasure or natural
choice alone. His liberty consists in being free from self; in being
liberated from the dominion of the world; in lying quietly and submis-
sively in the hands of God; in leaving himself, like clay in the hands of
the potter, to be molded and fashioned by the divine will. . . . . Spiritual
liberty implies, with the fact of entire submission to God, the great and
precious reality of interior emancipation. He who is spiritually free is
free in God. And he may, perhaps, be said to be free in the same sense
in which God is, who is free to do everything right, and nothing wrong.

"This is freedom indeed. This is the liberty with which Christ makes
free. This is emancipation which inspires the songs of angels—a freedom
which earth cannot purchase, and which hell cannot shackle" (pp. 56-62).

reason restored, and more than restored. The Divine
Spirit in the hearts of regenerate men seeks to work out
perfect obedience to the law of righteousness as taking
place by the bestowment of a new life in harmony with
the external law, it will be seen that the believer unfolds
in his spiritual life according to his own nature, and not
by means of outward compulsion. This inner law, therefore, amounts to self-government restored. It is the rule
of God's Spirit in a renewed self, according to the original idea of the Creator for man. Men are thus in their
new natures under the authority of the Holy Spirit, and
having their souls in subjection, they become a law unto
themselves, *not without law to God, but under the law
of Christ* (I Cor. 9:21). Thus the law is not made void,
but established through faith (Rom. 3:31). We are indeed delivered from the law of sin and death, but not
from the law of holiness and life. While the law is written upon the heart, it is still a law, and, therefore, necessitates the dignity of an external standard also, in conformity with the inner law of life. The fundamental
fact then, in Christian ethics, is the law of life, by which
man is delivered from outward compulsion, and given
the freedom to develop according to the new law of
his nature. Thus he keeps the law, by the unfolding of
his inner nature which is now in harmony with that
law. The keynote of this new nature is love, and thus
love is the fulfilling of the law.

The Law of Love. We have seen that holiness and
love are closely related in the nature of God. Holiness
is the divine nature interpreted from the standpoint of
self-affirmation, while Love is that same nature viewed
as self-communication. Both are, therefore, equally of
the essence of God. The holiness of God requires that
He always act out of pure love; while love seeks always
to impart Himself and that self is holy. (Cf. *Christian
Theology*, I, pp. 382ff.) We have seen, also, that the
Wesleyan conception of Christian Perfection is a purification of the heart from all that is contrary to pure
love. Considered from the standpoint of the inner Law
of Liberty, Christian Perfection is deliverance from sin;

considered from the standpoint of the royal law, Love is both the principle and the power of perfect consecration to God. Charity or divine love, which has its source in the nature of God, and which is imparted to the individual soul by the Holy Spirit through Christ, becomes, therefore, in its full ethical meaning, the substance of all obligation—whether to God or man. To the individual self, it is the fulfillment of a perfect character, for love is the *pleroma* (πλήρωμα) of religion as well as law. St. Peter makes it the crown of all graces introduced into the life and sustained by faith (II Peter 1: 5-7). Love thus becomes the sum of all interior goodness, and the bond of perfectness which unites and hallows all the energies of the soul. St. Paul makes love the end of the commandment in much the same sense that Christ is the end of the law for righteousness. (I Tim. 1: 5). Here charity or holy love is represented not only as the crowning grace of Christian character, but the point of transition in the relation of the individual to the social structure. It is, therefore, the ἀνακεφαλαίωσις or summing up of the law in perfect love which never fails (I Cor. 13: 8). It is a love, says Dr. Pope, "which neglects no injunction, forgets no prohibition, discharges every duty. It is perfect in passive as well as active obedience. It *'never faileth';* it insures every grace adapted to time or worthy of eternity. Therefore it is that the term perfect is reserved for this grace. Patience must *have her perfect work;* but love alone is itself perfect, while it gives perfection to him who has it." (POPE, *Compend. Chr. Th.,* III, p. 177).

Conscience as the Regulative Factor in Christian Experience and Conduct. We have discussed the law of liberty as an inward deliverance from the being and power of sin, and the law of love as the propulsive power of righteousness; it remains now for us to discuss conscience as the regulative factor in Christian experience and conduct. It is not our purpose, however, to discuss the place of conscience in philosophical ethics, but to use it in the Pauline sense as an integral part of vital religious experience. He says, *Now the end of the com-*

mandment is charity out of a pure heart, and of a good conscience, and of faith unfeigned (I Tim. 1:5). Here St. Paul analyzes Christian experience as follows: A stream of charity or divine love, flowing from a pure heart, regulated by a good conscience, and kept full and fresh and flowing, by an unfeigned faith. This faith refers, of course, to the constancy of trust in Christ, who by His Spirit sheds abroad the love of God in the hearts of the purified.

1. Conscience in ordinary usage "covers everything in man's nature that has to do with the decision and direction of moral conduct" (Standard Dictionary). While this may be a true description of conscience in popular speech, it is too vague for theological use. In our attempt to be more specific, however, we must constantly bear in mind the following facts: (1) Man is a moral being by virtue of being a person; for moral nature is an essential element in personality. (2) The spirit as the controlling factor in man's complex being, is a unit, and, consequently, is not divisible into parts. Being thus indivisible it always acts as a unity, and intellect, sensi-

As science means knowledge, so conscience etymologically means self-knowledge. In the moral being, conscience is the queen of every inward spring of action, will is her subject; and as all legislative function and delegated judicial authority emanates from the sovereign, so conscience is, objectively, the unwritten law of the heart, as founded on those eternal principles of right and equity and truth that are as rays from the throne of God; and, subjectively, it passes judgment upon the thoughts of the heart and the actions of the body. If conscience be obeyed, it approves, and then it is pure; but if it be dishonored and its voice disregarded, such disloyalty can only lay up materials for remorse. This authoritative principle of the mind and soul of man is referable only to the original gift of moral and spiritual life as the soul of man. "In the likeness of God made he him"; and as mental consciousness is our evidence of the existence of thoughts, desires, feelings, and other states of the mind, so conscience is a standing testimony of the divine genesis of the soul, as a direct afflatus from God. This fundamental element of man's moral being is proof to him of his religious relation to his Maker; it declares the mysterious intercommunication that subsists between the Spirit of God and the spirit of man; and it indicates the natural revelation of God's will made to man through reason. Conscience is the representative of this inner revelation, which, proceeding forth from the creative Spirit of God, infuses itself into the spirit of man, and as a plastic energy forms and molds him, by conveying to him the cognizance of God's will and of man's duties in His sight. Thus conscience is our moral sense continually held in check by the Spirit of God; it is the very soul of our loyalty to Him; it is the *religio* of a true communion.—WHEWELL, *Elements of Morality*, sect. 263.

bility and will are present in every activity. But while the
soul always moves as a unit, one form of activity may
so predominate at a given time, as to be discriminated
and defined. For this reason, we define the intellect as
the soul thinking; the sensibility, as the soul feeling; and
the will as the soul choosing or exercising volition. So,
also, if we restrict our definition of conscience to certain
modes of self-activity, we shall not be understood as
implying that the whole self is not active, but only that
the peculiar functions of the moral nature are predominant. We may, therefore, define conscience as "the
self passing judgment upon its conformity, or nonconformity, in character and conduct to moral law, that is,
as right and wrong, with the accompanying feeling or
impulse to obey the judgment of righteousness." (Robbins, *The Ethics of the Christian Life*, p. 79.) In this
view of conscience, the functions of discovery or annunciation of moral law are not attributed to it. It is
rather as Kant represents, to be regarded as a judge presiding over a court (Cf. *Christian Theology*, I, p. 307),
who decides that this desire, this affection, this purpose,
or this deed is in accordance with moral law, and therefore right. Upon this decision, a feeling corresponding
to the judgment follows, either impelling to action in
accordance with the decision, or dissuading from any
action which may not be in harmony with it.

2. Conscience derives its authority from the law
whose requirements it enforces. As it is the majesty of
the law which gives validity to the decisions of the
judge in civil courts, so it is the law of God which gives
validity to the decisions of conscience. Its province,
therefore, is not legislative but judicial. Its decisions are
always those of a just and incorruptible judge according
to the laws he is set to apply. Since then, the authority
of conscience is derived from the authority of the law
according to which its decisions are made; and since this
law is found primarily in the nature and constitution of
man, it follows that the authority of conscience is not
external but internal. Its voice does not come from
without, but rises from the depths of his innermost be-

ing. It is the whole of his being interpreting man to himself. The law by which it judges is the inner moral law of man's nature, and any external law derives its obligatory force from an appeal to this essential law of man's moral being.

3. From the view of conscience just stated, it follows that its decisions before the law will always be infallible, that is, they will always be in accord with the law of reason. This would be true if men were in their normal state. But another factor enters here. Man is not in his normal state. The law of his being is obscured and perverted as a consequence of original sin. Hence although conscience always makes its decisions according to the law, the latter being obscured or perverted, the decisions will in these instances be erroneous. For this reason, God has given to man an external law as a transcript of his own true inner life, and this law is found in the Word of God.

4. While conscience in the absolute sense is the utterance of God's voice in the soul, and is thus beyond the power of education or development (Cf. Volume I, p. 129); the term is also used in a relative sense as involving our own moral consciousness under the eye of God. In this sense, it is the positive assimilation within

W. Fleming in his *Manual of Moral Philosophy* mentions the defects of conscience as follows: "Conscience may be defective in respect to its law or rule, or in respect to its own certainty or clearness.

"First, in respect to its rule, conscience may be true, that is, it may be plainly and clearly in accordance with the will of God, or the ultimate and absolute rule of rectitude. It may be erroneous, that is, its decisions, instead of being in accordance with right reason and the revealed will of God, may be not in conformity with the one or the other. And this error may be vincible or invincible, according as it might and ought to have been removed, or as it could have been removed, by the diligent use of means to enlighten and correct the conscience. Conscience as erroneous has been denominated lax, when on slight grounds it judges an action not to be vicious which is truly vicious, or slightly vicious when it is greatly so; scrupulous, when on slight grounds it judges an action to be vicious when it is not truly vicious, or greatly vicious when it is not so; perplexed, when it judges that there will be sin, whether the action is done or not done.

"Secondly, in respect to its certainty, conscience is said to be certain or clear, when there is no fear of error as to our judgment of an action as right or wrong; probable when in reference to two actions, or courses of action, it determines that the probability is that the one is right rather than the other; doubtful, when it cannot clearly determine whether an action is or is not in accordance with the law of rectitude."

the soul, of those principles of truth and goodness necessary to bring man's will into conformity with the will of God. Two things are involved, (1) the inner impulse, and (2) the light of truth. The former is conscience proper which says "Find the right and do it"; the latter or moral judgment is strictly speaking no part of conscience, but the standard by which conscience operates. Since this moral judgment is true only insofar as it is enlightened by the Word of God, we are led to the conviction that in the Christian life, the Scriptures are the only authoritative rule of faith and practice. Further still, it will be seen that the conscience in this relative sense as involving the whole moral process, is subject to education and development, as conscience in the subjective sense is not. Hence the Scriptures refer to this relative aspect when they speak of a good or pure conscience; or of an evil and defiled conscience.

5. We are now prepared to understand the meaning of St. Paul when he speaks of a good conscience as

Conduct is based upon two things, namely, knowledge and conscience. Some teachers of psychology would prefer to say that conduct is based upon conscience alone, and then attribute to conscience two faculties. First, impulse, which is accepting or rejecting right or wrong when it appears; second, discrimination, which is the faculty of conscience that tells right from wrong. In this short discussion we prefer to hold that conduct is based upon two things, knowledge or light, and conscience, and then confine conscience to one function, namely, impulse, accepting or rejecting when right or wrong appear. In any case, we will all admit that some people have more knowledge or light than others have, and that some consciences, with proper training and education, have greater power of discrimination than others. These facts must be taken into consideration in the study of ethics.— R. T. WILLIAMS, *Sanctification, The Experience and Ethics*, pp. 51, 52.

Dr. Olin A. Curtis regards conscience as having two coworkers— the judgment, by which the man decides whether a given matter is right or wrong; and the will, by which the man makes a choice among the possible courses of action. In popular speech the judgment is considered a part of conscience; but, strictly speaking, there is no moral quality in the judgment; it is moral only in the loose sense that it is now dealing with moral matters. He points out, also, that in conscience proper, there are three features—moral distinction, moral obligation, and moral settlement. By moral distinction is meant the intuitive knowledge that there is a right and a wrong. Moral obligation follows immediately, for as soon as this distinction is made, Right says "You ought." When this sense of obligation is analyzed it will be found to contain three momenta, the obligation of allegiance, the obligation of search, and the obligation of action. Moral settlement follows personal volition under the sense of obligation. If the person has willed against his obligation, he has distress of spirit; if he has been true to his obligation, he has a flash of moral content.—CURTIS, *The Christian Faith*, pp. 31-33.

the regulative faculty of the soul. A good conscience is one which is enlightened by the Spirit of truth, and, therefore, always makes its decisions according to the standards of God's holy Word. Similarly, also, the conscience may be distinguished as pure (I Tim. 8: 9; II Tim. 1: 3); evil (Heb. 10: 22); defiled (Titus 1: 15); weak (I Cor. 8: 7); and seared (I Tim. 4: 2). To these are sometimes added such descriptions of conscience as steady or wavering, morbid or sound, enlightened or dark. In its objective sense, conscience may be distorted by ignorance or vice, and so form erroneous judgments; and as subjective, it may justify and bring peace as the effect of goodness; or it may condemn by the pangs of remorse. It is for this reason that the earlier moralists spoke of it as the συντήρησις or "inner guard" which kept watch over the hidden sources of the will.

William Whewell in his *Elements of Morality* gives the following two rules as being indispensable for the healthy action of conscience. (1) We should never undertake any action of moral import, much less embark on any course of action without first obtaining a distinct utterance from the conscience, in affirmation or derogation of the moral lawfulness of such action. We must not allow ourselves to act on a mere probable opinion, or doubt with respect to the right or wrong of the action. "He that doubteth is damned if he eat" (Rom. 14:23).

(2) It is an absolute rule, and one for universal observance, that we should never act contrary to the dictates of conscience; even though it be warped by error or prejudice. The moral tone of every action depends on its close dependence with the inner rule; and the morality of the agent maintains a relative proportion with respect for the decision of conscience, and an honest determination in following it out to its legitimate conclusion. To act contrary to conscience must always be wrong, irrespective of the abstract right or wrong of the action; and whether that wrong be capable of correction or not. For moral culture is the abiding duty of man; our position today must not be taken as a fixed point, but as a state of transition to something better. The law of the mind must be brought gradually into closer conformity with the law of God, that is absolutely "holy and just and good"; and converting the soul" in proportion as it seeks to assimilate its teaching. Conscience is never formed, but is always in the course of formation. Therefore, though for the present, we may err in following the guidance of a mistaken conscience, yet it is better to err for a while in this direction than to be disloyal to the inner rule, which would only weaken its check upon our actions, when conscience becomes more completely informed by the supreme rule. To be unconscientious is always to be immoral. He, therefore, whose conscience is clouded by error, must abide by the consequences of such error; but he sins not in the mere following of his conscience. But he whose conscience has a wrong direction, which with proper pains and regard for the truth might be adjusted, sins when he acts in accordance with its dictation (WHE-WELL, *Elements of Morality*, section 275).

PRACTICAL ETHICS

Practical ethics is the application of moral principles in the regulation of human conduct. Having discussed these principles, we must now consider their specific Christian application in the manifold and complex situations of life. Here as in other departments of theology, the methods of classification vary. Generally, however, the subject matter is arranged in the twofold division of (1) Duties to God, and (2) Duties to man; or the threefold classification of (1) Duties to God; (2) Duties to self; and (3) Duties to others. As to the order of treatment adopted here, we may say that since God is the foundation of all moral obligation, theistic ethics naturally comes first. Strictly speaking, all obligation must be to God as the Moral Governor, and all duties must, therefore, be duties to God. Here there is a parallel to the truth in dogmatics that all sin is ultimately against God. The duties to self come second in order, as essential to the formation of Christian character. This is necessary in a system which holds that the tree must first be made good if the fruit is to be good (Matt. 12: 33); and, also, that there can be no fruit except the branch abide in the vine (John 15: 4, 5). Christian character is unfolded only in loyal relation to the divine. Lastly, there is the regulation of the external conduct toward others, as having its source in, and flowing from the character of the individual. We shall then, in our treatment of Practical Ethics, observe the following outline: (I) Theistic Ethics: or Duties to God; (II) Individual Ethics: or Duties to One's Self; and (III) Social Ethics: or Duties to Others. Following this, we shall give brief attention to the Institutions of Christianity as being a part of Social Ethics, and yet differing in this, that they are more specifically corporate than individual in character. Here we shall mention (1) Marriage, and the duties of the family; and (2) The State, and the duties of citizenship. This will bring us to a consideration of the Church, which forms the subject matter of the two following chapters.

(I) THEISTIC ETHICS: OR DUTIES TO GOD

The three theistic virtues are faith, hope and charity. These, whether considered in themselves, in their effects, or in their growth and perfection, occupy the first place in the Christian life. Upon these, all other virtues depend. As compared with the so-called moral virtues—prudence, justice, courage and temperance, the theistic virtues constitute the end or objective of the Christian life; while the moral virtues are either the means by which this is attained or the consequences which flow from it. The theistic virtues are superior also, in that by them we are actually united to God—to God as truth by faith; to God as faithful, by hope; and to God as the supreme good, by love. Viewed from the ethical standpoint, we may analyze these virtues as follows: (1) Faith is at once an act and a habit, an act in that it is the outreach of the whole being toward another, consciously exercised; it is a habit, in that it is a conscious repose in the merits of another. Faith is sometimes distinguished from knowledge in this, that faith rests upon the authority or testimony of another; while knowledge arises from the perception of truth in the object itself. The sins against faith are infidelity, heresy and apostasy. Infidelity is unfaithfulness to God; heresy is unfaithfulness to truth or persistence in error; while apostasy is in its strictest sense, a defection from religion. (2) Hope is that divine virtue which furnishes the motive whereby we trust with unwavering confidence in the Word of God, and look forward to the obtainment of all that He has promised us. Like faith, hope may be viewed either as an act or a state, and in either instance, the motive and the objective are the same. Hope relates to the future and, therefore, implies expectation, but every expectation cannot be classified as hope. Only desirable objects can be hoped for. The sins against hope may be twofold—either despair or diffidence on the one hand, or presumption and false confidence on the other. Despair is the abandonment of all hope of salvation. Diffidence consists in hoping without due confidence. Presumption is taking advantage of God's goodness to commit sin; while false confidence is hoping in an inordinate manner. (3) Charity or divine love is the virtue whereby we give ourselves wholly to God as the sovereign good. It is a divinely infused virtue, the motive of which is God's goodness, and its object both God and our neighbor. Charity considered as an ethical virtue in its broadest sense signifies complacency in what is good. In a stricter sense, it is that affection which wishes well, or desires what is good, to another. If we desire good to another, not on his own account but for ours, we have the love of concupiscence, because it proceeds from a desire for our own advantage. If we wish well to another for his own sake, we have the love of benevolence; and if this is mutual, we have the love of friendship. Charity may be either perfect or imperfect. In order to be perfect it must (1) be inspired by a perfect motive; and (2) it must loyally adhere to God with the highest appreciation. If it fails in either of these aspects, it falls short of perfect love. Three things demand our attention in the further consideration of this subject: (1) Reverence as the Fundamental Duty to God; and (2) The Duty and Forms of Prayer; and (3) The Supreme Duty of Worship.

Reverence as the Fundamental Duty to God. Reverence has been defined as a "profound respect mingled with fear and affection," or a "strong sentiment of respect and esteem, sometimes with traces of fear." Coleridge defined it as a "synthesis of love and fear." As

Reverence is the supreme and eternal duty and grace of the created spirit. It is both the source and the issue of all godliness. The three passages, "Holy and reverend is his name" (Psalms 111:9); "Hallowed be thy name" (Matt. 6:9); "Sanctify the Lord God in your hearts" (I Peter 3:15), in their combination teach us first how awful is God in Himself, then that the coming of His kingdom is the universal acknowledgment of His majesty, and finally that this reverence must be the inmost sentiment of our individual hearts. Reverence is fear tempered by love. In the Old Testament the fear predominated, in the New Testament the love; but the sentiment of reverence pervades all religion on earth and in heaven. Whether as sacred dread or loving fear, it abideth always. As the spirit formed by religion it is universal in its influence. It is the habitual sense of the presence of God that gives dignity of life, and makes the character of him who cultivates it venerable. It extends to all divine things as well as to the name of God himself: to His Word, to His ordinances, to His created temple of the world, and to all that is His. In His presence more particularly it is awe.—POPE, *Compend. Chr. Th.*, III, pp. 225, 226.

such, reverence is the supreme duty of man the creature to God the Creator. It is the sentiment from which all worship springs. Awe adds to reverence the implication of solemn wonder mingled with dread, in view of the great and terrible presence of Deity, or of that which is sublime and sacred by virtue of that Presence. Reverence when expressed silently is known as adoration, and carries with it the added idea of homage or personal devotion. Praise is the audible expression which extols the Divine Perfections; and Thanksgiving is expressed gratitude for the mercies of God. The duty of the devout spirit, therefore, is to offer to God the adoration of a creature, the homage of a subject, and the praise of a worshiper. St. Paul in his enumeration of the works of the flesh, mentions two as violations of divine things— idolatry and witchcraft (Gal. 5:20). (1) Idolatry is commonly defined as the paying of divine honors to idols, images, or other created objects; but it may consist, also, in excessive admiration, veneration or love for any person or thing. Thus covetousness is regarded as idolatry (Col. 3:5). (2) Witchcraft is the practice of the arts of a sorcerer or sorceress, which was commonly believed to be the consequence of intercourse with

Superstition is not an excess of religion—at least in the ordinary sense of the word excess—as if anyone could have too much of true religion, but any misdirection of religious feeling, manifested either in showing religious veneration or regard to objects which deserve none; that is, properly speaking, the worship of false gods; or, in the assignment of such a degree, or such a kind of religious veneration to any object, as that object, though worthy of some reverence, does not deserve; or in the worship of the true God through the medium of improper rites or ceremonies. . . . . It may arise from a sense of guilt, from bodily indisposition, or from erroneous reasoning.—WHATELY.

Godlessness is practical atheism, or living as if there were no God. When it accompanies a knowledge and acknowledgment of God's existence and claims, it is the last and worst of all vices, as wilfully aiming the death-blow at man's highest being and mission. The perversion of religious culture, as manifested in the conduct, is perhaps more offensive than that in the views. Hypocrisy would cover the absence of true reverence for God by playing a part and putting on all the outward show of piety. Cant is hypocrisy as exhibited in language and air. Bigotry is the manifestation of an irrational or blind partiality for a particular party or creed. Fanaticism adds to the blind partiality of bigotry an equally blind hatred of all opposers, and a pretension to inspiration. These are all religious vices of the most insidious and dangerous character; hypocrisy and cant dethrone truth and make man a living lie; bigotry and fanaticism dethrone reason and moral principle and give the man over to prejudice and passion.—GREGORY, Christian Ethics, p. 210.

Satan. The injunction, therefore, forbids all enchantments, necromancy, spiritism, or other of the so-called black arts.

The Duty and Forms of Prayer. Prayer is a duty which is obligatory upon all men as an expression of the creature's dependence upon the Creator. It may be said that what the habitual sense of reverence is to adoration and praise, the spirit of dependence is to prayer. Dr. Wakefield defines prayer as "the offering of our desires to God through the mediation of Jesus Christ, under the influence of the Holy Spirit, and with suitable dispositions, for things agreeable to his will." (Wakefield, *Christian Theology*, p. 492). Desire is excited by a sense of want or a felt need, and leads immediately to prayer. *One thing have I desired of the Lord, that will I seek after* (Psalms 27:4). Without a proper appreciation of the importance of divine blessings, prayer will be unavailing. Hence *the kingdom of heaven suffereth violence and the violent take it by force*

Rev. Luther Lee points out that "the duty of prayer has its foundation in reason, and may be seen to be suited to our relation to God, and wonderfully adapted to the other parts of the economy of gospel salvation, and suited to promote piety and devotion." He calls attention to the following points. (1) Prayer is suited to the relation we sustain to God. God is the Author of all being, and the source of all blessedness; while we are His creatures, receiving all the good we enjoy from him. (2) Prayer, in its very exercise is admirably adapted to preserve a knowledge of the true God, and to keep man's erratic mind from running into idolatry. It has been seen that prayer implies an apprehension of God's universal presence and everywhere operative power. To pray is to bring God directly before the mind, in all the infinity of His attributes, so far as the human mind can grasp an idea of the infinite God. (3) The exercise of prayer must promote a sense of our dependence upon God, which it is all important to keep fully awake in the mind. It has been seen that prayer implies this sense of dependence, that there is no true prayer without it. (4) Prayer, upon the principles advanced above, must tend to promote devotion. It will produce this result as a mere mental habit, allowing it to be performed with honesty of intention. Devotion to the world, and constantly occupying the mind with worldly matters, will increase worldly mindedness; and so constant habit of abstracting the mind from matters of the world, and putting forth an effort to concentrate the thoughts and desires on god in prayer, must tend to lessen worldly mindedness, and increase a disposition to worship, and a deeper feeling of devotion, when we attempt it. (5) Prayer, as a required duty, is peculiarly adapted to help the exercise of faith, which in the gospel, is the fundamental condition of salvation. (6) The mental and moral state of the soul, which is necessary in order to offer acceptable prayer to God, is just that state which renders us proper recipients of His saving grace.—LUTHER LEE, *Christian Theology*, pp. 356, 357.

(Matt. 11:12). Prayer must be offered to God, through Christ, and in the Spirit, in order to be acceptable. Prayer must also be offered for things agreeable to the will of God, and the petitions must be presented with faith in His promises. Dr. Pope points out that "the formal acts of prayer are manifold, expressed by a number of terms common to both Testaments, and combining the spirit and the act. The leading word προσευχή is one of those. It is always prayer to God, and that without limitation. When St. Paul exhorts, in everything by prayer and supplication with thanksgiving let your requests be made known unto God, he distinguishes from this general prayer the δέησις or supplication for individual benefits. It is the difference between prayer and petition. The requests of the supplication, αἰτήματα, simply express the individuality of the prayer: the supplication noting our need (δεῖ), and the request the utterance of that need. When our Saviour said, *In that day ye shall ask me nothing* (John 16:23), He used another term signifying, in the case of the disciples, the interrogation of perplexity: there it is ἐρωτᾶν, which is changed for αἰτεῖν in what follows: *Verily, verily, I say unto you, Whatsoever ye shall ask the Father in my name, he will give it you.* The former word is used of our Lord's own prayer, never the latter: hence the former has in it more of familiarity, and is never used of human prayer. Save, indeed, in one passage, which leads us to the prayer of intercession. St. John changes αἰτήσει into ἐρωτήσῃ con-

On the general duty of secret prayer it may be remarked, (1) Every person, so far as circumstances will allow, should have some place which is to him his closet of prayer. The spirit of the command requires this. Without it, prayer will be likely to be neglected. (2) As no time is settled by the word, for the performance of this duty, it demands a reasonable construction and application, in this particular, on the part of Christians. The fact that no law prescribes how many times, and at what hours secret prayer shall be performed, shows the wisdom of the Law-giver. No rule could settle these points, which would not be impossible to some, or diminish devotion with others. These points are settled specifically by the law of Mahomet, and the result is, prayer with them has become a mere form. It being left by Christ to be settled by the enlightened judgment, under a sense of accountability to God, and a general rule requiring secret prayer, which judgment will be made in view of surrounding circumstances, and the strength of the feeling of piety, the tendency is to promote the spirit of devotion more than any specific rule could do.—LEE *Elements of Theology*, p. 359.

cerning the sin unto death, *I do not say that he shall pray for it* (I John 5:16): we may ask in confidence concerning every other sin, but concerning this we are to leave the ἐρωτᾶν to Christ. Intercessory prayer has no term to express our precise idea of it. The exhortation is generally to *supplication for all saints,* and *for all men,* after the example of the Lord's intercession. In the passage to Timothy St. Paul uses for once the word ἐντεύξεις, intercessions, which, however, means familiar and confident prayers, as coming from the word ἐν-τυγχάνειν literally to fall in with a person and enter into familiar speech with him. In the strength of Christ's intercession we also are commanded to intercede, or to speak confidently with God on behalf of others: save indeed with the one reservation mentioned above. Intercessory prayer must blend with all our supplications." (POPE, *Compend. Chr. Th.,* III, pp. 228, 229.)

The general duty of prayer is usually divided as follows: (1) Ejaculatory Prayer; (2) Private Prayer; (3) Family or Social Prayer; and (4) Public Prayer.

1. *Ejaculatory Prayer* is a term applied to "those secret and frequent aspirations of the heart to God for general or particular blessings, by which a just sense of our habitual dependence upon God and of our wants and dangers may be expressed while we are employed in the common affairs of life" (Wakefield). It denotes a devotional attitude of mind and heart in which a constant spirit of prayer is maintained. It includes all those impromptu expressions of prayer and praise which flow from a heart which is cultivated to *Rejoice evermore,*

In speaking of ejaculatory prayer, Dr. Wakefield says, "The cultivation of this spirit is clearly enjoined upon us by St. Paul, who exhorts us to 'pray without ceasing,' and 'in every thing' to 'give thanks'; and also to set our 'affection on things above,' exhortations which imply a holy and devotional frame of mind, and not merely acts of prayer performed at intervals. The high and unspeakable advantages of this habit are, that it induces a watchful and guarded mind; prevents religion from deteriorating into a lifeless form; unites the soul to God; induces continual supplies of divine influence; and opposes an effectual barrier, by the grace thus acquired, against the encroachments of worldly anxieties and the force of temptations. The existence of this spirit of prayer and thanksgiving is one of the grand distinctions between nominal and real Christians; and by it the measure of vital and effective Christianity enjoyed by any individual may ordinarily be determined.— WAKEFIELD, *Christian Theology,* p. 295.

pray without ceasing, and *In every thing give thanks* (I Thess. 5: 16-18). This form of prayer was held by the fathers as a distinguishing mark of genuine piety, but the habit needs to be guarded against any formality which would leave the impression of irreverence.

2. *Private Prayer* is expressly enjoined by our Lord in the words, *But thou, when thou prayest, enter into thy closet, and when thou hast shut thy door, pray to thy Father which is in secret; and thy Father which seeth in secret shall reward thee openly* (Matt. 6: 6). The duty of private prayer is further enforced by the example of our Lord and His apostles. The reason for the institution of private prayer is shown by our Lord's words, to be that of friendly and confiding communion with God in all those matters which pertain to the deeper feelings and interests of the individual. The strict performance of private prayer has ever been regarded as one of the surest marks of genuine piety and Christian sincerity.

3. *Family or Social Prayer* grows out of the nature of the social structure itself. Family prayer is basic as respects the whole system of Christian worship. The worship of patriarchal times was largely domestic; and the sacred office of father or master of the household passed from Judaism to Christianity. Early Christian worship was at first chiefly confined to the family, and only gradually took on wider significance. Hence family worship became an essential factor in the public services, by inculcating a spirit of devotion and by training in the forms of worship. Parents may as well conclude, therefore, that they are under no obligation to feed and clothe their children, or to educate them for lawful employment or one of the professions, as to conclude that they are under no obligation to afford them the proper religious instruction. Social prayer may be broader than the family; or it may be limited to a few individuals from different families. Here again we have the words of our Lord, *That if two of you shall agree on earth as touching any thing that they shall ask, it shall be done for them of my Father which is in heaven* (Matt. 18: 19). "From all these considerations, we conclude," says Dr.

Ralston, "that family prayer, though not directly enjoined by express precept, is yet a duty so manifest from the *general principles* of the gospel, the *character* of the Christian, the *constitution* of the family, the *benefits* it imparts, and the *general promises* of God, that it must be of binding obligation on every Christian who is the head of a household." (RALSTON, *Elements of Divinity*, p. 780.)

4. *Public Prayer* is used in a wide sense to include every branch of public worship, such as prayer, praise, the reading of the Scriptures, and the singing of psalms and hymns and spiritual songs. Public prayer was a part of the Jewish worship, at least from the time of Ezra, and was performed in the synagogues. Our Lord frequently attended and participated in these services, and by this means placed His approval upon the practice of public prayer. This duty, however, is also founded upon the express declaration of the Scriptures. In his instructions to Timothy, St. Paul says, *I exhort therefore, that, first of all, supplications, prayers, intercessions, and giving of thanks, be made for all men* (I Tim. 2: 1); and again, *I will therefore that men pray every where, lifting up holy hands, without wrath and doubting* (I Tim. 2: 8). The Epistle to the Hebrews contains a similar injunction also, *Let us consider one another to provoke unto love and to good works: not forsaking the assembling of ourselves together, as the manner of some is; but exhorting one another: and so much the more, as ye see the day approaching* (Heb. 10: 24, 25). Public worship is designed to benefit each individual worshiper, to keep alive the sense of dependence upon God as the Giver of every good and perfect gift, and to publicly express the grateful remembrance of every material and spiritual blessing.

The Supreme Duty of Worship. The union of all the offices of devotion constitutes divine worship. This is the highest duty of man. It includes the active offering to God of the tribute due Him, together with the supplication of His benefits. Both the active and passive phases are involved, as in the text, *The Lord is good unto them that wait for him, to the soul that seeketh him* (Lam. 3:25). Worship blends meditation and contemplation with prayer, and these through the spirit, strengthen the soul for its work of faith and labor of love. As worship marks the consummation of all ethical duty to God, so the end of all worship is spiritual union with God. This is the goal set for the church by our Lord in His high-priestly prayer. He prayed *that they all may be one; as thou, Father, art in me, and I in thee, that they also may be one in us* (John 17:21). This is not, however, a pantheistic union, as pagan mysticism taught, but a personal, spiritual union, in which the identity of the individual is preserved. It is a union of affection, of like-mindedness, and identity of purpose. "Worship is the recognition of Christ," says Bishop McIlvaine, "and the ascription to Him of everything which is beautiful and glorious and desirable. It is the necessary tendency of all true worship to assimilate the worshiper into the

Worship has played an important part, not only in the history of the Christian Church, but in the history of the world. Even in the most primitive forms of human life and civilization, worship has always been a prominent activity. As civilization advances, the forms of worship change, but the practice of worship never dies. The great moments of life, birth, marriage and death, have ever been the occasions for special acts of worship. It may be said that over the whole course of history, man has paid more attention to his worship than to any other activity. We need, therefore, to clearly distinguish its meaning, that we may better enter into this valuable experience. Intelligent participation in worship is more valuable than the unintelligent following of mere custom.

The following definitions of worship may be noted. "Worship is the adoration of God, the aspiration of supreme worth to God, and the manifestation of reverence in the presence of God."—SPERRY. "Worship is both a means and an end in itself. It is unquestionably the chief means of inspiring and motivating Christian conduct and character; and it is also a satisfying experience of self-expression, self-dedication and adoration for the glory of God."—FISKE.

Worship has been called the "I thank you" of the heart. It is an act of spiritual politeness, as reasonable and appropriate as it is improving and beautiful. A sense of decency and gratitude urges us to it, and the comfort and satisfaction it brings is proof of its propriety.—POTTS *Faith Made Easy*, p. 367.

Every truth contains within itself its peculiar duty. Every revelation of God is always a commandment, telling us something of him which we did not know before, and bidding us do for him that which we were not doing before. The truth is grasped and realized only in the performance of the duty; the duty must find its inspiration in the truth lying behind it. A man who aims faithfully and persistently to do the right will not long be kept in darkness as to what is right. A religion which is from God must touch practically upon human life at every point.—BISHOP MCILVAINE.

likeness of the being worshiped. Thus the public and private worship of Christ becomes one of the chief agencies in our redemption. The thoughts and feelings of the heart demand for their completeness, a corresponding expression. Faith finds this expression in the services of the church and the duties of the Christian life.

Evelyn Underhill points out that in the phenomena of worship, two currents of life meet—one proceeding from the transcendent God, the other flowing from the religious life of the subject. The descending current includes all forms of revelation, the ascending, all forms of prayer. Nor does the mutual action of the two currents exclude the primacy of the divine action; for this is manifest, not only in the descending current of the Word, of Revelation and the Sacraments, but also in its immanent action within the life of souls. This acknowledgment of our total dependence upon the free action of God, immanent and transcendent, is and must ever be a part of true worship. It is interesting to note that the term "prevenient grace" so popular in Arminian theology, is again coming into use, in connection with the idea of worship. Man could never have produced this disposition of the soul. It does not appear spontaneously from within the created order. The awed conviction of the reality of the eternal over against us—this sense of God in one form or another, is in fact a revelation of prevenient grace, proportioned to the capacity of the creature. It is something wholly other than ourselves, and not deducible from finite experiences, it is "the splendor and distinctness of God." The easy talk of the pious naturalist, therefore, as to man's approach to God, is irrational, impudent and irreverent, unless the priority of God's approach to man be constantly kept in mind. (Cf. EVELYN UNDERHILL, Worship.)

Our religious life requires giving. It withers under the constant desire to simply get. He who has not learned to worship inclines to the belief that there is no being more worthy of reverence than himself. He becomes as selfish as Shylock in that very exercise, one great design of which is to counteract the selfish tendencies of life. The essence of worship is, that in itself it is dethroned and God enthroned. By it we recognize Him as somewhat other than a very powerful person whom we may use for our convenience and benefit. A doubter who in his vast uncertainty changes his aim to giving, and away from himself, is the one whose gloom will lighten.—PRUDDEN. (Cf. POTTS, Faith Made Easy, p. 367.)

Worship rises high above all forms. If it attempts to find utterance through them it will set them on fire, and glow and burn in their consuming flame and rise as incense to God. If it starts out with the impartation and the receiving of the great thought of God; if it waits to hear His infinite will and eternal love, it spreads its pinions to fly to His bosom, there to breathe out its unutterable devotion. We have here the way of worship. They cry with a loud voice, saying, "Salvation to our God which sitteth upon the throne, and unto the Lamb" (Rev. 7:9-17). It is not the learning of some new thing; not a new shading of some thought which is a matter of interest; it is not the repeating, parrotlike, of some new form. But it is the cry of the soul, deep, earnest, intense, loud; the farthest removed from what might be regarded as cathedral service, with the intoning of prayer and praise, and where the light falls but dimly, the muffled music and sentiment rolling back upon the mind in subdued sensibility. I suppose this is about the best

(II) Individual Ethics: or Duties to Oneself

Individual ethics is that division of practical ethics which treats of the application of the moral law to the regulation of man's conduct insofar as it has reference to himself as an individual moral agent. There is a sense, of course, in which man's character is dependent upon his external obligations, but it will be simpler to treat individual ethics as forming the Christian character; and reserve the treatment of external obligations for the division of Social Ethics. Man's duty to himself is frequently summed up in Self-conservation, Self-culture, and Self-conduct. For the purpose of this work, however, with its emphasis upon the development of the Christian life, a simpler outline will be more appropriate. We shall, therefore, give attention to the following: (1) The Sanctity of the Body; (2) The Province of the Intellectual, Emotional, Moral and Aesthetic Powers of the Mind; and (3) The Development of the Spiritual Life.

The Sanctity of the Body. Since man's physical existence is essential to the fulfillment of his mission in this life, it is his first duty to conserve and develop all the powers of his being. Christianity regards the body, not as a prison house of the soul, but as a temple of the Holy Spirit. This gives sanctity to the body; and the preservation of this sanctity becomes a guiding principle in all matters of physical welfare. The specific duties pertaining to the body are as follows:

1. There must be the preservation and development of the bodily powers. This becomes a high and holy duty, for man's existence in the world depends upon this bodily organism. This is intuitively recognized as soon as the agent comes to realize the relation existing

earth-born, man-made form of worship one can find. But that which is here described is something altogether different. It is also equally far removed from a gathering of the people, who, without solemnity or soul earnestness wait to be sung at, and prayed at, and preached at, until the time comes when they can decently get away. The worship here seen rises from every soul; it is the outbursting passion of every heart; it breaks forth like a mighty tornado. One thing seems certain, the worship of the blood-washed company is not the still small voice (Dr. P. F. Bresee, *Sermons*, "The Lamb Amid the Blood-washed," pp. 166-67).

between the soul and the body. He who neglects his physical being, places his whole mission in jeopardy; and he who destroys it, brings his mission to an end. Hence self-murder is strictly prohibited. Wherever there is a morally enlightened conscience, men have agreed that suicide is contrary to the end for which life is given. So, also, self-mutilation is forbidden. This includes any bodily injury or dismemberment, such as disfigures the body or prevents the complete functioning of the physical organism. Christianity is opposed to ascetic practices also, such as were found among the mystics of the Middle Ages, and as they are practiced in pagan countries at the present time. The fasts and self-denials which Christianity enjoins upon men, are intended to invigorate rather than enfeeble the human system.

2. There must be the care and culture of the body through exercise, rest, sleep and recreation. Man was made for labor and for rest, and both are essential to his physical well-being. The mere possession of wealth does not exclude man from the duty of labor. The world owes no man a living who is able to earn it for himself. Holiness dignifies labor and makes it delightful, whether with the hands, the head or the heart. It also dignifies rest and makes the Sabbath a symbol of the spiritual "rest of faith." Too often there is a failure to discern the true meaning of the Sabbath which is not only for worship but also for repose. Many never give their bodies a Sabbath, Sunday being as laborious as the other days of the week. As the soil of Israel came into possession of its Sabbath by seventy years of captivity, so those who fail to make the Sabbath a day of worship and rest, may finally observe these Sabbaths by enforced rest through the providence of God. In the highly specialized forms of labor demanded by modern civilization, the tension of both mind and body is such that periods of rest and recreation become an essential factor in the preservation of the body. This recreation should be such as to renew the physical powers, and minister to both the mental and spiritual life of the individual.

3. The appetites and passions of the body must be subjugated to man's higher intellectual and spiritual interests. Some have assumed that holiness implies the destruction or near destruction of the physical appetites and pleasurable emotions. This is not according to the Scriptures. Holiness destroys nothing that is essential to man, either physically or spiritually. The appetites and passions remain, but they are freed from the incubus of sin. The early disciples ate *their meat with gladness and singleness of heart* (Acts 2:46); and one of the apostles warns against those seducing spirits who go about *forbidding to marry, and commanding to abstain from meats, which God hath created to be received with thanksgiving of them which believe and know the truth* (I Tim. 4:1, 3). Holiness, however, does not necessarily compel a normal condition of the appetites and passions. Sometimes perverted appetites exist for a time in those who have clean hearts, but who have not had as yet, any light on these specific matters. Both perverted and unnatural appetites are so subject to the power of God as to be instantly regulated or destroyed through faith. All appetite is instinctive and unreasoning. It knows nothing of right and wrong, but simply craves indulgence. It never controls itself, but is subject to control. Hence St. Paul says, *But I keep under my body, and bring it into subjection: lest that by any means, when I have preached to others, I myself should be a castaway* (I Cor. 9:27).

4. The care of the body demands proper clothing, not only for protection and comfort, but for propriety and decency. The question of dress, therefore, not only concerns the welfare of the body, but becomes, also, an expression of the character and aesthetic nature of the individual. It is for this reason made a matter of apostolic injunction. *In like manner also, that women adorn themselves* [κοσμεῖν] *in modest apparel* [ἐν καταστολῇ κοσμίῳ, in apparel becoming], *with shamefacedness* [μετὰ αἰδοῦς with modesty or shamefacedness] *and sobriety* [σωφροσύνης, soundness of mind]; *not with broided hair,* [πλέγμασιν, wreaths]; *but (which becometh*

women professing godliness) [ὃ πρέπει γυναιξὶν ἐπαγ-γελλομέναις θεοσέβειαν which is becoming for women undertaking the worship of God] *with good works* (I Tim. 2:9, 10). The second text bearing upon this subject is from St. Peter. *Whose adorning* [κόσμος] *let it not be that outward adorning of plaiting the hair* [ἐμ-πλοκῆς τριχῶν braiding of hairs], *and of wearing of gold* [περιθέσεως χρυσίων placing around of golden chains], *or of putting on of apparel; but let it be the hidden man of the heart, in that which is not corruptible, even the ornament of a meek and quiet spirit, which is in the sight of God of great price* (I Peter 3:3, 4). The root word which is here translated adorn, is κοσμέω and signifies to adorn (Luke 21:5; Titus 2:10; I Peter 3:5); to decorate or garnish (Matt. 12:44; 23:29; Luke 11:25); to trim a lamp (Matt. 25:7). It is used in three forms in the texts above mentioned, κοσμεῖν to adorn; κοσμίῳ becoming; and κόσμος adorning. With these interpretations before us, we may draw from them the following scriptural principles, which though directed primarily to women, are applicable in spirit to all. (1) Women are to adorn themselves with becoming taste in all matters of dress. This implies dress appropriate to the age, the occasion and the station in life. Here adorning is not condemned but beautifully commended as becoming the profession of holiness. (2) The highest artistic taste is to be found in modesty and sound-mindedness. Proper dress should accentuate the beauty and modesty of the wearer. (3) Ornaments of gold or pearl or other costly array are prohibited as being out of harmony with the spirit of meekness and modesty, and as unnecessary to true Christian adornment. We may say then that the Christian should dress in a manner that will not attract undue attention, either by expensive apparel or eccentric plainness; and that will leave upon observers, the impression of the wearer as being of a meek and quiet spirit.

5. The body must be preserved holy. Holiness may be said to belong to the body in two particulars: (1) It is holy according to the use to which it is put by the

spirit. To render the body impure by devoting it to unholy service is sin. To give it over loosely to its own appetites is sin also, whether these be natural or abnormal. Hence St. Paul says, *For this is the will of God, even your sanctification, that ye should abstain from fornication: that every one of you should know how to possess his vessel in sanctification and honour* (I Thess. 4: 3, 4); and again, *Flee fornication. Every sin that a man doeth is without the body; but he that committeth fornication sinneth against his own body* (I Cor. 6: 18). (2) The body is holy in itself, but only in a secondary sense. Holiness as it applies to the body is wholeness or healthfulness. The body in this sense is holy, as it is healthy. It is true that it is now under the consequences of sin, and hence is called an earthen vessel. But this tenement of clay, is an important and necessary link in the process of redemption, and the body of each saint will, in the resurrection be *fashioned like unto his glorious body* (Phil. 3: 21). During this life, the body must be the object of sanctified care, and true holiness always gives superior attention to it. But the supreme reason for the sanctity of the body, lies in the fact that it is the temple of the Holy Spirit. It is God's dwelling place. *What? know ye not that your body is the temple of the Holy Ghost which is in you, which ye have of God, and ye are not your own? For ye are bought with a price: therefore glorify God in your body, and in your spirit, which are God's* (I Cor. 6: 19, 20). The sanctity of the body, therefore, not only excludes the grosser sins—*adultery, fornication, uncleanness* and *lasciviousness*, but also the sins of intemperance—*drunkenness, revellings, and such like* (Gal. 5: 19, 21). We may say that whatever tends to injure the body or to destroy its sanctity as the temple of the Holy Spirit, is forbidden by Christian teaching and practice.

The Intellectual, Emotional, Moral and Aesthetic Powers of the Mind. The term *Mind* as used in psychology is generally limited to the intellectual powers; but in theology, it commonly refers to the life of the soul in contradistinction to the physical life of the body. As the bodily manifestations depend upon the deeper physical life, so the manifestations of the soul, whether intellectual, emotional or volitional, depend upon the deeper life of the spirit. Our Lord indicates the necessity of developing all the powers of the mind, in His statement of the first commandment. He says, *Thou shalt love the Lord thy God with all thy heart, and with all thy soul, and with all thy mind, and with all thy strength: this is the first commandment* (Mark 12:30). Here the *heart* refers to man's inmost being—the seat of his affections, with the emphasis upon adherence to principle and purpose. The love of the *soul* refers to the glow of feeling which attaches to it, and comes from communion with God through the beauty of His word and works. It is the Spirit in creation, seen and recognized by the Spirit within. The *mind* has reference to the intellectual powers, through which love is understood and interpreted. By the term *strength* as here used, is meant the full devotion to God of all the powers of personality as thus developed. We may say, then, that the love of the heart is purifying, the love of the soul enriching, and the love of the mind interpretative. The first has as its object God as the supreme Good; the second, God as supreme Beauty manifested in order and harmony; and the third, God as the supreme Truth or Reality. The varying emphasis upon the different phases of love found in this commandment, give rise to those anomalies of Christian experience so frequently observed in the church. There are those whose goodness is unquestioned,

These several factors, which together make up religion, limit and sustain one another; for, as the feelings, for example, are indebted to the will for true profundity, so, on the other hand, energy of will depends on depth of emotion. But these all unite together, and the central point of union we call faith. Faith is a life of feeling, a life of the soul, in God (if we understand by soul the basis of personal life, wherein, through very fullness, all emotion is still vague); and no one is a believer, who has not felt himself to be in God and God in him. Faith knows what it believes, and in the light of its intuition it views the sacred truths in the midst of the agitations and turmoil of this world's life; and though its knowledge is not a comprehensive knowledge, although its intuition is not seeing face to face: although in clearness it is inferior to these forms of apprehension, yet in certitude it yields to neither; for the very essence of faith is, that it is firm, confident certitude respecting that which is not seen. Faith, finally, is the profoundest act of obedience and devotion.—MARTENSEN, *Christian Dogmatics*, p. 11.

but who, nevertheless, are unduly narrow in their range of vision. There are those with brilliant intellectual powers, who have but little depth of emotion; and there are those who are both good and inspirational, who have never thought their way through the doctrines which they so dearly love.

1. The development of the intellect is essential to a useful Christian life. The desire to know is human and God-given, and in Christian experience, this desire is greatly intensified. Ignorance is no part of holiness. We may note, (1) That Christ is the truth, and hence the followers of Christ become "disciples" or learners. One who does not love truth, whether that truth be of a scientific, philosophical, or other cultural nature, has little appreciation of the wonderful works of God which has not a burning desire for spiritual truth, may seriously were created through Christ the eternal Logos. One who question, also, any claim to the gift of the promised Comforter, who is expressly stated to be the Spirit of Truth. (2) It is the intellect and the understanding which give vision to the soul. Hence only with the broadening of the intellectual horizons, and a spiritual insight into

The doctrine, which we propose to advance on this somewhat difficult subject, may be regarded as implying the admission of two things: First, that the mind, in some important and true sense, is departmental; that it exists in three departments of the Intellect, the Sensibilities, and the Will; and that the emotional or emotive states constitute a distinct and important subordinate division in these departments: and Second, that the operations of the Holy Spirit on the human mind are various; that they may embrace the whole of these departments, reaching and controlling the whole mind; or that, under certain circumstances, they may stop either at the intellectual department or at the emotive division of the sensitive department, producing certain important results, but leaving others without being realized. We proceed then to remark, in the first place, that it is the office of the Holy Spirit to operate, on the appropriate occasions of such operations, upon the human intellect; and especially by guiding it in the perception of the truth. The mode of the Spirit's operation upon the intellectual part, as it is upon other parts of the mind, is in many respects mysterious; but the ordinary results of His influence is the communication of truth; that is to say, the soul, when it is thus operated upon, knows spiritually what it did not know before. And it may properly be added, that the knowledge which is thus communicated will vary, both in kind and degree, in accordance with the nature of the subject or facts to be illustrated, and with the special circumstances, whatever they may be, which render a divine communication necessary. But it is not ordinarily to be expected that the operation, of which we are now speaking, will stop with the intellect.—UPHAM, *Interior Life*, pp. 138, 139.

truth, can there be the enrichment of the affectional nature, and the deepening of the spiritual life. In the more immediate relation to the spiritual life, however, this grace is administered through the truth in answer to faith, and is effected by the Spirit. (3) The discriminations of the heart are frequently communicated to the mind also. Rev. T. K. Doty points out that "the doctrine of holiness, before a jargon, is now more reasonable and plain, because the processes of reasoning are carried on from the standpoint and impulse of another experience. In the same way, semi-worldly practices, under a little instruction, and many times without it, become obnoxious, and are discarded. It is also true that the mind, formerly misdirected by sinful affections, is now occasionally hindered by the purified affections, because the latter lean toward those things already supposed to be proper and right. Such suppositions measurably prevent freedom of investigation." (T. K. Doty, *Lessons in Holiness*, p. 86.) (4) The breadth of understanding also makes for stability of character. Indecisions and instability are frequently the consequences of short-sightedness. Wide horizons and far distances, therefore, are essential to a continuity of purpose. St. Paul recognized this truth when he wrote that *our light affliction, which is but for a moment, worketh for us a far more exceeding and eternal weight of glory; while we look not at the things which are seen, but at the things which are not seen: for the things which are seen are temporal; but the things which are not seen are eternal* (II Cor. 4: 17, 18). Self-culture, then, requires the development to the highest degree possible, of the power to see, to think, to remember and to construct. This calls for exact and wide observation, profound thought, and the under-

---

We have said that man owes it to himself that to the extent of his ability he seek the perfection of his powers; especially that he so educate his intellect that he be a man of extensive information, of sound judgment, and a correct reasoner; that he so discipline his volitioning faculty that he may always hold his appetites, desires, and affections under control, keeping their gratification within the limits prescribed by our Creator, never allowing their gratification to peril a greater good than it confers.—RAYMOND, *Systematic Theology*, III, p. 104.

standing of things in their systematic order and completeness.

2. The emotions are closely related to the intellect and the will. "By an original law of our mental nature," says Dr. Upham, "the perception of truth which is the result of an intellectual act, is ordinarily followed by an effect upon that portion of the mind which is usually designated as the emotional or emotive susceptibility; a part of the mind which as it is subsequent in the time of its action, is sometimes figuratively described as 'being back of the intellect'." An emotion, considered from the religious standpoint, may be defined as a movement,

INTELLECTUAL VICES

Dr. Gregory in his *Christian Ethics* calls attention to the necessity of avoiding ignorance, stupidity, heedlessness, rashness, credulity and skepticism, as being fatal to any true mission. These vices all have their root in a vincible ignorance, and the agent is therefore bound to avoid them. He enumerates the following:

1. Ignorance may appear as want of knowledge as to the nature and consequences of any action, or want of knowledge of the mission of duty or any of its parts. In whatever form, it is reproach to the agent and a hindrance to his mission.

2. Stupidity is often not so much a defect of nature as of moral energy; and when it has this last origin it becomes immoral. The man refuses to awake to observation, reflection and judgment; and his native powers, therefore, become weak. . . . . Such stupidity is immoral and vicious in proportion to the neglected endowments and the lost opportunities.

3. Heedlessness is rather occasional disregard of the nature and consequences of actions than perpetual forgetfulness. When the man allows himself to become engrossed with a few things, and these perhaps unimportant, and loses sight of the many and more important things which should properly be kept in view in deciding his action, the consequences of evil overtake him unexpectedly, and he fails in his undertakings. Such heedlessness is evidently immoral and guilty.

4. Rashness is the hardy daring of consequences seen or unseen. The man is so intent on a particular end, that though he may have abundant occasion to anticipate evil consequences, he determines to risk them, and recklessly persists in his course until the blow falls. Passion is usually the leader in this vice. It is a worse vice than stupidity or heedlessness, for the depravity it manifests is in the fullest sense wilful, and shows the reckless determination to override the moral judgment and gratifying passion at whatever cost or hazard.

5. Credulity and skepticism are opposite forms of the same vice. Want of the proper intellectual culture leaves the agent weak in judgment, and, having little grasp of principles and less power of making safe deductions from facts, he gives or withholds his faith according to his own wishes or the opinions of anyone who may have influence over him. If he be of an ardent temperament, he will be ready to believe anything, or he will be credulous; if he be of an opposite temperament, or have an ambition to be thought brilliant or original, he will be equally ready to doubt everything, or, he will be skeptical.

sensibility, or excitement of the heart which is manifested in consciousness. It is immediately related to the intellect, being the glow of truth consciously realized and felt. All holy emotions, therefore, involve a divine as well as a human movement, but the spiritual sensibilities do not necessarily preclude those which are purely human. The ebb and flow of the emotional life is sometimes an occasion of stumbling to young or inexperienced Christians. When, however, it is seen that

THE SPRINGS OF POWER

Power of action depends upon power of motive, and, therefore, upon power of feeling. The feelings are as important and worthy of a part of man as the intellect or will. From the very nature of the human soul, there can be no powerful and persistent will in executing the mission of life unless there be powerful and sustained feeling. It is, therefore, man's duty to aim to develop all the natural affections and desires, in their proper proportion and harmony, in order that he may become a man with the full dignity of manhood, and may have a powerful motive-basis for his life. It is, therefore, man's duty to avoid all repression, perversion, or disproportionate development of the feelings. Insensibility and passion are alike immoral and vicious.

Insensibility holds the same relation to the feelings which stupidity holds to the intellect. It arises in a similar way, from the repression of feelings; so that the genesis already given of stupidity will apply to it. When it becomes general, it is one of the most deadening of vices. When it is confirmed and wilful, it becomes obduracy, and must appear both repulsive and guilty to every right-thinking being, and that whether it takes the form of insensibility to man's own highest interests and destiny, or to the claims of his fellows for affection and sympathy, or to God's claims.

Passion arises from the inordinate and ungoverned action of the affections and desires, as developed out of harmony and proportion, and made the end of action rather than its spring. When passion has completed its development, reason and will become its slaves, and the man loses his truest manhood.

It is obvious that under a wrong and evil culture each of the springs of action furnishes the germ of some passion. First, from Lower Feelings. In the undue development of the appetites and animal sensibilities arises the milder vice of sentimentality, which leads its victim to weep with equal ease over the agonies of a pet canary and a victim of the Inquisition; together with all those base and brutal vices of gluttony, intemperance, sensuality, which are usually designated by passion in its base sense. Second, from the Higher Feelings. In the proper development of the higher feelings there arises, from the side of the affections, pride, or that inordinate self-esteem which shows itself in the disposition to overrate what one possesses, and in haughtiness and loftiness of manners; egotism, which leads one to make himself prominent; vanity, which is allied to pride, egotism and conceit, self-praise and self-commendation, and which is manifested in a desire to attract notice and gain admiration in a small way, and which would, therefore, be ridiculed as weak if it were not condemned as immoral; and all other forms of selfishness — from the side of the desires — aimless restlessness, irrational curiosity, unbridled ambition, and base covetousness, which are all easily understood, and which are all condemned by mankind as vicious.—GREGORY, *Christian Ethics*, pp. 206, 207.

emotion depends upon the perception of new truth, or upon familiar truths seen in new aspects, the secret of stability and faith will have been learned. Truth seen and realized through the Spirit, brings the glow of emotion; but that same truth, even though it be fully incorporated in the spiritual life of the individual, may become familiar and hence lose its emotional glow. The essential thing, then, in the development of the emotional life is to search the Word for new truth, or to plead the Spirit's guidance into the deeper aspects of truths already known. Feeling apart from truth leads into dangerous fanaticism; truth which gives rise to strong emotion becomes a supreme power in the life of holiness. The man who moves others is the man who is himself moved upon by the truth. To act from principle is worthy, but to act from principle on fire, is the high privilege of every New Testament Christian. The emotional aspects of truth, however, are not lost when the conscious glow subsides. These have been built into the life—deeper down than temporary feeling, and as such give dominancy to motive, purpose and character. Under the New Testament dispensation, the whole process is lifted by the Spirit into what St. Paul calls, a being *changed into the same image from glory to glory* (II Cor. 3:18). "But the transfiguring glory, which changes the soul more fully into the divine image, is the work resulting from the manifestation in us of the divine

When the Lord sanctifies a soul, that soul knows what the conscious indwelling glory is, but it knows very little of what the outworkings of that glory are, in being and in life. Glory as a joy, as a flame kindling and burning in every sentiment and emotion is glorious, but glory in being, in character, in life is far more glorious. When Moses saw the flame in the bush and heard God talk to him, and removed his shoes because the place whereon he stood was holy ground, he was surely moved by emotions which he had never before felt, and a transfiguring glory came into his soul. But afterward on the Mount, the fire so continuously burned in him and about him that it permeated every part of his being. It was something more than emotion for he "wist not that his face shone." Out beyond emotion, there was a dominancy of divine glory—more than will, purpose, emotion, character. Somewhat like unto this there is a glory that transforms the affections, directs the purpose and strengthens the will. It is enclosed, so to speak, in a rough nonconducting, translucent manhood, but the transforming by the Spirit of God goes on and on, as we gaze into the glory of God as revealed in the face of Jesus Christ, in the mirror of His word.—DR. P. F. BRESEE, *Sermons*, "The Transferred Image," p. 149.

glory—more and more marvelous, ever more and more complete—and yet seemingly, more and more incomplete, because of the added revelation of our possibilities and privileges in Christ Jesus. There is no top to the divine heights; there is no shore to the ocean of God's perfections. The soul bathes and drinks, and drinks and bathes, and says, 'I know Him better and love Him more forever and forever and, yet, I stand awe inspired in the presence of the infinite glory, which, though I come nigh, is ever unapproachable; though I bathe my soul in it and am filled yet its measureless heights and depths and length and breadths overwhelm me.' "—Dr. P. F. Bresee, Sermon: The Transferred Image.

3. The moral nature requires development. Here we refer primarily to the discipline of the will with its obligation and responsibility. It is only by choices that moral character is formed, and conduct is wholly dependent upon moral character. Hence the impulses and volitions of the soul must be brought under the control of the will and subordinated to the highest good. Two things are involved—the adoption of correct moral standards, and the discipline of the will. (1) Correct moral standards are derived ultimately from the Word of God, and are communicated to the individual by means of the social structure. They may be learned from teachers, from a study of the Scriptures or other works bearing upon this subject, from the observance of correct social practices, from the examples of good men, and in some sense from native intuition. But they must be learned — they cannot be had otherwise. It is the duty of each individual, therefore, to cultivate the highest standards of ethical life, and to conscientious-

Spiritual emotions are expressed like all others. Their channels are natural, rather than supernatural. A lack of thoughtfulness regarding this truth has greatly hindered the work of salvation at many times and places. The multitude count it as a sin to appear spiritually moved, especially in some ways, and to any great degree. But, really, it may sometimes be sinful not to be so. If ordinary pleasures and pains be allowed to manifest themselves in the voice, and by various physical movements, there is no sound reason why purely spiritual pleasures and pains may not have the same privileges. The many attacks on these religious manifestations are really on religion itself. They are attempts to cramp it into frozen and unyielding forms that soon leave it empty and void.—T. K. DOTY, Lessons in Holiness, p. 95.

ly observe every rule of moral obligation. (2) The discipline of the will is effected only through controlled choices. Man learns to do by doing, and he gains facility only in constancy of action. Duty at first costs self-denial, and is determined only by severe conflict. There must be vigorous effort and eternal vigilance. However, with each duty done, new strength is acquired according to the law of habit, and the pathway of duty becomes easier and brighter. It is as the path of the just *that shineth more and more unto the perfect day* (Prov. 4:18). The province of discipline, whether by the self or by others, is exceedingly important. Without it there can never be developed that strength of purpose and ruggedness of character which becomes the true soldier of the cross. Too often through misguided

VICES CONNECTED WITH THE WILL

The vices more immediately connected with the will as distinguished from the intellect or emotions are servility and independence, fickleness and obstinacy.

Servility includes not only the assent to be a slave and obey a master who regards only his own ends, but all mean and cringing submission or fawning sycophancy. It includes the blind surrender of the will to any finite and fallible leader whatever, whether in fashion, business, politics, morals or religion; and the equally blind and irrational surrender of the will to perverse public sentiment in any of its aspects. It may manifest itself in hypocrisy, when the man does not dare openly to assert his freedom of opinion or action. It cringes to escape harm, flatters to win favor, makes a show of humility to procure praise, and indulges in false disparagement to gain compliments. It shows itself in general trimming and time-serving, in which the man sacrifices his manhood and becomes the mere plaything of circumstances. In all its forms and manifestations, servility must be acknowledged at once base and immoral.

Independence, in its immoral form, is the opposite of servility. It is obvious that there is an independence, which consists in proper self-assertion, and which is praiseworthy and virtuous. The improper and vicious independence consists in unnecessary and improper self-assertion, as against rightful authority or just law, or where it involves a culpable disregard for the opinions or feelings of others. A weakness, no less immoral than that exhibited in servility, may be shown in "speaking one's mind" on all occasions, without reference to timeliness of the utterance.

Fickleness and obstinacy are vices of opposite characters. In the former, the will changes constantly, without reference to any proper reasons or motives; in the latter the will remains fixedly the same, without any regard to any proper reasons or motives. Both are irrational. Both are likewise immoral, as it is man's duty to give heed to all consideration fitted to influence a rational being. Both prevent the accomplishment of man's mission; the one keeping him from turning his energies in any one direction long enough to accomplish anything, and the other turning them persistently in some wrong direction.—GREGORY, *Christian Ethics*, pp. 207, 208.

love, the youth are shielded from the responsibility of
their own choices, and, therefore, suffer from arrested
development. This is manifested not only in a lack of
self-discipline, but also in a failure to appreciate the just
obligations they owe to others. For this reason we are
exhorted to despise not the chastening of the Lord, nor
faint when we are rebuked of Him, *For whom the Lord
loveth he chasteneth, and scourgeth every son whom he
receiveth. . . . . Now no chastening for the present seem-
eth to be joyous, but grievous: nevertheless afterward
it yieldeth the peaceable fruit of righteousness unto
them which are exercised thereby* (Heb. 12: 6, 11).

4. Man has an aesthetical nature also, which requires cultivation. The various phases of personality,
such as the intellect, the sensibilities and the will, must
not only be given attention, but Christian character demands that these be developed in such proportions as to

The law of habit is one of the most powerful principles connected
with man's culture. First, it requires that the act, or exercise of the
power be repeated at regular and moderate intervals. Second, this
repetition results in inclination or tendency to the act repeated, although
at the outset it may be disagreeable and even repulsive. Third, this
tendency increases in power with the repetition of the act, and gives
increasing pleasure to him who complies with it, and growing pain to
him who resists it. Fourth, when the tendency is fully confirmed, the
agent comes at last to perform the accustomed act with no conscious
effort. His being has acquired a set in that accustomed direction of
action, which renders it certain that he will continue to perform the
act with ease and power, without even thinking of it.—GREGORY, *Christian Ethics*, p. 203.

The power of habit when perverted, becomes a destructive force.
In explanation of this, Dr. Bowen says, "The process is a simple one,
being merely a transference of the affections from the end to the means.
By the association of ideas that which was at first loved or practiced
only as an instrument becomes the leading idea and the chief object
of pursuit. Thus, in the downward course, money, at first desired only
as a means of gratifying the appetites, or of answering some higher
ends, becomes itself an appetite and passion, and the vicious habit of
avarice is formed. And so, in our upward progress, the honesty which
was at first practiced only because it was the best policy, the worship
of God which was first paid only as the price of heaven, becomes at
last the unbought and unselfish homage of the soul to uprightness,
holiness and truth."—BOWEN, *Metaphysics and Ethics*, p. 308.

Dr. Gregory in speaking of the law of habit says, "This beneficent
arrangement furnishes one of the greatest encouragements to parents
and instructors of the young. By firmly and prudently holding the
young to prescribed tasks and courses of conduct, which may at first
be irksome, but which are necessary and right, the proper habits are
formed; and what is done at first unwillingly and only from the
pressure of a superior will, comes to be done gladly and for its own
sake."—GREGORY, *Christian Ethics*, p. 203.

result in a balanced, harmonious and well-integrated personality. For this the psalmist prayed when he said, *Teach me thy way, O Lord; I will walk in thy truth: unite my heart to fear thy name* (Psalms 86: 11). The world not only has an aspect which we call the true, but also that which we call the beautiful. (Cf. *Christian Theology*, I, pp. 307, 308.) God reveals Himself through the latter as well as the former. *Strength and beauty are in his sanctuary,* and we are commanded to *worship the Lord in the beauty of holiness* (Psalms 96: 6, 9). The beautiful and the sublime, whether in nature or the works of art, are designed of God to elevate and ennoble the soul. Insensibility, therefore, to the beautiful is indicative of incomplete manhood, and it is the Christian's duty to avoid any repression or perversion in the development of his aesthetic nature. Instead, he is to cultivate a taste which is quick to discern beauty, correct in the judgment of it, and catholic in the sense of recognizing and appreciating beauty wherever found.

The Development of the Spiritual Life. The Scriptures abound with commands, instructions, injunctions

One's religious views may be held at second hand, that is, in a philosophical or aesthetic way. And just because religious perception deals with an objective element, that of thought and fancy, it may be sundered from its vital source in the affections, and be exercised in a merely aesthetic or philosophic way, independent of personal faith. Thus there are philosophers, poets, painters, and sculptors, who have represented Christian ideas with great plastic power, yet without themselves having a religious possession of those ideas; being brought into relation to them only through the medium of thought and fancy. Thus, too, a large proportion of men of the present time hold religious views only in an aesthetic way, or merely make them the subject of refined reflection; hold them only at second hand, because they know nothing of the personal feelings and the determinations of conscience which correspond to them; because, in other words, their religious knowledge does not spring from their standing in right religious relations. The adoption of religious notions, nay, even of a comprehensive religious view of life, is, therefore, by no means an infallible proof that a man is himself religious. The latter is the case only when the religious views are rooted in a corresponding inward state of the mind and heart; when the man feels himself in conscience bound to these views; in short, when he believes them. And even though a man, with the help of Christian views could achieve wonders in art and science, could prophesy, and cast out devils, yet Christ will not acknowledge him unless he himself stands in right personal relations to these views. It is especially necessary at the present time to call attention to this double manner in which religious notions may be entertained.—MARTENSEN, *Christian Dogmatics*, p. 10.

and exhortations concerning the development of the spiritual life. Three aspects of this development may be presented. (1) St. Peter closes his second epistle with the words, *But grow in grace, and in the knowledge of our Lord and Saviour Jesus Christ* (II Peter 3:18); and he marks out the stages of this progress as follows: *Giving all diligence, add to your faith virtue; and to virtue knowledge; and to knowledge temperance; and to temperance patience; and to patience godliness; and to godliness brotherly kindness; and to brotherly kindness charity. For if these things be in you, and abound, they make you that ye shall neither be barren nor unfruitful in the knowledge of our Lord Jesus Christ* (II Peter 1:5-8). Here the apostle makes all the Christian virtues to root in faith, and to find their perfect fruitage in charity or divine love. (2) St. James represents the *Chokmah* or Wisdom Literature of the New Testament and, therefore, makes spiritual development to spring from the wisdom of the Word. As the *doxa* or glory of God represents His nature and attributes as belonging to Himself, and yet in thought distinguishable from Himself; so the *chokmah* or wisdom of God, while dis-

Rev. J. A. Wood in his work entitled *Perfect Love* cites the following as evidences of advancement in holiness: (1) An increasing comfort and delight in the holy Scriptures. (2) An increasing interest in prayer, and an increasing spirit of prayer. (3) An increasing desire for the holiness of others. (4) A more heart-searching sense of the value of time. (5) Less desire to hear, see, and know for mere curiosity. (6) a growing inclination against magnifying the faults and weaknesses of others, when obliged to speak of their characters. (7) A greater readiness to speak freely to those who do not enjoy religion, and to backward professors of religion. (8) More disposition to glory in reproach for Christ's sake, and suffer, if need be, for Him. (9) An increasing tenderness of conscience, and being more scrupulously conscientious. (10) Less affected by changes of place and circumstances. (11) A sweeter enjoyment of the holy Sabbath, and the services of the sanctuary. (12) An increasing love for the searching means of grace. —WOOD, *Perfect Love*, pp. 311, 312.

Mr. Wesley mentions the following as hindering growth in holiness, in that they "grieve the Holy Spirit of God." (1) By such conversation as is not profitable, not to the use of edifying, not apt to minister grace to the hearers. (2) By relapsing into bitterness or want of kindness. (3) By wrath, lasting displeasure, or want of tender-heartedness. (4) By anger, however soon it is over; want of instantly forgiving one another. (5) By clamor or brawling, loud, harsh, rough speaking. (6) By evil speaking, whispering, talebearing; needlessly mentioning the fault of an absent person, though in ever so soft a manner.— WESLEY, *Plain Account of Christian Perfection*. p. 80.

tinguishable in thought from the nature of man, is yet such an impartation of the divine nature as works in him, holiness of heart and life. Hence we read that *the wsidom that is from above is first pure, then peaceable, gentle, and easy to be intreated, full of mercy and good fruits, without partiality, and without hypocrisy* (James 3:17). This wisdom is received through faith, and herein is the connection between the thought of St. James and that of St. Peter; it is administered by the Spirit, and this leads us to the position of St. Paul. (3) In the thought of St. Paul, the development of the spiritual life is accomplished through co-operation with the Spirit of God. *This I say then, Walk in the Spirit, and ye shall not fulfil the lust of the flesh. . . . . But if ye be led of the Spirit, ye are not under the law* (Gal. 5:16, 18). It is through the indwelling presence of the Spirit, therefore, that the soul is not only preserved in holiness, but is led into the deeper unfolding of grace and truth. It is for this reason the apostle prays that we *may be able to comprehend with all saints what is the breadth, and length, and depth, and height; and to know the love of Christ, which passeth knowledge, that ye might be filled with all the fulness of God* (Eph. 3:18, 19).

The literature of devotion which makes the greatest and most direct contribution to the spiritual life has been built up from the rich spiritual experiences of the saints in all ages. The Scriptures are, of course, the only inspired and authoritative literature on this subject; and even within the Scriptures themselves, the Psalms are usually regarded as belonging specifically to the devotional field. Here is a record of God's dealings with the souls of men, given to the church as an inspired language, by means of which, men have been enabled to voice the deepest emotions and highest aspirations of their souls. But as belonging properly to the field of devotion, we may note also, the spiritual flights of the ancient prophets, the gracious words which fell from the lips of our Lord himself, and the inspired utterances of His holy apostles—all of these enable the souls of men to enter more deeply into communion with their Lord through the Spirit. Outside the Scriptures, also, there has been built up a wide field of devotional literature, likewise born from the deep and rich experiences of men who have entered deeply into the knowledge of God. So important is this field that we give below a few of the more commonly known and accepted works in the devotional field.

Among the devotional writers, whose works have been generally accepted throughout the church, may be mentioned the following: Thomas a Kempis, *The Imitation of Christ; Theologica Germanica*, first discovered and published by Martin Luther; Francis de Sales, *Defence of the Standard of the Cross*, and *An Introduction to the Devout Life*. Among the Quietists we may mention, Molinos, *Spiritual Guide;* Madame Guyon, *Method of Prayer;* and Fenelon, *Maxims of the Saints*. Other writings more strictly Protestant are Bunyan, *Grace Abounding*, and *Pilgrim's Progress;* Bishop Andrewes, *Private Devotions;* Bishop Jeremy Taylor, *Holy Living* (1650) *and Holy Dying* (1651); Samuel Rutherford, *Letters*. Among the Friends are the writings of George Fox, Robert Barclay, William Penn and John Woolman. Following these we have William Law, the non-jurist, whose *Christian Perfection* (1726) was abridged by John Wesley (1740); also his *Serious Call* (1729); *The Spirit of Prayer* (1750) and *The Spirit of Love* (1754). Among the Methodists we have Wesley, *Journal; Sermons;* and especially his *Plain Account of Christian Perfection*. We may mention, also, as of exceptional devotional value, *The Journal of Hester Ann Rogers;* the *Life of William Bramwell; Memoirs of Carvosso*, and Fletcher's *Appeal*. Nothing is more conducive to the devotional life than the prayerful perusal of the writings of such eminently pious men as those mentioned above. Because of their peculiar value, we give in the following notes, the *Spiritual Reflections* of Mr. Wesley, and the *Religious Maxims* of Dr. Thomas C. Upham. The serious and prayerful perusal of these will prove of great value to the spiritual life.

SPIRITUAL REFLECTIONS

Mr. Wesley, in his *A Plain Account of Christian Perfection*, gives us the following spiritual reflections, which he recommends for deep and frequent consideration. The full text will be found on pp. 95ff in the work mentioned above.

(1) The sea is an excellent figure of the fullness of God, and that of the blessed Spirit. For as the rivers all return into the sea; so the bodies, the souls, and the good works of the righteous, return into God, to live there in His eternal repose.

The bottom of the soul may be in repose, even while we are in outward troubles; just as the bottom of the sea is calm, while the surface is strongly agitated.

The best helps to growth in grace are the ill-usage, the affronts, and the losses which befall us. We should receive them with all thankfulness, as preferable to all others were it only on this account, that our will has no part therein.

The readiest way to escape from our sufferings is to be willing they should endure as long as God pleases.

One of the greatest evidences of God's love to those that love Him is to send them afflictions, with grace to bear them.

(2) True resignation consists in a thorough conformity to the whole will of God, who wills and does all (excepting sin) which comes to pass in the world. In order to this we have only to embrace all events, good and bad, as His will.

We ought quietly to suffer whatever befalls us, to bear the defects of others and our own, to confess them to God in secret prayer, or with groans which cannot be uttered; but never to speak a sharp or peevish word, nor to murmur or repine but thoroughly willing that God should treat you in the manner that pleases Him.

We are to bear with those we cannot amend, and to be content with offering them to God. This is true resignation. And since He has borne our infirmities, we may well bear those of each other for His sake.

(3) There is no love of God without patience, and no patience without lowliness and sweetness of spirit.

Humility and patience are the surest proofs of the increase of love.

True humility is a kind of self-annihilation, and this is the center of all virtues.

(4) The bearing men, and suffering evils in meekness and silence, is the sum of a Christian life.

God is the first object of our love: its next office is to bear the defects of others. And we should begin the practice of this amidst our own household.

We should chiefly exercise our love toward them who most shock either our way of thinking, or our temper, or our knowledge, or the desire we have that others should be as virtuous as we wish ourselves to be.

(5) God hardly gives His Spirit even to those whom He has established in grace, if they do not pray for it on all occasions, not only once, but many times.

On every occasion of uneasiness, we should retire to prayer, that we may give place to the grace and light of God, and then form our resolutions, without being in any pain about what success they may have.

In the greatest temptations, a single look to Christ, and the barely pronouncing His name, suffices to overcome the wicked one, so it be done with confidence and calmness of spirit.

All that a Christian does, even in eating and sleeping, is prayer, when it is done in simplicity, according to the order of God, without either adding to or diminishing from it by his own choice.

Prayer continues in the desire of the heart, though the understanding be employed on outward things.

In souls filled with love, the desire to please God is a continual prayer.

(6) It is scarcely conceivable how straight the way is wherein God leads them that follow Him; and how dependent on Him we must be, unless we are wanting in our faithfulness to Him.

We ought to be in the church as the saints are in heaven, and in the house as the holiest men are in the church; doing our work in the house as we pray in the church; worshiping God from the ground of the heart.

We should be continually laboring to cut off all the useless things that surround us: and God usually retrenches the superfluities of our souls in the same proportion as we do those of our bodies.

We scarce conceive how easy it is to rob God of His due, in our friendship with the most virtuous persons, until they are torn from us by death. But if this loss produce lasting sorrow that is a clear proof that we had before two treasures, between which we divided our heart.

(7) If after having renounced all, we do not watch incessantly, and beseech God to accompany our vigilance with His, we shall again be entangled and overcome.

It is good to renew ourselves from time to time, by closely examining the state of our souls, as if we had never done it before; for nothing tends more to the full assurance of faith, than to keep ourselves by this means in humility, and the exercise of all good works.

To continual watchfulness and prayer ought to be added continual employment. For grace fills a vacuum as well as nature; and the devil fills whatever God does not fill.

(8) One of the principal rules of religion is, to lose no occasion of serving God. And since He is invisible to our eyes, we are to serve Him in our neighbor; which He receives as if done to Himself in person, standing visibly before us.

A constant attention to the work which God entrusts us with is a mark of solid piety.

Charity cannot be practiced right, unless, first, we exercise it the moment God gives the occasion; and second, retire the instant after to offer it to God by humble thanksgiving.—JOHN WESLEY, *Plain Account of Christian Perfection*, pp. 95-102.

RELIGIOUS MAXIMS

The following have been selected from the "Religious Maxims" of Dr. Thomas C. Upham found in his work entitled *Principles of the Interior Life*. Their perusal and observance will contribute much to the devotional life of those who seek a closer fellowship with God.

I.

Think much, and pray much, and let your words be few, and uttered with seriousness and deliberation, as in God's presence. And yet regard may be had to times and seasons. We may innocently act the child with children, which in the presence of grown persons would have the appearance of thoughtlessness and levity; and may perhaps at times express our gratitude to God, and our holy joys, with an increased degree of freedom and vivacity, especially in the company of those who bear the same image, and who know what it is to rejoice in the Holy Ghost.

II.

Be silent when blamed and reproached unjustly, and under such circumstances that the reproachful and injurious person will be likely, from the influence of his own reflections, to discover his error and wrong speedily. Listen not to the suggestions of nature, which would prompt a hasty reply; but receive the injurious treatment with humility and calmness; and He in whose name you thus suffer will reward you with inward consolation, while he sends the sharp arrow of conviction into the heart of your adversary.

III.

In whatever you are called upon to do, endeavor to maintain a calm, collected and prayerful state of mind. Self-recollection is of great importance. "It is good for a man to wait quietly for the salvation of the Lord." He who is in what may be called a spiritual hurry, or rather who runs without having evidence of being spiritually sent, makes haste to no purpose.

IV.

Seek holiness rather than consolation. Not that consolation is to be despised, or thought lightly of; but solid and permanent consolation is the result rather than the forerunner of holiness, therefore he who seeks consolation as a distinct and independent object will miss it. Seek and possess holiness, and consolation (not perhaps, often in the form of ecstatic and rapturous joys, but rather of solid and delightful peace) will follow as assuredly as warmth follows the dispensation of the rays of the sun. He who is holy must be happy.

V.

Be not disturbed because the eye of the world is constantly and earnestly fixed upon you, to detect your errors and to rejoice in your halting. But rather regard this state of things, trying as it may be, as one of the safeguards which a kind Father has placed around you, to keep alive in your own bosom an antagonistic spirit of watchfulness, and to prevent those very mistakes and transgressions which your enemies eagerly anticipate.

VI.

Do not think it strange when troubles and persecutions come upon you. Rather receive them quietly and thankfully, as coming from a Father's hand. Yea, happy are ye, if, in the exercise of faith, you can look above the earthly instrumentality, above the selfishness and malice of men, to Him who has permitted them for your good. Thus persecuted they the Saviour and the prophets.

VII.

"Be ye angry and sin not." The life of our Saviour, as well as the precepts of the apostles, clearly teaches us that there may be occasions on which we may have feelings of displeasure, and even of anger, without sin. Sin does not necessarily attach to anger, considered in its nature, but in its degree. Nevertheless, anger seldom exists in fact, without becoming in its measure inordinate and excessive. Hence it is important to watch against it, lest we be led into transgression. Make it a rule, therefore, never to give any outward expressions to angry feelings (a course which will operate as a powerful check upon their excessive action), until you have made them the subject of reflection and prayer. And thus you may hope to be kept.

VIII.

In the agitations of the present life, beset and perplexed as we are with troubles, how natural it is to seek earnestly some place of rest. And hence it is that we so often reveal our cares and perplexities to our fellowmen, and seek comfort and support from that source. But the sanctified soul, having experienced the uncertainties of all human aids, turns instinctively to the great God; and hiding itself in the presence and protection of the divine existence, it reposes there, as in a strong tower which no enemies can conquer, and as on an ever-

(III) Social Ethics: or the Duties We Owe to Others

As Christ summed up the first table of the law in one broad and comprehensive duty of love to God, so also, He did likewise with the second table in an equally comprehensive duty of love to man. To set the matter in proper relation to that which precedes it, we shall repeat the entire text. Jesus said unto him, *Thou shalt*

lasting rock which no flood can wash away. It knows the instructive import of that sublime exclamation of the psalmist, "My soul, wait thou only upon God; for my expectation is from him" (Psalms 62:5).

IX.

Speak not often of your own actions, nor even, when it can be properly avoided, make allusions to yourself, as an agent in transactions which are calculated to attract notice. We do not suppose, as some may be inclined to do, that frequent speaking of our actions is necessarily a proof, although it may furnish a presumption of inordinate self-love or vanity; but it cannot be denied that by such a course we expose ourselves to temptations and dangers in that direction. It is much safer, and is certainly much more profitable, to speak of what has been done for us and wrought in us—to speak, for instance, of ourselves as the recipients of the goodness of God—than to speak of what we ourselves have done. But even here, also, although it may often be an imperative duty, there is need of deliberation and caution.

X.

The divine life, which in every stage of its existence depends upon the presence of the Spirit of God, places a high estimate on mental tranquility. It is no new thing to remark that the Holy Spirit has no congeniality with and no pleasure in the soul where strife and clamor have taken possession. If, therefore, we would have the Holy Spirit with us always, we must avoid and flee, with all the intensity of our being, all inordinate coveting, all envying, malice and evil speaking, all impatience, jealousy and anger. Of such a heart, and such only, which is calm as well as pure, partaking something of the self-collected and sublime tranquillity of the Divine Mind, can it be said, in the truest and highest sense, that it is a temple fitted for the indwelling of the Holy Ghost.

THE TEN COMMANDMENTS OF THE NEW TESTAMENT

The Ten Commandments of the Old Testament as re-enacted in the New Testament have been tabulated by Rev. R. Crittenden as follows:

I. And Jesus answered him, The first of all the commandments is, Hear, O Israel; the Lord our God is one Lord (Mark 12:29).

II. For they themselves shew of us what manner of entering in we had unto you, and how ye turned to God from idols to serve the living and true God (I Thess. 1:9).

III. But I say unto you, Swear not at all (Matt. 5:34).

IV. And he said unto them, The sabbath was made for man, and not man for the sabbath (Mark 2:27).

V. Honour thy father and thy mother (Matt. 19:19).

VI. Thou shalt do no murder (Matt. 19:18).

VII. Thou shalt not commit adultery (Matt. 19:18).

VIII. Thou shalt not steal (Matt. 19:18).

IX. Thou shalt not bear false witness (Matt. 19:18).

X. And he said unto them, Take heed, and beware of covetousness (Luke 12:15).

love the Lord thy God with all thy heart, and with all thy soul, and with all thy mind. This is the first and great commandment. And the second is like unto it, Thou shalt love thy neighbour as thyself. On these two commandments hang all the law and the prophets (Matt. 22: 37-40). The First of the two Commandments has already been considered, and the second now demands our attention. We may be allowed also, to again call attention to the fact that in the Christian system, the love which forms the basis of duty to others, is not merely the affection of the natural heart alone, but that love which is shed abroad in the heart by the Holy Spirit, and which is perfected only as the heart is purified from sin. It is not pretended, however, that we are bound to love all men alike, irrespective of their character, or regardless of the relation which we sustain to them. This love, therefore, needs careful analysis. (1) We are required to love all men with the love of good will. We can wish no ill to any man, and must use all reasonable effort to promote the feeling of good will toward all our fellow creatures. (2) We are to love the unfortunate and distressed with the love of pity. This duty is enforced by our Lord in His description of the judgment (Matt. 25: 35-46); and specifically by St. Paul in the text: *Therefore if thine enemy hunger, feed him; if he thirst, give him drink: for in so doing thou shalt heap coals of fire on his head* (Rom. 12: 20). (3) We are to love good people with the love of complacency. This in its highest sense is Christian love, and can be felt toward none except such as are true Christians. We shall not transcend the teachings of Christ if we say that Christians are under obligations to each other, which do not bind them to other men. This obligation has its source in the "new Commandment" which Christ gave to His disciples. *A new commandment I give unto you, That ye love one another: as I have loved you, that ye also love one another* (John 13: 34). *By this shall all men know that ye are my disciples* (John 13: 35). The Commandment, *Thou shalt love thy neighbour as thyself* is found in the Old Testament (Lev. 19: 18); but this is to be distinguished from the new Commandment, in that the former was based on the love of benevolence, the latter on the love of complacency. The old Commandment required love to man as man; the new Commandment requires the love of character, or the love of a Christian as a Christian. Further still, the old Commandment was based upon the love of man for man as a creature of God; the love of the new Commandment is based upon the example of Jesus Christ as the Redeemer. The application of the law of love is stated in the Golden Rule. Here again Christ is His own best interpreter. He says, *All things whatsoever ye would that men should do to you, do ye even so to them: for this is the law and the prophets* (Matt. 7:12). The law of equal love therefore requires that a man treat every other as he himself would like to be treated in the same circumstances.

Violations of Brotherly Love. In this connection, St. Paul gives attention to those emotions, passions and practices which violate both in spirit and in conduct, the universal law of love. He mentions the following:

1. First of all, he calls attention to *anger*, which is a strong emotion of displeasure, excited either by a real or supposed injury; *wrath*, or deep and violent anger; and *hatred*—a strong aversion or abhorrence, coupled with ill will. These emotions or passions may or may not be expressed. They are not necessarily wrong in

This law of equal love to men is to be interpreted in consistency with all our manifest personal and domestic duties. Any other interpretation of it is wrong. In this view the subject is plain. Are you a husband? treat your wife as you would like to be treated if you were a wife. Are you a wife? treat your husband as you would like to be treated if you were a husband. Are you a parent? treat your child as you would like to be treated were you a child. Are you a child? treat your parents as you would like to be treated were you a parent. Are you a brother or sister? treat your brother or sister as you would like to have them treat you under like circumstances. Are you a ruler? treat your subjects as you would like to be treated were you in their place and they in yours. Are you a fellow citizen? treat your fellow citizens as you would like to have them treat you. Does a stranger cross your path? treat him as you would like to be treated were you a stranger. Do you find a fellow being in distress? treat him just as you would like to be treated were you in distress. In all this, the thing supposed is what you would require of your fellow being in perfect honesty.—Lee, *Elements of Theology*, p. 381.

themselves, but become so when they violate the law of love. Thus it is written that *God is angry with the wicked every day* (Psalms 7:11); and again, *The fear of the Lord is to hate evil* (Prov. 8:13). *Christ looked round about on them with anger, being grieved for the hardness of their hearts* (Mark 3:5). St. John speaks also of *the wrath of the Lamb,* and *of the great day of his wrath* (Rev. 6:16, 17). It is clear, therefore, that these emotions become evil, only as they are so misdirected and uncontrolled as to contravene the law of love. For this reason, when they are mentioned in the Scriptures it is generally in connection with other and more malevolent passions. Thus St. Paul says, *Let all bitterness, and wrath, and anger, and clamour be put away from you with all malice* (Eph. 4:31). Here anger and wrath are associated with bitterness and clamor. St. John tells us that *whosoever hateth his brother is a murderer* (I John 3:15); and our Lord himself declares that *whosoever is angry with his brother without a cause shall be in danger of the judgment* (Matt. 5:22).

2. Closely associated with the foregoing are *malice* (a malignant design of evil); *variance* (quarrels); *emulations* (jealousies); *wrath* (resentments); and *strife* (brawlings or altercations). These when brought into relation with civil government lead to sedition, which may be defined as conduct tending toward treason, but without the overt act; that is, discontent with, or resistance to, properly constituted government. In their application to the Church, they give rise to *heresies* or sects. The term signifies opinion as opposed to authorized doctrinal standards, especially when used to promote schism or divisions. Hence St. Paul says, *A man that is an heretick after the first and second admonition*

Holy wrath in human personality is an expression of the soul in its attitude toward wrong or supposed wrong. While it is somewhat mixed with various other emotions and may be faulty in the holiest of men because of its finite relationships, yet it is still a semblance to the infinite wrath of God in respect to its orderly procedure and control. As divine wrath or anger is majestic in its harmony with truth, and its expression is sanctioned by the entirety of every divine attribute, so also, holy anger in sanctified personality is a principle of life and expression which does not unbalance reason nor bring the various parts of selfhood into confusion.—PAUL S. HILL.

reject; knowing that he that is such is subverted, and sinneth, being condemned of himself (Titus 3:10, 11).

3. Growing out of the preceding, but with a more objective emphasis, are those violations of brotherly love which are occasioned by a lack of strict adherence to truth in conversation. Here may be mentioned: (1) All *censoriousness* and *evil speaking.* St. Paul commands that *all evil speaking, be put away* (Eph. 4:31); and St. James exhorts the brethren to *Speak not evil one of another* (James 4:11). Dr. Wakefield says of evil speaking, "It consists in relating that which is im-

Mr. Watson gives us an excellent statement of the law of love, as follows: "It excludes all anger, beyond that degree of resentment a culpable action in another may call forth, in order to mark the sense we entertain of its evil, and to impress that evil upon the offender, so that we may lead him to repent of it, and forsake it. This seems the proper rule by which to distinguish lawful anger from that which is contrary to charity, and therefore malevolent and sinful. It excludes implacability; for if we do not promptly and generously forgive others their trespasses, this is deemed to be so great a violation of that law of love which ought to bind men together, that our heavenly Father will not forgive us. It excludes all revenge; so that we are to exact no punishment of another for offenses against ourselves; and though it be lawful to call in the penalties of the law for crimes against society, yet this is never to be done on the principle of private revenge; but on the public ground that law and government are ordained of God, which produces a case that comes under the inspired rule, 'Vengeance is mine; I will repay, saith the Lord.' It excludes all prejudice; by which is meant a harsh construction of men's motives and characters upon surmise, or partial knowledge of the facts, accompanied with an inclination to form an ill opinion of them in the absence of proper evidence. This appears to be what the Apostle Paul means when he says, 'Charity thinketh no evil.' It excludes all censoriousness or evil speaking, when the end is not for the correction of the offender, or when a declaration of the truth is not required by our love and duty to another; for whenever the end is merely to lower a person in the estimation of others, it is resolvable solely into a splenetic and immoral feeling. It excludes all those aggressions, whether petty or more weighty, which may be made upon the interests of another, when the law of the case, or even the abstract right, might not be against our claim. These are always complex cases, and can but occasionally occur; but the rule which binds us to do unto others as we would they should do unto us, binds us to act upon the benevolent view of the case, and to forego the rigidness of right. Finally, it excludes, as limitations to its exercises, all those artificial distinctions which have been created by men, or by providential arrangements, or by accidental circumstances. Men of all nations, of all colors, of all conditions, are the objects of the unlimited precept, 'Thou shalt love thy neighbour as thyself.' Kind feelings produced by natural instincts, by intercourse, by country, may call the love of our neighbor into warmer exercise as to individuals or classes of men, or these may be considered as distinct and special, though similar affections superadded to this universal charity; but as to all men, this charity is an efficient affection, excluding all ill will and all injury" (WATSON, *Theological Institutes,* IV, 255-56).

proper or wrong in an absent person when duty or truth does not require it. For, whenever the end is merely to lower a person in the estimation of others, it is resolvable into a splenetic and immoral feeling" (WAKEFIELD, *Christian Theology*, p. 517). (2) All corrupt communications. *Let no corrupt communication proceed out of your mouth, but that which is good to the use of edifying, that it may minister grace unto the hearers* (Eph. 4: 29). This is not limited to obscenity only, but to all forms of corrupting speech—words tinged with envy or jealousy; tones which indicate anger or impatience; and everything which is either corrupt in form or unholy in spirit. (3) *Lying* and *deceptiveness*. Deceptiveness may be regarded as the root of the depraved nature, and lying as its corrupt expression. Hence St. Paul says, *Lie not one to another, seeing that ye have put off the old man with his deeds* (Col. 3: 9). Lying strikes at the very foundation of the social structure, sets man against man, and nation against nation. It destroys the only foundation for confidence and faith, and for this reason St. John passes severe judgment upon all who indulge in it. He says, *All liars shall have their part in the lake that burneth with fire and brimstone* (Rev. 21: 8); and again, in speaking of the holy city, *There shall in no wise enter into it anything that defileth, neither whatsoever worketh abomination, or maketh a lie* (Rev. 21: 27).

4. Revenge is prohibited by express command. While it is lawful and right that offenders against society should be punished by properly constituted authority, private revenge is not permissible. The divine injunction is, *Recompense to no man evil for evil* (Rom. 12: 17); and *Avenge not yourself, but rather give place unto wrath: for it is written, Vengeance is mine; I will repay, saith the Lord* (Rom. 12: 19). An implacable or unforgiving spirit is also a great violation of the law of love. *If ye forgive not men their trespasses*, says our Lord, *neither will your Father forgive your trespasses* (Matt. 6: 15).

But brotherly love not only has its prohibitions, it
has its positive assertions as well. Consequently, it maintains that true brotherliness must have due regard to
the rights and privileges of others. These are generally
summed up as the right to (1) life, (2) liberty and (3)
property.

   1. Man has the right to live. This not only refers to
actual bodily existence, which we have already discussed
in our treatment of the sanctity of the body; but all that
it means as our Lord interpreted it when He said, *I am
come that they might have life, and that they might have
it more abundantly* (John 10:10). Human culture not
only includes the enjoyment of physical values, but also
the apprehension of the true and the appreciation of
the beautiful. Hence society is under obligation to provide the individual with the opportunity to secure proper
food, clothing and shelter; and also the opportunity for
the cultural advantages of intellectual and spiritual development. "The underlying principle postulated in all
these cases is the doctrine of equality, equality of rights,
not equality of condition. That is to say, every man has
the same right to use the means of happiness providentially within his reach as any other man has to use the
means of happiness providentially within his reach.
These rights have respect to life, liberty and reputation"
(RAYMOND, *Systematic Theology*, III, p. 150).

   2. Man has a right to personal liberty. As generally
received, this liberty consists in freedom from compulsion or restraint, and applies to both body and mind.
"Liberty of person," says Dr. Wakefield, "consists in
exemption from the arbitrary will of our fellowmen, or
in the privilege of doing as we please, so as not to tres-
pass on the rights of others. This kind of liberty belongs
to men in a social state, and can be maintained only by
established laws. Hence, liberty of person, as it recognizes the rights of every member of society, and depends upon the restraints of law, is evidently included
in what we call civil liberty" (WAKEFIELD, *Christian
Theology*, p. 521). Civil liberty includes also the freedom of speech, the freedom of the press and the freedom

of assembly; and to this must be added, religious freedom, or freedom to worship God according to the dictates of one's conscience.

3. Man also has a right to private property. The right of private property is of inestimable value, and any violation of it is to be justly condemned. It is secured to men by the divine commandment, *"Thou shalt not steal"* (Exodus 20:15). In the New Testament the Commandment *"Thou shalt not covet"* (Exodus 20:17) is carried up into the principle of justice in the heart, from which corrupt affection arises every injury done to the property of men. St. Paul expressly declares also,

Liberty of person must be distinguished from what is sometimes called natural liberty. This is supposed to consist in a freedom to do in all things as we please, without any regard to the interests of our fellowmen. To such liberty, however, we have no just right, either natural or acquired. The liberty to rob and to plunder may be the natural right of the wolf or tiger; but if mankind are by nature fitted and designed for the social state, which will hardly be denied, it cannot be the natural right of men. When, therefore, we speak of liberty as a natural right, we mean that kind of liberty which is in accordance with the rights of all men.

Liberty of speech and of the press is the right of every citizen "freely to speak, write, and publish his sentiments" on all suitable subjects. The word "press" is here employed in its most comprehensive sense, denoting the general business of printing and publishing. Hence the liberty of the press is the liberty to publish books and papers without restraint, except such as may be necessary to guard the rights of others. Men are not at liberty in all cases to speak or publish against others what they please. Without some restraint they might, by false reports or malicious publications, injure the reputation, the peace, or the property of their fellowmen. It is therefore proper, while the civil authorities guarantee to every man freedom of speech and of the press, that it should hold him responsible for the abuse of this right. For a person to defame another by a false or malicious statement or report is either slander or libel. When the offense consists in words spoken, it is slander; when in words written or printed, it is called libel. The latter, because it is generally more widely circulated than the former, and is, therefore, likely to do greater injury, is supposed to be the greater offense.

Liberty of conscience, or religious liberty, consists in the unrestrained privilege of adopting and maintaining whatever religious opinions our judgment may approve, and of worshiping God according to the dictates of our conscience.

Thus we have seen that the proper administration of justice will secure to us the three great natural rights of man—life, property and liberty. But these rights may be forfeited by crime. If a man commits murder he forfeits his life, and lawfully suffers death. If he is guilty of rebellion, his estate may be seized and confiscated. If he steals, he loses his right to liberty, and is justly imprisoned. How far the natural rights of every man may be restrained by public authority is a point, however, on which different opinions have been held.—WAKEFIELD, *Christian Theology*, pp. 521-23.

That no man go beyond and defraud his brother in any matter: because that the Lord is the avenger of all such, as we also have forewarned you and testified (I Thess. 4: 6). Theft consists in taking property without the knowledge or consent of the owner. *Robbery* is taking property from its lawful possessor by violence; and *fraud* is the injury of our neighbor through deception. These common forms of dishonesty are all violations of justice, and are forbidden by the Eighth Commandment.

In addition to the rights of life, liberty and property involved in ethical justice, Christianity requires also

The right of property is of incalculable value to human beings. It enables them to secure happiness in a great measure proportionable to their skill, economy, and moral virtues. It multiplies objects of enjoyment, and lays a foundation for voluntary industry and enterprise. It is one of the main pillars of civilization. It leads to the perfection of all those arts and sciences which are connected with civilized life, and is the basis of all mechanical, mercantile and manufacturing pursuits. The protection of men by the state in the enjoyment of the rights of property is only second, therefore, to their protection in the enjoyment of personal rights and liberties.—WAKEFIELD, *Christian Theology*, p. 520.

The right to property may be acquired: (1) directly by the gift of God. A man who enters unappropriated lands and continues to occupy and improve the same, acquires thereby a right to said lands that is exclusive of all others, which right he may transfer by gift or sale. If he leave without a transfer of his right, the lands then become unappropriated, and may be entered upon by others; but while he or his successors remain in actual possession they may not be disturbed. (2) The right of property may be acquired directly by labor. Whatever is the product of one's own labor is his to the exclusion of all others. When products are the resultants of combined labor each party is evidently entitled to only that part of the product which his own labor has produced. Capital is the result of past labor; when, therefore, the laborer uses the capital of another, he and the capitalist must share the product in just proportion to the labor each has bestowed. In the arrangements of civilized society the just distribution of products among laborers and capitalists has been, in all ages, and is still, a question of great difficulty. We have not the assurance to attempt the solution of a problem which the philosophers and statesmen of the ages have failed to solve. (3) The right of property may be acquired by exchange, by gift, by will, by inheritance, by accession and by possession. When one delivers property to another for a consideration, it is called exchange; if he receive other commodities, it is barter; if money, sale; when he disposes of his property without a consideration, it is a gift; when he directs as to the disposition of his property after death, his heirs are said to acquire their right by will. If a man die without a will, being possessed of property, the government divides his estate, as it supposes he would have done had he made a will. Whatever value one's property produces is his—this is called property acquired by accession. If a man have peaceable possession of property for a term of years, this peaceable possession entails upon others the moral obligation to leave him undisturbed (cf. RAYMOND, *Systematic Theology*, III, pp. 134-137).

the exercise of benevolence toward all men. "Benevolence is not merely a negative affection, but brings forth rich and varied fruits. It produces a feeling of *delight* in the happiness of others, and thus destroys envy; it is the source of *sympathy* and *compassion;* it opens its hand in *liberality* to supply the wants of the needy; it gives *cheerfulness* to every service undertaken in the cause of our fellowmen; it resists the wrong which may be inflicted upon them, and it will run hazards of health and life for their sake. Benevolence has special respect to the *spiritual interests* and *salvation* of men. It instructs, persuades and reproves the ignorant and vicious; it counsels the simple; it comforts the doubting and perplexed; and it rejoices in those gifts and graces of others by which society may be enlightened and purified" (WAKEFIELD, *Christian Theology*, pp. 523-24). It will

In addition to the above statement, Dr. Wakefield points out (1) that true Christian benevolence is disinterested. "Thou shalt love thy neighbour as thyself." We do not say that it implies an absence of all reference to our own good. A total disregard of our own gratification is obviously impossible; for such a state of feeling would contradict the most active and efficient principles of human nature. But though, strictly and philosophically speaking, benevolence may not divest us of all reference to our own interests, yet it implies those feelings which render our happiness dependent on promoting the happiness of others. To be kind to men simply because they are kind to us, or to alleviate their wants merely because it contributes to our own interest, is not benevolence, but selfishness. (Cf. Luke 6:32, 33.) (2) True benevolence is unrestricted in its objects. Disdaining the dictates of a narrow and calculating policy, it inclines us, to the utmost of our ability, to promote the happiness of others. . . . . Unrestricted by the ties of consanguinity, the habits of association, circumstances of locality, or natural sympathy, Christian charity extends its benignant wishes to our entire race. Dissolving the fetters of sectarian bigotry, overleaping the boundaries of political proscription, and renouncing the system of a selfish reciprocity, its aspirations are bounded only by the residence of man. (3) Benevolence is self-sacrificing and laborious. The zeal of apostles, the patience of martyrs, the travels and labors of evangelists in the first ages, were all animated by this affection; and the earnestness of Gospel ministers in all ages, and the labors of private Christians for the benefit of the souls of men, with the operations of those voluntary associations which send forth missionaries to the heathen, or distribute Bibles and tracts, or conduct schools, are all its visible expression before the world. (4) True benevolence manifests itself in acts of practical mercy and liberality, to the needy and the miserable. This fruit of benevolence is more particularly denominated charity, the field for the exercise of which is very extensive. . . . . The entire neglect to exercise this practical benevolence is highly inconsistent with the character of a good man. "Whoso hath this world's good, and seeth his brother have need, and shutteth up his bowels of compassion from him how dwelleth the love of God in him?" (I John 3:17). (Cf. WAKEFIELD, *Christian Theology*, pp. 523-26.)

be seen that the duties of benevolence differ greatly from those of simple reciprocity. (1) Benevolent services are outside the range of obligation, and therefore our fellow-men may neither demand them of us, nor censure us if we do not render them. Here the duty and responsibility are purely to God and not to them. (2) Benevolence demands upon the part of the recipient an obligation of gratitude toward the donor. This is not true in the case of reciprocity. No gratitude is due for the payment of an honest debt. (3) The duties required by reciprocity may be enforced by civil authority, but the

WATSON ON PROPERTY RIGHTS

Property is not disposable at the option of man, without respect to the rules of the divine law; and here, too, we shall perceive the feebleness of the considerations urged, in merely moral systems, to restrain prodigal and wasteful expenditure, hazardous speculations, and even the obvious evil of gambling. Many weighty arguments, we grant, may be drawn against all these from the claims of children and near relations, whose interests we are bound to regard, and whom we can have no right to expose even to the chance of being involved in the same ruin with ourselves. But these reasons can have little sway with those who fancy that they can keep within the verge of extreme danger, and who will plead their "natural right" to do what they will with their own. In cases, too, where there may be no children or dependent relatives, the individual would feel less disposed to acknowledge the forces of this class of reasons, or think them quite inapplicable to his case. But Christianity enjoins "moderation" of the desires, and temperance in the gratification of the appetites, and in the show and splendor of life, even where a state of opulence can command them. It has its admonitions against the "love of money"; against "willing to be rich," except as "the Lord may prosper a man" in the usual track and course of honest industry—authoritative cautions which lie directly against hazardous speculations; and it warns such as despise them of the consequent "temptations" and "spiritual snares" destructive to the habits of piety, and ultimately to the soul, into which they must fall—considerations of vast moment, but peculiar to itself, and quite out of the range of those moral systems which have no respect to its authority. Against gambling, in its most innocent forms, it sets its injunction, "Redeeming the time"; and in its most aggravated cases, it opposes to it not only the above considerations, as it springs from an unhallowed "love of money"; but the whole of that spirit and temper which it makes to be obligatory upon us, and which those evil and often diabolical excitements, produced by this habit, so fearfully violate. Above all, it makes property a trust, to be employed under the rules prescribed by Him, who as Sovereign Proprietor, has deposited it with us, which rules require its use certainly (for the covetous are excluded from the kingdom of God); but its use, first for the supply of our wants, according to our station, with moderation; then, as a provision for children, and dependent relatives; finally, for purposes of charity and religion, in which "grace," as before stated, it requires us "to abound"; and it enforces all these by placing us under the responsibility of accounting to God Himself, in person, for the abuse or neglect of this trust, at the general judgment (Watson, *Theological Institutes*, IV, 275-76). (Cf. LEE, *Elements of Theology*, pp. 435-36.)

obligation of benevolence rests entirely upon the good which may be accomplished. Great caution, however, is always needed in the administration of benevolences, lest we unwittingly encourage idleness and dependence; but it is better to err on the side of liberality, than to lean toward stinginess and hardness of heart.

THE INSTITUTIONS OF CHRISTIANITY

Man not only has duties to God, to himself and to other men, but he is a part of a social structure which demands certain organizations for the perpetuity of the race, for its conservation, and for its spiritual illumination and guidance. These are the Family, the State and the Church. Viewed from the divine standpoint, these are three departments of God's one invisible government; viewed from the human standpoint, they are the means by which the individual enlarges his personality and usefulness. Here we shall give attention to the Family and the State only, reserving our discussion of the Church for later chapters.

(I) MARRIAGE AND THE FAMILY

Marriage is the earliest form of human relationships, and therefore the source and foundation of all others. Historically, both the Church and the State are but the outgrowth of the family, which in each instance is the unit of the social structure. Marriage may be defined as the voluntary compact between one man and one woman, based upon mutual affection, whereby they agree to live together as husband and wife, until separated by death. Several important factors must be taken into account:

1. Marriage is primarily a divine institution. This is clear (1) from the distinction of sex in creation (Gen. 1: 7); (2) from the divine declaration (Gen. 2: 18); (3) from the fact that the husband and wife acknowledge its divine origin in making their vows of mutual fidelity before God; and (4) from the added fact that its existence before the origin of civil society in the broader sense, proves it to be a divine institution. Since the essence of

the marriage contract is the mutual vows taken in the sight of God and the presence of witnesses, it should not be entered into unadvisedly, "but reverently, discreetly and in the fear of God." The ceremony should be performed by a minister of Christ, for he alone is authorized to represent the law of God, and to receive and register the vows made in the divine presence. God, having instituted marriage at the beginning, it is clearly the duty of man in general, to live in the wedded state. There are, however, grounds for exception in particular instances.

In regard to the duty of every person to marry, Mr. Watson says, "There was no need of the law being directed to each individual as such, since the instincts of nature and the affection of love planted in human beings were sufficient to guarantee its general observance. The very bond of marriage, too, being the preference founded upon love, rendered the act one in which choice and feeling were to have great influence; nor could a prudent regard to circumstances be excluded. Cases were possible in which such a preference as is essential to felicity and advantages of that state might not be excited, nor the due degree of affection to warrant the union called forth. There might be cases in which circumstances might be inimical to the full discharge of some of the duties of that state; as the comfortable maintenance of a wife, and proper provision for children. Some individuals would also be called by Providence to duties in the church and in the world, which might better be performed in a single and unfettered life; and seasons of persecution, as we are taught by St. Paul, have rendered it an act of Christian prudence to abstain even from this honorable estate. The general rule, however, is in favor of marriage; and all exceptions seem to require justification on some principle grounded upon an equal or paramount obligation."—WATSON, *Theological Institutes*, II, p. 543.

Dr. Gregory states the "Prerequisites of the Marriage Compact" as follows: "Bodily defect and mental imbecility, hereditary disease, and extreme old age have been thought sufficient to prevent those who labor under them from entering upon the married state. But, beyond this, it is evident that morality must require: First, that the parties shall be capable of giving a voluntary and deliberate consent. Hence, all forced marriages are immoral, as the compact is not voluntary. All marriages, entered into before the age at which it may reasonably be supposed that the parties fully understand the conditions, duties and responsibilities of the marriage state, are immoral, as the compact is not deliberate. Secondly, that the relations of consanguinity and affinity previously subsisting between the parties shall not be too near. By the Roman law, marriages were declared incestuous, 'when the parties were too nearly related by consanguinity—that is, being of the same blood, as brother and sister; or by affinity—that is, by being connected through marriage, as father-in-law and daughter-in-law.' The Levitical law corresponded closely to the Roman in this respect. That marriages between those who are thus closely related are unnatural, and hence immoral, may be shown by the following considerations: (1) the natural affections which relatives have is incompatible with conjugal love; (2) the prohibition of such marriages is requisite to domestic purity, and to health and welfare, bodily and mental, of the children; (3) the prohibition is necessary that the ties which bind society together may be multiplied by marriages between those who are not previously related.

2. **Marriage is also a civil contract.** This arises from its connection with civil society in the following or like instances. (1) A Christian state recognizes marriage as a matter of public morality, and a source of civil peace and strength. The peace of society is promoted especially by the separation of one man and one woman to each other, and the civil law protects them in their mutual rights and obligations. (2) Marriage distributes society into families, and the law takes cognizance of this, by making the head of the family responsible in a large measure for the conduct of those under his influence. (3) Property rights are also involved in marriage and its issue, and these must be secured by the state. (4) The state by common moral consent, has the pre-

Thirdly, that neither of the parties be already united in marriage, or obligated to marriage, to another. The betrothal is only less sacred than the marriage, and interposes an effectual barrier to marriage with another person. It should be borne in mind, however, that the betrothal is not marriage, but a mutual promise of future marriage; and that it must therefore be governed, not by the law of marriage, but by the law of promise. Fourthly, that there be mutual affection as the only true basis of a moral, peaceful and happy domestic life.

"The manner in which marriage has been sanctioned and celebrated has been very different in different countries and ages. It is evident that the preservation of a pure morality requires some proper public sanction at the entrance into the marriage relation, by the ministers of religion, or by authorized officers of the civil law. Laxness in this respect always tends to immorality."—Gregory, *Christian Ethics*, pp. 271, 272.

Whether marriage be a civil or religious contract has been a subject of dispute. The truth seems to be that it is both. It has its engagements to men, and its vows to God. A Christian state recognizes marriage as a branch of public morality, and a source of civil peace and strength. It is connected with the peace of society by assigning one woman to one man, and the state protects him, therefore, in her exclusive possession. Christianity, by allowing divorce in the event of adultery, supposes, also, that the crime must be proved by proper evidence before the civil magistrate; and lest divorce should be the result of unfounded suspicion, or be made a cover for license, the decision of the case could safely be lodged nowhere else. Marriage, too, as placing one human being more completely under the power of another than any other relation, requires laws for the protection of those who are thus exposed to injury. The distribution of society into families also, can only be an instrument for promoting the order of the community, by the cognizance which the law takes of the head of a family and by making him responsible, to a certain extent, for the conduct of those under his influence. Questions of property are also involved in marriage and its issue. The law must, therefore, for these and many other weighty reasons, be cognizant of marriage; must prescribe various regulations respecting it; require publicity of the contract; and guard some of the great injunctions of religion in the matter by penalties.—Watson, *Theological Institutes*, II, p. 546.

rogative of determining what marriages are lawful; to require publicity of the contract, and to prescribe various regulations respecting it. It is evident from the above reasons, that marriage cannot be left entirely to religion, thus shutting out the cognizance and control of the state. But neither can it be left wholly to the state. Marriage is a solemn religious act, and the vows are made to God; so that when the rite is properly understood, they agree to abide by all the laws with which He has guarded the institution.

3. Marriage is the union of one man and one woman. It is, therefore, not only opposed to polygamy, but to all other forms of promiscuity. That the Christian form of marriage is monogamic is based on the following considerations: (1) That God constituted marriage in the beginning, as the union of one man with one woman (Gen. 2: 18, 21-24). (2) That the primary ends of marriage are best secured by this form—such as mutual affection, mutual interest in the children, and provision for their proper training. (3) That any other form of marriage divides the affections of the parents, and reduces women from wives and companions to slaves and drudges. But the highest authority which the Church has for its belief in monogamic marriage is to be found in the confirmatory words of our Lord himself, when He said, *Have ye not read, that he which made them at the beginning made them male and female, and said, For this cause shall a man leave father and mother, and shall cleave to his wife: and they twain shall be one flesh? Wherefore they are no more twain, but one flesh. What therefore God hath joined together, let not man put asunder* (Matt. 19: 4-6).

4. Marriage is a permanent institution, and can be dissolved naturally only by the death of one of the parties. There are, however, unnatural methods by which this relation is severed. (1) It is dissolved by adultery. Christ's teaching at this point is specific. *But I say unto you, That whosoever shall put away his wife, saving for the cause of fornication, causeth her to commit adultery: and whosoever shall marry her that is divorced com-*

mitteth adultery (Matt. 5:32). (2) Protestantism has quite generally interpreted St. Paul to teach that wilful desertion also dissolves the marriage bond. He says, *But if the unbelieving depart, let him depart. A brother or sister is not under bondage in such cases: but God hath called us to peace* (I Cor. 7:15). Dr. Gregory points out, however, that "It is probable, from the tenacity with which the Scriptures elsewhere adhere to adultery as the proper ground of divorce, that desertion justifies divorce only as it implies adultery, as the two doubtless always went together in that licentious age" (GREGORY, *Christian Ethics*, p. 273). It seems clear, therefore, that the gospel does not allow divorce except for the single cause of adultery. As to the positive con-

Marriage is an indissoluble compact between one man and one woman. It cannot be dissolved by any voluntary act of repudiation on the part of the contracting parties; nor by any act of the church or state. "Those whom God hath joined together no man can put asunder." The compact may, however, be dissolved, although by no legitimate act of man. It is dissolved by death. It is dissolved by adultery, and, as Protestants teach, by wilful desertion. In other words, there are certain things which from their nature work a dissolution of the marriage bond. All the legitimate authority the state has in the premises is to take cognizance of the fact that the marriage is dissolved; officially to announce it; and to make suitable provision for the altered relation of the parties.—HODGE, *Systematic Theology*, III, pp. 393, 394.

As it respects divorce, the Christian law cannot be understood without reference to the Mosaic legislation, which it generally comprises. Our Lord makes very express reference to the matter: correcting ancient traditional errors on this subject, just as He corrected traditional errors on the subject of adultery. He could not have declared more absolutely than He did that marriage is a permanent compact, which neither the parties concerned nor any human power can dissolve; save on the conditions appointed by God himself. Whatever those conditions might have been in the days of the people's hardness of heart (Matt. 19:8) it is clear that our New Lawgiver has decreed that only one offence, fornication, shall dissolve the marriage bond: Whosoever shall put away his wife, except it be for fornication, and shall marry another, committeth adultery" (Matt. 19:9; Mark 10:11, 12). Under the old law, the penalty of adultery was death; our Lord's legislation tacitly abolishes that: moreover, He gives πορνεία the same meaning as μοιχεία, which generally signifies the same offence committed by a married person. A remarkable phase of the same question occurs in connection with the new relations between married persons of differing faith. Our Lord had intimated that the divorced might marry again. St. Paul, in his treatment of the question as to the desertion, deliberate and final, of an unbelieving partner, says that the forsaken one is free: "let him depart: a brother or a sister is not under bondage in such cases" (I Cor. 7:15). What the extent of this freedom is Scripture does not say; but it has generally been held that desertion is, equally with adultery, valid ground of divorce under the New Law.— POPE, *Compend. Chr. Th., III*, p. 240.

siderations in favor of the permanency of marriage, we may note the following: (1) It must be permanent in order to the accomplishment of the moral and spiritual ends of the individuals entering into this compact. (2) Permanency is demanded in order to the establishment of the interesting and influential relations of acknowledged children and parents, from which the purest and most endearing affections result. (3) It is necessary, also, to the proper training of children in obedience and virtue within the home, and to their affectionate advice and direction when they go out from the home. (4) Lastly, God has declared, both by His law in man's nature with its growing affections, and by explicit statement in His Word, that marriage is and ought to be a permanent estate.

Dr. Charles Hodge has the following excellent treatment of Divorce: Its Nature and Effects. He says, "Divorce is not a mere separation, whether temporary or permanent, a mensa et thoro. It is not such a separation as leaves the parties in the relation of husband and wife, and simply relieves them from the obligation of their relative duties. Divorce annuls the vinculum matrimonii, so that the parties are no longer man and wife. They stand henceforth to each other in the same relation as they were before marriage. That this is the true idea of divorce is plain from the fact that under the old dispensation if a man put away his wife, she was at liberty to marry again (Deut. 24:1, 2). This of course supposes that the marriage relation to her former husband was effectually dissolved. Our Lord teaches the same doctrine. The passages in the Gospels referring to this subject are Matt. 5:31, 32; 19:3-9; Mark 10:2-12; and Luke 16:18. The simple meaning of these passages seems to be, that marriage is a permanent compact, which cannot be dissolved at the will of either of the parties. If, therefore, a man arbitrarily puts away his wife and marries another, he commits adultery. If he repudiates her on just grounds and marries another, he commits no offense. Our Lord makes the guilt of marrying after separation to depend on the ground of the separation. Saying, 'that if a man puts away his wife for any cause save fornication, and marries another, he commits adultery'; is saying that 'the offense is not committed if the specified ground for divorce exists.' And this is saying that divorce, when justifiable, dissolves the marriage tie. Although this seems so plainly to be the doctrine of the Scriptures, the opposite doctrine prevailed early in the church, and soon gained the ascendancy. Augustine himself taught in his work 'De Conjugiis Adulterinis,' and elsewhere, that neither of the parties after divorce could contract a new marriage. In his 'Retractiones,' however, he expresses doubt on the subject. It passed, however, into canon law, and received the authoritative sanction of the Council of Trent. . . . . The indisposition of the mediaeval and Romish Church to admit of remarriages after divorce is no doubt to be attributed in part to the low idea of the marriage state prevailing in the Latin church. It had its ground, however, in the interpretation given to certain passages of scripture. In Mark 10:11, 12, and in Luke 16:18, our Lord says without any qualification: 'Whosoever putteth away his wife, and marrieth another, committeth adultery; and whosoever marrieth her that is put away from her husband committeth adultery.' As, however, there is no doubt of the genuineness of the passages in Matthew, they cannot be overlooked. One expression of the will of Christ is as authoritative and as satisfactory as a thousand repetitions could make it. The exception stated in Matthew, therefore, must stand. The reason for the omission in Mark and Luke may be accounted for in different ways. It is said by some that the exception was of necessity understood from its very nature, whether mentioned or not. Or having been stated twice, its repetition was unnecessary. Or what perhaps is most probable, as our Lord was speaking to Pharisees, who held that a man might put away his wife when he pleased, it was enough to say that such divorces as they were accustomed to did not dissolve the bonds of marriage, and that the parties remained as much man and wife as they were before. Under the Old Testament, divorce on the ground of adultery, was out of the question, because adultery was punished by death. And, therefore, it was only when Christ was laying down the law of His own kingdom, under which the death penalty for adultery was to be abolished, that it was necessary to make any reference to that crime."—Hodge, *Systematic Theology*, III, pp. 391-393.

The Roman Catholic Church regards marriage as a sacrament, which Protestantism denies. The Roman Catholic Church also denies the right of remarriage to all divorced persons, regardless of the grounds of divorce. It claims the right, however, to establish impedimenta, or causes why certain parties cannot lawfully be joined in matrimony, and, therefore, the right of annulment. Of these impediments, some are merely forbidding (*impedimenta impedientia*); others are annulling (*impedimenta dirimentia*). The former make the marriage illicit, the latter render it also invalid. The annulling impediments are (a) error regarding the person's identity; (b) violence or compulsion; (c) blood relationship in direct line indefinitely; collaterally as far as the fourth degree; spiritually, between godchildren and godchildren's parents; affinity arising from marriage to the fourth degree. Betrothal constitutes an impediment extending only to the first degree. (d) Solemn profession of religious and sacred orders; (e) disparity of religion, when one of the contracting parties is not baptized; (f) crime, such as adultery with the mutual promise of marriage; (g) violent abduction and detention of a woman with a view to marriage; (h) clandestinity, wherever the decree of the Council of Trent in reference to this matter is promulgated. The decree requires the marriage to be celebrated before the parish priest, or some other lawfully delegated priest and two or three witnesses. (Cf. Wilmers, *Handbook of the Christian Religion*, pp. 376, 377.)

Due to the fact that in Mark 10:11, 12 and Luke 16:18, our Lord asserts without qualification that remarriage after divorce is adultery, there have always been those in the church who make a sharp distinction between divorce and remarriage—allowing the first for the cause of adultery, but denying the second in any case. This view makes divorce merely a separation without breaking the *vinculum matrimonii*. However, the exception made by our Lord, though stated but once, must be regarded as having full authority, and the term divorce as He used it, must be admitted in its widest acceptation. But the divorce evil is of such magnitude, that it demands drastic though wise action on the part of the church, and utmost caution on the part of the ministry. Even though it be granted that the innocent party is according to the Scriptures free to remarry, there are other considerations that must be taken into account. There is ever the possibility that the guilty party may be converted, in which event there is a possibility of healing the estrangement and preserving the original agreement. Then there is the necessity of social adjustment on the part of the children, which

5. The purpose of marriage as a public institution is, according to Mr. Paley, to promote the following benefits: (1) The private comfort of individuals. (2) The production of the greatest number of healthy children, their better education, and the making of due provisions for their settlement in life. (3) The peace of human society, by assigning one woman to one man, and protecting his exclusive right by sanction of morality and law. (4) The better government of society, by distributing the community into separate families, and appointing over each the authority of master of a family, which has more actual influence than all civil authority put together. (5) The additional security which the state receives for the good behavior of its citizens from the solicitude they feel for the welfare of their children, and from their being confined to permanent habitations. (6) The encouragement of industry. These benefits are so evident that they need but little comment. Since they are chiefly economic, they will be given further consideration in our discussion of the duties of the married state. It is sufficient here to mention only the moral and spiritual benefits which accrue to the individuals and to the community at large. Mr. Watson has well said of marriage, that "It is indeed scarcely possible even to sketch the numerous and important effects of this sacred institution, which at once displays, in the most affecting manner, the divine benevolence and the divine wisdom. It secures the preservation and tender nature of children, by concentrating an affection upon them, which is dissipated and lost wherever fornication prevails. It creates conjugal tenderness, filial piety, the attachment of brothers and sisters, and of collateral relations. It softens the feelings, and increases the benevolence of society at large, by bringing all these affections to operate powerfully within

must be given serious consideration. While divorce usually takes place when the parties are sinners, remarriage makes great problems for them, if later they become Christians. These problems are perhaps the most serious that ministers are called upon to face in their pastoral work. While faithfulness is demanded, in no case should these peculiarly perplexing problems be treated with severe legality and harshness. In many instances, only the providences of God can untangle the tangled skein.

each of those domestic and family circles of which society is composed. It excites industry and economy; and secures the communication of moral knowledge, and the inculcation of civility, and early habits of submission to authority by which men are fitted to become the subjects of a public government, and without which, perhaps, no government could be sustained but by brute force, or it may be, not sustained at all. These are some of the innumerable benefits, by which marriage promotes human happiness, and the peace and strength of the community at large" (WATSON, *Theological Institutes*, II, pp. 543, 544). This brings us to a consideration of the so-called domestic duties as follows: (1) The Duties of Husbands and Wives; (2) the Duties of Parents and Children; and in a limited sense (3) Duties of Masters and Servants.

Duties of Husbands and Wives. The marriage state demands first of all, the duty of mutual affection. This requires that the husband and wife shall preserve the same tender regard for each other, as that which furnishes the basis of the marriage compact. Where this principle is duly regarded, mutual affection increases with the years, and becomes deeper and stronger as each seeks to become more unselfish, more self-sacrificing and more lovely for the sake of each other. No higher standard of the marriage relation is conceivable, than that found in the holy Scriptures. This we anticipated in our discussion of creation (Cf. *Christian Theology*, II, pp. 13, 14), but must now give it further considera-

Dr. Robbins in his *Ethics of the Christian Life* in commenting on the injunction "Husbands love your wives even as Christ also loved the church and gave himself for it" (Eph. 5:25) points out that here is the thought of God, and not the thought of man. "How pure! How lofty! How ennobling! What dignity it puts upon the wife! With what moral beauty, a reflection from the radiance of the unapproachable Master himself, it clothes the husband! He loves not for what selfishly he can get, but for what he can get by unselfishly giving, giving to the wife, giving to the children, not in material gifts alone nor chiefly, but in the far better and more costly gift of a constant self-sacrifice, manifested in countless ways, gladly made to secure the best culture of mind and heart of all who are brought within the charmed circle of this earthly paradise. . . . . He alone who as husband loses sight of self-will knows what exhaustless resources of benediction lie in wifehood, and who as father trains sons and daughters in his own likeness of self-sacrificing service to others will discover the possibilities of blessing in fatherhood" (pp. 55, 56).

tion from the ethical viewpoint. The standards mentioned are given to us by St. Paul in connection with the symbolism of Christ and the Church in the Epistle to the Ephesians (Eph. 5: 22-33); and in a briefer enunciation of principles found in His Epistle to the Colossians (Col. 3: 18, 19). The latter is as follows: *Wives, submit yourselves unto your own husbands, as it is fit in the Lord. Husbands, love your wives, and be not bitter against them.* Here there seems to be an emphasis upon the active and passive phases of love; the former, that of the husband in his active care for the entire range of wifely needs; the latter, that of the wife in confiding in his strength; using with prudence and economy, the means of support, "and to be herself the chief joy and attraction in a home made attractive by thrift and the gentle ministries of a true womanly and wifely affection" (GREGORY, *Christian Ethics*, p. 280). If we examine these principles in the light of St. Paul's larger statement, we shall find (1) That the supreme duty of the husband to the wife is love. Womankind lives by love; and this love is what a pure woman craves from her husband above all else. In the absence of this, no degree of care, comfort or adornment will prove satisfying; with it, even the humblest abode is illumined with peculiar glory. Nothing can take the place of appreciative love. (2) This love is not a mere sentiment. In St. Paul's view, the husband is a living sacrifice in giving himself to the best interests of his wife, even as Christ also loved the Church and gave himself for it. (3) He is to provide for the comfortable support of his wife, protect her from injury and insult, and to devote his powers to elevate and bless her. For this reason he is called *the saviour of the body.* (4) Lastly, St. Paul submits as a test of the quality of this love, that men ought *to love their wives as their own bodies. He that loveth his wife loveth himself. For no man ever yet hateth his own flesh; but nourisheth and cherisheth it, even as the Lord the church* (Eph. 5: 28, 29). The climax of this devotion is found in the perfect union of hearts and lives, and hence St. Paul says, *For this cause shall a man leave his father and mother, and shall be joined unto his wife, and they two shall be one flesh* (Eph. 5:31). The duties of the wife are likewise expressed. For the love shown to her by her husband, she is to submit herself in confidence and love to him. This is qualified by the expression, "as it is fit in the Lord." The plain meaning is this, that the wife is to submit herself unto her husband with the same affectionate and submissive love, which they both bear to their Lord. Coarse natures have sometimes conceived of this text as demanding subordination of the wife to the mere will and whim of the husband, but this is carnal selfishness, not love. Love finds its truest liberty in the service of its object. The mutual love of husband and wife prompts each to serve the other "in the gladness of mutual captivity. The weakness of the wife waiting on the strength of the husband becomes strengthened by a might which holds him in a bondage more complete than slave ever knew, for it is the bond-

But apart from the mystical fellowship which it illustrates, no higher tribute to marriage is conceivable than this. It carries the dignity and sanctity of the marriage relation to the highest point short of making it a sacrament. It is the most intimate and sacred union conceivable; the mutual complement necessary to the perfection of man and woman, and one which cannot be supposed to subsist with more than one person. As an institution for continuing the human race it is as pure in its own sphere as that union between the Bridegroom and the Bride to which the spiritual increase of the Church itself is due. This sheds a strong light upon the various kinds of dishonor done to the ordinance. The violations of ethical obligation refer to the two final causes of marriage. First, in all those tempers and acts which interfere between the persons to impair the perfection of their unity, Christ's union with the Church being always in view: "Wives, submit yourselves unto your own husbands, as unto the Lord; for the husband is the head of the wife, even as Christ is the head of the church. . . . . Husbands, love your wives, even as Christ also loved the church (Eph. 5:22, 25). Here there is much to ponder. The inmost grace of the wife as such is the love of submission: the earthly reflection of that loyal homage of devotion which the man was commanded to offer: "He is thy Lord; and worship thou him" (Psalms 45:11). The inmost grace of the husband is perfect self-sacrificing love. The two are one; and their union is sacred. Their communion, therefore, down to the slightest offices of affection, must be pure. Thence arise interior ethics which need not be dwelt upon; a hint of which, however, St. Paul gives when he says, "Defraud ye not one the other, except it be with consent for a time . . . . that Satan tempt you not for your incontinency" (I Cor. 7:5). This leads to the other class of offenses: the sinful indulgence of those lusts which war against the second primary purpose of marriage: adultery, with all the train of vices that precede, accompany, and follow it.—POPE, *Compend. Chr. Th.*, III, p. 239.

age of a willing spirit" (ROBBINS, *The Ethics of the Christian Life,* pp. 334, 335).

1. The mutual affection of husband and wife demands strict fidelity to the marriage contract. It especially forbids every violation of the law of chastity, as destroying the purity and harmony of the home, and corrupting society at large. Hence in all ages, and by all laws of God and man, it has been treated as an aggravated and serious offense. In Jewish law, the crime of unchastity was punished with death (Lev. 20:10). But fidelity to the marriage compact not only forbids criminal relations, but whatever tends to weaken the mutual esteem of husband and wife. Here may be mentioned especially, the want of mutual kindness and attention, or the preferring of the society of others to that of each other.

2. Mutual co-operation is essential on the part of husband and wife, if the family is to accomplish its highest mission. The two must recognize a common purpose and labor together in a common cause. "The so common estrangement of husband and wife," says Dr. Gregory, "often begins just here. The two recognize no common mission, sympathy, and work; the man becomes absorbed in his business or his profession, and the woman in fashion or household cares; they cease to look for common thoughts, common interests, and common joys; their love loses its height and purity and unselfishness, and wedded life loses its attractiveness and grandeur and becomes a commonplace and base thing, shorn of all noble aspiration and true inspiration. Mutual sympathy and co-operation in the one great work of life furnish the true preventive of such evils. In the one chosen pursuit along which the husband makes his way in the world, the wife must bring to bear her powerful aid, in the inspiration of intelligent wifely interest, sympathy, and effort; and so the two, 'thought in thought, purpose in purpose, will in will,' may together accomplish tenfold more than would be possible to the man alone" (GREGORY, *Christian Ethics,* p. 279).

3. The marriage relation demands organization. In all organized societies, whether in church or state, there must be a head—some responsible party; so also it must be in the family. Here the husband is the constituted head. This is clearly taught, both by the law of nature and by the Scriptures (Eph. 5:22-33; Col. 3:18, 19; I Peter 1:7). The outside contacts of the home demand that someone be responsible for the family as a whole. Each family must have a head, and God has seen fit to make the husband the head of the home. For this he is better fitted by nature than the wife who requires more seclusion, protection and appreciative love. Within the home, the wife rules as queen. By her kindness of heart, the depth of her feelings and affections, and the delicate discrimination and insight which she possesses, she is eminently fitted for rule in the domestic realm which is her chief glory. Here she must ever be the mistress and the central object of attraction. The husband is better fitted for the harder and more public pursuits of life. God has made him stronger physically, and thereby better qualified him to be the leader, supporter and defender of the home. He is the natural protector of his wife. Upon him, therefore, devolves the duty and responsibility of providing for the

Some may talk of man's superiority by nature, but that is only a dream of the imagination. The doctrine here advocated, is not based upon man's supposed superiority, but upon nature's law of adaptation. Man is doubtless superior to woman in some respects; as a general rule, he can stand under greater weight, run with greater speed, and clamber over rocks and mountains with greater ease, but in point of all that can delight the eye of God and holy angels, he is not woman's superior. But he is better adapted to the sphere our doctrine assigns him, and she is better adapted to the sphere assigned her by the same doctrine. The natural qualities of women, aided by their position in society, tend powerfully to develop correct moral and religious principles; and immorality is less frequent, and piety more common among them than among men. The position of woman as the subject of the conjugal and maternal relations, gives her the almost entire control of the care each successive generation is intrusted in the earliest periods of its existence. From her the first impressions on the susceptible mind of infancy are received. The infant character is molded and modified in many respects by her hand. Her gentleness, whether exalted or grovelling, is the school of childhood. In this maternal school we take our lessons; under this discipline we form our characters for time and eternity. The maternal office is, therefore, an office of the greatest dignity and usefulness, and challenges our highest admiration and esteem.—LEE, *Elements of Theology*, p. 390.

home, and this is exacted of him by the laws of both God and man. It is written that *if any provide not for his own, and especially for those of his own house, he hath denied the faith, and is worse than an infidel* (I Tim. 5:8).

Duties of Parents and Children. In this relation, the first duty devolves upon the parents. But as the children increase in years and understanding, they become involved in the obligation of duties to parents. The duty of parents to children cannot of course be adequately stated, but may be summed up in general, as follows: (1) Parental affection; (2) Parental care and training; and (3) Parental government and direction.

1. The first duty of parents to children is that of parental affection, upon which all else depends. It is the motive from which springs the obligation to protect and rear the children as worthy members of the social structure. It becomes the duty of parents, therefore, to cherish this affection in its purest and most unselfish form, for upon it depend the character and destiny of the children.

2. The second duty is that of parental care and training. This of necessity includes the proper nourishment of the body, and a wholesome physical environment; the education of the mind in accordance with the gifts and abilities of each particular child; and the de-

The origin and growth of such affection are provided for in the constitution of the family itself. It has its first natural root in the mutual affection of husband and wife, and is not to be expected in any proper measure where this does not exist. It has its second natural root in the relation of the children to the parents as "bone of their bone and flesh of their flesh." Paul presents a principle of universal application when he declares that "no man ever yet hated his own flesh; but nourisheth and cherisheth it." It has its third natural root in the innocent helplessness of the child, which makes the bosom of its parents so long its place of security and rest. This is the most powerful of all influences for the development of the fatherly and motherly tenderness; and the parents, who turn the children over to the almost exclusive care of menials and hirelings, place themselves in measure beyond its reach, and so make the highest and purest and most intense development of parental affection impossible. It has its fourth root in right and adequate views of the immortal existence and boundless possibilities of the child nature, and of the grandeur of training it for immortal goodness and glory. The parental love that does not strike deep root in this is of the earth and time only, and furnishes no fit motive to the training of the children for the highest mission.— GREGORY, *Christian Ethics*, p. 281.

velopment of high moral standards. Hence St. Paul commands parents to bring up their children *in the nurture and admonition of the Lord* (Eph. 6:4). The importance of early training is set forth in the proverb, *Train up a child in the way he should go; and when he is old, he will not depart from it* (Prov. 22:6). All this will be of little avail, unless the child is brought early to a knowledge of Christ's saving power, and experiences the divine grace which changes the heart and implants within it the principle of obedience to God. Childhood conversion may appear to many as being narrow in its range of experience, but the essential, the change of the heart, is the same, whether in children or mature persons.

3. The third parental duty is that of family government. Children are without the knowledge necessary to direct themselves, and it becomes the duty of the parents therefore to exercise wise control in the direction of their conduct. This authority must be absolute in infancy and early childhood, but will be relaxed proportionately to the ability of youth to govern itself. That family government should be firm, but kind and liberal, is implied in the words of St. Paul, *And, ye fathers, provoke not your children to wrath* (Eph. 6:4); and *Fathers, provoke not your children to anger, lest they be discouraged* (Col. 3:21).

The duties of children to their parents are to be found in the reciprocation of the parental duties, and may be summed up under two general heads, (1) Obedience,

The character of the parent must itself have been formed upon his teaching to make it effective upon his child. If a father would have his son live as in the presence of the unseen and eternal, if he would have him live above the world while living in it, if he would have him use the world as not abusing it, if he would have him attain to self-mastery, if he would have him live for the kingdom of God, the parent must himself exemplify these virtues. In a word, let both father and mother manifest the power of the new life hid with Christ in God in the unrestrained and familiar intercourse of family life; let this object lesson be reinforced by judicious instruction and admonition, then, in that case, the ancient proverb will be verified, "Train up a child in the way he should go; and when he is old, he will not depart from it" (Prov. 22:6). Children are continually, though unconsciously to themselves, taking snapshots of the characters of their elders, and will carry their spiritual photographs as unfading impressions on their souls.— ROBBINS, *The Ethics of the Christian Life*, p. 336.

and (2) Reverence. As to obedience, the scriptural injunction is. *Children, obey your parents in the Lord: for this is right* (Eph. 6:1); and *Children, obey your parents in all things: for this is well pleasing unto the Lord* (Col. 3:20). It is the child's duty to yield cheerfully to the instruction and direction which the superior wisdom of the parents may dictate. Parents are God's constituted officers to administer the government of their respective families; and to obey them in the exercise of their legitimate authority is to obey God. Like

Children are committed to the care of their parents in a state of helpless dependence, from whom they must receive every care, and be nurtured by the most tender hand, to keep alive the feeble vital spark with which their existence is first kindled, until the fires of life shall burn stronger. Each of the parents has an appropriate work to perform, but the mother's gentle hand and heart of love are put in immediate requisition, and have most important purposes to answer. An immortal being is in her arms and on her bosom; a soul with boundless faculties of thought and feelings hangs upon her lips of tenderness, and drinks intelligence from her kindling eye. Faculties capable of angelic intelligence, and heavenly virtue are slumbering in her arms and reposing on her breast. She must first call them into exercise, and give them impulses which they will never cease to feel. By the kindness of her heart, by the delicacy of her feelings and sentiments, and by her nice discrimination and accurate judgment, she is well fitted for her task. She plies her labors with unwearied assiduity. As months roll away, her immortal charge improves under her care, till the laughing lips and kindling eye respond to her own deep sympathies, and love and happiness fill the soul and expand its powers. This tender and watchful care has to be continued for years, but it is soon merged in other and sterner duties, as the infant becomes a prattling child, and as the child becomes a youth. This prepares the way for a second branch of duty. It is the duty of parents to govern their children. This is a work of great importance, and often of great difficulty. It is a work in which both parents must take a part, and co-operate to sustain each other's influence and authority. After the mother's tuition has been in progress for some time, the child comes under the sterner authority and severer influence of the father. The mother's tenderness and exquisite sensibility are necessary in the earlier stages of improvement; but, at a later period, the more vigorous modes of paternal discipline are equally requisite to a proper formation of character. The mother operates earliest, and continues her kind and sympathizing attentions to the last. The Father commences his appropriate influences after a certain degree of progress has been attained, and contributes to give manliness and energy to the character.—LEE, *Elements of Theology*, pp. 391, 392.

The true conception of the design of parental authority sets in their true light the loose views of some of the most popular of the would-be moral and religious teachers of the present day. The most certain way to undermine all morality, to corrupt the family, the society, the state, and the race, and to bring in the reign of vice and crime and godlessness, is to lower the public estimate of the sacred character of parental authority, by holding up to ridicule the strictness of the parental training to which these very teachers owe everything they are that is not base and contemptible, and which was moreover in accordance with God's Word.—GREGORY, *Christian Ethics*, p. 284.

other rulers, parents may abuse their power, but in such a case the child is to obey only *"in the Lord."* As to reverence, this includes the deference and respect due all superiors, and especially parents. So important is this, that it is enforced by one of the Commandments of the Decalogue: *Honour thy father and thy mother: that thy days may be long upon the land which the Lord thy God giveth thee* (Exod. 20: 12). St. Paul calls this *the first commandment with promise* (Eph. 6: 2). The word honor as here used, includes affection and obedience; and we may say also gratitude. It seeks, therefore, to requite in every way, the parental love so lavishly bestowed, and to provide generously for the parents when age with its helplessness and infirmity, overtakes them. Herein especially is the spirit of Christianity manifested.

Duties of Masters and Servants. The terms *master* and *servant* in the broad sense apply to the various forms of voluntary labor performed for a consideration. In the Old Testament, hired servants were regarded as a part of the household; and in the time when St. Paul wrote slavery existed in the Roman empire. This accounts for his reference to the *bond* and the *free.* The terms *employer* and *employee* as used in modern times express the same scriptural idea. Due to the various forms of specialized labor, and the growth of large capitalistic corporations, this relation has in modern times become exceedingly complex and difficult. For our purpose, however, it is sufficient to mention only the underlying principles given us in the Scriptures; which if properly observed would doubtless do much toward solving some of the more acute problems of the present time. To the servants or employees, St. Paul gives the following instructions: *Servants, be obedient to them that are your masters according to the flesh, with fear and trembling, in singleness of your heart, as unto Christ; not with eyeservice, as menpleasers; but as the servants of Christ, doing the will of God from the heart: with good will doing service, as to the Lord, and not to men; knowing that whatsoever good thing any man doeth, the same shall he receive of the Lord, whether he be bond or free* (Eph. 6: 5-8). Christianity thus considers even the most humble service as worthy of reward, if it be performed cheerfully and faithfully as unto the Lord. Concerning masters or employers, he says, *And, ye masters, do the same things unto them, forbearing threatening: knowing that your Master also is in heaven; neither is there respect of persons with him* (Eph. 6: 9). Here the duty of exercising control in the spirit of brotherly kindness is made imperative. The Christian spirit forbids harshness or cruelty, whether brutal or refined, all tyrannical measures or unjust demands, all threatening or reprisals. On the contrary, it demands that employees be given their just rights and prerogatives, proper and wholesome environment for working conditions, and fair wages proportioned to the skill of the laborer and the cost of living.

(II) The State; or Civil Government

The chief design of the state is to furnish man a wider sphere of social activity. Since man's moral nature is in disorder, his unregulated development must of necessity lead to unjust interference with the rights of other men. Civil government, therefore, is intended to protect its citizens from all violence, and to secure to each individual the peaceable enjoyment of all his rights, to the best of its ability. The state must in the very nature of the case, exercise authority in regulating public conduct; and this it does by laws based upon the immutable law of right. Penalty must be used in the enforcement of the law if need be; guilt must be made dangerous, and crime must become serious even to the criminal. It is important to note, however, that the sovereignty of civil authority lies in the state itself, and not in any king or ruler whatever. This is established by the fact that the state exists before all rulers, and by the additional fact, that rulers are at the most, but its instruments. With the development of civilization, civil government has become complex and embraces the fields of political science, economics, constitutional and industrial history, law, education and sociology in all its ramifications. It is sufficient for our purpose, therefore, as in the preceding section, to briefly state the underlying Christian principles concerning civil government. We mention the following: (1) Prayer for rulers. *I exhort therefore, that, first of all, supplications, prayers, intercessions, and giving of thanks, be made for all men; for kings, and for all that are in authority; that we may lead a quiet and peaceable life in all godliness and honesty* (I Tim. 2:1). (2) Obedience to those in authority. *Put them in mind to be subject to principalities, and powers, to obey magistrates, to be ready to every good work, to speak evil of no man, to be no brawlers, but gentle, shewing all meekness unto all men* (Titus 3:1, 2). (3) Government is ordained of God. *Let every soul be subject unto the higher powers. For there is no power but of God: the powers that be are ordained of God. Whosoever therefore resisteth the power, resisteth the ordinance of God: and they that resist shall receive to themselves damnation* (Rom. 13:1, 2). (4) Rulers must enforce the penalties of the law. *For rulers are not a terror to good works, but to the evil. Wilt thou then not be afraid of the power? do that which is good, and thou shalt have praise of the same: for he is the minister of God to thee for good. But if thou do that which is evil, be afraid: for he beareth not the sword in vain: for he is the minister of God, a revenger to execute wrath upon him that doeth evil* (Rom. 13:3, 4). (5) Christians must be subject to government for conscience' sake. *Wherefore ye must needs be subject, not only for wrath, but also for conscience' sake* (Rom. 13:5). (6) Government must be supported. *For this cause pay ye tribute also: for they are God's ministers, attending continually upon this very thing. Render therefore to all their dues: tribute to whom tribute is due; custom to whom custom; fear to whom fear; honour to whom honour* (Rom. 13:6, 7). St. Paul, therefore, applies the principle of love to the affairs of state in the same manner that he does to those of domestic and social life. He sums up the whole matter in these words, *Owe no*

*man any thing, but to love one another: for he that lov-
eth another hath fulfilled the law* (Rom. 13:8).
The relation of divine authority to human government is a question of vital importance, especially in
times like the present, when the very foundations of
human government are being restudied and reappraised.
Two statements are found in theological science which
may well be regarded as classical. The first is that of
Dr. Charles Hodge (1797-1878) entitled, *Obedience
Due to Civil Magistrates;* the second is that of Dr. William Burton Pope (1822-1903) entitled *Political Ethics.*
Both of these are given in the appended notes—the first
in greatly abbreviated form. They are worthy of careful study as representing the scriptural teaching on this
important subject.

OBEDIENCE DUE TO CIVIL MAGISTRATES

The whole theory of civil government and the duty of citizens to their
rulers, are comprehensively stated by the apostle in Romans 13:1-5. It
is there taught: (1) That all authority is of God. That civil magistrates are ordained of God. (3) That resistance to them is resistance to
Him; they are ministers exercising His authority among men. (4)
That obedience to them must be rendered as a matter of conscience, as
a part of our obedience to God. From this it appears:

First, that civil government is a divine ordinance. It is not merely an
optional human institution; something which men are free to have, as
they see fit. It is not founded on any social compact; it is something
which God commands. The Bible, however, does not teach that there is
any one form of civil government which is always and everywhere
obligatory. The form of government is determined by the providence
of God and the will of the people. It changes as the state of society
changes.

Second, it is included in the apostle's doctrine, that magistrates de-
rive their authority from God; they are His ministers; they represent
Him. In a certain sense they represent the people, as they may be
chosen by them to be the depositaries of this divinely delegated authority; but the powers that be are ordained by God; it is His will that they
should be, and that they should be clothed with authority.

Third, from this it follows that obedience to magistrates and to the
laws of the land, is a religious duty. We are to submit to "every
ordinance of man," for the Lord's sake, out of our regard to Him, as
St. Peter expresses it; or for "conscience' sake," as the same idea is
expressed by St. Paul. We are bound to obey magistrates not merely
because we have promised to do so; or because we have appointed them;
or because they are wise and good; but because such is the will of
God. In like manner the laws of the land are to be observed, not because we approve of them, but because God has enjoined such obedience. This is a matter of great importance; it is the only stable foundation of civil government and of social order.

Fourth, another principle included in the apostle's doctrine is, that
obedience is due to every *de facto* government, whatever its origin or
character. His directions were written under the reign of Nero, and
enjoined obedience to him. The early Christians were not called to

examine the credentials of their actual rulers, every time the praetorian guard chose to depose one emperor and install another.

Fifth, the Scriptures clearly teach that no human authority is intended to be unlimited. Such limitation may not be expressed, but it is always implied. . . . . The principles which limit the authority of civil government and of its agents are simple and obvious. The first is that governments and magistrates have authority only within their legitimate spheres. As civil government is instituted for the protection of life and property, for the preservation of order, for the punishment of evil doers, and for the praise of those who do well, it has to do only with the conduct, or external acts of men. It cannot concern itself with their opinions, whether scientific, philosophical or religious. . . . . The magistrate cannot enter our families and assume parental authority, or our churches and teach as a minister. Out of his legitimate sphere a magistrate ceases to be a magistrate. A second limitation is no less plain. No human authority can make it obligatory on a man to disobey God. If all power is from God, it cannot be legitimate when used against God. The apostles when forbidden to preach the gospel, refused to obey. When the three Hebrew children refused to bow down to the image which Nebuchadnezzar had made; when the early Christians refused to worship idols and when the protestant martyrs refused to profess the errors of the Romish church, they all commended themselves to God, and secured the reverence of all good men. On this point there can be no dispute. It is important that this principle should not only be recognized, but also publicly avowed. The sanctity of law, and the stability of human governments depend on the sanction of God. Unless they repose on Him, they rest on nothing. They have His sanction only when they act according to His will; that is in accordance with the design of their appointment and in harmony with the moral law.

Sixth, another general principle is that the question, When the civil government may be, and ought to be disobeyed, is one which every man must decide for himself. It is a matter of private judgment. Every man must answer for himself to God, and, therefore, every man must judge for himself, whether a given act is sinful or not. Daniel judged for himself. So did Shadrach, Meshach, and Abednego. So did the apostles, and so did the martyrs. An unconstitutional law or commandment is a nullity; no man sins in disregarding it. He disobeys, however, at his peril. If his judgment is right, he is free. If it be wrong, in the view of the proper tribunal, he must suffer the penalty. There is an obvious distinction to be made between disobedience and resistance. A man is bound to disobey a law, or a command, which requires him to sin, but it does not follow that he is at liberty to resist its execution. The apostles refused to obey the Jewish authorities; but they submitted to the penalty inflicted. So the Christian martyrs disobeyed the laws requiring them to worship idols, but they made no resistance to the execution of the law. . . . . When a government fails to answer the purpose for which God ordained it, the people have a right to change it. A father, if he shamefully abuses his power, may rightfully be deprived of authority over his children.—Hodge, *Systematic Theology*, III, pp. 357-360.

POLITICAL ETHICS

Divine revelation has from the beginning been bound up with government, and the social and political affairs of the world. Its history shows the sanctification of every form of developing rule among men; from the primitive household and family, its simplest and typical form, to the most violent form of imperial despotism. We have now to do with the final teaching of the New Testament, about which there is little room for doubt. Its general principles are very plain, both as to the rulers and as to the ruled.

I. The institution of government is divine: not founded on any compact or agreement among men, as the modern figment is. The more carefully we examine the basis of tribal and national distinctions among men—in other words what goes to constitute a distinct people— the more clearly shall we perceive that it is conditioned by a certain relation to God whose worship was the original bond of unity to every race, and whose representative the earthly ruler was. Government was made for man and man was also made for it. The form of that government is not prescribed rigidly and definitely: certainly not in the Christian legislation. Every form of valid authority is sanctified in the Old Testament. The New Testament introduces a universal monarchy in the spiritual economy of things: and only in a very subordinate way deals with the kingdoms of this world. But the foundations of civil and political society for earth were laid in heaven: "the powers that be are ordained of God" (Rom. 13:1). Human magistrates represent the Supreme Judge: being in the state His deputies. "He is the minister of God to thee for good" (Rom. 13:4); for the protection and peace of the law-abiding, He is the minister of God, a revenger to execute wrath; for the administration of divine justice on transgressors. These principles are indisputable. The same term is used concerning the representation of ecclesiastical authority in the church and in the world: they are both διάκονοι and λειτουργοί, or ministers.

II. Obedience to magistrates and the government of the land is made part of the Christian law: expressly included in His ethics by our Lord on the broad ground of the duty to render therefore unto Caesar the things which are Caesar's, though the Caesar of that day held the land in bondage. St. Paul recognized in his own person, and commands all men to recognize, what was at best a despotic and cruel authority.

1. The duty of submission is, first, in a certain sense, passive. Whosoever, therefore, resisteth the power, resisteth the ordinance of God; and they that resist shall receive to themselves damnation (Rom. 13:2). This forbids, negatively, personal insurrection and resistance. How far submission is to be carried, at what point resistance is permitted—not to the individual as such, but to a people—is a question which our present ethics do not contemplate. *Inter arma leges silent.* The obligation comes in, however, before the arms are taken up. No individual Christian may resist without betraying his trust, and losing the meekness of his wisdom. When the question is concerning the law of God (Dan. 6:5), the servant of Jehovah must resist, but not until submission has had its perfect work.

2. Positively, obedience to the government requires that diligence be given to uphold the honor of the law at all points, and that for conscience' sake (Rom. 13:5-7). Much emphasis is laid both by our Lord and by His apostles on paying tribute to whom tribute is due: a principle which involves very important issues. "For this cause pay ye tribute also." Let it be observed that St. Paul's ethics of submission to government follow and are, as it were, incorporated with his sublimest and most comprehensive doctrine of Christian morality.

3. The Bible, from beginning to end, inculcates and honors patriotism. It has been sometimes said that neither the sentiment of love to country nor that of personal friendship finds a place in Christian ethics. It is true that the supreme devotion to a kingdom which is not of this world (John 18:36) everywhere has the pre-eminence; and that the individual sympathies of friendship are merged in brotherly love. But both these sentiments are really inculcated and encouraged. There is no profane history that surpasses or equals its annals in examples of both, and Christianity must have the benefits of the old religion of which it is in a certain sense a continuation.—POPE, *Compendium of Christian Theology*, III, pp. 251-253.

PART V. THE DOCTRINE OF THE CHURCH

CHAPTER XXXI

THE CHURCH: ITS ORGANIZATION AND MINISTRY

The work of the Holy Spirit necessarily demands an objective economy. This new economy is the Church, or the mystical body of Christ. It represents a new order of spiritual life on earth, was created by the advent of Christ, and is preserved by the perpetual indwelling of the Holy Spirit. The word *church* as found in the New Testament, is from the Greek word *ecclesia* (ἐκκλησία), and in its simplest connotation, means an assembly or body of called out ones. The English word church comes from another Greek term, that of *kuriakos* (κυριακός) or the Lord's house. The church, therefore, may be regarded as at once the sphere of the Spirit's operations, and the organ of Christ's administration of redemption. As a corporate body, it was founded by our Lord Jesus Christ, and is invested with certain notes and attributes which are representative of His agency among men. It is (1) the *ecclesia*, or assembly of called out ones, and is made up of the divinely adopted sons of God. It is not, therefore, merely a human organization. Christ is its Head. From Him it receives its life through the indwelling Spirit, and as such, discharges a twofold function—as an institute of worship, and as a depository of the faith. It is (2) the *Body of Christ*, as constituting a mystical extension of the nature of Christ, and consequently is composed of those who have been made partakers of that nature. The relation between Christ and the Church is organic. As such, it embodies and affords on earth, the conditions under which, and by means of which, the Holy Spirit supernaturally extends to men, the redemptive work of Christ. In it and from it, Christ communicates to the membership of this body, the quickening and sanctifying offices of the Holy Spirit, for the extension of His work among men.

THE FOUNDING OF THE CHRISTIAN CHURCH

The Christian Church is linked historically with the Jewish—sometimes known as the "church in the wilderness" (Acts 7:38). When our Lord at the opening of His ministry, proclaimed that the kingdom of heaven was at hand, He by this means, related His own work to the Jewish theocracy as to its inner spirit, though not as to its outward form. In order to the establishment of the church, there was of necessity a gradual preparation for it, previous to, and during the earthly ministry of our Lord. This preparation is based upon the presupposition of a fundamental human society, or what Dr. Gerhart calls "the law of social integration," which he says, "demands and begets religious organization, an organization corresponding to the plane on which the religious life moves, whether lower or higher. Christianity recognizes and conserves every original law. Hence Christian life becomes organized life; Christian activity becomes organized activity; and, we may add, if human nature were not an organism, if it did not by virtue of the social principle spontaneously develop into some form of social organization, Christian life would not develop in the form of the 'kingdom of heaven'" (GERHART, *Institutes of the Christian Religion*, II, p. 455). In the development of this organization, we may note three distinct stages: (1) The Positive Preparation in the Old Testament; (2) The Intermediate Community during the earthly life of Christ; and (3) The Immediate Formation of the Church at Pentecost.

The Positive Preparation in the Old Testament. The church of the Old Testament was the first representative of the *ecclesia* or called out ones. The Hebrew word *kahal* which is derived from the verb meaning to call together, signifies an assembly, or a congregation convened for any purpose, but especially for religious wor-

Dr. Dorner includes the following subjects in his discussion of the church: (1) the genesis of the church, through the new birth of the Spirit, or Regeneration; (2) the growth and persistence of the church through the continuous operation of the Spirit in the means of grace, or Ecclesiology proper, as others call it; (3) the completion of the church, or Eschatology.

ship. The word *kahal* is translated *ecclesia* seventy
times in the Septuagint. While presupposing the natural
law of social integration, the Old Testament church must
nevertheless be distinguished (1) from all natural human
organizations, such as the family and the State; and (2)
from all pagan religions, by the fact that it was built upon
the *protevangelium* or primeval promise that the *seed
of the woman should bruise the serpent's head.* This
promise took definite form in the Abrahamic covenant.
The law which was added four hundred and thirty years
after the confirmation of the covenant, St. Paul regarded
as a pedagogic institution—a schoolmaster to bring men
to Christ (Gal. 3:16, 17, 24, 25). The Old Testament
church was, therefore, a community of the Spirit; and
while manifesting itself through natural and social laws,
was nevertheless a supernatural organization. As such,
it made a direct and positive contribution to the Christian Church, *first,* in that it cultivated and matured the
religion which should finally issue in the kingdom of
God; *secondly,* and chiefly, because it was the community that gave Christ to the world. *Who are the
Israelites,* inquires St. Paul in a rhetorical question which
he answers by saying, *to whom pertaineth the adoption,
and the glory, and the covenants, and the giving of the
law, and the service of God, and the promises; whose
are the fathers, and of whom as concerning the flesh
Christ came, who is over all, God blessed forever* (Rom.
9:4, 5).

The Intermediate Community. The second step in
preparation for the church, was the formation of the
"little flock" by our Lord himself. This must be regarded
as an intermediate community, in that it stood midway
between the Mosaic economy and Pentecost. We may
distinguish two stages in its formation, as recorded in
the Gospels. (1) The first comprised the group of disciples which clustered about John the Baptist as the
forerunner of Jesus. In John, the old economy drew to
a close. Hence the words, *He must increase, but I must
decrease* (John 3:30) The one who said of himself,
I indeed baptize you with water unto repentance, must

give place to Him of whom it was said, *He shall baptize you with the Holy Ghost, and with fire* (Matt. 3:11). (2) The second comprised the group which clustered about Jesus himself, being bound to Him by a common sympathy and devotion. In this latter group, three classes may be mentioned, (a) the Twelve Apostles; (b) the Seventy; and (c) an indefinite number of devout Jews—about five hundred. These were animated by a common belief that Jesus was the Christ, and were fused into an informal organization by their love for the Master and their faith in His words. Thus they were spiritually qualified to receive the gift of the Holy Spirit on the Day of Pentecost, and became thereby, the true nucleus of the Christian Church. During this period of earthly instruction, two things are noticeable in the development of the intermediate community. (1) A new meaning is injected into the teaching concerning the kingdom. It was revealed to the disciples, that the kingdom of God was to be Messiah's kingdom also, but only in the sense of the kingdom of heaven. The kingdom on earth must await His Second Coming. It was in this sense that Jesus interpreted the kingdom when He said, *the kingdom of God cometh not with observation* (Luke 17:20); *the kingdom of God is within you* (Luke 17:21); and *My kingdom is not of this world* (John 18:36). He taught, however, that there was to be in the consummation of all things, a kingdom of both heaven and earth, and therefore taught His disciples to pray specifically, *Thy kingdom come, Thy will be done in earth, as it is in heaven* (Matt. 6:10). (2) To the institution embodying the kingdom in this limited sense, our Lord gave the new name "My church" (Matt. 16:18). This statement, introduced as it is in the midst of St. Matthew's collection of parables on the kingdom, is significant, not only as indicating the name which should apply to it during the present age, but as indicating also, the relation which the church should bear to the kingdom. Twice only, does Jesus use the term *church*, in speaking of it as "founded upon this rock," which seems to be a reference to the "house of prayer for all nations" (Matt. 16:18; cf. Mark 11:17); and as a visible assembly of people, gathered in one place for the administration of its laws (Matt. 18:17). Here is a reference to both the visible and invisible church. In the last discourses, including the high priestly prayer, Jesus gives us further insight into His teachings concerning the church. This is especially true concerning the provision made for the sacraments, one as an initiatory rite, and the other as a memorial of perpetuity. In the high priestly prayer, the church was formally dedicated to God, in what Dr. Pope significantly calls "the first prayer in His own house." Always, even in this prayer, Jesus regards the church as yet to come. He laid the foundations Himself, and left a body of instruction, but this must await the Day of Pentecost, and the coming of the Comforter, before it could be disclosed in the fullness of its meaning.

The Formation of the Church at Pentecost. Pentecost was the birthday of the Christian Church. The prepared disciples in obedience to the command of their Lord, were assembled with one accord in Jerusalem, when suddenly the Holy Spirit fell upon them, making the intermediate community, in the truest sense of that term, "the new temple of the Triune God." As under the older economy, Pentecost was marked by the presentation of the fruits of the harvest, so in the new dispensation it marks the ushering in of the fullness of the Spirit. Furthermore, though not by divine enactment, Pentecost celebrated the giving of the law at Sinai; so also, it now represents the fullness of the New Covenant, in which the law of God is written upon the heart by the Spirit. Pentecost placed the Christian community under the jurisdiction of the Holy Spirit, who represents the invisible Head of a body now visible.

THE SPIRITUAL CHARACTER OF THE CHURCH

The Church is the creation of the Holy Spirit. Referring again to our discussion of the office of the Holy Spirit in relation to the church (Chapter XXVI), we indicated there, that the Holy Spirit administering the life of Christ is said to make us members of His spiritual body; and that ministering in His own proper personality as the Third Person of the Trinity, He is said to dwell in the holy temple thus constructed. The church, therefore, is not merely an independent creation of the spirit, but an enlargement of the incarnate life of Christ. The two most prominent symbols of the church then, are those of the body and the temple. The first represents the active side, or the church as an institute of evangelism; the second represents the passive side, or the church as an institute of worship.

The Church as the Body of Christ. Under this aspect of the church, there are three leading features to be considered—its unity, its growth and the sources of its ascendency. (1) The unity here mentioned is "the unity of the Spirit." It is something more than merely natural ties, whether of family, nation or race. No tie of outward relationship is capable of expressing this inward unity of the members of the church, or their entire oneness of life, and hence our Lord made His own Oneness with the Father an illustration of it. He prayed *that they all may be one; as thou, Father, art in me, and I in thee, that they also may be one in us* (John 17:21). Thus our Lord found no union short of that in the divine life, by which to express His thought. They were to be one through the Spirit. The Holy Spirit being the bond of union in the Godhead, becomes likewise, the source of union in the Church, uniting the members to one another, to their exalted Head, and to Himself. St. Paul uses three symbols of unity in a gradually deepening significance, to express this spiritual relationship. (a) Filial unity, or that of a common parentage or origin. Christ is the first born among many brethren—the Only Begotten being infinite, those made in His likeness, finite. (b) Conjugal unity as expressed by the marriage relationship, because of its closeness of union, its fruitfulness, its indissoluble character, and its complete interchange of goods. (c) Organic unity, or that of the head and the body, both of which are permeated by a common life. But St. Paul's most perfect illustration is like that of his Master, patterned after the Trinity. He gives us a trinity of trinities—one body, one Spirit, one hope; one Lord, one faith, one baptism; one God and father of all, who is above all, and through all, and in you all. (Eph. 4: 4-8.) In all as a life-giving and sanctifying Spirit; through all as a charismatic or gift-bestowing Spirit; above all, as an anointing or empowering Spirit. (2) Growth is the second factor of this organism. This growth is through the truth as ministered by the Spirit. Hence St. Paul says, *But speaking the truth in love, may grow up into him in all things, which is the head, even Christ: from whom the whole body fitly joined together and compacted by that which every joint supplieth, according to the effectual working in the measure of every part, maketh increase of the body unto the edifying of itself in love* (Eph. 4: 15, 16). Here it is indicated that the growth of the individual spiritually, is to be interpreted, not by an increasing independency of action, but by a deeper and more joyful co-operation with other members of the body. And it is to be further noted that the growth of the body is through the individual contributions of its members. (3) The elements of ascend-

Dr. Hutchings points out the following interesting points of comparison between the mystery of the incarnation and the mystery of Pentecost.

1. In each of these there is a personal coming, (a) in Nazareth, Mary in a hidden life is prepared for the marvel that was to be wrought in her; (b) in Jerusalem, the disciples with prayer and supplication, in secret withdrawal await the promised Comforter.

2. In Nazareth, the eternal Word descends from the bosom of the Father, to take into union with Himself, our nature in order to redeem it. In Jerusalem, the Third Person of the Trinity descends to dwell in our nature in order to sanctify it. As the creation of the body of Jesus was by the Holy Spirit, so He creates the Church as the visible organism of His Presence. (It behoveth the Holy Ghost to come among us in a bodily manner, as the Son had conversed with us in a body.—GREGORY NAZIANZEN.)

3. In both unions, the same love is the moving cause; but in the second, love takes on a new degree of prominence and intensity. It is the second divine gift, and that after the first had been abused. It is the gift now, not of personal wisdom, but of personal love; and it is the gift which makes love and not fear, the ruling motive of obedience.

4. In both mysteries, the fellowship with created life is so close that divine actions are imputed to man, and human properties ascribed to God; in both, heaven vouchsafes a divine Person, and earth contributes a vessel for His presence. (Cf. HUTCHINGS, *Person and Work of the Holy Ghost,* p. 127.)

ency are likewise given us by the same apostle. He tells us that the great gift of the ascended Christ to the Church is that of the ministry in its various types— apostles and prophets as the foundational ministry; evangelists, pastors and teachers as the proclaiming or instructional ministry. The purpose of these officers he further states, is *the perfecting of the saints, for the work of the ministry, for the edifying of the body of Christ;* and the goal of attainment is, *Till we all come in the unity of the faith, and of the knowledge of the Son of God, unto a perfect man, unto the measure of the stature of the fulness of Christ* (Eph. 4: 12, 13). This phase of the spiritual nature of the Church will be the foundation for further treatment, as embracing (I) The Organization of the Church; and (II) The Church and Its Ministry.

The Church as the Temple of the Holy Spirit. The second aspect of the spiritual church is represented by the symbol of a temple. While St. Paul's "great metaphor" is that of the body, he refers to the Church also as a temple—*In whom all the building fitly framed together groweth unto an holy temple in the Lord: in whom ye also are builded together for an habitation of God through the Spirit* (Eph. 2: 21, 22). As referring to individuals, he uses both figures in a single chapter: *Know ye not that your bodies are the members of Christ* (I Cor. 6: 15); and *Know ye not that your body is the temple of the Holy Ghost* (I Cor. 6: 19). St. Peter, however, uses this figure in a more elaborate manner. He says, *Ye also, as lively stones, are built up a spiritual house, an holy priesthood, to offer up spiritual sacrifices, acceptable to God by Jesus Christ* (I Peter 2: 5). The apostles understood clearly that the Lord Jesus Christ was Himself the Head of the Church, and not the Spirit. In instructing them concerning the coming of the Comforter, He had reserved His own dignity as One who should never be absent from them. He had said, *I will not leave you comfortless: I will come to you* (John 14: 18). Hence they saw by faith, that the great High Priest was interceding within the veil for them, and that the Spirit was present by no direct communication, but only through the mediatorship of Christ. As He was the temple of the Spirit, who dwelled in Him without measure, so the Church as His body is the temple of the Spirit communicated to it through its living Head. And further, as Christ was the image of the invisible God, so the church is to be the image of the invisible Christ; and when it is glorified, its members shall be like Him, for they shall see Him as He is.

This aspect of the Church will be given further consideration as an "Institute of Worship" and will include in its scope, (1) The Worship of the Church; (2) The Means of Grace; and (3) The Sacraments.

Notes and Attributes of the Church

Having considered the spiritual nature of the Church in its active aspect as the *Body of Christ,* or the organ of His manifestation in the world; and in its passive aspect as the *Temple of the Holy Spirit,* or sphere of worship, we must now give attention to those attributes which combine both in their unity. By the term "attributes" we mean those characteristics of the Church which are set forth in the Scriptures; while the "Notes" are those attributes transformed into tests by which the true Church is supposed to be known. In the earlier creeds, such as the Apostles' and Nicene, four of these notes are mentioned—one, holy, catholic and apostolic. Cardinal Bellarmine (1542-1621), in an effort to defend the Roman Church, set up fifteen notes, and excluded every Christian society from all claim to the character of a church, which lacked any one of these as follows: "Catholicity, antiquity, duration, amplitude, episcopal succession, apostolic agreement, unity, sanctity of doctrine, efficacy of doctrine, holiness of life, miracles, prophecy, admission of adversaries, unhappy end of enemies, and temporal felicity." Over against these have been set up other notes and attributes which express more truly the Protestant idea of the Church. Dr. Pope mentions seven, and treats them in contrast with their opposites, as follows: (1) One and manifold;

(2) sanctity and imperfection; (3) visible and invisible; (4) catholic and local; (5) apostolic and confessional; (6) indefectible and mutable; and (7) militant and triumphant. Dr. Summers is more controversial in his approach. He follows in general, the outline of Bellarmine, but opposes his positions, seeking to set forth the Protestant view on these important points. Our discussion must be brief, and we shall present only the four notes of the creeds, with their opposites, including in these some of the more important subdivisions.

1. Unity and Diversity. Unity is properly a note of the Church. There is one body, one Spirit, one hope, one Lord, one faith, one baptism. But this unity is one of manifoldness. The Scriptures nowhere speak of an outward or visible unity. There is no intimation of uniformity. The Scriptures never speak of the church of a province, but always of the churches. It is true that the churches were under a common bond of joint superintendency by the apostles, but there is even then, no evidence of a primacy among them. The unity is that of the Spirit; and the diversity includes anything that is not out of harmony with that spiritual unity.

2. Holiness and Imperfection. The term *hagia* (ἁγία) or *sancta* is applied both to the body of Christ and to the members which compose that body. In either instance, it signifies to be set apart from the world and devoted to God. In the case of the individual person, there must of necessity be a preliminary work of spiritual cleansing in order to this full devotement. The organization itself is regarded as holy on account of the purpose and end for which it exists. This implies an absolute and a relative holiness. The former applies to the membership of the Church having entered into the fullness of the new covenant privileges, and therefore holy through the blood of Christ. The latter applies to the organization as such, which though holy in purpose and end, may yet include those who have not individually been made holy. This is evident from the apostolic epistles, which though addressed to "saints" contain much in rebuke of that which is unholy. The

same is true of our Lord's own epistles to the churches, which He holds in His hands, and yet finds much which needs amendment.

3. Catholic and Local. The word *catholic* is not found in the earlier creeds. In the symbols of Jerome, Tertullian and other western creeds, the statement is simply the "holy church." It appears first in the early creeds of the east, especially those of Jerusalem and of Alexandria, but soon came to be incorporated in the Latin creeds also. The word was added to the Apostles' Creed about the close of the fourth or the beginning of the fifth century. The idea of catholicity at first included merely the universality of the Church in design and destiny, and was used in opposition to the Jewish conception of the church as local and national. But the term was never used in the sense of excluding the local churches, and hence we read of the church in Jerusalem, the churches of Galatia, and the seven churches of Asia (Cf. Acts 2:47; Gal. 1:2; Rev. 1:4). The varying emphasis upon these two notes has given rise to widely different conceptions of church organization. About the middle of the second century, the term *catholic* began to be used in a sense more ecclesiastical than scriptural, as referring to the body of the Church in opposition to the numerous smaller sects which arose at that time. The latter came to be known as schismatics and heretics, and hence were not regarded as a part of the catholic body. When the eastern and western churches divided, Rome assumed the name of *catholic,* and regarded all dissentients from the see of St. Peter, even the eastern church itself, as being outside the one only catholic church. The eastern church did not as-

Bishop Pearson gives this definition of catholicity. "This catholicism of the Church consisteth generally in universality, as embracing all sorts of persons, as to be disseminated through all nations, as comprehending all ages, as containing all necessary and saving truths, as obliging all conditions of men to all kinds of obedience as curing all diseases, and planting all graces in the souls of men."—PEARSON, on the Creed.

"The term schism (σχίσμα) means division viewed as to the corporate body, the term heresy (αἵρεσις) makes prominent the private judgment which leads to it. But the history of Christianity shows that the words must be applied with discrimination: they have been more abused than almost any others."—POPE, *Higher Catechism,* p. 328.

sume the use of the term *catholic*, preferring to be known as *orthodox* and *apostolic*.

Included in the note of catholicity, we may mention also the church as *visible* and *invisible*. By the invisible Church, is meant the mystical body of Christ as animated by His Spirit. This mystical fellowship is therefore, ·in its deepest and most profound character, a spiritual and unseen reality. The term *catholic* may be applied to either the invisible or the visible church. As applying to the former, it is simply the universal body of believers. Thus in the creed we have a statement concerning the general Church as follows: "The Church of God is composed of all spiritually regenerate persons, whose names are written in heaven" (Creed, Part II, Art. I). However, the invisible Church is frequently regarded as including, not only those now living, but those of every age—past, present and future. As applying to the latter, it includes within the visible church, all those particular constituencies which make up the total body of professed believers in Jesus Christ. The particular errors which attach to these notes are due to the overemphasis upon one to the minimizing or exclusion of the other. Roman Catholicism while believing technically in an invisible Church, so exalts the visible aspect as to suppress almost entirely, its invisible character. Hence it makes *exclusiveness* a note of the visible instead of the invisible church, and, therefore, holds that there can be no salvation outside of it. The opposite error is found in those smaller bodies

To obtain an accurate conception of the Christian Church, it is necessary that we distinguish properly between the ideal and the reality, between the inner nature and the external manifested form of the subject—in a word, between church and congregation. Conceived as a moral religious society, the Church embraces, without exception, all who are called by the name of Christ; viewed as a spiritual body, the congregation is the union of those who by a living faith are personally united to Christ, whether they belong to the Church militant on earth, or to the Church triumphant in heaven. The distinction between the visible and invisible Church is therefore correct in principle, and must be firmly held, as a matter of deep importance. Where it is arbitrarily drawn out into irreconcilable antithesis, sectarianism at once appears, which divides and weakens the Church, without being able to supply its place for a continuance.—VAN OOSTERZEE, *Christian Dogmatics*, II, p. 702.

which emphasize the invisible church, to the minimizing or exclusion of all external organization. Nothing is clearer in the Scriptures, however, than its teachings concerning external organization, and this in itself is a sufficient refutation of this error. Another question in this connection has been the source of much controversy. "What constitutes a visible church?" The position of Protestantism as found in the various creeds is essentially this, "The visible Church of Christ is a congregation of faithful men, in which the pure Word of God is preached, and the sacraments duly administered, according to Christ's ordinance, in all those things that are of necessity requisite to the same" (Wesley's revision of Anglican Creed). "The churches severally," we say, "are composed of such regenerate persons as by providential permission, and by the leadings of the Holy Spirit, become associated together for holy fellowship and ministries" (Creed, Part II, Art. II).

Another aspect of catholicity is that which regards the church as *militant* and *triumphant*. The church militant is the one body waging war with principalities and powers; and the church triumphant is the one body of believers, who having passed through death are now in Paradise with Christ, awaiting that more perfect state which the church shall enter at the end of the age.

The marks of a true church according to the Methodist Article (XIII) as given above is a revision of the Anglican Creed (Article XIX). Mr. Wesley adopted the first part of the article but rejected the second paragraph. The Anglican article is supposed to be derived from Article VII of the Augsburg Confession. Both of these articles are given below.

ARTICLE XIX of the Anglican Creed. The visible Church of Christ is a congregation of faithful men, in the which the pure Word of God is preached, and the sacraments duly ministered according to Christ's ordinances, in all those things that of necessity are requisite to the same.

As the Church of Jerusalem, Alexandria, and Antioch, have erred; so also the Church of Rome hath erred, not only in their living and manner of ceremonies, but also in matters of faith.

Article VII of the Augsburg Confession. "They likewise teach there will always be one holy Church. The Church is the congregation of the saints, in which the gospel is correctly taught and the sacraments are properly administered. And for the true unity of the Church nothing more is required than agreement concerning the doctrines of the gospel and the administration of the sacraments. Nor is it necessary that the same human traditions—that is, rites and ceremonies instituted by men—should be everywhere observed. As Paul says, 'One faith, one baptism, one God and Father of all, who is above all, and through all and in you all.'"

The simple, spiritual relation existing between the church militant and triumphant, which proved a source of courage and inspiration to the early martyrs, was soon corrupted. From the time of Origen, there was a tendency to interpose an intermediate state between the two, known as purgatory, which was neither wholly militant nor yet triumphant. With the widening of this gap, there developed a false position as to the offices of prayer—intercession for the dead on the part of those still living; intercession on the part of the saints in heaven for both those on earth, and those believed to be still in purgatory. This teaching is not only unscriptural, but anti-scriptural.

4. Apostolic and Confessional. The church is apostolic in the sense that it is *built upon the foundation of the apostles and prophets, Jesus Christ himself being the chief corner stone* (Eph. 2: 20). It is confessional in that it requires for membership, a confession of faith in Jesus Christ as Saviour and Lord. *For with the heart man believeth unto righteousness; and with the mouth confession is made unto salvation* (Rom. 10: 10). The errors which gradually arose in the church concerning these notes are marked, (1) by the theory which merged the apostolic authority of the Twelve into that of St. Peter; and (2) by the development of the so-called apostolic succession which resulted in the papacy. There are other churches, however, apart from Rome, which hold to an apostolic succession and profess to trace their orders through episcopal hands to the apostles. At the opposite extreme is the error, which holds that the church has had the apostolate restored to it, with the miraculous gifts and endowments which pertained to the original apostles. Both St. John and St. Paul seem to indicate, however, that the apostolate would be withdrawn from the church. Protestantism in general, has substituted belief in the Scriptures for living apostolic authority. "Hence we may lay down our dogma" says Dr. Pope, that "the Church is apostolic, as being still ruled by the apostolical authority living in the writings of the apostles, that authority be-

ing the standard of appeal in all the confessions that hold the head" (Pope, *Compend. Chr. Th.*, III, p. 285).

THE ORGANIZATION OF THE CHURCH

The organization of the church, in the strictest sense, belongs to the study of church polity. Here we can give only a brief survey of the several factors which enter into and constitute the church, a visible organization. We shall discuss (1) The Preliminary Forms of Organization; (2) Organization of the Christian Church; (3) Types of Organization; (4) The Churches as Local and Voluntary Organizations; (5) Conditions of Membership, and (6) The Function of the Church.

Preliminary Forms of Church Organization. The visible forms which the invisible Church has assumed from age to age, have been the consequence largely, of the historical struggles, and the various circumstances under which it has been forced to maintain itself. We may note the following: (1) The Patriarchal Form; and (2) The Theocratic Form.

1. The Patriarchal form of the church dates from the beginning of time. Before the fall, it was unsullied and perfect. What the form of organization would have been, had this state continued, we need not inquire. But after the fall, imperfection characterized the church, and will continue to do so, until the consummation of all things, when it shall again be presented faultless before the throne with exceeding joy. In its earliest form, the creed was simple—the *protevangelium* or redemptive promise being the sole condition of membership. The only official was a priest. Apparently the priesthood was not limited to the head of the family, for both Cain and Abel offered sacrifices. The church was individualistic in the extreme. With the call of Abraham, the individualistic form of organization gave way to that of the family, and the patriarchal form of government in its truest sense began. Abraham was the priest of his own family, and was succeeded in turn by Isaac and Jacob.

2. The Theocratic form of government began with Moses, who reorganized the church at Sinai, giving it an elaborate constitution, both civil and ecclesiastical. It was not designed, however, to be a state fulfilling churchly offices, but a church assuming the functions of the state. The religious idea permeated the whole social structure. Theoretically, this must ever be the true ideal for the church—not indeed the identification of church and state, but such a coalescence of the two as shall bring both to their highest efficiency. Such an ideal, however, can never be realized, until He who is Prophet and Priest shall also become King. Then He shall be not only the Lord of the church but the Ruler of the nations—He shall be King of kings, and Lord of lords (Rev. 11:15).

Organization of the Christian Church. Nothing is more clearly taught in the Scriptures than the fact of an external organization of the church. This is shown from (1) the stated times of meeting (Acts 20:7), and the exhortation to not forsake the assembling of themselves together (Heb. 10:25); (2) a regularly constituted ministry known as bishops (ἐπίσκοποι), elders or presbyters (πρεσβύτεροι) and deacons (διάκονοι) (Phil. 1:1; Acts 20:17, 28), with standards of eligibility (I Tim. 3:1-13); (3) formal elections (Acts 1:23-26; 6:5, 6); (4) a financial system for the local support of the ministry (I Tim. 5:17), and for the more general interests of charity (I Cor. 16:1, 2); (5) disciplinary authority on the part of ministers and churches (I Tim. 5:17; I Peter 5:2; Matt. 18:17; I Cor. 5:4, 5, 13); (6) common customs (I Cor. 11:16) and ordinances (Acts 2:41, 42; I Cor. 11:23-26); (7) qualifications for membership (Matt. 28:19; Acts 2:47); (8) register of widows (I Tim. 5:9); (9) official letters of commendation (Acts 18:27; II Cor. 3:1); and (10) the common work of all the churches (Phil. 2:30).

There are three general views concerning church organization. The first holds that the church is exclusively a spiritual body and, therefore, needs no external organization. This position is illogical and is held by only a few of the minor sects. It should be observed that a simple form of government does not necessarily imply a written creed; it may exist in oral form. Such an organization may exist also without written records, lists of members, or formal choice of officers. After all, these things must be regarded as aids and not essentials. The second theory is at the other extreme, and maintains that the Scriptures give us a formal plan of organization for the church. But even with those who hold this position, there is much controversy as to the form of government prescribed. It is held by both those who advocate the episcopal form of government on the one hand, and pure congregationalism on the other. There is a third and mediating theory, which holds that the New Testament lays down general principles of organization, but prescribes no specific form of church government. This is the position generally taken by the Protestant churches. Mr. Watson adopting the language of Bishop Tomline, says, "As it hath not pleased our Almighty Father to prescribe any particular form of government for the security of temporal comforts to his rational creatures, so neither has he prescribed any particular form of ecclesiastical polity as absolutely necessary to the attainment of eternal happiness. Thus the Gospel only lays down general principles, and leaves the application of them to free agents." Dr. Bangs takes the same posi-

Mr. Wesley who was always a firm believer in the episcopal form of government, makes this admission. "As to my own judgment, I still believe the episcopal form of church government to be scriptural and apostolic. I mean well agreeing with the practice and writings of the apostles. But that it is prescribed in Scripture, I do not believe."

Dr. Thornwall states the distinguishing features of Presbyterianism as follows: (1) That the church is governed by representative assemblies. (2) Those assemblies constitute two houses, or two elements, the preaching and ruling elder. (3) The parity of eldership, all elders, preaching and ruling, appearing in our church courts with the same credentials, and having the same rights. (4) The unity of the church, as realized in the representative principle. (5) The ministerial and declarative power of the representative Presbyteries, Synods and Assemblies, as against mandatory power.—THORNWALL, *Writings*, IV, p. 234.

"Thus a further confirmation is furnished of the view that has been taken: namely, that it was the plan of the sacred writers to lay down clearly the principles on which Christian Churches were to be formed and governed, leaving the mode of application of those principles undetermined and discretionary."—WHATELY, *The Kingdom of Christ*, p. 98.

tion. "No specific form of church government," he says, "is prescribed in the Scriptures and it is, therefore, left to the discretion of the church to regulate these matters as the exigencies, of time, place and circumstance shall dictate to be most expedient, always avoiding anything that God has prohibited." Dr. Miley holds that "the question of chief importance, is the adaptation of the polity to the attainment of the spiritual end for which the church is constituted. This should always be the determining principle. The principle means that the constitution of a polity is left to the discretion of the church; but it also means that the construction must be made in the light of her mission, and with a view to its very best accomplishment. The discretionary power of the church appears in the light of three facts: (1) the church must have a polity; (2) there is no divinely ordered polity; and (3) consequently it is left to the church and to each church rightfully existing as such, to determine her own polity" (MILEY, *Syst. Th.*, II, pp. 416, 417).

Types of Church Organization. In general, we may say that there are five leading types of organization, or forms of church government, held by professed Christians. These are concerned primarily, with the rightful authority of the visible church. (1) The Roman Catholic Church holds that the supreme and final authority is with the pope and is, therefore, a papacy. (2) At the other extreme, the Congregational Churches hold that the authority is vested in the separate congregations, and hence are known as independents. Between these extremes are the mediating positions. (3) The Episcopalians hold that the authority is vested in a superior order of the ministry; (4) The Presbyterians hold that it rests with the ministry and laity jointly; and (5) the Methodists hold that it is vested mainly in the elders of the church. These types may be reduced to three—the Episcopal, in which the authority is vested in the ministry; the Congregational in which it is vested in the congregation; and the Presbyterian, in which it is vested in both ministry and laity. "It is our opinion," says

Bishop Weaver, "that the form of government in the New Testament was not exclusively Episcopal, Presbyterian, or Congregational, but a combination of certain elements of all. . . . . From a careful review of the whole question, we conclude that it is nearest in harmony with the practice and writings of the apostles to say that the authority in the visible church is vested in the ministry and laity taken together." Emphasis upon the extremes mentioned above, has given rise to sharply divergent views of the nature of Christianity itself. (1) According to the one, the Church is constituted by a divinely commissioned clerical order, who through apostolical succession, is alone authorized to transmit the blessings of the Christian religion through the sacraments. According to this view, the church depends wholly upon the ministry, and where there is no apostolic ministry, there is no church. (2) According to the other view, the church is constituted by the acceptance, on the part of individuals, of Christ as Saviour and Lord. These individuals through voluntary association, form the churches, which in turn appoint their own "ministers" or "servants," for the more effective discharge of its functions. In this view, the ministry depends upon the church. Both views are equally unscriptural.

The Churches as Local and Voluntary Organizations. We have seen that there are two widely different views of church organization—views so extreme as to affect even the concept of Christianity itself. These are (1) the papacy which regards the church as the one and entire visible organization throughout the world, and as such, ruled by one visible head — the pope. According to this theory, the local bodies are not churches in truest sense of the word, but only parts of the one church. (2) At the other extreme is congregationalism, or independency, which holds strictly to the autonomy of the local church, and denies the title to any superimposed organizations. According to this view, the local body only is the church; and the universal church is merely a general term to express the totality of the churches, each perfect in itself and entirely independent.

The apostolic churches were voluntary associations. Those who joined themselves to them, did so freely and of their own accord. In this is to be found the outward expression of that inner life and freedom which char-

The question of philosophical theory enters largely into the matter of organization, whether of church or state. Philosophy deals with such questions as the absolute and the individual, the general and the particular, unity and plurality. As applied to the State, we have absolute monarchy and pure democracy, and between these extremes, all shades and degrees of political organization. As applied to the church, we have the extremes of episcopacy and congregationalism, or more properly, the papacy and independency. Church organization always tends toward one of these extremes, but the church that insists upon the one to the exclusion of the other has at most only a half truth. Provision must be made for the freedom of the individual, but this can be done only by providing for a proper relation to others.

It is generally conceded to be impractical to aim at oneness in the visible church save in the fundamentals of faith, worship and discipline. It must be obvious to every dispassionate mind that there never has been since the times of the apostles any other unity than that which God alone can discern. . . . . The Congregational theory which admits only of voluntary aggregation of churches, and neither has nor desires any guaranty for more than that, goes to an extreme but in a right direction.—POPE, *Compend. Chr. Th.*, III, p. 273.

Dr. A. A. Hodge has this interesting statement concerning the importance of variety in the church. "I do believe that God's purpose, on the contrary, has been to differentiate His church without end. You know that the very highest form of beauty of which you can conceive, the very highest form of order, is multiplicity in unity and unity in multiplicity. . . . . Now what has God been doing? He has broken humanity up into infinite varieties . . . . through all time . . . . simply to build up variety, which constitutes beauty in unity, to build up the rich, inexhaustible variety, which constitutes the beauty in unity of this great, infinite church of the first-born. . . . . We do desire comprehensively to work together toward unity, but mongrelism is not the way to get it. It is not by the uniting of types, but by the unity of the Spirit; it is not by the working from without, but from within outward."—A. A. HODGE, *Popular Lectures*, p. 212ff.

Mr. Wesley says, "Originally every Christian congregation was a church independent of all others." Dr. Adam Clarke takes the same position. "In the proper use of this word," he says, "there can be no such thing as the church exclusively; there may be a church, or the churches." So also Mr. Watson says, "Through the greater part of the second century the Christian churches were independent of each other."

"We are agreed on the necessity of a superintendency, which shall foster and care for churches already established, and whose duty it shall be to organize and encourage the organizing of churches everywhere." "We are agreed that authority given to superintendents shall not interfere with the independent action of a fully organized church, each church enjoying the right of selecting its own pastor, subject to such approval as the General Assembly shall find wise to institute; the election of delegates to the various assemblies; the management of their own finances; and of all other things pertaining to their local life and work."—Basis of Union, *Manual, Church of the Nazarene*, p. 18.

acterizes the Church of Christ. The apostles made no provision for any visible head of the one supposedly visible church. There appears to have been no primate even in the apostolic college, although St. James presided over the Jerusalem council. On the contrary, the apostles provided for the government of the churches which they founded, in a totally different manner, that is, by raising up within the churches themselves, those whom they ordained as ministers. The only unity of which the apostles speak is the unity of the whole church in Christ its invisible Head. This unity is that of faith and fervent charity through the indwelling Spirit. Furthermore, the best ecclesiastical historians are agreed that during the greater part of the second century, the churches were independent bodies, and only toward the close of this century were the larger associations formed. But this independency of the early Christian churches must not be regarded as identical with that of the churches which in modern times are called independent. It is evident from the Scriptures that the churches were founded by the apostles and evangelists, who during their lifetime, exercised control over them. This proves that the first churches were not marked by a complete independency. The Epistles to Timothy and Titus make it clear, also, that

It may be allowed that some of the smaller and more insulated churches might, after the death of the apostles and evangelists, have retained this form for some considerable time; but the large churches in the chief cities, and those planted in populous neighborhoods, had many presbyters, and as the members multiplied they had several separate assemblies or congregations, yet all under the same common government. And when churches were raised up in the neighborhood of cities, the appointment of "chorepiscopi," or country bishops, and of visiting presbyters, both acting under the presbytery of the city, with its bishop at its head, is sufficiently in proof that the ancient churches, especially the larger and more prosperous of them, existed in that form which in modern times we should call a religious connection, subject to a common government.—WAKEFIELD, *Christian Theology*, p. 544.

Mosheim, a Lutheran, in a statement concerning the churches in the first century, says, "All the churches, in those primitive times, were independent bodies, or none of them subject to the jurisdiction of any other. For though the churches which were founded by the apostles frequently had the honor shown them to be consulted in difficult and doubtful cases, yet they had no such judicial authority, no control, no power of giving laws. On the contrary, it is clear as the noonday, that all Christian churches had equal rights, and were, in all respects, on a footing of equality."

St. Paul committed to others, the authority to ordain elders in the churches, and to exercise a general supervision over their affairs. From this it appears that the type of organization established by the apostles, was a form of connectionalism, in which the local churches retained largely, the control of their own affairs, but were subject nevertheless in a general manner to a common government. This alone, seems to conform to the scripture teachings and historical facts concerning the organization of the early churches.

Conditions of Membership. "The churches severally are to be composed of such regenerate persons as by providential permission, and by the leadings of the Holy Spirit, become associated together for holy fellowship and ministries" *(Creed, Part II, Art. II).* While regarding the church as a voluntary and visible organization, we nevertheless insist upon the divine and invisible element also and, therefore, make regeneration the basic condition of membership. Since the church is the fellowship and communion of believers, a confession of faith in the Lord Jesus Christ, becomes the one essential requirement for admission to the visible organization. This confession Protestantism has interpreted to mean a "conscious Christian experience and life." The various denominations have generally adopted

Morris in his Ecclesiology, p. 93, reduces saving belief to its several elements, and thus discovers four essential qualifications for membership. These qualifications are (1) a spiritual knowledge of God, especially as revealed in the gospel, as Father, Son and Holy Spirit. (2) Repentance for sin as committed against God, and trust in the divine mercy, especially as that mercy is manifested in and through Christ as a Redeemer. (3) Obedience to God and cordial devotion to His interests and kingdom, culminating under the Christian dispensation in personal conformity with Christ and loyal consecration to His service. (4) A public declaration of such faith and devotion and a holy covenant with God to be His servant, followed and confirmed by voluntary communion with His people, and under the gospel, with some branch of the Christian church.

Church members are those who compose or belong to the visible church. As to the real church, the true members of it are such as come out from the world (I Cor. 6:17); are born again (I Peter 1:23); or made new creatures (II Cor. 5:17); whose faith works by love to God and all mankind (Gal. 5:6; James 2:14, 26); who walk in all the ordinances of the Lord blameless. None but such are members of the true Church; nor should any be admitted into any particular church without some evidence of their earnestly seeking this state of salvation. —WATSON, *Dictionary, Art. Church.*

some form of a covenant, including agreed statements of belief and practice, to which the applicant must be willing to conform. It is the duty of every Christian, not only openly to profess his faith in Christ, but to enter into fellowship with the body of believers in his community, and to take upon himself the responsibilities of church membership.

It is evident that the same difficulties which we discovered in our discussion of the visible and invisible church, attach also to the conditions of membership. Several leading errors may be mentioned. (1) Where the church is regarded solely as a visible organization, membership will be conditioned merely by subscription to outward forms of admission. In some Protestant churches, the partaking of the sacraments alone, is regarded as sufficient for church membership. (2) Where a confession of faith is required, another error has at times been dominant in the church. It is held that since men do not know the hearts of those who profess faith in Christ, no one has a right to make inquiry or question the profession of another. This is a mistaken principle, and where it has obtained, the church has been spiritually impoverished by a membership knowing nothing of a conscious Christian experience and life. For this reason, spiritual churches have guarded their membership by requiring that all candidates for admission be required to show evidence of salvation from their sins by a godly walk and vital piety. (Cf. *General Rules V*). (3) at the other extreme is to be found the error of those who look for and expect to

About 313 another schism broke out in Africa, owing to a dispute about the character of a bishop, and the validity of an ordination performed by him. The dissidents, called Donatists, from their leader, Donatus, inherited many of the opinions of the Montanists, the local remnant of which set they seemed to have absorbed. They strongly insisted on the absolute purity of the Church, accounting it sinful to exercise any forbearance toward unworthy members. They did not, however, like the Montanists and Novatians, refuse readmission to penitents. Their specialty was a belief that ministerial acts were invalid if performed by a person who either was, or deserved to be, excommunicated; and as a consequence, they claimed that valid sacraments were the exclusive possession of their own pure Church. The schism lasted through several generations, and before its extinction, ran into the wildest fanaticism.—CRIPPEN, *Hist. Chr. Doct.*, pp. 181, 182.

find, the purity of the invisible church, in the visible organization. This was the error of the early Donatists, who endeavored by rigid discipline to secure an absolutely pure ecclesiastical organization, refusing fellowship with all whose practice was more tolerant. Thus to maintain the outward semblance of purity, the inward sanctity of spiritual freedom was broken down, and in its stead, there developed a narrow, uncharitable and sectarian spirit. (4) Closely related to this is the error of attempting to carry on the operations of the invisible church in the world, without a visible organization. Finding it impossible to maintain an outwardly pure church, some have resorted to the expedient of denying the necessity of external organization. This error has been previously mentioned, and can exist only because of a mistaken view of the nature of organization itself.

The Function of the Church. The function of the church, considered as the body of Christ, is that of a missionary institute, or more properly an "Institute of Evangelism." As Christ assumed a body and came into this world, to reveal God and redeem men, so the Church as His body exists in the world for the spread of the gospel. It is the sphere of the Spirit's operation, and finds its highest expression in the great commission, given to the church by our Lord himself. *Go ye therefore, and teach all nations, baptizing them in the name of the Father, and of the Son, and of the Holy Ghost; teaching them to observe all things whatsoever I have commanded you: and, lo, I am with you alway, even unto the end of the world. Amen* (Matt. 28:19, 20). A word must be said also, as to the relation of the church to the kingdom. The kingdom is not to be narrowed down to the church, nor is the church to be broadened out to include the kingdom. "To do the first," says Dr. Taylor, "is to set up a monstrous ecclesiasticism; to do the second is to destroy the organism through which the kingdom manifests itself and does its work in the world." As the new dispensation began with the preaching of the kingdom, so it is the final form in which all the churches shall be absorbed at the end of the age. Only at the coming of the Lord, will the kingdom which had its preparatory stage in Israel, and its New Testament fulfillment in both Israel and the Gentiles, find its glorious consummation. Then shall the prophecy be fulfilled, *The kingdoms of this world are become the kingdoms of our Lord, and of his Christ; and he shall reign for ever and ever* (Rev. 11:15).

THE CHRISTIAN MINISTRY

The Christian ministry may be said to discharge a twofold function, according as the church is viewed under the aspect of the Body of Christ, or as a Temple of the Spirit. In the first, as an institute of evangelism, the ministerial function is that of preaching the gospel and administering the affairs of the church; in the second, as an institute of worship, it has reference to the conduct of public worship and the administration of the sacraments. Before considering this subject more in detail, it is necessary to give some attention to the different conceptions of the office as held by Roman Catholicism and Protestantism. The former holds to a priestly or sacerdotal ministry; the latter to a prophetic or preaching ministry. The principle adopted by the Reformers, is that of "the universal priesthood of believers."

The Universal Priesthood of Believers. In the early church, the ministers were known indifferently as bishops, presbyters or elders. The Old Testament conception of a priesthood, exercised at first, but little influence upon the churchly idea of the office. The sacrifices were abolished, and there could be no priest without a sacrifice. Consequently the whole congregation regarded itself as a body of priests to offer up spiritual sacrifices through Jesus Christ, its one great High Priest. Gradually, however, there grew up an unscriptural distinction between the clergy and the laity, the former being known as *sacerdotes,* to whom pertained a priestly function. With this distinction established, it was impossible to prevent the Old Testament conception of the priesthood from having its influence upon the Christian ministry. Since in the temple service, the priests offered up sacrifices *for* the people, and thereby became mediators between them and God; so in the church, the sacrifice soon came to be offered *for* the people instead of *by* the people. As long as the faithful themselves offered up the spiritual sacrifices through the one high priest, there was no need for a sacerdotal order. Consequently the idea of a universal priesthood was dominant in the church. With the gradual change in the idea of the ministry and its functions, there came a changed conception of the eucharist, from a simple memorial feast to the sacrifice of the mass. This in turn strengthened the belief in the priestly character of the ministry; and thus, as Peter Lombard indicates in his *Sentences*, the priestly character of the higher clergy, and the sacrificial character of the mass, were transmitted to the medieval church and accepted as axiomatic. With the coming of the Reformation, however, the idea of the universal priesthood of believers was again brought to the front, and has been the dominant characteristic of Protestantism since that time. As such, it teaches the essential equality of all true believers, and their direct relation to Christ through the Spirit, and thus preserves the true dignity of the individual Christian and the sanctity of corporate worship. It has at times unwisely been used against belief in a distinct ministerial order and, therefore, needs to be properly guarded.

The Divinely Constituted Ministry. Since the church is a divinely appointed institution, that is, it is the will of God that men organize themselves into societies for mutual edification and divine worship, so it is the will of God that individual persons be appointed to perform the duties and administer the sacraments of the church. In order to the more effective administration of the office, those who devote themselves exclusively to religious work are required to separate themselves from the ordinary vocations of secular life. This duty the Scriptures teach both directly and indirectly. In the Mosaic dispensation, Aaron and Levi were separated to do the work of the priesthood by divine commandment. The prophets were called of God, and spoke by divine commission (Ezek. 3:17). The divine order of the ministry is set forth even more clearly in the New Testament. The apostles were directly called and ordained by our Lord himself. *And when it was day, he called unto him his disciples: and of them he chose twelve, whom also he named apostles* (Luke 6:13); *And he ordained twelve, that they should be with him, and that he might send them forth to preach* (Mark 3:14). The Seventy were likewise appointed and sent forth. (Luke 10:1). St. Paul was specifically called to the ministry—*a chosen vessel unto me, to bear my name before the Gentiles, and kings, and the children of Israel* (Acts 9:15; cf. 27:16-18). It is recorded in the Acts also, that the apostles ordained elders in every church (Acts 14:23).

In this connection, it is well to point out that the ministry is a vocation or calling and not merely a profession. As it is the will of God that churches be formed, so it is His will also that particular persons be called to serve as ministers of these churches. As to what constitutes a divine call, nothing is better than the test of "gifts, grace and usefulness" which served the early fathers so well in their choice of candidates for the ministry.

The Distinctive Offices of the Church. St. Paul enumerates the following classes in the New Testament ministry, as given to the church by our ascended Lord. *And he gave some, apostles; and some, prophets; and some, evangelists; and some, pastors and teachers* (Eph. 4:11). From a further study of his epistles we learn also, of bishops, elders or presbyters, and deacons. Some of these terms, however, pertain to the same person, that is, the person may be designated sometimes by one, and sometimes by another of these official terms. The five offices mentioned by St. Paul, may be arranged in two main divisions, (1) The Extraordinary and Transitional Ministry, and (2) The Regular and Permanent Ministry.

1. The Extraordinary and Transitional Ministry includes the apostles, the prophets and the evangelists. The church was founded by a specially chosen and qualified body of men. Their ministry was transitional, continuing as it did, the extraordinary ministrations of the Holy Spirit under the old economy, and bringing them to their full consummation in the service of the new order. (1) The *apostles* were those who had been commissioned by our Lord in person, and were chosen to bear witness of His miracles and His resurrection. Their mission was to lay the broad foundations of the church in doctrine and practice, and to this end they were endowed with the gift of inspiration, and given the credentials or miracle working power. (2) The *prophets* included those who in some instances foretold the future (Acts 11:28; 21:10, 11), but the term generally refers to that body of extraordinary teachers who were raised up for the purpose of establishing the churches in the truth, until such time as they should be under qualified and permanent instructors. Like the apostles, they spoke under the immediate inspiration of the Spirit; and while uttering truth immediately revealed to them for the instruction of the church, their revelations in only a few

The apostles were ambassadors to the world; their credentials were a direct mission from the Lord in person, confirmed by miraculous powers. Their office was to preach the gospel to all men, in the name of the risen Lord, whose resurrection they proclaimed; and everywhere to lay the foundation of churches, or to sanction the foundation laid by others, to be the models for all the future. As the Spirit was the invisible representative of the Lord, so the apostles were the visible. Their absolute authority is indicated in two ways: first, as teachers of Christianity, by word and writing, they had the gift of inspiration; and, second, as founders of the Church, they had the power of the keys, of binding and loosing, that is, of uttering the unchangeable decrees of ecclesiastical government. Their sway everywhere is seen to be uncontrolled, and from their word there is no appeal. They had, and could have, no successors: they form a body of men chosen to lay the foundation of the universal Church built upon the foundation of the apostles and prophets (Eph. 2:20), and to commit to it the final documents of Scripture. A succession of such men would not have been in harmony with the will of Christ, which we may interpret as purposing to leave a fellowship with a settled organization, and a finished doctrine, and a natural development under the supreme guidance of the Holy Ghost. But being dead they yet speak in their writings, which are the only representatives of the apostolical company in the visible community. It is from St. Paul, the one apostle of the Gentiles that we gather our fullest information concerning the apostolical prerogative.—Pope, *Compend. Chr. Th.*, III, pp. 338, 339.

instances are preserved. It was to this class that the pentecostal promise pertained, *And on my servants and on my handmaidens I will pour out in those days of my Spirit; and they shall prophesy* (Acts 2:18). This promise was abundantly fulfilled, and consequently we find references to numerous prophets in the Acts and Epistles. From the Epistle to the Corinthians, it is evident that the gift was exercised by both men and women, that it was occasional, and that it was frequently exercised in the congregation. (Cf. Acts 21:9; I Cor. 14:24, 25, 29-33, 37). St. Paul defines the office of the prophets as speaking *unto men to edification, and exhortation, and comfort* (I Cor. 14:3); and assigns a high prerogative to the order by asserting that the church is *built upon the foundation of the apostles and prophets* (Eph. 2:20 cf. 3:5). It is in the sense of a foundational ministry only, that the order was transitory, as a proclamation of the truth, it abides in the church in the form of the regular ministry. (3) The *evangelists* were the assistants of the apostles, and performed the apostolic offices of preaching and founding churches. Their power was delegated to them by the apostles, to whom they were amenable, and under whose supervision their duties were performed. Timothy and Titus are representatives of this class. They were given the power to ordain bishops or elders in the churches, but since they had no authority to ordain their successors, the office must be regarded as temporary. It passed away with the apostolate upon

With the passing away of the apostles, the passing of the evangelist as an assistant of the apostle, also passed away; but as an irregular and proclaiming ministry of the church it continued, and must continue, if the church is to extend her borders. Eusebius, the learned bishop of Cæsarea, gives us an account of the evangelists who lived and labored during the reign of Trajan (A.D. 98-117). "Leaving their own country," he says, "they performed the office of evangelists to those who had not heard the faith; whilst with a noble ambition to proclaim Christ, they also delivered to them the books of the Holy Gospels. After laying the foundations of the faith in foreign parts as the particular object of their mission, and after appointing others as shepherds of the flocks, and committing to these the care of those who had been recently introduced, they went again to other regions and nations, with the grace and cooperation of God. The Holy Spirit also wrought many wonders as yet through them; so that as soon as the gospel was heard, men voluntarily in crowds, and eagerly embraced the true faith with their whole minds" (EUSEBIUS, *Eccl. Hist.*, III, p. 36).

which it depended. The evangelists had the gift of prophecy, as is shown by St. Paul's statement of Timothy's ordination, in which he speaks of *the prophecies which went before on thee* (I Tim. 1:18); and exhorts him to *Neglect not the gift that is in thee, which was given thee by prophecy* (I Tim. 4:14). The office was not only linked, therefore, to that of the prophets above it, but formed the transition to that of the regular ministry below it; and this in a twofold sense, as embracing both the administrative ·and instructional functions, which became permanent in the order of pastors and teachers. Eusebius seems to have been the first to apply the term evangelist to the writers of the Gospels. As used generally in later church history, evangelists represent that irregular ministry which is gifted in proclaiming the gospel to the unchurched, whether in new fields, or in reaching the unsaved through the means of established churches.

2. The regular and permanent ministry was appointed to care for the church after the apostolic supervision should be withdrawn. Two classes of office are mentioned—the *pastorate,* pertaining especially to the spiritual oversight of the church; and the *diaconate,* to the management of its temporal affairs. Those who served in the first office, were known as elders or presbyters (πρεσβύτεροι), and bishops (ἐπίσκοποι); those in the second, as deacons (διάκονοι).

The office of the pastorate has a twofold function— administrative and instructional; hence those chosen to fill this position were known as "pastors and teachers." Since the term pastor implies the duties of both instruction and government; and since elders or bishops were

There is therefore no office of eldership as such, but there is of course an ἐπισκοπή. . . . . It is remarkable, however, that no episcopate is alluded to, in the sense of a collective body of bishops; but once we read of a Christian Presbytery, as having ordained Timothy, after the pattern of the Jewish. . . . The elders of Judaism were seniors in age, chosen as assessors in the Sanhedrin with high priests and scribes. The elders of Christianity formed a body, generally but not always seniors in age, who presided over the Christian community as the only directing and governing authority. The term presbytery, therefore, runs up to the most reverend antiquity, and is invested with a dignity quite unique.— POPE, *Compend. Chr. Th.,* III, p. 343.

ordained in the various churches by the apostles or evangelists, it is evident that these are the pastors to which St. Paul refers in his Epistle to the Ephesians. The term *elder* was taken from Judaism, and had reference to age or dignity; that of *bishop* came from the Greeks, and had reference to office. We are to understand by the use of the term elder, not so much an *office*, as an *order* in the ministry. Hence we read of the ordination of Timothy, by the *laying on of the hands of the presbytery* (I Tim. 4:14). In apostolic times, it appears that the larger churches had several presbyters or elders, as in the church at Jerusalem (Acts 15:4); the church at Ephesus (Acts 20:17); and the prophets and teachers mentioned by name in Acts 13:1. When these elders met together for consultation or devotion, they would of necessity elect someone as moderator or presiding officer. Such an officer, we know from church history, was common during the second century, and was known as the προεστως or president of the church. It is not unlikely that it was to this that our Saviour referred when He addressed His epistles to the "angels" of the churches. This supposition is made more probable by the fact that in Judaism, the elder who officiated in the public prayers, was known as "the angel of the congregation." Whether the terms bishop and presbyter referred to the same office, or whether they express two distinct and sacred orders in the ministry has been the subject of much con-

Mr. Watson states that "the argument which is drawn from the promiscuous use of these terms in the New Testament, to prove that the same order of ministers is expressed by them, appears incontrovertible. When St. Paul, for instance, sends for the 'elders' or presbyters, of the church of Ephesus to meet him at Miletus, he thus charges them, 'Take heed to yourselves, and to all the flock, over which the Holy Ghost hath made you overseers,' or bishops. That here the elders or presbyters are called 'bishops' cannot be denied, and the very office assigned to them, to 'feed the church of God,' and the injunction, to 'take heed to the flock,' show that the office of elder or presbyter is the same as that of 'pastor' in the passage just quoted from the Epistle to the Ephesians. St. Paul directs Titus to 'ordain elders (presbyters) in every city,' and then adds, as a directory of ordination, 'a bishop must be blameless' plainly marking the same office by these two convertible appellations. 'Bishops and deacons' are the only classes of ministers addressed in the Epistle to the Philippians; and if the presbyters were not understood to be included under the term 'bishops,' the omission of any notice of this order of ministers is not to be accounted for."— WATSON, *Institutes*, II, pp. 575, 576.

troversy in the church. It cannot be doubted that the distinction between the terms arose at an early period, but "This," says Mr. Watson, "gives not the least sanction to the notion that bishops are a superior order of ministers to presbyters, invested in virtue of that order, and by divine right, with powers to govern both presbyters and people, and with exclusive authority to ordain to the sacred offices of the church" (WAKEFIELD, *Chr: Th.*, p. 542).

The office of the diaconate was concerned with the administration of the temporal affairs of the church. The appointment of the first deacons in the Christian church is distinctly recorded (Acts 6:1-16). The term *deacon* is derived from the Greek work διάκονος which denotes a "servant who attends his master, waits on him at table, and is always near his person to obey his orders." It was considered a more creditable form of service, than that implied in the term δοῦλος or slave. Our Lord used both terms in Matt. 20.26, 27, although these are somewhat veiled in the English translation. The qualifications of deacons and their wives are given by St. Paul in I Tim. 3:8-13. Christian women were invested with this office also, of whom Phoebe of Cenchrea, was one of the number (Rom. 16:1). The word *wives* (I Tim. 3:11) is sometimes translated *deaconesses*. It is probable, also, that St. Paul was speaking of the deaconesses when he

The manner in which the distinction between bishop and presbyter came into the church is pretty fully explained by Jerome, in his commentary on Titus 1:6: "A presbyter is the same as a bishop; and before there were, by the instigation of the devil, parties in religion, the churches were governed by joint councils of presbyters. But afterward it was decreed throughout the whole world that one chosen from among the presbyters should be put over the rest, and that the whole care of the church should be committed to him." Jerome proceeds to support his opinion, as to the original equality of presbyters and bishops, by commenting on Phil. 1:1, and on the interview of Paul with the Ephesian elders, and then adds, "Our design in these remarks is to show that among the ancients presbyter and bishop were the very same. But by degrees, that the plants of dissension might be plucked up, the whole concern was devolved upon an individual. As the presbyters, therefore, know that they are subjected, by the custom of the church, to him who is set over them, so let the bishops know that they are greater than presbyters more by custom than by any real appointment of Christ." In his Epistles to Evangelus and Occanus, Jerome assumes and maintains the same positions as in the foregoing passage.—POND, *Christian Theology*, p. 657.

describes the ministering widows (I Tim. 5:5-10). According to Calmet, "they served the church in those offices which the deacons could not themselves exercise, visiting those of their own sex in sickness, or when imprisoned for the faith. They were persons of advanced age, when chosen; and appointed to the office by imposition of hands." The word διακονία is a comprehensive term for ministry, and is once applied by our Lord to Himself (Matt. 20:28). In modern times, the word "minister" which is equivalent to "deacon" has come into common use as a substitute for the word elder or presbyter. For this reason, the deacon, in some churches is merely a presbyter on trial—a first step toward ordination as an elder.

Ordination of Ministers. The Scriptures clearly teach that the early church ordained elders or presbyters, by a formal setting apart to the office and work of the ministry. While it may be true that no particular form is prescribed, it seems evident from numerous references that the elders were set apart by the imposition of hands. Furthermore, it is evident from the Scriptures that the power of ordination rested in the eldership itself; and that all candidates were to be adjudged as worthy or unworthy of the office only by those who had been themselves ordained. Ordination, therefore, is to be regarded as in some sense, a divinely authorized and prescribed form of investiture or inauguration to a particular order. But ordination does not make the elder an officer in a particular church. This can be done only as he is elected

In the time of the apostles, who were endowed with special gifts, the concurrence of the people in the appointment of men to the sacred office was not, perhaps, always formally taken; but the directions to Timothy and Titus imply a reference to the judgment of the members of the church, because from them only it could be learned whether the party fixed upon for ordination possessed those qualifications without which ordination was prohibited. When churches assumed a more regular form, it was usual for the people to be present at ordinations and to ratify the action by their approbation. Sometimes also they nominated persons by suffrages, and thus proposed them for ordination. The mode in which the people shall be made a concurrent party is a matter of prudential regulation; but they had an early, and certainly a reasonable right to a voice in the appointment of their ministers, though the power of ordination was vested in ministers alone, to be exercised on their responsibility to Christ.—WAKEFIELD, *Chr. Th.,* p. 546.

by the church, and freely accepts this election. Thus, the eldership is an order of the ministry, from which only pastors can be elected, but until so elected they are not pastors of particular churches. This does not prevent a licensed minister from serving in the capacity of a pastor, but until ordained as an elder, he is not invested with all the rights and privileges of the ministry, and therefore cannot in the fullest sense meet the requirements of the office. What is true of the pastorate, is true also of other and various offices of the church. We may safely maintain, therefore, that there is one order in the ministry, but many and various offices. The qualifications for bishops or elders, and deacons are fully stated by St. Paul in his Epistles to Timothy and Titus (I Tim. 3: 1-13; Titus 1: 5-9).

Administrative and Disciplinary Functions. The church through its ministers exercises three forms of administrative power. (1) There is what the older theologians called the *potestas ordinans,* or διατακτική: by which is meant the power of the church in relation to the laws of order and government. The fact that the church is an institution made up of human beings, implies that it must have laws, and that these must be properly administered. These laws must be *scriptural,* that is, they must be drawn immediately from the Scriptures, or indirectly by inference; "so that whatsoever is not contained therein is not to be enjoined as an article of faith." They must be *spiritual.* The church has no voice in civil and secular matters, and, therefore, has no right to dictate to its members only in so far as moral and religious questions are involved. Again, these laws must be purely *ministerial.* Those through whom the government of the church is administered, are not the lords over God's heritage, but ensamples to the flock. (2) There is the *potestas* δογματική, or the didactic functions of the church. Since the church is the depository of the Scriptures, its ministers are required to defend them as a precious heritage. It is further required of them to preach the Word, and to use every possible means for its promulgation. This includes the instruction of the youth, the use of the Scriptures, psalms, hymns and spiritual songs in the public services, and the conserving of sound doctrine in the church. (3) there is the *potestas δια-κριτική*, or disciplinary function of the church. Ministers are not only required to teach, but to exercise proper discipline in the congregation. Neither the church nor its ministers, however, have power to use civil authority in even the severest cases of discipline. They have no right to inflict pain, to imprison individuals, or to confiscate property. Their power is limited to censure, suspension, or excommunication. Failure to observe this, has sometimes led to extravagant lengths in dealing with offenders against the church.

The authority of the church in matters of doctrine is thus summarized by Mr. Watson: (1) To declare the sense in which it interprets the language of Scripture on all the leading doctrines of Christianity; . . . . (2) To require from all its members, with whom the right of private judgment is by all Protestant churches left inviolate, to examine such declarations of faith, with modesty and respect to those grave and learned assemblies in which all these points have been weighed with deliberation; receiving them as guides to truth, not implicitly, it is true, but still with docility and humility; (3) To silence within its own pale the preaching of all doctrines contrary to its received standards. Nor is there anything in the exercise of this authority contrary to Christian liberty; because the members of any communion, and especially the ministers, know beforehand the terms of fellowship with the churches whose confessions of faith are thus made public; and because also, where conscience is unfettered by public law, they are neither prevented from enjoying their own opinions in peace, nor from propagating them in other assemblies.—WATSON, *Institutes*, II, p. 598.

Generally speaking, nothing is more unreasonable than the view that the state, the most comprehensive of all earthly institutions, and the one which so decidedly plays a chief part in the world's history, should be withdrawn from the influences of Christianity, and thus excluded from that transformation of things temporal which Christianity is designed to effect. The necessity for the Christian character of states is mainly founded on the fact that the state does not exist for the sake of this or that subordinate aim, but for the sake of human nature itself; that its vocation is to furnish and work out those external conditions which are indispensable to human culture and prosperity. It is for this very reason that there can be no constitution or government worthy of the name, which is not pervaded by a thorough understanding of the nature and destination of man, of the history of the race, and the ultimate object of human history. This ultimate object is above the state, nay, reaches beyond the sphere of the state. But the state must, nevertheless, regard itself as subservient thereto, and should in all its institutions keep it in view as a last resort. The object of the state will ever be erroneously viewed, so long as it is not consciously placed in relation with the object and aim of the race.—MARTENSEN, *Christian Ethics*, II, pp. 98, 99.

CHAPTER XXXII

THE CHURCH: ITS WORSHIP AND SACRAMENTS

Having considered the organization and ministry of the church, we must now turn our attention to its worship and ordinances. Here we have a changed aspect—not now the Church as the body of Christ, or an institute of evangelism; but as the temple of the Spirit, and hence an institute of worship. So, also, there is a changed aspect of the ministry, which is not now regarded as the focal point of the church's contact with the world, but with God—not as a priestly substitution, but as a prophetic leadership. The subject matter embraces not only the nature and forms of worship, but a consideration also of (1) the Sabbath; (2) the Means of Grace; and (3) the Sacraments, with a special consideration of (4) Baptism; and (5) the Lord's Supper.

The Worship of the Primitive Church. The worship of the early church was patterned in a general way, after the forms used in the Jewish synagogues. In the time of our Lord, this service included, (1) the *Shema,* preceded

The subject of worship, as to its order and form, belongs properly to practical rather than systematic theology. It is, however, vitally related to biblical theology which gives it the concept of God upon which all true worship must rest. Christian worship, we may say, is a conscious act based upon a conviction of God as revealed through Jesus Christ. For this reason the subject demands some discussion in any balanced system of dogmatics.

The ministry of the Word and the ministry of the Sacraments—"these two," says Thomas a Kempis, "may be called the two tables set on either side in the spiritual treasury of the holy church. The one is the table of the holy altar, having this holy bread, that is the precious body of Christ. The other is the table of the laws of God, containing the holy doctrine, instructing man in right faith, and leading him into the inward secrecies that are called *sancta sanctorum,* where the inward secrets of scripture be hid and contained (Bk. IV, chapter 11).

Robert Will points out that there are two currents of life in the phenomena of worship, one proceeding from the transcendent reality, the other flowing from the religious life of the subject. The descending current includes all forms of revelation, the ascending, all forms of prayer. Nor does the mutual action of the two currents exclude the primacy of the divine action, for this is manifest, not only in the descending current of the Word and the Sacraments, but in the immanent action within the life of souls.

and followed by benedictions; (2) prayers, probably not set forms at this time; and (3) lessons from the law and the prophets. Here the service originally ended; but as Hebrew ceased to be the spoken language, there was added later, (4) a translation or paraphrase of the readings into the vernacular; and (5) an exposition, not necessarily a sermon, which was frequently delivered in a sitting posture. In the Christian Church, previous to A.D. 100, the service consisted of the *Eucharist* or Lord's Supper, preceded by the *agape* or love feast, and followed by what Duchesne calls "the liturgy of the Holy Spirit." It seems probable, that at first the *agape* was a real meal, which the people ate until they were satisfied; and that following this, certain portions of the bread and wine having been set apart, were eaten solemnly as the Eucharist. Thus in the *Didache*, there is this statement, "After ye are filled, then give thanks." Early abuses, however, soon attached to this part of the service (Cf. I Cor. 11: 20-22), and it seems to have been finally merged into the Eucharist. It is for this reason that the early worship is commonly stated to be twofold—the eucharist service, and the free worship. (1) The first part of the service included the reading of the Scriptures and prayer, as well as the consecration and distribution of the elements. The sermon also formed a part of the service, as did the singing of psalms, hymns and spiritual songs. The letters of the apostles were read,

The earliest account of Christian worship after the close of the canon, is from the letters of Pliny, who was proconsul of Bithynia about A.D. 110. He states that the Christians were accustomed to meet together on a set day, before dawn, and sing responsive hymns to Christ as their God, and to pledge themselves in a sacrament to abstain from every form of evil, to commit no theft, rapine, or adultery, to falsify no word, and betray no trust. At a later period in the day they met together again, and joined in a harmless supper.—PLINY TO TRAJAN, Letter 95.

Justin Martyr in his first Apology, says "On the day called Sunday, all the Christians of a neighborhood meet together in one place, and listen to the reading of the gospels and the prophets. The presiding bishop preaches a sermon, exhorting them to holy living. All stand up, and pray. Bread is then brought in, with wine and water, the sacramental wine being invariably diluted. After further prayers, to which the people respond with audible "Amens," the body and blood of Christ are distributed. Portions are sent to the sick, and a collection is taken for the poor.

during the *agape,* or just before the communion service. (2) The second part, or so-called "free worship" held a very large place in the Christian service, as it is represented to us by the most ancient documents. After the Eucharist, inspired persons began to speak before the assembly, and to manifest the presence of the Spirit which inspired them. The exercise of the prophetic gift seems to have been most in evidence. Duchesne in his *Origines* says, "There is as it were a liturgy of the Holy Spirit, a real liturgy, with real presence and real communion. The inspiration can be felt; it thrills the organs of some privileged persons; but the whole congregation is moved, edified, and even ravished to a greater or less extent, and transported, in the divine spheres of the Paraclete." It is to this evidently, that St. Paul refers (I Cor. 14: 23); and abuses leading to disorder having crept in, he seeks to correct these by further instruction (I Cor. 14: 26-33).

Corporate and Individual Worship. Christian worship is both individual and social. Worship in its very nature is profoundly personal, but it is also the act of a person who is essentially social. The first words of the "Lord's Prayer" remind each individual worshiper of these social relationships. It is as "our" Father, not "my" Father, that he comes into the divine presence. However lonely the individual worshiper may appear to be, he yet stands as a member of the whole family of God. Corporate worship emphasizes the unity of the church. It exalts the body of Christ, rather than the free exercise of its many members. It checks religious egotism, breaks down devotional barriers, and confers the supporting and disciplinary benefits of life in a family. For this reason, corporate worship is exceedingly important, whatever may be its outward form or manner of expression. On the other hand, individual worship is basic. There is a true secret of worship which belongs to every child of God. Advocates of corporate religion have sometimes revealed a tendency to regard these hidden and personal lives of prayer, as lacking in social value, or as being spiritually selfish. But this is a superficial view of the matter, for it is the character of the personal life that gives strength to corporate worship. The value of the prophetic or charismatic aspect of worship, lies in the fact that it stresses the spiritual exercises of the individual, and gives a strong ethical basis to Christian character. It is one of the tragedies of church history, that the balanced form of worship as found in the apostolic church, was so soon lost. Separated from one another, the corporate or sacramental form of worship, tended toward ritualism — a cultus, with cathedral, altar and priest; while the prophetic, or free individual worship, improperly governed, frequently resulted in the wildest forms of fanaticism. Thus from the simple, but twofold character of primitive worship with its balanced elements of the corporate and the free, a dualism arose, which through the centuries has developed into the two general types of Christianity which we now know as the catholic and the evangelical. The simplicity of worship as found in the apostolic church, had in it, both the sacramental phase with its emphasis upon unity, and the prophetic, with its freedom, its enthusiasm, its personal spontaneity, and its intense ethical demands. It will be seen then, that emphasis upon individual experience, must be carefully guarded and conserved, by a corresponding emphasis upon corporate worship. The warning, "not to

Evangelical worship as re-established by the Reformers, was not intended to be an innovation, but a restoration of the ancient balance between the Word and the Sacraments, and thus bring back the soul into a direct and immediate spiritual relation with God. The free churches have certain ideas of worship in common: (1) the higher the type of worship, the less importance is attached to external matters; (2) that an overemphasis upon the means of worship detracts from the highest communion with God; and (3) that the worthiest worship is that which is richest in ethical content. But as we have shown, this soon falls into the formal and commonplace without the balancing influence of corporate worship.

Evelyn Underhill in her book entitled *Worship* points out that the prophetic element, although hidden in the corporate life, never dies out, but reappears in every "revival" as a protest against the supposed formality and unreality of the liturgic routine; reasserting the freedom and direct action of the Spirit, the priesthood of the individual, the prophetic office of "preachers of the Word," and the call to personal consecration. Wherever the institutional life becomes standardized, there is always a reaction toward the primitive group enthusiasm and the prophetic ministry described in the New Testament.

forsake the assembling of yourselves together," has a philosophical as well as a religious basis.

The Order and Forms of Worship. The order of divine worship has reference to the principles, according to which it must be conducted. These principles are fully set forth in the Holy Scriptures. (1) Worship must be offered to the Triune God. This is a fundamental principle. Whatever of worship is paid to one member of the Trinity, must be offered to all—or must be offered to the One in the unity of the other Two. (2) Worship must be mediatorial—*spiritual sacrifices, acceptable to God through Jesus Christ.* It is only through these mediatorial offices that we have the boldness (or liberty) to *enter into the holiest by the blood of Jesus* (Heb. 10:19); and it is *"through him"* that we have *access by one Spirit unto the Father* (Eph. 2:18). (3) Worship must be spiritual—that is, it must be inspired by the Spirit to be acceptable unto God. *God is a Spirit: and they that worship him must worship him in spirit and in truth* (John 4:24). It is the touch of God upon the soul that is the source of all true worship. The forms of worship are also left to the discretionary powers of the church, in so far as they conform to the Scriptures. (1) The time of worship is to be set by the church, but public worship must not be allowed to interfere with, or infringe upon, the rights of the family and the individual. The church may appoint special seasons for prayer and fasting, for preaching, and for thanksgiving. (2) The law of decency and order requires that public services be regulated. Spontaneity flowing from the presence of the Spirit in fresh anointing, is to be commended, but all mere caprice is to be put away as out of harmony with the dignity which should attach to divine service. (3) Simplicity must characterize the various forms of public service. An elaborate ritual which distracts the soul from its one true function of spiritual worship is detrimental; but a careless and indifferent spirit is death to any form of spiritual worship.

The Sabbath

The institution of the Sabbath is regarded as one of the permanent and divine ordinances of the church. It is, for this reason, sometimes treated by theologians in connection with the means of grace. Introduced as it was, at the time of man's creation, the Sabbath belongs to the race generally and in perpetuity. Its original design was a rest from physical labor, and with it a spiritual design, that man, thus ceasing from other occupations, might hold communion with his Creator. A right understanding of the Sabbath as an institution, therefore, must regard it as a period of rest after six days of labor. It consists of two parts, the *holy rest,* and the *day* on which this rest is observed. The first part belongs to the moral law, the second is purely positive. Thus as Dr. Wakefield indicates, God "did not bless and hallow the day *as the seventh,* but only as being the day on which the Sabbath, or holy rest, was to be kept. While, therefore, the Sabbath itself is a perpetual institution, morally binding upon all men, the law which determines the time of its observance is purely positive, and consequently may be changed. But though the day might be altered, without altering the substance of the institution, yet it could be altered only by divine authority. The same authority which instituted the Sabbath, appointed

Dr. Pond says that "neither the original institution of the Sabbath, nor the command in the decalogue, confines or fixes its observance to the seventh day of our week. God made the world in six days, and sanctified and blessed the seventh; but there is no certainty that this day corresponds to our seventh day, or Saturday, or that it corresponded to the seventh day of the ancient Jews. The command in the decalogue, also, requires us to labor six days, and to keep the seventh; but, as it does not fix upon any precise day from which the reckoning shall commence, it is impossible to determine, merely from this command, what particular day is to be observed."—POND, *Chr. Th.,* p. 632. "The institution of the Sabbath obviously consists of two parts; first, the appointing of one day in seven to be kept holy to the Lord; and, secondly, the fixing of a particular day to be observed. It is the first of these points which is settled in the original institution, and in the Fourth Commandment. The second has been settled, from time to time by other intimations of the divine will. The Sabbath began on the seventh day from the commencement of the creation, or on the first day after the creation of man. In the time of Moses it was observed on the seventh day of the Jewish week. Under the present dispensation, the Sabbath is fixed . . . . on the first day of our Christian week.—POND, *Chr. Th.,* pp. 632, 633.

also the day on which it was to be observed; and no other authority is competent to change either the one or the other." Two considerations then, demand our attention, (1) The Sabbath as a universal and perpetual obligation; (2) the change of the day as divinely authorized. To these must be added (3) the manner in which the Sabbath is to be observed.

The Sabbath as a Universal and Perpetual Obligation. When our Lord said, "The Sabbath was made for man," He referred to its original institution as a universal law, and not merely to the Jewish Sabbath as an enactment of the law of Moses. It belongs to all mankind, forms a part of the moral law as expressed in the Ten Commandments, and was never abrogated. It is sometimes stated that the law under the Mosaic dispensation was formulated into nine moral precepts, with a Sabbath commandment added, making ten in all. But there is no reason to suppose that the statement concerning the Sabbath is not so much a moral commandment as the other nine. The setting apart of a seventh of man's time to physical rest is essential to his well-being, if not his existence; and the devotement of this time to God, is a perpetual memorial of his spiritual mission, without which the social order would have no meaning. That the Sabbath is a moral obligation is seen from the argument of St. Paul concerning the relation of the law to faith. *Do we then make void the law through faith? God forbid; yea, we establish the law* (Rom. 3:31). It is evident that St. Paul is not referring to the civil or ceremonial law of the Jews, but to the fundamental law as expressed in the Ten Commandments. Thus in Romans 7:7 he says, *I had not known sin but by the law; for I had not known lust, except the law had said, Thou shalt not covet.* The law which is mentioned here is that of the Decalogue, and it is this which Christianity establishes. If so, then the law of the Sabbath being a part of the Decalogue, is as binding upon Christians as formerly it was upon the Jews. We may say then with conviction that whoever denies the obligation of the Sabbath, denies the whole Decalogue. Christians observe the Sabbath as truly as did the Jews, but they celebrate it on another day. That this day was changed by our Lord, is our next question for consideration.

The Change of the Day as Divinely Authorized. When Jesus declared that "the Son of man is Lord also of the sabbath," He doubtless intended them to understand that He had power to change the day on which the holy rest should be observed. The Scriptures clearly indicate that the Sabbath has been celebrated on different days, and this subject now demands our consideration.

1. The primitive and patriarchal Sabbath. The first notice of the Sabbath is found in Genesis 2: 3, *And on the seventh day God ended his work which he had made. . . . . And God blessed the seventh day, and sanctified it: because that in it he had rested from all his work which God created and made* (Gen. 2: 2, 3). Here, in the institution of the Sabbath, it is distinctly declared to be a day of holy rest after six days of labor; and further, it is stated in this instance, to be a memorial of creation. Now it is evident that God's seventh day would not be man's seventh day. "The seventh day which God blessed in Eden," says Dr. Whitelaw, "was the first day of human life, and not the seventh day; and it is certain that God did not rest from His labors on man's seventh day, but on man's first." Hence Adam's first day, and each suc-

Man is the last of the geological series, such as fish, reptiles and mammalia, and is the crown and consummation of God's creative work. His existence, then, began at or near the close of the sixth creative day, so that God's Sabbath rest was man's first full day. If he began the calculation of the week from that time, then the first day of the week, and not the seventh, was the primitive and patriarchal Sabbath. "The holy rest day was the seventh from the first, in the count of God's works for man; but it was the first day in his created history. He appeared before his Maker on that day, in possession of all good, and in the probationary prospect of a confirmation of it forever. The day was therefore blessed and sanctified to man, as containing in its present and promised good his everlasting inheritance. No bloody rites and typical shadows had conducted him to the enjoyment of that glorious day; it arose to him as the rest of God. All was very good, and all was very satisfactory, to both God and man. But from this lofty probation he fell by transgression under the curse of the whole law. All good was lost, and all threatened evil was incurred, and we must now keep our eye fixed upon this day of the Lord, till its lost blessing shall be recovered through His mediation" (AKERS, *Biblical Chronology*. Cf. POTTS, *Faith Made Easy*).

ceeding eighth day, would be his Sabbath—a reference strikingly similar to our Lord's appearances on the first and eighth days.

2. The Jewish Sabbath. The next mention of the Sabbath is in connection with the giving of the manna (Ex. 16:14-31). Here the manna is stated to have fallen for six days, that is, from the sixteenth to the twenty-first day of the second month; and that the day following, or the twenty-second, was the first seventh day Sabbath celebrated in the Wilderness of Sin. *See,* said Moses, *for that the Lord hath given you the sabbath, therefore he giveth you on the sixth day the bread of two days. . . . . So the people rested on the seventh day* (Exod. 16:29, 30). That the Sabbath as a holy rest was re-established at this time, there can be no doubt; that it was celebrated on the same day as that of the patriarchal Sabbath, has been a matter of controversy. Thus if the twenty-second was a Sabbath day, the fifteenth should have been a Sabbath also. That it was not, seems to be indicated by the fact that they marched on that day (Exod. 16:1). Dr. W. H. Rogers holds that "the only change of the Sabbath by God's authority is for the Jews between the giving of the manna and the resurrection of Christ. The first day of the week, but always the seventh after six working days, was the day of the holy rest from Adam to Moses. The Sabbatism was separated from idolatry by changing it from Sunday to Saturday among the chosen people 'throughout their generations,' fifteen hundred years (Cf. Exod. 31:13, 14; Ezek. 20: 12). At Christ's resurrection expired by statute limitation this peculiarity of exceptional change, leaving the divine rule for all mankind, requiring first-day Sabbath keeping, as had been the case for the first twenty-five hundred years of human history." It should be noted also that to the memorial of creation which the Sabbath represented, there was added also during this period, a secondary memorial—that is, a remembrance of their deliverance from the land of Egypt. This memorial was to last only "through their generations," and as indicated above expired by the statute of limitations. With the

coming of "the last Adam" the Sabbath was restored to the original day on which it was celebrated by the first Adam.

3. The Christian Sabbath or "Lord's Day." That the Christian Sabbath was restored, or at least changed to the first day, has been the teaching of the church since apostolic times. As such it came early to be known as the "Lord's Day" to distinguish it from the Jewish Sabbath. That this change was divinely authorized is shown (1) by the example of Jesus; (2) by the authority of the apostles; and (3) by the practices of the early church. To this may be added (4) the testimony of the early apostolic fathers.

(1) Jesus placed approval upon the first day of the week, by meeting with His disciples on this day. The resurrection took place on the morning of the first day of the week. The four accounts of the evangelists agree that the Saviour arose early "the first day of the week" (John 20:1). His first meeting with the body of His disciples was on the evening of the resurrection day (John 20:19); and the second on the evening of the eighth day, which would of course, be the following first day of the next week. There were three more "first days" before the ascension, but it is not said whether Jesus met with His disciples on any or all of them. There were, however, three more appearances—to the five hundred brethren, to James, and to the apostles (I Cor.

Concerning the instructions given by Jesus to the apostles during the forty days, Justin Martyr in giving his reasons for keeping the first day, says, "Because it is the first day on which God, having wrought a change in the darkness and matter, made the world; and Jesus Christ our Saviour, on the same day arose from the dead. For He was crucified on the day before Saturn (Saturday); and on the day after that of Saturn, which is the day of the Sun, having appeared to His apostles and disciples, He taught them these things, which we have submitted to you also for your consideration." This shows clearly that the belief was current among the early fathers who associated with the apostles, that they had been given the authority to celebrate the Sabbath on the first day of the week, as a memorial not only of the first creation, but of the new creation by the resurrection of Jesus Christ from the dead.

Ignatius, a disciple of St. John who wrote about 100 A.D. and therefore only about ten years or less after the death of St. John says this, "If those who were concerned with old things have come to newness of hope, no longer keeping (Jewish) Sabbaths, but living according to the Lord's Day, in which our life has arisen again through Him and His death."

15: 1-4). (2) The apostles authorized the change, doubt-less due to the unrecorded instructions of Jesus during the forty days (Cf. Acts 1: 2). Twenty-five years later St. Paul preached at Troas, *upon the first day of the week, when the disciples came together to break bread* (Acts 20: 7), which indicates his approval of the day of worship. About one year later, he wrote to the Corinthians saying, *As I have given order to the churches of Galatia, even so do ye. Upon the first day of the week let every one of you lay by him in store, as God hath prospered him, that there be no gathering when I come* (I Cor. 16: 1, 2). This clearly indicates that the apostle sanctioned the first day as the Christian Sabbath. (3) The practices of the early churches are further proof of worship on the first day of the week. This is shown by the passages just cited, and also by St. John's reference to the Sabbath as the "Lord's day" (Rev. 1: 10). Since he uses the phrase without any reference to the first day, it is evidence that when the Apocalypse was written, the "first day" was generally known as the "Lord's day" in contradistinction to the Jewish seventh day.

We can give only a few of the references to the fathers. Irenæus says, "On the Lord's day every one of us Christians keeps the Sabbath; meditating in the law, and rejoicing in the works of God." Justin Martyr states that "on the day called Sunday there is a gathering in one place of all who reside either in the cities or country places, and the memoirs of the apostles and the writings of the prophets are read." The Didache has this direction for the saints, "But on the Lord's day do ye assemble and break bread, and give thanks, after confessing your transgressions, in order that your sacrifice may be pure." Clement of Alexandria says that "a true Christian, according to the commands of the gospel, observes the Lord's day by casting out all bad thoughts, and cherishing all goodness, honoring the resurrection of the Lord, which took place on that day." Tertullian says, "Sundays we give to joy," "to observe the day of the Lord's resurrection." Origen wrote that the Lord's day was placed above the Jewish Sabbath. Eusebius has this decisive passage, "The Word (Christ) by the new covenant translated and transferred the feast of the Sabbath to the morning light, and gave us the symbol of true rest —the saving Lord's day—the first (day) of light in which the Saviour obtained the victory over death. On this day, which is the first of the light, and of the true Son, we assemble, after an interval of six days, and celebrate the holy and spiritual Sabbath; even all nations redeemed by Him throughout the world, assemble and do those things according to the spiritual law which was decreed for the priests to do on the Sabbath (that is the Jewish Sabbath) these we have transferred to the Lord's day, as more appropriately belonging to it, because it has the precedence, and is the first in rank, and more honorable than the Jewish Sabbath."

(4) Since some of the early apostolic fathers were associated with the apostles, their writings from the historical standpoint, furnish conclusive evidence as to the current thought of that time. Here we may mention Ignatius, Polycarp, Irenæus, Justin Martyr, Tertullian, Clement of Alexandria, Theodoret, Eusebius, Origen, the Didache or "Teachings of the Twelve" and many other authorities. All of these indicate that the first day of the week was the Lord's day, and that it was set apart and distinguished from other days in that it was the day of the resurrection. It was, therefore, a holy day, or a holy Sabbath.

The Manner in Which the Sabbath Is to Be Observed. Since the Sabbath as a holy rest day is enjoined upon the church as a perpetual obligation, the manner of its observance should be given brief consideration. The original commandment is *Remember the sabbath day, to keep it holy.* To this, both in the Exodus account, and in that found in Deuteronomy, there is the added explanation which forms the basis of the memorial aspect of the day. *Six days shalt thou labor, and do all thy work: but the seventh day is the sabbath of the Lord thy God: in it thou shalt not do any work, thou, nor thy son, nor thy daughter, thy manservant, nor thy maidservant, nor thy cattle, nor thy stranger that is within thy gates: for in six days the Lord made heaven and earth, the sea, and all that in them is, and rested the seventh day: wherefore the Lord blessed the sabbath day, and hallowed it* (Exodus 20:9-11; cf. Deut. 5:12-15 where deliverance from Egypt is made a secondary memorial for the Jewish dispensation.) We are to understand from this that the day is to be set apart for the worship of God and devoted to the spiritual interests of mankind. For this reason, all secular work is prohibited, except that which is commonly known as a work of necessity or mercy. This truth is brought out clearly by Isaiah also, as follows: *If thou turn away thy foot from the sabbath, from doing thy pleasure on my holy day; and call the sabbath a delight, the holy of the Lord, honorable; and shalt honor him, not doing thine own ways, nor finding thine own pleasure, nor speaking thine own words* (Isa. 58: 13). Thus the Old Testament fixes the Sabbath day as a time of worship and communion with God. It is a cessation of labor, whether of the body or the mind, in order to permit time for spiritual things. Our Lord gives us in the New Testament, two principles also, which parallel the twofold aspect of the Sabbath as found in the Old Testament. The first has reference to the holiness of the day, *God is a Spirit: and they that worship him must worship him in spirit and in truth* (John 4: 24). Here the true inwardness of the Sabbath is seen—a spiritual rest of the soul, from which flows that worship which is in Spirit and in truth. The second, concerns man's interests, *And he said unto them, The sabbath was made for man, and not man for the sabbath: therefore the Son of man is Lord also of the sabbath* (Mark 2: 27, 28). Here it is clearly taught, that those things which pertain to man's highest welfare, that is, his spiritual interests, are to be permitted on the sabbath day; and this is a true and sure test as to the kind and extent of secular labor on the Sabbath day.

The Means of Grace

The means of grace, or the *media gratiæ* of the theologians, are the divinely appointed channels through which the influences of the Holy Spirit are communicated to the souls of men. They are sometimes defined as "the ordinances and institutions appointed of God for the establishment and spread of the kingdom of grace among men" (MacPherson); or "the motives or means by which holy and gracious affections are awakened in the soul" (Pond). The Protestant doctrine stands midway between the exaggerated supernaturalism of the Roman Catholic church, which holds that the ordinances have power in themselves to confer grace; and the abstract position of the mystics who seek to do away with all external means. In a general sense, therefore, it is proper to regard all spiritual helps as means of grace, but theology has usually stated these as (1) the Word of God; and (2) Prayer—these being known as the universal means of grace. Following this is (3) the fellowship of the saints; and (4) the sacraments—these being known as the economic means of grace.

The Word of God as the Universal Means of Grace. The Scriptures claim to be the universal channel of grace. Their sufficiency is everywhere declared, both in the Old and the New Testaments. The Word of God is the *sword of the Spirit*—the instrument by which He operates in converting and sanctifying the souls of men. Christians are said to have been begotten *through the gospel* (I Cor. 4:15); to have been *born again, not of corruptible seed, but of incorruptible, by the word of God, which liveth and abideth forever* (I Peter 1:23); and to *sanctify them through thy truth* (John 17:17). St. Paul makes the word a means of grace by linking it directly to faith—*faith cometh by hearing, and hearing by the word of God* (Rom. 10:17). Resting securely on the basis of God's Word, faith opens the door of access to God, and lays hold of the purchased blessings. Here the importance of the ministry is seen in a new light. It is through the preached word that grace is administered to the hearers—not primarily now, to win men to God, but to deepen their love to Christ. The goal which St. Paul sets is that they *being rooted and grounded in love, may be able to comprehend with all saints what is the breadth, and the length, and the depth, and height; and to know the love of Christ, which passeth all knowledge, that ye might be filled with all the fulness of God* (Eph. 3:17-19). It is of course highly

A church consciousness which does not seek by means of preaching to submit itself to the testing of God's Word, and by its fullness to be edified, will very soon find itself reduced to an indistinct, powerless spiritualism, which knows no difference between the sayings of men and the saving doctrine of Christ. And the preacher who makes himself only "the mouth of the congregation," and who does not prepare himself, if need be alone—fortifying himself with Holy Scripture and the ecumenical testimony—to speak against the erring consciousness of the congregation, infected as it is with the spirit of the day, will soon become the servant of the church in such a sense, that he can no longer be the Lord's servant. The preacher, therefore, is rightly called "the minister of the Word"; and it is also in harmony with the Word of God, that the church shall test and prove that which they hear, according to the pattern of the apostolic church. "Let the prophets," says St. Paul, "speak two or three, and let the others judge" (I Cor. 14:29).— MARTENSEN, *Christian Dogmatics*, p. 414.

important to bear in mind the relation of the Holy Spirit to the Word. The preaching of the Word is to be *in demonstration of the Spirit and of power* (I Cor. 2:4). Apart from the Spirit's operation upon the hearts of men, the Word has no power. It derives its efficacy as a means of grace, only as it becomes the instrument of the Spirit. This truth taught with such accuracy by the theologians of the Reformation, must not be neglected or set aside. Again, the Word must be preached in all its offices, or spiritual growth will be retarded. The Scripture is given for *doctrine,* or instruction in the truths of the gospel; for *reproof,* of neglect or failure; for *correction,* of wrong tendencies, and for *instruction in righteousness, or the art of holy living* (II Tim. 3:16). Not only are the Scriptures to be read and studied privately, but they are to be read in the family (Deut. 6:6, 7; cf. II Tim. 1:5; 3:15); and also in the public services of the church (Deut. 31:12; Joshua 8:34, 35; Luke 4:16-18 furnishes examples of this practice. It is expressly enjoined in I Tim. 4:13).

Prayer or Communion with God. Prayer as combined with the Word is also a universal means of grace. When the promises of the Word are pleaded in prayer, they become effective in the spiritual life of the Christian; and when the sacraments are received in faith, they become likewise, channels of blessing. Thus prayer appears to be the concomitant of all other means of grace. Prayer is defined by Mr. Watson as "the offering of our desires to God through the mediation of Jesus Christ, under the influence of the Holy Spirit, and with suitable dispositions, for things agreeable to His will." Thus to

There has never been wanting a tendency to make the Scriptures sufficient of themselves, without any supernatural accompanying influence, to effect the salvation of men. The ancient Pelagians and semi-Pelagians regarded the Word of God as the intellectual and moral discipline which best suits the spiritual nature of man, its honest use leading sincere inquirers to perfection. As human nature retains its original elements unimpaired, its natural powers are supposed to be sufficient under the influence of truth to guide to salvation. Modern rationalism has the same general estimate of the Word of God: not regarding it as in any specific sense the means of grace, but only as one among many instruments of moral discipline.—POPE, *Compend. Chr. Th.,* III, p. 297.

be acceptable to God prayer must be offered through the mediation of Christ; it must be offered in faith and in a spirit of humility; and it must be according to the will of God. The elements of a well-ordered prayer are usually classified as (1) *adoration,* which ascribes to God the perfections which belong to His nature, and which should be uttered in deep devotion, reverence, confidence and affection; (2) *thanksgiving,* or the pouring forth of the soul in gratitude; (3) *confession,* or deep penitence, submission and humility; (4) *supplication,* or a prolonged and earnest looking to God in dependence, for needed blessings; and (5) *intercession,* or a pleading for our fellowmen, with sincere desires for their spiritual welfare. Four of these elements are mentioned by St. Paul in a single verse (I Tim. 2:1). As in the case of the Word as a means of grace, prayer is classified as (1) private prayer; (2) family prayer; (3) public

Devotion is the first step in raising up the soul to God, a relation of intercourse, of contemplation, a union with God, in edifying thought. But worship is an act; and the exercise of contemplation must lead on to a practical surrender of the will, in the offering of the heart. This, as a definite act of worship, takes place in prayer. Prayer, therefore, demands a deeper and more weighty inwardness than devotion, and many may be devotional who are not yet really prayerful. For in devotion man's relation to God is for the most part only an edifying reflection; a relation in which God is certainly present, and in which the soul certainly feels God's nearness, but in which withal, God is present, so to speak, in the third person only; in prayer, on the other hand, God is immediately present in the second Person, as a personal Thou, corresponding to the human I. In devotion, the man's relation to God is of a general kind, as the God of creation and of the whole church; in prayer that general relation is narrowed into one purely individual and direct between the man and God. In prayer, I hold communion with the God of all creation and of the church universal, as my God, the God of the individual man. This immediate relation between God and the soul, when the soul breathes forth its longings for the light of God's countenance, and calls upon Him, and when God himself gives His Holy Spirit to the suppliant, this union, *"unio mystica,"* is the essence of all true prayer. But the distinctive thing about Christian prayer is that it is prayer in the name of Jesus" (John 16:23, 24).—MARTENSEN, *Chr. Dogm.,* p. 415.

"Prayer," says Dr. Ryland, "has divided seas, rolled up flowing rivers, made flinty rocks gush into fountains, quenched flames of fire, muzzled lions, disarmed vipers and poisons, marshaled the stars against the wicked, stopped the course of the moon, arrested the sun in his rapid race, burst open iron gates, recalled souls from eternity, conquered the strongest devils, commanded legions of angels down from heaven. Prayer has bridled and chained the raging passions of man, and routed and destroyed vast armies of proud, daring, blustering atheists. Prayer has brought one man from the bottom of the sea, and carried another in a chariot of fire to heaven. What has prayer not done?"

prayer; to which is added another (4) ejaculatory prayer. By this is meant those short, occasional expressions of prayer or praise, flowing from a devotional frame of mind, or what is commonly known as a "spirit of prayer." Prayer is an obligation—a duty devolving upon all men. If it be neglected or omitted, there can be no advance in spiritual things.

Christian Fellowship. The Christian community is everywhere represented as a means of grace, both in the creeds and in the Scriptures. "The privileges and blessings which we have in association together in the Church of Jesus Christ are very sacred and precious. There is in it such hallowed fellowship as cannot otherwise be known. There is such helpfulness with brotherly watchcare and counsel as can be found only in the church. There is the godly care of pastors, with the teachings of the Word, and the helpful inspiration of social worship. And there is co-operation in service, accomplishing that which cannot otherwise be done." (*Covenant, Manual,* pp. 214, 215). The scriptures command us to *exhort one another daily, ... lest any of you be hardened through the deceitfulness of sin* (Heb. 3: 13); and to *obey them that have the rule over you, and submit yourselves: for they watch for your souls, as they that must give an account, that they may do it with joy, and not with grief: for that is unprofitable for you* (Heb. 13: 17). St. Paul exhorts the church to assist those who are tempted. He says, *Brethren, if a man be overtaken in a fault, ye which are spiritual, restore such an one in the spirit of meekness; considering thyself, lest thou also be tempted* (Gal. 6: 1).

The Sacraments. In this connection we shall treat the sacraments in a general way as the economic means of grace, reserving other important questions concern-

Christian fellowship is a privilege of church membership, and one of large spiritual profit. We are constituted for society, and are accordingly endowed with social affections. Life would be utterly dreary without its social element. But in no sphere is there deeper need of this element than in the religious. The Christian life would be lonely and lacking in spiritual vigor without the fellowship of kindred minds. On the other hand, the communion of souls alive in Christ is a fruition of grace. Here is a means of much spiritual profit.—MILEY, *Syst. Th.,* II, p. 389.

ing them for later consideration. In some sense, the sacraments are similar to all other means of grace, but in another, there are marked differences. These differences are due to the fact that they are not only individual but federal transactions; that is, they are signs and seals of a covenant. It is for this reason that they are known as the economic means of grace. Since a covenant implies the condescension of God in entering into relations with His people, the signs and seals must be mutual. By them, both the divine and human fidelity are pledged in sacred agreement. It is for this reason that a peculiar sacredness has always attached to these ordinances. Their efficacy, however, like that of the other means of grace, depends upon the Holy Spirit working in and through the faith of the believer.

The Sacraments

The term *sacraments* as used in theology, signifies an outward and visible sign of an inward and spiritual grace given unto us, ordained by Christ himself, as a means whereby we receive the same, and a pledge to assure us thereof. This is the definition of the Methodist Catechism. According to the Westminster Larger Catechism, "A sacrament is an holy ordinance instituted by Christ in His Church, to signify a seal, and exhibit unto those that are within the covenant of grace, the benefits of His mediation; to strengthen and increase their faith, and all other graces, to oblige them to obedience." The term *sacramentum* was originally applied to the money deposited in a sacred place by parties to a suit at law. Later it came to apply to any civil suit, and then to the oath taken by newly enlisted soldiers in the Roman army. From this it was carried over to the sacred ordinances of the church. Tertullian uses it in the twofold sense—first as applying to the army oath, and then to the Christian sacraments. As understood by the early Christians, the ordinances were religious rites which carried with them the most sacred obligation of loyalty to the church and to Christ. In the Greek church, the term *mystery* (μυστήριον) was used instead of sacrament, not, however, in the Pauline sense of a hidden truth revealed, but purely as an emblem. In ecclesiastical Latin, the term sacrament came to signify anything consecrated, while μυστήριον was used as a symbol or sign of a consecrated or sacred thing. Baptism, however, was held to represent more of the sacramental character as an oath of allegiance, while the Eucharist contained more of the mystery.

The Marks of a Sacrament. Since the Greek Orthodox and the Roman Catholic churches hold that there are seven sacraments, and the Protestant churches reduce the number to two, it is essential to understand what constitutes a sacrament. Dr. A. A. Hodge in his commentary on the Presbyterian Confession of Faith gives us the following marks. (1) A Sacrament is an ordinance immediately instituted by Christ. (2) A sacrament always consists of two elements: (a) an outward visible sign, and (b) an inward spiritual grace thereby signified. (3) The sign in every sacrament is sacramentally united to the grace which it signifies; and out of this union the scriptural usage has arisen of ascribing to the sign whatever is true of that which the sign signifies. (4) The sacraments were designated to represent, seal, and apply the benefits of Christ and the new covenant to believers. (5) They were designed to be pledges of our fidelity to Christ, binding us to his service, and at the same time badges of our profession, vis-

Dr. Pond gives the following marks of a sacrament. (1) It must be one of divine institution, it must be an ordinance of Christ. (2) It must be characterized by significance and appropriateness. It must not be an idle ceremony. It must have meaning—an important meaning. (3) It must hold intimate and vital connection with the church. It must be included in the covenant of the church, and be a rite of the church. (4) It must be of universal and perpetual obligation.

"Sacraments, ordained of Christ, are not only badges or tokens of Christian men's professions, but rather they are certain signs of grace, and God's good-will toward us, by the which he doth work invisibly in us, and doth not only quicken, but also strengthen and confirm our faith in Him." This is the first paragraph of Article XVI of Methodism, as revised by John Wesley. It is the same as Article XXV of the Anglican creed with the omission of the words "sure witnesses and effectual." These words were added to the creed originally, in order to counteract the teaching of Zwingli, and especially the Socinians, but the word "effectual" had to be used to support the *ex opere operatum* of the sacramental churches, and to this Mr. Wesley objected.

ibly marking the body of professors and distinguishing them from the world. Perhaps it is safe to say, that a rite in order to be properly termed a sacrament, must not only exhibit a general resemblance between the sign and the thing signified, but that there must be also the words of institution, and the promise which binds them together.

The Nature of a Sacrament. There are widely divergent opinions in the church, as to the manner in which divine power is attached to the outward and visible sign of the sacrament. (1) There is the sacramentarian view, according to which the sacraments contain the grace they signify; and when administered, convey this grace *ex opere operato*, that is, of necessity, apart from and independent of the faith of the communicant. (2) At the other extreme is the rationalistic view, which holds that the sacraments are purely symbolical, and that any power which attaches to them is to be found in the moral influence upon the mind, arising from meditation upon the events which they commemorate. This view is widely prevalent in the church. (3) There is a third or mediating view, which regards the sacraments as both signs and seals, signs as representing in action and by symbols, the blessings of the covenant; seals, as pledges of God's fidelity in bestowing them. This is the position generally held by the Protestant churches.

Signs and Seals. There has been little difference of opinion in the church concerning the sacraments as

There should be a clear understanding of the formulas that distinguish the different positions concerning the sacraments "To produce grace *ex opere operato*, says Bailly, "is to confer it by the power of the external act instituted by Christ, provided there is no hindrance. But to produce grace *ex opere operantis* is to confer it on account of the merits and dispositions of the receiver or minister."

Augustine held that the sacraments were *verba visibilia* or "visible words"; while Chrysostom said of them "one thing we see, another we believe." These statements have been received by the church generally as rightly indicating the meaning of the emblems.

The sacramentarian churches make a distinction between the matter and the form in the administration of the sacraments. The matter, refers to the physical elements and actions; the form, to the formula used in the consecration of the elements. The *res sacramenti* refers to the holy eucharist alone, and means the invisible substance present in the sacrament and constituting it the real vehicle of grace. The *virtus sacramenti* is applied to the efficacy of the sacrament, *ex opere operato* when validly performed.

signs, but widespread controversy concerning their character as seals. Overemphasis upon the former, as we have seen, led to the rationalistic view of the sacraments as mere symbols; undue emphasis upon the latter, to the sacramentarian view of the seals as reservoirs of grace. During the middle ages, two views were held as to the communication of this grace. Thomas Aquinas held to what is commonly known as the *ex opere operato,* or the view that the sacraments are channels of grace apart from any faith on the part of the communicant. Duns Scotus on the other hand, held to the *ex opere operantis,* which does not regard the sacraments as having power in themselves, except by a certain concomitance, the power accompanying them producing the sacramental effect through faith on the part of the communicant. The former developed into the doctrine of the Roman Catholic church as elaborated by the Council of Trent; the latter is essentially that held by the Protestant churches. Perhaps the simplest and most thorough explanation of the signs and seals, is the classic passage in Watson's *Institutes,* generally cited as an authoritative statement by Protestant theologians of the Arminian type. He says (1) "They are the signs of divine grace. As such they are visible and symbolical expositions of the benefits of redemption. In other words, they exhibit to the senses, under appropriate emblems, the same benefits that are exhibited in another form in the doctrine and promises of the Word of God." (2) "They are also seals. A seal is a confirming sign, or, according to theological language, there is in a sacrament

The importance attached to the *ex opere operato* by the Roman Catholic church is shown in Canons VI, VII, and VIII of the Tridentine Decrees. "Whoever shall affirm that the sacraments of the new law do not contain the grace they signify, or that they do not confer the grace on those who place no obstacle in its way, as if they were only external signs of grace or righteousness received by faith, and marks of Christian profession, whereby the faithful are distinguished from unbelievers; let him be accursed." "Whoever shall say that grace is not always given by these sacraments, and upon all persons, as far as God is concerned, if they be rightly received, but that it is only bestowed sometimes and on some persons: let him be accursed." "Whoever shall say that grace is not conferred by the sacraments of the new law, by their own proper *ex opere operato,* but that faith in the divine promise is all that is necessary to obtain grace: let him be accursed."

a *signum significans,* and a *signum confirmans;* the former of which it is said, *significare,* to notify or declare;
the latter, *obsignare,* to set one's seal to, to witness. As
therefore, the sacraments, when considered, as *signs,*
contain a declaration of the same doctrines and promises
which the written Word of God exhibits, but addressed
by a significant emblem to the senses; so also as *seals,*
or pledges, they confirm the same promises which are
assured to us by God's own truth and faithfulness in His
Word (which is the main ground of all affiance in His
mercy), and by His indwelling Spirit by which we are
'sealed,' and have in our hearts 'the earnest' of our
heavenly inheritance. This is done by an external and
visible institution; so that God has added these ordinances to the promises of His Word, not only to bring
His merciful purpose toward us in Christ to mind, but
constantly to assure us that those who believe in Him
shall be and are made partakers of His grace." (WAT-
SON, *Institutes,* II, pp. 611, 612. Cf. WAKEFIELD, *Christian Theology,* p. 555.) The true Protestant doctrine,
therefore, avoids the excesses of Roman Catholicism on
the one hand, and the deficiencies of rationalism on the
other, embodying in its doctrine of the signs and seals,
all the truth that is contained in other views of the sacraments.

The sacraments are the seal of the covenant of grace, both on the
part of God and on the part of men. They are seals on the part of God
by which He declares His gracious intention of bestowing His favors
upon us, and by which He binds Himself to fulfill His covenant engagements. While we look upon these symbols we feel our minds impressed
with His condescension and love, our faith in His promises is confirmed,
and the most devout affections toward Him are excited. On our part
also they are seals by which we enter into the most solemn obligations
with Him, according to the term of the covenant which He proposes to
our acceptance. While, by the reception of these visible tokens, we profess to "lay hold upon the hope set before us," we seal the solemn contract, as with our own signature, that we will dedicate to God ourselves
and our all—that he will be His alone and His forever."—WAKEFIELD,
Chr. Th., p. 555.

Dr. Pope harmonizes the signs and seals as follows: "As signs, they
represent in action and by symbols, the great blessings of the covenant;
as seals they are standing pledges of the divine fidelity in bestowing
them on certain conditions, being the Spirit's instrument in aiding and
strengthening the faith which they require, and in assuring to that faith
the present bestowment of its object.—POPE, *Compend. Chr. Th.,* III.

Additions to the Sacraments. Protestantism admits but two sacraments—baptism and the Lord's Supper. All additions to these are regarded as pseudo-sacraments. In the early church, the term sacrament, translated as it was from the Greek word μυστήριον, came to be applied to all things where the word mystery was used. The Greek church early adopted the seven mysteries, and the Roman church at a later time, the seven sacraments, but these are not identical. During the middle ages, the schoolmen were divided as to the exact number, but the matter was finally settled by Peter Lombard, who fixed the number as seven, and states them in this order—baptism, the Lord's Supper, confirmation (of catechumens), ordination, extreme unction, auricular confession (penance), and wedlock. These were not established, however, as a dogma until the Council of Florence (A.D. 1442), and were later confirmed by the Council of Trent (A.D. 1547). The additional five so-called sacraments were rejected by the Protestant churches, either on the ground that they were not appointed such by our Lord, or that they were not true symbols of inner grace.

It is remarkable that the Greek and Roman communions, differing in so much besides, agree in accepting seven sacraments. Both base their acceptance on the authority of the church as interpreting the will of Christ, and vindicate them as enfolding and hedging round and sanctifying the whole of life at its several stages: Baptism is the sanctification of birth, confirmation of adult life, penance of the life of daily sin, the Eucharist of life itself, orders of legitimate authority, matrimony of the church's law of continuance and increase, and unction of the departure hence. . . . . They were variously illustrated and defended by the scholastics. It was supposed that each was symbolized by or symbolized one of the seven cardinal virtues, faith, love, hope, wisdom, temperance, courage, righteousness; they were explained by the analogy of the spiritual life with the physical, as birth, growth into adult age, nourishment, healing, reproduction, instruction, death . . . . baptism, confirmation, and orders, were held to have an indelible character, never effaceable, and never to be repeated.—Pope, *Compend. Chr. Th.*, III, pp. 305, 306.

The creed of Pope Pius IV regards the Seven Sacraments as binding upon every member of the Roman Catholic church. It reads as follows: "I profess that there are truly and properly seven sacraments of the new law, instituted by Jesus Christ our Lord, and necessary for the salvation of mankind, though not all for everyone, to wit, baptism, confirmation, Eucharist, penance, extreme unction, orders, and matrimony, and that they confer grace; and that of those, baptism, confirmation, and orders cannot be reiterated without sacrilege."

BAPTISM

"We believe that Christian baptism is a sacrament signifying acceptance of the benefits of the atonement of Jesus Christ, to be administered to believers, as declarative of their faith in Jesus Christ as their Saviour, and full purpose of obedience in holiness and righteousness.

"Baptism being the symbol of the New Testament, young children may be baptized, upon request of parents or guardians who shall give assurance for them of necessary Christian training.

"Baptism may be administered by sprinkling, pouring, or immersion, according to the choice of the applicant" (Manual, ¶18).

Definitions of Baptism. The above statements from the Creed do not of course, give us a formal definition of baptism, for this is presupposed. Webster, however, defines baptism as "the application of water to a person, as a sacrament or religious ceremony, by which he is initiated into the visible Church of Christ." Dr. Summers defines it as "an ordinance instituted by Christ, consisting in the application of water by a Christian minister to suitable persons, for their initiation into the visible Church, and consecration to the Father, Son, and Holy Ghost." Dr. Miley says that "Baptism is not only a sign of profession and mark of difference whereby Christians are distinguished from others that are not baptized, but it is also a sign of regeneration, or the new birth." Dr. Pope defines it as "the rite ordained by our Lord to be the sign of admission into the Church, and the seal of union with himself and participation in the blessings of the Christian covenant."

The Institution of Christian Baptism. The practice of water baptism as a sacred ordinance was not first in-

Dr. Dale points out that there "is one baptism—a thorough change of spiritual condition, assimilating the soul to the characteristic quality of the divine baptizer. (1) The baptism which John preached was this one baptism in swelling bud; the Holy Ghost and Lamb of God within it, not yet unfolded. (2) The baptism which John administered was this one baptism in symbol, making manifest, Jesus the Lamb of God which taketh away the sin of the world. (3) The baptism of Christianity is John's baptism unfolded, revealing the Lamb of God slain and the Holy Ghost sent. (4) The symbol baptism of Christianity is the perpetuation of the symbolism of the baptism John preached, and of the one baptism of inspiration.

troduced by Christ, but was long familiar to the Jews as a religious rite. The precise time when it came into use is not known; but it was one of the rites by which proselytes were inducted into the Jewish religion, and thereby became partakers of the benefits of the covenant. The second step in the development of the ordinance was the baptism of John, which differed both from the proselyte baptism which preceded, and the Christian baptism which followed it. John's baptism was not merely a rite by which proselytes were brought into the Jewish religion, but was "unto repentance" as a preparation for Christ and the New Covenant. The third step in its development was Christian baptism, which differed from that of John in that it does not look forward to the coming of the Messiah, but confesses that Jesus as the Messiah has come, and also the Holy Spirit in whose dispensation it is to be administered. Christ was born under the Old Testament, and by His identification with a sinful race, was brought under its condemnation. And while He knew no sin, He nevertheless declared that it was necessary to be baptized with John's baptism in order to fulfill all righteousness. Christian baptism was instituted by our Lord in a direct injunction—*baptizing them in the name of the Father, and of the Son, and of the Holy Ghost* (Matt. 28:19); an injunction which at once instituted the ordinance and prescribed the formula by which it was to be administered.

Following the Day of Pentecost, the rite of baptism was observed in connection with conversion as an indispensable ordinance, there being no recorded instance of conversion with which it is not connected. The full formula does not always occur, however, although it may be said to be implied even where it is not directly stated. In Acts 2:38 St. Peter in his pentecostal sermon exhorts the believers to be *baptized everyone of you in the name of Jesus Christ, and they that gladly received his word were baptized* (Acts 2:41); in Acts 8:16 it is stated that the Samaritans were *baptized in the name of the Lord Jesus;* while in Acts 10:48, St. Peter commands the household of Cornelius *to be baptized in the name of the Lord.* Likewise, also, the Ephesian disciples were baptized under the ministry of St. Paul (Acts 19: 4-6). It will be noticed, also, that once the disciples were baptized, and later received the gift of the Holy Ghost after the imposition of hands; and once, at the house of Cornelius, the disciples received the Holy Ghost and were later baptized with water. In the later apostolic times baptism was regarded as having superseded the Jewish rite of circumcision. As a national custom it continued to exist, but to the church this was a matter of indifference for the rite was interpreted spiritually. Thus St. Paul says, *In whom also ye are circumcised with the circumcision made without hands, in putting off the body of the sins of the flesh by the circumcision of Christ: buried with him in baptism, wherein also ye are risen with him through the faith of the operation of God, who hath raised him from the dead* (Col. 2: 11, 12).

Development of the Doctrine in the Church. Great importance was very early attached to the rite of baptism—not as a sign and seal of all Christian blessings, but in that it was regarded as the means of conveyance, by which those blessings were imparted. In the later Ante-Nicene age, it may be said that baptism was universally regarded as the rite of admission to the church; and since it was held that there could be no salvation apart from the church, baptism came to be associated with regeneration. At first it was looked upon solely as the completing act in the appropriation of Christianity— the seal of positive adoption into the family of God. By the middle of the second century, however, it was regarded as procuring full remission of all past sins, and consequently we find it spoken of as "the instrument of regeneration and illumination." The Fathers taught this doctrine, not in the modern sense of a grace bestowed, or a change wrought by means of regeneration, but that baptism was itself regeneration. Pseudo-Barnabas (c. 120) refers to "that baptism which leads to the remission of sins"; and adds, "we descend into the water full of sins and defilement, but come up bearing fruit in our heart." So also Hermas (c. 140) says, "They descend into the water dead, they arise alive." There were, however, some limitations which attached to the doctrine as it was held by such writers as Justin Martyr, Clement, Tertullian, Origen and Cyprian. They held to the earlier belief that baptism was efficacious only in connection with a right inner disposition and purpose on the part of the candidate. Origen says, "He who has ceased from his sins receives remission in baptism. But if anyone comes to the fount still harboring sin, he obtains no remission of his sins" (In. Luc. Hom. XXI). They held also, that baptism was not absolutely essential to the initiation of the new life in regeneration, but

Too early, however, we see with respect to the administration, as well as to the conception of holy baptism, the commencement of a sad declension from the genuine simplicity of the Apostolic Age. Baptism is already in the first few centuries exalted in a manner which is sufficiently intelligible, but which must inevitably give rise to dogmatic misunderstanding. Baptism is regarded by Justin Martyr as supranatural illumination, and by a much-loved allusion the Christian Church is compared to fishes which are born in the water, and now swimming after their great fish are saved in and by that water (Tertullian, de Bapt. c.i.). Cyprian asserts that the Holy Ghost was united in a supranatural manner with the water of baptism, even as at the creation He moved life-giving over the waters. Baptism was thus considered absolutely necessary to salvation; since it not only secured, but directly brought about, the remission of previous sins, the gifts of the Holy Ghost, and the pledge of a blessed immortality. Since sins committed after baptism were considered unpardonable, this holy act was by many postponed as long as possible; while, when it was administered, it was illustrated by a number of emblematical ceremonies. Among these were, since the fourth century, the abjuration of the devil; the anointing with the mystical oil; the churchly consecration of the baptismal water; and after baptism a new anointing, the laying on of hands, the kiss of peace, the clothing in white robes, the carrying of burning candles, the administration of milk and honey, the change of name and such like. Where should we end if we would name everything which in former or later days has been practiced with respect to sponsors, seasons for baptism, the baptism of bells, altars and so forth? Of much more importance is it that the entire idea of baptism, in connection with these different things, departed more and more from that of the apostles. By Augustine in particular, and since his time, infant baptism was brought into direct connection with the dogma of original sin, and considered as the means for purifying from it the child to be baptized; so that unbaptized children could not possibly be saved. . . . . Thus here was gradually formed, after the later scholastic development of doctrine, the conception which the Romish Church now recognizes as her own. To her baptism is the sacrament of regeneration, by means of water in the Word, by which the grace of God is imparted in a supranatural manner to the person baptized for the forgiveness of all (inherited and actual) guilt, and for the sanctification of the life, and thus its administration is absolutely necessary—VAN OOSTERZEE, Christian Dogmatics, II, pp. 750, 751.

only as a completing process, as previously mentioned. Tertullian in speaking of baptism says, "The washing is a sealing of faith, which faith is begun and is commended by the faith of repentance. We are not washed in order that we may cease sinning, but because we have ceased, since in the heart we have been bathed already" (De. Poenit. VI).

The Nicene and Post-Nicene periods witnessed a further crystallization of the earlier positions, and hence the idea universally prevailed that the divine life dwelt in the corporate body of the church, and could be transmitted to its members only through the instrumentality of the sacraments. Baptism, therefore, as the rite of initiation took on added importance, and came to be regarded as essential to salvation. Ambrose (c. 397) understood John 3:5 to mean that "None can ascend into the kingdom of heaven except by the sacrament of baptism; indeed, it excepts none, neither infant nor him that is prevented by any necessity." Augustine's position, like many other of his doctrines, was of a twofold character. From his earlier viewpoint, baptism was regarded as symbolical. It was the external rite of entrance into the church, but the inner spiritual union was effected only by the Spirit through faith. He held also, that in infant baptism, the sponsors merely assumed the responsibility for the Christian education of the child, their confession being before God, the confession of the child. His later viewpoint was widely different. He maintained that baptism carried with it not only the forgiveness of actual sins, but of original sin also. While he held that concupiscence still remained in the heart, he maintained that its complexion was changed. In the unbaptized it was sin; but in the baptized, it was a sickness, the perfect cure of which could be wrought only in heaven. His views concerning infant baptism also underwent a marked change. He held that the church furnished a substitutive faith, and the Holy Spirit implanted in the unconscious babe the germ of a new life; so that regeneration was wrought in the heart before the conscious conversion of the child. It was this idea of passive receptivity advanced by Augustine, which later became in the Roman Catholic Church, the basis of the *opus operatum*, against which Protestantism so violently reacted. It will be necessary, therefore, to consider the later development of this doctrine in (1) The Roman Catholic Church; (2) The Lutheran Church; and (3) The Reformed Church.

1. *The Roman Catholic Doctrine.* Since baptism was regarded as operating solely for the remission of past sins, there grew up very early a system of penance for sins committed after baptism. Later this became a separate ordinance or sacrament. Likewise, also, it had been a custom from earliest times to accompany baptism with the laying on of hands in imitation of the apostles (Cf. Acts 8:17; 19:6), and also to anoint with oil as a symbol of the anointing from the Holy One (I John 2:20-27). This came to be known as "Confirmation" and in the fourth century was universally recognized as a separate sacrament. Later it was insisted that the validity of the rite depended upon the consecrating of the oil by a bishop; and gradually in the West, the whole ceremony came to be regarded as the peculiar function of the bishop. The schoolmen of the Middle Ages did little more than to elaborate the positions advanced by

The effect of the baptism proper was affirmed (as by Augustine) to consist in absolution from the guilt of all foregoing sin, original and actual, and in such an impartation of grace as modifies, but does not wholly eradicate, the corruption or concupiscence in the moral nature. . . . . As regards the grace which ameliorates the inward corruption, and works a renewal in the heart, it was apprehended by different writers that this might be experienced in virtue of repentance and faith anterior to baptism. It was maintained, however, that in such case there was still ample occasion for baptism, since there was left a certain obligation to punishment, and baptism could remove this as well as confer an increase of positive grace.—SHELDON, *History of Christian Doctrine,* I, p. 392.

Bellarmine summarizes the teachings of the church on baptism as follows: (1) Infants have no actual faith; (2) Nor spiritual manifestations; (3) They are justified absolutely without faith; (4) The habitus of faith, love and hope, is imparted to them; (5) They practically believe, partly because baptism itself is an actual confession of faith, and partly because of the vicarious faith of others. Habitus is defined as the condition which includes in itself at the same time a power to act. It may be infused, and then it is the condition of all corresponding activity; or acquired, and then it is the result of actions already performed (Cf. SCHAFF-HERZOG, *Encyclopedia,* Art. Baptism).

Augustine. They distinguished between the material and the form of baptism—the material being the water, and the form being the formula by which it was administered. St. Thomas especially followed Augustine in maintaining that baptism impressed an indelible character upon the soul through regeneration. On the negative side, baptism was held to cleanse from all sin, actual and original; and on the positive side to incorporate the recipient with Christ, and bestow all the gifts and graces of the new life. On the question of infant baptism also, he held with Augustine that babes do not believe through their own act, but through the faith of the church in which they are baptized. This faith comes from the Holy Spirit as the inner unity of the church, who makes equal distribution of her spiritual life, so that infants share in it potentially, though not then in the exertion of its spiritual power. Confirmation also was believed to confer "an indelible character," which, however, presupposed that imparted in baptism. The doctrinal decisions and ritualistic prac-

In the middle of the eighth century, an ignorant priest in Bavaria was accustomed in place of the regular baptismal formula which he intended to use, to utter a jargon of Latin words without intelligible meaning. Pope Zachary, to whom the case was referred, acknowledged the validity of these baptisms on the ground of the priest's intention. from this decision two startling conclusions were drawn by some later Roman Catholic divines: That, as the validity of a sacrament depends on the intention of the administrator, that is no sacrament, however ritually correct, in which the intention is lacking; and that, inasmuch as sectaries and heretics intend to baptize into the true church, the Roman Church, which is the only true church, has rightful jurisdiction over all persons so baptized.—CRIPPEN, *History of Christian Doctrine*, pp. 190, 191.

Baptism, together with the other two sacraments incapable of repetition, namely, confirmation and holy orders, was regarded as giving a certain indelible signature, or character to the recipient. "In these (three sacraments)," says Bonaventura, "a triple character is impressed, which is not obliterated. In accordance with the first arises the distinction of believers from unbelievers; in accordance with the second, distinction of the strong from the infirm and the weak; and in accordance with the third, the distinction of the clergy from the laity."— SHELDON, *History of Christian Doctrine*, I, p. 393.

In the third century heretical baptism was a matter of earnest controversy. Cyprian denied its validity, on ecclesiastical principles, but the authority of the Church at Rome prevailed: resting its plea on the ground of the objective value of the rite, by whosoever performed in the name of the Holy Trinity.—POPE, *Comp. Chr. Th.*, III, p. 319.

St. Boniface (755), "The apostle of Germany," introduced the practice of baptizing conditionally those whose former baptism was doubtful."— CRIPPEN, *History of Christian Doctrine*, p. 191.

tices which had long been current in the Roman Catholic Church, were confirmed by the Canons and Decrees of the Council of Trent (1545-1563).

2. *The Lutheran Doctrine.* The Protestant teaching, both Lutheran and Reformed, had for its starting point a valid objection to the *ex opere operato* of the Roman Catholic Church, or the doctrine that the mere administration of baptism saved the baptized person. The Reformers also contended that the "concupiscence remained after original sin had been pardoned in baptism, was really sin." They insisted that faith was necessary on the part of the recipient in order to make the ceremony a means of grace. Luther's teaching on this subject is usually traced through three stages: (1) Following Augustine's earlier position, he distinguished between the sign and the thing signified, and between them put faith as the means by which men realized the meaning of the sign. The sign is the outward baptism with water, the seal is the new birth, and faith makes real this spiritual baptism. (2) In the second stage, Luther considered baptism as a sign and a seal, to which God added His Word as a promise of divine strength and comfort. The chief thing, however, is the promise, and those who believe it and are baptized will be saved. (3) In the third stage, he more closely identified the water and the Word, teaching that to the sign and the Word, were added the command and ordinance of God; and that the former were given together in such a manner that the water of baptism is converted into the divine element. This position, however, does not appear in the Confessions except in the German original of the Schmalkald Articles. The Augsburg Confession represents Melanchthon's position, that baptism is a perpetual witness that the forgiveness of sins and the renewing of the Holy Ghost belong especially to the baptized —the operating cause of this condition being faith. For these reasons Lutheranism has always held a high

The Augsburg Confession (1530) Article IX is as follows: "Baptism is necessary to salvation, by (it) the grace of God is offered; and children are to be baptized, who by baptism, being offered to God, are received into God's favor."

theory of the sacraments, and ordinarily regards baptism as essential to salvation, since through it by divine appointment, the blessings of remission and regeneration are conveyed by means of faith and the Word.

3. *The Reformed Doctrine.* The Reformed Churches started with the idea that salvation is not conditioned upon any external work or ceremony, and therefore saved themselves from much confusion in the development of their doctrine. To them, baptism was but the initiatory sign which marks one as the follower of Christ. Zwingli attributed no sanctifying power to baptism *per se*, but only to faith. Thus he did away entirely with the mystery, and viewed the sacraments partly as acts of confession, and partly as commemorative signs. Calvin adopted the principles of Zwingli, but in his development of them, more nearly approached the Lutheran conception. To him, they were not merely memorials, but also pledges of grace—that is, they were accompanied with an invisible gift of grace. Since Lutheranism, especially the school of Melanchthon, also

The Reformed position is expressed in the Second Helvetic Confession (1566) as follows: "Baptism is instituted by Christ. There is only one baptism in the church: it lasts for life, and is a perpetual seal of our adoption. To be baptized in the name of Christ is to be enrolled, initiated, and received into the covenant, into the family and the inheritance of the sons of God, that, cleansed from our sins by the blood of Christ, we may lead a new and innocent life. We are internally regenerated by the Holy Ghost; but we receive publicly the seal of these blessings by baptism, in which the grace of God inwardly and invisibly cleanses the soul, and we confess our faith, and pledge obedience to God. Children of believers should be baptized; for to children belongs the kingdom of God: why, then, should not the sign of the covenant be given to them?"

The Belgic Confession (1561 was revised and approved by the Synod of Dort (1619). The statement is as follows: "Baptism is the substitute for circumcision: by it we are received into the Church of God. As water washeth away the filth of the body when poured upon it, as is seen on the body of the baptized when sprinkled upon him, so doth the blood of Christ, by the power of the Holy Ghost, internally sprinkle the soul, cleanse it from its sins, and regenerate us from children of wrath unto children of God. Not that this is effected by the external water, but by the sprinkling of the precious blood of the Son of God. Baptism avails us through the whole course of our life. Infants of believers ought to be baptized, and sealed with the sign of the covenant. Christ shed His blood no less for the washing of the children of the faithful than for adult persons; and therefore they ought to receive the sign and sacrament of that which Christ hath done for them. Moreover, what circumcision was to the Jews, that baptism is to our children. And for this reason Paul calls baptism the circumcision of Christ.

regarded the sacraments as pledges of grace, a point of union was formed between Calvin and Luther. Bishop Martensen who takes his stand upon the point of agreement between Luther and Calvin, makes it clear that there is after all an essential difference between them arising out of the different conceptions of predestination. "According to Calvin's doctrine," he says, "there is no real connection between predestination and baptism. The twofold election has been settled from eternity; and baptism, therefore, can be of no avail to those who have not been elected in the hidden decrees of God. Lutheran predestination, on the other hand, obtains its true expression in baptism. For baptism, according to Luther, is the revelation of the consoling decree that 'God will have all men to be saved, and to come to the knowledge of the truth.' We do not need in agony to inquire after a hidden decree, according to which we are either elected or rejected; for every one may read in his baptism his election to blessedness" (MARTENSEN, *Christian Dogmatics*, p. 424). We may say then, that in general, less stress was laid upon the necessity of baptism in the Reformed Church than in the Lutheran; and that the Reformed position, through the medium of the Thirty-Nine Articles of the Anglican Church, became essentially the teaching of Methodism.

4. *Later Doctrinal Developments.* (1) The Anglican doctrine as expressed in the Thirty-Nine Articles is a combination of the Lutheran and Reformed creeds. There are, however, two views as to the interpretation of the formularies—those who are more Lutheran and sacramentarian, and therefore suppose that the soul is renewed by an infusion of life; and those who more nearly approach the Reformed position of a change in relations only. (2) The Baptist doctrine differs from Christianity at large on two points—it maintains that baptism as a rite, belongs solely to adults as an expression of their faith; and that the only valid mode of baptism is immersion in water. (3) The Methodists hold to a mediating position. On the one hand, they repudiate the Socinian view that baptism is merely a

sign or badge of a Christian profession; and on the other, they reject the rite as an impressive ritualistic emblem of the washing away of sin. They hold that baptism is both a sign and a seal, and therefore is not without its accompanying grace to the recipient who complies with the conditions of the covenant. This position will be given further consideration in our discussion of the meaning, mode and subjects of baptism.

The Nature and Design of Christian Baptism. From the history of baptism, and the scriptural statements concerning it, we are able to arrive at the nature and

The Westminster Confession of Faith (1647), Cap. XXVIII is as follows: "Baptism is a sacrament of the New Testament, ordained by Jesus Christ, not only for the solemn admission of the party baptized into the visible church, but also to be unto him a sign and seal of the covenant of grace, of his ingrafting into Christ, or regeneration, of remission of sins, and of his giving up unto God, through Jesus Christ, to walk in newness of life. By the right use of this ordinance, the grace promised is not only offered, but really exhibited and conferred by the Holy Ghost, to such (whether of age, or infants) as that grace belongeth unto, according to the counsel of God's own will, in his appointed time."

Dr. Charles Hodge sums up the Reformed doctrine in three points: (1) The sacraments are real means of grace, that is, means appointed and employed by Christ for conveying the benefits of His redemption to His people. They are not as the Romanists teach, the exclusive channels; but they are channels. A promise is made to those who rightly receive the sacraments that they shall thereby and therein be made partakers of the blessings of which the sacraments are the divinely appointed signs and seals. The word "grace," when we speak of the means of grace, includes three things: 1. An unmerited gift, such as the remission of sin. 2. The supernatural influence of the Holy Spirit. 3. The subjective effects of that influence on the soul. Faith, hope, and charity, for example, are graces. (2) The second point in the Reformed doctrine on the sacraments concerning the source of their power. On this subject it is taught negatively that the virtue is not in them. The word virtue is of course here used in the Latin sense for power or efficiency. What is denied is that the sacraments are the efficient cause of the gracious effects which they produce. The efficiency does not reside in the elements, nor in the office of the person by whom they are administered . . . . nor on the character of the administrator in the sight of God; nor upon his intention; that is, his purpose to render them effectual. . . . . The affirmative statement on this subject is, that the efficacy of the sacraments is due solely to the blessing of Christ and the working of His Spirit. . . . . God has promised that His Spirit shall attend His Word; and He thus renders it an effectual means for the sanctification of His people. So He has promised, through the attending operation of His Spirit, to render the sacraments effectual to the same end. (3) The third point included in the Reformed doctrine is, that the sacraments are effectual as means of grace only, so far as adults are concerned, to those who by faith receive them. They may have a natural power on other than believers by presenting truth and exciting feeling, but their saving or sanctifying influence is experienced only by believers.— HODGE, *Systematic Theology*, III, pp. 499, 500.

design of the ordinance. It is a solemn sacrament "signifying the acceptance of the benefits of the atonement of
Jesus Christ"; and it is a pledge with "full purpose of
obedience in holiness and righteousness." From the
divine standpoint, it is also a pledge of the bestowal of
grace. Dr. Wakefield defines baptism and indicates its
four essential elements as follows: "Baptism, as a Christian ordinance, may be defined to be the application of
pure water to a proper subject, by a lawful administrator, in the name of the sacred Trinity. (1) It is the
application of pure water, as the language of the apostle
clearly indicates, *Having our hearts sprinkled from an
evil conscience, and our bodies washed with pure water*
(Heb. 10:22). (2) The water must be applied to a
proper subject; not to an inanimate object, but to a
human being under certain circumstances. (3) The ordinance must be performed by a lawful administrator;
and as the commission to baptize was given to ministers
of the gospel alone, no others have a right to perform
this office. And, (4) It must be administered in the
name of the sacred Trinity, *baptizing them in the name*

The Heidelberg Catechism defines the sacraments as follows: "They
are holy, visible signs and seals, ordained by God for this end, that He
may more fully declare and seal by them the promise of His gospel unto
us: to wit, that not only unto all believers in general, but unto each of
them in particular, He freely giveth remission of sins and life eternal,
upon the account of that only sacrifice of Christ, which He accomplished upon the cross."

The Church of England in Article XXV has this expression: "Sacraments ordained of Christ be not only badges or tokens of Christian
men's profession, but rather they be sure witnesses, and effectual signs
of grace, and God's will toward us, by the which He doth work invisibly in us, and doth not only quicken, but also strengthen and confirm our faith in Him."

The Protestant Episcopal Church, Article XXVII is as follows: "Baptism is not only a sign of profession, and mark of difference, whereby
Christian men are discerned from others that be not christened, but it is
also a sign of regeneration, or new birth, whereby, as by an instrument,
they that receive baptism rightly are grafted into the church; the promises of forgiveness of sin, and of our adoption to be the sons of God by
the Holy Ghost, are visibly signed and sealed; faith is confirmed, and
grace increased, by virtue of prayer unto God. The baptism of young
children is in any wise to be retained in the church, as most agreeable
with the institution of Christ."

The Methodist Episcopal Church, Article XVII has this statement
concerning baptism: "Baptism is not only a sign of profession, and
mark of difference, whereby Christians are distinguished from others
that are not baptized, but it is also a sign of regeneration, or the new
birth. The baptism of young children is to be retained in the church."

of the Father, and of the Son, and of the Holy Ghost (Matt. 28:19, 20). "Two things concerning baptism stand out clearly here (1) Its universal and perpetual obligation; and (2) Its sacramental import.

1. The universal and perpetual obligation of baptism is indicated by two things—our Lord's express command (Matt. 28:19, 20); and the apostolic practice (Acts 2:38, 41; 8:12). Baptism is a solemn ordinance which should be strictly observed. It is clearly evident from the above scriptures, that the apostles administered baptism immediately upon profession of faith; and if it was deemed necessary then, it can be no less so now.

"What is the Lutheran doctrine on this subject? The Lutherans agreed with the Reformed churches in repudiating the Romish doctrine of the magical efficacy of this sacrament as an *opus operatum.* But they went much farther than the Reformed in maintaining the sacramental union between the sign and the grace signified. Luther in his Smaller Catechism says baptism "worketh forgiveness of sins, delivers from death and the devil, and confers everlasting salvation on all who believe"; . . . . that "it is not the water indeed which produces these effects, but the Word of God which accompanies and is connected with the water, and our faith, which relies on the Word of God connected with the water. For the water without the Word is simply water and no baptism. But when connected with the Word of God, it is a baptism, that is, a gracious water of life, and a washing of regeneration.

"What was the Zwinglian doctrine on this subject?" That the outward rite is a mere sign, an objective representation, having no efficacy whatever beyond that due to the truth represented.

"What is the doctrine of the Reformed churches . . . . on this subject?" They all agree (1) that the Zwinglian view is incomplete. (2) That besides being a sign, baptism is also the seal of grace, and, therefore, a present and sensible conveyance and confirmation of grace to the believer who has the witness in himself, and to all the elect a seal of the benefits of the covenant of grace, to be sooner or later conveyed in God's good time. (3) That this conveyance is effected, not by the bare operation of the sacramental action, but by the Holy Ghost, which accompanies His own ordinance. (4) That in the adult the reception of the blessing depends upon faith. (5) That the benefits conveyed by baptism are not peculiar to it, but belong to the believer before or without baptism, and are often renewed to him afterward.—A. A. HODGE, *Outlines of Theology,* pp. 500, 501.

That our Lord intended baptism to be the initiating ordinance into His visible Church is evident from the fact that He connected it, by positive injunctions with that grand commission which He gave to His apostles to "preach the gospel to every creature." This initiatory character of baptism is alluded to by the apostle when he inquires of the Corinthians, "Were ye baptized in the name of Paul?" (I Cor. 1:13). Here he evidently assumes the principle that if he had baptized any persons in his own name, he would thereby have represented himself as the head of a sect. But as they were baptized in the name of Christ, they were thereby united to His Church by this initiatory rite."—WAKEFIELD, *Christian Theology,* p. 560.

But when they believed Philip preaching the things concerning the kingdom of God, and the name of Jesus Christ, they were baptized, both men and women (Acts 8: 12). Baptism is an ordinance of perpetual obligation. Some have argued that because Christ baptizes with the Holy Ghost, water baptism is no longer necessary. That it superseded John's baptism, is doubtless true; but we have already indicated that there is a wide distinction between John's baptism with water as a preparatory rite, and Christ's baptism with water as a sign and seal of an inward work of grace. Nor does the text (Heb. 9: 10) which refers to "divers washings, and carnal ordinances" present any argument against Christian baptism. The Christians rejected these Jewish rites, it must be admitted, but water baptism was administered by the apostles after the opening of the Christian dispensation, which clearly indicates that baptism was not included in the rites of which the apostle here speaks. Baptism being an initiatory rite is to be administered only once. It establishes a permanent covenant and is not therefore to be repeated. The baptized one may fall away, but the gracious promise of God still stands. It cannot be made of none effect. If he falls away, he needs to repent and believe, and the Father stands ready to restore him, but he does not need to be rebaptized. As an initiatory rite also, baptism is the visible act by which members are admitted into the Church of Christ as a visible society. This has been the faith of the church from the beginning, and to deny it is to deny that the church has any initiatory ordinance.

2. The sacramental import of baptism is to be found in the fact that it is a sign and seal of the covenant of grace. (1) As a sign, it represents spiritual purification. *Then will I sprinkle clean water upon you, and ye shall be clean: from all your filthiness, and from all your idols, will I cleanse you. A new heart also will I give you, and a new spirit will I put within you* (Ezek. 36: 25, 26). So also our Lord declares, *Except a man be born of water and of the Spirit, he cannot enter into the*

kingdom of God (John 3:5). Here, evidently, the sign is the outward baptism with water, and the thing signified is the inner work of the Spirit. St. Paul refers to

WATSON ON BAPTISM AS A SIGN AND A SEAL

Baptism as a sign of the new covenant, corresponds to circumcision. Like that, its administration is a constant exhibition of the placability of God to man; like that, it is the initiatory rite into a covenant which promises pardon and salvation to a true faith, of which it is the outward profession; like that, it is the symbol of regeneration, the washing away of sin, and "the renewing of the Holy Ghost"; and like that, it is a sign of peculiar relation to God, Christians becoming, in consequence, "a chosen generation, a peculiar people"—His Church on earth, as distinguished from "the world." "For we," says the apostle, "are the circumcision," we are that peculiar people and Church now, which was formerly distinguished by the sign of circumcision, "which worship God in the spirit, and rejoice in Christ Jesus, and have no confidence in the flesh."

But as a sign, baptism is more than circumcision; because the covenant, under its new dispensation, was not only to offer pardon upon believing, deliverance from the bondage of fleshly appetites, and a peculiar spiritual relation to God, all of which we find under the Old Testament; but also to bestow the Holy Spirit, in His fullness, upon all believers; and of this effusion of "the power from on high," baptism was made the visible sign; and perhaps for this, among some other obvious reasons, was substituted for circumcision, because baptism by effusion or pouring, was the natural symbol of this heavenly gift. The baptism of John had special reference to the Holy Spirit, which was not to be administered by him, but by Christ, who could come after him. This gift honored John's baptism only once, in the extraordinary case of our Lord; but it constantly followed upon the baptism administered by the apostles of Christ, after His ascension, and the sending of the promise of the Father. . . . . For this reason Christianity is called "the ministration of the Spirit"; and so far is this from being confined to the miraculous gifts often bestowed in the first age of the Church, that is, it made the standing and prominent test of true Christianity to "be led by the Spirit."

As a seal also, or confirming sign, baptism answers to circumcision. By the institution of the latter, a pledge was constantly given by the Almighty to bestow the spiritual blessings of which the rite was the sign, pardon and sanctification through faith in the future seed of Abraham; peculiar relation to Him as "his people" and the heavenly inheritance. Of the same blessings, baptism is also the pledge, along with that higher dispensation of the Holy Spirit which it especially represents in emblem. Thus in baptism there is on the part of God a visible assurance of His faithfulness to His covenant stipulations. But it is our seal also; it is that by which we make ourselves parties to the covenant, and thus "set to our seal, that God is true." In this respect it binds us, as, in the other, God mercifully binds Himself for the stronger assurance of our faith. We pledge ourselves to trust wholly in Christ for pardon and salvation, and to obey His laws; "teaching them to observe all things whatsoever I have commanded you"; in that rite also we undergo a mystical death unto sin, a mystical separation from the world, which St. Paul calls "being buried with Christ in [or by] baptism"; and a mystical resurrection to newness of life, through Christ's resurrection from the dead. . . . . If we bring all of these considerations together, we shall find it sufficiently established that baptism is the sign and seal of the covenant of grace under its perfected dispensation.—WATSON, *Theological Institutes*, II, pp. 626-628.

the twofold work of the Spirit—*the washing of regeneration, and renewing of the Holy Ghost* (Titus 3:5). As a sign, therefore, baptism not only symbolizes regeneration, but also the baptism with the Holy Spirit which is the peculiar event of this dispensation. Accordingly the pouring out of the "Spirit upon all flesh," as prophesied by Joel, is in the New Testament called a baptism. It is to this that John the Baptist referred when he said, *He shall baptize you with the Holy Ghost, and with fire* (Matt. 3:11); and to which Jesus himself referred when He said to His disciples, *Ye shall be baptized with the Holy Ghost not many days hence* (Acts 1:5). (2) Baptism is also a seal. "It is," says Dr. Shedd, "like the official seal on a legal document. The presence of the seal inspires confidence in the genuineness of the title-deed; the absence of the seal awakens doubt and fears. Nevertheless, it is the title-deed, not the seal, that conveys the title" (SHEDD, *Dogmatic Theology*, II, p. 574). On God's part, the seal is the visible assurance of faithfulness to His covenant—a perpetual ceremony to which His people may ever appeal. On man's part, the seal is that act by which he binds himself as a party to the covenant, and pledges himself to faithfulness in all things; and it is also the sign of a completed transaction—the ratification of a final agreement.

The Mode of Baptism. This subject has been one of long and serious controversy. From the days of the Anabaptists of Reformation times, and the Baptists of a later day, it has been asserted that immersion is the only valid mode of baptism; while others, the great body of the Church in all ages, have ever maintained that it may be administered by sprinkling or pouring, or to use a term which includes both, by effusion. The question is not, whether immersion is a valid baptism—this has never been denied, but whether it is the only form of baptism authorized by the Scriptures. Our position as a church is clear, "Baptism may be administered by sprinkling, pouring, or immersion, according to the choice of the applicant." It is sufficient, therefore, to merely indicate briefly the arguments which are offered for and against immersion as the only valid mode of baptism. The arguments most frequently urged in favor of immersion are (1) The meaning of the word βαπτίζω, to baptize; (2) The circumstances which attended many of the recorded baptisms; and (3) the symbol of the burial. The church generally has regarded these propositions as insufficient to establish a belief in immersion as the only valid mode of baptism. Without any effort at controversy we may summarize the arguments as follows, referring the student for further study to the more elaborate treatises upon this subject.

1. It is contended that the word βαπτίζω always means *to dip* or *to plunge*. It is a fact, however, beyond all controversy, that the majority of lexicographers give it a broader meaning; and that the classical writers use it to express a variety of ideas. Dr. Dale states that βαπτίζω is a derivative, modifying the meaning of its root βάπτω. The word means (1) to do a definite act, *to dip;* (2) to effect a definite change of condition, *to dye;* (3) to effect a thorough change of condition by assimilating quality or influence, without color, *to temper, to steep, to imbue.* The classical writers, Plutarch, Hippocrates and Aristotle frequently used the word to signify nothing more than to moisten, tinge

The primary word βάπτω occurs four times in the New Testament (Luke 16:24; John 13:26; Rev. 19:13), but never in connection with the subject of Christian baptism. Its classical meaning was, (1) to dip; (2) to dye.—A. A. HODGE, *Outlines of Theology,* p. 483.

The early document known as "The Teaching of the Twelve Apostles" which dates back to the early part of the second century, makes it clear that either immersion or pouring was regarded as valid baptism at that early date. "And touching baptism thus baptize: having first declared all of these things, baptize in the name of the Father and of the Son and of the Holy Spirit, in living water. But if thou have not living water, baptize in other water; and if thou canst not in cold, then in warm. But if thou have neither, pour on the head water thrice in the name of the Father, Son and Holy Spirit" (Section VII). In the spread of the gospel to colder climes, baptism by sprinkling or pouring naturally commended itself as more practicable. In the case of the sick, baptism by immersion in most cases would be impossible.

Dr. Owen says that βαπτίζω signifies to wash, as instances out of all authors may be given"; and also, "No one place can be given in the Scriptures wherein βαπτίζω doth necessarily signify, either to dip or to plunge." "In this sense," he continues, "as it expresseth baptism, it denotes to wash only, and not to dip at all, for so it is expounded" (Titus 3:5ff) OWENS, *Works,* Vol. XXI, p. 557.

and sprinkle. That the word employed to designate Christian baptism is used in the Scriptures other than in the sense of immersion is very evident. *Except they [baptize] wash, they eat not* (Mark 7: 4); which as the previous verse indicates refers to the washing of the hands. The Pharisee (Luke 11: 38) marveled that Jesus sat down to eat without first baptizing or washing, as was the custom of the Pharisees. St. Paul declares that the Israelites were baptized unto Moses in the cloud and the sea (I Cor. 10: 1, 2), using the word baptize as referring to the passing between the waters, overshadowed by the cloud. That the word βαπτίζω is used in a broader meaning than that of to dip or to plunge, is a sufficient refutation of the claim that immersion is the only valid mode of baptism.

2. A study of the circumstances attending the recorded baptisms in the Scriptures, makes it clear also, that baptism does not always signify immersion. The cases usually cited in proof of immersion are the following: *Then went out to him Jerusalem, and all Judea, and all the region round about Jordan, and were baptized of him in Jordan* (Matt. 3: 5, 6); *and Jesus, when he was baptized, went up straightway out of the water* (Matt. 3: 16); *and they went down both into the water, both Philip and the eunuch; and he baptized him. And when they were come up out of the water, the Spirit of the Lord caught away Philip* (Acts 8: 38, 39). Here the whole strength of the argument depends upon the meaning of the original Greek prepositions, *en* (ἐν), *eis* (εἰς), *ek* (ἐκ) and *apo* (ἀπὸ). It is well known that these prepositions are used in the Scriptures with different meanings, thus *apo* means *from*, far more frequently than it does *out of*; that *ek* also means *from* as well as *out of*; and that *eis* means *to* or *unto* as well as *into*. From the meaning of the original words, therefore it would be as faithful a translation as the present one to say that Jesus came up straightway *from* the water; and that Philip and the enunch went down *to* the water, and came up *from* the water. Schleusner in his celebrated lexicon points out that *en* has thirty-six distinct

meanings; *eis,* twenty-six; *ek,* twenty-four; and *apo,* twenty. It is evident, therefore, that a true interpretation can be found only in a study of the historical circumstances and usages, and not necessarily in a literal interpretation of the prepositions. Here we may refer briefly to such scriptures as the baptism of Saul, where it is stated that he arose and was baptized (ἀναστὰς ἐβαπτίσθη) literally, standing up he was baptized (Acts 9:18); the baptism of Cornelius and his friends, where it is evident that they were baptized in the house where the Holy Spirit had fallen upon them, and further, it is implied in the words, "Can any man forbid water," that is, forbid water to be brought in order to the baptism (Acts 10:47, 48); and lastly, the baptism of the jailer and his household at night, which must necessarily have taken place in the jail, and could not therefore with certainty be said to be immersion (Acts 16:31-33).

3. The symbolism of the burial has been a favorite argument with the immersionists, and is based upon such scriptures as, *Therefore we are buried with him by*

Both Dr. Wakefield and Mr. Watson point out other scriptures which are sometimes used in an attempt to support a belief in immersion as the only valid mode of baptism. (1) "These things were done in Bethabara beyond Jordan, where John was baptizing" (John 1:28). Here it is only necessary to remark that the persons whom John baptized in Bethabara could not have been baptized in Jordan, for Bethabara was beyond Jordan. This receives additional support from the text which states that Jesus "went away again beyond Jordan into the place where John at first baptized; and there he abode" (John 10:40). It is impossible to escape the conclusion that John at first baptized in Bethabara beyond Jordan, and not in its waters. (2) Another passage cited is this: "And John also was baptizing in Aenon near to Salim, because there was much water there" (John 3:23). Here it is assumed that the "much water" spoken of was required only for baptism. . . . . The meaning of the terms employed in the original is in accordance with those historical facts which show that there was no lake or other body of water near Aenon. "Aenon is derived from the Hebrew *ayin,* the eye, and signifies, according to Parkhurst and others, a well, a fountain, or a spring of water. In the Greek phrase *hudata polla,* which is rendered 'much water,' but 'many waters'; conveying the idea of many fountains or springs, rather than a great quantity of water. Thus Matthew 13:3, "And he spake [*polla,* not much, but] many things unto them'; Mark 1:34, 'And cast out [*polla*] many devils'; John 8:26, 'I have [*polla*] many things to say'; Acts 2:43, 'And [*polla*] many wonders and signs were done'; Revelation 1:15, 'And his voice as the sound of [*hudaton pollon*] many waters'." We are therefore safe in the conclusion that Aenon did not contain a large quantity of water, and that it was insufficient for the numerous immersions which are supposed to have taken place in it.—WAKEFIELD, *Christian Theology,* pp. 579, 580.

baptism into death: that like as Christ was raised up
from the dead by the glory of the Father, even so we
also should walk in newness of life (Rom. 6:4); and
again, *Buried with him in baptism, wherein also ye are*
risen with him through the faith of the operation of God,
who hath raised him from the dead (Col. 2:12). The argument for immersion rests entirely upon the words
"buried with him 'by' or 'in' baptism"; and it is assumed that the apostle is here speaking of water bap-
Baptist interpreters insist that the Bible teaches that the outward
sign in this sacrament, being the immersion of the whole body in
water, is an emblem both of purification and of our death, burial and
resurrection with Christ. . . . . We object to this interpretation, (1) in
neither of these passages (Rom. 6:3, 4; Col. 2:12) does Paul say that
our baptism in water is an emblem of our burial with Christ. He is
evidently speaking of that spiritual baptism of which water baptism is
the emblem; by which spiritual baptism we are caused to die unto
sin, and live unto holiness, in which death and new life we are conformed unto the death and resurrection of Christ. . . . . (2) To be
baptized into his death is a phrase perfectly analogous to baptism
unto repentance (Matt. 3:11), and *for the remission of sins* (Mark
1:4), and *into one body,* (I Cor. 12:13), that is, in order that, or to
the effect that we participate in the benefits of his death. (3) The
Baptist interpretation involves an utter confusion in reference to the
emblem. Do they mean that the outward sign of immersion is an
emblem of the death, burial and resurrection of Christ, or of the
spiritual death, burial and resurrection of the believer? But the point
of comparison in the passages themselves is plainly "not between our
baptism and the burial and resurrection of Christ, but between our
death to sin and rising to holiness, and the death and resurrection of
the Redeemer." (4) Baptists agree with us that baptism with water
is an emblem of spiritual purification, that is, regeneration, but insist
that it is also an emblem (in the mode of immersion) of the death of
the believer to sin and his new life of holiness. But what is the distinction between regeneration and a death unto sin, and life in holiness? (5) Baptists agree with us that water baptism is an emblem
of purification. But surely it is impossible that the same action should
at the same time be an emblem of a washing, and of a burial and a
resurrection. One idea may be associated with the other in consequence
of their spiritual relations, but it is impossible that the same visible
sign should be emblematical of both. (6) Our union with Christ
through the Spirit, and the spiritual consequences thereof, are illustrated
in Scripture by many various figures, for example, the substitution of
a heart of flesh for a heart of stone (Ezek. 36:26); the building of a
house (Eph. 2:22); the ingrafting of a limb into a vine (John 15:5);
the putting off of filthy garments, and the putting on of clean (Eph.
4:22-24); as a spiritual death, burial and resurrection, and as being
planted in the likeness of His death (Rom. 6:3-5); as the application
of a cleansing element to the body (Ezek. 36:25). Now baptism with
water represents all these, because it is an emblem of spiritual regeneration, of which all these are analogical illustrations. . . . . Yet
it would be absurd to regard water baptism as a literal emblem of all
these, and our Baptist brethren have no scriptural warrant for assuming that the outward sign in this sacrament is an emblem of the one
analogy more than any of the other.—A. A. Hodge, *Outlines of Theology,*
pp. 482, 483.

tism, and, therefore, defining the mode. That these texts have no reference either to water baptism or to its mode is ably and concisely stated by Dr. Wakefield, as follows: "We conclude, therefore, from a very careful examination of the whole subject, that in the passages under consideration the apostle has no allusion whatever either to water baptism itself or to its mode; but that he is speaking of a *spiritual death, burial, resurrection,* and *life.* He inquires, Romans 6:2, *How shall we, that are dead to sin, live any longer therein?* and in this question he gives us a key to the whole passage *dead to sin.* And, therefore, being thus *dead to sin,* we should not *continue in sin. Know ye not, that so many of us as were baptized into Jesus Christ were baptized into his death?* that is, *so many of us as were* united to Jesus Christ by the baptism of the Holy Spirit were made partakers of the benefits of His death. *For by one Spirit are we all baptized into one body* (I Cor. 12:13). This moral change by which believers are united to Christ, and constituted living branches in 'the True Vine,' includes in it a death to sin, a burial of 'the old man,' and a resurrection from spiritual death to a new life of holy obedience. *Therefore we are buried with him by baptism into death;* that is, as Christ was buried in the grave, so we, by the baptism with the Spirit, are brought into this state of death to sin, *that like as Christ was raised up from the dead by the glory of the Father, even so we also should walk in newness of life.* Indeed, the whole argument of the apostle shows that he is speaking of the work of the Spirit, and not of water baptism. *For if we have been planted together in the likeness of his death, we shall also be in the likeness of his resurrection; knowing this, that our old man is crucified with him, that the body of sin might be destroyed, that henceforth we should not serve sin* (Rom. 6:5, 6). And again, *Likewise reckon ye yourselves also to be dead indeed unto sin, but alive unto God through Jesus Christ our Lord* (Rom. 6:11). Can water baptism accomplish the moral change of which the apostle is here speaking? Surely no one will affirm this, unless he has adopted the

wild notion that 'immersion is the regenerating act' "
(WAKEFIELD, *Christian Theology*, p. 582).

Mr. Watson in his "Institutes" gives the following argument against immersion as the only mode of baptism. "Although the manner in which the element of water is applied in baptism is but a circumstance of this sacrament, it will not be a matter of surprise to those who reflect upon the proneness of men to attach undue importance to comparative trifles, that it has produced so much controversy. The question as to the proper subjects of baptism is one which is to be respected for its importance; that as to the mode has occupied more time, and excited greater feeling, than it is in any view entitled to. It cannot, however, be passed over, because the advocates for immersion are often very troublesome to their fellow Christians, unsettle weak minds, and sometimes, perhaps, from their zeal for a form, endanger their own spirituality. Against the doctrine that the only legitimate mode of baptizing is by immersion, we may observe that there are several strong presumptions. (1) It is not probable, that if immersion were the only allowable mode of baptism, it should not have been expressly enjoined. (2) It is not probable, that in a r. ligion designed to be universal, a mode of administering this ordinance should be obligatory, the practice of which is ill adapted to so many climates, whether it would either be exceedingly harsh to immerse the candidates, male and female, strong and feeble, in water; or, in some places, as in the higher latitudes, for a greater part of the year, impossible. Even if immersion were in fact the original mode of baptizing in the name of Christ, these reasons make it improbable that no accommodation of the form should take place, without vitiating the ordinance. (3) It is still more unlikely, that in a religion of mercy there should be no consideration of health and life in the administration of an ordinance of salvation, since it is certain that in countries where cold bathing is little practiced, great risk of both is often incurred, especially in the case of women and delicate persons of either sex, and fatal effects do sometimes occur. (4) It is also exceedingly improbable, that in such circumstances of climate the shivering, the sobbing, and bodily uneasiness produced, should distract the thoughts, and unfit the mind for a collected performance of a religious and solemn devotion. (5) It is highly improbable that the three thousand converts at Pentecost, who, let it be observed, were baptized on the same day, were all baptized by immersion; or that the jailer and 'all his' were baptized in the same manner in the night. Finally it is most of all improbable, that a religion like the Christian, so scrupulously delicate, should have enjoined the immersion of women by men, and in the presence of men. In an after age, when immersion came into fashion, baptistries, and rooms for women, and changes of garments, and other auxiliaries to this practices came into use, because they were found necessary to decency; but there could be no such conveniences in the first instance; and accordingly we read of none."—WATSON, *Theological Institutes*, II, p. 647ff.

Those who suppose the apostle to speak of water baptism as a burial, and consequently by immersion, must admit the following consequences: (1) That it is impossible for persons to be dipped or plunged "into Jesus Christ," or "into his death." (2) That St. Paul and those to whom he wrote were at that very time living in the watery grave; for he does not say, we were buried, but "we were buried with him by baptism." Is it possible for a person to be buried and exhumed at the same time? (3) That if the burial of which the apostle speaks is a baptism, then one baptism is made to perform another baptism; for "we are buried with him by baptism"; or in other words, and in Baptist language, we are immersed by an immersion.

The Subjects of Baptism. All who believe in the
Lord Jesus Christ, and have been regenerated, are
proper subjects for Christian baptism. This is established by the direct statement of Jesus Christ, *He that
believeth and is baptized, shall be saved* (Mark 16:16).
The same fact is also taught by the apostle Peter, *Then
answered Peter, Can any man forbid water, that these
should not be baptized, which have received the Holy
Ghost as well as we? and he commanded them to be
baptized in the name of the Lord* (Acts 10:47, 48). Dr.
Wakefield points out that "this passage proves, in addition to the object for which it is here adduced, that men
may receive the Holy Ghost, and, consequently, may be
regenerated without being baptized. Therefore baptism cannot be the regenerating act, as is confidently
affirmed by some" (WAKEFIELD, *Christian Theology,*
p. 562). But in addition to adult believers the church
has always held that the children of believers are, likewise, the proper subjects of baptism; nor does it deny
baptism to the children of unbelievers. This position
was called in question by the Anabaptists of the Reformation period, and their followers still object to it. We
do not think the controversy demands any extended

Thus, one immersion is made to perform the other. (4) That the term
death is only another name for water; for the text says, "we are
buried by baptism into death." Is there no difference between water
and death? (5) That our Lord himself is immersed with each one of
His disciples, and rises with Him from the watery grave; for "we are
buried with him by baptism," and "are risen with him." And, (6)
That those who are immersed rise from the water by an exercise of
faith, and not by the arm of the administrator; for the apostle says,
that in baptism we "are risen with him through the faith of the operation of God." If these consequences are absurd and ridiculous, so is
that theory of which they are the legitimate results.—WAKEFIELD, *Christian Theology,* p. 581.

Two phrases of Scripture are regarded by the immersionist as quite
conclusive of his theory: "Therefore we are buried with him by baptism into death"; and "Buried with him by baptism." These phrases
must be interpreted in the light of the passages to which they belong;
for only in this manner can their true meaning be reached. In each
passage the ruling idea is the moral change wrought in the attainment of salvation. This change is expressed as a death, a crucifixion, a
burial, a resurrection. There is in these forms of expression, and for
the purpose of illustration, a comparison with the crucifixion, death,
burial, and resurrection of Christ. What then is the part of the baptism
in the expression of this moral change? Simply that of a sign; nothing
else. There is then no reference to the mode of baptism. Nor is there
in either phrase, the slightest proof of immersion.—MILEY, *Systematic
Theology,* II, p. 404.

treatment, since our church in harmony with the orthodox belief of both ancient and modern times, definitely
states its position in the creed. We shall consider briefly
the following subjects: (1) The History of Infant Baptism; (2) Objections to Infant Baptism; (3) Arguments
in favor of it from the Abrahamic Covenant.

1. The history of infant baptism reveals the fact
that the practice has existed in the church from the
earliest times. Justin Martyr, who was born about the
time of St. John's death, states that "there were many
of both sexes, some sixty and some seventy years old,
who were made disciples of Christ in their infancy,"
doubtless referring to baptism. Origen (185-254) expressly declares that "the church hath received the tradition from the apostles, that baptism ought to be administered to infants." About the middle of the third
century, Fidus, an African bishop, directed a question
to Cyprian, bishop of Carthage, as to whether or not the
baptism of infants might take place before the eighth
day. Cyprian placed this before the synod in 254 A.D.,
at which sixty-six bishops were present, and it was
unanimously decided that it was not necessary to defer
baptism until the eighth day. Augustine in the fourth
century says that "the whole church practices infant
baptism. It was not instituted by councils, but was always in use"; and again, "I do not remember to have
read of any person, whether Catholic or heretic, who

Dr. Wall sums up the history as follows: "First, during the first
four hundred years from the formation of the Christian Church Tertullian only urged the delay of baptism to infants, and that only in some
cases; and Gregory only delayed it, perhaps, to his own children. But
neither any society of men nor any individual, denied the lawfulness of
baptizing infants. Secondly, in the next seven hundred years there was
not a society nor an individual who even pleaded for this delay;
much less any who denied the right or the duty of infant baptism.
Thirdly, in the year eleven hundred and twenty, one sect of the
Waldenses denied baptism to infants, because they supposed them to
be incapable of salvation. But the main body of that people rejected
the opinion as heretical, and the sect which held it soon came to nothing. Fourthly, the next appearance of this opinion was in the year
fifteen hundred and twenty-two" (Cf. WAKEFIELD, Christian Theology,
p. 573).

Pelagius, the opponent of Augustine, was reported to have rejected infant baptism, but he denied the charge in strong terms. He
says, "Men slander me as if I denied the sacrament of baptism to
infants. I never heard of any, not even the most impious heretic who
denied baptism to infants."

maintained that baptism ought to be denied to infants."
It seems impossible to account for these historical statements unless the practice of infant baptism has come
down to us from the days of the apostles.

2. The objections to infant baptism are usually
made on the following grounds: (1) That the practice
has no express warrant in the Scriptures; (2) That the
Scriptures declare that belief must precede faith, and
since infants cannot believe, therefore, they should not
be baptized; (3) That infants cannot consent to the
covenant of which baptism is the seal, and, therefore,
should not be bound by this ordinance; and (4) that
baptism can do infants no good, and, therefore, it is useless to baptize them. These objections will be answered
in the positive argument which follows.

3. Infant baptism is connected immediately with
the Abrahamic covenant, and can be fully understood
only in the light of the Old Testament teachings. (1)
God has but one Church. It is built upon the protevangelium, and first took its visible form in the covenant
with Abraham. Thus St. Paul declares that *the scripture, foreseeing that God would justify the heathen
through faith, preached before the gospel unto Abraham, saying, In thee shall all nations be blessed* (Gal.
3: 8). The promise made to Abraham and his seed, not
only included temporal blessings, but the Messiah himself, *and in thy seed shall all the nations of the earth
be blessed* (Gen. 22: 18). The temporal blessings were
fulfilled in the human posterity of Abraham, but Christ
as the divine seed is the source of the universal spiritual
blessings. *He saith not, And to seeds, as of many; but
as of one, And to thy seed which is Christ* (Gal. 3: 16).
*And if ye be Christ's, then are ye Abraham's seed, and
the basis of this promise that St. Peter in his sermon at
Pentecost, made the universal offer of salvation, *For
the promise is unto you, and to your children, and to all
that are afar off, even as many as the Lord our God
shall call* (Acts 2: 39). (2) The covenant made between
heirs according to the promise (Gal. 3: 29). It was on
Abraham and his seed was sealed by the rite of circum-

cision. *This is my covenant, which ye shall keep, be-tween me and you and thy seed after thee; every man child among you shall be circumcised* (Gen. 17:10). The child which was not circumcised on the eighth day was to be cut off by a special judgment of God, as having broken the covenant. Hence the rite was the constant publication of the covenant of grace among the descendants of Abraham, and its repetition the constant confirmation of that covenant. (3) The Christian Church is the continuation of the Abrahamic covenant in its universal unfoldings. The promise implicit in the covenant is unfolded in the rich fullness of the blessing of Christ. Hence we read that Abraham *received the sign of circumcision, a seal of the righteousness of the faith which he had yet being uncircumcised: that he*

In order to perceive the bearing of this passage (Acts 2:39) upon the question before us, it is only necessary to consider the resemblance that there is between the declaration of Peter, "the promise is to you, and to your children," and the promise of God to Abraham. This resemblance is seen in two particulars: (1) Each stands connected with an ordinance by which persons were to be admitted into the visible church; in the one case by circumcision, in the other by baptism. (2) Both agree in phraseology. The one knows that seed and children are terms of the same import. It follows, therefore, from these two points of resemblance, that the subjects in both cases are the same; and as it is certain that in the promise of God to Abraham both parents and infant children were included, it must be equally certain that both are included in the announcement of Peter. Here, then, we have an express warrant for infant baptism.—WAKEFIELD, *Christian Theology*, p. 571.

That children were included in this covenant is too plain a fact to be questioned. They were initiated by the same rite whereby the promises of the covenant were sealed unto Abraham. Their initiation was not made a matter of the divine sufferance, but a matter of the divine command. Why then should they be denied the rite of baptism, which in the Christian Church occupies the place that circumcision occupied in the Abrahamic covenant? It will be no answer to ask in objection, what benefit can baptism render infants? because the same objection would work equally against their circumcision under the Abrahamic covenant. If the reply should be that the children are not in the spiritual state which baptism signifies, the answer is that the same objection would have excluded them from the rite of circumcision. Again, if the reply should be that infants are incapable of the faith, on the condition of which the blessings of the gospel are offered, the answer is that they were equally incapable of the mental exercises which in the case of adults were conditional to the spiritual blessing of the Abrahamic covenant. Infant circumcision under that covenant warrants the right of infants to baptism under the Christian covenant—which indeed, is not another, but the very same in its full development. On the ground of such facts only a divine order could annul the right of infants to Christian baptism; but no such order has been given.—MILEY, *Systematic Theology*, II, pp. 406, 407.

might be the father of all that believe, though they be not circumcised; that righteousness might be imputed unto them also; and the father of circumcision to them who are not of the circumcision only, but who also walk in the steps of that faith of our father Abraham, which he had being yet uncircumcised (Rom. 4: 11, 12). *That the blessing of Abraham might come on the Gentiles through Jesus Christ; that we might receive the promise of the Spirit through faith* (Gal. 3: 14). Thus as we have indicated, the Abrahamic covenant is carried out to its highest degree in the gospel dispensation. (4) Baptism supersedes circumcision. The initiatory rite of circumcision passed away with the rites and ceremonies peculiar to the Old Testament phase of the covenant, and baptism becomes in its place, the initiatory rite of the New Testament. That baptism carries with it the same federal and initiatory character is clear from the statement of St. Paul that *ye are complete in him, which is the head of all principality and power: in whom also ye are circumcised with the circumcision made without hands, in putting off the body of the sins of the flesh by the circumcision of Christ: buried with him in baptism, wherein also ye are risen with him through the faith of the operation of God; who hath raised him from the dead* (Col. 2: 10-12). Here the rite of circumcision is brought into immediate connection with baptism as a New Testament ordinance, and this baptism is expressly stated to be "the circumcision of Christ." We may now sum up the arguments concerning the scriptural warrant for the practice of infant baptism, in the words of Dr. Wakefield. "We have shown that the Abrahamic covenant was the general covenant of grace; that children were embraced in that covenant,

It is sometimes urged, by way of objection, that if infants are baptized they should also be admitted to the Lord's Supper. To this our reply is, that as baptism is passively received, it may be administered to all infants; but to partake of the supper requires an agency of which many of them are physically incapable. Again, as the Lord's Supper is to be a memorial to each participant, infants are intellectually incapable of receiving it according to its intention. To this we have an exact parallel in the Jewish Passover; and though all Jewish children were circumcised at eight days old, yet they did not eat the Passover until they could comprehend its design.—WAKEFIELD, *Christian Theology*, p. 571.

and were admitted into the visible church by circumcision; that Christianity is but a continuation, under a new form, of that covenant which God made with Abraham; and that baptism is now the sign and seal of the covenant of grace, as circumcision was under the former dispensation. From these premises it necessarily follows that as the infant children of believing parents, under the Old Testament, were proper subjects of circumcision, so the infant children of Christian believers are proper subjects of baptism" (WAKEFIELD, *Christian Theology*, pp. 569, 570). To this may be added the fact that in three different instances, it is said that households were baptized—that of Lydia (Acts 16:15), the

St. Peter preserves the correspondence between the act of Noah in preparing the ark as an act of faith by which he was justified, and the act of submitting to Christian baptism, which is also obviously an act of faith, in order to the remission of sins, or the obtaining a good conscience before God. This is further strengthened by his immediately adding, "by the resurrection of Jesus Christ": a clause which our translators by the use of a parenthesis, connect with "baptism doth also now save us"; so that their meaning is, we are saved by baptism through the resurrection of Jesus Christ; and as he "was raised again for our justification," this sufficiently shows the true sense of the apostle, who, by our being "saved," clearly means our being justified by faith. The text, however, needs no parenthesis, and the true sense may be thus expressed: "The antitype to which the water of the flood, baptism, doth now save us; not the putting away of the filth of the flesh, but that which intently seeks a good conscience toward God, through faith in the resurrection of Jesus Christ." But however a particular word may be disposed of, the whole passage can only be consistently taken to teach us that baptism is the outward sign of our entrance into God's covenant of mercy; and that when it is an act of true faith, it becomes an instrument of salvation, like that act of Noah, by which when moved with fear, he "prepared an ark to the saving of his house," and survived the destruction of an unbelieving world.—WATSON, *Theological Institutes*, II, p. 625.

Mr. Wesley was trained to believe in a possible regeneration of infants. In his sermon on "The New Birth" he says, "It is certain our church supposes that all who are baptized in their infancy are at the same time born again." "Nor is it an objection of any weight against this, that we cannot comprehend how this work can be wrought in infants. For neither can we comprehend how it is wrought in a person of riper years." For himself he never distinctly defined this: "But whatever be the case with infants, it is sure all of riper years who are baptized are not at the same time born again." His views of the preliminary grace signified by the new birth of infants have been more fully expressed by later expositors of Methodist doctrine. Mr. Watson's summary may be accepted as giving their meaning. "To the infant child it is a visible reception into the same covenant and church, a pledge of acceptance through Christ, the bestowment of a title to all the grace of the covenant as circumstances may require, and as the mind of the child may be capable of receiving it." "It secures, too, the gift of the Holy Spirit in those secret spiritual influences by which the actual regeneration of those children who die in infancy is effected; and which are a seed of life in those who are spared."—POPE, *Compend. Chr. Th.*, III, p. 324.

THE CHURCH: ITS WORSHIP AND SACRAMENTS 189

Philippian jailer (Acts 16:33), and that of Stephanus (I Cor. 1:16). While there is of course no positive proof, we may regard the above statements as at least presumptive evidence that there were children in the households of those who were baptized. Further still, we have from the lips of our Lord himself, the declaration that children belong to the kingdom of God (Mark 10:4); and if so, they are entitled to this recognition as a witness to the faith of the parents in the words of their Lord. We maintain, therefore, that there is a warrant for infant baptism, and that the arguments just given are a sufficient answer to the objections previously mentioned. If it still be maintained that only believers are to be baptized, and infants excluded, then we insist that the argument proves too much. If only those who believe and are baptized will be saved; and if children cannot believe and therefore cannot be baptized, then by force of the argument, the logical conclusion is that they cannot be saved. This we think no one will allow, for it is in direct opposition to the words of our Lord mentioned above (Mark 10:4). When Christ made the statement, *He that believeth and is baptized shall be saved* (Mark 16:16), He was speaking of adult believers, to whom the disciples were sent with the gospel, and who were therefore capable of responding to their preaching. His words have no reference in this place, to the question of infant baptism.

THE LORD'S SUPPER

"We believe that the Memorial and Communion Supper instituted by our Lord and Saviour Jesus Christ, is essentially a New Testament sacrament, declarative of His sacrificial death, through the merits of which believers have life and salvation, and promise of all spiritual blessings in Christ. It is distinctively for those who are prepared for reverent appreciation of its significance, and by it they shew forth the Lord's death till He comes again. Being a Communion feast, only those who have faith in Christ and love for the saints should be called to participate therein" (*Manual, Church of the Nazarene,* "Articles of Faith," XIV).

The Institution of the Lord's Supper. The circumstances under which this sacrament was instituted, were solemn and impressive. It was the night of His betrayal, as Jesus and His disciples celebrated the Passover together. *And as they were eating, Jesus took bread, and blessed it [εὐλογήσας], and brake it, and gave it to the disciples, and said,, Take, eat; this is my body. And he took the cup, and gave thanks [εὐχαριστήσας], and gave it to them, saying, Drink ye all of it; for this is my blood of the new testament, which is shed for many for the remission of sins* (Matt. 26: 26-28; Cf. Mark 14: 22-24; Luke 22: 19, 20). The preceding references are historical, and describe the events connected with the holy institution. The following verses set forth St. Paul's doctrinal interpretation of the institution. *The cup of blessing which we bless, is it not the communion of the blood of Christ? The bread which we break, is it not the communion of the body of Christ? For we being many are one bread, and one body; for we are all partakers of that one bread* (I Cor. 10: 16, 17). *For I have received of the Lord that which also I delivered unto you, That the Lord Jesus the same night in which he was betrayed took bread: and when he had given thanks, he brake it, and said, Take, eat: this is my body, which is broken for you: this do in remembrance of me. After the same manner also he took the cup, when he had supped, saying, This cup is the new testament in my blood: this do ye, as oft as ye drink it, in remembrance of me. For as often as ye eat this bread, and drink this cup, ye do shew the Lord's death till he come* (I Cor. 11: 23-28).

As baptism was substituted for circumcision, so also, the Lord's Supper superseded the Passover. Under the old covenant, the Passover was the eminent type of our Lord's redemptive sacrifice, which from age to age had

This sacrament is called the Lord's Supper because the Lord himself appointed it, and because it was first instituted in the evening, and at the close of the paschal supper. It is called the communion, as herein we hold communion with Christ and with His people. It is also called the eucharist, a thanksgiving, because Christ, in the institution of it, gave thanks; and because we, in participation of it, are required to be thankful.—WAKEFIELD, *Christian Theology,* p. 590.

represented the faith and hope of the ancient people. And since Christ himself as the true Passover was about to fulfill the Old Testament symbol, a new rite was necessary to commemorate this spiritual deliverance and confirm its benefits. At the Feast of the Passover, the head of each family took the cup of thanksgiving, and with his family gave thanks to the God of Israel. So also, when Jesus had finished the usual paschal ceremony with His disciples, He proceeded to a new and distant action. *He took bread* [the bread from the paschal table], *and gave thanks, and brake it, and gave unto them, saying, This is my body which is given for you: this do in remembrance of me. Likewise also the cup after supper* [the paschal cup], *saying, This cup is the new testament in my blood, which is shed for you* (Luke 22:19, 20). Thus there exists a continuity of symbolism in the Old and New Testaments; and yet the old was brought to a sharp close, and the new rite which superseded it had an equally distinct beginning. That this rite was intended to be permanent is evident from the fact that St. Paul received of the Lord the word which enjoined upon him, the necessity of establishing it in all the churches which he founded (I Cor. 11:23).

During the apostolic age there were a number of terms used to express the meaning of the Lord's Supper, at least five of these words being found in the New Testament. (1) It was called the Eucharist (εὐχαριστέω, to give thanks), referring to Christ's taking the cup and giving thanks. Sometimes also the *eulogesas*

Mr. Watson in commenting on I Cor. 11:23-26 says, "From these words we learn, (1) That St. Paul received a special revelation as to this ordinance, which must have had a higher object than the mere commemoration of an historical fact, and must be supposed to have been made for the purpose of enjoining it upon him to establish this rite in the churches raised up by him, and of enabling him rightly to understand its authority and purport, where he found it already appointed by the first founders of the first churches. (2) That the command of Christ, 'This do in remembrance of me,' which was originally given to the disciples presented with Christ at the last Passover, is laid by St. Paul upon the Corinthians. (3) That he regarded the Lord's Supper as a rite to be 'often' celebrated, and that in all future time until the Lord himself should 'come' to judge the world. The perpetual obligation of this ordinance cannot therefore be reasonably disputed."— WATSON, *Theological Institutes*, II, pp. 661, 662.

(from εὐλογέω, to praise, or bless), as in the reference to Jesus' act in blessing the bread. The two words were often interchanged also. Thus St. Paul speaks of "the cup of blessing." On account of the appropriateness of the term "Eucharist" it has always been popular among English speaking people. As such it is a solemn thanksgiving for the blessings of redemption. (2) It was known also as the Communion. The Acts of the Apostles joins together "the breaking of bread" and "the fellowship" (Acts 2:42). The fellowship meal, however, was in itself regarded as a communion and was sealed by the kiss of peace. (Rom. 16:16; I Cor. 16:20; II Cor. 13:12; I Thess. 5:26; I Peter 5:14). St. Paul emphasizes this

The following is a summary of Dr. Pope's excellent discussion of the Lord's Supper in relation to the Passover: (1) Now the ancient rite was an annual commemoration of the typical redemption of the Hebrew people; and the Lord's Supper is the solemn act of the Church's commemoration of the redeeming death of the Saviour of the world. St. Paul adds "in remembrance of me" to the giving of the bread as well as the cup. . . . . Our Saviour blessed the elements and gave thanks: offering the praise of His own atonement which His people continue forever. Hence the rite is the great expression of the Church's gratitude for the gift of Christ, and especially His atoning death. It is the feast of thanksgiving within the Christian assembly, and it is the feast of testimony before the world, "Showing forth" His death. (2) The ancient Passover was also the annual ratification of the covenant between God and His people. . . . . When our Lord substituted His Supper, He used language that included all, and specially referred to the solemn covenant transaction in which Moses divided the blood of atonement into two parts: half of the blood he sprinkled on the altar, to denote the propitiation of God; with the remainder he sprinkled all the people, to signify to them the divine favor, and the book of the covenant also, to signify the ratification of the covenant of which that book was the record: "This is the blood of the testament which God hath enjoined unto you." These words of Moses our Lord connect with the new Passover of His new covenant: "Drink ye all of it: for this is my blood of the new testament which is shed for many for the remission of sins." . . . . The Holy Spirit uses this sacramental ordinance for the assurance of faith: hence the meaning of the term Sacrament as applied to this solemnity. (3) But the ancient Passover was the rite that kept in annual remembrance the birth of the people as such and their community life in the bond of the covenant. When our Lord ordained His Supper, He distributed to each and laid emphasis on the All. . . . . The Supper is the sacrament of union with Jesus the True Vine; and of union with one another in Him; hence it might seem that the elements represent not only the sacrificed body of Christ, but the spiritual body itself saved by that sacrifice and made a part of Himself. The real bond of union, however, is not the bread and the wine; it is the common participation of life in Christ by the Spirit. But the sacramental eating and drinking together is the outward and visible sign of that union. The Supper therefore is the perfect badge of common discipleship: the mutual pledge of all the offices of brotherly love.— POPE, *Compend. Chr. Th.*, III, pp. 326, 327.

communion with one another as being inseparable from the communion with Christ. He notes that we are one body as we partake of the one loaf which is the body of Christ (I Cor. 10:16). Jesus emphasizes the same aspect of communion in His Parable of the Vine and the Branches (John 15:1-8). (3) It was regarded as a Memorial Feast, a commemoration of the death of Jesus. This phase was not greatly stressed at first, for to the early Christians, Christ was not a dead hero, but the One who was alive forevermore. The memorial aspect, therefore, was more closely associated with the redemptive death of Christ and the eschatological hope. *For as often as ye eat this bread, and drink this cup, ye do shew the Lord's death till he come* (I Cor. 11:26). (4) It was looked upon as a Sacrifice ($\theta\nu\sigma\iota\alpha$). As such, it not only commemorated the sacrifice of Christ, but was itself regarded as a sacrifice. This distinction must be kept clearly in mind—the interpretation of the death of Jesus as a sacrifice, and the interpretation of the community meal as a sacrifice. Christ's sacrifice was once for all (Heb. 9:25, 26), and could not be repeated. It superseded all animal sacrifices, and was regarded as something new and final for men. The community meal was called a Sacrifice, in that it was itself a thank-offering or a "sacrifice of praise" (Heb. 13:15. Cf. Phil.

Apart from matters of doubtful interpretation, these passages plainly teach, First, that the Lord's Supper is a divine institution of perpetual obligation. Second, that the material elements to be used in the celebration, are bread and wine. Third, that the important constituent parts of the service are: (1) The consecration of the elements. (2) The breaking of the bread and pouring of the wine. (3) The distribution and the reception by the communicants of the bread and wine. Fourth, that the design of the ordinance is, (1) to commemorate the death of Christ. (2) To represent, to effect and to avow our participation in the body and blood of Christ. (3) To represent, effect and avow the union of believers with Christ and with each other. And (4) to signify and seal our acceptance of the new covenant as ratified by the blood of Christ. Fifth, conditions for profitable communion are: (1) Knowledge to discern the Lord's body. (2) Faith to feed upon Him. (3) Love to Christ and to His people. The main points of controversy concerning the ordinance are: (1) The sense in which the bread and wine are the body and blood of Christ. (2) The sense in which the communicant receives the body and blood of Christ in this ordinance. (3) The benefits which the sacrament confers, and the manner in which those benefits are conveyed. (4) The conditions on which the efficacy of the ordinance is suspended.—HODGE, *Systematic Theology*, III, p. 612.

2:17; 4:18); and also because it was attended by almsgiving for the poor. (5) Finally, it was called the Presence, or the Mystery (μυστήριον). The first carried with it the idea of Christ as a host at His table, and is drawn from the Emmaus account, where Christ's presence was made known in the breaking of Bread. The second emphasizes more especially, the sacred food as a channel of grace and power. St. John is the primary witness here. Christ is the "bread of life" (Cf. John 6:53). The apostle does not depart from spiritual conceptions, however, and we are not to conclude that he held to any benefit from the flesh apart from the Word. There were other terms expressive of the Lord's Supper also, but the five mentioned above represent the principal phases of the sacrament as set forth in the Scriptures.

The Development of the Doctrine in the Church. Following the apostolic age, there began very early a tendency to depart from the symbolical interpretation of the elements and actions as set forth in the New Testament, and to substitute in its stead a realistic interpretation of the Lord's Supper. This trend was found especially in the Greek Fathers—Justin Martyr, Irenæus

There are other terms also by which the Lord's Supper was sometimes designated. It is called προσφορά or "offering" because of the gifts and offerings made to the poor in connection with this service. It is called Σύναξις "the assembly" because the nature of the service implied an assembly of the believers. It is called the "missa" or Mass, probably from the words used in the dismissal of the congregation. The term "Mass," however, was used long before it took on the meaning which attaches to it in the Roman Catholic Church.

Concerning the origin of the term "Mass" Dr. Charles Hodge gives us the following: "This word has been variously explained; but it is almost universally, at the present time, assumed to come from the words used in the dismission of the congregation. (*Ita, missa est*, 'Go, the congregation is dismissed.') First the unconverted hearers were dismissed, and then the catechumens, the baptized faithful only remaining for the communion service. Hence there was in the early church a *missa infidelium*, a *missa catechumenorum*, and finally a *missa fidelium*. There seems to have been a different service adapted to these several classes of hearers. Hence the word *missa* came to be used in the sense of the Greek word λειτουργία or service. As under the Old Testament the offering of sacrifice was the main part of the temple service, so in the Christian Church, when the Lord's Supper was regarded as an expiatory offering, it became the middle point in public worship and was called emphatically the service, or mass. Since the Reformation this has become universal as the designation of the eucharist as celebrated in the Church of Rome."—Hodge, *Systematic Theology*, III, p. 614.

and Gregory of Nyssa. With their bent toward mysticism, their tendency was naturally toward the realistic view, according to which the bread became the actual body of Christ, and the wine His blood. The history of this doctrine may be best summed up by considering it in the following stages of development. (1) The Patristic Period; (2) The Nicene and Post-Nicene Periods; (3) The Mediæval Period; and (4) The Reformation Period. Following this we shall consider the Nature of the Lord's Supper, and in the discussion we shall deal more fully with the Reformation theories and their later developments.

1. The Patristic Period. This period marked the beginnings of doctrinal development along two lines which afterward were united: (1) the sacramental Presence in the Communion, which later developed into the doctrine of transubstantiation; and (2) the sacrificial offering in the Eucharist which later became the Mass. The earlier Fathers took but little cognizance of the distinctions which later were regarded as important, and consequently their statements are often ambiguous. Both Ignatius and Irenæus indicate a trend away from symbolism in such statements as "His body is reckoned to be in bread," and "He made it His own body by saying, 'This is my body, that is, the figure of my body.'" Clement of Alexandria (220) states that the wine is "a symbol of the blood." Cyprian often speaks of the bread and wine as the body and blood of Christ, yet at other times apparently regards the elements as symbols or emblems.

2. The Nicene and Post-Nicene Periods. The lines of development were more marked during these periods and may be indicated as follows: (1) Chrysostom and others began to speak of the Eucharist as a repetition of that great oblation of Christ. At first this was merely an oblation of gratitude for the gifts of God in nature and grace, but the resemblance was soon carried farther. It soon came to be identified with consubstantiation or a coexistence of the actual body and blood of Christ with the consecrated elements, which seems to have prevailed very early in both the East and the

West. This is found in the writings of Hilary (368), Cyril (386), Gregory of Nyssa (395), Ambrose (397), and Chrysostom (407). Some of these lean far toward the doctrine of transubstantiation or a change in the substance of the elements. Eusebius (331), Athanasius (373), Gregory Nazianzen (391) and Nilus (457) make a more or less clear distinction between the sign and the thing signified. (2) The next step in the development of transubstantiation is found in Gregory the Great (604) who speaks of "the daily sacrifice." Thus the sacrifice which Cyprian mentioned as being "the Lord's passion which we offer" came to be regarded as the "atoning sacrifice" which was to be repeated at every celebration. (3) In 818 A.D. Paschasius Radbertus formally propounded the doctrine that the material elements are by divine power through the prayer of consecration, literally changed into the very body that was born of Mary; and consequently after the prayer of consecration, the outward appearance of the bread and wine is a mere veil that deceives the senses. Rabanus Maurus (825) and Ratramus (832) opposed this position and Gerbert (1003) defended it — the matter finally resulting in one of the greatest controversies of the Western Church.

3. The Middle Ages. During the Middle Ages the schoolmen gave much attention to the subject of the sacraments. (1) In 1030 A.D., Berengarius wrote a treatise affirming that the body of Christ is present in the Eucharist, though not in essence, only in power; that the elements are not changed in substance; and to secure this power, there must not only be the prayer of consecration, but faith on the part of the recipient as well. He was opposed by Humbert (1059) and Lanfranc (1089), and later was compelled to retract his statements by Gregory VII. (2) The doctrine of Radbertus and Humbert was defined under the title of transubstantiation by Hildebert of Tours (1134) and was imposed as an article of faith by the Fourth Lateran Council in 1215 A.D. At the same time, the Mass was decreed as the bloodless repetition of the one sacrifice,

and its efficacy to avail for the quick and the dead. (3) Thomas Aquinas (1274) popularized the doctrine of transubstantiation by means of four hymns. Together with other schoolmen, he held to a distinction between substance and accident, the substance being that which underlies all properties and accidents those properties which are discernible by the senses. (4) Peter Lombard (1164) taught that the substance of the bread was converted into Christ's body, and the wine into His blood, but yet the whole Christ was present on the altar under each species. Along with the growth of this sentiment, which Thomas Aquinas afterward termed "concomitance," there grew up also a sentiment favoring communion in one kind. Robert Pulleyn (1144) first suggested withholding the cup from the laity on the ground of sacrilege through the possible spilling of "the very blood of Christ." This was sanctioned by Alexander of Hales (1245), Bonaventura (1274) and Aquinas, and was confirmed by the Council of Constance in 1415 A.D. Thomas Aquinas also elaborated the doctrine of concomitance by teaching that the elements were converted into the body and blood of Christ, and that His soul is united to the body, and His divinity to the soul. This prepared the way for the practice of Eucharistic adoration. As early as 1217, Pope Honorius III had instituted the "elevation of the host" or the lifting up of the sacramental elements as an act of reverence, but in 1264, the Adoration of the Host was established as a sacrifice. The Eastern Church differed from the Western in that it maintained communion in

One of the numerous theories concerning the eucharist prevalent more or less in the early church, was that which is known in the history of doctrine as impanation. As in man the soul is united to the body imparting to it life and efficiency without itself becoming material, or rendering the body spirit; and as the Eternal Logos became flesh by taking to Himself a true body and a reasonable soul, without receiving anything human into His divine nature, or imparting divinity to His humanity; so the same Logos becomes united with a consecrated bread, without any substantial change in it or in Him. His relation to the bread, however, is analogous to that of the soul to the body in man and of the Logos to humanity in the person of our Lord. As the assumption of our nature by the Son of God is expressed by the word "incarnation," so His assumption and union with the bread in the Lord's Supper is called "impanation."—HODGE, *Systematic Theology*, III, p. 648.

both kinds for the laity, used leavened instead of unleavened bread, and retained infant communion.

4. *The Reformation Period.* The Reformers revolted
against the doctrine of transubstantiation, and the sacrifice of the mass. Three lines of development may be
distinctly traced: (1) that in Germany under Luther;
(2) that in Switzerland under Zwingli; and (3) that
under Calvin the Genevan reformer, also in Switzerland.
The first issue was in the doctrine of consubstantiation as
held by the Lutheran Church; the second, in the commemorative idea as held by the Reformed churches
with a strong tendency toward Socinianism; and third,
the more orthodox doctrine of the Reformed churches
as expressed in the signs and seals. The Anglican formularies are a combination of the Lutheran and Reformed
doctrines, both Zwinglian and Calvinistic. The Roman
Catholic teaching is renounced. Article XXVIII states

The Roman Catholic Doctrine is given in the Canons and Decrees
of the Council of Trent (1551). "In the Eucharist are contained truly,
really, and substantially, the body and blood, together with the soul and
divinity of our Lord Jesus Christ, and consequently the whole Christ."
—Canon 1.

"The whole substance of the bread (is converted) into the body,"
and "the whole substance of the wine into the blood."—Canon 2.

"The whole Christ is contained under each species, and under every
part of each species, when separated."—Canon 3.

"The principal fruit of the most holy Eucharist is the remission of
sins."—Canon 5.

"In the Eucharist, Christ is to be adored."—Canon 6.

"All and each of Christ's faithful are bound to communicate every
year."—Canon 9.

"Sacramental confession is to be made beforehand, by those whose
conscience is burdened with mortal sin."—Canon 11.

The authoritative teaching of the Lutheran Church is to be found
in the Augsburg Confession (1530) Article X. "The true body and
blood of Christ are truly present under the form of bread and wine,
and are there communicated to and received by those that eat in the
Lord's Supper." Later, Melanchthon changed this article, a departure
which occasioned much controversy. This change is expressed in the
Formula of Concord (1540) as follows: "We believe, teach, and confess that in the Lord's Supper the body and blood of Christ are truly
and substantially present, and that they are truly distributed and taken
together with the bread and wine."

The Thirty-Nine Articles of the Church of England (1562), Article
XXVIII. "The Supper of the Lord is not only a sign of love that Christians ought to have among themselves one to another; but rather it is
a sacrament of our redemption by Christ's death: insomuch that to
such as rightly, worthily, and with faith, receive the same, the bread
which we break is a (heavenly and spiritual) partaking of the body of
Christ; and likewise the cup of blessing is a partaking of the blood
of Christ."

that "Transubstantiation (or the change of the substance of bread and wine) in the Supper of the Lord, cannot be proved by Holy Writ; but is repugnant to the plain words of Scripture, overthroweth the nature of a sacrament, and hath given occasion to many superstitions. The body of Christ is given, taken and eaten in the Supper, only after a heavenly and spiritual manner. And the means whereby the body of Christ is received and eaten in the Supper, is faith. The Sacrament of the Lord's Supper was not by Christ's ordinance reserved, carried about, lifted up, or worshiped." Article XVIII of the Methodist Creed is identical with the above except that the word "it" is dropped in the first paragraph, as a comparison of the full text of the creeds will show. The Westminster Confession of the Presbyterian churches is substantially the same also. These views will be considered more fully in the following section.

The Nature of the Sacrament. The various views concerning the nature of the Lord's Supper, are determined largely by the construction put upon the words, *This is my body,* and *This is my blood* (Matt. 26: 26-28). These varying interpretations give us (1) The Roman Catholic doctrine of Transubstantiation; (2) The Lutheran doctrine of Consubstantiation; (3) The Zwinglian doctrine of Commemoration; and (4) The Calvinistic doctrine of the Signs and Seals.

1. The doctrine of Transubstantiation is held by the Roman Catholic Church, and the steps in its historical

The Heidelberg Catechism (1563). "What is it to eat of the crucified body and drink the shed blood of Christ? It is not only to embrace with a believing heart all the sufferings and death of Christ, and thereby to obtain the forgiveness of sins and life eternal, but moreover, also, to be so united more and more to His sacred body by the Holy Ghost, who dwells both in Christ and in us, that although He is in heaven, and we are upon the earth, we are nevertheless flesh of His flesh, and bone of His bone, and live and are governed forever by one Spirit, as members of the same body are by the one soul."

The Westminster Confession of Faith (1647) Article XXIX. "The Lord's Supper (is) to be observed for the perpetual remembrance of the sacrifice of Himself in His death, the sealing of all benefits thereof which true believers, their spiritual nourishment and growth in Him, their further engagement in, and to all duties which they owe unto Him; and to be a bond and pledge of their communion with Him, and with each other, as members of His mystical body." "Worthy believers do inwardly by faith, really and indeed, yet not carnally and corporally, but spiritually receive and feel upon Christ crucified, and all the benefits of His death."

development have already been indicated. Here the words *This is my body* and *This is my blood,* are taken in the most literal sense possible. It is believed that when our Lord pronounced these words, He changed the bread and wine upon the table into His own body and blood, and delivered it into the hands of the apostles. Since that time it is held that the priests through apostolic succession, have the power of making a similar change by means of the prayer of consecration and the pronouncement of the same words. The accidents of the bread and wine remain, that is, the bread tastes like bread, and the wine like wine; but the substance underlying these accidents is regarded as being changed, so that the bread is no longer bread, but the body of Christ; and the wine is no longer wine, but the blood of Christ. Since the blood is included in the body, the laity receive only the bread, and the priest the wine. There are several important consequences which attach to this doctrine. (1) The bread and the wine, having been changed into the body and blood of Christ, are by the priest presented to God as a sacrifice. While this sacrifice differs from others as being without the shedding of blood, it is nevertheless regarded as a true propitiatory offering for the sins of both the living and the dead. (2) This body and blood contain within them the grace they signify, and therefore confer it *ex opere operato,* that is, they have intrinsic value in themselves and this grace is imparted to all through the mere partaking of the sacrament. No special disposition is necessary on the part of the recipient, not even faith, for the sacrament operates immediately upon all who do not obstruct it by mortal sin. (3) The bread having been changed into the body of Christ, any unused portion was sacredly kept as the "reserved host." (4) Since

The only ground of such a doctrine lies in the assumption of a literal sense of the words "This is my body," "This is my blood," transubstantiation itself is a mere inference from this assumption. The bread and wine must be changed into the flesh and blood of Christ if they are really present in the supper, because there is no other way of accounting for their presence. This is the manner in which the doctrine is constructed. Without a literal sense of the words of institution it has not the slightest ground in Scripture.—MILEY, *Systematic Theology,* II, p. 413.

Christ's divinity was attached to His body, it was regarded as highly proper to worship them upon the altar; and further, to carry them about that they might receive the homage of all who met them. Against this unscriptural doctrine, Protestants not only objected, but revolted, and hence the Reformation doctrine is more simple and scriptural.

THE TRIDENTINE DOCTRINE

In the first place the holy Synod teaches, and openly and simply professes, that, in the august sacrament of the holy eucharist, after the consecration of the bread and wine, our Lord Jesus Christ, true God and true man, is truly, really, and substantially contained under the species of those sensible things. For neither are these things mutually repugnant—that our Saviour himself always sitteth at the right hand of the Father in heaven, according to the natural mode of existing, and that nevertheless He be, in many other places, sacramentally present to us in His own substance by a manner of existing, which, though we can scarcely express it in words, yet can we, by the understanding illuminated by faith, conceive, and we ought most firmly to believe, to be possible unto God: for thus all our forefathers, as many as were in the true Church of Christ, who have treated of this most holy sacrament, have most openly professed that our Redeemer instituted this so admirable a sacrament at the last supper when, after the blessing of the bread and wine, He testified, in express and clear words which—recorded by the holy evangelist, and afterward repeated by St. Paul, whereas they carry with them that proper and most manifest meaning in which they were understood by the Fathers—it is indeed a crime the most unworthy that they should be wrested, by certain contentious and wicked men, to fictitious and imaginary tropes, whereby the verity of the flesh and blood of Christ is denied, contrary to the universal sense of the Church, which as the pillar and ground of truth, has detested, as satanical, these inventions devised by impious men; she recognizing, with a mind ever grateful and unforgetting, the most excellent benefit of Christ.—SCHAFF, *Creeds of Christendom*, II, pp. 126, 127.

Dr. Charles Hodge in his *Systematic Theology* (III, pp. 688 ff.) has an excellent discussion of the Protestant objections to the Roman Catholic position. We can only give a brief summary here. "Protestants reject the doctrine that the eucharist is a true propitiary sacrifice: (1) Because it is not only destitute of all support from the Scriptures, but is directly contrary to the whole nature of the ordinance, as exhibited in its original institution and in the practice of the apostolic church. (2) Because it is founded on the monstrous doctrine of transubstantiation. If the whole substance of the bread be not changed into the substance of Christ's body, and the whole substance of the wine into the substance of His blood, and if the whole Christ, body, soul, and divinity be not really and truly present under the form (or species) or appearance of the bread and wine, then the priest in the mass has nothing to offer. He in fact offers nothing, and the whole service is a deceit. (3) The Romish doctrine is that the apostles were priests, and were invested with authority and power to continue and perpetuate in the Church the priestly office by ordination and the imposition of hands by which the supernatural gifts of the Holy Spirit are conveyed. All this is unscriptural and false. First, because a priest is a man appointed to be a mediator between God and other men. But there is no such office under the Christian dispensation, save in the person of

2. The doctrine of Consubstantiation was adopted by Luther respecting the presence of Christ in the sacrament. While protesting against the Roman doctrine of transubstantiation, he yet felt the need of conserving in an objective manner, the saving significance of the ordinance. He accepted, therefore, the words of institution in their literal significance, but denied that the elements were changed by consecration. He maintained that the bread and the wine remained the same, but that in, with and under the bread and the wine, the body and blood of Christ were present in the sacrament for all partakers and not merely for believers. With the bread and wine, therefore, the body and blood of Christ are literally received by all communicants. Since Christ's presence is only in the use of the elements, the remnants are only so much bread and wine. It is in the use also, that the blessing is given to those who partake in faith. Luther's doctrine of consubstantiation is closely bound up with his Christological teaching concerning the ubiquity of the glorified body of Christ. It is this that makes possible his belief in the real presence, and relates it in some sense to the doctrine of the logos.

Jesus Christ. Second, Christian ministers are never called priests in the New Testament. Third, Christ and the apostles uniformly assume that the way is open for the return of every sinner to God without human intervention. (4) The Romish doctrine is derogatory to the sacrifice of the cross. It opposes that the work of Christ in making satisfaction for the sins of men, needs to be constantly repeated. (5) The doctrine of the sacrificial character of the eucharist, is an integral part of the great system of error, which must stand or fall as a whole. Romanism is another gospel. Moehler, whose philosophical and mitigated Romanism, has called down upon him no little censure from his stricter brethren, represents the doctrine of the eucharist as the point in which all the differences between the Romanists and Protestants converge."

Dr. Joseph Stump insists that the Lutheran Church does not teach the doctrine of consubstantiation, although she is frequently accused of doing so. He holds that consubstantiation means the combining of the body and blood of Christ into a third substance, and this the Lutheran Church does not teach. He further insists that neither impanation nor subpanation is taught by the Lutherans, the former holding that the body and blood are locally included or inclosed in the bread and the wine, the latter that they are located under them. They teach rather, that the body and blood of Christ are not locally, but sacramentally connected with the bread and the wine; and that only during their actual use by the communicant, are the body and blood present. Hence there can be no reserved host, for before and after the actual administration, the elements are only bread and wine.—STUMP, *The Christian Faith*, pp. 353, 354.

The mind of Luther so powerful to throw off dogmas which had nothing but human authority to support them, was, as to the sacrament, held in the bonds of early association. He concluded that the body and blood of Christ are really present in the Lord's Supper; but aware of the absurdities and self-contradictions of transubstantiation, he laid hold of a doctrine which some writers in the Romish church itself, had continued to prefer to the papal dogma above stated. This was designated by the term consubstantiation, which allows that the bread and wine remain the same after consecration as before. Thus he escapes the absurdity of contradicting the very senses of men. It was held, however, by Luther, that though the bread and wine remain unchanged, yet that, together with them, the body and blood of Christ are literally received by the communicants. Some of his immediate followers did not, however, admit more on this point, than that the body and blood of Christ were really present in the sacrament; but that the manner of that presence was an inexplicable mystery. Yet, in some more important respects, Luther and the Consubstantialists wholly escaped the errors of the Church of Rome as to this sacrament. They denied that it was a sacrifice; and that the presence of the body and blood of Christ gave to it any physical virtue acting independently of the disposition of the receiver; and that it rendered the elements the objects of adoration. Their error, therefore, may be considered rather of a speculative than of a practical nature; and was adopted probably in deference to what was conceived to be the literal meaning of the words of Christ when the Lord's Supper was instituted. —Watson, *Theological Institutes*, II, pp. 663, 664.

If we would get at the idea which lies at the foundation of the Lutheran doctrine regarding the Lord's Supper, we must bear in mind that it is an idea independent of those scholastic forms, in which the old theology endeavored to develop it, and especially independent of that doctrine regarding Christ's unlimited ubiquity, the one-sidedness of which we have referred to in our Christology. It is, in fact, the idea of Christ as the head of that new creation whose final end is redemption and perfecting of human nature as a whole, as undivided body and soul. As Christ is not a spirit only, but the incarnate logos; as man, created in God's image, is in the true conception of Him, the center in which spirit and nature unite; as the resurrection of the body is the last eschatological event which Christianity presents; the Lord's Supper is an act of union with Christ, as the principle of that holy marriage of spirit and nature which is the final end of creation. The Lutheran view of the Lord's Supper is thus, in the truest sense of the expression, prophetically Christian, that is, it recognizes in the Eucharist the actual anticipation of that union with the Saviour, the perfection of which will be reached in the consummation of all things. It sees, accordingly, in the Lord's Supper, not only, like Calvin, an aliment for the soul but an aliment for the whole new man, for the future man of the Resurrection, who is germinating and growing in secret, and who shall be manifested in glory, in exact likeness with the glorified humanity of his Lord. Holy Scripture itself thus associates the doctrine concerning the last things with the Lord's Supper, not only in the words of the Apostle Paul, "Ye do shew forth the Lord's death till he come" (I Cor. 11:26); but in the words of our Lord himself, "I will not drink henceforth of this fruit of the vine, until that day when I drink it new with you in my Father's kingdom" (Matt. 26:29; Mark 14:25; Luke 22:16-18). However these words may be interpreted as regards particulars, they plainly give us to understand that the Lord's Supper is an actual prophecy, type, and anticipation of the Union with the Saviour, which will take place in the realm of bliss; and not only of union with the Lord, but of the inward fellowship of love by which believers shall be united to one another in that blessed kingdom. For in the Lord's Sup-

3. The doctrine of the Lord's Supper as a Commemorative rite was advanced by Zwingli, the Swiss reformer and contemporary of Luther. He objected to the literal interpretation of the words of institution as taught by Luther, and maintained instead, that when Jesus said, "This is my body, this is my blood," He employed a common figure of speech, in which the sign is put for the thing signified. Instead of the elements representing the real presence, they are rather, the signs of the absent body and blood of Christ. The Lord's Supper, therefore, is to be regarded as merely a religious commemoration of the death of Christ with this addition, that it is naturally adapted to produce helpful emotions and reflections, and to strengthen the purposes of the will. This is the view generally held by the So-

per believers are all united together into one body, because, as the apostle says, they are partakers of one bread. (I Cor. 10:17).—MARTENSEN, *Christian Dogmatics*, pp. 436, 437.

Zwingli asserted as strongly as Calvin the spiritual presence of Christ in the sacrament, denying with him the carnal and corporeal presence, either in the form of transubstantiation or consubstantiation. "Christ," he says, "is spiritually present in the consciousness of the believer. In the recollection of His sufferings and death, and by faith in these, His body is spiritually eaten. We trust in the dying flesh and blood of Christ, and this faith is called the eating of the body and blood of Christ." . . . . Zwingli regarded the sacrament of the Supper as a means of grace and sanctification, because of its didactic character; because, by evidently setting forth before the eyes Jesus Christ crucified (Gal. 3:1), it teaches in a vivid and special manner the great truth of Christ's atonement and redemption, and confirms the soul of the believer in it. It is an object lesson. In this respect, the function of the sacrament is like that of the Word. Gospel truth is taught in both alike. Both alike are employed by the Holy Spirit in enlightening, strengthening, and comforting the mind of the believer.—SHEDD, *Dogmatic Theology*, II, pp. 370, 371.

The Lutheran asserts that Christ is "spiritually present in the sacrament of the Supper as to the manner, but corporeally as to the substance." That is to say, the substance of Christ's spiritual and glorified body as it once existed on earth, is actually present in and with the sacramental emblems. Consequently, the spiritual and glorified body of Christ is present in the bread and wine, wherever and whenever the sacrament is administered. This requires the ubiquity of Christ's glorified body, whereby it can simultaneously be in heaven and on earth. But the glorified body of Christ, like that of His people, though a spiritual body, has form, and is extended in space. The description of Christ's body after His resurrection and ascension proves this. But one and the same form cannot occupy two spaces at one and the same moment. Christ's glorified body can pass from space to space instantaneously, but cannot fill two spaces at the same instant. When Christ's body passed through, the "doors being shut" (John 20:26), and stood in the midst of the disciples, His body was no longer on the outside of the doors, and could not be.

cinians; and while it escapes the errors of the two former theories, it nevertheless falls short of the full truth.

4. The last theory to be mentioned, is that of the Reformers as taught by Calvin. This is a mediating position between Luther and Zwingli, and is now the generally accepted creed of the Reformed churches. Calvin renounced both transubstantiation and consubstantiation. He taught that the body and blood of Christ were not locally, but only spiritually present in the elements. "It is not the blessing pronounced which makes any change in the cup; but to all who join with becoming affection in the thanksgiving then uttered, in the name of the congregation, Christ is spiritually present, so that they may truly and emphatically be said to be partakers of His body and blood; because His body and blood being spiritually present, convey the same nourishment to their souls, the same quickening to their spiritual life, as bread and wine do to the natural life. According to this system the full benefit of the Lord's Supper is peculiar to those who partake worthily. For while all who eat the bread and drink the wine may be said to show forth the Lord's death, and may also re-

THE REFORMED DOCTRINE

Dr. Shedd gives the chief points in the Reformed teaching as follows: "(1) the believer in worthily partaking of the Lord's Supper, consciously and confidently relies upon Christ's atoning sacrifice for the remission of his sins. This is meant by the phrase, 'Feed upon Christ crucified.' The Lord's Supper can have no meaning, if His vicarious sacrifice is denied. (2) The 'presence' of Christ is not in the bread or the wine, but in the soul of the participant. Christ, says the Westminster Confession, is 'present to the faith of believers,' and faith is mental and spiritual. The statement of Hooker upon this point is explicit and excellent. 'The real presence of Christ's most blessed body and blood is not to be sought for in the sacrament, but in the worthy receiver of the sacrament.' And again he remarks, 'No side denieth but that the soul of man is the receptacle of Christ's presence. Whereby the question is driven to a narrower issue, nor doth anything rest doubtful but this, whether, when the sacrament is administered, Christ be whole (wholly) within man only, or else His body and His blood be also externally seated in the very consecrated elements themselves. Which opinion, they that defend are driven either to consubstantiate and incorporate Christ with elements sacramental, or to transubstantiate and change their substance into His; and so the one holds Him really, but invisibly, molded up with the substance of those elements, the other to hide Him under the only visible show of bread and wine, the substance whereof, as they imagine is abolished, and His succeeded in the same room."—SHEDD, Dogmatic Theology, II, pp. 665, 666.

ceive some devout impressions, they only to whom Jesus is spiritually present share in the spiritual nourishment which arises from partaking of His body and blood" (HILL's *Lectures,* quoted in WAKEFIELD, *Christian Theology,* p. 594). The Reformed doctrine is expressed in Article XXIII of the First Helvetic Confession (1536), as follows: "The bread and wine (of the Supper) are holy, true symbols, through which the Lord offers and presents the true communion of the body, and blood of Christ for the feeding and nourishing of the spiritual and eternal life."

The doctrine which we hold, is well summed up by Dr. Ralston in the following statement. He says, "We conclude that, in this ordinance: (1) No change is effected in the elements; the bread and the wine are not literally the body and blood of Christ. (2) The body and blood of Christ are not literally present with the elements, and received by the communicants. (3) But the elements are signs, or symbols, of the body and blood of Christ, serving as a memorial of His sufferings on the cross and a help to the faith of the communicant. (4) The elements also possess a sacramental character, being a divinely appointed seal of the covenant of redemption. As the blood of the paschal lamb served as a seal of this covenant under the old dispensation, point-

The true Protestant doctrine may be stated thus: The body and blood of Christ are not corporeally present in the ordinance, nor are they received in any corporeal sense; nor are the bread and wine in any sense expiatory, nor do they feed the soul. The body and blood of Christ are received only in a spiritual manner, the benefits of His atonement communicated to the soul by the Holy Spirit, being the only manner in which we can be said to receive the body and blood of Christ in the Supper. Also faith is the medium through which the benefits of the atonement are received; nor are the bread and wine a channel through which this grace is received, only so far as they are received by faith as Christ's appointed symbols of His body and blood, and so far as they, being received in this light, are a help to our faith. This exposition of the light in which the Supper is to be regarded, falls below what appears to be implied in much of the language employed on the subject, in the old standards and formulas, but if they mean anything more than has been expressed above, they lean too far toward Romish doctrine. If Christ, when He said, "This is my body," meant anything more than "this represents my body," he must have meant that it was His real body, for there can be no medium sense. If He meant no more than "this represents my body," then the exposition which has been given above, is all that is implied in the language, and in all the rational ends to be secured by the institution itself.—LEE, *Elements of Theology,* pp. 575, 576.

ing the faith of the Israelite to the coming Redeemer, it was fit that, as the old dispensation was now to be superseded by the new, the seal of the covenant should be correspondingly changed; hence at the conclusion of the last authorized Passover, the Holy Supper is instituted, as a perpetual memorial and abiding seal of the covenanted mercy and grace of God, till the Saviour 'shall appear the second time without sin unto salvation.' " (RALSTON, *Elements of Divinity*, p. 997). As will be easily seen, the above is in perfect agreement with Article XIV of our own creedal statement, as well as those of Protestantism in general.

The Administration of the Lord's Supper. A few things need to be noted in connection with the proper administration of the Lord's Supper.

1. The elements are bread and wine. While many of the older denominations used fermented wine, and some used leavened bread, our special rules state that "Only unfermented wine and unleavened bread should be used in the sacrament of the Lord's Supper."

2. The sacramental actions are symbolical also. These are: (1) The Prayer of Consecration which includes (a) the giving of thanks to God for the gift of His Son; (b) the preparation of the hearts of the communicants for the solemn service on which they are attending; and (c) the consecration of the elements. (2) The breaking of the bread is significant also as representing the broken body of our Lord Jesus Christ. It is not essential, however, that it be broken as served. It is the common custom to pass it already broken to those who participate in the service. The cup is to be passed also, as an emblem of His shed blood. (3) The manner of distribution of the elements is also significant, Christ gives; while the disciples, each for himself, receives and partakes of the offered gifts.

3. The Lord's Supper is for all of His people. Hence the invitation is, "Let all those who have with true repentance forsaken their sins, and have believed in Christ unto salvation, draw near and take these emblems, and, by faith, partake of the life of Jesus Christ,

to your soul's comfort and joy. Let us remember that it is the memorial of the death and passion of our Lord; also a token of His coming again. Let us not forget that we are one, at one table with the Lord."

4. The Perpetuity of the Lord's Supper. Since this sacrament was ordained for perpetual observance to commemorate the Saviour and especially His death and His coming again, it is the privilege and duty of all who believe in Christ to participate in it. "The habitual neglect of this ordinance," says Dr. Wakefield, "by persons who profess a true faith in Christ is highly censurable. In this case a plain command of Christ is violated, though not perhaps with direct intention; and the benefit of this singularly affecting means of grace is lost, in which our Saviour renews to us the pledge of His love, repeats the promises of His covenant, and calls for invigorated exercises of our faith, only to feed us more richly with the bread that comes down from heaven. If a peculiar condemnation falls upon them who partake 'unworthily,' then a peculiar blessing must follow from partaking worthily; and it therefore becomes the duty of every minister to explain the obligation, and to show the advantages of this sacrament, and earnestly to enforce its regular observance upon all those who give satisfactory evidence of 'repentance toward God, and faith in our Lord Jesus Christ.'" (WAKEFIELD, *Christian Theology*, p. 596).

PART VI. THE DOCTRINE OF LAST THINGS

CHAPTER XXXIII

ESCHATOLOGY OR THE DOCTRINE OF LAST THINGS

Eschatology, as the term indicates, is the doctrine of Last Things. In preparation for the kingdom of God in its completeness, certain events must take place which are of vital interest, from both a theological and a practical viewpoint. We have seen that the doctrines of Christianity all point to a final consummation, and that these all converge in one glorious hope—the Second Advent of our Lord. As preceding this event, the questions of Death and the Intermediate State must claim our attention; as following it, those of the Resurrection and Final Judgment. "The high importance of the eschatological problems," says Dr. Van Oosterzee, "scarcely needs to be formally indicated. The question, 'What shall be the end?' slumbers deep in every Christian heart; and it becomes of so much the greater significance, in proportion as for some and for all the end is nearer at hand. As all other articles of Dogmatics presuppose and prepare the way for Eschatology, so does this in turn shed the light of eternity on every cloud which yet rests upon the parts already traversed of the sanctuary of this science" (VAN OOSTERZEE, *Christian Dogmatics*, II, p. 777). It should be observed also, that since the distance between the actual and the ideal is so

We spoke of the means of grace, by which the Holy Spirit calls forth and strengthens the life of faith, and cannot doubt that by a devout use thereof it is possible for each believer, and for the whole Church, to rise to a comparatively high degree of spiritual growth. Yet Scripture and experience equally proclaim that perfection (in the sense of deliverance from the consequences of sin) itself is never attained on this side of the grave; and the Israel of the New Covenant is on this account, like that of the Old, emphatically a people of the future. Thus then this last chapter also of the doctrine concerning salvation stands in direct connection with that which immediately precedes. . . . . The necessity for understanding something of the things of the future is indeed so universal that every form of religion, of any degree of development, has its own eschatological expectations.—VAN OOSTERZEE, *Christian Dogmatics*, II, p. 775.

great in the kingdom of God, it can never be filled up on this side of the grave. Consequently the life of faith and love on the part of the believer, necessarily becomes a life of hope also. To this *lively hope,* we have been begotten again, *by the resurrection of Jesus Christ from the dead* (I Peter 1:3). It is, therefore, to the Word of God that we must turn for all authoritative information, not only concerning the individual, but also as to the consummation of all things.

DEATH

The word "death" in the Christian system, carries with it a wide variety of interpretation. (1) It is a penalty imposed upon the human race because of sin, and in this sense the subject has already received ample treatment. (2) Physical death, or the separation of the soul from the body, must be viewed as the last event in the probationary history of man. (3) There is a realm of the dead, or death as a state, commonly known as the intermediate state, and (4) there is death, spiritual and eternal. The first three of these events precedes the Second Advent of Christ; the last follows it, and is bound up with the consummation of all things. In this chapter we shall consider physical death and the intermediate state as events of eschatological significance, reserving the subject of "eternal Death" for later consideration.

Death as a penalty, whether physically or spiritually considered, is abolished in the gospel of our redemption. (1) In the widest possible sense it is negatived or done away. There is no restriction in the words used to signify the Saviour's endurance of death in the stead of the human race. He underwent in dying the curse of the law; received the wages of sin not due to Himself; and all mankind are delivered as a whole from the original sentence. For the entire family of Adam it is virtually and provisionally abolished. Our Lord tasted death for every man (Heb. 2:9). . . . . (2) It is really abolished to all who are found in Christ. "He that believeth on the Son had everlasting life." . . . . It is true that the abolition is conditional, and gradually revealed both in the soul and in the body; even as the full revelation of the death from which we are saved is gradual. "We are saved by hope." This law runs through the Christian economy; we receive only the first fruits, every blessing and every deliverance being at best given in its earnest alone "until the redemption of the purchased possession." But the day will come when every trace of this sentence shall be effaced. "The last enemy that shall be destroyed is death (I Cor. 15:26). It was also the first enemy destroyed.—POPE, *Compend. Chr. Th.,* III, p. 373.

The Nature of Physical Death. Death never means annihilation. It was not existence which was forfeited by the original sin, but the separation of the soul from the body, and in a spiritual sense, the separation of both from God. Dr. Hodge speaks of it as "the suspension of personal union between the body and the soul, followed by the resolution of the body into its chemical elements, and the introduction of the soul into that separate state of existence which may be assigned to it by its Creator and Judge" (A. A. HODGE, *Outlines of Theology*, p. 430). Dr. Pope calls it "the introduction to another world, and therefore as an event in the history of fallen and redeemed man: the separation of the soul from the body" (POPE, *Higher Catechism of Theology*, p. 361). In the Scriptures physical death is mentioned as being *gathered unto thy people* (Deut. 32:50); a going *the way of all the earth* (Joshua 23:14); a being *gathered unto their fathers* (Judges 2:10); a return of the dust *to the earth as it was,* and the spirit returning *unto God who gave it* (Eccl. 12:7); a giving up, or a yielding up of the ghost (Acts 5:5, 10); a dissolving of *our earthly house of this tabernacle* (II Cor. 5:1); and a being *absent from the body* and *present with the Lord* (II Cor. 5:8).

Death as a Penalty Abolished in Christ. The Scriptures teach that as by one man *sin entered into the world, and death by sin; and so death passed upon all men, for that all have sinned* (Rom. 5:12). Thus death is the penalty for sin, death physical, spiritual and eternal. But the Scriptures teach with equal clearness that death as a penalty is abolished in Christ. *Therefore as by the offence of one judgment came upon all men to condemnation; even so by the righteousness of one the free gift came upon all men unto justification of life* (Rom. 5:18). Consequently, death as a penalty, whether considered physically or spiritually, is abolished by Christ, and this in two ways: (1) It is abolished provisionally for all mankind. When Christ underwent the curse of the law, and received the sentence of condemnation, He tasted death for every man (Heb. 2:9), and thus removed the specific condemnation from the race. (2) It is actually abolished for all who are in Christ. *He that believeth on the Son hath everlasting life: and he that believeth not the Son shall not see life; but the wrath of God abideth on him* (John 3:36). This abolition is both conditional and gradual, even as the revelation of the death from which we are saved is gradual. This is the deep meaning of St. Paul's words, *We are saved by hope* (Rom. 8:24). The law of the Christian economy is, that we receive here only the first fruits, as the earnest of *our inheritance until the redemption of the purchased possession* (Eph. 1:14). But we look forward in hope to the day when every trace of death shall be removed from God's created universe. Death is at once the first enemy, and the last enemy that shall be destroyed—such is the infinite sweep of this great salvation.

In this gradual abolition of death we may note the following stages: (1) Physical death is now bound up with the divine purpose concerning the destiny of mankind. What that development would have been, had sin not entered the world, we cannot know, but the eternal counsel concerning the human race now is, that *It is appointed unto men once to die* (Heb. 9:27). Thus death is retained as a law in the divine government. (2) Christian death becomes a part of the probationary discipline of believers, and is hallowed as a ground of fellowship with Christ. *It is a faithful saying: For if we be dead with him, we shall also live with him* (II Tim. 2:11). Man by his federal relation with the first Adam dies that he may rise again with the last Adam. (3) Physical death for the Christian is now transfigured into a simple departure from this life to another. *For we know that if our earthly house of this tabernacle were dissolved, we have a building of God, an house not made with hands, eternal in the heavens. . . . . For we that are in this tabernacle do groan, being burdened: not for that would we be unclothed, but clothed upon, that mortality might be swallowed up of life* (II Cor. 5:1, 4). With the curse removed, death for the believer in Christ becomes a means to a blessed end. It is the door through which he enters into the new life, the method by which he receives in the resurrection which follows, a new and glorified body as the eternal habitation of his redeemed soul.

IMMORTALITY

The question of immortality first arises in connection with the nature of the divine image in man. It was therefore briefly, and in a preliminary manner discussed in our treatment of this subject (Vol. II, p. 34). Now, however, the problem appears in a different light and must be given further consideration. Every man believes in the immortality of his own soul, although he can neither demonstrate it nor disprove it. This fundamental conviction is the strongest proof of immortality outside the teachings of the Holy Scriptures. It is

"A solemn murmur of the soul
    Which tells of a world to be,
As travelers hear the billows roar
    Before they reach the sea."

The life of man never ceases to be. As we have shown, the grave is only the tunnel through which men pass in order to reach the life beyond. The nature of this future existence is determined by personal character; and this in turn by the attitude of the soul toward

The Christian thought of being unclothed is an advance upon any former revelation: the body is the only clothing which, folded in the grave, will be hereafter refashioned for the naked spirit. Death is rest, as of old: but rest in the ceaseless service of the Lord. It is sleep: but it is sleep in Jesus. It is still the penalty of sin: but no longer only a penalty. For to those who believe in Jesus death is no more death: not only is its sting gone, but itself is already as to its terror—which is its shadow following it, the second death—annihilated: "whosoever liveth and believeth in me shall never die" (John 11:26). Finally, it is more than the Old Testament "going the way of all the earth" (Joshua 23:14); it is a departure or decease, for these two words are one. Such it was in the case of our Lord: Moses and Elias spoke of the decease "which he should accomplish at Jerusalem" (Luke 9:31). And among the last allusions to death in the New Testament it is regarded as only a removal to another sphere: "the time of my departure is at hand" (II Tim. 4:6); which is the simplest and sublimest description of it given to our faith and hope.—POPE, Compend. Chr. Th., III, pp. 375, 376.

the atoning work of Jesus Christ. To the believer, it is eternal life; to the unbeliever, eternal death.

The Philosophical Arguments for Immortality. The philosophical arguments are, after all, less convincing than the inalienable conviction of immortality which every man has in his own breast; and hence the most that can be said of them is, that they are attempts to clarify this deep, underlying conviction. We present them, therefore, merely as a list of the traditional arguments commonly offered in support of immortality. (1) *The Psychological Argument* is based on the nature of the soul as simple, immaterial essence, indivisible and hence indestructible. This argument tends to show that the soul is self-existent, and therefore will

It may be considered to be universally acknowledged in our day that no independent proof can be given of the immortality of man, but that the doctrine of immortality must be derived from the contemplation of life as a whole. In the Christian view of life, immortality appears on every hand. It is implied in the doctrine of a special providence, in the doctrine of the eternal individuality of Christ, in the election of grace, in prayer, in baptism, in the Lord's Supper, all of which owe their true import to the presupposition of the destiny of the individual to eternal salvation; but the general and fundamental idea lies in the doctrine that man is created in the image of God. All questions concerning human immortality may be traced back to our idea of God. The true conception of man is, that he is the organ of revelation for the Godhead. If God be merely the impersonal spirit of the world, as Pantheism maintains — an impersonal universality — this impersonal spirit needs only impersonal instruments, intermediate channels for his universal life, which possess only a transitory immortality, an immortality limited to that moment only when the eternal Spirit shines through them, and like the rainbow which is formed in the clouds, only for a moment in the presence of the sun. The pantheistic Godhead can have no care for the personal and monadic, because it is itself impersonal. The personal God, on the contrary, cannot find a perfect form for the revelation of Himself in beings which are only impersonal mediums, but only in beings in His own image who are appointed to be permanent witnesses of His eternal power and Godhead. The God of Revelation is Love, and He therefore has interests in the monadic, the minute and individual.—MARTENSEN, *Christian Dogmatics*, p. 452.

My belief in the immortality of the soul springs from the idea of activity; for when I persevere to the end in a course of restless activity I have a sort of guaranty from Nature, that, when the present form of my existence proves itself inadequate for the energizing of my spirit, she will provide another form more appropriate. When a man is seventy-five years old, he cannot avoid now and then thinking of death. This thought, when it comes, leaves me in a state of perfect peace; for I have the most assured conviction that our soul is of an essence absolutely indestructible—an essence that works on from eternity to eternity. It is like the sun, which to our earthly eyes sinks and sets, but in reality never sinks, but shines on unceasingly.—GOETHE.

exist forever. (2) The Teleological Argument holds that the human soul does not, and cannot fulfill all its promise in this world; and hence necessitates another world and continued existence, in order to achieve its full complement of blessedness. (3) The Cosmical Argument is based on the fact, that in the natural realm there is the law of gravitation which binds the heavenly bodies together, and yet, there is no basis for the communion of the people of those other worlds. Hence there must be another mode of existence in order to fulfill the possibilities of human life. This argument was used by Kant, Herder, Lange, Chalmers and others. (4) The Analogical Argument is drawn from analogies in the

The history of primitive religion shows that the hope of immortality is not peculiar to the Christian, but finds expression in religions of the lowest order. Among the Karens the souls of the dead are supposed to assume different aspects as determined by their previous life. Some become divine spirits, while others especially those guilty of murder or adultery assume the forms of monstrous animals. The good go to join their ancestors, while the bad wander about as restless phantoms. The Dyaks of Borneo believe that, as the smoke of the funeral pyre of a good man rises, the soul ascends to the sky; and that the smoke from the pyre of a bad man descends, and with it, his soul is borne down to the earth, and through it to the regions below. The Krumans maintain that the soul of the dead tarries for a while around a fire which is built on the occasion of a death, in order to warm and prepare itself to appreciate the new life into which it has been born. "The idea of a future life," says Pressense, "is inseparable from the idea of God in the credo of the savage."

Victor Hugo (1802-1885) has this sublime passage concerning his own faith in immortality. "I feel in myself the future life. I am like a forest which has been more than once cut down. The new shoots are stronger and livelier than ever. I am rising, I know, toward the sky. The sunshine is on my head. The earth gives me its generous sap, but the heaven lights me with the reflection of unknown worlds. You say the soul is nothing but the resultant of bodily powers. Why, then, is my soul the more luminous when my bodily powers begin to fail? Winter is on my head, and eternal spring is in my heart. Then I breathe, at this hour, the fragrance of the lilacs, the violets, and the roses as at twenty years. The nearer I approach the end, the plainer I hear around me the immortal symphonies of the worlds which invite me. It is marvelous, yet simple. It is a fairy tale, and it is history. For half a century I have been writing my thoughts in prose, verse, history, philosophy, drama, romance, tradition, satire, ode, song—I have tried all. But I feel that I have not said the thousandth part of what is in me. When I go down to the grave I can say, like so many others, "I have finished my day's work,' but I cannot say, 'I have finished my life.' My day's work will begin again the next morning. The tomb is not a blind alley; it is a thoroughfare. It closes in the twilight to open with the dawn. I improve every hour, because I love this world as my fatherland. My work is only a beginning. My monument is hardly above its foundation. I would be glad to see it mounting and mounting forever. The thirst for the infinite proves infinity."

organic world. The seed dies, and yet perpetuates its identity; the chrysalis bursts and the butterfly emerges as a new order of being, totally unlike its former mode of existence. (5) The Moral Argument is presented in both its individual and social aspects. It is essentially this—man in this world does not always receive justice. Mere annihilation would not permit degrees of punishment corresponding to the different degrees of guilt. Hence this is an argument from the justice of God to the continued existence of the wicked. Furthermore, in many of its moral aspects life would appear to be a mockery were there no world to come. Thus St. Paul reasoned when he said, *If in this life only we have hope in Christ, we are of all men most miserable* (I Cor. 15:19).

The Doctrine of Immortality as Revealed in the Scriptures. The only authoritative teaching which we have concerning immortality, is that found in the Holy Scriptures. It is sometimes asserted that the immortality of the soul is not emphasized in the Old Testament, but as a matter of fact this teaching permeates both the Old and the New Testaments. No Hebrew writer, either inspired or uninspired, ever doubted the immortality of the soul, and this, not in a pantheistic but in an individual sense. The scriptures previously cited in disproof of annihilation, serve likewise as proofs of the immortality of the soul. In addition to these, we may note the following: *Who knoweth the spirit of man that goeth upward, and the spirit of the beast that goeth downward to the earth?* (Eccl. 3:21). Dr. Clarke says that the literal translation of this text is, "Who considereth the immortal spirit of the sons of Adam, which ascendeth. It is from above: and the spirit or breath of the cattle, which descendeth? It is downward unto the earth, that is, it tends to the earth only." Here the spirit of a man is distinguished from that of an animal, as tending in different directions. That man's spirit goes upward, clearly denotes, not only continued but more elevated existence, and hence survives bodily death. Again, *For I know that my redeemer liveth, and that he shall stand at the latter day upon the earth: and though after my skin worms destroy this body, yet in my flesh shall I see God* (Job 19:25, 26). Here is a certainty of conviction that there is a life beyond. The psalmist also declared that *The days of our years are threescore years and ten; and if by reason of strength they be fourscore years, yet is their strength labour and sorrow; for it is soon cut off, and we fly away* (Psalms 90:10). The argument hangs on the words "We fly away." The figure itself is borrowed from the belief that man has a soul which departs when the body dies, and can mean nothing other than that the soul exists after death. In the New Testament we cite only a representative text. *And fear not them which kill the body, but are not able to kill the soul* (Matt. 10:28). From this it is evident that the soul and the body are not identical, and that to kill the body does not kill the soul. This argument from the words of our Lord is conclusive. There are many other Scriptures bearing upon this subject, as the following list of references will show. (Cf. Luke 12:4,5; Matt. 17:3; Matt. 22:31, 32; Luke 16:22,23; Luke 23:43, 46; Acts 7:59; Rom. 8:35, 38, 39; II Cor. 5:1, 6, 8; II Cor. 12:2, 3, 4; Phil. 1:21, 23, 24; Rev. 6:9).

Dr. James H. White has grouped the Bible passages which indicate the soul's continuous existence, by words and phrases descriptive of its conditions and belongings, as follows:

1. It has an existence that is independent of the body, and therefore continuous beyond the death of the body. Man can kill the body, but cannot kill the soul (Matt. 10:28). The soul lives when the body is dead (Matt. 22:32). The soul is capable of suffering when the body is dead and buried (Luke 16:23). The body dead, and the soul in paradise (Luke 23:43). Stephen dies, and his soul is received into heaven (Acts 7:59). The soul may be absent from the body, and present with the Lord (II Cor. 5:8). Such a state is better than the present (Phil. 1:23).

2. Its existence is continuous, because it may suffer eternal or always continuing punishment (Cf. Matt. 18:8 and 25:41). "These shall go away into everlasting punishment"; literally, always enduring punishment (Matt. 25:46). The Revised New Testament in this verse gives us "eternal punishment" and "eternal life" (Cf. also, Mark 3:29; II Thess. 1:9; Jude 13; and Rev. 14:11).

3. Its existence is continuous, because it may enjoy an always enduring life. The passages are numerous wherein eternal and everlasting are connected with the future life and joy of the saints. I need give but a few: Matt. 25:46; John 6:27; Gal. 6:8; Titus 3:7; Hebrews 9:15; and II Peter 1:11. These are enough. God would not have us ignorant "concerning them which are asleep," and to this end He has given us the sure testimony of His Word. (Quoted in POTTS, *Faith Made Easy*, p. 448).

The Christian Victory

The doctrine of immortality comes into its clearest light through the resurrection of Jesus Christ from the dead. The ancient writers of the Church unanimously maintained that death as a consequence of sin, was a merciful provision of the Creator; since it was a means by which the spiritual results of sin might cease, and the holy dead no longer be included in the category of sinners. This could not be as long as they were in bodies capable of ministering to sin and under the penalty of death. But with the death and resurrection of Christ, there is a triumph over death, and consequently a changed attitude toward it. Christ's resurrection, therefore, was not only His own personal triumph over death, it was the triumph of His people also. This is expressly stated in the Epistle to the Hebrews as follows: *Forasmuch then as the children are partakers of flesh and blood, he also himself likewise took part of the same; that through death he might destroy him that had the power of death, that is, the devil; and deliver them who through fear of death were all their lifetime subject to bondage* (Heb. 2:14, 15). It is this changed attitude toward death through Jesus Christ, that we must now consider.

Death in Relation to Jesus Christ. Our discussion must include three important facts: (1) Christ asserts the original law and the original purpose of God for men, not only as to His life on earth, but as to His exit from earth also. He overcame wrong by doing right; He overcame sin by fulfilling the law of holiness; and He overcame death through the law of the Spirit of life (Rom. 8:2). (2) Christ was made a curse for us, in that He brought Himself under the penalty of a fallen race (Gal. 3:16). But He not only died vicariously for sin, He also died unto sin (Rom. 6:10). For a time therefore, death had dominion over Him; but in subjecting Himself to death under the condemnation of the law, the penalty was fully satisfied, and all organic connection with the world of evil, at once and forever dissolved. Thus His death became an epoch of judicial peace, and

an eternal triumph over the curse of the law. (3)
Through the offering of Himself upon the cross, Christ
endured in reality, the curse entailed by sin, but it be-
came for Him also, a birth into a new order of being.
It was the resolution of His earthly life into a post-
earthly form of human existence. For this reason He is
called *the firstborn from the dead* (Col. 1:18); and again
He is said to be *the first begotten of the dead* (Rev. 1:5).
By His bearing of our sins in His own body on the tree
(I Peter 2:24; Gal. 3:13), He not only fulfilled the positive demands of the divine law, but He realized also in
Himself, the perfection of human life—both of these
being demonstrated by the fact of the resurrection. This
mystery of the cross is thus stated by St. Peter as *being
put to death in the flesh, but quickened by the Spirit*
(I Peter 3:18). According to the flesh, Christ died a
real death under condemnation; but according to the
new law of the life-giving Spirit, He was like the grain
of wheat which is quickened while it dies. Thus in sur-
mounting death by the giving of His spirit, He at the
same time advanced into a new stage of triumphant
life. "This mysterious process of the vegetable kingdom," says Dr. Gerhart, "our Lord employs to set forth
the more mysterious process of His spiritual kingdom.

The exit of "the spiritual man" from the present world and the
exit of "the natural man" are not in kind the same. The exit of each is
an epoch in the history of human existence. Neither is the extinction
or cessation of being; but the one is an epoch governed by the law of
life in Christ Jesus, while the other is an epoch determined by the
operation of the law of sin. The exit of "the natural man" is properly
denoted by the word "death." Death and sin as to kind are the same,
sin being the seed of death, death the bitter fruit of sin. An epoch of
transition from the present world to the future world is not in itself
abnormal or unnatural. Sound Christian speculation, justified by the
history of the Son of Man, may teach that a transition was ordained by
the divine idea of human history. It is typified by the translation of
Enoch and of Elijah, and demonstrated by the ascension of our Lord.
That normal epoch of departure became abnormal in consequence of
the entrance of the vitiating power of sin; and because abnormal, the
change has the false character which we call death. . . . . The life of
Jesus, on the contrary, is the ideal human life. He asserts the original
law and the original teleology of man as formed in the image of God,
both in His history on earth and in His exit from the earth. His exit
was in one respect the normal epoch of transition from the lower to
the higher realm which the original law of humanity anticipated and
demanded. Considered under this aspect, the epoch is to be regarded
as the organic resolution of the earthly order into the heavenly order
of ideal human existence.—GERHART, *Institutes of the Christian Religion,*
II, pp. 773, 774.

The one is a fact confronting natural perception; the other a fact concerning spiritual perception" (GERHART, *Institutes of the Christian Religion*, II, p. 776).

Christ as the Author of Eternal Life. Christ having triumphed over death, becomes the author of life to every believer. Death, therefore, which will eventually be swallowed up of life, is now a conquered enemy. This fact alone makes necessary a changed attitude toward death on the part of the believers. Eternal life as manifested in Christ is in the individual Christian marked by stages and degrees corresponding to the several fundamental epochs in the life of Christ on earth. We may note here three clearly marked periods in the history of the incarnate Christ: (1) From His conception and birth to His death and burial—the ordinary span of a man's life: (2) From His death and burial to His resurrection, including the descent into Hades. This marks a stage in the progress of the new creation, in which our Lord, through death, overcame him who had

Dr. Olin A. Curtis in his chapter on the "Christian Meaning of Death," treats the subject of bodily death (1) as to its Personal Significance; (2) its Moral Significance; and (3) its Racial Significance. First, as to the personal significance of bodily death, he states that the province of the body to furnish man with the machinery of personal expression—a point, which if kept clearly in mind takes on large personal significance. In the experience of bodily death, man undergoes for the first time, the experience of being absolutely alone. As long as he remained in the body, there was something to hear or touch. A man may cease to have fellowship with other men, and as a consequence think that he has exhausted the torture of loneliness. But he has not exhausted it, for he can still see the sun, or hear the thunder, or feel the wind in his face. These things do not of course, meet his personal need at all, but they do occupy his attention, and thus protect him from the solitude of the profoundest introspection. But it is in death that the body is torn away, and no protection whatever is left to the man. All he has is his own isolated poverty of person—a solitary personality all alone in the reaches of the Infinite. Second, man in death is not absolutely alone only, but alone with his own conscience. Not one thing can for a moment shelter him from the violence of the moral smiting. Now, of all times, this lonely sinner needs the presence of God, but death is empty of the friendly God. His death expresses the holy anger of God. The man must now meet the insistence of God's moral concern closely and finally, before the last door of destiny is closed. Third, the death of the body has a racial significance also, since the body is the racial nexus. Not only does physical death isolate the individual person, but it also breaks him off from the race. He is now a man without a race—the solidarity of the Adamic race as the groundwork of relations being destroyed by bodily death. One by one men are wrenched out of their racial relations by death, and flung out into the isolation of bare personal existence, to await as responsible persons, the final judgment.—CURTIS, *The Christian Faith*, pp. 295, 296.

the power of death, and thus secured deliverance for His people (Heb. 2:14, 15). (3) His life on earth during the forty days between the resurrection and the ascension. This marks the establishment of a new order of being— the resolution of the earthly into the resurrected state, with freedom from weakness, mortality and corruption for all His people.

Since the experiences and achievements of Christ are to be made those of His people also, we may likewise discern three stages in the progress of eternal life as manifested in the individual Christian. (1) The first is that life communicated in the new birth. As Christ became incarnate of the Holy Ghost by the virgin Mary, so the Spirit of God infuses into the soul of the believer, the new life in Christ. (2) The second is that spiritual transformation which is symbolized by the death and resurrection of Christ. *For in that he died, he died unto sin once: but in that he liveth, he liveth unto God. Likewise reckon ye also yourselves to be dead unto sin, but alive unto God through Jesus Christ our Lord* (Rom. 6:10, 11). This is accomplished through

Of Jesus Christ as the Head of the new race we therefore predicate only life. "I am the life." By the realization in humanity of the law of holiness Christ annuls the law of sin; by quickening and perfecting the eternal life Christ destroys death. "The spiritual man," being a member of the destroyer of sin and death, lives the life of the ascended Conqueror. The end of his earthly history is not death, but an epoch which on the one hand is victory over the curse of sin, and on the other hand is the transition from a lower to a higher plane of eternal life.—GERHART, *Institutes of the Christian Religion*, II, p. 777.

Christian death is abundantly and most impressively brought to light as not abolished absolutely; but as taken up into the divine plan for the individual just as it is for the race. It enters into the probationary discipline of believers. Hence it is hallowed and dignified as part of the fellowship of their lot with Christ. . . . . That unknown element in His suffering which negatived the sinner's eternal death is of necessity unshared, but His physical surrender to death admits us to a fellowship with it. . . . . There is no grace of Christian life which is not made perfect in death; not that death is the minister of the Spirit to destroy sin, but the last earthly act and oblation of the sinless spirit in which the sacrifice of all becomes perfect in one. Therefore it is the appointed end of human probation. Other methods of placing a limit to the probationary career, especially in relation to the unfallen creature, may be imagined: this is the appointed end since sin and redemption began. The very execution of doom is made the goal of destiny, in which the sentence is finally reversed. And thus in a certain sense death is the preliminary and decisive judgment for every individual on earth who knows the connection between sin and deliverance.—POPE, *Compend. Chr. Th.*, pp. 374, 375.

the baptism with the Spirit. Both of these stages are included in Soteriology, and have been previously treated in connection with the Person and Work of the Holy Spirit (*Christian Theology*, II, pp. 321-326). (3) The third stage belongs properly to Eschatology and has to do with the resurrection of the body. This is commonly known as glorification. Christ departed this life under the curse, but in such a manner as to dissolve His organic connection with the world of moral evil, and thereby realize the perfection of human life in a new order of being. Consequently the curse was removed and death resolved into victory. As in dying, Christ destroyed death in relation to Himself, so His people in dying likewise destroy death in relation to themselves. The curse being lifted, the Christian emphasis is placed upon the inner spirit of life. Hence death to the Christian believer is not now an abnormal event, but the operation of the law of the spirit of life in Christ Jesus. The whole process is taken up and glorified. Like the preceding stage, this is also a death to sin, but in a different sense. That was a death to sin as a ruling principle in the individual believer; this is death to sin as an eternal possibility. Consequently the Scriptures now regard physical death as in some sense a birth—not a spiritual birth into the kingdom of God, but a bursting forth of life into the post-earthly realm, a birth into the kingdom of glory. *But if the Spirit of him that raised up Jesus from the dead dwell in you, he that raised up Christ from the dead shall also quicken your mortal bodies by his Spirit that dwelleth in you* (Rom. 8:11).

THE INTERMEDIATE STATE

The fact of the immortality of the soul having been established, the question next in order is concerned with its conscious existence between the death and the

Dr. Olin A. Curtis objects to the idealization of death as a friendly and even beautiful event, as is done by some philosophical and poetical writers. "This poetic idealization," he says, "is not to be explained by the natural temper of the poet, ... but rather by the fact that he is (with notable exceptions) a heathen mystic made superficially hopeful by a Christian atmosphere. He is an easy optimist who has never paid the ethical price of a profound optimism."—CURTIS, *Christian Faith*, p. 281.

resurrection of the body. All who accept the teaching of the Scriptures as the Word of God, accept also the fact of an intermediate state; but the point on which opinions differ is the question as to the nature of this state. (1) *Sheol* is derived from the Hebrew word "to ask" and expresses probably the sense of the English proverb—the "grave crieth give, give." The word sometimes means indefinitely, the grave, or place or state of the dead; and at others, definitely, a place or state of the dead into which the element of misery, and punishment enters: but never a place or state of happiness, or good after death (Cf. BLUNT, *Dictionary*). (2) *Hades* is a Greek word derived from α privative and ἰδεῖν and signifies the invisible world of departed spirits. It was used by the authors of the Septuagint to translate the Hebrew word *Sheol*, as in Psalms 16: 10 and Acts 2: 27. Dr. A. A. Hodge points out that the word occurs only eleven times in the New Testament (Matt. 11: 23; 16: 18; Luke 10: 15; 16: 23; Acts 2: 27, 31; I Cor. 15: 55; Rev. 1: 18; 6: 8; 20: 13, 14); and that in every case except I Cor. 15: 55, where the more critical editions of the original substitute the word θάνατε in the place of ἅδης, hades is translated hell, and certainly always represents the invisible world as under the dominion of Satan, and as opposed to the kingdom of Christ (Cf. A. A. HODGE, *Outlines of Theology*, p. 435). (3) *Paradise*, from the Greek word παράδεισος, was adopted into both Greek and Hebrew from some oriental language. The

Throughout the Scriptures, from Genesis to Revelation, the departed souls of men are represented as congregating in one vast receptacle, the interior conditions of which differ much in the two Testaments and vary in each respectively. On their estate a steady increase of light as revelation proceeds, though even in its final disclosures leave much obscurity which only the Lord's coming will remove. It is, however, made certain that the intermediate state is under the special control of the Redeemer as the Lord of all the dead who have ever passed from the world; that those who have departed in unbelief are in a condition of imprisonment waiting for the final judgment, while those who have died in the faith are in Paradise, or rather with Christ, waiting for their consummation; and that the universal resurrection will put an end both to death and to the state of the disembodied dead. Some few hints which the New Testament gives as to the conscious personality of the subjects of the Lord's kingdom in Hades have been made the basis of doctrinal determinations and ecclesiastical institutions and speculative theories which belong to the department of historical theology.—POPE, *Compend. Chr. Th.*, III, p. 376.

word means a park, or pleasure garden, and was used by the translators of the Septuagint to represent the garden in Eden (Gen. 2: 8ff). It occurs only three times in the New Testament (Luke 23: 43; II Cor. 12: 4; and Rev. 2: 7), and the context shows that it is connected with the "third heaven" in one instance; and in the others with the "Garden of God" in which grows the tree of life—all three necessarily referring to a life beyond physical death.

In our discussion of this doctrine we shall consider (I) the historical development of the doctrine; and (II) some of its theological implications.

I

In historical theology, the idea of Hades has undergone a number of modifications. These we shall consider in the following order: (1) The Patristic Doctrine of the Intermediate State; (2) The Heretical Doctrine of Soul Sleeping; (3) The Roman Catholic Doctrine of an Intermediate Place; and (4) The Protestant Doctrine of an Intermediate State.

The Patristic Doctrine of the Intermediate State. While the doctrine of the immortality of the soul is taught in the Old Testament, the Hebrew people generally seem to have held it in a more or less perverted form. The common belief appears to have been this, that all souls descended at death into Sheol or Hades, which was a gloomy, subterranean abode; and where the inhabitants were shades, existing in a weak, powerless and dreamy state. At other times, Sheol is represented as divided into two departments—Paradise, a place of positive bliss, and Gehenna, a place of positive torment. In the former or Abraham's bosom, were the Jews, or at least those who had been faithful to the law; in the latter were the Gentiles. It was held, further, that at the coming of the Messiah, the faithful Jews would be resurrected and have a part in His glorious kingdom; while the Gentiles would be left forever in the abode of darkness. The doctrine of an Intermediate State was prevalent in the early church, as is shown by the numerous references to it in the writings of the Fathers. In the main, their teachings were similar to those of later Judaism. Hades, or the invisible region, was an underworld, or realm of the dead. It was a place of partial rewards and punishments. Justin Martyr says of it, that "the souls of the pious are in a better place, those of the unjust and wicked in a worse, waiting for the time of judgment." Tertullian (220) states that "no one, becoming absent from the body, is at once a dweller in the presence of the Lord, except by the prerogative of martyrdom, whereby he gets at once a lodging in Paradise, not in Hades." Cyprian (258) appears to have taken a different view from that of Tertullian, and intimates that the departed saints come immediately into the presence of Christ. Origen (d. 254) taught that since the resurrection of Christ, Hades no longer

The opinions of the early fathers concerning the residence of the soul in its disembodied state, between death and the resurrection, were somewhat fluctuating. The idea of Hades, or underworld, where departed spirits dwell, was familiar to the Hebrew mind as it was to the Greek, and so far as this idea passed over to Christianity it tended to the doctrine of a state intermediate between this earthly life and the everlasting abode of the soul assigned to it in the day of judgment. Justin Martyr represents the souls of the righteous as taking up a temporary abode in a happy, those of the wicked in a wretched place; and stigmatizes as heretical the doctrine that souls are immediately received into heaven at death. Tertullian held that the martyrs went at once to the abode of the blessed, but that this was a privilege peculiar to them, and not granted to other Christians. Cyprian, on the other hand, says nothing of an intermediate state, and expresses the confident belief that those who die in the Lord, by pestilence or by any other mode, will be at once taken to Him. In the Alexandrian school, the idea of an intermediate state passed into that of a gradual purification of the soul, and paved the way for the later doctrine of purgatory. The doctrine of an intermediate state not only maintained itself, but gained in authority and influence during the polemic period (A.D. 250-730). Ambrose taught that the soul is separated from the body at death, and after the cessation of the earthly life is held in an ambiguous condition, awaiting the final judgment. Augustine remarks that "the period which intervenes between the death and the final resurrection of man contains souls in secret receptacles, who are treated according to their character and conduct in the flesh." "The majority of ecclesiastical writers of this period," Hagenbach remarks, "believed that men do not receive their full reward till after the resurrection of the body. Here and there, however, there was a dissenting voice. Gregory Nazianzen supposed that the souls of the righteous prior to the resurrection of the body, are at once admitted into the presence of God; in which opinion he seems supported by Gennadius and Gregory the Great. Eusebius also declares that Helena, the mother of Constantine, went immediately to God and was transformed into an angelic substance. In the Middle Ages and the Papal Church, the doctrine of an intermediate state was, of course, retained and defended in connection with that of purgatory.—SHEDD, *History of Christian Doctrine*, II, pp. 400-403.

holds the souls of the righteous—those of the former
ages having been transported by Christ to Paradise.

The Doctrine of Soul Sleeping. According to this
doctrine, the soul during the intermediate period is
either in a state of unconscious sleep known as *Psycho-
pannychism* (from παννυχίζειν, to spend all night long,
and ψυχή the soul); or that it is in a state of actual death
known as *Thnetopsychism* (from θνήσκω, death and
ψυχή the soul). In neither form has the doctrine been
extensively adopted in the church, and therefore has
always been regarded as heretical. However, it has had
its advocates in every age. Origen in the third century
wrote against a small sect which held this doctrine; Calvin wrote against it in the sixteenth century, and the
Roman Catholic Church condemned it in several councils, notably that of Trent (1545-1563). The doctrine
is based upon a misapprehension of those passages of
Scripture which refer to death as a sleep. Furthermore,
the doctrine presupposes that the soul cannot know
itself, or in any sense energize except through the instrumentality of the body. It is for this reason that the
soul during its disembodied state is regarded as dorm-
ant, or as virtually dead. This position, however, is
philosophically, pure assumption. Because the soul
cannot function except through the body in its relation
to material things, it is assumed that it cannot function
apart from the body in spiritual things. This error is
refuted by the arguments commonly urged against materialism. From the standpoint of exegesis also, the
doctrine is false. By no allowable interpretation, can the
discourse concerning Dives and Lazarus be made to

Dr. E. Y. Mullins points out that there is no basis in the New
Testament, for what is known as the doctrine of "soul-sleeping." There
are indeed passages which refer to death as a sleep, but it is nowhere
said that the soul sleeps. The reference is to the personality as a
whole, and the figure of sleep must be interpreted in harmony with
the general teachings of the New Testament. Sleep means "not alive
to surroundings." A man asleep knows nothing of the activities about
him. So death is a sleep in the sense that men become alive to a new
set of surroundings and cut off from those of the present life. In one
passage the idea of death as a sleep and that of conscious fellowship
with Christ are combined in a single statement. In I Thessalonians
5:10 the apostle refers to Christ "Who died for us, that, whether we wake
or sleep, we should live together with him." (MULLINS, *The Christian
Religion*, p. 461.)

support the doctrine of soul sleeping; nor can the words of Jesus to the thief on the cross have any meaning unless he was to be consciously with Him in Paradise. Furthermore, the statement of St. Paul in regard to being absent from the body and present with the Lord, cannot be understood, if an interval of unconsciousness is to elapse between the two events.

The Roman Catholic Doctrine of an Intermediate Place. Since the time of Gregory the Great (c. 604), there has been connected with the belief in Hades as an intermediate state, a belief also, in Purgatory as an intermediate place. Purgatory, as the doctrine is elaborated by the Roman Catholic Church, insofar as the souls of departed human beings are concerned, seems to comprise the following departments.

1. The *Limbus Patrum* is a term referring to the state of the righteous dead, previous to the First Advent of Christ. It is held that when Christ descended into Hades after His crucifixion, He delivered the souls of the patriarchs and carried them in triumph to heaven. This is, of course, similar to the common Jewish teach-

The doctrine that the soul exists, during the interval between death and the resurrection, in a state of unconscious repose, properly supposes the soul to be a distinct substance from the body. It is therefore to be distinguished from the materialistic theory, which assumes that as matter in certain states and combinations exhibits the phenomena of magnetism or light, so in other combinations it exhibits the phenomena of life, and in others the phenomena of mind, and hence that vital and mental activity are as much the result of effect of the molecular arrangements of matter, as any physical operations in the external world. As in this view it would be absurd to speak of the sleep or quietude of magnetism or light when the conditions of their existence are absent, so it would be equally absurd on this theory, to speak of the sleep of the soul after the dissolution of the body. . . . . "The more philosophical view as to the nature of the connection between life and its material basis, is the one which regards vitality as something superadded and foreign to the matter by which vital phenomena are manifested. Protoplasm is essential as the physical medium through which vital action may be manifested; just as a conductor is essential to the manifestation of electric phenomena, or just as a paint brush and colors are essential to the artist. Because metal conducts the electric current, and renders it perceptible to our senses, no one thinks therefore of asserting that electricity is one of the inherent properties of a metal, any more than one would feel inclined to assert that the power of painting was inherent in the camel's hair or in the dead pigments. Behind this material substratum, in all cases, is the active and living force; and we have no right to assume that the force ceases to exist when its physical basis is removed, though it is no longer perceptible to our senses" (Cf. NICHOLSON, in HODGE, *Systematic Theology*, III, p. 731).

ing concerning the Old Testament saints. Many hold that this compartment ceased to exist after the ascension, but others maintain that the souls of the departed since that time, are still confined in this intermediate place, awaiting deliverance at the Second Advent.

2. The *Limbus Infantum* refers to the supposed abode of the souls of unbaptized infants. This is not regarded as a place either of suffering or happiness. Thomas Aquinas states that although unbaptized infants are deprived forever of the happiness of the saints, they suffer neither sorrow nor sadness in consequence of the privation.

3. Purgatory is regarded as the intermediate abode of those who die in the peace of the church, but who need further purification before entering the final state of heaven. The doctrine of Purgatory as held by Romanists is fairly summed up by Dr. Charles Hodge as follows: "They teach: (1) That it is a state of suffering. The commonly received traditional, though not symbolical, doctrine on this point is, that the suffering is from material fire. The design of this suffering is both an expiation and purification. (2) That the duration and intensity of purgatorial pains are proportioned to the guilt and impurity of the sufferers. (3) That there is no known or defined limit to the continuance of the soul in purgatory, but the day of judgment. The departed may remain in this state of suffering for a few hours or for thousands of years. (4) That souls in purgatory may be helped; that is, their sufferings alleviated or the duration of them shortened by the prayers of the saints, and especially by the sacrifice of the Mass. (5) That purgatory is under the power of the keys. That is, it is the prerogative of the authorities of the church, at their discretion, to remit entirely or partially the penalty of sins under which the souls there detained are suffering (HODGE, *Systematic Theology*, III, pp. 749, 750). This erroneous doctrine arises from the belief of the Roman Catholic Church, that the atonement of Christ is available for us only in respect to original sin and the exposure to eternal death. That is, Christ

delivers us only from the *reatus culpae*, or culpability, not from the *reatus poenae*, or liability to punishment. For sins after baptism, the offender must make satisfaction by penance or good works. This satisfaction must be complete in this life if the soul is to enter heaven; if not, then this purification must be completed in purgatory. The Eucharist or Mass is the propitiatory sacrifice intended to secure the pardon of sins committed after baptism; and since this takes effect according to the intention of the priests, he may if he so desires, by his intention, make it effective for souls in purgatory. The pope, being the vicar of Christ on earth, has full power to forgive sins in this sense—he may exempt offenders from the obligation to make sacrifices for their offenses. This is the doctrine against which Protestantism took such a vigorous stand.

4. Heaven is defined to be the place and state of the blessed where God is, where Jesus is enthroned in majesty, and where the angels and the spirits of just men are made perfect. It is the place of the highest blessedness. Into this state of perfect blessedness, the

Article VIII of the Tridentine Profession of Faith is as follows: "I firmly hold that there is a purgatory, and that the souls therein detained are helped by the suffrages of the faithful. Likewise, that the saints reigning with Christ are to be honored and invoked, and that they offer up prayers to God for us, and that their relics are to be had in veneration." This is a general statement and no mention is made as to whether these souls exist in a state of misery or happiness. However, in the catechism of the Council of Trent, drawn up by order of the Fathers, the statement is more explicit. "There is a purgatorial fire, where the souls of the righteous are purified by a temporary punishment, that entrance may be given them into their eternal home, where nothing that is defiled can have a place. And of the truth of this doctrine, which holy councils declare to be confirmed by the testimony of Scripture and of apostolic tradition, the pastor will have to declare more diligently and frequently, because we are fallen on times in which men will not endure sound doctrine (*Catech. Trident.* Chap. VI).

Purgatory, as an assumed Christian doctrine, is peculiar to Romanism. It has no place in the creed of any other church, though in some it may be held by individual members. In Romanism Christians compose two classes: the imperfect, and the truly good. The former have impurities which must be cleansed away, and venial sins which must be expiated in penal suffering, in order to a meetness for heaven. Even the truly good, while free from the guilt of mortal sins, yet have deserts of temporal punishment which must be expiated. Purgatory provides for both classes, as in its penal and purifying fires both may attain to a fitness for heaven. But it provides only for such as the Romish Church recognizes as Christians: therefore it has no connection with the doctrine of a second probation.—MILEY, *Systematic Theology*, II, p. 438.

Romanists hold that only a few, even of true believers, enter immediately at death. Instead, both the righteous and the wicked remain in an intermediate state, which for the righteous is known as Paradise or Abraham's Bosom, and for the wicked is called Purgatory. From this intermediate state the righteous go to their final reward, and the wicked to their eternal doom, at the last judgment. It is maintained, however, that there are two classes which may enter heaven previous to the resurrection—those who are perfectly pure at the time of death; and those who, although not perfect when they leave this world, have become perfect in purgatory.

5. Hell is defined as a place or state, in which wicked angels and the finally impenitent among men suffer forever the punishment of their sins. The sufferings of the lost are due to two things: (1) those of loss or deprivation, in which they are denied the vision, favor and presence of God; and (2) those of positive infliction, such as the sufferings arising from remorse, wicked passions and despair. The Romanists differ, however, as to whether the fire mentioned in this connection is literal or symbolical. Gousset says that on this subject the church has given no decisions. "It is of faith," he says, "that the condemned shall be eternally deprived of the happiness of heaven, and that they shall be eternally tormented in hell; but it is not of the faith that the fire which causes their suffering is material. Many doctors, whose opinion has not been condemned, think that as 'the worm which never dies' is a figurative expression, so also is 'the fire that is never quenched'; and that the fire means a pain analogous to that by fire rather than the real pain produced by fire. Nevertheless the idea that the fire spoken of is real material fire is so general among Catholics, that we do not venture to advance a contrary opinion" (Cf. HODGE, *Systematic Theology*, III, pp. 747, 748).

The Protestant Doctrine of an Intermediate State. Protestantism retains the idea of an intermediate state, but rejects generally the idea of an intermediate place. We may state the common Protestant doctrine as follows: (1) That at the death the souls of the righteous go immediately into the presence of Christ and of God. The Scriptures make no mention of a long delay; instead it is clearly taught that to be absent from the body is to be present with the Lord (II Cor. 5: 6). (2) The souls of the departed exist in a state of consciousness. In referring to the righteous, St. Paul declares that nothing shall separate us from the love of Christ (Rom. 8: 38); that is, the moral and spiritual relationship to Christ is continuous and unbroken. No provision is made for an interrupted period of consciousness. (3) Not only are the righteous dead conscious, but they are in a state of blessedness and rest (Rev. 14: 13). (4) The intermediate state is not the final state of believers. Man is body as well as spirit, and hence in his disembodied state there is an element of imperfection which can be supplied only by the resurrection. This belief in an intermediate state is perfectly consistent with the teaching of Protestantism, that after the Second Advent and the resurrection of the dead, the state of the soul will be still more exalted and blessed. What has been said of the righteous dead, is equally applicable to the state of the wicked: (1) That at death the souls of the wicked are banished from the presence of the Lord; (2) that the wicked exist in consciousness; (3) that this consciousness is one of suffering and unrest; and (4) that the state of the wicked is not final— they too will be raised, but to everlasting shame and contempt; and the judgment will fix their eternal doom.

In the Protestant Church the doctrine of purgatory was rejected; but some difference of sentiment appears respecting the intermediate state. Calvin combated the theory of a sleep of the soul between death and the resurrection, which had been revived by some of the Swiss Anabaptists, and argues for the full consciousness of the disembodied spirit. The second Helvetic Confession expressly rejects the notion that departed spirits reappear on earth. Some theologians endeavored to establish a distinction between the happiness which a disembodied spirit enjoys, and that which it will experience after the resurrection of the body. They also distinguish between the judgment which takes place at the death of each individual, by which his destiny is immediately decided, and the general judgment at the end of the world. Speaking generally, the doctrine of an intermediate state has found most favor in the Lutheran division of Protestants. In the English Church, since the time of Laud, the doctrine has found some advocates, chiefly in that portion of it characterized by high church views, and a Romanizing tendency. The followers of Swedenborg adopt the tenet in a highly gross and materializing form.—Shedd, *History of Christian Doctrine*, II, pp. 402, 403.

II

Growing out of the preceding historical discussion, there are certain questions which, because of their theological implications, demand further consideration. We refer especially to such questions as: (1) Is there an intermediate place as well as an intermediate state? and what are the theological and practical implications which are involved. (2) Is the intermediate state a period of future probation? and (3) Is the intermediate state one of progress and development? These are but a few of the questions which arise in connection with this important subject.

Is there an Intermediate Place as well as an Intermediate state? This is a question which has engaged the interest of many learned and pious men; and yet it is without value, except for its practical implications. The Scriptures leave the question undecided, some texts appearing to favor one view, and some another. As favoring the idea of an intermediate place, there is the account of Dives and Lazarus (Luke 16:19-31), and also the words of Christ to the dying thief, *Today shalt thou be with me in paradise* (Luke 23:43). The word Paradise is sometimes used in a lower sense than that of heaven; and besides Jesus did not ascend into heaven on that day as His words to Mary indicate, *for I am not yet ascended to my Father* (John 20:17). As opposed to the idea of an intermediate place, we may cite such

According to the doctrine of the New Testament, therefore, there is no third place, or medium, between heaven and hell or between being happy and miserable, although there are very different degrees both of the one and the other. The intermediate condition of which we have spoken must not be understood to imply anything like this. Still an opinion like this got footing very early in the Christian Church. And this gave rise to the custom of praying for the dead, since men were foolish enough to imagine that there is room to obtain an alteration in the yet undecided destiny of departed spirits, while in truth their destiny must depend solely upon their own actions during the present life. This custom had become very general in the fourth century, and was at that time opposed by Aerius, presbyter of Pontus, as we learn from the testimony of Epiphanius, who is very indignant against him on this account. It was also opposed by the Spanish presbyter, Vigilantius, in the fifth century, in reply to whom Hieronymus wrote a violent book. The doctrine was afterward brought into connection with that respecting purgatory, and then followed masses for souls, as sacrifices for the departed. There are also some traces of prayers for the dead, even among Grecian Jews (Cf. II Mac. 12:43-46).—KNAPP, *Christian Theology*, p. 350.

texts as the words of St. Stephen, *Lord Jesus, receive my spirit* (Acts 7:59); and those of St. Paul, *to be absent from the body, and to be present with the Lord* (II Cor. 5:8). These passages seem to indicate that the good at death go immediately into the presence of the Lord.· But the question may be asked, Does not an intermediate state necessarily imply an intermediate place? We think not. It is the general belief of the church, that during the intermediate state the persons of men are incomplete while their souls and bodies are separated, but this incompleteness is due to the state or condition, and not to the place. That is, the righteous and the wicked each go to their place of final abode, but do not thereby enter upon their eternal state. This latter can take place only at the final judgment. The early church seems to have held to a belief in an intermediate place, due to Jewish influence.

This view was held at a later time also, being strongly supported by the Roman Catholic doctrine of purgatory. The churches of the Reformation, however, rejected it, both because of their revolt against the abuses which

The saints who are in life and death united to Him are spoken of as those who "sleep in Jesus"; He is their κοιμητηρίον or Cemetery, where sleep is life while life is sleep. The current language of the Epistles refers to their death as departure "to be with Christ," the entering "an house not made with hands, eternal in the heavens," and the attainment of an almost consummate state in "the general assembly and church of the firstborn which are written in heaven," where are "the spirits of just men made perfect." All this seems inconsistent with a locality in any sense corresponding to the underworld of Sheol: in fact the term Hades would be all but lost, save in the symbolical Apocalypse, were it not for the explicit declaration that in the resurrection its victory will be taken away: "O Hades, where is thy victory?" With the Lord's resurrection Paradise seems to have risen also into a lower heaven: as it were the third heaven if not the seventh. Of the elevation of Paradise some hint was given when "many bodies of the saints which slept arose, and came out of the graves after his resurrection"; these may have been the mysterious symbolical first-fruits, whose spirits reunited to their bodies "appeared unto many" on their way with Christ from Paradise to heaven. The disembodied ungodly are never spoken of save as being generally or by implication in Hades.— POPE, *Compend. Chr. Th.*, III, pp. 379, 380.

But though there is no intermediate place in which the soul is confined between death and the resurrection—no *limbus patrum*, just below heaven; no *limbus infantum* for unbaptized children, or purgatory, just above hell, for unsanctified Christians, as the Papists dream—yet there is an intermediate state, which some have strangely confounded with the intermediate place—the hades, grave, or dormitory of souls—of which the Bible is silent.—SUMMERS, *Systematic Theology*, I, p. 351.

attached to the doctrine of purgatory, and because of
the theological implications involved in it. Dr. Enoch
Pond sums up these theological implications as follows:
"I have examined, in as few words as possible, the question of an intermediate place, and find no foundation
for it in the Word of God. It is of heathen and not Christian origin, and better becomes a believer in the mythology of Greece and Rome than a disciple of the Saviour.
I regard the theory, too, as of dangerous influence. Could
it be generally received by evangelical Christians, it
would be followed, I have no doubt, in a little time, with
prayers for the dead, and with the doctrine of a future
probation and restoration—perhaps with all the superstitions of purgatory. This is the course which things
took in the ancient church, and in all probability they
would take the same again. Let us, then, 'hold fast the
form of sound words' on this subject—the words of
Scripture and of most of our Protestant confessions of
faith, and not be 'driven about by every wind of doctrine' " (POND, *Christian Theology*, p. 552).

*Is the intermediate State a Period of Future Pro-
bation?* To this question we must reply that there can
be no future probation for the wicked beyond the grave.
This is evident for the following reasons: (1) It is unreasonable because it is unnecessary. God can extend
probation in this life to any extent He pleases, and to
suppose another probation, gives rise to more problems
than it solves. (2) The very abundance of light and
truth would seem to make the next world unfit for a
period of trial. The outshining of truth with such efful-
gence and glory would be compelling rather than probationary. There the very devils believe and tremble,
even though afar off from the realms of glory. (3) If
the wicked are on probation in the next world, why not
the righteous also? If the wicked can be saved after
death, then by a parity of reasoning the righteous may
fall away and perish. (4) Sinners sometimes finish their
probation before leaving this present world, as in the
case of those who have committed the "unpardonable
sin." (5) Those who believe in a future restoration,

must of necessity regard the punishments of the next world as wholly disciplinary, that is, as designed for the sufferer and not for the public good. If this be true, then they are not a curse but a blessing. But the inhabitants of hell are said to be under the curse of God (Jude 7), and objects of His vengeance (II Thess. 1: 8, 9). (6) If it be said that previous to their restoration sinners suffer all that they deserve, then they are saved by works and not by grace—a position entirely out of harmony with the teachings of the New Testament. (7) The Scriptures teach that it is *appointed unto men once to die, but after this the judgment* (Heb. 9: 27). Here it is evident that between death and the judgment there are no important changes, which indicates that only while men are in the body are they on probation (II Cor. 5: 10). Besides, if sinners are not reclaimed in the judgment, of what value is a second probation? (8) There will be no opportunity for the wicked to return to God through a Mediator, for at the judgment the mediatorial kingdom will come to an end, insofar as it is a provision for the salvation of the lost (I Cor. 15: 24-28). We may add also, that the idea of a probation beyond the grave and preceding the final judgment, is out of harmony with the general tenor of the Scriptures, but this subject must be reserved for further treatment in connection with the final state of the wicked.

Is the Intermediate State one of Progress and Development? This is not merely a speculative question, but is bound up with psychological and philosophical theory concerning the soul and its relation to the body. While Protestantism rejects the doctrine of a purgatory,

The Scriptures make no announcement of any probation after the present life. The merest suggestion of such a state is all that may reasonably be claimed; and rarely is anything more actually claimed. As to any explicit utterance in favor of a second probation, there is a dead silence of the Scriptures. How is this? Probation, with its privileges and responsibilities, very deeply concerns us. No period of our existence is fraught with deeper interest. The Scriptures are replete with such views of our present probation. They constantly press it upon our attention as involving the most solemn responsibilities of the present life and the profoundest interests of the future life. In a future probation there must be a renewal of all that so deeply concerns a present probation; yet there is not an explicit word respecting it. Such silence of the Scriptures is utterly irreconcilable with the reality of such a probation. —MILEY, *Systematic Theology,* II, p. 435.

the soul's activity in a disembodied state is a question which has been peculiarly attractive to philosophically minded theologians. The breaking off of the soul from the body as the racial nexus, and the tearing away of the veil of the flesh, furnishes the "aloneness" which underlies Dr. Olin A. Curtis' chapter on "The Christian Meaning of Death" (CURTIS, *The Christian Faith*, Chap. XX). Bishop Martensen fairly states the problem as follows: "The departed are described in the New Testament as souls, or spirits (I Peter 3:19, 20); they are divested of corporeity, have passed away out of the whole range of full daylight activity, and are waiting for the new and perfect body with which they shall be 'clothed upon.' That state immediately following death must therefore be the direct contrast of the present. In contrast with the present state, it must be said that the departed find themselves in a condition of rest, a state of passivity, that they are in 'the night wherein no man can work' (John 9:4). Their kingdom is not one of

Dr. Olin A. Curtis says, "Whatever one may think of the doctrine of the intermediate state from a merely religious standpoint, it has large Christian importance. For no one can see total Christianity, no one can grasp the philosophy of the Christian faith, until he has caught the peculiar significance of that personal experience between death and the resurrection. The systematic theologian is wont to consider the intermediate state as a doctrinal fragment of eschatology; but to me the profounder connection is soteriological." He notes five things that must be considered in a constructive doctrine: (1) The ethical spirit of the New Testament must be protected; (2) We should give this earthly life a full philosophical significance; (3) In the same spirit of Christian economy we must give also to the intermediate state a full philosophical significance; (4) The view of personality and bodily life, already gained, must be maintained watchfully; and (5) the doctrine must be so constructed as to protect the awful Christian emphasis upon death.—CURTIS, *Christian Faith*, pp. 397, 398.

As long as man is in this present world, he is in a kingdom of externals, wherein he can escape from self-contemplation and self-knowledge by the distractions of time, the noise and tumult of the world; but at death he enters upon a kingdom the opposite of all this. The veil which this world of sense, with its varied and incessantly moving manifoldness, spreads with soothing and softening influence over the stern reality of life, and which man finds ready to his hand to hide what he does not wish to see—this veil is torn asunder from before him in death, and his soul finds itself in a kingdom of pure realities. The manifold voices of this worldly life, which during this earthly life sounded together with the voices of eternity, grow dumb, and the holy voice now sounds alone, no longer deadened by the tumult of the world; and hence the realm of the dead becomes a realm of judgment. "It is appointed unto men once to die, but after this the judgment."—MARTENSEN, *Christian Dogmatics*, p. 458.

works and deeds, for they no longer possess the conditions upon which works and deeds are possible. Nevertheless, they live a deep spiritual life; for the kingdom of the dead is a kingdom of subjectivity, a kingdom of calm thought and self-fathoming, a kingdom of remembrance in the full sense of the word, in such a sense, I mean, that the soul now enters into its inmost recesses, resorts to that which is the very foundation of life, the true substratum and source of all existence" (MARTENSEN, *Christian Dogmatics*, pp. 457, 458). Dr. Curtis denies that the intermediate state is one of a second or even continued probation, but holds that its province is that of adjusting a person's mental life to his moral meaning. This world is planned for an ethical test, but we all reach death holding various sorts of false or fragmentary opinions. These opinions do not determine our central intention or influence our moral ideals; but they do confuse the expression of intention, and entire consistency at the point of judgment. "Therefore in the intermediate state," he says, "our relation to truth and reality is to be fully cleared up. No longer will a perfect purpose be held back by an imperfect judgment. No longer can any man's moral meaning be hidden under a false opinion" (CURTIS, *Christian Faith*, p. 402).

After death, the difference in principle, which existed here below, between the children of light and the children of darkness, is thus ever more developing; and the man finds himself placed in a very real and just state of retribution, although a state of retribution as yet only in its beginning, in relation to God and to himself. Upon the broad as upon the narrow way, falls the impenetrable curtain of death; but the first step after borders immediately upon the last step, before this curtain. Death alters our condition and our surroundings, but in our personality, nothing. Individuality, self-consciousness, memory, remains.—VAN OOSTERZEE, *Christian Dogmatics*, II, p. 781.

Dr. Pope states that the Scriptures indicate "a progress in blessedness and in the development of moral energy during the disembodied state. They have the discipline of hope; and of hope as not yet eternal in the heavens, though no longer probationary. They wait for the consummation, their Lord's and their own. And their progress in the spiritual life is not simply that which after the judgment will go on forever, but an advance from stage to stage peculiar to the intermediate state. Time is behind them; time is also before them; the day of eternity is not yet fully come."—POPE, *Compend. Chr. Th.*, III, p. 384.

Steffens calls attention to the fact that what is an evolution within the thoughts—that is a growth and development, must in the intermediate state perfect itself by becoming an involution ever more intense.

It is further pointed out that the clearing up of the mental life may result in a new formal adjustment to Jesus Christ.

Here again we must turn to the Scriptures for our authoritative teaching on this subject. Nor do they leave us without any light on this important subject. In the Apocalypse we are told that the spirits of the redeemed from among men, *follow the Lamb whithersoever he goeth* (Rev. 14:4); and that having washed their robes and made them white in the blood of the Lamb, they *serve him day and night in his temple* (Rev. 7:15). There is one instance also, in which the rapid development in the intermediate state is clearly set forth. St. John having heard the messenger of God says, *I fell at his feet to worship him. And he said unto me, See thou do it not: I am thy fellowservant, and of thy brethren that have the testimony of Jesus: worship God* (Rev. 19:10). So transformed was the messenger, that St. John did not recognize him as a martyr, but supposed him to be a divine being to be worshiped. We may well believe then, on the authority of the Scriptures, that the intermediate state will be one of progress in righteousness for the righteous, and in wickedness for the wicked.

THE DOCTRINE OF PURGATORY

I. History of the Doctrine. The idea of purification by fire was familiar to the Greek mind, having been taken up and made a part of his philosophy by Plato. He taught that no one could become perfectly happy after death until he had expiated his sins; and that if they were too great for expiation, his sufferings would have no end. That this doctrine passed from the Greeks to the Jews is inferred from the fact that Judas Maccabeus sent money to Jerusalem to pay for sacrifices to be offered for the sins of the dead. Also from the fact that the Rabbins taught that children by means of sin offerings could alleviate the sufferings of their deceased parents. Paradise, it seems, was regarded as encompassed by a sea of fire, wherein the blemishes of souls must be consumed before their admission to heaven. For this reason they taught that all souls not perfectly holy must wash themselves in the fire-river of Gehenna; and while the just would soon be cleansed, the wicked would be retained in its torments indefinitely.

The doctrine of purgatorial purification first began to be approached in the third century by Clement of Alexandria, who speaks of a spiritual fire in this world; and was followed by Origen, who held that this purifying fire continues beyond the grave. There were two theories in the early church, which although they differed from each other, were not necessarily exclusive, and may have been held together in many cases. (1) There was the judgment day purgatory which was based upon the words of St. Paul taken literally, that the "fire shall try every man's work"; and that even those who had built with wood, hay and stubble, would be saved if they had built upon the right foundation —saved as by fire (I Cor. 3:11-15). Both Hilary and Ambrose speak of the severity of the judgment day purification. Origen often speaks of judgment day fire through which even St. Peter and St. Paul must pass, though they shall hear the words, "When thou passest through the fire, the flame shall not harm thee." Basil says that baptism may be understood in three senses—in the one of regeneration by the Holy Spirit; in another, of the punishment of sin in the present life; and in a third, of "the trial of judgment by fire." Both Gregory of Nyssa and Gregory Nazianzen mention the fire of the judgment. This judgment day purgation differs widely from the Roman Catholic doctrine of purgatory. (2) There was the doctrine of a purification in the intermediate state, or a temporary punishment between death and the resurrection. This was held chiefly by the Western divines, who followed Augustine and developed the Roman Catholic doctrine as it is now understood. Augustine taught with respect to purgatory, first, that the souls of a certain class of men who are ultimately saved, suffer after death; and second, that they are aided through the Eucharist, and the alms and prayers of the faithful. Cæsarius of Arles (543) further developed the idea of purgatory by making a distinction between mortal crimes and lesser sins, holding that the latter might be expiated by good works in this life, or the cleansing fire in the life to come.

Gregory the Great (604) gathered together the vague and conflicting views of purgatory, and brought the doctrine into such shape that it became effective both for discipline and for income. For this reason he is commonly known as "the inventor of purgatory." "It is believed," he says, "that there is, for some light faults, a purgatorial fire before the judgment." However, the idea must have been vaguely entertained as early as the time of Perpetua, or even Augustine tacitly admitted the truth of her vision. From the eighth century on through the Middle Ages, the doctrine of purgatory took fast hold upon the popular mind, and was one of the most prominent topics of public conversation. Both scholastics and mystics were explicit and vivid in their descriptions of purgatory, and the belief was supported by a multitude of dreams and visions. Among these were the visions of Fursey and Drycthelm mentioned by Bede (736). Thomas Aquinas, Bonaventura, Garson and other great men of the Middle Ages held that the fires of purgatory were material, although Aquinas admitted the difficulty of understanding how literal fire could inflict pain on disembodied spirits. He held, also, that only those would go to purgatory who required it, but the saints would go at once to heaven, and the wicked to perdition.

The Greek Church never fully accepted the views of purgatory held in the West, and at the Council of Florence (1439) it was one of the irreconcilable differences between them. The mystic Wessel (1489) allegorized the popular language as "a spiritual fire of love, which purifies the soul of its remaining dross, and consists in the longing after union with God." John Tauler rejected the popular trifling with the doctrine, and maintained that "to behold the glory of God is Paradise." The Cathari, Waldenses and Wycliffe (1384) rejected the doctrine. The Reformers unanimously denounced the doctrine in unmeasured terms. The Council of Trent on the other hand, pronounced an anathema against all those who reject the doctrine.

II. Objections to the Doctrine of Purgatory. As indicated, the Reformers rejected the whole purgatorial theory as out of harmony with the teachings of the Scriptures, and the fundamental doctrines of grace. Excellent treatises on this subject may be found in the writings of the Reformed theologians. The following is Dr. Charles Hodge's summary of his own teaching on the subject. He says: (1) That it is destitute of scriptural support. (2) That it is opposed to many of the most clearly revealed and most important doctrines of the Bible. (3) That the abuses to which it has always led and which are its inevitable consequences, prove that the doctrine cannot be of God. (4) That the power to forgive sin, in the sense claimed by the Romanists, and which is taken for granted in their doctrine of purgatory, finds no support in the words of Christ, as recorded in John 20:23 and Matt. 16:19, which are relied on for that purpose. (5) The fifth argument against the doctrine is derived from its history, which proves it to have had a pagan origin, and to have been developed by slow degrees into the form in which it is now held by the Church of Rome (Cf. HODGE, *Systematic Theology*, III, p. 766).

CHAPTER XXXIV

THE SECOND ADVENT

In approaching the subject of our Lord's Second Advent, we are about to enter one of the most delicate and controversial fields of theology. The differences of opinion which have occasioned these controversies, are not merely speculative. They touch the deeper springs of the heart, and are vitally related to the experiences of men. It is a theme, also, which has periodically agitated the Church, always coming to the front when man feels most his need of divine help. In times of disaster, war, pestilence or persecution, the hope of His coming has always occupied the thoughts of men. Furthermore, this doctrine cannot be considered as merely one among many; it is rather a viewpoint—a determining principle by which men shape all their beliefs in logical order. Whether one believes in a "personal return of Christ," or merely in an increasing spiritual effusion," is not a matter of indifference. These positions reach back into the whole history of redemption, and affect some of the most commanding points in Christian theology. What he believes is the culminating point of his entire scheme of faith. It determines the whole character of his theology. The importance of the subject therefore demands the most careful and conscientious consideration.

The glory of Christianity, as over against the ethnic religions, is nowhere more manifest than in its eschatology. In our discussion of the Nature and Existence of God, we endeavored to show that the idea of God is a fundamental concept in religion, and therefore a determinative factor in theological thought. But the religious knowledge of God cannot rest in abstract thought. It must take shape in a comprehensive view of the world, of nature, of human history, of heaven and of hell. The history of religion reveals the fact that no religion has ever come into prominence without developing some form of a world order. The imagination blends the primitive religious concepts into mythology —hence we have the Greek religion of beauty, and the stronger Germanic conceptions embodied in the myths of the North. Bishop Martensen maintains that mythology is the attempt of the cosmical spirit or principle to embody itself in human history, and hence the ethnic religions must be regarded as the embodiment of the relative rather than the real—the spirit of the world manifested in heathendom which honors not God. He says, "As the created universe has, in a relative sense, life in itself—including as it does, a system of powers, ideas and aims, which possess a relative value—this relative independence, which ought to be subservient to the aims of the kingdom of God, has become a false 'world autonomy.' Hence arises the scriptural expression 'this world,' ὁ κόσμος οὗτος, whereby the Bible conveys the idea that it regards the world not only ontologically, but in its definite and actual state, the state in which it has been since the fall. 'This world' means the world content with itself, in its own independence, in its own glory; the world which disowns its dependence on God as its Creator. 'This world' regards itself not as the κτίσις, but only as the κόσμος, as a system of glory and beauty which has life in itself and can give life. The historical embodiment of 'this world' is heathendom, which honoreth not God as God. In the consciousness of heathendom the visible and invisible κόσμος is taken to be the highest reality; and the development of this consciousness displayed in heathen mythology, is a reflection of the universe, not of God, an image of the world, not the manifestation of the true image of the Lord. The darkness of heathen consciousness does not consist in the total absence of any enlightening idea of what is really true and universally excellent, but in the fact that it does not see that idea reflected in God. It is not the contrast between the idea and the want of it—between the spirit and the spiritless—which must guide us in judging of heathenism; it is rather the contrast between idea and idea, between spirit and spirit,

between the holy aim and the world's aim, between the
Holy Spirit and the spirit of the world (MARTENSEN,
Christian Dogmatics, pp. 183, 184). Over against this
purely relative expression, it is the glory of Christianity that it presents a revelation of reality. It finds its
highest expression in the return and reign of the God-
man, who as the Christ or Anointed One, Creator and
Redeemer, will establish Himself in a perfect world
order—the kingdom of God in a new heavens and a
new earth, wherein dwelleth righteousness.

We shall consider this subject under two general
heads—the Personal Return of Our Lord; and The Order of Events Connected with His Return. The first is
of course, the more important. The personal return of
Christ has been frequently denied by a rationalistic
philosophy and a faithless church, and must be defended
by an appeal to the Scriptures as our sole authority.
The second is concerned largely with the development
of the various millennial theories in the history of the
Church. These have always had a peculiar fascination
for the curious minded, but are not vital to Christian
experience in the same sense as is a belief in the personal
return of Christ. The more specific divisions of this
chapter will be as follows: (1) The Personal Return of
Our Lord; (2) The Development of the Doctrine in the
Church, including a review of the various millennial
theories; (3) Modern Types of Millennial Theory; and
(4) The Parenthetic View of the Millennium.

Bishop Martensen points out that the ὁ κόσμος οὗτος or "this world"
as used in the Scriptures, is "not confined exclusively to the old heathenism; it is wherever that kingdom does not exercise its guiding influence.
This world is ever striving after an earthly state which does not make
itself subordinate to God's rule; it develops a wisdom which does not
retain the living God in its knowledge; its forms for itself an excellency
which is not the reflection of His glory. And this glittering pantheistic
world-reality is not a mere imaginary thing, for the powers of the universe are really divine powers. The elements, the materials with which
this world builds its kingdom, are of the noblest kind, their want of
genuineness lies in the ethical form given to them; or in the false relation between the glory of this world and the will of man."—MARTENSEN,
Christian Dogmatics, p. 184.

The Personal Return of Our Lord

The Scriptures clearly teach that as Christ once came into the world to effect man's redemption, so also, He will come again to receive His redeemed Church to Himself. This is expressly stated in the words, *Christ was once offered to bear the sins of many; and unto them that look for him shall he appear the second time without sin unto salvation* (Heb. 9:28). This Second Coming will be personal, visible and glorious. *Behold, he cometh with clouds; and every eye shall see him, and they also which pierced him; and all kindreds of the earth shall wail because of him. Even so, Amen* (Rev. 1:7). It is evident from this that the appearance of Jesus will not be merely to the eye of faith, but in the sight of heaven and earth—the terror of His foes, and the consolation of His people. This is confirmed by the incident on the Mount of Ascension. *And when he had spoken these things, while they beheld, he was taken up; and a cloud received him out of their sight. And while they looked steadfastly toward heaven as he went up, behold two men stood by them in white apparel;*

The Christian belief in the coming again of Christ is the expression of the well-grounded expectation, that He will ever increasingly make manifest before every eye the splendor of His dominion, and one day visibly appear as King of the Church, and Judge of the world, forever to end the present dispensation, and to complete, in a manner worthy of Himself, the kingdom of God founded by Him. . . . That the New Testament really teaches such a visible final coming again cannot be seriously denied. The Lord repeatedly says that He shall appear in splendor, and visible to the eyes of all—in a glorified body, therefore—upon the clouds of heaven, in the full radiance of His kingly majesty (Luke 17:24; Matt. 24:30; 25:31). He compares Himself to a nobleman who goes away in order to receive a kingdom, and then again to return (Luke 19:12). In other parables, also, He gives us to understand the same thing (Matt. 13:40, 41, 49; Luke 18:8); and His last prolonged discourse (Matt. 24, 25) is devoted to the unveiling of the mysteries of the future.—Van Oosterzee, *Christian Dogmatics,* II, pp. 577, 579.

The Second Coming of our Lord is the one all-commanding event of prophecy and the future: itself supreme, it is always associated with the universal resurrection, the judgment of mankind, and the consummation of all things. Though these epochs and crises are in the style of prophecy presented together in foreshortened perspective, they are widely distinct. But while treating them as distinct, we must be careful to remember their common relation to the Day of the Lord; which is a fixed and determinate period, foreshadowed in many lesser periods to which the same term is applied, but the issue and consummation of them all.—Pope, *Compend, Chr. Th.,* III, p. 387.

which also said, Ye men of Galilee, why stand ye gazing up into heaven? this same Jesus, which is taken up from you into heaven, shall so come in like manner as ye have seen him go into heaven (Acts 1: 9-11). According to Dr. Whedon, "This passage is an immovable proof text of the actual, personal, Second Advent of Jesus. It is the same personal, visible Jesus which ascended that shall come. The coming shall be in like manner with the going. A figurative or spiritual coming would clearly not be a coming of the same Jesus, and still more clearly not a coming in like manner." Dr. Hackett in his comment on this verse says that the words ὅν τρόπον mean in this place, visible and in the air; and that the expression is never employed to affirm merely the certainty of one event as compared with another. By the analogy of the first coming of Christ as literal and vis-

Christ always spoke of His coming as that of the Son of man. By this He himself taught the same truth with which afterward the angel at the ascension reassured the disciples who stood "gazing up into heaven," namely, that He that shall come then shall be the "same Jesus" which was taken up. It will then be in human form that He will appear, and with the same sympathizing human as well as divine love toward His own which He so wonderfully displayed while on earth. But the Apostle Peter, at Pentecost, said, "Therefore let all the house of Israel know assuredly, that God hath made that same Jesus whom ye have crucified both Lord and Christ" (Acts 2:36). Hence the apostles, almost exclusively, speak of Christ as Lord in connection with His Second Coming. This was their common name for Christ, and they recognized the glorious reward bestowed upon Him for the salvation wrought for them, and the "all power" given unto Him in heaven and earth.—BOYCE, *Abstract of Systematic Theology*, p. 453.

The Creedal statements concerning the Second Advent are as follows: "He ascended into heaven, and sitteth on the right hand of God the Father Almighty: from thence he shall come to judge the quick and the dead."—The Apostles' Creed. "And he shall come again, with glory, to judge both the quick and the dead; whose kingdom shall have no end."—The Nicene Creed. "Christ did truly rise again from death and took again His body, with flesh, bones, and all things appertaining to the perfection of man's nature; wherewith He ascended into heaven, and there sitteth, until He return to judge all men at the last day."—Art. IV of the Thirty-Nine Articles of the Anglican Church. "Christ did truly rise again from the dead, and took again His body, with all things appertaining to the perfection of man's nature, wherewith He ascended into heaven, and there sitteth until He return to judge all men at the last day."—Art. III of the Twenty-Five Articles of Methodism. "We believe that the Lord Jesus Christ will come again; that we who are alive at His coming shall not precede them that are asleep in Christ Jesus; but that, if we are abiding in Him, we shall be caught up with the risen saints to meet the Lord in the air, so that we shall ever be with the Lord."—Art. XI of the Articles of Faith of the Church of the Nazarene.

ible, so also we must expect the Second Coming to be likewise literal and visible.

Modern theology has frequently been too much inclined to deny the personal, visible return of our Lord, and to substitute instead, a belief in His spiritual presence only. William Newton Clarke may be regarded as a representative of this modern viewpoint. In a summary of his teaching on the Second Coming of Christ he says, "No visible return of Christ to the earth is to be expected, but rather the long and steady advance of His spiritual kingdom. The expectation of a single dramatic advent corresponds to the Jewish doctrine of the nature of the kingdom, but not to the Christian. Jews, supposing the kingdom of the Messiah to be an earthly reign, would naturally look for the bodily presence of the king: but Christians who know the spiritual nature of His reign may well be satisfied with a spiritual presence, mightier than if it were seen. If our Lord will but complete the spiritual coming that He has begun, there will be no need of visible advent to make perfect His glory on the earth" (WILLIAM NEWTON CLARKE, *An Outline of Christian Theology*, p. 444). But the terms *paraclete* and *parousia* must not be confused. The former, or *paracletos* (παράκλητος), means an advocate or an intercessor, and is the term applied by Christ to the Holy Spirit—the Paraclete or Comforter. It therefore represents Christ as spiritually and invisibly present in the Holy Spirit, while *parousia* (παρουσία or presence), signifies His personal, visible presence. It is sometimes argued that *parousia* simply means presence with, and therefore does not denote an act of coming. This position cannot be substantiated as the following

There are some signs of a present tendency of thought away from the traditional doctrine of a personal, visible advent, in favor of a merely spiritual or providential manifestation. The prevalence of the new view would carry with it a recasting of the traditional doctrines of the general resurrection and the final judgment, or, rather, the elimination of these doctrines. We see no sufficient reason for the acceptance of this view, and therefore adhere to the manner of the advent so long held in the faith of the Church. That the Scriptures set forth the coming of Christ as in a personal, visible manner can hardly be questioned. Indeed, such expression of it seems so definite and clear as to leave no place for the opposing view.—MILEY, *Systematic Theology*, II, p. 440.

passages of Scripture will show (I Cor. 16: 17; II Cor. 7: 6, 7; and II Peter 3: 12). Since these passages cannot be rendered other than as a coming or arrival, so also we may believe that there must be a coming of Christ in order to His presence with us. The full meaning of the word *parousia* is generally understood to be such a coming that His presence shall be abidingly with His people, and His absence shall have passed away forever. There are two other terms used in connection with the Second Advent. The first is *apocalypsis* (ἀποκάλυψις), from which our word apocalypse is derived, and in its simplest form means an unveiling. As used in connection with the Second Advent, it means a disclosure or manifestation of Himself from the heaven which had received Him. The second word is *epiphaneia* (ἐπιφάνεια) from *epiphaino* (ἐπιφαίνω), a verb signifying *to give light to* (Luke 1: 79), or in the passive, *to become visible*, or to *appear* (Acts 27: 20). In its simplest sense, therefore, the word means an *appearance* or a *manifestation*. St. Paul uses it in reference to the First Advent in these words, *But is now made manifest by the appearing* [ἐπιφανείας] *of our Saviour Jesus Christ, who hath abolished death, and hath brought life and immortality to light through the gospel* (II Tim. 1: 10). He uses it in connection with the Second Advent when he enjoins Timothy to *keep this commandment without spot, unrebukable, until the appearing* [ἐπιφανείας] *of our Lord Jesus Christ* (I Tim. 6: 14). It is hardly probable that

The word ἐπιφάνεια occurs in the New Testament six times, namely in the following passages: I Tim. 6:14 "the appearing of our Lord Jesus Christ." II Tim. 1:10, "the appearing of our Saviour Jesus Christ." II Tim. 4:1, "at his appearing." Verse 8, "love his appearing." Titus 2:13, "glorious appearing of the great God," and II Thess. 2:8, "destroy with the brightness [that is, the appearing] of his coming." H. Bonar in his comments on the last verse says, "the word ἐπιφάνεια which the apostle uses here occurs just six times in the New Testament. In one of these it refers to the First Advent, which we know was literal and personal. In four it is admitted to refer to the literal and personal Second Coming: the fifth is the one under discussion, and it is the strongest and most unambiguous of all the six. Not one of these others is so explicit, yet no one thinks of explaining them away. Why then fasten upon the strongest, and insist on spiritualizing it? If the strongest can be explained away so as not to prove the Advent at all. If the antimillennarian be at liberty to spiritualize the most distinct, why may not the Straussian be allowed to rationalize or mythologize the less distinct.— Bonar, *Coming and Kingdom*, p. 343.

the apostle would use the word to express a personal coming of Christ in the first instance, and not use it in the same sense concerning the Second Coming. St. Paul uses all three words in his Second Epistle to the Thessalonians, to set forth or describe the influence of the coming of Christ upon the Wicked or Lawless One. He says, *When the Lord Jesus shall be revealed* [ἀποκαλύψει] *from heaven* (II Thess. 1: 7) .... *then shall that Wicked be revealed* [ἀποκαλυφθήσεται], *whom the Lord shall consume with the spirit of his mouth, and shall destroy with the brightness* [ἐπιφανείᾳ, by the appearing] *of his coming* [τῆς παρουσίας αὐτοῦ, of the presence of himself] (II Thess. 2: 8). To the unbiased student of the Holy Scriptures, there can be but one conclusion concerning the Second Advent, that is—a personal, visible, glorious return of our Lord to this earth. However, it may be well to note at this time, that while these words clearly indicate a personal return of our Lord as over against the theory of a purely spiritual effusion, the fact that they are often used interchangeably, would seem to render futile any attempt to build a theory of the Second Advent on a distinction of terms—the παρουσία as referring to one phase of His appearing, and the ἀποκάλυψις to another.

With this general survey of the subject we must now turn our attention to the more important details of the doctrine, as follows: (1) The Scriptural Basis of the Doctrine; (2) The Sign of His Coming; (3) The Manner of His Coming; and (4) The Purpose of His Coming.

Scriptural Basis of the Doctrine. The most direct, and what in this sense may be regarded as the primary

The word παρουσία is used in the New Testament twenty-four times, the following being all of the passages in which it is found: Matt. 24:3, "sign of thy coming"; v. 27, "the coming of"; v. 39, "the coming of the Son of man"; I Cor. 15:23, "Christ's at his coming"; 16:17, "coming of Stephanus, and Fortunatus, and Achaicus"; II Cor. 7:6, "coming of Titus"; v. 7, "by his coming"; 10:10, "his bodily presence"; Phil. 1:26, "by my coming"; 2:12, "my presence only"; I Thess. 2:19, "at his coming"; 3:13, "at the coming"; 4:15, "coming of the Lord"; 5:23, "coming of our Lord"; II Thess. 2:1, "coming of our Lord"; v. 8, "brightness of his coming"; v. 9, "him, whose coming"; James 5:7, "coming of the Lord"; v. 8, "coming of the Lord"; II Peter 1:16, "coming of our Lord"; 3:4, "promise of his coming"; v. 12, "the coming of"; and I John 2:28, "at his coming."—TAYLOR, *The Reign of Christ on Earth*, p. 389.

revelation, is to be found in the words which fell from the lips of our Lord himself. Following a solemn warning to the Jews, He declared, *Behold, your house is left unto you desolate. For I say unto you, Ye shall not see me henceforth, till ye shall say, Blessed is he that cometh in the name of the Lord* (Matt. 23:38, 39). Immediately following this, His disciples called His attention to the buildings of the temple which had been erected with consummate architectural skill, but He only replied, *See ye not all these things? verily I say unto you, There shall not be left here one stone upon another, that shall not be thrown down* (Matt. 24:2). Seated upon the Mount of Olives, *the disciples came unto him privately, saying, Tell us, when shall these things be? and what shall be the sign of thy coming, and of the end of the world?* (Matt. 24:3). These questions were the occasion of the remarkable eschatological discourses found in the Gospel of Matthew (chapters 24 and 25); and in a more condensed form in the Gospels of Mark and Luke. The climactic utterance, however, is that before

Inasmuch as this subject involves, almost exclusively, the use of prophecy, it may be well to note in brief some of the principles which apply to this department of biblical study. The first prophecy, or what is commonly known as the Protevangelium (Gen. 3:14-19), is not only the foundation of all prophecy, but includes within itself, all the prophecies touching the conflict between the serpent and the seed of the woman. It suggests also, both the nature of the conflict and the final outcome. In the words to the serpent are contained the spiritual issues, in those to the woman, the social order, and in those to Adam, the physical consequences. There is nothing in time or eternity—spiritual, social or physical—that is outside the scope of this foundational and all inclusive prophecy. With this as a basis, all prophetic utterance and all historic development may rightfully be viewed as a detailed explanation of what is here contained in germ form. The promises to Abraham, the words of the dying Joseph, the elaborate system of religion set up under Moses, and all the period of the Old Testament, must all be regarded as the unfolding of this primitive prophecy. The Old Testament prophecies may be analyzed as follows: (1) those that were fulfilled before the incarnation; (2) those that were fulfilled by the incarnation; and (3) those that extended into the New Testament and church periods. In the New Testament, prophecy would again be regarded as threefold: (1) an explanation of those prophecies already fulfilled in and by the incarnation; (2) an explanation of those prophecies projected from the Old Testament into the time period succeeding the incarnation; and (3) a new set of prophecies beginning with the New Testament period and looking forward to the time of the end. This latter would include the foundational statements of Christ, such as the Sermon on the Mount, and those specific counsels which guided the Church in its development, as over against the background of the Gentile and pagan world.—Rev. Paul S. Hill.

the judgment seat of the high priest, and is **expressed** in these words, *Hereafter shall ye see the Son of man sitting on the right hand of power, and coming in the clouds of heaven* (Matt. 26: 64).

It is not surprising, therefore, that these predictions fixed the truth of the Second Coming firmly in the mind of the Church; and that the apostles should constantly present it as an incentive to holy living. With this insight into prophetical truth also, the apostles were enabled to lift out of the Old Testament certain mysterious passages and interpret them in the light of the new dispensation. Thus St. Peter in his sermon at Pentecost, quotes the prophecy of Joel, assigning that portion referring to the promise of the Holy Spirit to the opening of the dispensation, and that concerning *the great and terrible day of the Lord* to its close, or the time of the *Second Advent* (Cf. Joel 2: 28-31; Acts 2: 16-21). St. Jude, likewise, quotes a prophecy of Enoch, the seventh from Adam, saying, *Behold, the Lord cometh with ten thousands of his saints, to execute judgment upon all, and to convince all that are ungodly among them of all their ungodly deeds* (Jude 14, 15). Whatever doubts may be had in regard to the passages in the Old Testament which are sometimes presented as proofs of this doctrine, the New Testament cannot be called in question. To the early Christians it was the *blessed hope, and the glorious appearing of the great God and our Saviour Jesus Christ* (Titus 2: 13). St. Paul further

We can touch only on the ground forms and main lines—not on the complete filling up—of the Christian eschatological doctrinal structure. The foundation for this structure can be no other than that which a true God has revealed in His infallible Word concerning the things of the future. While the philosophy of religion in general may apply itself to the examination as to what human reason by its own light proclaims concerning immortality and external life, Christian Dogmatics avails itself of another torch in this mysterious obscurity. Here it emphatically presupposes the truth of that which has already been earlier treated of, such as the supranaturalistic Theistic conception of God; the existence of a particular revelation of salvation; the trustworthiness of the words of the Lord and of His first witness concerning things unseen and eternal. It consequently has not to return to the question as to the continued existence of the spirit, which was already treated of in connection with Anthropology; and just as little to that as to the nature of death, which was already entered into in connection with Hamartiology.—VAN OOSTERZEE, *Christian Dogmatics,* II, p. 776.

states that *our conversation is in heaven; from whence also we look for the Saviour, the Lord Jesus Christ: who shall change our vile body, that it may be fashioned like unto his glorious body* (Phil. 3:20, 21). St. Peter gives us this exhortation, *Wherefore gird up the loins of your mind, be sober, and hope to the end for the grace that is to be brought unto you at the revelation of Jesus Christ* (I Peter 1:13); while St. James gives a like exhortation, *Be patient therefore, brethren, unto the coming of the Lord, ... stablish your hearts: for the coming of the Lord draweth nigh* (James 5:7, 8). Perhaps the most loved text is that of St. John, *Let not your heart be troubled: ye believe in God, believe also in me. In my Father's house are many mansions: if it were not so, I would have told you. I go to prepare a place for you. And if I go and prepare a place for you, I will come again, and receive you unto myself; that where I am, there ye may be also* (John 14:1-3). Two generations after His ascension, our Lord appeared to His disciple in Patmos, and closed the revelation of Himself with the words, *Surely I come quickly* (Rev. 22:20), the very last words which men were to hear from Him who spake not only on earth but also from heaven.

The Sign of His Coming. In His reply to the question of the disciples, *What shall be the sign of thy coming, and of the end of the world?* (τοῦ αἰῶνος, or the age), our Lord did not hesitate to describe the vicissitudes of the Church in the present age. In His reply, there is a prediction of three classes of events, which we understand from the remainder of His discourse, are not to be regarded as distinct epochs set off from each other, but as being in a large measure coincident

Dr. Blunt gives this interesting note in connection with his article on the Second Advent. He says, "In association with the sign of the Son of man and the coming as lightning, it is observable that lightning has frequently been known to leave the mark of the cross upon the persons and garments of those whom it has struck. Bishop Warbuton gives some indubitable instances of this." He therefore regards "the sign of His coming" as a celestial Labarum which will herald the immediate approach of Christ. He says, "All will then see Christ's cross stretched forth in the midst of the darkness as the bright standard of the King of Kings, and will at once know that it is set up as the token of His coming to reign in judgment."—BLUNT, *Dictionary*, Article. Second Advent.

in time. (1) There will be an age of tribulation, in which there will be disturbances in the physical world, great political upheavals and social disintegration. *For nation shall rise against nation, and kingdom against kingdom: and there shall be famines, and pestilences, and earthquakes, in divers places* (Matt. 24: 7). These our Lord declares *are the beginning of sorrows* (Matt. 24: 8). From the words, *but the end is not yet* (Matt. 24: 6), we may infer that this beginning of sorrows will precede the Second Advent by a considerable space of time. But our Lord predicts the deepening shadows of a greater tribulation as the end of the age approaches. This He introduces with warnings and exhortations of great moment (Matt. 24: 15-20) and concludes by saying, *For then shall be great tribulation, such as was not since the beginning of the world to this time, no, nor ever shall be. And except those days should be shortened, there should no flesh be saved: but for the elect's sake those days shall be shortened* (Matt. 24: 21, 22). (2) The Preparation of the Church and the Evangelization of the World, mark the second prediction of our Lord. The circumstances of the world will serve to discipline the Church, and only those that endure to the end shall be saved. At our Lord's coming He will exact an account of all His stewards. Those who are found faithful will be rewarded, and those who have been untrue to their trust will be punished for their negligence or infidelity. This stewardship is immediately related to the dissemination of the gospel, as given to the disciples in the Great Commission (Matt. 28: 19, 20). To preach the gospel and to bear witness of Christ is the supreme duty of the Church in this age, over against which idle and curious questions concerning the future were regarded by our Lord as of little importance (Acts 1: 7, 8). Hence we are told that *this gospel of the kingdom shall be preached in all the world for a witness unto all nations; and then shall the end come* (Matt. 24: 14). (3) The third prediction is that of an apostasy or falling away due to the deceptiveness of sin. *And then shall many be offended, and shall betray one another, and shall hate one another. And many false prophets shall rise, and shall deceive many. And because iniquity shall abound, the love of many shall wax cold* (Matt. 24:10-12). Our Lord seems to indicate also, that as the tribulation deepens toward the end of the age, so also the deceptiveness of sin increases. *Then if any man shall say unto you, Lo, here is Christ, or there; believe it not. For there shall arise false Christs, and false prophets, and shall shew great signs and wonders; insomuch that, if it were possible, they shall deceive the very elect. Behold, I have told you before* (Matt. 24:23-25). The progressive unfolding of divine truth concerning the Antichrist is very marked in the Scriptures. Here our Lord speaks of false Christs and false prophets, as indicating all those who are in opposition to Christ and the truth. These, of course, could find no place in history until after the appearance of the true Christ. St. John likewise speaks of a plurality of antichrists. *Little children, it is the last time: and as ye have heard that*

Dr. Blunt points out that "the great object of Antichrist will be to set himself up as the object of men's worship instead of Christ; the great means by which the seduction of his worshipers is accomplished will be the supernatural power which he will be able to oppose to the supernatural power of Christ." His coming will therefore be preceded by a manifestation of the power of Satan communicated to the Antichrist. It is recorded that Satan said to our Lord in the second temptation, "All this power will I give thee, and the glory of them: for that is delivered unto me; and to whomsoever I will give it. If thou therefore wilt worship me, all shall be thine" (Luke 4:6, 7). It is to this evidently that St. Paul refers when in speaking of the Antichrist, he says, "His coming [παρουσίας] is after the working of Satan, with all power, and signs, and lying wonders" (II Thess. 2:9). "It thus seems," Dr. Blunt continues, "that the supernatural power of working miracles will be accompanied by a universal authority or kingdom, won, perhaps, by means of them. Thus the opposition of Antichrist to Christ will consist in setting up a person instead of Him as the object of worship, in working miracles such as characterized Christ's First Advent, and in establishing a universal empire in the place of the church. The elements of seduction contained in such a power are sufficiently evident, and perhaps they will possess all the greater strength in proportion to the high developments of a civilization uninfluenced by love of God. Men will be attracted to become followers of Antichrist first by his accumulation of universal empire, reverencing in its extreme development (Rev. 13:4ff) that success which is said to be the most successful of all things. They will be attracted also by his supernatural power, the visible exercise of which subdues at once. . . . . After the chains of such seductions have bound the minds and affections of mankind, they will be easily prevailed upon to take the last step in apostasy, 'Fall down and worship me.' Such, it seems, will be the course of the great apostasy, the last stage in the preparation for Christ's Second Advent" (Cf. BLUNT, *Dict. of Doct. and Hist. Theology*, Art. Second Advent).

antichrists shall come, even now are there many anti-christs: whereby we know that it is the last time (I John 2:18). But St. John goes farther than this. He says, *Every spirit that confesseth not that Jesus Christ is come in the flesh is not of God: and this is that spirit of antichrist, whereof ye have heard that it should come: and even now already is it in the world* (I John 4:3). St. Paul also reveals the fact, that while there will be a great falling away in the last time, there will be also the revelation of a "man of sin" who with wicked presumption, will assume the place of God and lay claim to the honor of divine worship. *Let no man deceive you by any means: for that day shall not come, except there come a falling away first, and that man of sin be revealed, the son of perdition; who opposeth and exalteth himself above all that is called God, or that is worshipped; so that he as God sitteth in the temple of God, shewing himself that he is God* (II Thess. 2:3, 4). Here, then, in the eschatological discourses of our Lord do we find a delineation of the events which shall characterize the present age, and therefore serve as a sign of His coming. It is sometimes said that this emphasis upon the increase of wickedness tends to inculcate a belief in

The many false Christs or even the spirit of the Antichrist as specifically opposed to the true Christ, could find no place of importance in history until after the real Christ had made His first appearance. The story of the rise of many who claim to be the Christ is well known. They were numerous in the days of the early church, as our Lord had predicted. They were in the deserts and in the secret places. The spirit of these pretenders was of course opposed to the real Christ, and thus they became the forerunners of the whole antichristian program of the New Testament period. Doubtless there will be an increasing intensity of this spirit, which shall reach its culmination and final defeat in the last great conflict.—Rev. Paul Hill.

The climax of the misery of the last days is attained in the appearing of the Antichrist, whom the prophetic word leads us to expect. The reference to the rise and development of this expectation must be left by Christian Dogmatics to the Biblical Theology of the Old and New Testaments. Here it can only be said, that for him who interprets the Scriptures without preconceived views, and allows his thoughts to be brought into captivity to the obedience of the Word, there can be no doubt that a personal Antichrist will yet arise before the close of the world's history. . . . . If we see already in the history of the world colossal figures arise in the service of the powers of darkness; and if already in connection with many a name there was heard from sundry lips the question whether this was the Antichrist; nothing prevents our seeing in their appearance the preparation for a future central personality, in whom the spirit of evil will as it were embody itself, and display its full power.—Van Oosterzee, *Christian Dogmatics*, II, p. 796.

the gradual and necessary decline of Christ's kingdom; and consequently begets a passive and hopeless attitude toward sin. To this we reply, that Christ does not teach, nor does the Church believe that His kingdom shall decline. Our Lord teaches that the same harvest season which ripens the wheat, ripens the tares also; that there is, therefore, a progress in wickedness as well as in righteousness; and that both the wheat and the tares are to grow together—not one grow and the other decline. But the true motive for evangelism as found in the Church, is not in the glory of outward success, but in a deep sense of obedience to a trust, and a fervent love for her Lord. As the end of the age approaches, we may expect an increase in righteousness and in wickedness, and the Church must gird herself for an aggressive and constant warfare against sin until Jesus comes.

The Manner of His Coming. Here again our Lord's discourses must be the source of our authority concerning this great eschatological event. Having warned against the deceptiveness of false Christs and false prophets, He instructs the disciples concerning the manner of His coming, in these words, *Wherefore if they shall say unto you, Behold, he is in the desert; go not forth: behold, he is in the secret chambers; believe it not. For as the lightning cometh out of the east, and shineth even unto the west, so shall also the coming of the Son of man be* (Matt. 24: 26, 27). He indicates also, that there shall be disturbances of a cataclysmic nature in the physical universe, preceding the Second Advent.

As to the Antichrist, whose coming was expected to precede the final consummation, it was a common opinion that he should be a being of supernatural origin. . . . . Another opinion was, that he already had appeared in the person of Mahomet, that the apocalyptic "Number of the Beast," 666, denoted the duration of his power, and that his downfall might be looked for toward the end of the thirteenth century. This expectation seems to have assisted in producing the enthusiasm of the Crusades, which declined as the expected time passed by, and the Mahometan power continued to flourish. Others, again, discerned Antichrist in the various sects, which in the twelfth and thirteenth century, refused submission to the pope; while these in turn, applied to him the same title. This was done as early as 1204, by Amalric of Bema; and Louis of Bavaria, Emperor of Germany, about 1327, so designated Pope John XXII. Wycliffe (1384) and the Lollards also denounced the pope as Antichrist.—CRIPPEN, *History of Christian Doctrine,* pp. 233, 234.

*Immediately after the tribulation of those days shall the
sun be darkened, and the moon shall not give her light,
and the stars shall fall from heaven, and the powers of
the heavens shall be shaken: and then shall appear the
sign of the Son of man in heaven: and then shall all the
tribes of the earth mourn, and they shall see the Son
of man coming in the clouds of heaven with power and
great glory. And he shall send his angels with a great
sound of a trumpet, and they shall gather together his
elect from the four winds, from one end of heaven to
the other* (Matt. 24: 29-31).

Our Lord teaches also, that a certain unexpected-
ness will attend His coming. The time of the Second
Advent is veiled in mystery. *But of that day and hour
knoweth no man, no, not the angels in heaven, but my
Father only* (Matt. 24: 36). He instructs His disciples,
therefore, to give the utmost attention to watchfulness
and faithfulness in the things of the kingdom. *Watch
therefore: for ye know not what hour your Lord doth
come* (Matt. 24: 42); and again, *Therefore be ye also
ready: for in such an hour as ye think not the Son of man
cometh* (Matt. 24: 44). He further declares that at the
time of His Second Coming the world will be pursuing
its ordinary course, unmindful of the great event which
will take place suddenly and without special warning.
*But as the days of Noe were, so shall also the coming of
the Son of man be. For as in the days that were before
the flood they were eating and drinking, marrying and
giving in marriage, until the day that Noe entered into
the ark, and knew not until the flood came, and took*

It is obvious that the Supreme Prophet of His own dispensation
has made it a law of His kingdom that its final consummation shall
forever be uncertain as to its date. Hence in His eschatological discourses He answered the disciples' double question, "Tell us, when
shall these things be? in such a manner as to prevent their attempting to define either the date of the nearer end of the world, the destruction of Judaism, or that of the more distant end of all things.—
POPE, *Compend. Chr. Th.,* III, p. 391.

Under both dispensations, patient waiting for Christ was intended to
discipline the faith and to enlarge the conception, of God's true servants. The fact that every age since Christ ascended has had its Chiliasts
and Second Adventists should turn our thoughts away from curious
and fruitless prying into the time of Christ's coming, and set us at
immediate and constant endeavor to be ready, at whatsoever hour He
may appear.—STRONG, *Systematic Theology,* III, p. 1007.

them all away; so shall also the coming of the Son of man be (Matt. 24: 37-39). This does not apply solely to the wicked, for then shall two be in the field; the one shall be taken, and the other left. Two women shall be grinding at the mill; the one shall be taken, and the other left (Matt. 24: 40, 41). We may confidently believe then, that the Second advent will be a sudden and glorious appearance of our Lord, bursting in upon the ordinary course of the world as an unexpected catacylsmic event. To the righteous, who have through faith in His Word prepared themselves and are watching for His return, this appearance will be hailed with supreme joy; to the wicked who have rejected His words, saying *Where is the promise of his coming?* It will be a time of consternation and condemnation.

The Purpose of His Coming. Our Lord sets forth the purpose of His coming in the latter part of this eschatological discourse, by means of two familiar parables— that of the Ten Virgins, and that of the Talents. In the former He emphasizes more especially the lack of a proper preparation for His coming, while in the latter He condemns the violation of a trust. Both emphasize the sins of omission rather than those of commission. The outstanding truth, however, which is set forth in these parables is the same—that of a coming judgment in which the righteous shall be rewarded and the wicked punished. Hence it is, that following the second parable, our Lord clearly states the purpose of His Second Coming as that of judgment. His words are unmistakable. *When the Son of man shall come in his glory, and all the holy angels with him, then shall he sit upon the throne of his glory: and before him shall be gathered all nations: and he shall separate them one from another, as a shepherd divideth his sheep from the goats: and he shall set the sheep on his right hand, but the goats on the left. Then shall the King say unto them on his right hand, Come, ye blessed of my Father, inherit the kingdom prepared for you from the foundation of the world* (Matt. 25: 31-34). Following this He depicts in vivid colors the scene of judgment, in which He pronounces

sentence upon those on his left hand, saying, *Depart
from me, ye cursed, into everlasting fire, prepared for
the devil and his angels* (Matt. 25:41); and concludes
the discourse with the solemn words, *And these shall
go away into everlasting punishment: but the righteous
into life eternal* (Matt. 25:46). From these words of
our Lord concerning the Second Coming as directly related to judgment, there can be no appeal.

There are two of our Lord's earlier parables which
express this idea of judgment also, that of the Tares,
and that of the Drag Net. In His interpretation of the
former, Jesus states that *the field is the world; the good
seed are the children of the kingdom; but the tares are
the children of the wicked one; the enemy that sowed
them is the devil; the harvest is the end of the world*
[αἰών or age]; *and the reapers are the angels* (Matt.
13:38-39). In the application of the parable, we are told
that *The Son of man shall send forth his angels, and they
shall gather out of his kingdom all things that offend,
and them which do iniquity; and shall cast them into a
furnace of fire: there shall be wailing and gnashing of
teeth. Then shall the righteous shine forth as the sun in
the kingdom of their Father* (Matt. 13:41-43). While
judgment is expressed, it is evident that the dominant
thought of the parable is the purification of the kingdom
from those things which hinder its progress and which
veil the true character of its subjects. In the second parable—that of the Drag Net and the separation of the
good and bad fishes, the application is the same with the
emphasis more especially upon the judgment. *So shall
it be at the end of the world: the angels shall come
forth, and sever the wicked from the just, and shall cast
them into the furnace of fire: there shall be wailing and
gnashing of teeth* (Matt. 13:49-50).

Turning from the Gospels to the Epistles, we find the
Second Advent presented in the light of its concomitants
—the resurrection, the judgment, and the consummation
of all things. These subjects must receive consideration
later. It is sufficient here, to mention only a few of the
scriptures in which the Second Advent is given promin-

ence. St. Paul places it in close time relation to the resurrection, making the resurrection of the righteous dead to precede immediately the translation of the living saints. *For if we believe that Jesus died and rose again, even so them also which sleep in Jesus will God bring with him. For this we say unto you by the word of the Lord, that we which are alive and remain unto the coming of the Lord shall not prevent them which are asleep. For the Lord himself shall descend from heaven with a shout, with the voice of the archangel, and with the trump of God: and the dead in Christ shall rise first: then we which are alive and remain shall be caught up together with them in the clouds, to meet the Lord in the air: and so shall we ever be with the Lord* (I Thess. 4:14-17). Here it is evident that the coming of Jesus *with* His saints (the dead in Christ whose souls have already gone to be with Him), and the coming of Jesus *for* His saints (those that are alive and remain) must be associated not only with the same event, but must be regarded also, as indicating the order of the happenings in that event. "That the return of the Lord will not be simply a momentarily becoming visible from heaven, but a return to earth, is according to the Scriptures beyond doubt. Those dwellers on the earth, who, according to I Thess. 4:17, are caught up to meet Him in the air, must certainly be conceived of as then returning with the heavenly host again to the earth. They form an escort to the King, who personally comes to this part of His royal domain. Simultaneously with the coming of Christ takes place the first resurrection. The believers, who live to witness this appearing of Christ upon earth, are without dying, by an instantaneous change, made meet for the new condition; and the departed who are ripe for the life of resurrection, live and reign with Christ on earth" (VAN OOSTERZEE, *Christian Dogmatics,* II, pp. 798, 799). St. Peter places the Second Advent in a time relation to the *consumatio seculi* or final consummation of the present order. *But the day of the Lord will come as a thief in the night; in the which the heavens shall pass away with a great noise, and the elements shall melt with fervent heat, the earth also and the works that are therein shall be burned up. Seeing then that all these things shall be dissolved, what manner of persons ought ye to be in all holy conversation and godliness* (II Peter 3: 10, 11). Here the Second Advent is connected with the day of the Lord, which introduces another phase of the subject.

We may conclude, then, that as an event the Second Coming of Christ will be associated in time with the resurrection, the judgment and the final consummation. As directly related to the work of Jesus Christ, it may be summed up in a threefold purpose. (1) It is a part of His total mission of redemption. As the incarnate Son in heaven, He is still subordinate to the Father, and consequently is sent of the Father on this final mission. *And he shall send Jesus Christ, which before was preached unto you: whom the heaven must receive until the times of the restitution of all things, which God hath spoken by the mouth of all his holy prophets since the world began* (Acts 3: 20, 21). (2) It marks the day of the Lord. "Thus it is the coming, in one sense, in another, it is the Second Coming, or the coming again of the Lord. Hence also, (3) the scripture rises above both these phrases, and speaks of that future event as *his day,* or *that day,* or *the day of Jesus Christ* (Cf. Luke 17: 24; II Tim. 1: 18; Phil. 1: 6), which is in the new economy all that the day of Jehovah was in the old. The day of the Lord is the horizon of the entire New Testament: the period of His most decisive manifestation in a glorious revelation of Himself which could not be, and is never, predicated of any but a divine Person" (POPE, *Compend. Chr. Th.,* III, p. 388).

DEVELOPMENT OF THE DOCTRINE IN THE CHURCH

Our study of the scriptural basis of the Second Advent has made it clear that this doctrine had an apostolic emphasis. Three things characterized their teaching: (1) the prominence which they gave to eschatological subjects; (2) their association of the hope of eternal life with the Person of the risen Christ and His prom-

ised return; and (3) that this hope of eternal life reached
out beyond this period of earthly development to a new
heaven and a new earth. Furthermore, the New Testament seems to indicate that the apostles themselves expected a speedy return of their Lord, and the Church
evidently shared with them in this hope. It is for this
reason that Dr. Dorner calls the Second Coming the
oldest Christian dogma. Consequently, the Church during its persecutions and martyrdoms, opposed heathenism by a complete renunciation of the world and a firm
confidence of final triumph when Christ should come
again. It is not surprising, therefore, that we find this
same note in the writing of the earlier Fathers. Clement
of Rome (c. 95) in his First Epistle says, "Of a truth,
soon and suddenly shall His will be accomplished, as
the Scriptures also bear witness, saying 'Speedily will
He come, and will not tarry:' and 'The Lord shall suddenly come to His temple, even the Holy One, for whom
ye look'" (XXIII, 5). Ignatius of Antioch (d.c. 107) in
a letter to the church says, "The last times are upon us.
Let us therefore be of a reverent spirit, and fear the long-
suffering of God, that it tend not to our condemnation"
(*To the Ephesians*, XI, 1). We may say, then, that the
attitude of the earlier Fathers was one of expectancy, one
of watching and praying for the soon coming of Christ,
their Lord.

In one of the anonymous writings of this period, generally attributed to Barnabas and sometimes dated as early as A.D. 79, we find
the following: "Therefore, my children, in six days, that is, in six
thousand years, all things will be finished. 'And he rested on the
seventh day.' This meaneth: when His Son, coming again, shall destroy
the time of the wicked man, and judge the ungodly, and change the
sun, and the moon, and the stars, then shall He truly rest on the
seventh day" (XV, 5).

From one of the visions in the Shepherd of Hermas, we have the
following: "You have escaped from great tribulation on account of
your faith, and because you did not doubt in the presence of such a
beast. Go, therefore, and tell the elect of the Lord His mighty deeds,
and say to them that this beast is a type of the great tribulation that
is coming. If then ye prepare yourselves, and repent with all your
heart, and turn to the Lord, it will be possible for you to escape it,
if your heart be pure and spotless, and ye spend the rest of the days
of your life in serving the Lord blamelessly" (*Visions*, IV, ii, 4-5).

Ignatius writes to Polycarp saying, "Weigh carefully the times.
Look for Him who is above all time, eternal and invisible, yet who became visible for our sakes."

The personal return of Christ was very early associated with the idea of a millennium (from the Latin *mille*, a thousand) or a reign of Christ on earth for the period of a thousand years. Those who embraced this doctrine were known as Chiliasts (from the Greek χιλιάς, a thousand). The development of the doctrine of the Second Advent must, therefore, in a large measure include a treatment of the various theories of the millennium which have developed in the history of the Church. The history of millennialism falls into three main periods: (1) The Earlier Period, from the Apostolic Age to the Reformation; (2) The Reformation Period, to the middle of the eighteenth century; and (3) The Modern Period, from the middle of the eighteenth century to the present.

The Earlier Period. It is commonly agreed by historians that, from the death of the apostles to the time of Origen, Chiliasm, or what is now known as premillennialism, was the dominant, if not the generally accepted faith of the Church. Two fundamental affirmations characterized this doctrine—that the Scriptures teach us to look for a millennium, or universal reign of righteousness on the earth; and that this millennial age will be introduced by the personal, visible return of the Lord Jesus. It is very frequently asserted that this theory was brought over from Judaism, and to a certain extent, doubtless, this is true; for it appears far more prominently among the Jewish Christians than in the Gentile churches. But Christian Chiliasm must be distinguished, both from Judaism on the one hand, and a pseudo-chiliasm on the other. Over against Judaism it maintained: (1) that the inheritance of the kingdom

Dr. Blunt gives this description of Chiliasm. "The Millenarians, or Chiliasts, accepting this prophecy literally (Rev. 20:1-7), hold, that after the destruction of the powers symbolized by the beast and the false prophets, Satan will be 'bound,' that is, his power will be suspended for the period of a thousand years, or for the period represented by a thousand years; that there will be a first resurrection of martyrs, and of those worthy to share in the martyr's crown; that for the thousand years these will live and reign with Christ on earth, in free communion with the heavenly powers; that after this will be the general resurrection. There are on both sides many shades and varieties of teaching, but the crucial point is that of the first and second resurrection."

is conditioned solely by regeneration, and not by race or ritual observances; (2) that the nature of the kingdom is not carnal or materialistic, but suited to a sanctified spirit, and to a body at once spiritual and incorruptible; and (3) that the millennium is only a transitional stage and not the final state of the world. For this reason, Dr. Dorner maintains that so far from being derivable from it, it may in part be more justly regarded as a polemic against Judaism (Cf. DORNER, *Doctrine of the Person of Christ*, I, p. 408). Over against the false and fanatical theories, the Church maintained that the millennium is to be introduced by the return of Christ, and condemned all attempts of the pseudochiliasts to institute this reign of righteousness by material force. Nitzsch points out also, that the doctrine was already received by the Gentile Christians before the close of the first century, and was expressly rejected during the first half of the second century by the Gnostics only. Millennialism received a fresh impulse, doubtless, from the persecutions which came upon the Church, during which the saints took comfort in looking forward to a speedy deliverance by the return of Christ. The doctrine is first mentioned in the Epistles of Barnabas (c.

Semisch holds that the ultimate root of millenarianism is the popular notion of the Messiah current among the Jews. The prophecies of the Messiah had affirmed that a period of peace and triumph of Israel would follow the establishment of His kingdom. The fancy of the Jewish people, misinterpreting these prophecies, reveled in dreams of an external kingdom, in which the Messiah should reign from Jerusalem, and inaugurate an era of inexpressible happiness. Some of these thoughts passed over to the Christians, who, however, made this period of the visible reign of the Messiah on earth only the prelude of a second and final stage of heavenly glory.

Professor Moses Stuart calls attention to the fact, "That the great mass of Jewish Rabbins have believed and taught the doctrine of the resurrection of the just in the days of the Messiah's development, there can be no doubt on the part of him who has made any considerable investigation of this matter. The specific limitation of this to the commencement of the millennium, seems to be peculiar to John" (Commentary on the Apocalypse, I, p. 177).

Joseph Mede says, "Though the ancient Jews had no distinct knowledge of such an order in the resurrection as first and second, but only of the resurrection in gross and general . . . . yet they looked for such a resurrection, wherein those that rose again should reign some time upon the earth. . . . . In fine, the second and universal resurrection, with the state of the saints after it, now so clearly revealed in Christianity, seems to have been less known to the ancient church of the Jews than the first, and the state to accompany it (Cf. MEDE, *Works*, II, p. 943).

120). Hermas (c. 140), Papias (c. 163), Justin (c. 165) and Irenaeus (c. 202) all interpreted the twentieth chapter of Revelation in a literal manner, and therefore held that between the two resurrections Christ should reign over Jerusalem, either literally or spiritually, for a thousand years. Justin says, "I and others, who are right-minded Christians on all points, are assured that there will be a resurrection of the dead and a thousand years in Jerusalem, which will then be built, adorned and enlarged.....There was a certain man with us whose name was John, one of the apostles of Christ, who prophesied, by a revelation made to him, that those who believed in our Christ would dwell a thousand years in Jerusalem; and that thereafter, the general, and in short the eternal resurrection and judgment of all men would likewise take place." (Trypho LXXX and LXXXI) Papias wrote extravagantly of the millennial fertility and fruitage of the earth, and these were reproduced in some measure by Irenaeus. The latter places the coming of Antichrist just before the inauguration of the millennial reign. He teaches that the just will be resurrected by the descended Saviour, and dwell in Jerusalem with the remnant of believers in the world, being there disciplined for the state of incorruption which they are to enjoy in the New Jerusalem which is from above, and of which the earthly Jerusalem is an image. Tertullian (d. 240) says, "Of the heavenly kingdom, this is the process. After its thousand years are over, within which period are completed the resurrection of the saints, who rise sooner or later, according to their deserts, there will ensue the destruction of the world and the conflagration of all things at the judgment." No trace of millennialism is found in the writings of Clement of Rome, Ignatius, Polycarp, Tatian, Athenagoras or Theophilus. Hippolytus (c. 239) wrote an elaborate treatise on the rise and overthrow of Antichrist, whose manifestation was generally regarded as preceding the Second Advent. Cyprian (c. 258) does not express any well-defined views on the subject.

The third century was the flowering period of chiliasm, but the doctrine was carried to extreme lengths by the Ebionites, a Jewish sect of Christians, and later by the Montanists. It is easy to understand how this doctrine would be open to perversion and misunderstanding. The new heavens and the new earth would naturally be described in the language of temporal felicity, such as is found in the Old Testament, and this could easily be perverted to mean a carnal kingdom. Thus Dr. Blunt says that "there can be no doubt that some, perhaps many, held the doctrine in a carnal sense, but it is a misrepresentation to attribute that sense to such writers as, for example, Irenaeus." Cerinthus, a Gnostic with Judaistic tendencies, and the opponent of St. John, is said to have perverted this doctrine by promising a millennium of sensual luxury. Mosheim, however, endeavors to show that this originated with Caius and Dionysius, who, to suppress the doctrine, made it appear that Cerinthus was the author of it. The Montanists began as a reform movement in Phrygia, during the latter part of the second century under the leadership of Montanus, who seems to have regarded it as a special mission to complete in himself and by his system, the perfection of the Church. He was regarded by his followers as one to whom the Holy Spirit had made special revelations. Rebelling against the secularism of the Church, Montanism presented a model of church discipline such as they conceived the nearness of Christ's coming demanded. Long and stringent fasts were established, celibacy enjoined and a rigid penitential system set up.

Origen (185-254) was the chief opponent of the earlier chiliasm, and Augustine (353-430) its later opponent. Origen in his "De Principiis" says that those "who receive the representations of Scripture according to the understanding of the apostles, entertain the hope that the saints will eat indeed, but that it will be the bread of life. . . . . By this food of wisdom the understanding is restored to the image and likeness of God, so that . . . . the man will be capable of receiving instruction in that Jerusalem, the city of the saints."

Augustine was at one time a chiliast, but abandoned the doctrine, it is said, because of the influence and misrepresentations of his enemies, particularly, Eusebius. He then developed what is now known as the Augustinian view of the Millennium, which afterward became prevalent.

Montanism was the occasion of the opposition to the millennial theory which arose in the earlier part of the third century. Caius of Rome (c. 210) is said to have been the first to write against it, and greatly embarrassed the situation by referring to those who held this doctrine as heretics. The chief opposition, however, came from the Alexandrian School. Origen, who re-

Lactantius gives a rather detailed account of his doctrine of the Second Advent in the Epitome (LXXII). He says, "Then the heaven shall be opened in a tempest, and Christ shall descend with great power, and there shall go before Him a fiery brightness and a countless host of angels, and all the multitude of the wicked shall be destroyed, and torrents of blood shall flow, and the leader himself shall escape, and having often renewed his army, shall for the fourth time engage in battle, in which, being taken, with all the other tyrants, he shall be delivered up to be burnt. But the prince also of the demons himself, the author and contriver of evils, being bound with fiery chains, shall be imprisoned, that the world may receive peace, and the earth, harassed through so many years, may rest. Therefore, peace being made, and every evil suppressed, that the righteous king and conqueror will institute a great judgment on earth respecting the living and the dead, and will deliver all the nations into subjection to the righteous who are alive, and will raise the righteous dead to eternal life, and will Himself reign with them on earth, and will build the holy city, and this kingdom of the righteous shall be for a thousand years. Throughout that time the stars shall be more brilliant, and the brightness of the sun shall be increased, and the moon shall not be subject to decrease. Then the rain of blessing shall descend from God at morning and evening, and the earth shall bring forth all her fruit without the labor of men. Honey shall drop from rock, fountains of milk and wine shall abound. The beasts shall lay aside their ferocity and become mild, the wolf shall roam among the flocks without doing harm, the calf shall feed with the lion, the dove shall be united with the hawk, the serpent shall have no poison; no animal shall live by bloodshed, for God shall supply to all abundant and harmless food. But when the thousand years shall be fulfilled, and the prince of demons loosed, the nations will rebel against the righteous, and an innumerable multitude will come to storm the city of the saints. Then the last judgment of God will come to pass against the nations, for He will shake the earth from its foundations, and the cities shall be overthrown, and He shall rain upon the wicked fire with brimstone, and hail, and they shall be on fire, and slay each other. But the righteous shall for a little space be concealed under the earth, until the destruction of the nations is accomplished, and after the third day they shall come forth, and see the plains covered with carcasses. Then there shall be an earthquake, and the mountains shall be rent, and valleys shall sink down to a profound depth, and into this the bodies of the dead shall be heaped together, and its name shall be called Polyandrion (a name sometimes given to cemeteries because many men are borne thither). After these things, God will renew the world, and transform the righteous into forms of angels, that, they may serve God forever and ever; and this will be the kingdom of God, which shall have no end. Then also the wicked shall rise again, but not to life, but to punishment, for God shall raise these also, when the second resurrection takes place, that, being condemned to eternal torments and delivered to eternal fires, they may suffer the punishments which they deserve for their crimes."

garded matter as the seat of evil, referred to the view of an earthly kingdom of Christ, full of physical delights, as "an empty figment," and "a Judaizing fable." Nepos, a bishop in Egypt revived the doctrine, holding that the promises in the Bible should be interpreted as the Jews understood them. He supposed that there would be a certain millennium of material luxury on this earth. His work entitled, *A Refutation of the Allegorists*, was answered by Dionysius in another entitled *On the Promises*. Methodius, bishop of Tyre (d. 311) defended the millennial doctrines against Origen, but the decline had set in, and the last apology for it, was a pamphlet by Apollinarius of Laodicea against the positions of Dionysius. In the West, the doctrine was maintained for a longer period, its chief exponents being Lactantius (c. 320) and Victorinus, bishop of Petau, who flourished c. 290 A.D.). Even Jerome did not dare to condemn the position on chiliasm. The fate of the doctrine, however, for this period, was settled by Augustine (De Civitate Dei xx, 7-9), who declared that the Church was the kingdom of God on earth. Eschatological questions sank into insignificance, once the Church had won the protection of the state. As to the thousand years mentioned in the Apocalypse, Augustine suggests that they denote either the last thousand years of the world's history, or the whole duration of the world—the number one thousand being a reference not so much to a definite period as to the totality of time. By the reign of the saints during the millennial period, he means nothing more than the dominion which pertains to the Church. "The Church even now is the kingdom of Christ, and the kingdom of heaven. Accordingly, even now His saints reign with Him, though otherwise than as they shall reign hereafter" (De Civitate Dei, XX, 7-9). The first resurrection according to Augustine was the spiritual resurrection of the soul from sin. For the remainder of this period, millennialism was practically an obsolete doctrine. The clergy possessed the kingdom for a thousand years in the Church as triumphant over kings and princes. Semisch says that "the

circles which were prophetic of the reformation period
looked for the regeneration of the Church, not from the
visible coming of Christ, but in a return to apostolic
poverty and piety, or to the enthronement of a righteous pope. Peter de Olivia explained the Second Coming by the operation of the Holy Ghost in the heart."

From the time of Augustine to the Reformation, the
doctrines of chiliasm were given but little prominence.
The Apostles' Creed—an early document, but dating
in its unchanged form from c. 390; the Nicene Creed
as revised at Constantinople (381); and the Athanasian
Creed (c. 449) to which an anathema is attached, were
the accepted standards of the Church. However, these
were interpreted in opposition to the millennial theory,
for Rome was anti-chiliastic. But Dr. Blunt cites the
Formula Doctrinae by Gelassius Cyzicenus of the Council of Nicea, to show that the Scriptures were understood by that body, to teach that the saints received their
reward under the reign of Christ on earth; and that the

The reference to the Formula Doctrinæ of the Council of Nicea is
as follows: "We look for new heavens and a new earth, when there
shall have shown the appearing and kingdom of the great God, and
our Saviour Jesus Christ: and then, as Daniel saith, the saints of the
Most High shall take the kingdom. And the earth shall be pure, holy,
the earth of the living, and not of the dead (which David foreseeing
with the eye of faith, exclaims, I believe verily to see the goodness of
the Lord in the land of the living), the earth of the gentle and lowly.
For, blessed, saith the Lord, are the meek, for they shall inherit the
earth; and the prophet saith, the feet of the poor and needy shall
tread it" (Cf. art. "Millennium," in Blunt's Dictionary).

Some of the sects catalogued as heretical, are such only on certain doctrines. Many of them, such as are mentioned above were in
reality prophets of the Reformation, and were classified as heretics solely
because of their opposition to what they regarded as the secularization
of the Church. Thus Mr. Wesley speaks of Montanus as "not only a
good man, but one of the best men then upon earth" (Works, XI, p.
485). Doubtless this was true as to purpose and intent, but the historical records of the excesses of the Montanists cannot be denied, although many of these were excrescences and not typical of the movement as a whole. Hurst, Milner and other church historians take practically the same position in regard to the Waldenses, the Cathari and
similar sects, seeing in them the precursors of the Reformation.

From the tenth to the fourteenth century the notion prevailed that
the end of the world was at hand. The state establishment of Christianity by Constantine was thought to be intended by the figure of the
first resurrection; the thousand years' reign was conceived of as actually
passing, and drawing to a close; Antichrist would then appear, and
the end of all things would promptly ensue. These expectations find
their expression in the devotional literature of the period.—CRIPPEN,
Hist. Chr. Doct., p. 233.

Nicene statement, "He shall come again, with glory, to judge both the quick and the dead: whose kingdom shall have no end," is to be interpreted in the light of a millennial reign. In spite of the opposition, Harnack points out that the doctrine "still lived on in the lower strata of society." It was preserved in the teachings of the Waldenses, the Paulicians, the Albigenses, the Cathari, and many of the Mystics, although in those dark ages, connected with much that was erratic and unorthodox.

The Reformation Period. The beginning of the Reformation is generally dated from the time when Luther began his public labors, or about A.D. 1517. During this period the doctrine of the millennium which had fallen into disrepute was again revived. Several things were conducive to this renewed emphasis. *First,* there was a growing decline of the papacy, which was regarded as one of the sure signs of the soon coming of Christ. The Reformers generally held that the pope was the Antichrist. *Second,* there were many strange natural occurrences during this period, such as comets

As we have shown, there was very little taught concerning a future millennium during the period from Augustine to the Reformation. Chiliasm was almost annihilated. From the time when the Council of Rome under Pope Damascus formally denounced it in A.D. 373, its condemnation was so effective. Baronius, a Roman Catholic historian of the sixteenth century, writing concerning the millennialists views of the fifth century says, "Moreover the figments of the Millenaries being now rejected everywhere, and derided by the learned with hisses and laughter, and being also put under the ban, were entirely extirpated!" This was the general attitude of the Church at the beginning of the Reformation.

Elliott in his *Horæ Apocalypticæ,* a learned and exhaustive treatise in four volumes, sums up the millennial view at the beginning of the Reformation as follows: "That the Millennium of Satan's binding, and the saints' reigning, dated from Christ's ministry, when He beheld Satan fall like lightning from heaven; it being meant to signify the triumph over Satan in the hearts of true believers; and that the subsequent figuration of Gog and Magog indicated the coming of Antichrist at the end of the world—the one thousand years being a figurative numeral, expressive of the whole period intervening. It supposed the resurrection taught, to be that of dead souls from the death of sin to the life of righteousness; the beast conquered by the saints, meant the wicked world; its image, a hypocritical profession; the resurrection being continuous, till the end of time, when the universal resurrection and the final judgment would take place." Dr. Elliott points out that this view prevailed from Augustine's time among certain writers to the Reformation; and also that it was held, although in a more ecclesiastical sense and with certain modifications, after the Reformation, by Luther, Bullinger, Bale, Pareus and others (Cf. Taylor, *The Reign of Christ on Earth,* pp. 114-116).

and earthquakes.   Then, too, there were many national
changes—all of which produced an unrest and a nervous
tension which resulted in many and various forms of
mass hysteria. The Anabaptists determined to prepare
the way by violence and consequently established a new
Zion at Muenster in 1534, organized along communistic
lines. All these things seemed to be indicative of the
approaching end of the world. The Reformers shared
in this expectation of the soon coming of Christ, but
kept themselves free from fanatical teachings. Also,
they appeared to studiously avoid all millennial doctrines. The Helvetic and Augsburg Confessions condemn the excesses of the Anabaptists, as does also the
English Confession of Edward VI, from which the
Thirty-nine Articles were condensed. It is commonly
stated that these creeds condemn premillennialism as
merely a Jewish opinion, brought over without due
warrant, into the Christian Church. A careful consideration of the articles in question, does not seem to sustain this position. Article XVII of the Augsburg Confession as translated by Philip Schaff, is as follows:
"They condemn others, also, who now scatter abroad
Jewish opinions, that, before the resurrection of the
dead, the godly shall occupy the kingdom of the world,
the wicked being everywhere suppressed. (SCHAFF,
Creeds of Christendom). Melanchthon, who wrote the
Confession, explains Article XVII as follows: "The
Church in this life is never to attain to a position of universal triumph and prosperity, but is to remain de-

Sheldon sums up the attitude toward chiliasm during the Reformation period as follows: "By all the larger communions chiliasm or
millenarianism was decidedly repudiated. It had, however, considerable
currency among the Anabaptists. Some of the mystical writers taught
kindred views. The English Mede and the French Calvinist, Jurieu, held
the early patristic theory. In the days of the Rebellion and the Com-
monwealth, quite a number of the sectaries were millenarians. Such
was the party designated as Fifth Monarchy Men. John Milton believed
in a future visible appearing and reign with Christ upon earth—a reign
of a thousand years. Near the close of the period, William Peterson attracted attention as an enthusiastic advocate of the same doctrine. At
the same time, a departure from the interpretation of Augustine began
to be made by some who, like him, did not believe in the visible reign
of Christ on earth. Instead of placing the beginning of the millennium
in the past, they located it in the future. Whitby and Vitringa were
prominent representatives of this view" (SHELDON, *Hist. Chr. Doct.*, II,
p. 213).

pressed, and subject to afflictions and adversities, until the time of the resurrection of the dead (Corpus Reformatorum XXVI, p. 361). From this it is evident that the Article does not condemn premillennialism unless a prior or first resurrection be denied; otherwise it condemns in strong words, the theory of postmillennialism which looks for an era of spiritual triumph previous to the Second Advent of Christ.

Beginning with the seventeenth century, millennialism again came into prominence, due perhaps to the religious wars in Germany, the persecution of the Huguenots in France, and the Revolution in England. The immediate occasion of the interests in millennial studies, was the publication of the *Clavis Apocalypticae* by Joseph Mede (1586-1638), commonly known as "the illustrious Mede." Dr. Elliott states that "his works have generally been thought to constitute an era in the solution of Apocalyptic mysteries, for which he was looked upon and written of, as a man almost inspired." In Germany Jacob Spener was regarded as holding millennial views. Jacob Boehme, the mystic, (1624) warmly

There were many in this period who held to a firm belief in the Second Advent, and who were known to have held millennial views, but have written to no great extent on the subject. Some like Samuel Rutherford (1600-1661); Jeremy Taylor (1613-1677); Richard Baxter (1615-1691) and Joseph Alleine (1623-1668) were devotional writers, and their views of the Second Advent are largely expressed in their heart-longings for the return of their Lord. John Bunyan (1628-1688) "the Prince of Dreamers"; John Milton (1608-1674) "the Christian Homer"; Matthew Henry (1663-1714), the celebrated commentator; John Cocceius (d. 1669), professor of theology at Bremen; Isaac Newton (1642-1727) and a host of others. The following list of names may be helpful—Joseph Farmer, Peter Sterry, John Durant, Simon Menno (founder of the Mennonites), John Alstead, and Robert Maton.

Interpretations of the Book of Revelation are divided into three classes: (1) the Praeterist (held by Grotius, Moses Stuart and Warren), which regards the prophecy as mainly fulfilled in the age immediately succeeding the time of the apostles (666=Neron Kaisar); (2) the Continuous (held by Isaac Newton, Vitringa, Bengel, Elliott, Kelly, and Cumming), which regards the whole as a continuous prophetical history, extending from the first age until the end of things (666=Lateinos); Hengstenberg and Alford hold substantially this view, though they regard the seven seals, trumpets, and vials as synchronological, each succeeding set going over the same ground and exhibiting it in some special aspect; (3) the Futurist (held by Maitland and Todd), which considers the book as describing events yet to occur, during the times immediately preceding and following the coming of the Lord.—STRONG, *Systematic Theology*, III, p. 1000.

advocated millennialism, as did the Lutheran Bishop Peterson at a later date (1705). Among the outstanding premillennialists associated more or less closely with Mede, may be mentioned Dr. William Twisse (1575-1646), a pupil of Mede, and the first moderator of the Westminster Assembly of Divines; Nathaniel Homes, whose *Revelation Revealed* was published in 1653; Thomas Burnet (1635-1715), known for his *Sacred Theory of the Earth,* published in Latin (1681) with an English translation (1684-1689); Thomas Goodwin (1600-1679) an independent minister of the rigid Calvinistic type (Works in five volumes, 1681-1704) and Joseph Perry, whose work entitled *The Glory of Christ's Visible Kingdom,* was published in 1721.

The dominant type of premillennialism, held by the writers of this period may be summed up in the following general statements: (1) They identified in point of time, the rapture, the revelation, the first resurrection, the conflagration, and the creation of the new heavens and the new earth, and taught that all these events occurred before the millennium. (2) They taught that the church was complete before the millennium—the wicked having been destroyed by the brightness of His coming; and (3) they identified the millennium and the period of the investigative judgment. On the second and

Mede comments on I Thess. 4:14-18 as follows: "After this, our gathering together unto Christ at His coming, we shall henceforth never lose His presence, but always enjoy it. . . . . The saints being translated into the air, is to do honor to their Lord and King at His return . . . . and they may be preserved during the conflagration of the earth, and the works thereof: that as Noah and his family were preserved from the deluge by being lifted up above the waters in the ark, so should the saints at the conflagration be lifted up in the clouds, unto their ark, Christ, to be preserved there from the deluge of fire, wherein the wicked shall be consumed." In II Peter 3:8 he says, "But whereas, I mentioned the day of judgment, lest ye might mistake it for a short day, or a day of few hours, I would not, beloved, have you ignorant that one day is with the Lord as a thousand years, and a thousand years as one day . . . . these words are commonly taken as an argument why God should not be thought slack in His promise, but the first Fathers took it otherwise, and besides it proves it not. For the question is not whether the time be long or short in respect of God, but whether it be long or short in respect of us, otherwise not only a thousand years, but an hundred thousand years, are in the eyes of God no more than one day is to us, and so it would not seem long to God if the day of judgment should be deferred till then (Cf. Joseph Mede, *Works,* III, p. 611; IV, p. 776).

third points, there were more or less differences in opinion. Mede held that a distinction must be made between the state of the New Jerusalem, and the state of the nations which walk in the light of it. The New Jerusalem is not the whole Church but the metropolis of it. He says, "I make this state of the Church to belong to the Second Advent of Christ, or the day of the judgment, when Christ shall appear in the clouds of heaven to destroy all the professed enemies of His Church and kingdom, and deliver the creature from that bondage of corruption brought upon it for the sin of

Nathaniel Homes was a Puritan writer of great ability, and a contemporary of Joseph Mede. In his *Revelation Revealed,* he says, "In that new creation Christ restores all things to their perfection, and every believer to his; to the end that all believers may jointly and co-ordinately rule over the whole world, and all things therein, next under Christ their Head. I say all, and not a part, as some unwarily publish. And I say jointly, and not one part of the saints to usurp authority over all the rest, as many dream. And co-ordinately, all upon equal terms, not some saints to rule by deputies made of the rest of the saints, as men seem to interpret." Concerning those who are "reserved out of the fire to be an appendix of the new creation, as Lactantius, Sixtus, Senensis, and Dr. Twisse understand," he says that these "by virtue of the Adamic covenant, shall be restored in soul and body to the natural perfection which Adam had in the state of innocency; but being mutable, they shall fall, when in like manner they are assaulted by Satan. Out of these shall spring the brood of Gog and Magog. . . . . The Church, being now as heaven on earth, the false-hearted spawn of the future Gog and Magog, shall be remote on earth near their future hell. . . . . But if these hypocrites were nearer the Church, might they perhaps be converted? We answer, No; for it is (if we may use the word) the fate of the millenary period, I mean, God's righteous peremptory sentence, that as all that time there shall be no degenerating of believers, so no more regenerating of any believers."—HOMES, *Revelation Revealed,* pp. 279, 282.

Thomas Burnet agreed with both Mede and Homes as to the time of the conflagration and the new heavens and the new earth, and also with the completion of the Church which should reign in a resurrection state on the new earth. "Neither is there any distinction made," he says, "that I find by St. John, of two sorts of saints in the millennium, the one in heaven (in resurrection bodies), the other upon earth (in a mortal state). This is such an idea of the millennium as to my eye hath neither beauty nor foundation in Scripture." He admits the difficulty of accounting for the wicked, who at the close of the millennium, will compass the camp of the saints and the beloved city (Rev. 20:7-9). His own solution is as follows: "It seems probable that there will be a double race of mankind in the future earth, very different from one another. . . . . The one born from heaven, sons of God and of the resurrection, who are the true saints and heirs of the millennium: the others born of the earth, sons of the earth, generated from the slime of the ground and heat of the sun, as brute creatures were at the first. This second progeny, or generation of men, in the future earth, I understand to be signified by the prophet under these borrowed or feigned names of Gog and Magog."—BURNET, *Theory of the Earth,* IV, p. 7.

man." Mede also taught that this state is neither before nor after, but is itself the day of judgment; and that the Jews never understood the expression to mean otherwise than a period of many years' continuance. Homes differed from Mede in holding that only the open and obstinate of the ungodly would be destroyed by the conflagration, the rest being reserved out of the fire as "an appendix of the new creation." Burnet taught that all the wicked would perish in the conflagration; while Perry went still farther and denied the existence of either saints or sinners in the flesh during the millennium. Since these writers all maintained that the Church was complete at the time of the Second Advent, their problem was to explain the appearance of the wicked at the close of the millennium. Homes held, that those who escaped the conflagration would be restored in body and soul to the natural perfection which Adam had in the state of innocency, but being mutable, would likewise fall when assaulted by Satan. Burnet was forced to adopt the position of a double race, which he regarded as being very different from each other—the one sons of God by resurrection, the other, sons of the earth generated from the slime of the ground and the heat of the sun. Since Perry maintained that the earth

On the subject of the completion of the Church, Perry states that "It is certain that when Christ personally comes from heaven will be the time of the open solemnization of the marriage glory between Him and His Spouse; and, if so, then the Bride must be ready against that time, as it is expressed in this text, 'And his wife hath made herself ready'; which cannot be if they were not all converted before Christ comes. For this I think is undeniable that by the 'wife,' 'bride' or 'spouse' of Christ, the whole elect must be understood. . . . . How can it be thought that Christ when He comes from heaven to celebrate that marriage feast between Himself and His people, that He should have a lame and imperfect bride, as she must be, if some should be with Christ, in a perfect and glorified state, and some of His mystical body at the same time in an imperfect and unglorified condition."—JOSEPH PERRY, *The Glory of Christ's Visible Kingdom*, pp. 225, 226. Perry also states that "The last restitution, or the restitution of all things, will not be, as I conceive, until Christ's personal coming. As the heaven received Him, so it will retain Him until this time, in which all things shall be restored. . . . . When though this restitution of all things takes in the restitution of the creation unto its paradisiacal state; yet it is certain that the bringing in of the elect by regenerating grace, and completing the whole mystical body of Christ, is the principal part of that restitution, they being principally concerned in it, and for whose sake all other creatures are to be restored; all which shows that there will be no conversion when Christ is come" (*Ibid.*, p. 224).

during the millennium would be in the exclusive possession of men in the resurrected state, he resorts to an explanation "which he knows is out of the common road of almost all expositors," that is, that the Gog and Magog who will rise at the end of the thousand years, "will consist of the number of all the wicked when raised out of their graves." These are but a few of the difficulties which arose in connection with this subject, and which formed the basis of further discussion in the next period.

The Modern Period. Beginning with the middle of the eighteenth century, a new period in the history of millennialism was ushered in by the publication of Bengel's *Commentary on Revelation* (1740), and his *Sermons for the People* (1748). Attention was soon turned to the question of prophecy, and the study of Revelation became popular in pious churchly circles. The French Revolution at the end of the eighteenth century, gave a fresh impetus to prophetical studies, and premillennialism was adopted by many of great scholastic ability and high standing in the Church. Bengel

Bengel wrote, "Apart from all the details of chronological computation, we can but think ourselves approaching very near to the termination of a great period; neither can we get rid of the idea, that troublesome times will soon supersede the repose who have so long enjoyed. At the approaching termination of any great and remarkable period, many striking events have been found to take place simultaneously, and many others in quick succession; and this after a course of intermediate ages in which nothing unusual has occurred."—BENGEL, *Memoirs and Writings*, p. 311.

Dr. John Gill (1697-1771) was an English contemporary of Bengel. Concerning the Millennium or Personal Reign of Christ, he says, "I observe that Christ will have a special, peculiar, glorious, and visible kingdom, in which He will reign personally on earth. (1) I call it a special, peculiar kingdom, different from the kingdom of nature, and from His spiritual kingdom. (2) It will be very glorious and visible; hence His appearing and kingdom are put together (II Tim. 4:1). (3) This kingdom will be, after all the enemies of Christ and His people are removed out of the way. (4) Antichrist will be destroyed; an angel, who is no other than Christ, will then personally descend to bind Satan and all his angels. (5) This kingdom of Christ will be bounded by two resurrections; by the first resurrection, or the resurrection of the just, at which it will begin; and by the second resurrection, or the resurrection of the wicked, at which it will end, or nearly. (6) This kingdom will be before the general judgment, especially of the wicked. John, after he had given an account of the former (Rev. 20), relates a vision of the latter. (7) This glorious, visible kingdom of Christ will be on earth, and not in heaven; and so is distinct from the kingdom of heaven, or ultimate glory."

(1687-1751) it will be recalled, was the originator of
the modern Biblical Movement and the author of the
Apparatus Criticus (Cf. I, p. 90). Dr. Adam Clarke says
that "In him were united two rare qualifications—the
deepest piety and the most extensive learning"; and
Mr. Wesley is thought to have followed him in his interpretation of the Apocalypse.

Bengel held a peculiar position concerning the millennium, arguing from Revelation 20: that there is a
double millennium, namely, a thousand years' reign
on earth, followed by a thousand years' reign in heaven;
the first the seventh, and the second the eighth thousand
years from creation. He believed that the millennium
on earth would be a time of rulers, marriage, agriculture
and all the course of life as it is now known. His belief
concerning the completeness of the Church, led at length
to the adoption of the Bridehood theories, as limitations
of this completeness. A distinction is made, therefore,
between the "Church as the Bride," and the whole
number of the "saved" regarded as outside the bridehood—the "Church of the Afterborn" as contrasted with
the "Church of the Firstborn." Thus Dr. Bickersteth
says that the "Church which is to appear as a complete

Dr. Bickersteth says, "The Bride consists of all who have believed
up to the commencement of the millennium. These alone are the
mystical body of Christ. . . . . But after they are completed, at the
Second Advent, the earth will be peopled by nations of the saved, in
flesh and blood, friends, companions, servants of the Bridegroom—a
totally different party from the glorified Bride."—BICKERSTETH, *The
Divine Warning.*

According to the Duke of Manchester, "The gifts necessary for
the forming of Christ's mystical body were not conferred until after
the ascension of Jesus. . . . . We could not, therefore, say with propriety that the Church under the former dispensation was 'Christ.'
The Bride is the New Jerusalem. . . . . Now the great glory of the New
Jerusalem is, that it is the abode of Deity. But for the believer to be
a habitation of God, is the peculiar glory of the dispensation, founded
by the apostles, according to the promise, 'he dwelleth with you and
shall be in you.' "—DUKE OF MANCHESTER, *The Finished Mystery*, pp.
284-288.

Mr. Bonar differs from both the preceding positions. All the
saints redeemed amid toil and temptation, sorrow and warfare, shall
form the Bride at the Lord's coming; and this Bride shall reign with Him
a thousand years. Then as the saints who shall people the earth during these thousand years, they are as really saints and as simply dependent on their Head as any one of those already in glory.—A. A.
BONAR, *Redemption Drawing Nigh*, pp. 124ff.

and corporate body with Christ at His coming, is not all the saved, but only a peculiar portion of them called the "Bride," the Assembly of the Firstborn, the kings and priests unto God, the Holy City; whose blessedness is distinct and peculiar, not holiness and blessedness merely, but these in a peculiar form." This led immediately to the question, Who then constitutes the Bride? Dr. Bickersteth thinks that the Bride consists of all the saints who have believed up to the commencement of the millennium; the Duke of Manchester limits the Bride still further, by excluding from this company all those who lived prior to the ascension; while Mr. Bonar holds that the saints of the millennial age will be the same as all others, except that they will not have shared in the trials of the preceding saints, and therefore will not attain the dignity of the Bridehood, which is reserved exclusively for the tried saints. Here, again, we may say that speculative theories seem eventually to fall of their own weight. These theories, however, led to another type of premillennialism, which holds that the Church is incomplete at the time of the Second Advent, and consequently is followed by the millennium as a further period of salvation.

In addition to the premillennial development, there arose during this period an opposition movement known as postmillennialism. Daniel Whitby (1638-1726) reverted to the Augustinian view, that the millennium referred to the beginning and progress of the Church between the two Advents. This spiritual progress of the Church he viewed as ending in a final triumph over the world, or a millennial reign of righteousness preceding the Second Coming of Christ to judgment. Whitby is generally regarded, therefore, as the author of the postmillennial theory in modern times—a theory which he himself explained as "A New Hypothesis." He was followed by Vitringa, Faber and David Brown, the latter being especially able in his presentation and defense of the doctrine. These later developments must now be reviewed more fully as Modern Types of Millennial Theory.

Modern Types of Millennial Theory

We have attempted to trace in a brief way, the history of millennial theory from the patristic age to modern times, and shall conclude this historical survey with a review of some of its more prominent types. These fall into two main groups which may be classified as (1) Literalistic Theories; and (2) Spiritualistic Theories. These can be given only brief mention.

A. *The Literalistic Theories.* These include in general the premillennial theories of every type. As our historical statement has shown, the early church held universally to a belief in the personal return of Christ. This return soon took the form of a personal reign of Christ on earth for a thousand years, or during the millennium, which most writers regard as practically universal to the time of Augustine, when the spiritualistic theories came to the front and chiliasm sank into decline. With the Reformation, the premillennial theories again came to the front, especially during the seventeenth and earlier part of the eighteenth centuries. These theories as we have indicated regarded the Church as complete at the time of the Second Advent, and only later, was the millennium viewed as an extension of the Church age. Many and varied as these theories were, they have in modern times developed into two general types of premillennialism. (1) Those which regarded the Church as complete, and therefore identified in point of time, the Second Advent with its rapture and revelation, the first resurrection, and the conflagration, placing all these events before the millennium, devel-

---

Dr. Daniel Steele in his book entitled, *Antinomianism Revived,* deals with what he terms "The Plymouth Eschatology." His discussion is concerned with the eschatology of the Plymouth Brethren, but the theory discussed is the same as that which we have called "The Keswick Theory." That the modern Keswick movement is largely an outgrowth of the earlier Plymouth movement will not be questioned. While Dr. Steele discusses this premillennial position solely from the standpoint of a postmillennialist, his references to the underlying antinomianism are well taken. The repression theory of the millennium is but an extension of the repression theory of sin in the individual heart, a position decidedly in opposition to Wesleyanism. The emphasis upon election at times, as Dr. Steele points out, needs only the doctrine of a limited atonement to make the scheme of Calvinistic antinomianism complete.

oped into what is known at present as the Adventist Theory. (2) Those which regarded the Church as incomplete at the time of the Second Advent, have separated between the rapture and the revelation on the one hand, and the conflagration on the other, making the millennium to lie between these two terminal points. This we think may properly be termed the Keswick theory, at least, it will be granted that the Keswick people have been enthusiastic in their support of this position. We give now simply a general statement of these positions.

1. *The Adventist Theory.* The theory held by the Adventist people is generally characterized by the following positions. (1) The rapture, the revelation, and the conflagration are all identified in point of time. (2) The wicked are all destroyed at the coming of the Lord (I Thess. 1: 7, 8). (3) The righteous are taken to heaven (John 14: 2, 3; I Thess. 4: 17). (4) The earth is rendered void, an abyss or bottomless pit (Cf. Gen. 1: 1 with II Peter 3: 10). (5) Satan is bound through lack of opportunity to exercise his powers (Rev. 20: 1-3). (6) The millennium is in heaven and not on earth. The saints are engaged in the investigative judgment (Rev. 7: 9-15; 21-2). (7) The descent of the Holy City to judgment, and the resurrection of the wicked (Rev. 21: 2). (8) The apostate nations are the wicked dead resurrected, whom Satan rallies to attack the Holy City. Satan loosed because of opportunity to again deceive the wicked. (9) Satan's host defeated through fire from heaven which sweeps them away to the Great White Throne Judgment (Rev. 21: 11-13). (10) The punishment of the wicked by fire from heaven which destroys sin and annihilates the wicked in the lake of fire, which is the second death (Rev. 20: 14, 15). (11) The earth purified and made new through the fire which destroyed it at the Second Coming of Christ (II Peter 3: 12, 13). The righteous saved by being lifted above it. (Cf. Noah and the Ark (I Peter 3: 20, 21). (12) The Eternal State. The new heavens and the new earth become the abode of the saints. These are under-

stood to be the present heavens and earth purified by fire. Here it will be seen that the earlier theories as to the completion of the Church and the identification of the millennium with the day of judgment are continued; but the creation of the new heavens and the new earth are regarded as following, rather than preceding the millennium. It is to be regretted that the Adventist people have attached to this doctrine formerly regarded as orthodox, the untenable and unscriptural doctrine of the annihilation of the wicked.

2. *The Keswick Theory.* As the Adventist theory is built upon the supposition that the Church is complete at the time of the Second Advent, so the Keswick theory has as its presupposition, the idea of its incompleteness. The former links the millennial reign more closely to the eternal state; the latter regards it as an extension of the Church age. Here again, the variations in matters of detail are exceedingly numerous, but perhaps the best representative of this type of premillennialism is that of Dr. Joseph A. Seiss. This theory which was published in his work entitled *The Last Times,* and more fully discussed in his later works, is as follows: (1) Christ Jesus, our adorable Redeemer, is to return to this world in great power and glory, as really and as literally

W. W. Spicer in his work entitled, *Our Day in the Light of Prophecy,* gives us the following summary of the Adventist position. (1) The Millennium is the closing period of God's great week of time, a great Sabbath of rest to the earth and to the people of God. (2) It follows the close of the Gospel Age, and precedes the setting up of the everlasting kingdom of God on earth. (3) It completes what in the Scriptures is frequently spoken of as the "Day of the Lord." (4) It is bounded at each end by a resurrection. (5) Its beginning is marked by the pouring out of the seven last plagues, the Second Coming of Christ, the resurrection of the righteous dead, the translation of the saints to heaven; and its close by the descent of the New Jerusalem with Christ and the saints from heaven, the resurrection of the wicked dead, the loosing of Satan, and the final destruction of the wicked. (6) During the thousand years the earth lies desolate, Satan and his angels are confined here; and the saints with Christ sit in judgment on the wicked, preparatory to final punishment (Cf. Jer. 4:23-26; Earth desolate). (7) The wicked dead are then raised, Satan is loosed for a little season, and he and the host of the wicked encompass the camp of the saints and the Holy City, when fire comes down out of heaven and devours them. (8) The earth is cleansed by the same fire that destroys the wicked and the earth renewed becomes the eternal abode of the saints. (9) The millennium is one of the "ages to come." Its close will mark the beginning of the New Earth State.

as He ascended from it. (2) This Advent of the Messiah will occur before the general conversion of the world, while the man of sin continues his abominations, while the earth is yet full of tyranny, war, infidelity and blasphemy, and consequently before what is called the millennium. (3) This coming of the Lord will not be to depopulate and annihilate the earth, but to judge, subdue, renew, and bless it. (4) In the period of His coming He will raise the holy from among the dead, transform the living that are waiting for Him, judge them according to their works, receive them up to Himself in the clouds, and establish them in a glorious heavenly kingdom. (5) Christ will then also break down and destroy all present systems of government in church and state, burn up the great centers and powers of wickedness and usurpation, shake the whole earth with terrific visitations for its sins, and subdue it to His own personal and eternal rule. (6) During these great and destructive commotions the Jewish race shall be marvelously restored to the land of their fathers, brought to embrace Jesus as their Messiah and King, delivered from their enemies, placed at the head of the nations, and made the agents of unspeakable blessings to the world. (7) Christ will then re-establish the throne of His father David, exalt it with the heavenly glory, make Mount Zion the seat of His divine empire, and with the glorified saints associated with Him in His dominion reign over the house of Jacob and over the world in a visible, sublime, and heavenly Christocracy for the period of a "thousand years." (8) During the millennial reign in which mankind is brought under a new dispensation, Satan is to be bound and the world enjoy its long expected Sabbatic rest. (9) At the end of this millennial Sabbath the last rebellion shall be quashed, the wicked dead, who shall continue in Hades until that time, shall be raised and judged, and Satan, Death, Hades, and all antagonism to good, delivered over to eternal destruction. (10) Under these wonderful administrations, the earth is to be entirely recovered from the effects of the fall, the excellence of God's righteous providence vindicated, the whole curse repealed, death swallowed up, and all the inhabitants of the world thenceforward forever restored to more than full happiness, purity and glory which Adam forfeited in Eden.

The objection urged against this type of premillennialism, centers largely in its emphasis upon a continuance of the work of salvation during the millennium. The ground of this objection is found in those scriptures which seem to indicate that when Christ comes the Intercession will cease and the Judgment begin. It is in this work of the Intercession that the merit of Christ's death and the might of His Spirit find their logical connection, and by means of which the one

The Keswick theory holds that the work of salvation will continue throughout the millennium. Dr. Seiss further says, "I therefore hold it to be a necessary and integral part of the scriptural doctrine of salvation, that our race, as a self-multiplying order of beings, will never cease either to exist or to possess the earth." And again, "The earth, and generations and nations of earth, notwithstanding the momentous changes that are to happen, will extend through and beyond the thousand years, if not in some sort forever" (SEISS, *Millennialism and the Second Advent*). He holds, further, that these nations will exist in their present state as far as their mortality and inward depravity are concerned, but that there shall be established a new form of administration in which outward obedience shall be made compulsory. He says, "the so-called Millennium brings with it an altogether different dispensation from that under which we live. . . . . The great work and office of the Church now is to preach the gospel to every creature, and to witness for Christ to an adverse and gainsaying world; but there is not one word said about any such office in mortal hands during all that long period. In its stead, however, there is to be a shepherdizing of the nations with a rod of iron, an authoritative and invincible administration of right and justice on the part of immortal king-priests, and a potent disciplining of men and nations far beyond anything which the mere preaching of the gospel has ever wrought or was ever intended to do for earthly society. . . . . Now we can only beseech men in Christ's stead to be reconciled to God; then they will be compelled to take the instructions given them, to serve with fear and rejoice with trembling, to kiss, give the required adoration to the Son or perish from the way (Psalms 2:10-12). Now it is left to men's option to serve God or not, with nothing to interfere with their choice but the judgment to come; then they will be obliged to accept and obey His laws, or be smitten and blasted on the spot (Cf. SEISS, *Lectures on the Apocalypse*, III, pp. 346, 347). The discerning reader will hardly fail to see here the Keswick teaching of the repression of inbred sin in the individual heart, extended to the millennial reign in its external aspects. Those who hold that sin in the heart is not merely to be repressed but purged out, find it difficult to accept this external and repressive type of a millennial reign. If the carnal mind is not subject to the law of God now, how can it be during the millennium. This is one of the perplexing problems which attach to this form of millennialism.

passes into the other. The continuous Intercession makes possible the acknowledgment of Christ's right to receive and dispense the Spirit, without which salvation is admittedly impossible. This is the whole tenor of the New Testament, the deep undertone of the work of redemption. The force of this argument will be clearly seen by those who care to consider those Scriptures which bear upon the relation of the Spirit to Christ, such as, *I will pray the Father, and he shall give you another Comforter* (John 14: 16); *when the Comforter is come, whom I will send unto you from the Father* (John 15: 26); *Therefore being by the right hand of God exalted, and having received of the Father the promise of the Holy Ghost, he has shed forth this, which ye now see and hear* (Acts 2: 33); *he saved us, by the washing of regeneration, and renewing of the Holy Ghost; which he shed on us abundantly through Jesus Christ our Saviour* (Titus 3: 5, 6), and many others. But the scriptures which bear more directly and specifically upon the intercessory work of Christ are found

It is common for the advocates of this type of millennialism, to ground their objections to postmillennialism on the basis of the parable of the Tares and the Wheat. We may cite the following paragraph from Rev. A. Sims as an illustration. He says, "The current theory (referring to postmillennialism) is opposed to the spirit and teaching of the parable of the Wheat and the Tares. These are not to be separated, but are to grow together till the harvest, or the end of the age, when Christ shall come in judgment. But how can the growth of evil alongside the growth of good continue till the close of the dispensation if all are to be saved and a thousand years of righteousness are to take place before the Second Coming of Christ? The prevailing view of the millennium thus teaches that the wheat and the tares shall not grow together till the harvest, but that the tares shall all be converted into wheat, and it also puts off the Second Coming of Christ for a thousand years" (SIMS, *Deepening Shadows and Coming Glories*, p. 191). Here the writer objects to postmillennialism on the ground that it teaches a reign of absolute righteousness previous to the coming of Christ a reign in which all the tares shall be converted into wheat. If postmillennialists believe this, it would be a strong argument against them; that they do not, is evident from a careful perusal of their writings. But the argument is reactionary. The plain inference is, that the millennium which follows the coming of Christ will not be a mixed reign in which sinners and the righteous shall dwell together; but the tares having been destroyed, the people shall be all righteous. If this be not the inference, then there is no point to the argument against the postmillennialists. But does this type of millennialism thus teach? It most certainly does not. It holds that the work of salvation during the millennium will continue as before, and that there shall still exist an admixture of the wicked and the righteous, the tares and the wheat.

in Hebrews 7:25 and 9:12, 24-28. In the latter text three things are mentioned, each of which is termed an appearance, and to which the word "once" is attached either directly or indirectly. These are the incarnation, or the First Advent; the intercession, and the Second Advent. *Once in the end of the world hath he appeared* [πεφανέρωται] *to put away sin by the sacrifice of himself. By his own blood he entered in once into the holy place* .... *not into the holy places made with hands* .... *but into heaven itself, now to appear* [ἐμφανισθῆναι] *in the presence of God for us: so Christ was once offered to bear the sins of many; and unto them that look for him shall he appear* [ὀφθήσεται] *the second time without sin unto salvation.* This last statement according to Dr. Pope means that He shall appear "without any redeeming relation to the sin which He will still find, and for the complete and bodily salvation of those whom He has already saved in spirit (POPE, *Compend. Chr. Th.*, III, p. 389). So also, Dr. David Brown in commenting on this text says, "When the Advent arrives, the inter-

Dr. Pope in commenting on Hebrews 9:12, 24-28 says, "This is a cardinal text, and the variation in the phraseology, chosen with great precision, must be observed. In this verse the word is ὀφθήσεται (Heb. 9:28, appear the second time), while in another which says that 'He appeared to put away sin' it was πεφανέρωται, his manifestation between these two, 'now to appear in the presence of God for us,' ἐμφανισθῆναι. The first is the most visible exhibition of Himself as King, in the judicial form of His kingly office. He vindicates His atonement as against all who have despised it. Sin shall be finally punished as the rejection of Himself and His redemption. 'The Lord Jesus shall be revealed from heaven with his mighty angels, in flaming fire taking vengeance on them that know not God, and that obey not the gospel of our Lord Jesus Christ': upon all hearers of that gospel who shall then be found without evangelical knowledge of God."—POPE, *Compend. Chr. Th.*, III, p. 390.

Mr. Barker in his comment on Hebrews 7:25 says, "It is absolutely necessary to remember that the word 'ever' signifies continuity, not eternity of action; for the office of Christ as our Intercessor will have its close when He has brought all His people with Him."—BARKER, *Hope of the Apostolic Church*, p. 184.

The Duke of Manchester, an ardent premillennialist, takes the same position. He says, "When Messiah shall leave the 'Holy of Holies' where He has now entered, to 'appear in the presence of God for us'— intercession, which is peculiar to his being in the Holy of Holies, shall have ceased. .... Coincident with this, upon resigning the kingdom (that in which He now reigns, but which He will resign at the millennium), to the Father, He will leave 'the throne of grace,' on which He shall reign until the effectual application, by the Holy Ghost, of all His work toward 'the restitution of all things.'"—DUKE OF MANCHESTER, *Horae Hebraicae*, p. 90.

cession is done; and when the intercession is done, salvation is done. When Christ appears the second time *to us*, He will cease to appear in the presence of God *for us* (BROWN, *Christ's Second Coming*, p. 112). The argument against the continuance of salvation after the Second Coming of Christ, is not only urged against this type of premillennialism by the postmillennialists, but also by the premillennialists of the earlier type.

B. *The Spiritualistic Theories*. These theories are more abstract in nature, and while they date back to an earlier period, came into special prominence at the time of Augustine. Reacting from his earlier chiliastic views, Augustine taught that the reign of Christ referred to the Church age, and embraced the whole period of time

Joseph Perry, a strong advocate of the earlier type of premillennialism, rejects the idea of a continuance of salvation after the Second Advent, believing the Church to be complete previous to that time. He says, "There are some things that these last do hold, that I cannot by any means assent to; and that is, when Christ shall be established upon the throne of His glory, in His kingdom, and all the saints with Him, in a perfect incorruptible state of immortality, that then there shall be the preaching of the gospel, and conversion work go forward among the multitude of the nations that shall be found living when Christ cometh, according to the opinion of some good men. I say this is that which I cannot fall in with, but must profess my dislike against, because I cannot believe that the Lord Jesus Christ will come down from heaven, and leave that great work of intercession now at God's right hand, until the whole number of God's elect among the Jews and Gentiles are converted, and the mystical body of Christ completed. And if so, where is there any room for conversion work to go on after this?"—PERRY, *Glory of Christ's Visible Kingdom*.

Thomas Burnet declared that we can "as well open a lock without a key as interpret the Apocalypse without the Millennium." He identified the millennium with the period of the new heavens and the new earth, and therefore a period of unmixed righteousness. This he said, "was the doctrine of all the ancient millenaries, and we ought to be careful and locate it thus." He contends that the New Jerusalem state is the same as the millennial state, and is ushered in by the seventh trumpet and the judgment; and that during the millennium there will be a lustral appearance of Christ and the Shekinah. He affirms that placing the millennium in this earth before the renovation, was what brought the doctrine anciently into discredit and decay (Cf. TAYLOR, *The Reign of Christ on Earth*, p. 214).

The following analysis of Augustine's position is arranged from Elliott's abstract of the *City of God*, and is quoted in Silver's work entitled, *The Lord's Return*. (a) The first resurrection is the rising of dead souls into spiritual life, beginning with the ministry of Christ, from which the millennium dates. (b) The devil, the strong man armed, is bound and expelled from the hearts of the disciples of Christ. (c) The reign of saints is their personal victory over sin and the devil. Satan no longer deceives. (d) The 'beast' is the wicked world; his 'image' is hypocrisy. (e) The millennium will end in 650 A.D., terminating the six thousandth year period and introducing the rise of the Antichrist.

between the First Advent and the Second. He also taught that the millennium was the sixth period of one thousand years in the world's history. However, the Church rejected this theory, and held that the millennium was to be identified with the whole gospel dispensation. The number they held to be purely symbolical, and as signifying a totality, rather than a definite period of time. From this impetus given to the spiritualistic phase of the millennium, two types of theory have developed—the Roman Catholic, and the modern Post-millennial Theory.

1. *The Roman Catholic Theory*. The theory held by the Church is essentially that of Augustine, with this exception, they reject his position of the thousand years, and hold rather to his primary statement, that the millennium is identical with the reign of the Church on earth, and is to be followed by the judgment. Dr. Wilmers, S.J., in his *Handbook of the Christian Religion* states that "Christ shall come again to judge the living and the dead; and this general judgment will close the present order of things. No one can with certainty foretell the day of judgment. But we know that it will not come until certain signs and prophecies have been fulfilled. The gospel shall be preached over the whole world (Matt. 24:14); there will be a great apostasy in the Church (II Thess. 2:3); a great decadence in Christian life, great corruption of morals, manifesting itself in luxury and sensuality (Luke 17:26-30); finally, Antichrist shall appear (II Thess. 2:3, 4). The last day shall be preceded by war, pestilence, and famine (Matt. 24: 4, 5); and by diverse signs and catastrophes (Matt. 24:20; Luke 21:25, 26). The day of judgment will close the present order of things. The time of probation will have passed, and there will remain only two classes— the blessed in heaven, and the reprobate in hell. . . . . At the last judgment the whole visible world shall be changed (II Peter 2:11-14). That is to say, after the complete victory over sin, the earth, which till then shall be under the curse of sin, and the visible universe, shall be made to harmonize with the glorious existence

of the risen man. Even now, according to the apostle, nature sighs for the day of deliverance (Rom. 8:19)."

2. *The Postmillennial Theory.* This theory is so called because it regards the Second Advent as following, rather than preceding the millennium. As to the personal, visible return of our Lord, postmillennialists hold this belief as firmly, and cherish it as highly as do the premillennialists. The difference in the theories concerns only the order of events which attach to the Second Advent. Modern postmillennialism is generally attributed to Daniel Whitby (1638-1726), and as revived by him, is essentially a return to the Augustinian position. However, instead of adopting the modified Augustinianism which regards the millennium as being in the past; or identifying it with the entire

Dr. Charles Hodge presents this doctrine as follows: "The Common church doctrine is, first, that there is to be a second, personal, visible and glorious Advent of the Son of God. Secondly, the events which are to precede that Advent are: (1) The universal diffusion of the gospel; or, as our Lord expresses it, the ingathering of the elect; this is the vocation of the Christian Church. (2) The conversion of the Jews, which is to be national. As their casting away was national, although a remnant was saved; so their conversion may be national, although some may remain obdurate. (3) The coming of Antichrist. Thirdly, that the events which are to attend the Second Advent are: (1) The resurrection of the dead, of the just and the unjust. (2) The general judgment. (3) The end of the world. And (4) The consummation of Christ's kingdom."—HODGE, *Systematic Theology,* III, p. 792.

The Arminian theologians have almost without exception, been the exponents of the postmillennial theory. Here may be mentioned Richard Watson as the earliest Methodist theologian, Pope, Raymond, Wakefield, Miley, Summers, and Field. Among the Calvinistic or Reformed theologians, we may mention in addition to Charles Hodge, A. A. Hodge, Strong, Shedd and Boyce. Some of these, however, give little attention to the subject in their theological treatises.

Dr. Pope says, "No church having incorporated the doctrine (premillennialism) into its profession of faith, it has been in modern times confined to schools of thought within the several communions, influenced, for the most part, and led by individual students of prophecy. . . . . This belief has, during the present century, been incorporated into many systems, being almost the leading characteristic of some. Still it is generally speaking held only by individuals and private schools of interpretation: inconsistently by divines of the Lutheran, Anglican, Westminster, and some other Confessions; consistently by those alone who in other respects deny the analogy of the faith as expressed in the ancient creeds and the formularies of the Reformation and the general consent of the Catholic Church, being limited by no Confession.—POPE, *Compend. Chr. Th.,* III, pp. 397, 398.

Dr. I. A. Dorner and Bishop Martensen emphasize the importance of the Second Advent, and in some sense may be regarded as premillennialists, although their teachings more nearly approach in many instances, the postmillennial theory—or to them, the common teachings of the Confessions.

Church age, as does Roman Catholicism, he regarded the millennium as a reign of righteousness in the future. His doctrine appears to be only a restatement of what Dr. Charles Hodge calls, "the common doctrine of the Church" as expressed in the Reformed Confessions, with particular emphasis upon the final triumph. Dr. Elliott sums up the position of Daniel Whitby as follows: (1) The first resurrection is a revival of the cause, principles, doctrines, character and spirit of the early martyrs and saints. It is ecclesiastical, spiritual, national. (2) It lies in the future. The millennium will be preceded by

Dr. Van Oosterzee among the Dutch theologians holds to the pre-millennial theory. He says, "The term millennial kingdom has in many an ear so unpleasant a sound that, even from the believing standpoint, some courage is required to range oneself among the defenders of Chiliasm. If we do so, nevertheless, in obedience to faith in the Word, without which we know nothing of the future, we must begin with repudiating the Jewish form, in which this prospect is represented by some, in a manner which furnished a ready occasion to the Reformers to speak of *Judaica somnia*. For us also is the hope here treated of 'a real pearl of Christian truth and knowledge'; but it is so only after we have separated the pearl from the variegated shell, in which it is so often proffered us.—VAN OOSTERZEE, *Christian Dogmatics*, II, p. 799.

The post-millennial position is ably stated by Dr. Beckwith in his article on the Millennium in the new Schaff-Herzog Encyclopedia of Religious Knowledge.

1. Through Christian agencies the gospel gradually permeates the entire world and becomes immeasurably more effective than at present.

2. This condition thus reached will continue for a thousand years.

3. The Jews will be converted, either at the beginning or some time during this period.

4. Following this will be a brief apostasy and terrible conflict of Christian and evil forces.

5. Finally and simultaneously there will occur the Advent of Christ, general resurrection, judgment, the old world destroyed by fire, the new heavens and the new earth will be revealed.

It is well known that John Wesley followed Bengel in his interpretation of the Apocalypse. Dr. Owen also holds this view. They assert that there are two distinct periods of a thousand years spoken of in Rev. 20:1-7, and Dr. Steele remarks that the Greek article sustains this view. The first period is that during which Satan is bound for a thousand years, which as Bengel states, indicates the great period of prosperity in the Church. The second is that of the martyrs who lived and reigned with Christ a thousand years. Concerning this last, Bengel says, "Whilst Satan is loosed from his imprisonment of a thousand years, the martyrs live and reign, not on the earth, but with Christ; then the coming of Christ in glory at length takes place at the last day; then, next, there is the new heaven, the new earth, and the new Jerusalem." He further states that "the confounding of the two millennial periods has long ago produced many errors, and has made the name of Chiliasm hateful and suspected." Dr. Daniel Steele in commenting on the above positions says, "Thus Bengel and Wesley, instead of being premillenarians, were, in fact, what most modern Methodists are, post-millenarians."—STEELE, *Antinomianism Revived*. p. 241.

triumph over the Antichrist. (3) Satan no longer deceives; the doctrines of the martyrs and their spirit is revived like that of Elias in John the Baptist. (4) The Church will flourish and holiness will triumph for a thousand years. The world will enjoy paradisaical blessedness while martyrs and saints in heaven will sympathize with its joy. The triumph on earth will be universal.

"The term *millennium*," says Dr. Raymond, "long since came to be used in a generic sense. to signify the time when the kingdom of Christ on earth should be in the ascendant, should be in its highest power, exaltation and glory. All Christians now speak of a millennium in which they believe; all look forward to a time when the kingdom of Christ shall be perfected, shall be in completeness, when the highest earthly purposes contemplated in the gospel dispensation shall be accomplished. All believe in *a* millennium, though there is now, as there always has been, great diversity of opinion as to what will be the precise state of things when the millennium shall have fully come" (RAYMOND, *Systematic Theology*, II, p. 472). As to the nature of the millennium as held by postmillennialists, we may likewise look to Dr. Raymond for a typical example of this teaching. "To our thought," he says, "the idea of a millennium is the idea of a complete success,

Dr. Raymond also says, "Will all the inhabitants of the earth be true Christians in the time of the millennium? We think not; for to suppose they will be is to suppose that probation has ceased, and that men on earth have attained to the condition of their heavenly state. To affirm the certain salvation of a class requires the assumption of an agency which will secure results; such an assumption is the contrary of contingency. If the salvation of all living at any given time be certainly secured, their salvation is not a contingency; they are not probationers. The true millennium is gospel success; the gospel is preached unto moral agents, capable of accepting or rejecting. . . . . By what means are we to expect that the millennium will be ushered in? We have assumed that the present is the last time; the last dispensation of grace and probation provided for men; that Christ's coming is at the end of the world; that the resurrection of the dead, both of the just and the unjust, will be at the coming of Christ, the resurrection of the unjust in immediate succession after that of the just. This assumption is equivalent to an affirmation that the means of gospel success are the same as those now in operation, and that have been in operation from the beginning, changed only in that they shall be greatly increased in number and efficiency.--RAYMOND, *Systematic Theology*, II, pp. 490-492.

as to the Church as now constituted, and as to the enterprises of the Church now in operation, when that time has fully come, there will be but one religion, and that the Christian religion, upon the whole surface of the globe; all will have adequate educational and religious privileges; the mass of mankind will have attained a commendable moral character; the pious will be more eminently pious than were their ancestors; universal peace and general prosperity will prevail over all the earth; but some will refuse to obey, will persist in rebellion, and men who are the enemies of God and holiness will be found on earth when the Lord comes to raise the dead and judge the world" (RAYMOND, *Systematic Theology*, II, pp. 493, 494).

From what has been said, it must be evident, even to the casual reader, that premillennialism and postmillennialism represent opposite extremes of thought, and a totally different method of approach. One can sense the difference in the feeling tone. The millennium as postmillennialists conceive it, is the flowering age of the Church—a time in which righteousness shall reign and peace spread throughout the world. This condition will be brought about by the present means of evangelism, to which will be added, "the binding of Satan," or the restraining judgments of God. While the righteous are in the ascendancy, the millennium is, nevertheless, a mixed condition of saints and sinners—all in the flesh. Postmillennialists do not, therefore, regard the millennium as an absolute reign of righteousness, as some premillennialists argue; and furthermore, the inconsistency of the argument by those premillennialists who likewise regard the millennium as a mixed reign, must be evident to all.

What may be said to be the scriptural basis upon which this superstructure of postmillennialism rests? It is built upon two assumptions: (1) the spiritual nature of the first resurrection; and (2) the spiritual character of the reign of Christ during the millennium.

1. Postmillennialists generally, though not universally, maintain that the first resurrection is purely

spiritual, and that the second only, is bodily and literal. This argument for the two types of resurrection is drawn from the words of our Lord found in John 5: 24, 25 and 5: 28, 29, *Verily, verily, I say unto you, He that heareth my word, and believeth on him that sent me, hath everlasting life, and shall not come into condemnation; but is passed from death unto life. Verily, verily, I say unto you, The hour is coming, and now is, when the dead shall hear the voice of the Son of God: and they that hear shall live* (John 5: 24, 25). There can be no doubt that our Lord refers here to a spiritual resurrection, and that St. Paul also, uses the same figure in his epistles. *Marvel not at this: for the hour is coming, in which all that are in the graves shall hear his voice, and shall come forth; they that have done good, unto the resur-*

Dr. David Brown, a postmillennial writer of note says, "On opening your books (referring to Mr. Bickersteth's "Guide") we find you making the millennium the same Christian state that we expect it to be. The Jews you say, looking on their pierced Saviour will repent and believe, and be the missionary instruments of the Gentiles' conversion; and you speak of the spiritual blessedness of that period when 'the earth shall be full of the knowledge of the Lord, as the waters cover the sea,' when 'the kingdom and dominion under the whole heaven shall be given to the people of the saints of the Most High,' when 'men shall be blessed in Christ [with salvation of course], and all nations shall call him blessed.' Here, then, is the inextricable difficulty into which your system shuts you up; and yet you are either unaware of it, or will not face it. You expatiate with equal confidence upon two things, the one of which is destructive of the other. You rejoice that Christ will bring all His people with Him, before the millennium. You no less rejoice in the prospect of a world peopled with believing men for a thousand years after His coming!"—DR. DAVID BROWN, *Christ's Second Coming*, p. 78.

Dr. Daniel Steele makes the following statements concerning the views of John Wesley: "Wesley, in his 'Notes on the New Testament,' followed Bengel largely but definitely on the nearness of the binding of Satan and the millennium; also in the opinion that Rev. 20:1-11 included two thousand years, the first of which Satan will be bound and the Church and the world will have 'immunity from all evils and an affluence of all blessings'—the millennium. During the second thousand years Satan will be loosed, and 'while the saints reign with Christ in heaven, men on earth will be careless and secure.' After this second thousand years, according to Mr. Wesley, the Second Advent will occur. His words are unequivocal and decisive: 'Quickly he [Satan] will be bound; when he is loosed the martyrs will live and reign with Christ. Then follows His coming in glory' (Notes on Rev. 20:1-11). So, in his sermon on 'The Great Assize,' Wesley distinctly places the Second Advent at the judgment (Rev. 20:11-15), which the apostle says and all admit is after the millennium. These facts show conclusively that Wesley placed the Second Advent after the millennium. And in this parted from Bengel, if, as alleged, he placed the Advent before the millennium."—STEELE, *Antinomianism Revived*, pp. 273, 274.

rection of life; and they that have done evil, unto the resurrection of damnation (John 5:28, 29). This refers, of course, to a bodily or physical resurrection. In commenting on these scriptures Dr. Pope says, "Now we have seen that our Lord expressly speaks in one and the same discourse of a first resurrection, understood spiritually, and of a second resurrection understood physically. If we apply the same principle here, this much contested symbolical prophecy (Rev. 20:1-9) is made perfectly harmonious with the rest of Scripture, and the most substantial ground of the premillennial Advent is taken away (POPE, *Compend. Chr. Th.*, III, p. 898).

2. Postmillennialists uniformly regard the reign of Christ during the millennium as purely spiritual. Consequently they generally view the apocalyptic statement (Rev. 20:1-11) as purely symbolical or figurative. In a reference to premillennialism, Dr. Miley says, "The chief reliance of the theory is upon a single passage of scripture (Rev. 20:1-6). This may be said, first, that the passage contains not a word respecting any Advent of Christ, nor a word respecting his reigning personally on the earth. Further, it is in a highly figurative or symbolical book, and is itself highly symbolical. Consequently the construction of a theory of the Advent on such ground is without the warrant of any principle of doctrinal formation, and the more certainly so as there are many explicit texts on that subject" (MILEY, *Systematic Theology*, II, p. 442). The various attitudes which postmillennialists take toward the statement in the Apocalypse, and the different construction which they put upon it, must be reserved for the appended notes.

Dr. Raymond in his objections to premillennialism says, "The theory has no support but in a literal interpretation of the twentieth chapter of Revelation. If that chapter contained all the information we have on the subject, we might be compelled to concede that postmillenarianism is the eschatology of the Bible, but the Book of Revelation is confessedly highly figurative and symbolic, and its interpretation extremely difficult. It is an accepted rule of exegesis that the obscure is to be explained by the perspicuous, the figurative by the literal, and not the reverse.—RAYMOND, *Systematic Theology*, II, p. 478.

Here a difference emerges between the Revelation and the other New Testament writings. Whereas, the latter join the judgment and the consummation of the world to Christ's Second Advent, the Revelation interposes another phase. It makes a thousand years' reign of the rule of Christ fall into this earthly world period, and before the final decisive struggle and the victory of Christ. But the meaning of the passage is disputed. According to one interpretation, the martyrs and saints will be previously raised to life in a first resurrection with glorified bodies. According to others, their resurrection only means endowment with power in order to their reigning with Christ. It is further disputed, whether according to the Revelation Christ will be visible upon earth during the millennium, or will come again at the millennium only in the sense of the triumphant and glorious manifestation of the power of the gospel, upon which depends the other question, whether the joint reigning of the saints with Christ will take place invisibly and therefore spiritually in heaven, the earth remaining the old earth, or upon earth. After the millennium the Revelation makes Satan to be loosed once more for a short time, and Gog and Magog to march against the Holy City, in which representation the earthly relations in the millennium are viewed as essentially the same as the old ones. But this being so, it is improbable that the author is thinking of a visible government of Christ with saints raised in glorified bodies on the old earth. Neither Christ's visible return, nor a glorifying and transforming of the world, is promised in the Apocalypse for the thousand years' kingdom. The only characteristic of Christ's Second Advent mentioned with certainty is the joint reigning of the saints with Christ upon thrones and the temporary binding of Satan's authority, which latter may just as well take place on the outwardly unchanged earth as the time of the unchaining of his power. Only after the last conflict with the antichristian powers do the final judgment and the manifestation of Christ in glory follow (Rev. 20:10ff), with the account of the new heaven and new earth, with which cosmical changes the general resurrection is connected (Rev. 20:11-15, 21:1; Cf. II Peter 3:13).—DORNER, *System of Christian Doctrine*, IV, pp. 389, 390.

RICHARD WATSON'S STATEMENT OF POSTMILLENNIALISM

The following statement in regard to the millennium, and the blessings which shall be more particularly enjoyed during that period as marked out by prophecy, is from the writings of Richard Watson, the earlier theologian of Methodism. The article in its entirety can be found in Watson's Dictionary, Article, "Millennium."

1. It is expressly said of those who shall partake of the first resurrection, that they shall be "blessed and holy"; by which the inspired writer seems to denote that it will be a time of eminent holiness. This will constitute the peculiar glory and the source of the happiness of the millennial state (Zech. 14:20, 21).

2. There is reason to expect a remarkable effusion of the Spirit, about the commencement of this happy period, even as there was at the first setting up of Christ's kingdom in the world. Besides the promises of the Spirit, which were accomplished in the apostolic age, there are others which from the connection appear to refer to the time we are now speaking of. Thus Isaiah, after having described Christ's kingdom which was set up at His First coming, and then the succeeding desolate state of the Jews, represents this as continuing "until the Spirit be poured upon us from on high, and the wilderness be a fruitful field, and the fruitful field be counted for a forest" (Isaiah 32:15-19). (Cf. also Rom. 11:26, 27 and Isaiah 59:20, 21. Ezekiel 36:27; 39:28, 29; Zech. 12:10).

3. A universal spread of the gospel, diffusing the knowledge of the Lord throughout the world in a more extensive and effectual manner than ever it was before. This is repeatedly promised: "The earth shall be full of the knowledge of the Lord, as the waters cover the

sea"; and this shall take place in that day when the Gentiles shall seek to the branch of the root of Jesse, whose rest shall be glorious, and when "the Lord shall set his hand against the second time to recover the remnant of his people, ... and he shall set up an ensign for the nations, and shall assemble the outcasts of Israel, and gather together the dispersed of Judah from the four corners of the earth" (Isaiah 11: 9-12). The same promise of the universal knowledge of the glory of the Lord is repeated in the prophecy of Habakkuk 2:14. This will be attended with corresponding effects: "All the ends of the world shall remember and turn unto the Lord: and all the kindreds of the nations shall worship before thee" (Psalms 22:27); "yea, all kings shall fall down before him; all nations shall serve him," (Psalms 72:11). And although we may not imagine that all the inhabitants of the globe will have the true and saving knowledge of the Lord; yet we may expect such a universal spread of light and religious knowledge as shall root up pagan, Mohammedan, and the antichristian delusions, and produce many good effects upon those who are not really regenerated, by awing their minds, taming their ferocity, improving their morals, and making them peaceable and humane.

4. The Jews will then be converted to the faith of the Messiah, and partake with the Gentiles of the blessings of His kingdom. The Apostle Paul (Rom. 11) treats of this at large and confirms it from the prophecies of the Old Testament. He is speaking of Israel in a literal sense, the natural posterity of Abraham; for he distinguishes them both from the believing Gentiles and the Jewish converts of his time, and describes them as the rest who were blinded, had stumbled and fallen, and so had not obtained, but were broken off and cast away (Rom. 11:7, 11, 12, 15, 17). Yet he denies that they have stumbled that they should fall, that is, irrecoverably, so as in no future period to be restored; but shows that through their fall, salvation might come to the Gentiles, and that this again might provoke them to jealousy or emulation (v. 11). He argues that if their fall and diminishing was the riches of the Gentiles, and the casting away of them was the reconciling of the world, their fullness will be much more so, and the receiving of them be life from the dead (vs. 12, 15). He further argues, that if the Gentiles "were grafted contrary to nature into a good olive tree, how much more shall these which be the natural branches be grafted into their own olive tree?" (v. 24). Nor did he consider this event as merely probable, but as absolutely certain; for he shows that the present blindness and future conversion of that people is the mystery or hidden sense of prophecies concerning them; and he cites two of these prophecies where the context foretells both their rejection and recovery (Isaiah 59:20, 21; 27:9).

5. The purity of visible church communion, worship and discipline, will then be restored according to the primitive apostolic pattern. During the reign of Antichrist a corrupted form of Christianity was drawn over the nations, and established in the political constitutions of the kingdoms which were subject to that monstrous power. By this means the children of God were either mixed in visible religious communion with the profane world, in direct opposition to the Word of God, or persecuted for their nonconformity. In reference to this state of the things, the angel commands St. John to leave out the court which is without the temple, and not to measure it, for this reason, because "it is given unto the Gentiles: and the holy city shall they tread under foot forty and two months" (Rev. 11:2); that is, they shall pollute and profane the worship and communion of the Church during the one thousand two hundred and sixty years of Antichrist's reign, so that it cannot be measured by the rule of God's Word. But when the period we are speaking of shall arrive, the sanctuary shall be cleansed (Daniel 8:14); the visible communion, worship, order and discipline of the

house of God will then be restored to their primitive purity, and accord with the rule of the New Testament.

6. The Lord's special presence and residence will then be in the midst of His people. . . . . He also calls them to purity of communion and personal holiness, and promises to dwell in them and walk in them (II Cor. 6:16, 17); but this will be fulfilled in an eminent and remarkable manner during the millennial period. The Lord, having promised to raise Israel out of their graves, to gather them from among the heathen, and bring them into the Church and kingdom of Christ. as one fold having one shepherd, adds, "And will set my sanctuary in the midst of them for evermore; my tabernacle also shall be with them; yea, I will be their God, and they shall be my people" (Ezek. 37:11-27). . . . . It is intimated that there will be such visible tokens of the divine presence and residence among them as will fall under the notice of the world, and produce conviction and awe, as was in some measure the case in the first churches (Acts 2:47; 5:11, 13; I Cor. 24:25). . . . . Indeed this is represented by St. John as accomplished: "And I heard a great voice out of heaven saying, Behold, the tabernacle of God is with men, and he will dwell with them, and they shall be his people, and God himself shall be with them, and be their God" (Rev. 21:3).

7. This will be a time of universal peace, tranquility and safety. Persons naturally of the most savage, ferocious and cruel disposition will then be tame and harmless; so it is promised in Isaiah 11:6-10. Whether we consider the persons represented by these hurtful animals to be converted or not, it is certain they will then be effectually restrained from doing harm, or persecuting the saints. There shall be no war or bloodshed among the nations during this happy period; for we are told, that in the last days, when the mountain of the Lord's house shall be established in the top of the mountains, and shall be exalted above the hills, and all nations shall flow unto it; the Lord "shall judge among the nations, and shall rebuke many people; and they shall beat their swords into ploughshares, and their spears into pruning hooks: nation shall not lift up sword against nation, neither shall they learn war any more" (Isaiah 2:4). Though war has hitherto deluged the world with human blood, and been a source of complicated calamities to mankind, yet, when Satan is bound, his influence upon wicked men restrained, and the saints bear rule, it must necessarily cease.

8. The civil rulers and judges shall then be all maintainers of peace and righteousness. Though Christ will put down all that rule, power and authority which opposes the peace and prosperity of His kingdom; yet as rulers are the ordinance of God, and His ministers for good; some form of government seems absolutely necessary to the order and happiness of society in this world; it is thought that when the kingdoms of this world are become our Lord's and his Christ's, the promise will be accomplished, "I will also make thy officers peace, and thine exactors righteousness"; and in consequence of this, "violence shall no more be heard in thy land, wasting nor destruction within thy borders" (Isaiah 60:17, 18).

9. The saints shall then have the dominion, and the wicked shall be in subjection. This is clear from the united voice of prophecy: "The kingdom and dominion, and the greatness of the kingdom under the whole heaven, shall be given to the people of the saints of the most High" (Daniel 7:27, 28; Matt. 5:5; Rev. 5:10; 20:4). With regard to the nature of this reign, it will undoubtedly correspond in all respects with the spiritual and heavenly nature of Christ's kingdom, to the promotion of which all their power will be subservient.

THE MILLENNIUM AS A TRANSITIONAL PERIOD

In reviewing the historical development of the various millennial theories, we have had a twofold purpose: (1) to furnish factual information pertaining to this important subject; and (2) to enable the student through the perspective of history, to attempt an evaluation of the several theories. The amount and variety of the material submitted may seem confusing, but it must be borne in mind that the literature on this subject is enormous. However this confusion will prove to be a blessing to the reader if it serves to guard him against the short and easy methods proposed by those who in overconfidence and self-assertiveness declare to the well-read and informed that they have not as yet seen the problems, much less solved them. In our own thinking, we have come to view the millennium as a transitional period between the present temporal order, and the eternal order that shall be. We view this transition, as we shall later show, after the analogy of the First Advent and the earthly life of Christ. During this time the older dispensation was brought to a close and the new inaugurated—the one in some measure overlapping the other. We are indebted, first of all, to Dr. Gerhart for the seed thought of this position, which he has set forth in such an able manner in his *Institutes of the Christian Religion*. Then again, we acknowledge our indebtedness to Dr. J. A. Dorner and Bishop Martensen for the cosmological viewpoint which has shown us the necessity of a perfect fulfillment of the purposes of God—not only for the individual but for the social structure and its physical environment as well. If man is first redeemed from sin, and possesses this treasure in earthen vessels which later through death and the resurrection are to become immortal, incorruptible and glorious, why may not this earth out of which man's body was formed, likewise pass through a state of dissolution and emerge as the new heavens and the new earth? Lastly, we are indebted to the Dutch theologian, Dr. Van Oosterzee, himself a pronounced premillennialist, for a scholarly confirmation of this transitional theory of the millennium. He says, "Altogether there lies over this part of the expectation of the future a transparent cloud, which makes it impossible here to define more particularly; the millennium is a *period of transition*. The longest night is over, but still the *full* day has not yet come. Instinctively we think of the forty days between the resurrection and the ascension of Christ; His Church also has now its Calvary behind it, and its Olivet immediately before it, without having yet ascended this latter. Its enemies are driven back,

On the Lord's return an earthly glorification is also to be expected by His faithful Church, a glorification which is the worthy manifestation of its inner development. Without yet being wholly overcome, the antichristian power is bound for a certain time; until a last struggle leads to its complete overthrow, and therewith to the utter annihilation of every hostile power, finally also of the last enemy.—VAN OOSTERZEE, *Christian Dogmatics*, II, p. 798.

A pregnant eschatological element lies in the Christian faith, as such. Faith has experienced so much of Christ's effectual working, that in the presence of what is still lacking, however much this may be, it possesses not merely the hope, but the certainty, that the divine idea of the world will not remain simply a faith, but an impotent picture of the imagination.—DORNER, *System of Christian Doctrine*, IV, p. 377.

History must at some time reach its ἀκμή, its culminating point. There must be some climax which the human race and the Church may attain to, even within this present state and these earthly conditions, a period which shall present the highest blossoming and flowering of history. Christianity must necessarily and essentially be not only a suffering and struggling power in the world, but a world-conquering, a world-ruling power likewise. It is this idea of the universal triumph of Christianity, as far as this can be realized within the bounds of time and sense, which finds its expression in the millennial reign.—MARTENSEN, *Chr. Dogm.*, p. 470.

It is the peculiarity of the New Testament forecast that it strongly tends to mount above the earthly horizon into the sphere of glorified existence. As was noticed in the consideration of the subject of immortality, the national and preliminary character of the Jewish religion naturally dictated that it should deal somewhat scantily with the supramundane unfoldment of the divine kingdom. Both the Old Testament and the New are intensely prophetical; both show the impress of a divinely enkindled optimism; the great difference is that in the latter the light is upon a loftier horizon, illuminating a scene which is distinctly characterized as belonging to the region of incorruptibility and immortality.—SHELDON, *System of Christian Doctrine*, pp. 540, 541.

The Second Coming of our Lord is the one all-commanding event of prophecy and the future: itself supreme, it is always associated with the universal resurrection, the judgment of mankind, and the consummation of all things. Through these epochs and crises are in the style of prophecy presented together in foreshortened perspective, they are widely distinct. But while we treat them as distinct, we must be careful to remember their common relation to the day of the Lord; which is a fixed and determined period, foreshadowed in many lesser periods to which the same term is applied, but the issue and consummation of them all.—POPE, *Compend. Chr. Th.*, III, p. 387.

but not yet destroyed. It is evident that the kingdom of darkness cannot rest until it has made trial of a gigantic concentration of its remaining forces: to this the prophetic word points; but the unintelligent mode of interpretation which would read, as it were 'between the lines' the names of the nations here intended, is not and cannot be ours" (VAN OOSTERZEE, *Christian Dogmatics*, II, p. 800).

The Analogy of the First and Second Advents. The First Advent marked the transition from the Old Testament to the New—a period of brief duration in which the former dispensation reached its culmination, and the latter had its beginnings. Our Lord declared that the law and the prophets were until John, after which the kingdom of heaven is preached. But the new dispensation which had its inception in the incarnation, was fully inaugurated only with the gift of the Holy Spirit on the Day of Pentecost. And further, as the ministry of Jesus was preceded by the preparatory work of John, so also after Pentecost, there was a gradual decay of the Mosaic order until the destruction of Jerusalem (A.D. 70), which marked its close. At that time, "the church was released from the swaddling clothes of Judaism" and the gospel became the heritage of all nations and all peoples. As the First Advent marked the beginning of an intermediate transitional period, which was preceded by a prophetic preparation and followed by a time of judgment, so we may expect the Second Advent to be. Thus Dr. Gerhart points out, that "like the age of the First Advent, may be the age of the Second Advent — an indefinite, intermediate period between the present aeon and the transcendent aeon. Of the peculiar nature of each of these opposite aeons, the intermediate age may in a measure partake" (GERHART, *Institutes*, III, p. 814). It is due to the twofold aspect of this transitional period, that much confusion arises. This intermediate period is commonly known as the millennium. Being a transitional period it looks both ways, and conjoins in itself, two widely different orders. It marks the transition from the natural to the spiritual, from the temporal to the eternal, from the immanent to the transcendent, and from grace to glory. There are those who view the millennium solely from the temporal order, and therefore regard it as merely an extension of the church age; while others, viewing it from the eternal order, sometimes confuse it with the new heavens and the new earth.

Characteristics of the Second Advent. The analogy between the First and Second Advents demands further consideration. Three things stand out clearly in the life of Christ. (1) He came into the natural race of men, that He might be the last Adam of the old order, and the New Man of the eternal order. (2) He was born under the Abrahamic covenant of promise, and became the Seed to whom the promises were made. (3) He was born in the bosom of Mosaic economy, by means of which no flesh could be justified. He was therefore manifested to take away our sins. Each of these distinctions, as Gerhart has so ably pointed out, must also bear a relation to the Second Advent. Consequently we must consider the Second Advent as a movement "new in kind, new in relations, new as to its purposes" (GERHART, *Institutes,* II, pp. 806ff).

1. The Second Advent will be a movement new in kind. The First Advent was a coming into the race by means of the Virgin birth; the second will be His coming in kingly glory (Matt. 25:31). In the First Advent, He came as a ministering servant; in the Second, He will *sit upon the throne of his glory; and before him shall*

If the Lord is indeed highly exalted, it can but be the case that this glory should eventually be manifested before the eyes of all; and it is exceedingly worthy of God that the same earth which witnessed His deep humiliation, should also become the scene of His manifested glory. If He still continues to maintain a personal and truly spiritual relation to the Church and the world, wherefore should not here also "embodiment in outward form" be the end of the ways of God?" .... If He personally lives and reigns unto eternity, then the King cannot permanently remain unvisible, in the case where the kingdom is everywhere established; and just as little, from the nature of the case, can this appearing be anything else than a final judgment. The expectation of so great a catastrophe—whatever enigmas and questions it may leave unanswered—is, for man's reason itself, much more satisfactory than that of an everlasting continuance of the present economy, a sort of *progressio in infinitum,* or indeed a long-continued dying out of creation.—VAN OOSTERZEE, *Christian Dogmatics,* II, p. 580.

be gathered all nations (Matt. 25: 32). Let it be recalled that there were two great mysteries in Christ, "the union of human nature with the divine, and the un-measured fullness of the Spirit which dwelt in that holy nature the one administered through the other" (I, p. 330). Hence our Lord speaks of His coming as that of *the Son of man;* that is, He comes in His per-fected and glorified humanity. He came indeed, in a spiritual sense, at Pentecost, manifesting Himself through the Holy Spirit as the Third Person of the Trinity; but He comes the second time, in His own mode of existence—as the Second Person of the Trinity manifested through His glorified humanity. His Second Coming will institute a movement also, new in kind as to the redemption of man's environment, or the physi-cal universe. By this we mean, not only an ethical and spiritual movement, but a metaphysical restoration of organic nature in the structure of the universe. "The expectation of the future transformation of the earth into a heavenly establishment," says Lange, "of the con-junction of the spiritual kingdom in the other world with that in this, is to man a mere fancy, but to every earnest Christian is a great hope, an assurance of faith, a certain prediction" (*Breman Lectures,* p. 251).

2. The Second Advent will be a movement new in its relations. The First Advent was an entrance into the Abrahamic covenant of promise, conditioned upon obedience unto death, *even the death of the cross* (Phil. 2: 8). Our Lord came to a world lying in the Wicked

The New Testament does not countenance a theory which assumes merely a quiet, steadily growing interpenetration or subjugation of the whole world by Christianity in the course of history. This is the op-timistic view, which is unprepared for eclipses of the sun in the firma-ment of the Church. The New Testament foretells catastrophes to the life of the Church, so that in this respect, also, it is a copy of the life of Christ and indeed catastrophes arise not merely through persecu-tions on the part of heathen and Jews in its beginning, but also out of itself, that is, from its outward circle, on the ground of intimations of Christ (Matt. 7:21; 24:11, 12, 24; Mark 13:6, 22); according to John and Paul (I John 2:18, where antichrists are spoken of in the plural; II Thess. 2:3ff), when the Christianizing of the nations has advanced, false prophets and pseudo-Messiahs will arise, desiring to enter into con-federacy with Satan and to some extent with the world-power against Christians, and to seduce to the denial of Christ.—DORNER, *System of Christian Doctrine,* IV, pp 387, 388.

One (I John 5:19), and brought to man in His own Person, the gift of eternal life. In His humiliation, he was despised and rejected of men (Isa. 53:3); *He came unto his own and his own received him not* (John 1:11). But His Second Coming will be governed by the law of exaltation and not that of humiliation. He will come to a world where the law of sin has already been broken, and where Satan has been personally defeated in immediate conflict. His Second Advent, therefore, will not be marked by a rejection, but by His people rising with joy to meet Him in the air, and with an innumerable company of angels forming the convoy of their glorious Bridegroom in His return to earth. The unbelieving world shall quail before Him, and the wicked shall cry for the rocks and the mountains to fall upon them, and hide them *from the face of him that sitteth on the throne, and from the wrath of the Lamb* (Rev. 6: 14-17). At His Second Advent He will appear, not to be despised, but to be honored; not to suffer, but to judge; not to overcome death by His resurrection from the dead, but to abolish death (I Cor. 15:26); not to introduce the principle of eternal life in the midst of the dying world, but to emancipate the members of the new race from all the limitations of the current age; not to initiate a victorious conflict with the kingdom of darkness, but to put an end to the existing disorganization, transforming the cosmos into the new heavens and the new earth; not to found the Church and proclaim salvation, but to actualize the idea and fulfill the teleological law of the Church in the post-mundane perfection of His kingdom" (GERHART, *Institutes,* II, p. 810).

3. The Second Advent will be a movement new in its purposes. Christ not only came as the Seed to whom the Abrahamic promise should be given, but as a Deliverer from the bondage of the Mosaic law, as to both its guilt and its penalty. The purpose of the First Advent was the deliverance from the guilt, the power, and the being of sin; the purpose of the Second Advent is the removal of the consequences of sin. The first was wrought by means of a priestly sacrifice for sin, Him-

self the Priest and the Offering; the second will be accomplished through the "all power" given to Him as our glorious King. He will not only be present with His Church in the Spirit of communion, but as the Logos in nature, He will also transform the mystical body of His Church, and in its own order, the subhuman kingdoms as well. Nature will be fully restored and become the willing instrument of our Lord and His people. Dr. Dorner was right when he said that "redeemed humanity has another goal than that of common zoology, and that goal is the kingdom of the resurrection. Complete victor Christianity can never be, until nature has become an organ of its service, a willing instrument of the perfect man, that is, of the righteous who are raised from the dead" (DORNER, *Person of Christ*, I, p. 412). Likewise, Dr. Ellicott writes that "Man and the creature, bound together in one common feeling of longing and expectancy, are awaiting that redemption of the body which shall be the immediate precursor of the restitution of the world, and the consummation of all things in Christ" (ELLICOTT, *Destiny of the Earth*, p. 18).

The Day of the Lord. As indicated in our discussion of the days of creation (I, p. 455ff), the older Hebrew exegesis never regarded the days of Genesis as solar days, but as day periods of indefinite duration. The word "day" is frequently used in this sense in the New Testament also. Thus our Lord says, *Your father Abraham rejoiced to see my day* (John 8: 56) and again, *For as the lightning, that lighteneth out of the one part under heaven, shineth unto the other part under heaven; so shall also the Son of man be in his day* (Luke 17: 24). St. Peter speaks of *the day of the Lord* (II Peter 3: 10, 12, 13); and St. Paul mentions both *the day of the Lord* (I Thess. 5: 2, 4, 5), and *the day of Christ* (II Thess. 2: 1, 2). This day of the Lord is generally, if not always, associated with the idea of judgment, as the following

Throughout the ancient economy a future period called the day of Jehovah appears as the one perspective of all prophecy. In the New Testament this day is declared to have come; all the purposes of the divine mercy and judgment are regarded as accomplished in the Advent of Christ, which is the last time or the end of the world.--POPE, *Compend. Chr. Th.*, III, p. 387.

Old Testament references will show (Isa. 2: 12, 13; 13: 6-13; Joel 1: 15; Zeph. 1: 14; Malachi 4: 5). We may confidently believe, then, that the day of the Lord is a period of time, marked by opening, intervening and closing events. "Though these epochs are crises, are in the style of prophecy presented together in foreshortened perspective, they are widely distinct. But while we treat them as distinct, we must be careful to remember their common relation to the day of the Lord; which is a fixed and determined period, foreshadowed in many lesser periods to which the same term is applied, but the issue and consummation of them all. What the Old Testament prediction beheld as one undistinguished whole is now divided into times and seasons, which all, however, converge into one decisive and fixed event, the return of Jesus from the invisible world. There is a rich and steady light thrown upon the Christian day of Jehovah, which is variously described in relation to the final manifestation of the person of Christ, and the final consummation of His work (POPE, *Compend. Chr. Th.*, III, p. 387). St. Paul views this day in relation to its opening event, the coming of Christ; while St. Peter regards it as the closing event in Christ's ultimate and triumphant accomplishment. It is, therefore, a transitional period in which a time or season *kairos* ($\kappa\alpha\iota\rho\delta\varsigma$), is preceded by other times and seasons, *chronoi* ($\chi\rho\delta\nu o\iota$). For this reason it is often difficult to distinguish the preparatory events from those of the final consummation to which they lead.

In this prophetical day of the Lord, events appear as a confused whole. Prophecy, it has been said, "has no perspective." The seers looked forward to the great goals of the future, without clearly distinguishing the

Dean Farrar observes that "the main difficulties in our Lord's prophecy vanish when we bear in mind that prophecy is like a landscape in which time and space are subordinated to eternal realities, and in which events look like hills seen, chain behind chain, which to the distant spectator appears as one." To this J. F. Silver adds that "looking at two heavenly bodies in conjunction, one partially eclipses the other and both present the aspect of a single star. We see the feet of Christ on the Mount of Olivet in the foreground and far beyond we discern the rising mountains that border on the vast eternity. The Millennium lies between."—SILVER, *The Lord's Return*, p. 236.

intervening events. The classical example of this is Christ's reading of the scripture in the synagogue at Nazareth. Having read of His anointing *to preach the acceptable year of the Lord,* He closed the book, thus indicating that the remaining portion of the sentence, *the day of vengeance of our God* (Isa. 61:1, 2; Luke 4:19, 20), was not then to be fulfilled. We may note also, that the point of view determines the events which are emphasized by the several writers of the Scriptures. Thus the Apostle Paul comforts the saints with the thought of Christ's personal return; while St. Peter, looking forward to our Lord's ultimate triumph, sees in this day of the Lord, the consummation of all things.

If now we analyze the debatable or controversial points connected with Christ's return, we shall find that each is a transitional event. (1) There is the appearance of Christ with its confusion of rapture and revelation; (2) there is a first resurrection, and the resurrection of "the rest of the dead"; (3) there is a judgment set immediately following our Lord's return, wherein the twelve apostles are seated on twelve thrones, judging the twelve tribes of Israel; and yet another "great white throne judgment" when the heavens and the earth shall have fled away; (4) there is a gathering of the righteous, and a destruction of the wicked, and yet the nations later appear in a great apostasy; (5) there is a setting up of the kingdom, and yet again, a yielding up of the kingdom; (6) there is a time of restitution of all things, when creation itself shall be delivered from its bondage; and a final dissolution of the earth, out of which shall emerge the new heavens and the new earth; and (7) there is a passing away of the old and sinful order, and the inauguration of a new and eternal Sabbath of rest, when God *shall be all in all.*

The Order of Events in the Lord's Day

At the outset, I may say that I have had considerable hesitancy in discussing this phase of my subject. However, I have not felt free to pass it by without some more or less general statements concerning it. A subject that has caused such a variety of opinion should be approached cautiously, and this we have sought to do. On subjects which are not clearly revealed, one should speak with becoming modesty. Those who speak with such a degree of positiveness as to exclude the sincere thought of Bible students who hold different positions, are neither wise nor reverent. My design, therefore, is to present the material of this division, suggestively, rather than dogmatically, and we trust that the statements here made will serve to provoke further study and research. We may emphasize again, that we regard this whole period as of a transitional nature, one in which the temporal order merges into the eternal, and therefore as a period, partaking in a measure of both orders of existence. According to the law of prophetical reserve, there is enough given us in the Scriptures to furnish the Church with a glorious hope; but the events can never be untangled until prophecy passes into history, and we view them as standing out clearly in their historical relations.

The Rapture and the Revelation. The Second Coming of Christ is the opening event of the Lord's day. It will be attended by the resurrection of the righteous dead and the translation of the righteous living, both companies of the saints being caught up in the clouds meet the Lord in the air. Here a distinction is made between the Rapture and the Revelation. The Rapture is the catching away of the Lord's people to the meeting in the air; the Revelation is His return to earth accompanied by the convoy of saints and angels. The word "rapture" comes from the Greek verb ἁρπάζω which signifies to seize, to take by force, to snatch away, or to rescue. The word "meeting" is from ἀπαντάω and carries with it the idea of a going forth in order to return with. It is so used in Acts 28:15. The words used to express the idea of the Revelation have already been discussed, that is, *apocalypse* ἀποκάλυψις or an unveiling; *parousia* (παρουσία or an appearing); and *epiphaneia* (ἐπιφάνεια or becoming visible). As to the relation of the Rapture and the Revelation there are widely different opinions. Some identify them, maintaining that when He comes every eye shall behold him, the saints rising with joy to meet Him, and the nations of the earth wailing because of Him (Rev. 1: 7). Others separate between the Rapture and the Revelation, maintaining that the former is secret and known only to the saints; the latter alone being visible to the world. As to the time intervening between the two, most writers hold that it will be a period of three and one-half years. During this time the saints attend the marriage supper of the Lamb in the heavenlies, while the earth passes through a period of unparalleled tribulation at which time Antichrist assumes full authority. Here we must assert that the general fact of the Rapture and the Revelation is clearly scriptural; the details just mentioned must be a matter of individual opinion.

The Investigative Judgment. Immediately following the return of Christ, the investigative judgment will be set. For this we have the clear statement of our Lord Himself. *When the Son of man shall come in his glory, and all the holy angels with him, then shall he sit upon the throne of his glory: and before him shall be gathered all nations: and he shall separate them one from another, as a shepherd divideth his sheep from the goats: and he*

Postmillennialists identify the judgment mentioned in Matthew 25:31-46 with the general judgment at the last day. Premillennialists are divided in their opinion. (1) Writers like Dr. J. A. Seiss look upon this judgment scene as applying only to the nations living when Christ returns, and not caught up to Him in the rapture. Consequently this judgment becomes merely "a shepherdizing of the nations with a rod of iron," only the obdurate and rebellious being destroyed. This destruction, however, is regarded merely as a violent death, such as overtook the inhabitants of Sodom and Gomorrah, the dead being raised later for final judgment, as in the case of all who were deceased previous to the coming of the Lord. However, a careful study of this judgment scene mentioned by our Lord, reveals the fact that while it concerns the living nations, it is, after all, a judgment of the individuals. (2) Other premillennial writers, such as Dr. W. B. Riley, regard this statement or account as applying to the final judgment after the millennium. He states that many premillennialists have been led into a misinterpretation here, simply because God does not on every age of Scripture, put forth the full program of the ages. As in the case of our Lord, who broke into two parts the prophecy of Isaiah which He read at Nazareth, so here, the juxtaposition of sentences does not involve a closeness of events. The order of judgment is against the "children of the millennium" or the living rebels first; and later, against the unbelieving dead, raised to receive their sentence (Cf. RILEY, *The Evolution of the Kingdom,* pp. 174-176).

shall set the sheep on his right hand, but the goats on the left (Matt. 25: 31-34). *And Jesus said unto them, Verily I say unto you, That ye which have followed me, in the regeneration when the Son of man shall sit on the throne of his glory, ye also shall sit upon twelve thrones, judging the twelve tribes of Israel* (Matt. 19: 28). That this is in the investigative judgment of the living nations at the time of the Second Advent is further evidenced by our Lord's parable of the sower, previously cited. *The Son of man shall send forth his angels, and they shall gather out of his kingdom all things that offend, and them which do iniquity; and shall cast them into a furnace of fire: there shall be wailing and gnashing of teeth. Then shall the righteous shine forth as the sun in the kingdom of their Father* (Matt. 13: 41-43).

The Destruction of the Wicked. Closely associated with the investigative judgment is the destruction of the wicked. In addition to the scriptures previously cited, St. Paul gives us the following statement: *And to you who are troubled rest with us, when the Lord Jesus shall be revealed from heaven with his mighty angels, in flaming fire taking vengeance on them that know not God, and that obey not the gospel of our Lord Jesus Christ: who shall be punished with everlasting destruction from the presence of the Lord, and from the glory of his power; when he shall come to be glorified in his saints, and to be admired in all them that believe* (II Thess. 1: 7-10).

The Fall of Antichrist and the Binding of Satan. Included in the destruction of the wicked, at the time of the Second Advent, is the Antichrist, whom St. Paul calls that "Wicked" or the "Wicked One." *And then shall that Wicked be revealed, whom the Lord shall consume with the spirit of his mouth, and shall destroy with the brightness of his coming: even him, whose coming is after the working of Satan with all power and signs and lying wonders* (II Thess. 2: 8, 9). We may be permitted to refer at this time to the binding of Satan, *that he should deceive the nations no more, till the thousand years should be fulfilled: and after that he must be loosed a little season* (Rev. 20: 1, 3).

The Establishment of the Kingdom. The Church Militant, in its full New Testament sense, began with the Day of Pentecost, and will become triumphant with the rapture of the saints at the coming of the Lord. The Church will then in some sense be merged into the kingdom. In a mystical sense, *the kingdom of God is within you* (Luke 17: 21). St. Paul defines it as *not meat and drink; but righteousness, and peace, and joy in the Holy Ghost* (Rom. 14: 17). But Jesus looked forward also to a kingdom in the future when He said, *I will not drink henceforth of this fruit of the vine, until that day when I drink it new with you in my Father's kingdom* (Matt. 26: 29). *He said also, I appoint unto you a kingdom, as my Father hath appointed unto me; that ye may eat and drink at my table in my kingdom, and sit on thrones judging the twelve tribes of Israel* (Luke 22: 29,30). We may say, therefore, that we are now in the kingdom of God the Holy Spirit, or the mystical reign of Christ in the hearts of His people. The kingdom of God the Son will succeed this, when the inner mystical kingdom shall find expression in outward glory. Then follows the kingdom of God the Father, when the Son himself becomes subject to Him, that is, the Triune God, Father, Son, and Holy Spirit, may be all in all. From the Parable of the Pounds, it seems evident that some in the days of Jesus looked for the kingdom to immediately appear, and this erroneous view He sought to correct. *A certain nobleman went into a far country to receive for him-*

Concerning the use of the word "kingdom" in the Scriptures, Mr. West says, "In its fullness, it is past, it is present, it is to come; it is inward and spiritual existing now, it is outward and visible yet to exist; it is heavenly; it is a kingdom of grace; it is a kingdom of glory; it is earthly; it is temporal; it is everlasting. In its forms it is many, in its essence it is one. It has various dispensations. It is above, it is below, and its highest consummation is the realization of the will of God on earth as it is now realized in heaven; a consummation begun below, developed in the age to come, and completed in the eternal state."— WEST, *John Wesley and Premillennialism*, p. 46.

Trench says of this kingdom, that it is "not the unfolding of any powers which already existed in the world—a kingdom not rising, as those other kingdoms, 'out of the earth,' but a new power brought into the world from above.—TRENCH, *Notes on the Parables*, p. 160.

self a kingdom, and to return (Luke 19:12). Jesus, having overcome the world, is now seated on His Father's throne, awaiting the time when He shall return to be seated upon the throne of His glory (Matt. 25:31). He left a promise also, that *To him that overcometh will I grant to sit with me in my throne, even as I also overcame, and am set down with my Father in his throne* (Cf. Matt. 25:31; Rev. 3:21). Thus the Church as the Bride of Christ, anxiously awaits the return of the Nobleman, and daily prays, *Thy kingdom come. Thy will be done in earth, as it is in heaven* (Matt. 6:10). It is this kingdom of which the prophets spoke, which John and Jesus heralded, and which the apostles affirmed with confidence.

The character of the citizenship of this kingdom proves a perplexing problem to those types of premillennialism which maintain that the Church is incomplete at the time of the millennium. Postmillen-

In the Parable of the Pounds, it is interesting to note that when the nobleman having received the kingdom returns, it is to call his servants to judgment (Luke 12:19-27).

Dr. William B. Riley, in his book entitled, *The Evolution of the Kingdom*, takes the position that this future millennial kingdom is not made up of mortal men, for "flesh and blood cannot inherit the kingdom of God." At the first resurrection when Christ shall come, "corruptible must put on incorruption" and the life of these risen saints will not be dependent upon the heart-beat of flesh and blood, but rather like that in which their Lord lived again after His resurrection—a body of "flesh and bones" animated by the eternal spirit, "a spiritual body." He interprets the words in Luke "equal to the angels" to mean "angel-like." This does not mean bodiless, for every angel that has appeared on earth, has appeared in bodily form. They have sat at human tables, and have taken human food; they have exercised gracious missions for men in human forms. The great difference has been that they were not mortal; that their natural home was in a higher sphere. Yet he believes in the "ongoing of the nations" and looks for the restoration of Israel during the millennium. He further states that, "There is no indication either that converts made from the Jewish people and the nations during the millennium, under the personal reign of Christ, will be mortal men, and asserts that the scripture, "They that wait upon the Lord shall renew their strength; they shall mount up with wings as eagles; they shall run, and not be weary; and they shall walk, and not faint," refers to the children of the kingdom in the millennial age. He bases this upon the words of Christ, "he that believeth in me, though he were dead, yet shall he live," as referring to all the deceased; and "Whosoever liveth and believeth in me shall never die" as referring to all those who are alive when Christ comes, and all who believe during Christ's millennial reign. These shall escape the grave and be changed in the twinkling of an eye from the mortal to the immortal (Cf. RILEY, *The Evolution of the Kingdom*, pp. 128-133).

nialism which regards the millennium as merely the flowering period of the present age avoids this problem. Jesus specifically states that *they which shall be accounted worthy to obtain that world, and the resurrec-*

Bishop Martensen in referring to the millennium says, "But besides this purely spiritual view, and the literal, the carnal method of interpretation, we must notice a third form of belief which recognizes the historical points here enumerated; but at the same time maintains that as the millennial reign is an actual prophecy of the glory of perfection, nature also will exhibit prophetic indications, anticipating its future glorification; and though Christ will not be raised up in a literal and sensitive manner to His kingly dominion, yet His presence will not be merely spiritual; visible manifestations of Christ will, during this period, be granted to the faithful, like those to the disciples after the resurrection. According to this view, the thousand years' reign would correspond with the interval of forty days between the resurrection and the ascension, an interval which implies the transition from earthly existence to heavenly glory.—MARTENSEN, *Christian Dogmatics*, p. 471.

Jesus is the lawful successor, as the Son of man, to Adam's dominion; as the seed of Abraham, He is the lawful heir to the throne of David, and as the Son of God, the Father has been pleased to put in subjection to Him, "the world to come, whereof we speak" (οἰκουμένην the habitable or inhabited earth; τὴν μέλλουσαν that about coming; περὶ ἧς λαλοῦμεν concerning which we speak (Heb. 2:5). From the numerous passages of scripture referring to this event we select the following only: "And in the days of these kings shall the God of heaven set up a kingdom, which shall never be destroyed: and the kingdom shall not be left to other people, but it shall break in pieces and consume all these kingdoms, and it shall stand forever" (Dan. 2:44). "I saw in the night visions, and, behold one like the Son of man came with the clouds of heaven, and came to the Ancient of days, and they brought him near before him. And there was given him dominion, and glory, and a kingdom, that all people, nations, and languages, should serve him: his dominion is an everlasting dominion, which shall not pass away, and his kingdom that which shall not be destroyed" (Dan. 7:13, 14). "And the kingdom and dominion, and the greatness of the kingdom under the whole heaven, shall be given to the people of the saints of the most High, whose kingdom is an everlasting kingdom, and all dominions shall serve and obey him" (Dan. 7:27). "Of the increase of his government and peace there shall be no end, upon the throne of David, and upon his kingdom" (Isa. 9:7). "The Lord of hosts shall reign in Mount Zion, and in Jerusalem, and before his ancients gloriously" (Isa. 24:23). "And his dominion shall be from sea even to sea, and from the river even to the ends of the earth" (Zech. 9:10). "And the Lord shall be king over all the earth: in that day shall there be one Lord, and his name one" (Zech. 14:9). The prophecies of the kingdom found in the Old Testament are reaffirmed in the New, as the following instances will show: "He shall be great, and shall be called the Son of the Highest: and the Lord God shall give unto him the throne of his father David: and he shall reign over the house of Jacob for ever: and of his kingdom there shall be no end" (Luke 1:32, 33). "Therefore being a prophet, and knowing that God had sworn with an oath to him, that of the fruit of his loins, according to the flesh, he would raise up Christ to sit on his throne" (Acts 2:30). "The kingdoms of this world are become the kingdoms of our Lord, and of his Christ; and he shall reign for ever and ever" (Rev. 11:15).

tion from the dead, neither marry, nor are given in marriage: neither can they die any more: for they are equal unto the angels; and are the children of God, being the children of the resurrection (Luke 20:35, 36). St. Paul makes a similar statement that *flesh and blood cannot inherit the kingdom of God; neither doth corruption inherit incorruption* (I Cor. 15:50). Hence he says, *As we have borne the image of the earthy, we shall also bear the image of the heavenly;* and again, *this corruptible must put on incorruption, and this mortal must put on immortality* (I Cor. 15:49, 53). These are the plain statements of Scripture concerning the nature of the children of the resurrection or the kingdom, and any theory which does not take these facts into consideration cannot be regarded as scriptural.

The Regeneration of the Earth. It is a significant fact that our Lord connects the *regeneration* with His coming kingdom. *Verily I say unto you, That ye which have followed me, in the regeneration when the Son of man shall sit on the throne of his glory, ye also shall sit upon twelve thrones, judging the twelve tribes of Israel* (Matt. 19:28). This statement is very suggestive when we consider that regeneration in the sense of the "new birth from above" stands for the direct spiritual results which come from the grace of God considered personally; and that here it refers to the divine redemption of the earth, which when our Lord appears, shall certainly be delivered from the bondage of corruption. St. Peter speaks of this event as "the times of refreshing" or "restitution of all things," and connects it immediately with the Second Coming of Christ. *Repent ye therefore, and be converted, that your sins may be blotted out, when the times of refreshing shall come from the presence of the Lord: and he shall send Jesus Christ, which before was preached unto you: whom the heaven must receive until the times of restitution of all things, which God hath spoken by the mouth of all his holy prophets since the world began* (Acts 3:19-21). We have before referred to St. Paul's clear teachings on this subject, and need now to call attention to only one statement, *The*

*creature itself also shall be delivered from the bondage
of corruption into the glorious liberty of the children of
God* (Rom. 8: 21).

From the above scriptures it appears that the earth
must undergo certain changes at the Second Coming of
Christ. In the consideration of this subject, however,
we must take into account, a distinction of great importance, that is, we must distinguish between those
changes which take place when the curse is removed
and the earth restored to its pristine state; and those
which are connected with the final consummation of
all things, in which the present order shall through dissolution and a process of glorification, be changed into
the new and eternal order. The "regeneration" or the
"restitution," therefore, pertains to the removal of the
curse from the present earth; the consummation, to the
emergence of the new heavens and the new earth. The
former constitutes the transition to the latter, and it is
this period in its preparations and its eternal state to
which the prophets have looked forward, since the world
began.

The nature of the changes which take place in this
time of restoration cannot be certainly known, but the
prophets give us some foregleams of the miraculous
transformations which will occur. Isaiah the prophet is
peculiarly rich in his poetical descriptions of "that day."
We can cite but a few of the more familiar of his prophecies: (1) There will be an increase in the fertility
of the earth. To fallen Adam it was said, *Cursed is the
ground for thy sake; in sorrow shalt thou eat of it all
the days of thy life: thorns also and thistles shall it bring
forth to thee* (Gen. 3: 17, 18); but the prophet sees a
day, when, *Instead of the thorn shall come up the fir tree,
and instead of the brier shall come up the myrtle tree:
and it shall be to the Lord for a name, for an everlasting
sign that shall not be cut off* (Isa. 55: 13). There are now
large portions of the earth which are uninhabitable, but
in that day will become the abode of beauty and glory.
*The wilderness and the solitary place shall be glad for
them; and the desert shall rejoice, and blossom as the*

rose. *It shall blossom abundantly, and rejoice even with joy and singing: the glory of Lebanon shall be given unto it, the excellency of Carmel and Sharon, they shall see the glory of the Lord, and the excellency of our God. . . . . For in the wilderness shall waters break out, and streams in the desert. And the parched ground shall become a pool, and the thirsty land springs of water: in the habitation of dragons, where each lay, shall be grass with reeds and rushes* (Isa. 35: 1, 2, 6, 7). *I will plant in the wilderness the cedar, the shittah tree, and the myrtle, and the oil tree; I will set in the desert the fir tree, and the pine, and the box tree together: that they may see, and know, and consider, and understand together, that the hand of the Lord hath done this, and the Holy One of Israel hath created it* (Isa. 41: 19, 20). Amos the prophet sees an enrichment of the soil and increased harvest. *Behold, the days come, saith the Lord, that the plowman shall overtake the reaper, and the treader of grapes him that soweth seed; and the mountains shall drop sweet wine, and all the hills shall melt* (Amos 9: 13). (2) It appears that there will be a miraculous restoration of the wild animals to their normal instincts. *The wolf also shall dwell with the lamb, and the leopard shall lie down with the kid; and the calf and the young lion and the fatling together; and a little child shall lead them. And the cow and the bear shall feed; their young ones shall lie down together: and the lion shall eat straw like the ox. And the sucking child shall play on the hole of the asp, and the weaning child shall put his hand on the cockatrice' den. They shall not hurt nor destroy in all my holy mountain: for the earth shall be full of the knowledge of the Lord, as the waters cover the sea* (Isa. 11: 6-9). "Each animal is coupled with that one which is its natural prey—a fit state of things under the Prince of Peace. There is to be a restoration to man in the person of Christ of the

Postmillennialists usually regard these expressions as purely figurative. Thus Dr. Raymond says, "The lying down together of the lion and the lamb, of the leopard and the kid, can have no application to the heavenly state, and in the earthly must be figurative, or those animals must undergo a change of nature both as to species and genera."— RAYMOND, *Systematic Theology*, II, p. 480.

lost dominion over the animal kingdom, of which he had been designed to be the merciful vicegerent under God for the good of his animal subjects." (3) There will be an increased longevity of life. *There shall be no more thence an infant of days, nor an old man that hath not filled his days; for the child shall die an hundred years old; but the sinner being an hundred years old shall be accursed. And they shall build houses, and inhabit them; and they shall plant vineyards, and eat the fruit of them. They shall not build, and another inhabit; they shall not plant, and another eat: for as the days of a tree are the days of my people, and mine elect shall long enjoy the work of their hands. They shall not labour in vain, nor bring forth for trouble; for they are the seed of the blessed of the Lord, and their offspring with them* (Isa. 65:20-23). (4) It seems probable that there may be changes in the astronomical heavens in their relation to the earth. *Moreover the light of the moon shall be as the light of the sun, and the light of the sun shall be sevenfold, as the light of seven days, in the day that the Lord bindeth up the breach of his people, and healeth the stroke of their wound* (Isa. 30:26). The scriptures which we have just cited are fraught with intense spiritual significance, and have been the source of joy and strength to multitudes of God's holy people. While this is true, it does not necessarily forbid a conviction of their literal fulfillment also; nor does it detract from their spiritual meaning, but rather increases it.

The Final Consummation. The *consummatio seculi*, or destruction of the world, marks the close of the transitional period, and ushers in the new heavens and the new earth of the eternal order. It is the closing event of the "day of the Lord." As in the beginning of this period, there is the rapture with its resurrection of the righteous dead and the translation of the living saints, followed by the investigative judgment of the living nations; so also the day closes with an apostasy following the thousand years' reign, the resurrection of the wicked dead, the destruction of the heavens and the earth by fire, and the final judgment with its rewards and punishments. Beyond earth's fiery baptism is the new and eternal day, *a new heavens and a new earth wherein dwelleth righteousness*. However, we are concerned here only with the *consummatio seculi*—the discussion of the resurrection and the final judgment being reserved for the last chapter. As to the process of this renewal of the earth we are not left to guess. We have only to read, *But the heavens and the earth, which are now, by the same word are kept in store, reserved unto fire against the day of judgment and perdition of ungodly men* (II Peter 3:7). Dr. Eliott in his *Horae Apocalypticae*, states that these words literally translated should stand as follows: "The same heavens and earth which are now by the same word stored with fire, being reserved unto the judgment and perdition of ungodly men." Commenting upon this Dr. Cumming says, "Just as the earth of old was stored with the waters, whose fountains broken up overflowed the earth, so by the same word the earth, now stored, treasured up, or charged with fire, is ready when the repressive force is withdrawn, to burst forth, to burn up all things, and to cause the elements to melt with fervent heat" (CUMMING, *The Great Preparation*, p. 36). This appears to be the meaning of St. Peter's further statement that

Referring to the words of St. Peter, that this world is to be burned up, Bishop Merrill says, "The burning up of this world, if it be literally understood, cannot take place until the close of time, and, if we find it connected with the judgment as one of the incidents of the day of the Lord, it will follow that the judgment is subsequent to the gospel day. The Scriptures teach that when the gospel dispensation closes, and the Lord descends from heaven and calls the dead from their graves, the visible earth and heaven will be destroyed by fire, and afterward be renewed in righteousness. We accept this statement as pointing to a literal fact, and propose to test it in the light of the criticisms and objections offered by the opposers of a literal advent and future judgment."—MERRILL, *The Second Coming of Christ*, pp. 262ff.

Dr. Adam Clarke, in his comment on II Peter 3, writes as follows: "All these things will be dissolved, separated, be decomposed; but none of them will be destroyed. And as they are the original matter out of which God formed the terraqueous globe, consequently they may enter again into the composition of a new system, and therefore the apostle says, 'We look for a new heaven and a new earth'; the others being decomposed, a new system is to be formed out of their materials." Again he says, "The present earth, though destined to burn up, will not be destroyed, but renewed, and refined, and purged from all moral and material imperfections and made the endless abode of happy spirits. But this state is certainly to be expected after the day of judgment."

the heavens shall pass away with a great noise, and the
elements shall melt with fervent heat, the earth also
and the works that are therein shall be burned up; and
again, *looking for and hasting unto the coming of the*
day of God, wherein the heavens being on fire shall be
dissolved and the elements shall melt with fervent heat
(II Peter 3: 10, 12). The question is sometimes asked,
"Are these words to be taken in their strictly literal
sense? If the flood, to which this catastrophe is compared, was a literal and historic fact, then we must regard this cataclysmic event as a literal occurrence also.
It is evident, however, that St. Peter does not intend to
teach the annihilation of the world by its fiery baptism,
as he does not teach its destruction by a watery baptism.
Concerning the flood and its effects he uses the strongest possible expression, saying, *The world that then was,*
being overflowed with water, perished (II Peter 3: 6). So
also, concerning the coming cataclysmic event he says,
all these things shall be dissolved; and again, *the heav-*
ens being on fire shall be dissolved (II Peter 3: 11, 12).
The word dissolved as used here is in the first instance
λυομένων, and in the second λυθήσονται, both being from
the root verb λύω which means to unloose, or to loose, to
unfasten, to unbind, but never to annihilate. It is used
in Luke 19: 30, 33 concerning the untying of the colt; in
John 1: 27 concerning the loosing of a shoe latchet; and
it is applied to the ship in which St. Paul was wrecked.
It is said that the ship was dissolved ἐλύετο in the sense of
being broken up or destroyed (Acts 27: 41). The dissolving of the earth, therefore, is not its annihilation, but the
breaking of its bonds, the loosing of it to before what it
was originally intended to be—its deliverance from the
bondage of corruption. We regard this loosing as an
exact parallel of the transformation of the earthly elements in the human body. In the same manner as a
man's body is dissolved by death and becomes the subject of decay, out of which it shall be raised immortal,
incorruptible, in power and glory; so this earth as man's
habitation shall likewise be dissolved, but out of it shall
appear in a comparable resurrection, the new heavens

and the new earth wherein dwelleth righteousness (II Peter 3: 13). *Then cometh the end, when he shall have delivered up the kingdom to God, even the Father; when he shall have put down all rule and all authority and power. For he must reign, till he hath put all enemies under his feet. The last enemy that shall be destroyed is death. For he hath put all things under his feet. But when he saith all things are put under him, it is manifest that he is excepted, which did put all things under him. And when all things shall be subdued unto him, then shall the Son also himself be subject unto him that put all things under him, that God may be all in all* (I Cor. 15: 24-28).

CHAPTER XXXV

THE RESURRECTION AND THE JUDGMENT

The resurrection which follows as an immediate effect of the Second Advent must be considered as at once a distinctive and an elementary truth of the Christian system. The doctrine of the resurrection, however, must be clearly distinguished from that of the immortality of the soul. It is possible to believe in the continuous existence of the soul after death without believing in the resurrection of the body. Frequently the two are identified, and belief in one made to stand or fall with the other. This was the case of the Sadducees who identified the two and denied both. Thus our Lord in reasoning with them said, *As touching the dead, that they rise: have ye not read in the book of Moses, how in the bush God spake unto him, saying, I am the God of Abraham, and the God of Isaac, and the God of Jacob?* (Mark 12: 26). Here Christ meets the real objection without meeting it verbally. However, since He refers only to the continuance of the soul after death, some have inferred that He meant to teach only a spiritual resurrection, that is, that the soul does not die with the body but rises to a new and higher life. St. Paul in the elaborate argument found in his epistle to the Corinthians (I Cor. 15: 12-58) seems to regard the denial of the resurrection as tantamount to a denial of immortality. Here again, this has been suggested as a basis for belief; that the only resurrection which the Bible teaches is the resurrection of the soul when the body dies. It becomes necessary, therefore, to first of all examine the Scriptures as to their teaching concerning the resurrection of the body.

The Scriptures Teach the Resurrection of the Body. The term resurrection signifies a rising again, that is, a rising of that which was buried. It signifies also a restoration of life of that which was dead. Now since the soul does not die with the body, it cannot therefore be the subject of a resurrection, except in an antithetical sense as opposed to spiritual death, which is not now the question. This definition sets at nought also, the doctrine of those who, like the Swedenborgians, hold that man in this life has two bodies—an external or material body, and an internal or psychical body. The former dies and remains in the grave, the other does not die, but in union with the soul enters in upon a future state of existence. It is to the Scriptures, however, that we must turn for any authoritative teaching upon the subject. We, therefore, call attention to (1) The Idea of the Resurrection as found in the Old Testament; and (2) The New Testament teaching concerning the Resurrection.

1. The Old Testament makes a distinction between the immortality of the soul and the resurrection of the body. We may believe on the authority of our Lord himself, that the resurrection was everywhere presupposed in the economy of the Old Testament. "As the *children of God,* so called in the Saviour's new terminology, are *the children of the resurrection* (Luke 20: 36), so the ancient fathers were, and are, and will ever be His in their integrity: His now in their spirit, hereafter in spirit and body. The key thus put into our hands by the Master, His apostles have instructed us to use freely" (POPE, *Compend. Chr. Th.,* III, p. 402). The author of the Epistle to the Hebrews states that Abraham offered up Isaac, *accounting that God was able to raise him up . . . . from whence also he received him in a figure* (Heb. 11: 19); and again, that the patriarchs desired *a better country, that is, an heavenly* (Heb. 11: 16). There are passages in the Psalms which rise to the hope of a redemption from Hades, as *God will redeem my soul from the power of the grave: for he shall receive me* (Psalms 49: 15). Here the context shows that the object of this hope is the psychical soul animating a body as well as the spiritual soul delivered from imprisonment. While the prophecies found in Isaiah 25: 8 and Hosea 13: 14 refer to the state of the Church as a whole, that found in Isaiah 26: 19 can refer only to

the resurrection of the individual, or the resumption by the soul of bodily existence. It is to the Church, however, that this wonderful prophecy is addressed. *Thy dead men shall live, together with my dead body shall they arise. Awake and sing, ye that dwell in the dust: for thy dew is as the dew of herbs, and the earth shall cast out the dead* (Isa. 26:19). Here the dead are called "my" because they sleep in Him, their disembodied souls existing safely in His keeping. It may be admitted also, that the future restoration of the Church as vividly portrayed in Ezekiel's well known vision of the "valley of dry bones," could not have been presented under the symbolism of a dead body raised to life, had not the idea of the resurrection been familiar, both to the prophetic and the common mind (Cf. Ezekiel 37:1-15). The fact that the prophets nowhere use language which would imply that the idea of the resurrection was new to the people, together with the fact that belief in this doctrine by the Pharisees must have been an inheritance and not the outgrowth of inspired teaching, furnishes a strong argument for the Old Testament belief in a bodily resurrection. The doctrine of the resurrection, however, is explicitly taught in the Book of Daniel. *And many of them that sleep in the dust of the earth shall awake, some to everlasting life, and some to shame and everlasting contempt* (Daniel 12:2). Here "the many" is the great company of the dead as contrasted with those who are alive at the time of the end; and "the dust of the earth" indicates that the reference is to the body. Doubtless it is to this that Jesus refers when he speaks of the resurrection of life and the resurrection of damnation (John 5:29). Taken in connection with the verse which follows, Daniel gives us a long range vision of the resurrection, of both the just and the unjust, the general judgment and the eternity which follows. *And they that be wise shall shine as the brightness of the firmament; and they that turn many to righteousness as the stars for ever and ever* (Daniel 12:3).

2. The New Testament is permeated with the truth of the resurrection, but here it is presented on a far higher level. St. Paul speaks of *the appearing of our Saviour Jesus Christ, who hath abolished death, and hath brought life and immortality to light through the gospel* (II Tim. 1:10). We must understand, therefore, that only through the gospel does the Christian conception of the resurrection and the complete destruction of death find its highest expression. Here is to be found the proclamation which counteracts death in all its manifestations. The basic testimony of the New Testament is found in the words of our Lord himself. Referring evidently to the prediction of Daniel, He says, *The hour is coming, and now is, when the dead shall hear the voice of the Son of God: and they that hear shall live* (John 5:25). This refers, of course, to a spiritual resurrection, or the making alive of souls that are dead in trespasses and sins (Cf. Eph. 2:1). Immediately following this in the same discourse, He says, *Marvel not at this: for the hour is coming, in the which all that are in the graves shall hear his voice, and shall come forth; they that have done good, unto the resurrection of life; and they that have done evil, unto the resurrection of damnation* (John 5:28, 29). The gospel announcement, therefore, includes the idea of a resurrection of the whole man, and of the whole race of men to an endless existence. Again, the resurrection is associated immediately with our Lord's Person and work. He says, *I am the resurrection, and the life: he that believeth in me, though he were dead, yet shall he live: and whosoever liveth and believeth in me shall never die* (John 11:25, 26). The *I am* as here used must be taken in connection with John 5:26, which indicates that there is in the Son a life and power deeper than the purely mediatorial function, *For as the Father hath life in himself; so hath he given to the Son to have life in himself.* Hence it is God's appointment that man must pass through a resurrection in order to the future life, that is, he must know both the power of the spiritual resurrection for the soul, and then the resurrection of the

body. For this reason, the resurrection of Christ is the first fruits, or pledge of the resurrection of His people.

Further still, Christ's resurrection is the Pattern after which the bodies of the saints will be raised. This St. Paul indicates in the words, *Who shall change our vile body, that it may be fashioned like unto his glorious body* (Phil. 3:21). It is union with the risen Christ as the source of life for both soul and body, that is the secret ground and condition of the resurrection of believers. The resurrection of Christ, however, is never represented as standing in the same relation to the unbeliever. The bodies which unbelieving souls inhabit after the intermediate state will indeed be immortal, but in this respect only are they like those of the saints. Hence the resurrection of the just is unto everlasting life; that of the wicked unto shame and everlasting contempt. St. Paul in answering before Felix the accusation of the Jews, speaks of his *hope toward God, which they themselves also allow, that there shall be a resurrection of the dead, both of the just and unjust* (Acts 24:15). Other scriptures bearing immediately upon this subject are the following: *But if the Spirit of him that raised up Jesus from the dead dwell in you, he that raised up Christ from the dead shall also quicken your mortal bodies by his Spirit that dwelleth in you* (Rom. 8:11): *For if we believe that Jesus died and rose again, even so them also which sleep in Jesus will God bring with him* (I Thess. 4:14); and, *I saw the dead, small and great, stand before God. . . . . And the*

Dr. Pope in commenting on Phil. 3:20, 21 says, "There are two words here of great importance: the σύμμορφον suggests the same idea as 'conformable unto his death'; the body is to be subject to the blessed law of our predestination to be *conformed to the image of his Son* (Rom. 8:29). This word 'change' is not the same as in the Corinthian chapter: here it is μετασχηματίσει which refers only to the new fashion of the risen body; there it is ἀλλαγησόμεθα, 'we shall be changed,' which refers to the entire transformation of the already existing bodies. Now it is of this latter only that our Saviour was the pattern. He 'saw no corruption'; and consequently could not be a perfect example at all points of our restoration from death, any more than He is the pattern at all points of our redemption from the final penalty of sin. There is an analogy here with His example of holiness: He leads not the way in the process of attainment; but is the consummate exemplar only of what we are to attain. We shall live in glorified bodies like His; but in our redemption from the dust He has no part with us."—POPE, *Compend. Chr. Th.*, III, p. 405.

sea gave up the dead which were in it; and death and hell delivered up the dead which were in them: and they were judged every man according to their works (Rev. 20: 12, 13).

The Nature of the Resurrection Body. It is to divine revelation that we must turn for an understanding of this important subject. St. Paul in his Corinthian discourse tells us that *It is sown in corruption; it is raised in incorruption; it is sown in dishonour; it is raised in glory: it is sown in weakness; it is raised in power: it is sown a natural body; it is raised a spiritual body. There is a natural body, and there is a spiritual body* (I Cor. 15: 42-44). Two distinct questions are involved in this statement: (1) What is the principle of identity which links the future body to the present one? and (2) What is the nature of the perfected body in its resurrected state?

1. It is evident that identity is involved in the very nature of the resurrection itself. The church has always held that the bodies, whether of the righteous or the wicked, will be identical with the bodies which they occupy in this world. *"It is sown a natural body,"* says

In former times it was commonly thought necessary to affirm a material identity between the future body and that of the present. But Paul, while he intimates that there is some bond of connection between the one and the other, is far from affirming a material identity (I Cor. 15:35-38). The only ground for inferring this identity is the association of the resurrection with the grave, and this is by no means of compelling force. The earth is the common grave of the race. In death men universally give back their bodies to the mass of physical nature. Suppose, then, that one should wish to express in vivid rhetorical phrase the fact that out of the mass of physical nature the constituents of new bodies will be taken through the marvelous working of God's power; what better could he do than to speak of the grave as yielding up its dead? This is the fitting equivalent in popular discourse for the declaration of the physical nature which receives the old body is to be the source of the new and far more perfect body which is forever to mirror the glory of the indwelling spirit. In reconstituting man's physical being material identity is of no consequence whatever. One set of molecules is just as good as another of the same order. It is therefore enormously improbable that God has devised an intricate and far-reaching economy for conserving from each body the quantity of matter necessary for physical perfection, and has undertaken to gather together in the day of the resurrection the scattered particles which are comprised in this quantity. Sameness of type, resulting from the operation of the same organizing principle, provides for the proper identity of the body through the changes of earthly life; and there is no occasion to suppose any further basis of identity in the future state.— SHELDON, *System of Christian Doctrine*, pp. 563, 564.

St. Paul, *"it is raised a spiritual body."* Here the "it" or subject, is the same in each instance; and it is this principle of identity upon which the church bases its doctrine of the resurrection. But what is this principle of identity? That identity depends upon very different conditions is generally admitted. In the inorganic realm, identity depends upon substance and form. If a stone be pulverized and scattered abroad, the substance remains but the form is destroyed, and, therefore, the identity of the object. If water be frozen or heated, the form is changed into ice or steam, but it is still water. If, however, the water be separated into its constituent elements, oxygen and hydrogen, it is no longer water. In the organic world of living substance, identity is something higher. The acorn grows into the oak, and the infant into the man, but here the principle of identity does not appear to lie in either the substance or the form, for both are constantly undergoing change. That there is a continuity between the seed and the plant, the infant and the man, cannot be doubted. So also, although it cannot be explained, it is perfectly rational to assert a continuity between our present and our future bodies, even though we admit that we do not know in what this

In our study of Anthropology (Vol. II, pp. 23, 24) we referred to "the immaterial principle" of Agassiz, which he maintained, determines the future bodily form of the organism. Agassiz says, however, that when the individual dies, this immaterial principle ceases to exist. Dr. Julius Mulleron, on the other hand, held that this vital organizing force continues in union with the soul, but is not operative between death and the resurrection. "It is not the σάρξ, the mass of earthly material," he says, "but the σῶμα, the organic whole, to which the Scriptures promise a resurrection. The organism, as the living form which appropriates matter to itself, is the true body, which in its glorification becomes the σῶμα πνευματικόν."

The object of the resurrection, as the active exertion of the divine-human power, is the body. But this formula must be understood in a wide latitude of meaning. It must include the perfect or undivided integrity of the man raised up; the actual sameness or unity of the body as the organ of the spirit; and the change that adapts it to its new state when raised. Hence three terms are the watchwords of our doctrine: the integrity, the identity, the glorification of the flesh raised in the last day. The main, or at least the most important teaching of Scripture is that of the return of the whole man to existence, that is, in the integrity of the nature which in the idea of the Creator was that of a spiritual being using a bodily organization. Man suffers in death the penalty of a dissolution which will then be repaired. He is perfect only as spirit, soul and body. . . . . The man in his entireness is the man before his Maker, both now and hereafter.--POPE, *Compend. Chr. Th.,* III, p. 406.

identity consists. The Church, therefore, asserts that
the body will rise, and that it will be the same after the
resurrection that it was before; but neither the Bible
nor the Church determines wherein this sameness consists.

2. As to the nature of the perfected resurrection
body, we can of course know but little. Our Lord's revelation of Himself to the disciples, both on the Mount of
Transfiguration and after His resurrection, made a profound impression upon them. Of the first St. Peter says,
*We have not followed cunningly devised fables, when
we made known unto you the power and coming of our
Lord Jesus Christ, but were eye-witnesses of his majesty* (II Peter 1:16; Cf. 1:17, 18). It may be well to
notice at this time, two negative statements which must
be considered in our treatment of this subject. There is,
first of all, the statement of our Lord addressed to the
Sadducees: *The children of this world marry, and are
given in marriage: but they which shall be accounted
worthy to obtain that world, and the resurrection from
the dead, neither marry, nor are given in marriage:
neither can they die any more: for they are equal unto
the angels; and are the children of God, being the children of the resurrection* (Luke 20:34-36). The second
is that of St. Paul to the Corinthians, *Flesh and blood
cannot inherit the kingdom of God; neither doth corruption inherit incorruption* (I Cor. 15:50). "There

Dr. Lange, whose imagination often dominates him, teaches that
the soul was created to be incarnate; and therefore was endowed with
forces and talents to that end. In virtue of its nature, it as certainly
gathers from surrounding matter the materials for a body, as a seed
gathers from the earth and air the matter suited to its necessities. He
assumes, therefore, that there is in the soul "a law or force, which
secures its forming for itself a body suited to its necessities and sphere;
or more properly," he adds, "the organic identity" may be characterized as the *Schema des Leibes*, which is included in the soul, ...
or a *nisus formativus* which belongs to the human soul. The soul
while on earth forms for itself a body out of earthly materials; when it
leaves the earth it fashions a habitation for itself out of the materials
to be found in the higher sphere to which it is translated; and at the
end of the world, when the grand palingenesia is to occur, the souls of
men, according to their nature, will fashion bodies for themselves out
of the elements of the dissolving universe. "The righteous will clothe
themselves with the refined elements of the renovated earth; they shall
shine as the sun. The wicked shall be clothed with the refuse of the
earth; they shall awake to shame and everlasting contempt.—HODGE,
Systematic Theology, III, p. 779.

seem to be plainly three things implied or asserted in these passages," says Dr. Charles Hodge, (1) That the bodies of men must be specially suited to the state of existence in which they are to live and act. (2) That our present bodies, that is, our bodies as now organized, consisting as they do of flesh and blood, are not adapted to our future state of being. And (3) That everything in the organization or constitution of our bodies designed to meet our present necessities, will cease with the life that now is. If blood be no longer our life, we shall have no need of organs of respiration and nutrition. So long as we are ignorant of the conditions of existence which await us after the resurrection, it is vain to speculate on the constitution of our future bodies. It is enough to know that the glorified people of God will not be encumbered with useless organs, or trammeled by the limitations which are imposed by our present state of existence (HODGE, *Systematic Theology*, III, p. 780).

St. Paul broadly outlines the nature of the resurrection body in the following series of contrasts: (1) *It is sown in corruption; it is raised in incorruption.* Here the word incorruption signifies, not merely that the body will never decay, but that it is not susceptible to corruption in any form. Consequently, it will not only be free from dissolution and death, but free from every

John Wesley in his sermon on the "Resurrection of the Dead" (Vol. II, p. 507) says, "The plain notion of a resurrection requires that the self-same body that died should rise again. Nothing can be said to be raised again but that very body that died. If God gives to our souls at the last day a new body, this cannot be called the resurrection of our body; because that word plainly implies the fresh production of what was before."

Dr. Miley points out that the difficulties concerning the resurrection of the body centers in two points: (1) the wide dispersion of the particles which composed the living body, and (2) the possibility that in the course of time some may belong to different bodies. To this he replies, "The apparent magnitude of these difficulties is far greater than the real, especially if we view them, as we should, in the light of the divine providence. The dispersion of the particles is real only in our own view. However widely scattered or deeply mingled with other matter, they remain as near to the omniscient eye and omnipotent hand of God as if placed in an imperishable urn at the foot of His throne. Nor is there any probability, even on natural grounds, that in any case so much matter could become common to two bodies as would be necessary to a proper identity of either. When we place the subject in the light of God's providence, whose purpose it is to raise the dead, all difficulties vanish."—MILEY, *Systematic Theology*, II, p. 455.

thing that tends toward that end—disease, pain and suffering. (2) *It is sown in dishonour; it is raised in*

The following particulars, however, may be inferred with more or less confidence from what the Bible has revealed on this subject: (1) That our bodies after the resurrection will retain the human form. God we are told, gave to all His creatures on earth each its own body adapted to its nature, and necessary to attain the end of its creation. Any essential change in the nature of the body would involve a corresponding change in its internal constitution. . . . . (2) It is probable that the future body will not only retain the human form, but that it will also be a glorified likeness of what it was on earth. We know that every man has here his individual character—peculiarities mental and emotional which distinguish him from every other man. We know that his body by its expression, air and carriage more or less clearly reveals his character. This revelation of the inward by the outward will probably be far more exact and informing in heaven than it can be here on earth. How should we know Peter or John in heaven, if there were not something in their appearance and bearing corresponding to the image of themselves impressed by their writings on the minds of all their readers? (3) This leads to the further remark that we shall not only recognize our friends in heaven, but also know, without introduction, prophets, apostles, confessors and martyrs, of whom we have read or heard while here on earth. (a) This is altogether probable from the nature of the case. If the future body is to be the same with the present, why should not that sameness, whatever else it may include, include a certain sameness of appearance. (b) When Moses and Elias appeared on the mount with Christ, they were at once known by the disciples. Their appearance corresponded so exactly with the conceptions formed from the Old Testament account of their character and conduct, that no doubt was entertained on the subject. (c) It is said that we are to sit down with Abraham, Isaac and Jacob in the kingdom of heaven. This implies that Abraham, Isaac and Jacob will be known; and if they are known surely others will be known also. (d) It is promised that our cup of happiness will then be full; but it could not be full, unless we met in heaven those whom we loved on earth. Man is a social being with a soul full of social affections, and as he is to be a man in heaven, is it not likely that he will retain all his social affections there? (e) The Bible clearly teaches that man is to retain all his faculties in the future life. One of the most important of these faculties is memory. If this were not retained there would be a chasm in our experience. The past for us would cease to exist. We could hardly, if at all, be conscious of our identity. We should enter heaven, as creatures newly created, who had no history. Then all the songs of heaven would cease. There could be no thanksgiving for redemption; no recognition of all God's dealings with us in this world. Memory, however, is not only to continue, but will doubtless with all our faculties be greatly exalted, so that the records of the past may be as legible to us as the events of the present. If this be so, if men are to retain in heaven the knowledge of their earthly life; this of course involves the recollection of all social relations, of all the ties of respect, love and gratitude which bind men in the family and in society. (f) The doctrine that in a future life we shall recognize those whom we knew and loved on earth, has entered into the faith of all mankind. It is taken for granted in the Bible, both in the Old Testament and in the New. The patriarchs always spoke of going to their fathers when they died. The Apostle exhorts believers not to mourn for the departed as those having no hope; giving them the assurance that they shall be reunited with all those who die in the Lord.—Hodge, *Systematic Theology*, III, pp. 781, 782.

glory. The new body will be immortal. While incorruption is a negative term signifying immunity from decay, the word immortality has more of a positive content, and implies the perpetuity of life, forever redeemed from the empire of death. But the word glory carries the thought still farther, as that which excites wonder and delight. The disciples were overwhelmed with Christ's glory at the transfiguration; the keepers of the tomb became as dead men at the resurrection of our Lord; St. Paul beheld His glory as a light above the brightness of the sun at midday; and St. John declares that His countenance was as the sun shineth in his strength. St. John also declares that *when he shall appear, we shall be like him; for we shall see him as he is* (I John 3:2). It was for this reason that the apostle exhorted true believers not to mourn unduly for their pious dead, for they were to see them again, arrayed in beauty and glory beyond the power of human comprehension. (3) *It is sown in weakness; it is raised in power.* The present body is vitiated by the presence of sin, and its senses are weakened both in quality and extent. Perhaps in the perfected resurrection body, new and exalted capabilities will be discovered, and most certainly those now in use will be immensely increased. However high our expectations may be, they will doubtless fall far short of the full reality of this glorious change. (4) *It is sown a natural body; it is raised a spiritual body. There is a natural body, and there is a spiritual body.* The words *natural* and *spiritual* as here used, are most commonly interpreted to mean the adaptation of the body to its environment. Thus a natural body is that by means of

The specific resurrection of the flesh; and the express revelation of Scripture is, that the same bodies shall rise from the graves. But the identity of the body is not the identity of the man: nor is the identity of the body dependent upon the continuation of the particles in their union which were deposited in the grave. A brief reference to Scripture examples and testimonies is sufficient to obviate misconception on this point. If appeal is made to our Lord's resurrection body, it must be remembered that there is no analogy. We have seen that death never finished its work of dissolution on Him: His bodily organization was inviolate. The only permissible argument is that, as His glorification took place upon a physical frame, so also will ours. But it is not said that we shall be raised as He was, in order to be afterward glorified: "it is raised a spiritual body"; raised immediately as such.—POPE, *Compend, Chr. Th.,* III, p. 407.

which the soul adjusts itself to the present state of existence; while a spiritual body is that which the soul will use to adapt itself to the new conditions of the future life. "It is a remark which must occur to every person," says Dr. Wakefield, "that a *spiritual* body is an apparent contradiction; and we are therefore under the necessity of taking the word *spiritual* in an unusual sense. The apostle does not mean that the resurrection body, like the immortal spirit, will be immaterial; for then it could not be the same body that dies. Nor does he mean that it will be so sublimated or etherealized as not to be a *body* in the proper sense of the word. It will be 'a body' ($\sigma\hat{\omega}\mu\alpha$), but it will be so far spiritual as to be without the mere animal functions which are essential to the *natural* body. The meaning of the apostle seems to be this: As the soul has an existence independent of animal functions, living without nourishment, and incapable of decay, sickness or death, so will be the body in the resurrection. It will be destitute of the peculiar physical organization of flesh and blood; for flesh and blood cannot inherit the kingdom of God (I Cor. 15:50). It must therefore undergo a new modification in consequence of which, though still material, it will be very different from what it now is. It will be a body without the vital functions of the animal economy,

When Paul asserts that "flesh and blood cannot inherit the kingdom of God," he means only to deny that a corrupt and mortal body can thus inherit, and not to assert that such inheritance is not true of a glorified body of material substance, from which all corruption and mortal elements have been removed. We consequently see what he means by the spiritual body in vs. 44-46, where he contrasts it with the "natural," and declares the resurrection body to be "spiritual." It is not spiritual in the sense that it is not material; for it is composed of matter. But it is spiritual, as being fitted for the spiritual life hereafter, as it had previously been natural, as fitted for the animal life of this world. This is the pneumatic body as opposed to the psychical. As the first body had been suited to the present life, and could not be used in the life to come without change; so the resurrection body is suited to the life to come, and not to the present stage of being. Hence it is that the change, with or without death, does not take place until the time of reunion in which the pneumatic life is to begin.—BOYCE, *Abstract of Systematic Theology*, p. 457.

For as spirit that serves the flesh is called carnal, so flesh that serves the spirit is called spiritual; not because it is converted into spirit, but because it is subject to spirit with a supreme and marvelous facility of obeying, having no sense of weariness, no liability to decay, and no tardiness of motion.—AUGUSTINE, *De Civitate Dei, XIII*, 20, 22.

living in the manner in which we conceive spirits to live, and sustaining and exercising its powers without waste, weariness, decay, or the necessity of having them recruited by food and sleep" (WAKEFIELD, *Christian Theology*, pp. 620, 621). While there are a few writers who regard the resurrection body as purely spiritual and in no sense material, the commonly accepted view is that which we have just stated.

The General Resurrection. The term "general resurrection" refers to the belief commonly held in the Church, that at the Second Coming of Christ, all the dead, both the righteous and the wicked, shall be raised simultaneously and immediately brought to judgment. It is in this sense also, that the creeds are commonly interpreted. Thus the Apostles' Creed has the simple statement, "I believe in . . . . the resurrection of the body." The Nicene Creed has it, "I look for the

While the body shall be marvelously changed in the resurrection, it shall still be material in substance. The terms "natural body" and "spiritual body" mean simply different states, not any distinction of essence. In a word, the resurrection is a transformation, not a transubstantiation. The latter would mean a future body of the same essence as the spirit of which it shall be a corporeal investment. The incongruity of such a state of things disproves it. The materiality of the resurrection body is entirely consistent with its immortality. The common tendency of material things to dissolution or death is wholly from their interior constitution or exterior condition, or from both. The constitution and condition may be such that both interior forces and exterior agencies shall be efficaciously operative toward the dissolution or death of the body; but just the opposite is also possible with respect to both. Surely God can so constitute and condition the resurrection body that all interior forces and external influences shall work together for its immortality. So far the resurrection bodies of the righteous and the wicked will be without distinction, the immortality of the body being no more determinative of future destiny than the immortality of the soul.—MILEY, *Systematic Theology*, II, p. 453.

It is sown a natural body, it is raised a spiritual body. When words are thus used antithetically, the meaning of the one enables us to determine the meaning of the other, we can, therefore, in this case learn what the word "spiritual" means, from what we know of the meaning of the word "natural." The word ψυχικόν translated "natural," is derived from ψυχή which means sometimes life; sometimes the principle of animal life which men have in common with the brutes; and sometimes the soul in the ordinary and comprehensive sense of the term; the rational and immortal principle of our nature; that in which our personality resides. . . . . Such being the signification of the ψυχή, it is plain that the σῶμα ψυχικόν, the psychical, or natural body, cannot by possibility mean a body made out of the ψυχή. In like manner it is no less plain that the σῶμα πνευματικόν cannot by possibility mean a body made of spirit. That indeed would be such a contradiction in terms, as to speak of a spirit made out of matter.—HODGE, *Systematic Theology*, III, pp. 783, 784.

resurrection of the dead"; while the Athanasian Creed declares, "At whose coming all men shall rise again in their bodies, and shall give an account for their works. And they that have done good shall go into life everlasting, and they that have done evil into everlasting fire." Neither the Thirty-nine Articles of the Anglican Church, nor the Twenty-five Articles of Methodism has a statement concerning the resurrection, other than that which refers to Christ. Our own creed is as follows: "We believe in the resurrection of the dead, that the bodies of both the just and the unjust shall be raised to life and united with their spirits—'they that have done good, unto the resurrection of life; and they that have done evil, unto the resurrection of damnation'" (Article XII, Section 1). That the resurrection of the righteous and the wicked is simultaneous, is the general opinion of both Reformed and Arminian theologians. Dr. Wakefield, who interprets the Wesleyan theology of Richard Watson, makes the following statement: Under the head of the resurrection as general or universal, he says, "On this subject the language of our Lord is very express. *For the hour is coming, in the which all that are in their graves shall hear his voice, and shall come forth; they that have done good, unto the resurrection of life; and they that have done evil, unto the resurrection of damnation* (John 5: 28, 29). So St. John tells us that he *saw the dead, small and great, stand before God* (Rev. 20: 12). So also St. Paul, in contrasting the benefits of redemption with the evils brought upon man by the sin of Adam, bears witness to the doctrine of a general resurrection. *For since by man came death, by man came also the resurrection of the dead. For as in Adam all die, even so in Christ shall all be made alive* (I Cor. 15: 21, 22)" (WAKEFIELD, *Christian Theology*, p. 614).

It will appear evident, however, even to the casual reader, that with the exception of the Athanasian statement, the creeds may be interpreted as teaching a general or universal resurrection, that is, a resurrection of both the righteous and the wicked, without regarding the two events as simultaneous. This may be urged on the ground (1) that the distinction in the statement itself seems to imply a distinction in the resurrection, both as to character and time. If it is an arbitrary interpretation to separate the two, it is no less so to combine them. (2) The statement in Revelation 20: 3-7, even if regarded as figurative, as it is by most of the interpreters who identify in point of time the two phases of the resurrection, yet nevertheless, reveals the fact that its author regarded a distinction in time as permissible to proper interpretation of Daniel 12: 2; Mark 12: 25; Luke 20: 35, 36 and in harmony with his own statement in John 5: 28, 29. The Emphatic Diaglot gives the literal translation of John 5: 29 as follows: "Those having done good things to a resurrection of life (εἰς ἀνάστασιν ζωῆς); and those having done evil things, to a resurrection of Judgment (εἰς ἀνασάτασιν κρίσεως)." (3) A study of the phrase ἐκ νεκρῶν, out of, or from the dead, and its characteristic use in connection with the resurrection of the righteous, strongly indicates a distinction in time. The phrase ἐκ νεκρῶν denotes that the individuals or the groups (τάγματα, or bands) are chosen out from the many who yet remain in the realm of the dead.

This last statement concerning the use of the phrase ἐκ νεκρῶν deserves further treatment. We are told that the phrase occurs forty-nine times in the New Testament, and not once is it applicable to the resurrection of the wicked, or to the resurrection when considered as embracing both the righteous and the wicked. (1) It is used thirty-four times in connection with Christ's resurrection, which certainly was out from among the dead (Cf. Notes). (2) It is used three times concerning John the Baptist, who as Herod thought, had been raised out of the dead (Mark 6: 14, 16; Luke 9: 7). (3) Three times the phrase is used in connection with Lazarus, who likewise was raised out from among the dead (John 12: 1, 9, 17). (4) Three times it is used in a figurative sense to indicate spiritual life out of the death of sin (Rom. 6: 13; 11: 15; Eph. 5: 14). (5) Once it is used in the discourse concerning Dives and Lazarus (Luke 16: 31); and (6) It is used once concerning Abraham's faith (Heb. 11: 19). There are four passages remaining to be considered, Mark 12: 25; Luke 20: 35, 36; Acts 4: 1, 2, and Philippians 3: 11. These require brief mention. (1) In Mark 12: 25, Jesus says *When they shall rise from the dead* [ἐκ νεκρῶν], *they neither marry, nor are given in marriage; but are as the angels which are in heaven;* and in Luke 20: 35, 36, *They which shall be accounted worthy to obtain that world, and the resurrection from the dead* [τῆς ἀναστάσεως τῆς ἐκ νεκρῶν], *neither marry nor are given in marriage; neither can they die any more: for they are equal unto the angels; and are the children of God, being the children of the resurrection.* Here Jesus holds out to His disciples as the hope of the righteous, that they shall be resurrected out from among the dead, which in itself necessarily implies a distinction in the time order. It is further evident, that it is to this St. John refers when he says, *But the rest of the dead lived not until the thousand years were finished. This is the first resurrection. Blessed and holy is he that hath part in the first resurrection: on such the second death hath no power* (Rev. 20: 5, 6). (2) In Acts 4: 1, 2, it is stated that the Sadducees were grieved because the apostles Peter and John *preached through Jesus the resurrection from* [ἐκ νεκρῶν] *the dead.* If now we take into account the statement in Mark 9: 10, that the disciples were perplexed as to *what the rising from the dead should mean,* we have a clue to the disturbing doctrine. Jesus had spoken of His own resurrection as out from among the dead. When this had become an established

The thirty-four texts referring to Christ's resurrection out from the dead are as follows: Matt. 17:9; Mark 9:9, 10; Luke 24:46; John 2:22; 20:9; 21:14; Acts 3:15; 4:10; 10:41; 13:30; 13:34; 17:3; 26:23; Rom. 1:4; 4:24; 6:4-9; 7:4; 8:11; 10:7, 9; I Cor. 15:12, 20; Gal. 1:1; Eph. 1:20; Col. 1:8; 2:12; I Thess. 1:10; II Tim. 2:8; Heb. 13:20; I Peter 1:3, 21.

Compare also, the following references where the "ek" or out of, is not used. Matt. 22:31; Acts 17:32; 23:6; 24:15, 21; I Cor. 15:12, 13, 21, 42, and especially John 5:28, 29 (R.V.), "Marvel not at this: for the hour cometh, in which all that are in the tombs shall hear his voice, and shall come forth; they that have done good, unto the resurrection of life; and they that have done evil, unto the resurrection of condemnation."

fact in history, the disciples understood that there was
to be an order in the resurrection. This order, St. Paul
says, is *Christ the first fruits; afterward they that are
Christ's at his coming* (I Cor. 15: 23). The resurrection
which the disciples preached, therefore, was out from
among the dead, and for those only who were accounted
worthy through Christ. The Jews believed in a resurrection of the dead at "the last day"; but that there
should be a resurrection out from among the dead, for
either Jesus or His anointed ones, was a doctrine obnoxious to them, especially to the Sadducees who questioned the fact of any bodily resurrection. (3) In Philippians 3: 11, St. Paul emphasized that phase of Christ's
teaching which regarded the resurrection out from the
dead, as a goal to be attained by those only who were accounted worthy. He therefore sought by every possible
means to attain unto the resurrection of the dead, that
is, τὴν ἐξανάστασιν τὴν ἐκ νεκρῶν or the out-resurrection
of the dead. Tischendorf's text includes the preposition
ἐκ making it, the out-resurrection from the dead. It was
for this reason that the apostle said, *I press toward the
mark for the prize of the high calling of God in Christ
Jesus* (Phil. 3: 14). It must be evident to all, that this
question is vital to the whole millennial theory. Those
who fail to make a distinction between the two resurrections are shut up either to *post* or *nil* millennialism.
The position taken in our discussion of the Second Advent necessarily determines and is determined by, this
view of the resurrection.

The Development of the Doctrine in the Church.
The questions which arose in the apostolic church were
carried over into the subapostolic period. In his first
apology Justin Martyr (c 138-166) says, "We put up
prayers that we may have a resurrection to incorruptibility through our faith in Him." This incorruptibility,
however, was not merely a spiritual body, for "in the
resurrection the flesh shall arise perfect and entire."
Origen (185-254) writes, "Differences of opinion obtain,
but the true opinion is that which has been transmitted
in orderly succession from the apostles. This teaching

is clearly that there is to be a resurrection, when this body, now *sown in corruption,* shall rise in *incorruption.* . . . . What rises at the resurrection is a spiritual body. . . . . We are not to think that bodies of flesh and blood, with passions of the senses, but rather that incorruptible bodies will be given." There developed very early a conflict between the literalistic and spiritualistic views of the resurrection, the former being held primarily in the West, the latter in the East. Irenaeus (c. 202), Tertullian (c. 220), and Cyprian (c. 258) all followed Justin in the literal interpretation, as did also at a later period Methodius (c. 312), Epiphanius (c. 403), Theophylus of Alexandria (c. 404), Prudentius (c. 405) and Jerome (c. 419). In the East, Origen led the way and was followed by Basil (c. 375), Gregory Nazianzen (c. 376), Gregory Nyssa (c. 395) and Chrysostom (c. 407). These alternating views continued until the time of Augustine (353-430), who succeeded in laying down a middle course, which in a large measure determined the position of later thought. His position was stated in these words: "Spiritual bodies will yet be bodies, not spirits; having the substance, but not the unwieldiness and corruption of the flesh; being animated, not by the living soul but by the quickening spirit. This body is now worn by Christ in ˋanticipation of what we shall wear." During the Middle Ages the schoolmen took opposite sides and dogmatized after their manner concerning the resurrection body. Erigena seems to have been inclined toward the Origenistic views, and Thomas Aquinas followed Augustine. The Protestant theologians were faithful to the ancient creeds. The Lutherans with their peculiar Christological doctrines and strongly sacramental emphasis, taught that "our bodies were framed in Adam for immortality; by the incarnation of the Son of God they were taken into affinity with Him; in His resurrection they began to be glorified; they were washed from sin in the laver of regeneration; by faith they became members of His mystical body, the temple of the Spirit; and fed and sanctified by the body and blood of Christ unto eternal life." Dr. Charles Hodge sums up the doctrine of the Reformers as follows: "(1) That the resurrection body is to be numerically, and in substance, one with the present body. (2) That it is to have the same organs of sight, hearing, and so forth, as in this life. (3) Many held that all the peculiarities of the present body as to size, stature and appearance, are to be restored. (4) As the bodies of the righteous are to be refined and glorified, those of the wicked, it was assumed, would be proportionately repulsive. The later Protestant theologians, as well Lutherans as Reformed, confine themselves more strictly within the limits of Scripture (HODGE, *Systematic Theology*, III, p. 789). This brings us to the next important subject of Eschatology, the Final Judgment.

THE FINAL JUDGMENT

By the final judgment, we understand a general judgment of all the righteous and all the wicked in one vast public assembly. This has been denied by some who think that the judgment of each man occurs at death; and by others who think that only the wicked will be judged at the last day. But the general judgment is very different from the individual or particular judgment which is passed upon each man, or which he passes upon himself at death. There are many scriptures which substantiate the latter, but which do not go to the extent of establishing the former. However, it is also true that the Scriptures make frequent mention of a day of judgment; and a comparison of these passages makes it clear that they do not refer to death, but to a specific period or day which is to synchronize with the conflagration at the end of the world. *The heavens and the earth, which are now, by the same word are kept in store, reserved unto fire against the day of judgment and perdition of ungodly men* (II Peter 3:7). It is expressly declared that *he hath appointed a day, in the which he will judge the world in righteousness* (Acts 17:31). It is also referred to as *the day of wrath and revelation of the righteous judgment of God* (Rom. 2:5); *the day when God shall judge the secrets of men by Jesus Christ* (Rom. 2:16); *the day of judgment* (II Peter 2:9); *the great day* (Jude 6); and *the great day of his wrath* (Rev. 6:17). These scriptures clearly prove three things: (1) there is to be a general judgment; (2) this is to take place at a fixed time; and (3) this great and terrible day is in the future.

As to the duration of the judgment, the indefinite use of the term "day" forbids any statement of even its probable length. This has already been discussed in connection with the Second Advent. Mr. Wesley says that "the time, termed by the prophet, 'the great and terrible day,' is usually, in Scripture, styled *the day of the Lord.* The space from the creation of man upon the earth to the end of all things, is *the day of the sons of men:* the time that is now passing over us is properly *our day;* when this is ended, *the day of the Lord* will begin. But who can say how long it will continue? 'One day is with the Lord as a thousand years, and a thousand years as one day' (II Peter 3:8). And from this very expression, some of the ancient fathers drew the inference, that, what is commonly called the day of judgment would be indeed a thousand years: and it seems they did not go beyond the truth; nay, probably they did not come up to it. For, if we consider the number of persons who are to be judged, and of actions which are to be inquired into, it does not appear that a thousand years will suffice for the transaction of that day; so that it may not improbably comprise several thousand years. But God shall reveal this also in its season." (WESLEY, Sermon: *The Great Assize*). At the other extreme is the opinion of Dr. Pond who says, "The process of judgment will continue long enough to answer all the purposes for which it was instituted;

The judgment is emphatically the final revelation of the Judge: as such the consummation of a judicial work that has ever been going on in the world. It will be executed by Christ as God-man, in strict connection with His coming to raise the dead; and its range will be universal and individual. The principles of the judgment will be the application of sundry and just tests, which will reveal the characters of all, to be followed by a final and eternal judgment distinction or severance. In the case of the ungodly this judgment will be condemnation in various degrees but eternal; and in the case of the godly their everlasting confirmation in glory and the rewards of heaven.—POPE, *Compend. Chr. Th.,* III, p. 412.

but I see no necessity for supposing that it will continue for a very long period, perhaps no longer than a literal day. At the sound of the last trumpet the dead are to be raised, 'in a moment, in the twinkling of an eye.' In a very little time the thrones can be set, and the books opened, and the worlds assembled before their final Judge. An unerring separation can be made. And by some mysterious process, there may be such a general unfolding of character, that 'every work shall be brought into judgment, with every secret thing, whether it be good or whether it be evil.' We know not, at present, how such an exhibition of character is to be made; but who will say that it cannot he made, and made suddenly; so that the whole process of the judgment may pass away in comparatively a little time?" (POND, *Christian Theology*, pp. 571, 572).

Particular and General Judgment. The Scriptures make a distinction between particular or private judgment which takes place at death, and a general or public judgment which takes place at the last day. (1) That there is a *particular judgment* is shown by the following scriptures: *Then shall the dust return to the earth as it was: and the spirit shall return unto God who gave it* (Eccl. 12:7). Here it is implied that the soul is self-conscious in the presence of God, and hence, of necessity, has a knowledge of its own moral state. St. Paul affirms this position in the words, *Now I know in part; but then shall I know even as also I am known* (I Cor. 13:12). We must believe, then, that every man at death has such a self-knowledge as to know accurately his own moral character. In another statement of St. Paul it is implied that what takes place in the day of judgment, takes place also in every man's consciousness at death, *Their conscience also bearing witness,*

Dr. Boyce says, "It has been argued that, from the vast numbers to be judged, and the many events connected with the life of every man, it will comprise a long period of time. But the rapidity with which, in some conditions, the mind will run over the course of a long life, in a moment of time, shows that a period of even exceeding brevity may suffice for a full revelation and judgment of all persons and events. The indefiniteness of the word should, however, caution us against the assumption that the day must be of only a few hours' duration."—BOYCE, *Abstract of Syst. Th.*, p. 462.

and their thoughts the mean while accusing or else excusing one another (Rom. 2:15). In the Epistle to the Hebrews there is this specific text, *It is appointed unto men once to die, but after this the judgment* (κρίσις). Here the word "judgment" is *anarthrous,* and hence no article being employed it should read, *after this, judgment,* or *a judgment.* It is not *the* judgment, in the sense of the general judgment that follows immediately after death, but a judgment—*a* particular, private judgment. (2) There is also a general or public judgment, as we have defined it above, clearly taught in the Scriptures. In the Old Testament, we may note the following: *But know thou, that for all these things God will bring thee into judgment* (Eccl. 11:9); *For God shall bring every work into judgment, with every secret thing, whether it be good, or whether it be evil* (Eccl. 12:14); *the judgment was set, and the books were opened* (Cf. Daniel 7:9, 10); *And many of them that sleep in the dust of the earth shall awake, some to everlasting life, and some to shame and everlasting contempt* (Daniel 12:2). The New Testament distinctly teaches a day of public judgment. Our Lord frequently made mention of it in words that cannot be misunderstood. *It shall be more tolerable for Tyre and Sidon at the day of judgment, than for you* (Matt. 11:22, cf. v. 24); *The men of Nineveh shall rise in judgment with this generation, and shall condemn it* (Matt. 12:41). The scene of judgment is vividly portrayed by Christ at the close of His parable on the talents (Matt. 25:31-46). St. Paul in his address on Mars' Hill declared that God *hath appointed a day, in the which he will judge the world in righteousness by that man whom he hath ordained;* (Acts 17:31); and again, *In the day when God shall judge the secrets of men by Jesus Christ according to my gospel* (Rom. 2:16). So also St. Jude says, *Behold, the Lord cometh with ten thousands of his saints, to execute judgment upon all* (Jude 14, 15). In the Apocalypse, after the account of the millennium and the great defection at its close, the writer says, *I saw a great white throne, and him that sat on it, from whose face the earth and the heaven fled away; and there was found no place for them. And I saw the dead, small and great, stand before God: and the books were opened: and another book was opened, which is the book of life: and the dead were judged out of those things which were written in the books, according to their works. And the sea gave up the dead which were in it; and death and hell delivered up the dead which were in them: and they were judged every man according to their works. . . . . . And whosoever was not found written in the book of life was cast into the lake of fire* (Rev. 20: 11-13, 15). Here is a plain and uncontestable prediction of a general judgment, at which all the dead and all the living are to be assembled. That both the righteous and the wicked will be present is evident from the fact that those whose names are written in the book of life will be saved, and those whose names are not found there, will be cast into the lake of fire.

The Person of the Judge. God alone is competent to perform the office of Judge in the last great assize. He, only, is all-wise and to Him alone are known the innermost secrets of men's lives. He understands not only their actions, but their inward thoughts and hidden

But at the judgment seat of Christ will be assembled all men, to be judged according to the deeds done in the body; from Adam, the first of the human race, down to the very last one of his numerous posterity. All, all will be there. In that vast multitude ranks and distinctions, such as now exist, will be unknown. Those whom birth, or office, or wealth, or talents placed at a distance from one another, will then stand upon the same level. The great will be without their ensigns of dignity, and the poor without their marks of abasement; for then moral distinctions alone will be regarded. The oppressor and the oppressed will be there; the former that his violence may be returned upon his own head, and the latter that his wrongs may be redressed. Jews and Gentiles, Mohammedans and Christians, the learned and the illiterate, the bond and the free, the high and the low will be there, to render an account to Him who is no respecter of persons, and whose omniscient eye will distinguish each individual in the immense throng as easily as if he were alone. Not one of the righteous will there be forgotten, and not one of the wicked shall find a hiding-place from the eye of the Judge.—WAKEFIELD, *Chr. Th.*, pp. 625, 626.

Every man, every woman, every infant of days, that ever breathed the vital air, will then hear the voice of the Son of God, and start into life, and appear before Him. And this seems to be the natural import of that expression, 'the dead, small and great:' all universally, all without exception, all of every age, sex or degree; all that ever lived and died, or underwent such a change as will be equivalent with death.—JOHN WESLEY, *The Great Assize.*

motives—even their natures and the possibilities of those natures. But this judgment is not by God as God, *For the Father judgeth no man, but hath committed all judgment unto the Son: that all men should honour the Son, even as they honour the Father* (John 5: 22, 23). The reason for this is, that the Son is not only divine but human, and his relation to humanity peculiarly qualifies Him for this office. Indeed it seems evident that the judgment is to be exercised peculiarly by Christ as man, for St. Peter declares that *he commanded us to preach unto the people, and to testify that it is he which was ordained of God to be the Judge of quick and dead* (Acts 10: 42). Specific utterances to this effect are found in Matt. 16: 27, 28 and 25: 31-34. St. Paul preached to the Athenians that God would *judge the world in righteousness by that man whom he hath ordained* (Acts 17: 31); and in his epistle to the Corinthians declares that *we must all appear before the judgment seat of Christ; that every one may receive the things done in his body, according to that he hath done, whether it be good or bad* (II Cor. 5: 10). The judgment of the world is represented as the last mediatorial act of Christ. After the execution of the final sentence, when the rewards of the righteous are bestowed, and the penalties of the wicked determined, He will deliver up the mediatorial kingdom to the Father, that God may be all in all (I Cor. 15: 24-28).

It is manifestly proper that He who is the Saviour of men should be their final judge. It is fit that the promises which He has made and the threatenings which He has uttered should be carried into effect by Himself; that from His hand those who have submitted to His law should receive their reward, and those who have been disobedient their punishment. It is fit that He should bring to a close the remedial dispensation which He established by His own personal interposition. But in addition to this, as the general judgment is intended to be a public manifestation of the righteousness of the divine administration, it will be necessary that there should be a visible judge, whose proceedings all shall see, and whose voice all shall hear. The proper person, therefore, is Jesus Christ, who being both God and man, will appear as our visible judge in His glorified humanity.—WAKEFIELD, *Christian Theology*, p. 625.

Christ is the most proper person to judge. (1) He is in favor of the prisoners. (2) He is righteous, not to be bribed. (3) He is omniscient, not to be deceived. (4) He is almighty; none can escape the sentence dire.—POTTS.

Development of the Doctrine in the Church. **There** is very little of detail in the teachings of the earliest fathers concerning the judgment. They were generally content with insisting upon its certainty. Justin (c. 165) says that "Plato used to say that Rhadamanthus and Minos would punish the wicked who came before them; and we say the same thing will be done, but at the hand of Christ; and upon the wicked, in the same bodies united again to their spirits, which are now to undergo everlasting punishment." The fathers built their doctrine chiefly upon the imagery of the Scriptures, and their writings were often lurid paraphrases or poetic descriptions. This is especially true of those commonly but perhaps improperly attributed to Tertullian (c. 220) and Hippolytus (c. 239). Origen (c. 254) explains Romans 2:13-16 as follows: "When the soul has gathered together a multitude of evil works, and abundance of sins against itself, at a fitting time all that assembly of evil boils up to punishment. The mind . . . . will see a kind of history of all the foul, shameful and unholy deeds which it has done exposed before its eyes. Then the conscience . . . . pierced by its own goads, becomes an accuser against itself." Here it will be noted, the emphasis is placed upon the particular or individual judgment. Augustine sought to reduce the truth found in the scripture imagery to dogmatic statement. His summary of the doctrine is this: "The whole Church confesses that Christ will come from heaven to judge the living and the dead; this we call the last day of divine judgment. But how many days this judgment will be held is uncertain, for that it is the manner of Holy Scripture to put 'day' for time, no one who has read the Scripture, however carelessly, can be ignorant. And

The later fathers indulged in rhetorical descriptions of the coming of Christ to judgment. Lactantius (c. 325) said that "Christ, before He descends, will give this sign, there shall suddenly fall from heaven a sword." According to Cyril of Jerusalem (c. 386), the sign of His coming will be the appearance of a cross in the sky. The descriptions of the judgment found in Basil (c. 375) and Gregory Nazianzen (c. 376) are more or less ornate. Augustine in the Enchiridion held that the fire that is to try every man's work (I Cor. 3:13) takes place in this probationary life, but afterward thought that it might in some sense take place after this life. This is the hint out of which the Roman Catholic doctrine of purgatory developed, as we have previously indicated.

therefore, when we speak of the day of judgment, we add 'the last'; for He judges now, and has judged since the human race began. . . . and even if no one had sinned, not without a good and right judgment would He retain every rational creature, perseveringly cleaving to its good, in eternal blessedness. He judges not only of the race of men and demons as a whole, that they should suffer according to the merits of their former sins, but also of each one's own work, which he has done by his own will." During the Middle Ages, opinions varied greatly, but generally the judgment was interpreted on the principle of the grossest literalism—an example of which is found in the account of Thomas Aquinas (c. 1274). The theologians of the Reformation simply affirmed the scriptural doctrine, but were careful to distinguish between the final judgment (*judicium universale et manifestum*), which takes place at the end of the world, and the individual judgment (*judicium particulare et occultum*), which is passed upon each one at death. The purpose of the former was understood in the sense of a public vindication of the divine justice, in the final awards and punishments.

The Principles of Judgment. St. Paul enumerates the principles of judgment as follows: *To them who by patient continuance in well doing seek for glory and honour and immortality, eternal life: but unto them that are contentious, and do not obey the truth, but obey unrighteousness, indignation and wrath, tribulation and anguish, upon every soul of man that doeth evil, of the Jew first, and also of the Gentile: but glory, honour, and peace, to every man that worketh good, to the Jew first, and also to the Gentile: for there is no respect of persons with God* (Rom. 2: 7-11). Dr. Wakefield in referring to the statement "the books were opened" (Rev. 20: 12) supposes that these are the different dispensa-

Thomas Aquinas says, "How will the Lord come to judgment? Like an emperor entering his city, wearing his crown and other insignia, whereby his coming may be known; thus Christ will come to judgment, in the same form in which He ascended, with all the orders of angels. Angels, bearing His crown, will go before Him; with voice and trumpet they will awaken the dead to meet Him. All the elements will be disturbed, a tempest of mingled fire and frost everywhere raging."

tions under which men have been placed, and according
to which justice requires that they should be tried. That
portion of the divine will which men know, or might
know, will therefore be the standard of trial. (1) The
heathen will be judged by the law of nature, or the
law originally given to man as the rule of his conduct.
Some portion of this law has been preserved among
them, partly by tradition and partly by reason; and
though the traces of it are in some instances obliterated,
and in others greatly obscured, yet enough remains to
render them accountable beings, and to be the foundation of a judicial trial. *For when the Gentiles, which
have not the law, that is, the written law as the Jews
had it, do by nature the things contained in the law,
these, having not the law, are a law unto themselves;
which shew the work of the law written in their hearts,
their conscience also bearing witness, and their thoughts
the mean while accusing or else excusing one another*
(Rom. 2:14, 15). (2) The Jews will be judged by the
law of Moses and the teaching of the prophets. Our
Lord's own words will be the standard for His own generation—*the word that I have spoken, the same shall
judge him in the last day* (John 12:48). (3) Christians
in general will be judged by the Scriptures of the Old
and New Testaments—especially the gospel as it confers
on men superior privileges. If the Gentile who sins
against the light of nature is justly punishable; if he who
despised the law of Moses "died without mercy," *Of*

Only faith in Christ can justify a sinner, but his works must justify
him before men. And this faith is not an inoperative principle, an intellectual recognition of the fact that divine justice requires an atonement, but it is such a heart-appreciation of this divine verity as makes a
complete change in the whole state and character of the man, as well as
his condition before God, which will not only clothe him with the
righteousness of Christ, but will infuse into him the holy principles of
the Lord of glory.—PRENTISS.

Dr. Boyce points out that in the wonderful combination by which
the created spirit, and even created matter, were, through the making
flesh of the divine Word (John 1:14) enabled to do that work which
neither man nor God could do separately. Where, but on the throne of
judgment, could this personage be seen by any except those who are
made partakers of His glory? How fit is His appearance to fill with
anguish those who have rejected Him, and with exultation and praise
all those who have trusted in Him. . . . . The judgment day will clearly
exhibit these perfections, and their harmony, to all the intelligences of
God. —BOYCE, *Abstract of Systematic Theology*, p. 467.

how much sorer punishment, suppose ye, shall he be thought worthy, who hath trodden under foot the Son of God, and hath counted the blood of the covenant, wherewith he was sanctified, an unholy thing, and hath done despite unto the Spirit of Grace? (Heb. 10:29). We may say, then, that the measure of revealed truth granted to men will be the standard by which they are judged in the last day. To this also, we may add the words of our Lord—*For unto whomsoever much is given, of him shall be much required* (Luke 12:48).

In connection with these principles, we call attention also, to the fact that the judgment is the third or executive department of the moral law—the first being the legislative, and the second, the judicial. As to the origin of moral law, we may say that it issues from the absolute holiness of God, and is exactly suited to the moral nature of man. This is important; for if moral

Dr. Pope states the principles of the judgment as follows: "The principles of the judgment may be exhibited and summed up in the following five watchwords: The test applied according to various measures of probationary privileges; the revelation of character; the separation of classes; the execution of the condemning sentence; and the confirmation or ratification of the acceptance of the saved. All these will be combined in one result. The omniscient Lord will justly apply His unerring tests.

The foregoing principles are amplified as follows: (1) Self-revelation. In both the Old and New Testaments the day of judgment is represented as the final manifestation of all secrets, whether as such unknown fully to man, or as known only to himself, or as designedly kept hidden by him and known only to God. (2) Separation. The idea of separation or discrimination inheres in the Greek term κρίσις, and in all the disclosures of judgment. It will be the final separation or sifting of the world. This separation will be in two senses twofold: a broad separation between two classes: and also a discrimination within those classes themselves. Everywhere this division into two vast masses is maintained: acceptance or rejection of Christ being the alternative. But within these great masses the same process of sifting discrimination goes on. For every man there will be a distinct judgment, succeeding or included in the former, by which his position and degree either in salvation or perdition will be determined. (3) Condemnation. There can be no doubt that the term judgment is most frequently connected with condemnation: this, in fact, is the more common meaning of κρίσις. Judgment determining the sentence, condemnation pronouncing it, and execution administering it, are almost synonymous terms in regard to the wicked: in Scripture, as in the common language of human justice. It is κατάκρισις. (4) Confirmation. It is part of the dignity of the saints that the judgment in their case will be only a ratification of a previous decree in their favor and already known to themselves. Though judged, in the more general sense of that administrative, they shall not come into condemnation. But their place and order in the state of salvation has yet to be determined (Cf. POPE, *Compend. Chr. Th.,* III, pp. 416-423).

law be in any wise unsuited to the probationary period of man, then its judicial application and its final execution must of necessity, be unjust. If, however, the law is "good" as St. Paul affirms that it is, then in its judicial aspect it is applicable to every transgression. Only on this basis can the execution of the sentence be conducted on the plane of absolute holiness. This execution is now delayed under, and because of, the sway of prevenient or restraining grace. But the wrath of God is constant in the Divine Being, and will move with all its terribleness in the executive department of moral law, when at last grace is finally spurned and no longer mitigates the sentence. The matter of moral law can be understood, therefore, only in relation to the holiness and righteousness of God. Thus the whole question of future punishment is saved from the fallacy of unconditional election, and the "true and righteous judgments" of God fully vindicated.

The Purpose of the General Judgment. In order to understand the purpose of the general judgment, it must be considered (1) in relation to God; (2) in relation to Christ; and (3) in relation to man. *First,* the judgment will furnish a worthy arena for the display of the divine attributes. In the presence of the assembled universe, it will be seen that "the judge of all the earth will do right"; and the sentence, whether of acquittal or condemnation, will be sanctioned by countless myriads of angels and men. "Then will appear," says Dr. Boyce, "the wisdom of His purpose, the truth and faithfulness

We have thus presented the rational argument for the most severe and unwelcome of all the tenets of the Christian religion. It must have a foothold in the human reason, or it could not have maintained itself against all the recoil and opposition which it elicits from the human heart. Founded in ethics, in law, and in judicial reason, as well as unquestionably taught by the Author of Christianity, it is no wonder that the doctrine of eternal retribution, in spite of selfish prejudices and appeals to human sentiment, has always been a belief of Christendom. From theology and philosophy it has passed into human literature, and is wrought into its finest structures. It makes the solemn substance of the Iliad and the Greek Drama. It pours a somber light into the brightness and grace of the Aeneid. It is the theme of the Inferno, and is presupposed by both of the other parts of the Divine Comedy. The epic of Milton derives from it, its awful grandeur. And the greatest of the Shakespearean tragedies sound and stir the depths of the human soul, by their delineation of guilt intrinsic and eternal.—SHEDD, *Dogmatic Theology,* II, pp. 747, 748.

of His promise, His power to accomplish His will, His universal benevolence, His sacrificing love, His unbounded mercy, His delivering power, His conquering grace, and, not to attempt to enumerate further, everything that can be imagined as constituting that holiness which, in one word, embraces all moral perfection." (BOYCE, *Abstract of Systematic Theology*, p. 466.) *Second,* the glory of Christ's work will then appear—not only as Judge, but as Lord and King. As Lord, His dominion is now seen to be universal, and as King who has reigned in the hearts of His people, He now welcomes them into His joy, and invites them to participate in His glory. Third, as it concerns man, the judgment is necessary for the following reasons: (1) It is the testimony of conscience in both Christian and pagan lands, that final judgment awaits the deeds of men. How can this be accounted for, except to say that it is "the

The general judgment is not so much an investigative judgment for the determination of character, as it is the summing up and manifestation of man's total moral history. It will (1) reveal every man's true character to all; and (2) vindicate the righteous judgment of God in the final rewards and punishments.

"But will the sins of the redeemed be remembered in that day, and made known in the great congregation? Some suppose they will not, as they are all forgiven in Christ, and as the Scriptures represent them as being blotted out, covered, cast into the depths of the sea, and remembered no more. Others suppose that they will be published to the assembled universe, that all may know from what a depth of sin and misery the grace of God has delivered them. Of this much, however, we may be sure, that the righteous will be far from feeling any painful sorrow or shame for past transgressions. It will be enough for them to know that these were all washed away in the blood of the Lamb, and that they shall be remembered against them no more."—WAKEFIELD, *Christian Theology*, p. 627.

Mr. Wesley holds that not only the good deeds of the righteous, but their evil deeds also before their justification will be remembered in that day. He says, "It is apparently and absolutely necessary, for the full display of the glory of God—for the clear and perfect manifestation of His wisdom, justice, power and mercy toward the heirs of salvation—that all the circumstances of their life should be placed in open view, together with all their tempers, and all the desires, thoughts, and intents of their hearts: otherwise, how would it appear out of what depth of sin and misery the grace of God had delivered them? . . . . And in the discovery of the divine perfections, the righteous will rejoice with joy unspeakable; far from feeling any painful sorrow or shame, for any of those transgressions which were long since blotted out as a cloud, washed away by the blood of the Lamb. It will be abundantly sufficient for them, that all the transgressions which they had committed shall not once be mentioned unto them to their disadvantage; that their sins and transgressions, and iniquities shall be remembered no more to their condemnation.—WESLEY, Sermon, *The Great Assize*.

voice of God in man." God does not mock His creatures, and as conscience points to a day of future reckoning, so most certainly that day will come. (2) The condition of the righteous in this world is frequently such that without the awards of the future, the justice and equity of God cannot be vindicated. (3) But we are not to understand that the general judgment is concerned solely with the acts of men. Men are not only individuals responsible for their own acts, they are also social creatures responsible for others. They exert an influence either for good or evil, and this influence lives on after the present life of the individual. His work, therefore, is not done when he dies. His deeds live after him, and will continue to do so, until history is brought to a close. Only in the final judgment, can the total influence of his life be summed up—either for good or evil. Hereditary and solidarity forces must be reckoned with in the general judgment. (4) The supreme purpose of the general judgment is, therefore, not so much the discovery of character, as it is its manifestation. St. Paul

WAKEFIELD ON THE GENERAL JUDGMENT

That men enter upon a state of retribution immediately after death is evident from our Lord's declaration to the penitent thief, the parable of the rich man and Lazarus, and St. Paul's "desire to depart and to be with Christ." This fact, however, does not set aside the necessity of a general judgment at the end of time; for, though we do not pretend fully to understand why God has appointed a day in which he will judge the world, yet there are obvious reasons which seem to justify such an appointment.

(1) Man, in his present state, is composed of soul and body. In this compound state he forms his moral character; and hence it is fitting that his whole nature should be the subject of future retribution. But this it cannot be, until the body is raised from the dead, which involves the necessity of a general resurrection in order to a final judgment.

(2) We must not suppose that when a man dies his entire moral history is concluded. The influence of his actions may continue to operate, either for good or evil, long after his earthly career is closed. Thus men, though dead, may continue to speak, even to the end of time; and as retribution cannot precede the moral conduct to which it has respect, and on which it is based, it is proper that a general judgment should close the earthly history of the human race.

(3) The circumstances of a general judgment will be declarative of the glory of God. "The Judge of all the earth," clothed in the habiliments of heavenly light, and seated upon "the throne of his glory," will summon before him the multiplied millions of our race to receive their final allotments. In the decision of that tremendous day His wisdom, justice, goodness, and truth will shine out in sunlight brilliancy, and be acknowledged by every moral creature.—WAKEFIELD, Christian Theology, pp. 627, 628.

says, *We must all appear* [φανερωθῆναι or be made manifest] *before the judgment seat of Christ; that each may receive the things done in his body, according to that he hath done, whether it be good or bad* (II Cor. 5:10). In the judgment, God discriminates between the righteous and the unrighteous, and separates them from each other, that He may uncover or make manifest their true character. Men are saved by faith, but they are rewarded according to their works, and these works spring out of the true nature of faith. As we are justified now by faith without works in the sense of merit, but by a faith that is always evidenced in works; so will it be in the final judgment, when the righteousness which is by faith will be vindicated by the works which flow from it.

The Circumstances Attending the General Judgment. The Scriptures describe the final judgment as a scene of awful solemnity and grandeur. The circumstances attending it, witness to the solemnity of the occasion. What these circumstances are, the Scriptures alone reveal. Mr. Wesley gives us the following summary of the events connected with this great and terrible day. He says, "(1) Let us, in the first place, consider the chief circumstances which precede our standing before

God will not be mocked and cannot be deceived; the character of every man will be clearly revealed. (1) In the sight of God. (2) In the sight of man himself. All deception will be banished. Every man will see himself as he appears in the sight of God. His memory will probably prove an indelible register of all his sinful acts and thoughts and feelings. His conscience will be so enlightened as to recognize the justice of the sentence which the righteous judge shall pronounce upon him. All whom Christ condemns will be self-condemned. (3) There will be such a revelation of the character of every man to all around him, or to all who know him, as shall render the justice of the sentence of condemnation or acquittal apparent. Beyond this the representations of Scripture do not go—HODGE, *Systematic Theology*, III, p. 849.

That the works are, throughout the New Testament, made so prominent as the judicial test has many reasons. It is the standing and most solemn rebuke of all Antinomianism. It has also reference to that final and full manifestation of the divine righteousness, against all who might impugn it, which is made so prominent everywhere. And, finally, as will be seen hereafter, the works will be the standard by which the various degrees of reward will be determined. Gradations will be as manifold then as now: these will not be decided by faith but by works. "My reward is with me, to give every man according as his work shall be" (Rev. 22:12); this is our Lord's last testimony on the subject.—POPE, *Compend. Chr. Th.*, III, p. 418.

the judgment seat of Christ. And, first, God will show 'signs in the earth beneath'; (Acts 2:19) particularly he will 'arise to shake terrible the earth.' 'The earth shall reel to and fro like a drunkard, and shall be removed like a cottage' (Isa. 24:20). There shall be earthquakes, κατὰ τόπους (not in divers only, but) in all places; not in one only, or a few, but in every part of the habitable world (Luke 21:11); even 'such as were not since men were upon the earth, so mighty earthquakes and so great.' In one of these, every island shall flee away and the mountains will not be found (Rev. 16:20). Meantime all the waters of the terraqueous globe will feel the violence of these concussions; 'the sea and the waves roaring' (Luke 21:25) with such an agitation as had never been known before, since the hour that 'the fountains of the great deep were broken up,' to destroy the earth, which then 'stood out of the water and in the water.' The air will be all storm and tempest, full of dark vapors and pillars of smoke (Joel 2:30); resounding with thunder from pole to pole, and torn with ten thousand lightnings. But the commotion will not stop in the region of the air; 'the powers of heaven also shall be shaken. And there shall be signs in the sun, and in the moon, and in the stars' (Luke 21:25, 26); those fixed, as well as those that move round them. 'The sun shall be turned into darkness, and the moon into blood, before the great and terrible day of the Lord come' (Joel 2:31). 'The stars shall withdraw their shining' (Joel 3:15), yea, and fall 'unto the earth' (Rev. 6:13), being thrown out of their orbits. And then shall be heard the universal shout, from all the companies of heaven, followed by the 'voice of the archangel,' proclaiming the approach of the Son of God and man, 'and the trumpet of God' sounding an alarm to all that sleep in the dust of the earth (I Thess. 4:16). In consequence of this, all the graves shall open, and the bodies of men arise. The sea also shall give up the dead which are therein (Rev. 20:13) and every one shall rise with 'his own body': his own in substance, although so changed in its properties as we cannot now conceive.

'For this corruptible' will then 'put on incorruption, and this mortal must put on immortality' (I Cor. 15:53). Yea, 'death and hades,' the invisible world, shall deliver up the dead that are in them (Rev. 20:13). So that all who ever lived and died, since God created man, shall be raised incorruptible and immortal. (2) At the same time, the Son of man 'shall send his angels' over all the earth; and they shall 'gather together his elect from the four winds, from one end of heaven to the other' (Matt. 24:31). And the Lord himself shall come with clouds in his own glory, and the glory of his Father, with ten thousand of his saints, even myriads of angels, and shall sit upon the throne of his glory. 'And before him shall be gathered all nations: and he shall separate them one from another . . . . and he shall set the sheep, [the good], on his right hand, but the goats, [the wicked], upon the left' (Matt. 25:31ff). Concerning this general assembly it is that the beloved disciple speaks thus: 'And I saw the dead,' all that had been dead, 'small and great, stand before God; and the books were

The final judgment must have been appointed for some great and important object—an object worthy of the vastness and grandeur of the scene. The object was not, certainly, to satisfy God how His creatures had acted; or to satisfy them, individually, as to their own character and state: for God will learn nothing new respecting His creatures, in the light of the judgment; and each one of them may be as well satisfied as to his own character and state before the judgment as afterward. The grand object of the judgment must be something vastly higher than all this. It is, probably, to afford to the Divine Being an opportunity to vindicate His own character before the universe; to show each and every one of His creatures that He has done right—in respect not only to that one, but to all the rest. In the judgment, God will show to me that He has treated all my fellow creatures right; and to all my fellow creatures that he has treated me right. He will show to each individual of the countless myriads who surround His throne, that He has treated not only themselves, but all others right; so that when the separation is made, and the sentences pronounced, every mouth may be stopped and every conscience convinced that the award is, in every instance, right. We have here the grand object of the general judgment; the purpose to be answered by it; the reason why God has determined, at some period yet future, to bring His intelligent creatures, friends, and enemies, together, and try to judge them in the presence of each other. And certainly this is a most noble object— one altogether worthy of the grandeur and glory of the final day. . . . . And thus the grand drama of this world's history will be closed. Heaven will gather into its capacious bosom all that is holy and lovely from the earth—all that is meet for that blest abode; and hell will receive to its flaming prisons those only that are degrated, polluted, and vicious, on whose souls are found the stains of unforsaken, uncleansed, unpardoned guilt.—POND, *Christian Theology*, pp. 572, 573.

opened' (a figurative expression, plainly referring to the manner of proceeding among men), 'and the dead were judged out of those things which were written in the books, according to their works' " (Rev. 20: 12) (JOHN WESLEY, Sermon: *The Great Assize*). And when the judgment is closed, and all are prepared to hear the final sentence, He will say to those on His right hand, *Come, ye blessed of my Father, inherit the kingdom prepared for you from the foundation of the world* (Matt. 25: 34); and to those on the left, *Depart from me, ye cursed, into everlasting fire, prepared for the devil and his angels* (Matt. 25: 41). In that dreadful hour, also, sentence will be passed upon the angels who kept not their first estate but left their own habitation; and who are now, as St. Jude tells us, *reserved in everlasting chains under darkness unto the judgment of the great day* (Jude 6).

CHAPTER XXXVI

THE FINAL CONSUMMATION

Our Lord's return and the final judgment brings about the end of the world, or the *consummatio mundi*. This is the vanishing point to which all the rays of revelation converge. But this does not mean the utter destruction of all things—rather it is a new beginning on a higher level. The mediatorial reign of Christ as a means of salvation will cease, and the kingdom of grace will then merge into the kingdom of glory. With the cessation of the mediatorial reign, the estates of men will be eternally fixed. All spirits having reached the final result of their being, the faithful will enter into absolute blessedness, and the wicked into absolute misery. Thus, as it respects the redeemed, man will be restored to the ideal of his Creator, but the wicked will be banished into outer darkness. The consummation will not only affect the world of personal spirits, however, for nature itself shall witness the great transformation. Spiritual bodies demand a new and higher environment, and hence there shall be a new heaven and a

The re-established order will be so new that the old things shall hardly come to remembrance; but the relation between the new and the old is in many points a mystery reserved. Meanwhile, the combination of these is the only notion of Consummation, an end opening to a new beginning. The end of human development, combined of sin and redemption is but a contribution from one little section of what is to us an unlimited universe presided over by a Being whose infinite resources prepare our feeble minds for wonders which we cannot sketch, even in outline, to our imagination. Human science has taught us much of the amazing consummation which the physical universe has reached; the science of faith knows no limits to its hope. There is a third τετέλεσται of the divine economy, the fullness of time in the fullest sense, which we expect. The first was when the world was finished as the scene of redemption; the second was when the Lord's cry declared the new creation finished. We must reverently look at the dim reflection of the third as it is thrown upon us only from the word of God. The contemplation ought to be one of wonder and joy. As Abraham rejoiced to see the day of Christ in the distance, so may all the children of the faithful rejoice to see in the future the day for which all other days were made.—POPE, *Compend. Chr. Th.*, III, pp. 424, 425.

new earth. The subjects which now present themselves for consideration may be classified as follows: (1) The Future State of the Impenitent; (2) The Eternal Blessedness of the Saints; and (3) The Final Consummation of the World.

THE FUTURE STATE OF THE IMPENITENT

The general judgment not only makes possible the bestowment of eternal blessedness upon the saints, but necessitates also the sentence of endless punishment upon the finally impenitent and wicked. The consideration of this subject brings before us one of the most solemn themes in the entire range of Christian theology. Dr. Asbury Lowrey says, "The simple thought of misery after death strikes with dread. The severity of that misery, to accord with Scripture representations, immeasurably expands the idea of woe, while its absolute eternity is enough to confound the sense and overwhelm with horror. . . . . This consideration should suppress trifling, inspire caution, and wake concern. Nothing could be more unnatural and shocking than to make this doctrine a subject of jesting or the theme of vehement and vindictive declamation. Let none touch the question unless, with becoming solemnity, they can treat it as a note of alarm, sounded in the ear of guilty men for the sole purpose of impelling them to take refuge in Christ." (LOWREY, *Positive Theology*, p. 269.) In our treatment of this serious subject, we shall consider (1) The Development of the Doctrine in the Church; (2) Heretical Theories Concerning the Final State of the Wicked; (3) Scripture Terms Denoting the Place of Punishment; and (4) The Scriptural Doctrine of Eternal Punishment.

The Development of the Doctrine in the Church. In order to properly understand the objections that have

If we accept the truth of the Scriptures we must be loyal to their teaching on the question of future punishment, as on all others, and none the less so because of its fearful character. On no subject could the perversion of truth be more disastrous. While such perversion may neutralize the practical force of the truth, and induce a false sense of security, it is powerless to avert the doom of sin. Our only safety lies in the acceptance of the salvation in Christ Jesus.—MILEY, *Systematic Theology*, II, p. 462.

been raised against this doctrine, it is necessary to review briefly the catholic position, and the various heretical opinions that have risen from time to time in the
history of the Church. (1) In the ancient Church, it
was the common opinion among the fathers, that the
punishment of the wicked was of endless duration.
Justin says that "Gehenna is the place where those will
be punished who have lived wickedly"; Minucius Felix
(c. 208) that "There is neither measure nor termination of these torments"; Cyprian (c. 258) that "An
everburning Gehenna will burn up the condemned, and
a punishment devouring with living flame; neither will
there be any source whence at any time they may have
either respite or end of their torments"; while Lactantius (c. 325) says that "They shall be burnt forever with
perpetual fire in the sight of angels and the righteous."
The first and principal deviation from the catholic
view of endless retribution was in the Alexandrine
school, founded by Clement and Origen. Their position is thus stated, "The punishments of the condemned
are not eternal, but only remedial; the devil himself being capable of amelioration." Dr. Shedd points out that
the question reduces itself to this, "whether the suffering to which Christ sentences the wicked is for the
purpose of correcting and educating the transgressor, or
of vindicating and satisfying the law he has broken: a
question which is the key to the whole controversy. For
if the individual criminal is of greater consequences than

Minucius Felix says, "There is neither measure nor termination to
these torments. There the intelligent fire burns the limbs and restores
them, feeds on them and nourishes them. As the fires of the thunderbolts
strike on the bodies and do not consume them, as the fires of Etna and
Vesuvius glow, but are not wasted, so that penal fire is not fed by the
waste of those who burn, but is nourished by unexhausted eating of
their bodies."

Origen's Restorationism grew naturally out of his view of human
liberty. He held that the liberty of indifference and the power of contrary choice, instead of simple self-determination, are the substance of
freedom. These belong inalienably and forever to the nature of finite
will. They cannot be destroyed, even by apostasy and sin. Consequently, there is forever a possibility of a self-conversion of the will
in either direction. Free will may fall into sin at any time; and free
will may turn to God at any time. This led to Origen's theory of an
endless alternation of falls and recoveries, of hells and heavens; so that
practically he taught nothing but a hell.—SHEDD, *Dogmatic Theology*,
II, p. 669.

the universal law, then the suffering must refer principally to him and his interests. But if the law is of more importance than the individual, then the suffering must refer principally to it (SHEDD, *Dogmatic Theology*, II, pp. 668, 669). (2) The Mediaeval Church was almost a unit in holding to the doctrine of endless punishment. Erigena (c. 850), however, was inclined toward the views of Origen, maintaining that the consciousness of sin and helplessness would constitute the misery of the lost; but ultimately all things would be purified from evil, and return to God. Thomas Aquinas taught that Gehenna is situated under the surface of the earth, that darkness reigns there, and a real material fire. The orthodox mystics dwelt with painful elaboration on the subject of eternal torment. (3) The Reformers accepted the catholic belief in eternal punishment, but avoided all detail in their confessions. The Augsburg Confession (1530) contains only the simple statement that Christ "will give the pious and elect eternal life and perpetual joy, and will condemn impious men and devils to be tormented without end." Since the Reformation, Annihilationism, Universalism and Restorationism have been affirmed at different times, but have never been generally accepted by the Church. (4) In modern times, Universalism grew up with German rationalism, and like deism before it, vehemently opposed this evangelical truth. The anti-rationalistic and mediating theologians, however, did much to spread the idea of universal salvation under the form of restorationism. Schleiermacher and his school objected to the doctrine

Schleiermacher offers the following objections to eternal punishment. "(a) Christ's words in Matt. 25:46; Mark 9:44; John 5:29 are figurative. (b) The passage in I Cor. 15:25, 26, teaches that all evil shall be overcome. (c) Misery cannot increase, but must decrease. If it is bodily misery, custom habituates to endurance, and there is less and less suffering instead of more and more. If, on the other hand, it is mental suffering, this is remorse. The damned suffer more remorse in hell than they do on earth. This proves that they are better men in hell than upon earth. They cannot, therefore, grow more wretched in hell, but grow less so as they grow more remorseful. (d) The sympathy which the saved have with their former companions, who are in hell, will prevent the happiness of the saved. The world of mankind, and also the whole universe, is so connected that the endless misery of a part will destroy the happiness of the remainder." This is a fair sample of the rationalistic positions of that age.

of eternal punishment; Nitzsch taught restorationism, and Rothe contended for the doctrine of annihilation. Dorner concludes his discussion of endless punishment with the remark, that "We must be content with saying that the ultimate fate of individuals, namely, whether all will attain the blessed goal or not, remains veiled in mystery."

Heretical Theories Concerning the Final State of the Wicked. While these heretical theories concerning the future state of the wicked reach back in some instances to the earlier periods of Church history, they have had their chief development in modern times. Four theories may be mentioned—Destructionism, Universalism, Annihilationism and Restorationism.

1. Destructionism is a term which was formerly used to express the materialistic belief that the soul is mortal and perishes with the body. Materialism as we have indicated (Cf. Volume I, p. 275) is that form of philosophy which gives priority to matter as the ground of the universe, and hence regards the soul as only rarefied material essence. Being material, the soul is not immortal, and therefore perishes with the body.

2. Universalism is the doctrine that all men will be saved, and exists in several different forms. The earliest English congregation of Universalists was founded in 1760. The promoters of this doctrine were men who believed in the divinity and atonement of Jesus Christ, and that He suffered the penalty for all men. Hence they taught that sooner or later, in this world or in the next, all men would believe and be saved. This it will be noted is a form of universal restorationism. Another class of Universalists taught that sin would be punished but the sinner himself would be saved. They based their doctrine on the Scripture, *If any man's work shall be burned, he shall suffer loss: but he himself shall be saved; yet so as by fire* (I Cor. 3:15). A grosser form of universalism was found in that of the Necessarians or Fatalists, who denied any distinction between sin and holiness, and held that "one man does the will of God as much as another. Every man answers the end for

which he was made, and of course is a fair candidate for everlasting happiness." There are other forms of Universalism which are also Unitarian. They deny the divinity of Christ and the merit of His atonement. They admit that men are sinners in varying degrees, but hold that none are entirely so. Punishment of sin, they maintain, takes place in this life. They believe in a future life also, in which all will be gathered at the resurrection, and upon which all will enter, regardless of their characters formed upon earth. The scriptures already cited are a sufficient refutation of these false positions.

3. Annihilationism holds that the souls of the wicked will be punished by destruction, which is interpreted to mean annihilation. The form of this doctrine which is most popular in modern times, is based upon a belief in conditional immortality. Man's soul which survives his body, was created to be immortal, but by sin, this precious gift was forfeited. Christ died that men might

It may be stated in general, as to all the places which speak of destruction and death of the soul, that reference is made to its spiritual loss of God's favor and holiness, and not to the extinction of its being. This extinction would be contrary to the natural immortality conferred on spirit. It is not even true, so far as we can know, that even matter will ever be annihilated. What is called its destruction is simply such a change of form as makes it unfit for the uses for which it had been so formed. Thus we speak of the utter destruction of a house, of machinery, of an animal, not meaning the annihilation of the matter which composed it; but the destruction of the form in which that matter appeared, and which was essential for its use. In like manner, the death of the soul means its becoming unfit for the uses for which it was made, namely, for happiness, for holiness, for the service of God, for the complacent love of God and for the reflection of His image. Such an utter deprivation of all the faculties for which the moral nature of man was made, may well be called its death, even its utter destruction.—BOYCE, *An Abstract of Theology*, p. 491.

Many other objections to this hypothesis of annihilation might be mentioned, which do not affect theology so much as isolated interpretations of Scripture, and the psychological or physiological theories of human nature which it forces or tempts those who accept it to adopt. The student must be constantly on his guard as to both these points; otherwise he will be bewildered by the variety of plausible arguments with which both the heavier and the lighter literature on this subject abound. But, after all, it cannot be too habitually remembered that this solemn question does not depend upon isolated texts, nor upon speculations as to the nature of personality and consciousness. It is connected with the great principles and steadfast tendency of all the teaching of revelation, which everywhere speaks to man as an immortal being, having an eternal destiny, the issues of which are bound up with his use of the means provided of God for his salvation in this probationary state.—POPE, *Compend. Chr. Th.*, III, p. 444.

be saved, and all who accept His offer, will receive in the most literal sense, the gift of eternal life. This gift is the restoration of the forfeited immortality, and is bestowed upon believers only. Hence in the resurrection, both the righteous and the wicked appear before God, but only those who have the gift of immortality will enter into His eternal kingdom. The wicked not being immortal, will be annihilated. Some hold that this takes place immediately; others, that there will be a longer or shorter period of suffering—but all teach that ultimately the wicked will cease to exist. This theory claims support from such terms as ἀπώλεια, which is sometimes translated "perdition" and sometimes "destruction"; and ὄλεθρος, generally translated destruction (I Thess. 5: 3; II Thess. 1: 9; I Tim. 6: 9). These words, however, do not mean annihilation, as other scripture references clearly indicate. Thus, *If any man worship the beast and his image, and receive his mark in his forehead, or in his hand, the same shall drink of the wine of the wrath of God, which is poured out without mixture into the cup of his indignation; and he shall be tormented with fire and brimstone in the presence of the holy angels, and in the presence of the Lamb: and the smoke of their torment ascendeth up for ever and ever: and they have no rest day nor night, who worship the beast and his image, and whosoever receiveth the mark of his name* (Rev. 14: 9-11). There is no way to evade the force of such scriptures as these, without a direct denial of their teaching concerning eternal punishment. Without further discussion, we may say, (1) that the theory of annihilation contradicts the commonly received doctrine of immortality; (2) that annihilation cannot be regarded as a proper punishment for sin; (3) that it allows no degrees in punishment—a fact clearly expressed in the Scriptures; and (4) that the doctrine is out of harmony with general trend of scriptural truth.

4. Restorationism is based upon the principle that punishment of sin is not so much retributive as disciplinary and reformatory; and therefore teaches that sinners, however intensely they may suffer in the future,

will ultimately be brought to holiness and heaven. While this is a form of universal salvation, it differs from what is commonly known as Universalism, in that it does not limit the punishment of sin to this life. Restoration-ism lays claim to the support of such scriptures as the following: (1) the general promise to Abraham, that in his seed should all the nations of the earth be blessed

Dr. Wakefield gives the best refutation of annihilationism, in our opinion, of any of the Protestant theologians. We can give only a sum-mary of his position. He says:

1. That the term death, as applied to man in the Scriptures, ever means annihilation and that annihilation is the penalty of the divine law, are mere assumptions for which there is not the shadow of proof, and which we may very confidently deny. Indeed, to understand the term death in the sense of annihilation would turn many passages of scrip-ture into downright nonsense, as a few examples will show. Thus: "Precious in the sight of the Lord is the death [annihilation] of his saints" (Psalms 116:15). "We were reconciled to God by the death of his Son" (Rom. 5:10). "Who shall deliver me from the body of this death?" (Rom. 7:24). "He that loveth not his brother, abideth in death" (I John 3:14).

2. The theory is inconsistent with itself. Its advocates teach, not only that annihilation is the penalty of the law, but that it is the most dreadful of all punishments, even worse than endless suffering; and yet they maintain that the annihilation of the righteous between death and the resurrection is no punishment at all, but a real gain. Will the wicked suffer any more from annihilation between death and the resur-rection than the righteous? Certainly not. And if the annihilation of the righteous at death is not the penalty of the law, how can the an-nihilation of the wicked be? If in the former case there is no infliction of punishment, how can the punishment be so dreadful in the latter? The system teaches, therefore, that annihilation is the penalty of the law and not the penalty; that it is a most dreadful punishment, and no punishment at all; and that the only difference between the righteous and the wicked, as far as this matter is concerned, is that the former shall be annihilated once, the latter twice.

3. That annihilation will not be the future punishment of the wicked is evident from the absurdity of supposing that they shall be raised again into existence merely to be annihilated. If annihilation is true, all men lose their personal identity at death; for it would be per-fect folly to talk about continued existence of persons who are an-nihilated. If death is annihilation, a resurrection is impossible. There might be other moral beings created, but they could not be justly re-wardable or punishable for the moral conduct of annihilated generations of men.

4. If the future punishment of the wicked is to consist in anni-hilation, then all sinners will be punished alike; which is both unreason-able and unscriptural. But as there will be different degrees of future punishment, and as there cannot be different degrees of annihilation, therefore, annihilation cannot be that punishment. Again, to those who are suffering these supposed torments, annihilation would either be a curse or a blessing. If the former, a state of endless torment would be better for the sinner than a release from all suffering by annihilation; and if the latter, annihilation cannot be the penalty of the law, unless it can be made to appear that a penalty and a blessing are the same thing.—WAKEFIELD, *Christian Theology,* pp. 647, 648.

(Gen. 22:17, 18; 26:4; 28:14; Gal. 3:8-16); (2) that Christ tasted death for every man, and consequently is the Saviour of all men (Heb. 2:9; I Tim. 4:10); (3) that God wills the salvation of every man (I Tim. 2:4); (4) that every knee shall bow, and every tongue confess that Jesus Christ is Lord (Phil. 2:10, 11); and (5) that death itself shall be destroyed (I Cor. 15:26, 54). Reference is also made to the purpose of God to *gather together in one all things in Christ, both which are in heaven, and which are on earth; even in him* (Eph. 1:10); and also the pleasure of the Father *to reconcile all things unto himself; whether they be things in earth, or things in heaven* (Col. 1:19). A careful study of these scriptures and their contexts, however, makes it clear that they do not support the doctrine of restorationism.

The Scripture Terms Denoting the Place of Punishment. There are three words translated "hell" in the Authorized Version of the New Testament — Hades, Tartarus and Gehenna. (1) Hades refers to the realm of the dead, and the distinctions between place and state have already been discussed. (2) Tartarus appears only in the participle form of the verb ταρταρόω, which means to cast down to Tartarus. It is found only in II Peter 2:4 — *For if God spared not the angels that sinned, but cast them down to hell* [ταρταρώσας], *and delivered them into chains of darkness, to be reserved unto judgment.* We may, therefore, regard Hades as the

It would be easy to show, however, by careful examination of all such passages (the references cited above), that they do not prove the doctrine in support of which they are adduced; but such an examination is uncalled for at this point. It is only necessary to remark, (1) that the blessing which comes upon all men through the seed of Abraham, does not necessarily imply the actual salvation of all. (2) That though Christ died for all men, and is, in this respect as well as in others, the Saviour of all men, yet He is the special Saviour only "of those that believe." (3) That God wills the salvation of all men, but only in the appointed way, that is, "through sanctification of the Spirit and belief of the truth," and not whether they believe in Christ or not. (4) That all men shall bow to Christ and acknowledge Him, either by a voluntary reception of His grace and salvation, or by a constrained subjection to His avenging justice; and (5) That death shall be destroyed when "all that are in the graves shall hear" the voice of Christ "and shall come forth; they that have done good, unto the resurrection of life; and they that have done evil, unto the resurrection of damnation." —WAKEFIELD, *Christian Theology*, p. 644.

intermediate state of wicked men, and Tartarus as the intermediate state of wicked angels. (3) Gehenna is compounded from the two Hebrew words *Ge* and *Hinnom,* and means "the valley of Hinnom." In the New Testament it is called *Gehenna* (γέεννα), and appears twelve times (Matt. 5: 22, 29, 30; 10: 28; 18: 9; 23: 15, 33; Mark 9: 43, 45, 47; Luke 12: 5 and James 3: 6). In all of these places, the word refers to torture and punishment in the future world. In Matt. 18: 9 the word Gehenna is associated with the punishment to be meted out at the judgment; and in the preceding verse, the words "everlasting fire" are used as its equivalent. In Mark 9: 43, Jesus says, *It is better for thee to enter into life maimed, than having two hands to go into hell, into the fire that never shall be quenched* [ἄσβεστον or inextinguishable]: *where their worm dieth not, and the fire is not quenched* [οὐ σβέννυται]; in Luke 12: 5, the words of Christ are, *Fear him, which after he hath killed hath power to cast into hell* [Gehenna]. It is frequently pointed out, that of the twelve passages in the New Testament in which the word Gehenna occurs, all were used by Christ himself, except that in James 3: 6. The word "hell," therefore, in the sense of *Gehenna,* refers to the place provided for the final punishment of evil angels and impenitent men, after the day of judgment—the intermediate *Hades of the wicked, and the Tartarus* of the fallen angels, already anticipating the horrors of *Gehenna* in the same sense that *Paradise* anticipates the joys of heaven.

Bishop Weaver says, that in arriving at the meaning of any generic term, we must not only take the definition of the word, but it must be such a definition as will agree with the context. This general rule should be observed in determining the meaning of all generic words. Because the word "Gehenna" literally signifies the valley of Hinnom, we are not thence to conclude that it was never used in any other sense. The proper meaning must be determined by the connection in which it is used. The original meaning of the word "Paradise" is, "a place inclosed for pleasure and delight." In the Old Testament, it is used in reference to the garden of Eden. In the New Testament it is used as another name for heaven (Luke 23: 43; II Cor. 12: 4; Rev. 2: 7). If, because the word "Gehenna" literally signifies the valley of Hinnom, it never means anything else, then Paradise never means anything else than the garden of Eden, or a place on earth inclosed for pleasure and delight. (Cf. WEAVER, *Christian Theology,* p. 323.)

The Doctrine of Eternal Punishment as Taught in the Scriptures. As in all matters which concern the future, the Scriptures must be our sole authority. We shall, therefore, in our study of this subject, arrange the scriptures in answer to three important questions which commonly arise: (1) Do the Scriptures teach the doctrine of future punishment? (2) What is the nature of this punishment? and (3) Is this punishment eternal?

1. Do the Scriptures teach the doctrine of future punishment? The mere perusal of Christ's words, without any note or comment, should convince the unprejudiced reader that He taught the doctrine of future punishment. The following should be carefully studied. *Then will I profess unto them, I never knew you: de-*

Watson's Dictionary, Article Hell. This is a Saxon word, which is derived from a verb which signifies to hide or conceal. A late eminent Bible critic, Dr. Campbell, has investigated this subject with his usual accuracy; and the following is the substance of his remarks: In the Hebrew Scriptures the word sheol frequently occurs, and uniformly he thinks, denotes the state of the dead in general, without regard to the virtuous or vicious characters of the persons, their happiness or misery. In translating that word, the LXX have almost invariably used the Greek term αἵδης, hades, which means the receptacle of the dead, and ought rarely to have been translated hell, in the sense in which we now use it, namely, as the place of torment. To denote this latter object, the New Testament writers always make use of the Greek word γέεννα, which is compounded of two Hebrew words Ge Hinnom, that is, "The Valley of Hinnom," a place near Jerusalem, in which children were cruelly sacrificed by fire to Moloch, the idol of the Ammonites (II Chron. 33:6). This place was also called Tophet (II Kings 23:10) alluding, as is supposed, to the noise of drums (*toph* signifying a drum) there raised to drown the cries of helpless infants. As in process of time this place came to be considered as an emblem of hell, or the place of torment reserved for the punishment of the wicked in a future state, the name Tophet came gradually to be used in this sense, and at length to be confined to it. In this sense, also, the word gehenna, a synonymous term, is always to be understood in the New Testament, where it occurs about a dozen times. The confusion that has arisen on this subject has been occasioned not only by our English translators having rendered the Hebrew word *sheol* and the Greek word *gehenna* frequently by the term hell; but the Greek word hades, which occurs eleven times in the New Testament, is in every instance, except one, translated by the same English word, which it ought never to have been.

Stuart says, while the Old Testament employs *sheol*, in most cases to designate the grave, the region of the dead, the place of the departed spirits, it employs it also, in some cases, to designate along with this idea the adjunct one of the place of misery, place of punishment, place of woe. In this respect it accords fully with the New Testament use of hades. For though hades signifies the grave, and often the invisible region of separate spirits, without reference to their condition, yet in Luke 16:23, it is clearly used for a place and condition of misery. The word hell is also used by our translators for gehenna, which means the world of future punishment.—STUART, *Essay on Future Punishment.*

part from me, ye that work iniquity (Matt. 7:23); *And fear not them which kill the body, but are not able to kill the soul: but rather fear him which is able to destroy both soul and body in hell* (Matt. 10:28); *The Son of man shall send forth his angels, and they shall gather out of his kingdom all things that offend, and them which do iniquity; and shall cast them into a furnace of fire: there shall be wailing and gnashing of teeth* (Matt. 13:41, 42); *So shall it be at the end of the world: the angels shall come forth, and sever the wicked from among the just, and shall cast them into the furnace of fire: there shall be wailing and gnashing of teeth* (Matt. 13:49, 50); *Then shall he say also unto them on the left hand, Depart from me, ye cursed, into everlasting fire, prepared for the devil and his angels: and these shall go away into everlasting punishment: but the righteous into life eternal* (Matt. 25:41, 46); *For what shall it profit a man, if he shall gain the whole world, and lose his own soul?* (Mark 8:36); *And if thy hand offend thee, cut it off: it is better for thee to enter into life maimed, than having two hands to go into hell, into the fire that never shall be quenched: where their worm dieth not, and the fire is not quenched* (Mark 9:43, 44 cf. vs. 45-48); *The rich man also died, and was buried; and in hell he lift up his eyes, being in torments, and seeth Abraham afar off, and Lazarus in his bosom* (Luke 16:22, 23); and *Marvel not at this: for the hour is coming, in the which all that are in their graves shall hear his voice, and shall come forth; they that have done*

The miseries of the wicked, previous to the resurrection, must be purely spiritual; but, after that event, they will be, in part, corporeal. They will consist in the loss, the absence, of everything desirable, and in the infliction of positive, unmingled, sufferings. The rich man in hell is said to have received his good things; implying that no more good remained for him. Accordingly, he was denied a drop of water to cool his burning tongue. The wicked in hell are said to "have no rest day nor night." "The wine of the wrath of God is poured out without mixture into their cup" (Rev. 14:10). They will endure the tortures of an ever-accusing, stinging conscience. They will suffer from the indulgence of unsated malice, envy, revenge, rage, and every other hateful passion of which they are capable. They will suffer from perpetual disappointment, defeat, and despair. They will suffer from one another. They will suffer all that is implied in those awful figures, those appalling representations, by which the Holy Spirit has set forth their agonies.— POND, *Christian Theology*, p. 576.

good, unto the resurrection of life; and they that have done evil, unto the resurrection of damnation (John 5: 28, 29. The solemn truth taught in these scriptures is, that those who reject Christ and the salvation offered through Him, shall die in their sins and be separated from God forever. Many learned men have sought to explain away this truth as contrary to the goodness of God, but the simple fact still remains that *God is not mocked: for whatsoever a man soweth, that shall he also reap. For he that soweth to his flesh shall of the flesh reap corruption; but he that soweth to the Spirit shall of the Spirit reap life everlasting* (Gal. 6: 7, 8). This present life is one of probation, and following it must be the eternal consequences. This is no more than simple

It is an almost invincible presumption that the Bible does teach the unending punishment of the finally impenitent, that all Christian churches have so understood it. There is no other way in which the unanimity of judgment can be accounted for. To refer it to some philosophical speculation which had gained ascendancy in the Church, such as the dualism of good and evil as two coeternal and necessary principles, or the Platonic doctrine of the inherent immortality and indestructible nature of the human soul, would be to assign a cause altogether inadequate to the effect. Much less can this general consent be accounted for of the ground that the doctrine in question is congenial to the human mind, and is believed for its own sake, without any adequate support from the Scripture. The reverse is the case. It is a doctrine which the natural heart revolts from the struggles against, and to which it submits only under stress of authority. The Church believes the doctrine because it must believe it, or renounce faith in the Bible and give up all the hopes founded upon its promises. There is no doctrine in support of which this general consent can be pleaded, which can be shown not to be taught in the Bible.—HODGE, *Systematic Theology*, III, p. 870.

We have already admitted that the language of Scripture on this subject is more or less figurative; but whether it is figurative or otherwise, of one thing we may be sure, that it was intended to convey ideas strictly conformable to truth. God can no more make a false impression on the human mind by use of figures, than he can lead men into error by the plainest and most positive declarations; for both alike would be contrary to the divine veracity. Nor will his goodness, any more than his truth, allow him to alarm his moral creatures with groundless fears or to represent the consequences of sin as more dreadful than they really are. We may therefore safely conclude, that the future state of the wicked, as to its general character, will be one of intense suffering; for, to suppose that it will be more tolerable than absolute darkness, the agonies of death, and the action of fire, is virtually to charge God with the utterance of falsehood, and to set up our own standard in opposition to divine revelation. This intense suffering which will be the portion of the ungodly, will arise (1) from what is called the punishment of loss . . . . and (2) from the punishment of sense.—WAKEFIELD, *Christian Theology*, p. 642.

justice, and every person of sincerity must admit that the principles here laid down are eternally just.

2. What will be the nature of future punishment? The terms which are used in the Scriptures to express the idea of future punishment, must of necessity be in part figurative. Only by comparing it with that which is within our mental grasp, are we able to understand even in a small measure, something of this solemn truth. The following terms are used in the Scriptures to express the nature of future punishment: (1) It is called the *second death.* This is the term used by St. John in the Apocalypse. *But the fearful, and the unbelieving, and the abominable, and murderers, and whoremongers, and sorcerers, and idolaters, and all liars, shall have their part in the lake which burneth with fire and brimstone: which is the second death* (Rev. 21:8 cf. Rev. 20:14, 15). The fear of death brought the whole race of men into bondage (Heb. 2:15). It is surrounded with gloom and terror, and is the source of tormenting fears. Then sentence of death cannot be executed while the sinner lives, but comes as an unescapable consequence at the judgment, because of the withdrawal of the remedy of grace. During his lifetime, the corruption of his soul was mitigated by prevenient and restraining grace, but at death he becomes eternally exposed to the corruption of his own soul without this mitigation. Thus the second death is the only possible condition of the unregenerate in the world to come. We have pointed out that physical death is a change which indicates the corruption consequent upon sin; we may now reverse the order and say that the second death is that spiritual corruption of which physical death is the visible type. Physical death is soon over, but here is a death that never dies—where groanings shall never cease, and

"Depart from me, ye cursed, into everlasting fire" (Matt. 25:41). These words are not only pronounced against them by the Son of man, they echo against them from the depths of their own being, from the abused divine likeness in themselves, they echo against them from all ranges of the creation, which now unanimously bear witness for Him. There is no more peace in the glorified creation for those who are thus condemned; they must be separated therefrom, and to any inquiry concerning their state, we have no other answer than this, "outer darkness."—MARTENSEN, *Christian Dogmatics,* p. 474.

agony never end. (2) Our Lord speaks of future punishment as *outer darkness*. It is to be noted also, that in each instance, He associates this darkness with weeping and gnashing of teeth (Cf. Matt. 8: 12; 22: 13; 25: 30). St. Peter speaks of the *chains of darkness, and the mist of darkness reserved for the ungodly forever* (II Peter 2: 4, 17); while St. Jude speaks of the evil angels which are *reserved in everlasting chains under darkness unto the judgment of the great day* (Jude 6); and again, of the *blackness of darkness forever* (Jude 13). Dr. Wakefield speaks of this darkness as resembling "the deep midnight of the grave, lengthening onward from age to age, and terminated by no succeeding day." "Let this darkness be understood literally," says Dr. Ralston, "and it denotes a condition inexpressibly horrible. We have read of a darkness in Egypt so thick that it could 'be felt'; we have tried to imagine the cloud of gloom that would soon envelop our world, if the light of the sun and every star were to be instantly and completely quenched; but how indescribably inadequate must be these illustrations to portray the horrors of that 'outer darkness' into which the wicked will be driven, and by which they will be forever overwhelmed!" (RALSTON, *Elements of Divinity*, p. 520). (3) It is described as a state of positive punishment. Our Lord himself informs us that the wicked shall be cast *into a furnace of fire: there shall be wailing and gnashing of teeth* (Matt. 13: 42); while St. Paul speaks of the Lord as being *revealed from heaven with his mighty angels, in flaming fire taking vengeance on them that know not God, and that obey not the gospel of our Lord Jesus Christ* (II Thess. 1: 7, 8). Attempts have been made to tone down the severity of these scriptures by regarding them as purely

Dr. Charles Hodge states that "the sufferings of the finally impenitent, according to the Scriptures, arise: (1) From the loss of all earthly good. (2) From the exclusion from the presence and favor of God. (3) From utter reprobation, or the final withdrawal from them to the Holy Spirit. (4) From the consequent unrestrained dominion of sin and sinful passions. (5) From the operations of conscience. (6) From despair. (7) From evil associates. (8) From their external circumstances; that is, future suffering is not exclusively the natural consequence of sin, but also includes positive inflictions. (9) From their perpetuity."—HODGE, *Systematic Theology*, III, p. 868.

figurative. But the figure never fully portrays the reality; and the reasonable conclusion is, therefore, that the fire of future punishment, if not literal, will be infinitely more intolerable. (4) Future punishment is further described as *banishment from God*. This is the worst form of punishment conceivable—before which death, everlasting fire, and the blackness of darkness are as nothing. God is the author of every good and every perfect gift, and the loss of God is the loss of all good. The words, *Depart from me, ye cursed* (Matt. 25: 41) indicates a loss of light and love, of friendship, of beauty and song—the loss of even hope itself. To be banished from God is to be forever separated from heaven and all good. Such are the solemn representations which the Holy Spirit has seen proper to make concerning the state of the finally impenitent and the nature of their punishment.

3. Is future punishment eternal? Since this question has been answered in the negative by some, a careful consideration of the subject necessitates a study of the word αἰώνιος, which in the Scriptures is rendered *everlasting* or *eternal*. The word αἰών, as the substantive from which the adjective αἰώνιος is derived, signifies an "age," and denotes indefinite duration—that is, it does not of itself determine the length or duration of the age. Thus the Creator has an αἰών and the creature has an αἰών, but the former is infinite and the latter finite. *Behold, thou hast made my days as an handbreadth; and mine age is as nothing before thee* (Psalms 39: 5). Dr. Shedd, who made an excellent study of this question, says, that "In reference to man and his existence, The Scriptures speak of two, and only two αἰῶνες, or ages; one finite, and one infinite; one limited, and one endless; the latter succeeding the former. . . . . The two aeons, or ages known in Scripture, are mentioned together in Matt. 12: 32, *It shall not be forgiven him, neither in this world* [αἰών], *neither in the world* [αἰών] *to come;* in Mark 10: 30, *But he shall receive an hundredfold now in this time* [καιρός], ... *and in the world* [αἰών] *to come, eternal life;* in Luke 18: 30, *Who*

Since the word aeon (αἰών), or age, in Scripture, may denote either the present finite age, or the future endless age, in order to determine the meaning of "aeonios" (αἰώνιος), it is necessary first to determine in which of the two aeons, the limited or the endless, the thing exists to which the epithet is applied; because anything in either aeon may be denominated "aeonian." The adjective follows its substantive, in meaning. Onesimus, as a slave, existed in this world (αἰών) of "time," and when he is called "aeonian" or "everlasting" (αἰώνιος) servant (Philemon 15), it is meant that his servitude continues as long as the finite aeon in which he is a servant; and this is practically at an end for him, when he dies and leaves it. The mountains are denominated aeonian, or "everlasting" (αἰώνια), in the sense that they endure as long as the finite world (αἰών) of which they are a part endures. God, on the other hand, is a Being that exists in the infinite αἰών, and is therefore αἰώνιος in the endless signification of the word. The same is true of the spirits of angels and men, because they exist in the future aeon, as well as in the present one. If anything belongs solely to the present age, or aeon, it is aeonian in the limited signification; if it belongs to the future age, or aeon, it is aeonian in the unlimited signification. If, therefore, the punishment of the wicked occurs in the present aeon, it is aeonian in the sense of temporal; but if it occurs in the future aeon, it is aeonian in the sense of endless. The adjective takes its meaning from the noun. The English word "forever" has the same twofold meaning, both in Scripture and in common use. Sometimes it means as long as a man lives upon earth. The Hebrew servant that had his ear bored with an awl to the door of his master, was to be his servant "forever" (Exodus 21:6). Sometimes it means as long as the Jewish state should last. The ceremonial laws were to be statutes "forever" (Lev. 16:34). Sometimes it means, as long as the world stands. "One generation passeth away, and another generation cometh; but the earth abideth forever" (Eccl. 1:4). In all such instances, "forever" refers to the temporal aeon, and denotes finite duration. But in other instances, and they are the great majority in Scripture, "forever" refers to the endless aeon; as when it is said that "God is over all blessed forever." The limited signification of "forever" in the former cases, does not disprove its unlimited signification in the latter. That Onesimus was an "everlasting" (αἰώνιος) servant, and that the hills are "everlasting" (αἰώνια), no more disproves the everlastingness of God, and the soul; of heaven, and of hell; than the term "forever" in a title deed disproves it. To hold land "forever" is to hold it "as long as grass grows and water runs"; that is, as long as this world, or aeon, endures. The objection that because αἰώνιος, or aeonian, denotes "that which belongs to an age," it cannot mean endless, rests upon the assumption that there is no endless αἰών, or age. It postulates an indefinite series of limited aeons, or ages, no one of which is final and everlasting. But the texts that have been cited disprove this. Scripture speaks of but two aeons, which cover and include the whole existence of man, and his whole duration. If, therefore, he is an immortal being, one of these must be endless. The phrase "ages of ages," applied to the future endless age, does not prove that there is more than one future age, and more than the phrase "the eternities" proves that there is more than one eternity; or the phrase "the infinities" proves that there is more than one infinity. The plural in these cases is rhetorical and intensive, not arithmetical in its force (SHEDD, Dogmatic Theology, II, pp. 686-688). Dr. Shedd holds that an indefinite series of limited aeons with no final endless aeon, is a Pagan and Gnostic, not a biblical conception. The importation of the notion of an endless series of finite cycles, each of which is without finality and immutability, into the Christian system, has introduced error, similarly as the importation of the Pagan conception of Hades has (cf. SHEDD, Dogmatic Theology, II, p. 682, 683).

shall not receive manifold more in this present time [καιρός], *and in the world* [αἰών] *to come, life everlasting;* in Eph. 1:21, Above . . . . *every name that is named, not only in this world* [αἰών], *but also in that which is to come.* The *things present,* and the *things to come,* mentioned in Romans 8:38 and I Cor. 3:22, refer to the same two ages. These two aeons, or ages, correspond to the two durations of 'time' and 'eternity,' in the common use of these terms. The present age, or aeon, is 'time'; the future age, or aeon, is 'eternity.'" (SHEDD, *Dogmatic Theology,* II, pp. 682-686). The present or limited aeon is denominated in Scripture, "this world" (Matt. 12:32; 13:22; Luke 16:8; 20:34; Rom. 12:2, I Cor. 1:20; and 2:6). The future or infinite and endless aeon, is called "the future world," "the world to come," or "that world" (Cf. Matt. 12:32; Heb. 2:5; 6:5; Mark 10:30; Luke 18:30; and 20:35).

With this study of the words αἰώνιος and αἰών, we may now note their application in the following scriptures: *Wherefore if thy hand or thy foot offend thee, cut them off, and cast them from thee: it is better for thee to enter into life halt or maimed, rather than having two hands or two feet to be cast into everlasting* [αἰώνιον] *fire* (Matt. 18:8). St. Mark uses this same scripture but adds the words *into the fire that never shall be quenched: where their worm dieth not, and the fire is*

It is also the doctrine of Scripture, that this future punishment of the incorrigible shall be final and unlimited; another consideration of great importance in considering the doctrine of the atonement. This is a monitory doctrine which a revelation could only unfold; but being made, it has no inconsiderable degree of rational evidence. It supposes, it is true, that no future trial shall be allowed to man, the present having been neglected and abused; and to this there is much analogy in the constant procedures of the divine government in the present life. When many checks and admonitions from the instructions of the wise, and the examples of the froward, have been disregarded, poverty and sickness, infamy and death, ensue, in a thousand cases which the observation of every man will furnish; the trial of an individual, which is to issue in his present happiness or misery, is terminated; and so far from its being renewed frequently, in the hope of his finally profiting by a bitter experience, advantages and opportunities, once thrown away, can never be recalled. There is nothing, therefore, contrary to the obvious principles of the divine government as manifested in this life, in the doctrine which confines the space of man's highest and most solemn probation within certain limits, and beyond them cutting off all his hope.—WATSON, *Theological Institutes,* I, p. 211.

not quenched (Mark 9:43, 44). He also says, *But he that shall blaspheme against the Holy Ghost hath never forgiveness, but is in danger of eternal damnation* (Mark 3:29). St. John says, *He that believeth on the Son hath everlasting* [αἰώνιον] *life: and he that believeth not the Son shall not see life; but the wrath of God abideth on him* (John 3:36). In the description of the judgment found in Matthew 25:31-46, Jesus says to those on his left hand, *Depart from me, ye cursed, into everlasting* [αἰώνιον] *fire, prepared for the devil and his angels;* and the scene closes with the words, *And these shall go away into everlasting* [αἰώνιον] *punishment: but the*

Stuart in his "Exegetical Essays" states that "αἰώνιος is employed 66 times in the New Testament. Of these, 51 relate to the future happiness of the righteous; 7 relate to the future punishment; namely, Matt. 18:8; 25:41, 46; Mark 3:29; I Thess. 1:9; Heb. 6:2; Jude 6; 2 relate to God; 6 are of a miscellaneous nature (5 relating to confessedly endless things, as covenants, invisibilities; and one, in Philemon 15, to a perpetual service). In all the instances in which αἰώνιος refers to future duration, it denotes endless duration; saying nothing of the instances in which it refers to future punishment." The younger Edwards says that αἰών, reckoning the reduplications of it, to be single instances of its use, occurs in the New Testament in 104 instances; in 32 of which it means a limited duration. In 7 instances it may be taken in either the limited or endless sense. In 65 instances, including 6 instances in which it is applied to future punishment, it plainly signifies an endless duration. (Both of these notes are quoted in SHEDD, *Dogmatic Theology,* II, pp. 688, 689.)

The Greek words αἰών and αἰώνιος literally and properly denote endless duration. Their etymology (ἀεί and ὤν—being or existing always) shows this. Their ordinary use and signification show the same. They as properly denote an endless duration as our English words eternal and everlasting. They are sometimes used, like the English words, in a restricted sense—restricted by the nature of the subject to which they are applied; but in such cases the connection readily indicates the sense, so that there is little danger of error. But we are not left to the general meaning of these words, however satisfactory they may be. The word αἰώνιος is so used by our Saviour, in reference to the future punishment of the wicked, as to show, conclusively, that it must denote an endless duration. I refer particularly to the passage (Matt. 25:46) where the future punishment of the wicked, and the future happiness of the righteous are set over against each other, and the same term αἰώνιος is applied to both; thus indicating that the duration of both is equal and endless.—POND, *Christian Theology,* p. 581.

The materialistic interpretation of its figurative representations, as held in the earlier centuries, and particularly by the mediaeval church, is now discarded and replaced by a more rational and truthful interpretation. But through all these differences and disputations a very remarkable unanimity has remained respecting the duration of such punishment. On this question the best scholarship of today is in full accord with the historic doctrine of the Church. This is a significant fact, and the more so because such accordance is not from any predilection or preference, but simply by constraint of the plain sense of Scripture.—MILEY, *Systematic Theology,* II, pp. 470, 471.

righteous into life eternal [αἰώνιον]. If by these statements our Lord does not mean eternal punishment, what significance can possibly attach to them? The word αἰώνιος is the strongest word in the New Testament to express the duration of happiness. If, therefore, we limit the meaning of the word in relation to the wicked, we must also limit it in relation to the righteous, so that we shall then have neither a future heaven nor hell. "I have seen," says Dr. Adam Clarke, "the best things that have been written in favor of the final redemption of damned spirits, but I never saw an answer to the argument against the doctrine, drawn from this verse, but that sound learning and criticism should be ashamed to acknowledge."

The objections which are urged against eternal punishment may generally be reduced to these two: (1) It is objected that the punishment is disproportionate to the sin. This objection, as Dr. Asbury Lowrey points out, is based upon a low estimate of the nature of sin. He says, "The objection to the eternity of hell is made to appear contrary to divine justice and repugnant to the divine nature by two false assumptions: *first*, that sin, especially when it is connected with the moral life, possesses so little turpitude, that it may be regarded as a human frailty or weakness; and *second*, that sin will not disturb any principle of the moral government of the universal Ruler, except only so far as the province of earth and the human family are concerned." (LOWREY, *Positive Theology*, pp. 276, 277.) (2) It is objected that

Dr Luther Lee declares that "the sentence which will be passed upon sinners, by the righteous judgment of God, at the last day, will be irrevocable. This must appear from a consideration of the immutability of God, the Judge. Immutability is that perfection of God, which renders Him eternally unchangeable. The force of this is plain. No change by way of repentance and regeneration can take place in the sinner, after being condemned at the last judgment and sent to hell. The atonement of merits of Christ's death, and the advantages of His intercession, will after the day of judgment, no longer be available, and hence, all the benefits of the same, including the efficacy of prayer, and the agency of the Holy Ghost, will be forever lost. For God to condemn a sinner and send him to hell, at one time, and then revoke the sentence and recall him from his infernal prison, while he is yet the same in moral character, is to act differently at different times, in view of the same moral principles; which implies change or mutability.—LEE, *Elements of Theology*, p. 325.

God is too merciful to inflict everlasting punishment upon His creatures. Here, again, there is a low estimate of sin. God's mercy and His justice are never in conflict with each other. As previously indicated, Jesus Christ himself, during His earthly ministry, gave to the Church its severest declarations concerning this solemn truth. The opponents of the doctrine, therefore, are brought into direct opposition to Him who suffered—*the just for the unjust, that he might bring us to God* (I Peter 3:18).

THE ETERNAL BLESSEDNESS OF THE SAINTS

The Scriptures have more to say of the eternal blessedness of the saints, than of the final state of the wicked; but the subject being less controversial, has generally occupied less space in theology. God's grace which warns the wicked against the day of wrath, assures the righteous also, of their eternal blessedness. In our treat-

The Christian Gospel—the universal offer of pardon through the self-sacrifice of one of the Divine Persons—should silence every objection to the doctrine of endless punishment. For as the case now stands, there is no necessity, as far as the action of God is concerned, that a single human being should ever be the subject of future punishment. The necessity of hell is founded in the action of the creature, not of the Creator. Had there been no sin, there would have been no hell; and sin is the product of man's free will. And after the entrance of sin and the provision of redemption from it, had there been universal repentance in this life, there would have been no hell for man in the next life. The only necessitating reason, therefore, for endless retribution that now exists, is the sinner's impenitence. Should every human individual, before he dies, sorrow for sin, and humbly confess it, Hades and Gehenna would disappear.—SHEDD, *Dogmatic Theology*, II, p. 749.

Those who deny the position that sin is an infinite evil forget that the principle upon which it rests is one of the commonplaces of jurisprudence: the principle, namely, that crime depends upon the object against whom it is committed as well as upon the subject who commits it. The merely subjective reference of an act is not sufficient to determine whether it is a crime. The act may have been the voluntary act of a person, but unless it is also an offense against another person, it is no crime. To strike is a voluntary act; but to strike a post or a stone is not a culpable act. Furthermore, not only crime, but degrees of crime depend upon the objective reference of a personal act. . . . . One and the same act may be simultaneously an offense against an individual, a family, a state, and God. Measured by the nature and qualities of the offender himself, it has no degrees. But measured by the nature and qualities of these moral objects against whom it is committed, it has degrees of turpitude. As the first three are only finite in worth and dignity, the culpability is only certain degrees of the finite. As the last is infinite in worth and dignity, the culpability is infinite also. (SHEDD, *Dogmatic Theology*, II, p. 750 cf. EDWARDS: *Justice of God*, *Works*, IV, p. 228.)

ment of this subject, we shall consider (1) Heaven as a Place and a State; (2) The Blessedness of the Saints; (3) The Employments of Heaven; and (4) The Endless Duration of Heaven.

Heaven Is Both a Place and a State. That heaven is a state of eternal blessedness is admitted by all. But heaven is a place also. In our discussion of the Intermediate State, we pointed out the scriptural teaching that both heaven and hell are places, and that at death, souls enter the one or the other. There they await the judgment which shall fix their final state with its rewards or punishments. Heaven, therefore, as we must now view it, is the abode of the righteous in their final state of glorification. It is perhaps impossible to speak of place in reference to spiritual bodies, in the same sense that we use the term when speaking of the present bodies of flesh and blood. We know, however, that Jesus comforted His sorrowing disciples with the words, *In my Father's house are many mansions; if it were not so, I would have told you. I go to prepare a place for you. And if I go and prepare a place for you, I will*

There is a blessed state beyond this life, of which we cannot speak minutely as if we had seen it, but of which we can speak confidently because we know the principle of it. The man who has entered it is present with God and with Christ, in a clearer and truer consciousness of the divine presence than was possible on earth, and enters upon the higher stages of that divine life which has already been begun. He is living the life of progressive holiness; he is like his Lord and Saviour, and is ever growing more like Him, advancing to perfection. He is under the most holy and inspiring influences, where all that is best in him is constantly helped to increase. All characteristic activities of the Christlike life are open to him. The grade of being in which he finds himself is higher than that which he has left, and fresh opportunities of holy service and of holy growth and blessedness are constantly set before him. He is in the life that he loves and ought to love, and the course of free and Godlike activity stretches on before him without end.—CLARKE, *An Outline of Christian Theology,* pp. 471, 472.

God and blessed spirits are the exhaustless constituents of the life of bliss. Each spirit not only reflects God, but the entire kingdom of which he is a member. When God shall be all in all, it may be said that all are in all, in one another; and the multiplicity of charismata unfolds itself, in this unlimited and undarkened reflection of love and contemplation; in this ever new alteration of giving and receiving, of communication and receptivity. The medium by which the blessed in a spiritual manner communicate with each other, and are in each other, we designate as light (Col. 1:12), according to the indications given in Scripture, and we take this word in both a spiritual and corporeal sense. Thus we read of "the inheritance of the saints in light."—MARTENSEN, *Christian Dogmatics,* p. 488.

come again, and receive you unto myself; that where I am, there ye may be also (John 14: 2, 3). But we need not here discuss the relation of the spiritual body to space. The Scriptures speak of the physical heavens above us, but they also speak of a *third heaven,* where God dwells and where His presence is manifested in a peculiarly indescribable sense. St. Paul speaks of being caught up into this highest heaven—whether in the body or out of the body, he could not tell, and having heard there, words which could not be uttered. It is commonly supposed that this was the occasion when he saw the glorified body of Jesus (I Cor. 9: 1). Stephen *looked up steadfastly into heaven, and saw the glory of God, and Jesus standing on the right hand of God* (Acts 7: 55); and St. Paul tells us that *to be absent from the body is to be present with the Lord* (II Cor. 5: 8). We need not, therefore, think of the soul as having to travel long distances spatially, in order to enter heaven. The distance is not to be conceived in terms of physical space, but of changed conditions. At the ascension Jesus was taken up into heaven, and a cloud received Him out

The heaven of the saints will therefore not be a realm of shades, unsubstantial and indeterminate, but a kingdom substantial and real, where the faculties and functions of human personality will be active in the joy of righteous freedom. Like the capacities of the soul, the powers of the body will be commensurate with the law and vocation of the everlasting life. These are they which have come out of the Great Tribulation, and they washed their robes, and made them white in the blood of the Lamb. Therefore are they before the throne of God; and they serve Him day and night in His temple: and He that sitteth on the throne shall spread His tabernacle over them. They shall hunger no more; neither shall the sun strike upon them, nor any heat: for the Lamb which is in the midst of the throne shall be their shepherd, and shall guide them unto fountains of waters of life, and God shall wipe away every tear from their eyes.—GERHART, *Institutes of the Christian Theology,* II, p. 473.

When the teaching of the New Testament regarding the after life is carefully considered, the question naturally rises, "What difference is there between Paradise and heaven? What is the distinction between the life of departed believers before the judgment and after it?" The answer should embrace four particulars: in heaven a physical organism is bestowed upon the soul; the Church will be complete and perfected; the universe will be brought into harmony with the spiritual needs and longings of the Christian soul; a new and clearer vision of God will be opened to believers. At the resurrection and judgment the spirit will be clothed anew with a material framework which is so completely in harmony with the thoughts and desires of the Spirit that it is itself designated a spiritual body.—CLAPPERTON, *The Essentials of Theology,* p. 461.

of sight (Acts 1:9). Heaven, therefore, is just behind the veil, which so often but "thinly intervenes," as marking that which to us is visible, and that which is beyond the range of mortal sight. The word *apocalypse* means an unveiling, and at death, the righteous pass through this veil into the beatific vision of Christ. This to the redeemed soul is heaven. But as the cloud veiled Jesus from the sight of the disciples, so also, He will come again with clouds, that is, He will burst through the veil in an apocalypse, and be revealed from heaven in majesty and power. When also, St. Paul speaks of Jesus as having *ascended up far above all heavens, that he might fill all things* (Eph. 4:10), he is not speaking primarily of physical distance, but of his glorious majesty and the fullness of His redeeming grace. Heaven, therefore, will be a place, the eternal abode of all the redeemed of all the ages.

St. John states specifically, that he *saw the holy city, new Jerusalem, coming down from God out of heaven, prepared as a bride adorned for her husband* (Rev. 21:2); and again, he heard the words, *Come hither, I will show thee the bride, the Lamb's wife* (Rev. 21:9).

The Scriptures ever represent heaven as a place. This is so plain a fact that it hardly needs any illustration. Our Lord represented it as a place or mansion in His Father's house (John 14:1-3); St. Paul, as a building of God, a house not made with hands, eternal in the heavens (II Cor. 5:1). Again, it is the temple of God, the place of His throne and glory (Rev. 7:9-17); and a great city, the holy Jerusalem (Rev. 21:10). No doubt these are figurative representations of heaven; but that does not affect the underlying reality of place.—MILEY, *Systematic Theology*, p. 473.

Dr. Gerhart while regarding heaven as having substantial reality, emphasizes the difference between the present earthly order, and the future spiritual order. He says, "Heaven is the domain of uncreated glory, in which God, the Father, Son and Holy Spirit, lives the life of absolute love in fellowship with Himself. Heaven, the self-produced οἰκία of God, is eternal, supernatural, transcendent. It is not a part of the created universe. It may not be located. Heaven is the form of existence which differs essentially from the present economy of mankind or of the cosmos, as the Creator differs from His creation. . . . . Nor may we think of heaven as an abode which is separated from us conformably to the laws of nature-space or nature-time. Considered from this point of view, heaven is neither far from us nor near us. The conception is equally defective, whether we imagine the οἰκία of God to be locally present or locally distant. Like God himself, the sphere of His essential glory does not, objectively, exist under the conditions of any natural or earthly category.—GERHART, *Institutes of the Christian Religion*, II, pp. 889, 890.

These references clearly indicate that the apostle is speaking of the Church in her perfected glory. Other passages, however, seem to refer to the Church militant on earth. Thus, *they shall bring the glory and honour of the nations into it* (Rev. 21:26). One passage seems to blend the militant and triumphant aspects of the Church in a single statement—*And the nations of them which are saved shall walk in the light of it,* referring to the light which streams down from the Jerusalem which is above; *and the kings of the earth do bring their glory and honour into it*—referring to the Church Militant on earth (Rev. 21:24). Dr. Adam Clarke's comment is significant, as indicating the quick transition in thought from the Church Militant to the Church Triumphant. On Rev. 21:2 concerning the new Jerusalem he says, "This doubtless means the Christian Church in a state of great prosperity and purity"; while the declaration, "there shall be no more earth," he applies to the Church after the resurrection. Dr. Ralston thinks that the true interpretation of the last three chapters of the Apocalypse is this: "In the preceding part of Revelation a prophetic sketch had been given of the history of the Church to the commencement of Christ's millennial reign. In the last three chapters the millennial reign of Christ, the solemn events of the resurrection, the general judgment, and the glories of the future state, are depicted. As the millennial reign of Christ with His saints on earth will precede, and is typical of, His triumphant reign with them in the heavenly state, the most rational inference is, that both of these states are included. The burden of this description unquestionably relates to the heavenly state; yet, as both the millennial and heavenly glory are connected with the mediatorial reign of Christ, the one unfolding its greatest triumphs in this world and the other revealing its final issues in the world to come, it is but natural that the description of both should be blended. The triumphs of Christ's mediatorial reign on earth, and its rewards in heaven, are, in an important sense, one." (RALSTON, *Elements of Divinity,* pp. 535, 536.) As the one Church is sometimes viewed as militant, and at other times as triumphant, so if we mistake not, the concluding chapters of the Apocalypse, open up the prospect of a new and eternal order, in which the old boundary line between heaven and earth is effaced, and the latter inhabited by redeemed and glorified beings, has in itself become a part of heaven. Behold, the tabernacle of God is with men, *and he will dwell with them, and they shall be his people, and God himself shall be with them, and be their God* (Rev. 21:3).

The Blessedness of the Saints. While the nature of future happiness cannot be known in this life, the Scriptures give us many intimations of what God has prepared for them that love Him. (1) Heaven will be a place from which all sin and unrighteousness shall be banished forever. *There shall in no wise enter into it any thing that defileth, neither whatsoever worketh abomination, or maketh a lie* (Rev. 21:27). No unholy thing shall ever enter the abode of the blessed, nor shall the saints ever feel the sinister influence of Satan or wicked men. (2) It will be a place where the penal consequences of sin are all removed. *And God shall wipe away all tears from their eyes; and there shall be no more death, neither sorrow, nor crying, neither shall there be any more pain: for the former things are passed*

In referring to the description of the New Jerusalem, Dr. Ralston says, "But the question is often asked: Are these descriptions figurative, or are they literal? It is generally assumed that they are figurative. Perhaps they are. But we dare not affirm that they are entirely so. The human body, in the resurrection, will be the identical body that we have here: yet it will be changed into a 'spiritual body'; it will be 'fashioned like unto Christ's glorious body'; even so, for aught we know, when the new heaven and the new earth' shall be created, God may produce new substances of gold and precious stones, so refined and spiritualized, that they will far transcend those metals, as known on earth, as will the spiritual bodies of the saints the 'vile bodies' they now possess. And if this be correct (and who can say that it is not?) then the descriptions here given of the magnificent city which shall be the final habitation of the people of God may be different from the literal acceptation only in so far as the spiritual gold and precious stones, and rivers and trees, of the celestial world, shall excel in beauty, magnificence and purity, those substances on earth; just as the vile body of the saints on earth shall be excelled by that body which shall rise from the tomb, with all the undying energies and unfading beauties of immortality. But if we conclude that these descriptions are entirely figurative, then we are bound to infer that all these glowing descriptions must come far short of imparting a full conception of the glorious reality.—RALSTON, *Elements of Divinity*, pp. 536, 537.

away (Rev. 21:4). (3) Heaven will not only be characterized negatively by the absence of all evil, but the saints shall also enjoy the possession of all positive good. The curse having been removed, St. John says, *The throne of God and of the Lamb shall be in it; and his servants shall serve him: and they shall see his face; and his name shall be in their foreheads. And there shall be no night there; and they need no candle, neither light of the sun; for the Lord God giveth them light: and they shall reign for ever and ever* (Rev. 22:3-5). The scriptures just cited represent heaven as the perfect answer of every holy desire. For those who are weary, it is everlasting rest; for the sorrowing, it is a place where God shall wipe away all tears; for the suffering, there shall be no more pain; for the mistakes and blunders of a sincere but imperfect service, the throne of God shall be there, and His servants shall serve Him—every deed being performed in His presence and under His approving smile; for those who are perplexed and bewildered by the uncertainties and disappointments of this life, it is promised that there shall be no night there; for the Lord God giveth them light, and they shall reign with Him forever and ever.

Another source of blessedness to the saints, will be their communion with each other and with their common Lord. We may be sure that the distinct personality of every redeemed saint will be preserved inviolate; and that the social instincts which characterized them here, will not be obliterated there, but rather intensified. Hence the apostle says, *But ye are come unto mount Sion, and unto the city of the living God, the heavenly Jerusalem, and to an innumerable company of angels,*

Joy consists in that vivid pleasure or delight which results from the reception and possession of what is peculiarly grateful. The humble Christian, even in this vale of tears, may sometimes possess a "joy unspeakable and full of glory"; but the glorified in heaven shall realize a fullness of joy which never can be experienced in this life. It will be joy raised to its highest degree of perfection, and expressing itself in songs of heaven-inspired rapture and delight. They will unite in ascribing "glory and dominion unto him that loved us, and washed us from our sins in his own blood"; while the chorus of that multitude shall be heard "as the voice of many waters, and as the voice of mighty thunderings, saying, Alleluia for the Lord God omnipotent reigneth."—WAKEFIELD, *Christian Theology,* p. 635.

to the general assembly and church of the firstborn, which are written in heaven, and to God the Judge of all, and to the spirits of just men made perfect (Heb. 12: 22, 23). Our Lord says that they *shall come from the east and west, and shall sit down with Abraham, and Isaac, and Jacob, in the kingdom of heaven* (Matt. 8: 11). "They shall hold converse with prophets and righteous men of olden time. They shall listen to the orations of Enoch and Elijah, of Abraham and Job, of Moses and Samuel, of David and Isaiah, of Daniel and Ezekiel, of Peter and James, of Paul and John. If a few moments of Mt. Tabor, where Moses and Elijah talked with Jesus, so entranced the apostles, with what thrilling emotions must the souls of the redeemed be inspired, when on the eternal mount on high they shall listen to the sublime strains in which so many eloquent and immortal tongues shall comment on the stupendous wonders of redemption!" (RALSTON, *Elements of Divinity*, pp. 539, 540). Furthermore, the plain inference of scripture is, that the saints shall recognize and mingle with their loved ones of earth, who like themselves have been saved through the blood of the Lamb. "*Then shall I know,*" writes the Apostle Paul, "*even as also I am known* (I Cor. 13: 12). To the question, *Shall we know each other in heaven?* we may then, confidently answer in the affirmative. Since memory remains, and the theme of our song is redemption, we may be assured that we shall also retain the knowledge of persons, places and circumstances connected with our salvation. St. Paul appears to hold out to the Thessalonians the joy of this knowledge when he says, *For what is our hope, or joy, or crown of rejoicing? Are not even ye in the presence of our Lord Jesus Christ at his coming?* (I Thess. 2: 19).

Heaven will be replete with loving fellowships and holy worship. The imperfections which so often mar our present social life, even in its most spiritual forms, will have no place in those fellowships. There love shall be supreme. Through the headship of Christ saints and angels shall form a happy brotherhood. Yet the saints will have a song and a joy which angels can share only by the power of sympathy—the song of redemption and the joy of salvation. Holy love will make all duty a holy delight. The heavenly worship, kindled by the immediate presence and open vision of God and the Lamb, shall be full of holy rapture.—MILEY, *Systematic Theology*, II, p. 475.

If the apostle looked forward to meeting those who had been converted under his ministry, may not all cherish the same hope in respect to their own loved ones? But highest and best, it is promised that without dimming veil, *they shall see his face; and his name shall be in their foreheads* (Rev. 22:4); and St. John in an equally exultant strain exclaims, *Beloved, now are we the sons of God, and it doth not yet appear what we shall be: but we know that, when he shall appear, we shall be like him; for we shall see him as he is. And every man that hath this hope in him purifieth himself, even as he is pure* (I John 3:2, 3).

The Employments of Heaven. While heaven will be a place of rest, we are not to suppose that it will be a place of inactivity. The question, therefore, naturally arises, What will be the nature of the employments of heaven? We may well suppose that they will be first of all spiritual. God, who hath blessed us with all spiritual blessings in heavenly places in Christ Jesus (Eph. 1:3), will enable the souls of the redeemed to constantly expand in the ocean-fullness of divine love. He who hath redeemed them, shall dwell in the midst of them, and lead them to fountains of living waters. New views of divine grace, and fresh visions of His adorable person, will constantly burst in upon their enraptured minds and hearts. Their intellectual faculties will be enlarged and purified. "Before them shall lie the whole circle of creation," says Dr. Graham; "the system of providence and

Heaven must be a social state, because this is our nature. Our character and our history have been wrought out in connection with our relations to our fellowmen. This makes our life; we must lose ourselves, our identity, before we can find satisfaction in a solitary, subjective life. The friends we have known we must still know. . . . . The rest of heaven, then, is not cessation from activity, but relief from toil and hardship and the burdens of life; a difference like that between Eden and the world cursed and bringing forth thorns, so that in the sweat of our face we eat our bread. We must have activity and responsibility in heaven, because our nature requires these as conditions of blessedness. Heaven must be a progressive state, because growth, progress, is the law of our nature; and with an endless life before us, and a wide field of action opened to us, no limit can be set to progress in knowledge, in power, and in blessedness. That conception of heaven must be most true which is most wholesome, most effective, in its reaction, to beget a heavenly mind in those who cherish it.—FAIRCHILD, *Elements of Theology,* p. 334.

the character and attributes of God. His wisdom, love and power they shall be able to trace in the mysteries of

The intellectual life of heaven must infinitely transcend the attainments of the present life. The mental powers will there be free from any present limitations. In the new conditions they must have large development. There is no apparent reason why they should not have perpetual growth. Certainly they will be capable of a perpetual acquisition of knowledge, and a universe of truth will be open to their research. Many problems, now dark and perplexing, will there be solved. The ceaseless pursuit and acquisition of knowledge through all the realms of truth will be a ceaseless fountain of pleasure.—Miley, *Systematic Theology*, II, p. 475.

It is highly probable that the happiness of the redeemed in heaven, however full and perfect at first, will nevertheless be progressive. We know that the capacities of the soul for holy enjoyment are increased on earth by holy exercises; and may we not conclude that the continuance of such exercises, under more favorable circumstances, will still enlarge these capacities? Again, the desires of the soul for happiness are constantly increasing in this life, and will probably increase in eternity. Hence, as the capacities for enjoyment will be progressive, and the sources of gratification inexhaustible, an ever-growing happiness will necessarily follow.—Wakefield, *Christian Theology*, p. 636.

The perfection of heaven includes the body, not the present earthly corruptible body of flesh and blood, but the spiritual body which is incorruptible (I Cor. 15:42). As Christ now enthroned in glory is veritable man, in body as in soul, so will every saint be conformed to the body of his glory (Phil. 3:21). Of that spiritual body we are now not able to form a conception that is just and satisfying. Nor is such a conception a present necessity. What is chiefly a matter of importance is to recognize the life everlasting to be a reality comprehending the whole man. The spiritual body is the finite form of personal existence which will answer completely to the status of glorified manhood, not less real, but more real than the earthly body. Compared with corporeity during our present abnormal history, the spiritual body is the only true human body, of which our present material organization is but an imperfect type and prophecy.—Gerhart, *Institutes of the Christian Religion*, II, p. 910.

Heaven is a sphere of unique blessedness as being the sphere of a unique harmony. External nature, ordered as perfect and unchecked benevolence may dictate, is there completely adjusted, we may believe, to the spiritual bodies of the saints, and spreads out into a scene of transcendent beauty. Each member of the heavenly community, radiant with spiritual perfection, is an object of complacency and spontaneous delight to every other. Thus, mutually giving and receiving holy joys, all know the fruition of a society in which love is absolutely sovereign. As the center of this holy society, the ground of its harmony, the life of its life, sufficiently known to invite to full confidence and loving communion, sufficiently mysterious in the infinite depths of His being to afford a field of endless research and revelation, is He who is truly known as Immanuel, the ever-present One, who is above, and in, and through, all things, and by whom all things consist. Each heir of immortal life knows Him as the source of His own perfection, and sees His grace and beauty mirrored in all the rest of the heavenly host. So all are "perfected into one," and the prayer of Christ gains its ideal fulfillment. To the Church Militant, struggling through earthly vicissitudes and battling with foes, has succeeded the Church Triumphant, dwelling in unclouded light and secure in its eternal inheritance.
—Sheldon, *System of Christian Doctrine*, pp. 578, 579.

nature and providence which are now hidden from human eyes. . . . . The enjoyments of the mind must make up a great part of the blessedness of heaven. The freed and expanded reason will no doubt delight in tracing the laws of the material universe and the supreme wisdom which ordained them, the rise and progress of the various kingdoms and empires, nations and races, which constitute the dominion of God; in tracing the wisdom, love and goodness of the Creator in every department of being, from the insect on earth to the seraph before the throne. Oh, what a field for the intellect!" (GRAHAM, *On the Ephesians*, p. 72). Nor must we forget the bodily enjoyments also. A new physical framework or bodily organism will be given to the soul at the resurrection, which will so perfectly express the new redeemed and spiritual nature, that it is called a spiritual body. The soul and body were made for each other, and death which occasioned their separation in this life, will itself be destroyed in the world to come.

The Endless Duration of Heaven. The crowning excellency of heaven is, that its joys shall never end. Heaven is called "the city of God," *a city which hath foundations, whose builder and maker is God* (Heb. 11:10); it is called a *better country, that is, an heavenly* (Heb. 11:16); and it is spoken of as a *kingdom which cannot be moved* (Heb. 12:28). The word eternity or some of its forms, is frequently associated with heaven. *It is a house . . . . eternal in the heavens* (II Cor. 5:1); *eternal glory* (I Peter 5:10); *everlasting habitations* (Luke 16:9); and the *everlasting kingdom of our Lord and Saviour Jesus Christ* (II Peter 1:11). We have already considered the word αἰώνιος in its relation to future punishment, and the same world, as signifying endlessness, is used in connection with eternal life. In fact, the endlessness of the future life is essential to the life itself. The very possibility of an end would seriously mar the concept of its felicity and security. When the saints enter into that eternal glory, they enter upon a life that shall never be finished, and of which it may be said of them, as it is of God himself, that their "years shall have no end."

In mediating upon what is revealed of the conditions of heavenly existence two errors are to be avoided: (1) the extreme of regarding the mode of existence experienced by the saints in heaven as too nearly analogous to that of our earthly life; (2) the opposite extreme of regarding the conditions of the heavenly life as too widely distinguished from that of our present experience. The evil effect of the first extreme will, of course, be to degrade by unworthy associations our conceptions of heaven; while the evil effect of the opposite extreme will be in great measure to destroy the moral power which a hope of heaven should naturally exert over our hearts and lives, by rendering our conception of it vague, and our sympathy with its characteristics consequently distant and feeble. To avoid both of these extremes, we should fix the limits within which our conceptions of the future existence of the saints must range, by distinguishing between those elements of man's nature, and of his relations to God and other men, which are essential and unchangeable, and those elements which must be changed in order to render his nature in his relations perfect. The following must be changed: (1) all sin and its consequences must be removed; (2) spiritual bodies must take the place of our present flesh and blood; (3) the new heavens and the new earth must take the place of the present heavens and earth, as the scene of man's life; (4) the laws of social organization must be radically changed, since in heaven there will be no marriage, but a social order analogous to that of the "angels of God" introduced. The following elements are essential, and therefore unchangeable. (1) Man will continue ever to exist, as compounded of two natures, a spiritual and material. (2) He is essentially intellectual and must live by knowledge. (3) He is essentially active, and must have work to do. (4) Man can, as a finite creature, know God mediately, that is, through His works of creation and providence, the experience of His gracious work upon our hearts, and through His incarnate Son, who is the image of His person, and the fullness of the Godhead bodily. God will, therefore, in heaven continue to teach man through His works, and to act upon him by means of motives addressed to his will through his understanding. (5) The memory of man never finally loses the slightest impression, and it will belong to the perfection of the heavenly state that every experience acquired in the past will always be within the perfect control of the will. (6) Man is essentially a social being. This, taken in connection with the previous point, indicates the conclusion that the associations, as well as the experience of our earthly life, will carry all of their natural consequences with them into the new abode of existence, except as so far they are necessarily modified (not lost) by the change. (7) Man's life is essentially an eternal progress toward infinite perfection. (8) All the known analogies of God's works in creation, in His providence in the material and moral world, and in His dispensation of grace, indicate that in heaven saints will differ among themselves both as to inherent capacities and qualities, and as to relative rank and office. These differences will doubtless be determined (a) by constitutional differences of natural capacity, (b) by gracious rewards in heaven corresponding in kind and degree to the gracious fruitfulness of the individual on earth, (c) by the absolute sovereignty of the Creator.—A A. HODGE, Outlines of Theology, pp. 461, 462.

THE FINAL CONSUMMATION

The final consummation, sometimes known as the *consummatio seculi*, or *consummatio mundi*, marks the close of the history of this present world. In its place, there will be a new heaven and a new earth, wherein dwelleth righteousness—destined through eternity to be the seat of the kingdom of God in its perfection of beauty. In this triumphant kingdom Christ will lay down the mediatorial work of salvation from sin, for the last enemy shall have been overcome. He will not, however, cease to be the exalted one, for He shall still be the Firstborn among many brethren, our fountain of living waters, and our everlasting light. He shall forever be the mediate cause of our eternal life and light, our holiness and our happiness, even when He gives up the kingdom to the Father. The final consummation brings to a close: (1) the probationary history of the individual—the final consequences being the future

The final issues of our Lord's return may be said to be the consummation of all things. This, with reference to the Redeemer, will be the end of His mediatorial kingdom as such, while as it respects man it will be the finished redemption of the race, and its restoration to the divine ideal and primary purpose of the Creator. In regard to the scene of redemption, the world, it will bring in a renewal or transformation; and, as to the Church of Christ collectively and individually, it will seal the perfection in the eternal vision of God and blessedness of the heavenly state.—Pope, *Compend. Chr. Th.*, III, p. 424.

The Son has now advanced the kingdom of God to that point at which the love of the Father can be perfectly realized. He has given up the kingdom to the father, laid aside His mediatorial office, for by the perfect destruction of sin and death, no more place is found for the mediatorial work by making atonement and redemption, because all the saved are matured for the glorious liberty of the children of God. But the meaning of the apostle by no means is that the mediatorial office of Christ is in every sense terminated, for Christ abides eternally the Bridegroom, the Head of the blessed kingdom; all communications of blessings from the Father to His creatures pass through the Son, and now it is for the first time, in the full sense of the words, true that Christ is present in all creation, for He now fills all with His own fullness.—Martensen, *Christian Dogmatics*, p. 484.

The mediatorial kingdom will cease in its relation to the Triune God; the redemptional Trinity which introduced the economy of subordination in the Two Persons will be again the absolute Trinity. The Son incarnate will cease to mediate; as Incarnate He will be forever subordinate, but there will be nothing to declare His subordination: no mediatorial rule over enemies, no mediatorial service or worship of His people. The Triune God will be seen by all mankind in the face of Jesus Christ; and the mediation of grace will become the mediation of glory. The Intercessor will pray for us no more, but will reveal the Father openly forever.—Pope, *Compend. Chr. Th.*, III, p. 425.

punishment of the wicked and the eternal blessedness of the saints. (2) It marks also the perfection of the Church. Heaven will not be inhabited by an innumerable company of redeemed individuals only, but by the Church as an organic unity. However glorious the angels may be which in adoration hover about the throne, she will be the most precious jewel of heaven. Perhaps none, in an affectional sense, will be nearer the throne. For this reason, St. John speaks of the Church as the Bride of the Lamb, which he describes in the symbolism of a holy city—the New Jerusalem, coming down from God out of heaven (Rev. 21:2, 9, 10). No symbol is better adapted to express the complexity of social organization. In the present world, through the ill-adjustments of an imperfect social structure, the city becomes the seat of sin and wickedness, of want and penury, of pain and suffering. But in the city of God, the organization will be so perfect, as it affects the relation of the individual to the social order, that *there shall be no more death, neither sorrow, nor crying, neither shall there be any more pain: for the former things are passed away* (Rev. 21:4). The Church Militant on earth, becomes triumphant in heaven, but she will never lose her identity. And when the Church shall have reached this perfection, and every enemy has been subdued and death itself shall be no more, then it is that the mediatorial kingdom as an agency of salvation must of necessity cease, and be absorbed in the endlessly blessed kingdom of God the Father, God the Son, and God the Holy Ghost. (3) But the *consummatio mundi* includes the physical universe as well as the individual and the Church. There shall be a new heaven and a new earth— a subject to which we must now give brief attention in the final paragraphs of our treatise on Christian Theology.

The New Heavens and the New Earth. At the end of the present world, there shall be a new heavens and a new earth. The resurrected and glorified bodies of the saints demand a new and glorious environment. The form of the present world must be changed, and in its place will be a new and eternal order, as the sphere of the kingdom of glory. "While the path of eschatology," says Dr. Van Oosterzee, "is traced over against the highest mountain heights, we cannot be surprised that the loftiest peaks are bordered by the deepest chasms. This is notably the case with regard to those questions which yet remain. We saw, after the long working week of the history of our race, with the appearing of the Millennial Kingdom, the dawn of a Sabbath of rest, and after that Sabbath a last conflict, succeeded by perfect victory. Time now disappears from our eye, and that which further awakens our devout attention belongs wholly to the realm of eternity. Yet the question cannot be put aside: what will now become of the world itself, for whose inhabitants the eternal destiny has been forever decided? If the Christian consciousness can give no single decision on this point, yet it is something more than a question of mere curiosity; and we rejoice to say that the word of prophecy is not wanting even here in hints, although these in turn call forth a multitude of new questions (VAN OOSTERZEE, *Christian Dogmatics*, II, p. 804). The Scriptures of both the Old and the New Testaments look forward to a new creation, when the present heavens and earth shall have grown old, and are folded up as a vesture. Thus, *Of old hast thou laid the foundation of the earth: the heavens are the work of thy hands. They shall perish, but thou shalt endure: yea, all of them shall wax old like a garment; as a vesture thou shalt change them, and they shall be changed*

The kingdom will have a new beginning: new as the kingdom of the new heavens and a new earth made one. The Spirit of Christ will be the immanent bond between Him and us, between us and the Holy Trinity: "He that is joined unto the Lord is one Spirit" (I Cor. 6:17). The Incarnate Person will be glorified then as never before: His personality as divine will be no more veiled or obscured by any humiliation, nor will it be intermittently revealed. God shall be All in All: first in the Holy Trinity, and then through Christ in us.—POPE, *Compend. Chr. Th.*, III, p. 426.

The heaven of the saints will therefore not be a realm of shades, unsubstantial and indeterminate, but a kingdom substantial and real, where the faculties and functions of human personality will be active in the joy of righteous freedom. Like the capacities of the soul, the powers of the body will be commensurate with the law and vocation of everlasting life.—GERHART, *Institutes of the Christian Religion*, II, p. 914.

(Psalms 102: 25, 26; cf. Heb. 1: 10-12). "The earth as yet wears its working garb," says Martin Luther, "then the earth also will put on its paschal and pentecostal raiment." The Prophet Isaiah waxes eloquent in contemplation of the new creation: *And all the host of heaven,*" he says, "*shall be dissolved, and the heavens shall be rolled together as a scroll: and all their host shall fall down, as the leaf falleth off from the vine, and as a falling fig from the fig tree* (Isa. 34: 4)—a judgment against Idumea, which seems prophetic of the greater day of judgment to come. Again, *Lift up your eyes to the heavens, and look upon the earth beneath: for the heavens shall vanish away like smoke, and the earth shall wax old like a garment, and they that dwell therein shall die in like manner: but my salvation shall be for ever, and my righteousness shall not be abolished* (Isa. 51: 6); *For, behold, I create new heavens and a new earth: and the former shall not be remembered, nor come into mind. But be ye glad and rejoice for ever in that which I create: for, behold, I create Jerusalem a rejoicing, and her people a joy* (Isa. 65: 17, 18). In the New Testament, we are drawn to the plastic representation of St. Peter, *But the day of the Lord will come as a thief in the night: in the which the heavens shall pass away with a great noise, and the elements shall melt with fervent heat, the earth also and the work that are therein shall be burned up. . . . . Nevertheless we, according to his promise, look for new heavens and a new earth, wherein dwelleth righteousness* (II Peter 3: 10, 13). This seems to be in harmony with our Lord's own statement that *Heaven and earth shall pass away, but my words shall not pass away* (Matt. 24: 35). In our discussion of the events connected with the Second Advent, we pointed out that the word "dissolved" as here translated is from the Greek λύω which means to unloose, unfasten, unbind, but never

God and blessed spirits are exhaustless constituents of the life of bliss. Each spirit not only reflects God, but the entire kingdom of which he is a member. When God shall be all in all, it may be said that all are in all, in one another; and the multiplicity of charismata unfolds itself, in this unlimited and undarkened reflection of love and of contemplation; in this ever new alternation of giving and receiving, of communication and receptivity.—MARTENSEN, *Christian Dogmatics*, p. 488.

to annihilate. The Scriptures lead us to believe that God in time will set free these forces of earth which are now held in reserve, and use them to the purifying of that which has been defiled by sin. God destroys only that He may create something more beautiful; and upon the ruins of earth laboring under the curse, he will raise up another, which shall bloom in unfading splendor. This new heaven will be the consequence of dissolution and purifying—"the noblest gold, brought forth from the most terrible furnace heat."

The Restoration of All Things. The great consummation marks the restoration of harmony and order in the universe. It was to this, doubtless, that St. Peter referred when he said that the heaven must receive, or retain Jesus Christ, *until the times of restitution of all things, which God hath spoken by the mouth of all his holy prophets since the world began* (Acts 3:21). The doctrine of restorationism is known in theology as the *apokatastasis*, from the phrase ἀποκαταστάσεως πάντων which occurs only in the passage just mentioned. As a form of universalism based on the disciplinary idea of suffering, this subject has already been sufficiently discussed. In this connection, however, the subject presents a different aspect. Many of the finest and tenderest minds of the ages, have sincerely hoped that all men might eventually turn to God and be saved. Attractive as this doctrine is, however, these men have been compelled to confess the rugged truth of the Scriptures, that some will be finally impenitent, and consequently lost forever. "When we thus start from the idea of God's character," says Bishop Martensen, "and reason therefrom, we are led on to the doctrine of universal restoration ἀποκατάστασις; but the anthropological, psychological, and ethical methods, that is, life and facts, conduct us, on the other hand, to the dark goal of eternal damnation. For if man can by no means be made blessed by a process of nature, must it not be possible for the will to retain its obduracy, and forever to reject grace, and in this manner to elect its own damnation? If it be replied that this possibility of a progressive obduracy

implies also a continual possibility of conversion—this
is a rash inference. For our earthly life already bears
witness to that awful and yet necessary law according
to which evil ever assumes a more unchangeable character in the individual who chooses it." (MARTENSEN,
Christian Dogmatics, p. 478.) Dr. Raymond, who holds
firmly to the doctrine of eternal punishment says this:
"The idea of endless torment is, beyond question, the
most terrible idea ever conceived. It is the great burden
of religious thought. It is not strange that generous
minds have endeavored to avoid it. It is not *prima
facie* evidence of the love of sin, or of enmity to truth,
that man seeks grounds for belief that it will never become a fact of history. But on the other hand, it is
evidently vain for human philosophy to attempt decisive
proof on the negative of this question; no man can affirm
that endless torment will not be; it is not absurd or self-
contradictory to affirm that it will be." (RAYMOND,
Systematic Theology, II, p. 520). The Scriptures are
clear on this important subject, and our Lord to whom
all authority and power is committed, is a merciful and
faithful high priest. Christian theology has to do with
no other thoughts than those revealed by Himself. And
when the curtain is drawn on this present age, we hear
the words, *He that is unjust, let him be unjust still: and
he which is filthy, let him be filthy still: and he that is
righteous, let him be righteous still: and he that is holy,
let him be holy still* (Rev. 22:11). The consummation

Dr. Pope says that "there are some indications that the end of
human history will be the restoration of the universe; as if man will
then at length, perfectly redeemed, join with the other orders of intelligent creatures in the worshipping service of the eternal temple:
their harmony, without human voices, not being counted perfect. But
this does not sanction the speculative notion that the number of the
saved from the earth will precisely fill up the vacancy caused by the
fall of those who kept not their first estate. This speculation of the
Middle Ages introduces a predestinarian element into the final consummation which the Scriptures do not warrant. Nor does the testimony of Jesus by the Spirit of prophecy sanction the thought that the
consummation will unite all spirits with all men in the blessedness of
union in God. Discord will be suppressed, but not in that way. The
reconciliation of which St. Paul speaks (I Cor. 15:25-28); (Eph. 1:10)
is heaven and earth: it does not couple hell. And the union is effected
as the result of the atonement by the sacrifice of Jesus, which was offered
in human nature and in human nature alone."—POPE, *Compend. Chr.
Th.*, III, pp. 450, 451.

of the ages marks the glorious completion of the kingdom of God. Then the kingdom will have a new beginning, in a new heavens and a new earth made one. The glory of the divine Christ will no longer be obscured nor intermittently revealed, and His countenance is as the sun shineth in his strength (Rev. 1:16). His kingdom shall be an everlasting kingdom, *for the Lord God giveth them light: and they shall reign for ever and ever* (Rev. 22:5). But until that glorious and dread day shall come, when the destinies of men shall be fixed for weal or woe, for eternal life or endless death, the invitation of divine love rings clear and strong, *the Spirit and the bride say, Come. And let him that heareth, Come. And let him that is athirst come. And whosoever will, let him take of the water of life freely* (Rev. 22:17).

Now the God of peace, that brought again from the dead our Lord Jesus, that great shepherd of the sheep, through the blood of the everlasting covenant, make you perfect in every good work to do his will, working in you that which is well pleasing in his sight, through Jesus Christ; to whom be glory for ever and ever. Amen (Heb. 13:20-21).

GENERAL BIBLIOGRAPHY

The following bibliography includes a partial list of those books frequently cited as references in the study of theology. Its purpose is to acquaint the student with the literature of theology, and the books mentioned, therefore, do not necessarily express the views of the author. Their worth must be evaluated by the student himself. Whenever possible, the name of the publisher and the date of the work are both given. Since different editions are frequently published, these dates may vary in some instances.

PART I. INTRODUCTION: THE PROVINCE OF THEOLOGY

General Reference Works

William Burton Pope, *Compendium of Christian Theology* (3 volumes), Phillips & Hunt, Second Edition, 1880

John Miley, *Systematic Theology* (2 volumes), Eaton & Mains, 1892

Miner Raymond, *Systematic Theology* (3 volumes), Hitchcock & Walden, 1877

John J. Tigert, *Summers' Systematic Theology* (2 volumes), Nashville, 1888

Thomas N. Ralston, *Elements of Divinity* (Edited by T. O. Summers), Cokesbury, 1924

A. M. Hills, *Fundamental Christian Theology* (2 volumes), C. J. Kinne, Pasadena College, 1931

Emanuel V. Gerhart, *Institutes of the Christian Religion* (2 volumes), Funk & Wagnalls, 1894

Charles Hodge, *Systematic Theology* (4 volumes), Scribners, 1871, 1883

A. A. Hodge, *Outlines of Theology*, Carter & Brothers, 1860

Henry C. Sheldon, *System of Christian Doctrine*, Methodist Book Concern, 1903

Enoch Pond, *Lectures on Christian Theology*, Boston, 1867

James Petigru Boyce, *Abstract of Systematic Theology*, Wharton & Co., 1888

S. J. Gamertsfelder, *Systematic Theology*, Cleveland, Ohio, 1913

H. Martensen, *Christian Dogmatics*, T. & T. Clark, 1898

Joseph Stump, *The Christian Faith*, Macmillan, 1932

Francis J. Hall, *Dogmatic Theology* (10 volumes), New York, 1907-1922

Francis J. Hall, *Theological Outlines*, Morehouse, 1933

John MacPherson, *Christian Dogmatics*, T. & T. Clark, 1898

James H. Fairchild, *Elements of Theology*, Oberlin, 1892

Olin A. Curtis, *The Christian Faith*, Eaton & Mains, 1905

Edgar Y. Mullins, *The Christian Religion in Its Doctrinal Expression*, Judson Press, 1917

J. J. Butler and Ransom Dunn, *Lectures on Systematic Theology*, Boston, 1892

Samuel Sprecher, *The Groundwork of a System of Evangelical Lutheran Theology*, Philadelphia, 1879

William G. T. Shedd, *Dogmatic Theology* (2 volumes), Scribners, 1888

GENERAL BIBLIOGRAPHY 395

Henry B. Smith, *Introduction to Theology*, 1883; *Systematic Theology*, 1884, New York
William Adams Brown, *Christian Theology in Outline*, Scribners, 1906
William Newton Clarke, *An Outline of Christian Theology*, Scribners, 1905
Ezekiel Gilman Robinson, *Christian Theology*, 1894
J. J. Van Oosterzee, *Christian Dogmatics* (2 volumes), Scribners, 1874
William Burton Pope, *A Higher Catechism of Theology*, Hunt & Eaton
Alvah Hovey, *Manual of Christian Theology*, Silver Burdett & Co., 1900
Samuel Wakefield, *Christian Theology*, New York, 1869
Isaac A. Dorner, *A System of Christian Doctrine*, T. & T. Clark, 1888
A. W. Drury, *Outline of Doctrinal Theology*, Otterbein Press, 1914, 1926
Jonathan Weaver, *Christian Theology*, United Brethren Publishing House, 1900
J. T. Horger, *Fundamental Revelation in Dramatic Symbol.*
Miles Grant, *Positive Theology*, Boston, 1895
Theodore Haering, *The Christian Faith* (2 volumes), London, 1915
L. Berkhof, *Systematic Theology* (2 volumes), Eerdmanns, 1938
L. Berkhof, *Reformed Dogmatics*, Eerdmanns, 1937
W. Elert, *An Outline of Christian Doctrine*, Philadelphia, 1927
R. F. Weidner, *Dogmatic Theology*, based on Luthardt and Krauth (8 volumes), 1888-1915
A. G. Voigt, *Biblical Dogmatics*, Columbia, S. C., 1917
J. A. Singmaster, *A Handbook of Christian Theology*, Philadelphia, 1927
W. Hove, *Christian Doctrine*, Minneapolis, 1930.
C. E. Lindberg, *Christian Dogmatics*, Rock Island, 1922
P. L. Mellenbruch, *The Doctrines of Christianity*, New York, 1931
H. Schmid, *Doctrinal Theology of the Evangelical Lutheran Church*, Translated by Hay and Jacobs, Philadelphia, 1876, 1889
M. Valentine, *Christian Theology* (2 volumes), Philadelphia, 1906
H. E. Jacobs, *A Summary of the Christian Faith*, Philadelphia, 1905
A. H. Strong, *Systematic Theology* (3 volumes), Griffith & Rowland, 1907
Amos Binney, *Theological Compend Improved*, Nelson & Phillips, 1875
Asbury Lowrey, *Positive Theology*, Eaton & Mains, 1853
W. B. Godbey, *Bible Theology*, Cincinnati, 1911
E. P. Ellyson, *New Theological Compend*, 1905
Nels F. S. Ferre, *The Christian Faith*, Harper Brothers, 1942
Henry David Gray, *A Theology for Christian Youth*, Cokesbury, 1941
J. S. Whale, *Christian Doctrine*, Macmillan, 1941
Frank Hugh Foster, *The Fundamental Ideas of the Roman Catholic Church*, Philadelphia, 1899
W. Wilmers, *Handbook of the Christian Religion* (Roman Catholic), Benziger, 1891
John Dickie, *The Organism of Christian Truth*, London, 1930
William Edgar Fisher, *Sound Doctrine*, 1918
H. L. Smith, *Bible Doctrine*, Upland, 1921
John Milton Williams, *Rational Theology*, Chicago, 1888
J. M. Conner, *Outlines of Christian Theology*, Little Rock, 1896
Charles G. Finney, *Lectures on Theology*, 1878
Dabney, *Theology, Dogmatic and Polemic*, Richmond, 1885
Beard, *Lectures on Theology* (3 volumes), Nashville, 1871
Lewis French Stearns, *Present Day Theology*, Scribners, 1893
J. M. Pendleton, *Christian Doctrine*, Philadelphia, 1878
Wilhelm Herrmann, *Systematic Theology*, Macmillan, 1927

Wilhelm and Scannell, *A Manual of Catholic Theology* (2 volumes), London, 1890

A. G. Mortimer, *Catholic Faith and Practice* (2 volumes), New York, 1897, 1898

Henry R. Percival, *A Digest of Theology*, Philadelphia, 1893

E. A. Litton, *Introduction to Dogmatic Theology*, London, 1912

Darwell Stone, *Outlines of Christian Dogma*, London, 1905

T. A. Lacey, *The Elements of Christian Doctrine*, New York, 1901

Joseph Pohle and Arthur Preuss, *Dogmatic Theology*, St. Louis, 1911-1917

John P. Norris, *Rudiments of Theology*, New York, 1876

D. C. Macintosh, *Theology as an Empirical Science*, New York, 1919

Orchard, *Foundations of the Faith*, New York, 1926

Nathanael Burwash, *Manual of Christian Theology on the Inductive Method* (2 volumes), London, 1900

H. Maldwyn Hughes, *Basic Beliefs*, Abingdon Press, 1929

Edw. G. Selwyn, (Editor), *Essays Catholic and Critical*, New York, 1926

F. R. Tennant, *Philosophical Theology* (2 volumes), London, 1928, 1930

Hunter, *Outline of Dogmatic Theology* (3 volumes), Longmans Green & Co.

Moule, *Outlines of Christian Doctrine*, Hodder & Stoughton

James Denny, *Studies in Theology*, Hodder & Stoughton

B. H. Streeter, *Foundations*, London, 1913

T. B. Strong, *A Manual of Theology*, London

Norris, *Rudiments of Theology*, New York, 1876

Buell, *Systematic Theology* (2 volumes), New York, 1889

A. L. Graebner, *Outlines of Doctrinal Theology*, St. Louis, 1898

J. A. Clapperton, *Essentials of Christian Theology*, London, 1913

Older Works on Theology

John Dick, *Lectures on Theology*, Glasgow and New York, 1859

Joseph Bellamy, *Works* (1850 Edition, Boston)

Herman Venema, *Institutes of Theology*, Translated by Brown, T. & T. Clark, 1850

Alexander Vinet, *Outlines of Theology*, London, 1866

George Tomline, *Elements of Christian Theology* (2 volumes), London, 1812

Thomas Ridgley, *A Body of Divinity* (4 volumes), London, 1812

George Hill, *Lectures in Divinity*, Herman Hooker, 1844

Timothy Dwight, *Theology Explained and Defended in a Series of Sermons* (4 volumes), Harper Brothers, 1849

Samuel Hopkins, *The System of Doctrines Contained in Revelation, Explained and Defended*

Richard Watson, *Theological Institutes* (2 volumes), Lane & Scott, New York, 1851

John Calvin, *The Institutes of the Christian Religion* (2 volumes), New York, 1819 (Translated by John Allen, London, 1813)

James Arminius, *Works* (3 volumes), Translated from the Latin, Auburn and Buffalo, 1853

Thomas C. Thornton, *Theological Colloquies, or a Compendium of Divinity*, Lewis Coleman, 1837

Henry E. Jewett, *Analysis of Lectures delivered by Professor Park*, Andover, 1867-1868

S. H. Willey, *Notes of Lectures by Rev. H. White*, Professor of Systematic Theology, Union Theological Seminary, 1846

George Christian Knapp, *Lectures on Christian Theology*, Translated by Leonard Woods, Philadelphia, 1845

Nitzsch, *System of Christian Doctrine*, 1849

Robert J. Breckinridge, *The Knowledge of God Objectively Considered*, 1859; and *The Knowledge of God Subjectively Considered*, 1860

Chr. Ernst Luthardt, *Fundamental Truths of Christianity*, Translated by Sophia Taylor, T. & T. Clark, 1869: cf. also, *Dogmatics*, 1865, Seventh Edition, 1886

Dagg, *Manual of Theology*, Charleston, 1859

Randolph, *Lectures on Systematic Theology* (3 volumes), London, 1869

Granahan, *Introduction to the Theologica Summa of St. Thomas*, Zybura Herder Book Co., St. Louis

Thomas Aquinas, *Summa Theologica*

HISTORY OF CHRISTIAN DOCTRINE

K. R. Hagenbach, *History of Doctrine* (2 volumes), Edited by Henry B. Smith, New York, 1861

Adolph Harnack, *History of Dogma* (7 volumes), Translated by Buchanan, London, 1905

George P. Fisher, *History of Christian Doctrine*, New York, 1896

R. Seeberg, *Text-Book of the History of Doctrine*, Translated by C. E Hay (2 volumes), Philadelphia, 1905

J. F. Bethune-Baker, *An Introduction to the Early History of Christian Doctrine*, Methuen & Co.

T. R. Crippen, *A Popular Introduction to the History of Christian Doctrine*, T. & T. Clark, 1883

Henry C. Sheldon, *History of Christian Doctrine* (2 volumes), New York, 1886

William G. T. Shedd, *History of Christian Doctrine* (2 volumes), Scribners, 1884

Arthur Cushman McGiffert, *A History of Christian Thought* (2 volumes), Scribners, 1932

Augustus Neander, *History of Christian Dogmas* (2 volumes), Translated by J. E. Ryland, Edited by J. L. Jacobi, London, 1882

John Stoughton, *An Introduction to Historical Theology*, London

Charles A. Briggs, *History of the Study of Theology* (2 volumes), Scribners, 1916

Herbert B. Workman, *Christian Thought to the Reformation*, Scribners, 1911

Arthur Cushman McGiffert, *Protestant Thought Before Kant*, Scribners

Edward Caldwell Moore, *An Outline of the History of Christian Thought Since Kant*, Scribners

W. A. Butler, *Letters on the Development of Christian Doctrine*, Dublin, 1850

Bernard Otten, *A Manual of the History of Dogmas* (2 volumes), St. Louis, 1917, 1918

J. Tixeront, *History of Dogmas, English Translation* (3 volumes), St. Louis, 1910

J. F. Bethune-Baker, *An Introduction to the Early History of Christian Doctrine to the Time of the Council of Chalcedon*, London, 1903

Ante-Nicene Library (14 volumes), Christian Literature Edition, Edinburgh, American Reprint, New York, 1926

Ante-Nicene Fathers (10 volumes), New York, 1905

Nicene and Post-Nicene Library, First Series (14 volumes), New York, 1907

Nicene and Post-Nicene Library, Second Series (14 volumes), New York, 1904

Ante-Nicene Christian Library, T. & T. Clark, 1868

E. Hatch, *The Influence of Greek Ideas and Usages upon the Christian Church*, London, 1890, 1914

G. Uhlhorn, *The Conflict of Christianity with Heathenism*, Translated by Smyth and Ropes, New York, 1891

C. Bigg, *The Christian Platonists of Alexandria*, 1886

A. T. Drane, *Christian Schools and Scholars*, 1867, 1881, 1910

C. Kingley, *Alexandria and Her Schools*, 1854

E. Caird, *Evolution of Theology in Greek Philosophers* (2 volumes)

Cunningham, *Historical Theology* (2 volumes), Edinburgh, 1862

J. Donaldson, *A Critical History of Christian Literature and Doctrine from the Death of the Apostles to the Nicene Council* (3 volumes), London, 1864

R. Blakey, *Lives of the Primitive Fathers*, 1842

Douglas, *Christian Greek and Latin Writers* (Edited by F. A. March), New York, 1874-1880

Fred Watson, *The Ante-Nicene Apologies: Their Character and Value*, Cambridge, 1870

J. Bennet, *The Theology of the Early Christian Church Exhibited in the Quotations from the Writers of the First Three Centuries*, London, 1852

W. J. Bolton, *The Evidences of Christianity as exhibited in the Writings of its Apologists down to Augustine*, New York, 1854

John Wright Buckham, *Progressive Religious Thought in America*, Houghton-Mifflin, 1919

Earlier Period

The Ante-Nicene, Nicene and Post-Nicene Fathers (previously mentioned)

Migne, *Patrologia Latina* (An extensive work on the Literature of the Fathers)

J. F. Bethune-Baker, *An Introduction to the Early History of Christian Doctrine to the Time of the Council of Chalcedon*, London, 1903

Lightfoot, *Apostolic Fathers; Clement of Rome* (2 volumes); *Ignatius and Polycarp* (3 volumes)

F. J. A. HORT, *Six Lectures on the Ante-Nicene Fathers*

F. W. Farrar, *Lives of the Fathers* (2 volumes)

Kruger, *History of Ancient Christian Literature* (English translation)

Hall, *Papias*

Roberts and Donaldson (Editors), *Writings of Irenaeus*, T. & T. Clark,

Poole, *Life and Times of St. Cyprian*
    1868; *Writings of Hippolytus*, T. & T. Clark, 1868

J. W. Benson, *Life and Times of St. Cyprian*, 1898

J. Drummond, *Philo Judaeus* (2 volumes), 1888

C. Siegfried, *Philo V. Alexander*, Jena, 1875

Origen, *De Principiis*, Ante-Nicene Library, Vol. IV

William Fairweather, *Origen and the Greek Patristic Theology*, Scribners, 1901

C. H. Lommatzsch, *Origen,* English Translation by F. Crombie, Berlin, 1831-1848

T. Taylor, *Works of Plotinus,* 1794, with Notes by G. R. S. Mead, 1895

J. Patrick, *The Apology of Origen in Reply to Celsus,* 1892

G. Hartel, *Cyprian* (3 volumes), Vienna, 1868-1871

T. Whittaker, *Apollonius of Tyana,* 1906

G. R. S. Mead, *Apollonius of Tyana,* 1901

H. L. Mansel, *Gnostic Heresies,* 1875 (Edited by Bishop Lightfoot)

W. Wright, *Apocryphal Acts of Apostles* (2 volumes), 1871

F. Oehler, *Tertullian* (3 volumes), Leipsic, 1854

A. Robertson, *Selected Works of Athanasius translated into English,* Oxford, 1892

Augustine, *Enchiridion; De Doctrina Christiana; De Civitate Dei;* Nicene and Post-Nicene Library

Cunningham, *St. Austin and His Place in the History of Christian Thought*

Philip Schaff, *Life and Labors of St. Augustine,* 1851

A. Hatzfeld, *St. Augustine* (6th Edition), Paris, 1902

Erich Przywara, *An Augustine Synthesis*

Augustine, *Works, Nicene Fathers*

Athanasius, *C. Arianos,* Nicene and Post-Nicene Fathers; *C. Gentes; On the Incarnation*

H. M. Gwatkin, *Studies in Arianism,* 1882, 1900; *Arian Controversy,* 1896

J. H. Newman, *Arians of the Fourth Century,* 1871

J. de Soyres, *Montanism and the Primitive Church,* 1878

C. E. Raven, *Apollinarianism: An Essay of the Christology of the Early Church,* 1923

J. F. Bethune-Baker, *The Meaning of Homoousios in the "Constantinopolitan" Creed,* Cambridge, 1901; *Nestorius and His Teaching,* Cambridge, 1908

E. R. Goodenough, *The Theology of Justin Martyr*

W. Bright, *The Age of the Fathers* (2 volumes), 1903

J. A. Neander, *Antignosticus or Spirit of Tertullian,* Translated by Ryland, London, 1851

Lactantius, *Divinarum Institutionum Libri Septem; De ira Dei; De ave Phoenice,* Nicene and Post-Nicene Fathers.

John of Damascus, *De Fide Orthodoxa,* part of a larger work, *The Fountain of Knowledge.* (Works edited by LeQuien, Paris, 1712) English translation, Nicene and Post-Nicene Fathers

J. H. Lupton, *St. John of Damascus,* London, 1882

G. A. Jackson, *The Apostolic Fathers and the Apologists of the Second Century,* New York, 1879

W. G. T. Shedd (Editor), *The Confessions of Augustine,* Andover, 1860

J. Fitzgerald, *The Didache or Teaching of the Twelve Apostles,* John B. Alden, New York, 1884

Philip Schaff, *The Teaching of the Twelve Apostles,* 1885

F. Loofs, *Nestorius and His Place in the History of Christian Doctrine,* 1914

Driver and Hodgson, *The Bazar of Heracleides,* 1925 (The Apology of Nestorius)

H. Koch, *Pseudo-Dionysius Areopagita,* 1900

C. E. Rolt, *Dionysius the Areopagite on the Divine Names and the Mystical Theology,* 1920

Rufus M. Jones, *Studies in Mystical Religion*, 1909 (Chapter VI deals with Dionysius)
A. Robertson, *Selected Works of Athanasius*, Oxford, 1892
J. Patrick, *Clement of Alexandria*, 1914
R. B. Tollinton, *Clement of Alexandria*

The Mediaeval Period

Church, *St. Anselm*
Sykes, *Peter Abailard*, Cambridge University Press, 1932
E. H. Blakeney, *The Tome of Leo the Great*, London, 1923
Townsend, *The Great Schoolmen of the Middle Ages*
Maurice De Wulf, *History of Mediaeval Philosophy*, 1909; *Scholasticism Old and New*, Longmans Green & Company
West, *Alcuin*
Anselm, *Cur Deus Homo*, London, 1896; *Proslogium; Monologium*, Chicago, 1903
Deane, Translation of Anselm's *Proslogium, Monologium* and *Cur Deus Homo*
Storrs, *Bernard of Clairveaux*
Compayre, *Abelard*
E. A. Moody, *The Logic of William of Ockham*, New York, 1935
McKeon, *Selections from the Mediaeval Philosophers*, Scribners, 1929
Thomas Aquinas, *Summa Theologica* (8 volumes), Paris, 1880; English Translation (22 volumes); *Commentary on the Sentences of Peter Lombard*
E. I. Watkins, *St. Thomas, Angel of the Schools*, Translation by Scanlan, London, 1931
Vaughn, *Hours with the Mystics*
Eales, *Life and Works of St. Bernard* (2 volumes), London, 1889
Hugo of St. Victor, *Summa Sententiarum; De Sacramentis Fidei Christinnae*
Liebner, *Hugo von St. Victor*, Leipsic, 1832
Richard of St. Victor, *De gratia contemplationis*
Peter Lombard, *Libri sententiarum quattuor*, or "Four Books of Sentences."
Robert Pulleyn, *Sententiarum*
William of Champeaux, *De Origine Animae; De Eucharistia*
Abelard, *Introductio ad theologiam; Sic et Non*
John Scotus Erigena, *De Divisione Naturae*
Alexander of Hales, *Summa Universae Theologiae*
Albertus Magnus, *Summa Theologiae*
Bonaventura, *Breviloquium* (An exposition of Christian Dogmatics)
Duns Scotus, *Opus Oxoniense* (Comments on the Books of Sentences); *Opus Parisiense* (Notes on Lectures)

The Mystics

Meister Eckhart, *Works* (Edited by Franz Pfeiffer, Leipsic, 1857)
Johannes Tauler, *Sermons* (English translation by Winkworth), London, 1857, New York, 1858
Heinrich Suso, "*On Eternal Wisdom*," 1338
John Ruysbroeck, *Works* (5 volumes), by J. David Ghent, 1857-1869

Cf. Ullmann, *Reformers before the Reformation* (2 volumes); and Vaughn, *Hours with the Mystics* (2 volumes), London, 1880

Precursors of the Reformation

John Wycliffe, *Trialogus* (Edited by Lechler), Oxford, 1869; Translation of the Bible (Edited by Forshall and Madden), (4 volumes), Oxford, 1850
John Huss, *De Ecclesia*, "On the Church"
Johann Wessel, *Works* (Collected and published by Luther, 1522)

The Reformation Period

Martin Luther, *De Servo Arbitrio*, 1525
Philip Melanchthon, *Loci Communes*, 1521
Ulrich Zwingli, *Commentarius de Vera et Falsa Religione*
John Calvin, *Institutes of the Christian Religion*, London, 1813, Philadelphia
Krauth, *The Conservative Reformation and Its Theology*, Philadelphia, 1871
Cunningham, *The Reformers and the Theology of the Reformation*, Edinburgh, 1862

The Confessional Period

Leonard Hutter, *Compendium Locorum Theologicorum*, 1610 (Translation by Jacobs and Spieker, Philadelphia, 1881); *Loci Communes Theologici*, 1619
John Gerhard, *Loci Theologici*, 1610-1625 (9 volumes), Leipsic; *Meditationes Sacra* (English translation by John Winterton)
George Calixtus, *Epitome Theologiae*, 1619; *Life and Correspondence*, London, 1863. (See also, W. C. Dowding, *German Theology during the Thirty Years War*)
John William Baier, *Compendium Theologiae Positivae*, 1685 (Ed. C. F. W. Walther, St. Louis, 1879)
Johann Quenstedt, *Theologia Didactica Polemica*, 1685
A. Calovius, *Systema Locorum Theologicorum* (12 volumes), 1655-1677; *Biblia Illustrata* (4 volumes)
David Hollaz, *Examen Theologicum Acroamaticum*, 1707
Daniel Chamier (polemical writings), *Memoir of D. Chamier*, London, 1852; Read, *Daniel Chamier*, Paris, 1858
Francis Turretin, *Institutio Theologiae Elencticae* (3 volumes), Edinburgh, 1847
Jean Alphonse Turretin, *A Discourse Concerning the Fundamental Articles of Religion*, London, 1720
William Twisse, *Opera* (3 volumes), Amsterdam, 1652
Johannes Wolleb, *Compendium Theologiae Christianae*, 1626
M. F. Wendelin, *Compendium Christianae Theologiae*, 1634; *Christianae Theologiae Systema Majus*, 1656 (Published from manuscript after his death)
W. R. Bagnall, *The Writings of James Arminius* (3 volumes), Auburn and Buffalo, 1853
Bangs, *Life of Arminius*, New York, 1843
Simon Episcopius, *Institutiones Theologicae* and *Responsio ad Quaestiones Theologicas*. (Works in 2 volumes, the first edited by Curcellaeus and the second by Polenbrugh, 1665. See also, Calder, *Memoirs*

of *Simon Episcopius*, New York, 1837; Philip Limborch, *Life of Simon Episcopius*, Dutch and Latin, 1701

Hugo Grotius, *Defensio Fidei Catholicae de Satisfactione Christi*, 1617: *De Veritate Relig. Christianae*, 1627; also *Annotations upon the Old and New Testament*. (Grotius' theological works, *Opera Theologica*, were published at Amsterdam, 1644, and reprinted at London, 1660.) See also Butler, *Life of Hugo Grotius*, London, 1826

Philipp van Limborch, *Institutiones Theologiae Christianae*, 1686 (English translation by William Jones, London, 1702); *Historia Inquisitionis*, 1692, and *De Veritate Religionis Christianae*, 1687; (English translation by Samuel Chandler, London, 1731)

Etienne de Curcellaeus, *Vindicia Arminii*, 1645; *Defensio Blondelli*, 1657; *Dissertationes*, 1659; also edition of Greek New Testament (Collected works, Amsterdam, 1675)

Francis Gomarus, *Loci Theologiae*, 1644 (Opponent of Arminianism)

Johannes Macovius, *Loci Communes*, 1626 (Opponent of Arminianism)

Gysbertus Voetius (Opponent of Arminianism and Federalism)

Johannes Cocceius, *Summa Doctrinae*, 1648; *Summa Theologiae*. (Founder of the Federal or Covenant Theology)

Melchoir Leydecker, *De Aeconomia Trium Personarum*, 1682

Hermann Witsius, *De Aeconomia Foederum Dei cum Hominibus*, English translation "The Covenants" (2 volumes), London, 1837

The writers of this period in the Church of England were Hooker, Field, Jackson and Laud; Bull, Jeremy Taylor, Stillingfleet, Waterland, Beveridge, Pearson and Burnett. The Puritan writers were Charnock, Bunyan, Baxter, Owen and Howe. The works of these authors have been cited in other connections.

John Wesley, *Works* (7 volumes), Methodist Book Concern, New York. In addition to his *Sermons*, *Notes* and *Journals*, special mention may be made of his *Treatise on Original Sin* (a reply to Dr. Taylor); *Appeal to Men of Reason and Religion*, (a defense of Methodism); and *Plain Account of Christian Perfection*, 1766 (numerous later editions). The literature concerning Wesley and Wesleyanism is abundant. We mention but a few of the older sources: Biographies by John Hampson (3 volumes), London, 1791 (earliest published biography); Dr. Adam Clarke, Wesley Family, London, 1823; Henry Moore (2 volumes), London, 1824; Richard Watson, London, Tyerman (3 volumes), London, 1870; George J. Stevenson, *Memorials of the Wesley Family*, London, 1876; Abel Stevens, *History of the Religious Movement of the Eighteenth Century, called Methodism* (3 volumes), New York, 1859-1862

John William Fletcher (Vicar of Madeley), *Five Checks to Antinomianism; Scripture Scales to Weigh the Gold of Gospel Truth, Being an Equal Check to Pharisaism and Antinomianism*. Posthumous work, *Portrait of St. Paul*. First complete edition of works (8 volumes), London, 1803; *The Works of the Rev. John Fletcher* (4 volumes), Methodist Book Concern, New York. There are lives of Fletcher by John Wesley, London, 1786; L. Tyerman, 1882; Macdonald, 1885. See also Stevens, *History of Methodism;* and Ryle, *Christian Leaders of the Last Century*, London, 1865

W. P. Harrison, *The Wesleyan Standards* (Sermons by the Rev. John Wesley) with notes and analysis, 1886, Nashville, 1894.

The Modern Period

F. D. E. Schleiermacher, *The Christian Faith*, T. & T. Clark

Nitzsch, *System of Christian Doctrine* (Fifth edition translated into English, Edinburgh, 1849)

Tweston, *Dogmatics* (2 volumes), 1838

Karl August Hase, *Evangelical Dogmatics*, Leipsic, 1826; *Hutterus Redivivus*, Leipsic, 1883 (12th edition)

Daniel Schenkel, *Christian Dogmatics* (2 volumes), 1858-1859 (German)

Richard Rothe, *Theologische Ethik* (Considered most important work next to that of Schleiermacher); *Christian Dogmatics* (2 volumes), Edited by Schenkel, Heidelberg, 1870

Isaac August Dorner, *System of Christian Doctrine*, T. & T. Clark, 1888; *History of the Development of the Doctrine of the Person of Christ*, 1835 (See also J. A. Dorner); *Foundation Ideas of the Protestant Church; Christian Ethics*

Bishop H. L. Martensen, *Christian Dogmatics*, T. & T. Clark, 1898

J. P. Lange, *Christian Dogmatics*, Heidelberg, 1849-1852; (Also editor of Lange's *Commentary*, and author of the *Life of Christ* (6 volumes)

J. H. Ebrard, *Christian Dogmatics* (2 volumes), 1851. Second edition, 1862

H. J. M. Voight, *Fundamental Dogmatics*, Gotha, 1874

Heinrich Schmid, *The Doctrinal Theology of the Evangelical Lutheran Church*, (Translated by Hay and Jacobs), Philadelphia, 1876, 1889

Gottfried Thomasius, *Christ's Person and Work* (2 volumes), Erlangen, 1886-1888

K. F. A. Kahnis, *Lutheran Dogmatics* (2 volumes), Leipsic, 1874-1875

F. A. Philippi, *Kirchliche Glaubenslehre* (9 volumes), 1883

A. F. C. Vilman, *Dogmatics* (2 volumes), 1874

F. H. R. Frank, *Die Theologie der Concorddienformel* (4 volumes), Considered standard work on the Theology of the Formula of Concord

Christoph Ernst Luthardt, *Apologetic Lectures on the Fundamental Truths of Christianity*, T. & T. Clark, 1869; *Apologetic Lectures on the Saving Truths of Christianity*, 1868; *Apologetic Lectures on the Moral Truths of Christianity*, 1875; *Compendium of Dogmatics*, 1893

S. L. Bring, *Outlines of the Christian Doctrine of Faith* (Lund), 1869-1877

Gisle Johnson (Norway), *Outlines of Systematic Theology*

Axel F. Granfelt (Finland), *Christian Dogmatics*

Carl Olof Bjorling (Sweden), *Christian Dogmatics according to the Confessions of the Lutheran Church*, 1866

Ralph Wardlaw, *System of Theology* (3 volumes), 1856-1857 (posthumous work)

A. Ritschl, *Justification and Reconciliation*

Julius Kaftan, *Das Wesen der Christlichen Religion*, 1881

Richard Adelbert Lipsius, *Lehrbuch der Evang. Prot. Dogmatik; Dogmatische Beitraege*, 1878 (Third Edition, 1893)

Theodore Haering, *The Christian Faith* (2 volumes), London, 1915

The British and American works on theology will be found in the General Reference list and need not be repeated here.

Contemporary Theology

Walter Marshall Horton, *Theism and the Modern Mood; Realistic Theology*, 1934; *A Psychological Approach to Theology*, 1931; *Contemp-*

orary *English Theology; Contemporary Continental Theology*, 1938, Harper Brothers

Karl Barth, *The Word of God and the Word of Man*, Pilgrim Press, 1928; *The Christian Life*, London, 1930; *Epistle to the Romans*, Oxford, 1933; *God in Action*, Round Table Press, 1936; *Credo*, Scribners, 1936; *The Doctrine of the Word of God*, T. & T. Clark, 1936 (Prolegomena to Church Dogmatics) See also, *The Resurrection of the Dead*, Revell, 1933; *The Knowledge of God and the Service of God*, Scribners, 1939

Emil Brunner, *The Theology of Crisis*, Scribners, 1929; *The Word and the World*, Scribners, 1931; *The Mediator*, MacMillan, 1934; *God and Man*, MacMillan, 1936; *Philosophy of Religion*, Scribners, 1937; *The Divine Imperative*, MacMillan, 1937; *The Christian Understanding of Man* (Oxford Conference Books)

H. R. Mackintosh, *Types of Modern Theology*, London, 1937

A. Keller, *Karl Barth and Christian Unity*, MacMillan, 1933

A. Nygren, *Agape and Eros*, MacMillan, 1932

J. S. Zybura, *Present-day Thinkers and the New Scholasticism*, St. Louis, 1926

N. Berdyaev, *The End of Our Time*, Sheed & Ward, 1935; *The Fate of Man in the Modern World*, London, 1935; *The Meaning of History*, Scribners, 1936; *The Destiny of Man*, Scribners, 1937; *Freedom and the Spirit*, Scribners, 1939

J. Baillie, *Our Knowledge of God*, Scribners, 1939

P. A. Bertocci, *The Empirical Argument for God in Late British Thought*, Harvard University Press, 1938

E. E. Aubrey, *Present Theological Tendencies*, Harper Brothers, 1936

G. P. Conger, *The Ideologies of Religion*, Round Table Press, 1940

S. Bulgakov, *The Orthodox Church*, London, 1935; *The Wisdom of God*, Paisley Press, 1937

CREEDS AND CONFESSIONS

Philip Schaff, *Creeds of Christendom* (3 volumes), Harper Brothers, 1877

W. A. Curtis, *History of Creeds and Confessions of Faith*, Scribners, 1912

Charles A. Briggs, *Theological Symbolics*, Scribners, 1914

E. H. Klotsche, *Christian Symbolics*, Eerdmanns, 1929

J. L. Neve, *Introduction to Lutheran Symbolics*, Burlington, 1917

J. A. Moehler, *Symbolism, or the Exposition of Doctrinal Differences between Catholics and Protestants*, Translated by J. A. Robertson, London, 1906

T. Herbert Bindley, *Ecumenical Documents of the Faith*, London, 1906

J. R. Lumby, *The History of the Creeds*, London, 1873

T. E. Schmauk and C. T. Benze, *The Confessional Principle and the Confessions*, Philadelphia, 1897

A. C. McGiffert, *The Apostles' Creed*, Scribners

T. Zahn, *The Articles of the Apostles' Creed*, Hodder & Stoughton, 1890

McFayden, *Understanding the Apostles' Creed*, MacMillan, 1927

Arthur Cushman McGiffert, *The Apostles' Creed*, Scribners, 1903

J. Kunze, *The Apostles' Creed and the New Testament*, Funk & Wagnalls, 1912

John Pearson, *An Exposition of the Creed*, London, 1824

A. E. Burns, *The Apostles' Creed*, New York, 1906; *The Nicene Creed*, New York, 1909

Thomas, Richey, *The Nicene Creed and the Filioque*, New York, 1884

John H. Skrine, *Creed and the Creeds*, London, 1911

C. A. Heurttley, *Harmonica Symbolica: A Collection of Creeds belonging to the Ancient Western Church, and to the Mediaeval English Church*, Oxford, 1858

S. S. Schmucker, *Lutheran Manual on Scriptural Principles*, Philadelphia, 1855

M. Loy, *The Augsburg Confession*, Columbus, 1908

J. H. W. Stuckenberg, *The History of the Augsburg Confession*, Philadelphia, 1869

R. W. Jelf, *The Thirty-Nine Articles of the Church of England*, London, 1873

C. Hardwick, *A History of the Articles of Religion, with Documents*, London, 1859

Bishop A. P. Forbes, *An Explanation of the Thirty-Nine Articles*, London, 1866

T. P. Boultbee, *An Introduction to the Theology of the Church of England in an Exposition of the Thirty-Nine Articles*, London, 1871

Edward Bickersteth, *Questions Illustrating the Thirty-Nine Articles*, Philadelphia, 1845

Henry Blunt, *Discourse on the Doctrinal Articles of the Church of England*, Philadelphia, 1839

E. J. Bicknell, *A Theological Introduction to the Thirty-Nine Articles of the Church of England*, Longmans Green, 1919 (Last impression, 1936)

Bishop George Tomline, *Christian Theology, an Exposition of the Thirty-Nine Articles of Religion*, London, 1843

W. Baker, *A Plain Exposition of the Thirty-Nine Articles*, London, 1883

Bishop E. Harold Browne, *Exposition of the Thirty-Nine Articles*, Oxford, 1847

Bishop Gilbert Burnet, *Exposition of the Thirty-Nine Articles*, New York, 1845

B. J. Kidd, *The Thirty-Nine Articles: Their History and Explanation*, New York, 1901

Edgar C. S. Gibson, *The Thirty-Nine Articles of the Church of England Explained*, London, 1904

John Macpherson, *The Westminster Confession of Faith*, New York, 1881

R. L. Cloquet, *Exposition of the Thirty-Nine Articles*, London, 1885

E. Terrel Green, *The Thirty-Nine Articles and the Age of the Reformation*, London, 1896

A. A. Hodge, *Commentary on the Confession of Faith*, Philadelphia, 1869

Silas Comfort, *An Exposition of the Articles of the Methodist Episcopal Church*, New York, 1847

Henry Wheeler, *History and Exposition of the Twenty-Five Articles of Religion of the Methodist Episcopal Church*, New York, 1908

A. A. Jimeson, *Notes on the Twenty-Five Articles*, Cincinnati, 1855

G. W. Bethune, *Expository Lectures on the Heidelberg Catechism* (2 volumes), New York, 1864

RELIGION

History of Religion

E. B. Tylor, *Primitive Culture*, 1871

Allan Menzies, *History of Religion*, MacMillan, 1910, Scribners, 1927

M. Jastrow, *The Study of Religion*

C. P. Tiele, *Elements of the Science of Religion* (2 volumes), 1897
A. Lang, *Myth, Ritual and Religion*
F. B. Jevons, *Introduction to the Study of Comparative Religion*, Mac-Millan, 1916
Frazer, *The Golden Bough* (one volume edition), New York, 1926
Brinton, *Religions of Primitive Peoples*
De la Saussaye, *Handbook of Religions*
George F. Moore, *History of Religions* (2 volumes), Scribners, 1913, 1919
Lowrie, *Primitive Religions*, 1925
Marett, *Sacraments of Simple Folk*, 1933; *Faith, Hope and Charity in Primitive Religion*, 1932
Murray, *Five Stages in Greek Religion*, 1925
Nilsson, *A History of Greek Religion*
Radin, *Monotheism and Primitive Peoples*, 1924
Schmidt, *The Origin and Growth of Religion*
Spencer and Gillen, *Native Tribes of Central Australia*, 1898
Thomas, *History of Buddhist Thought*, 1933
Gowen, *A History of Religion*, Morehouse
S. M. Zwemer, *The Origin of Religion*, 1935
S. Cave, *Christianity and Some Living Religions of the East*, 1929
Albert Schweitzer, *Christianity and the Religions of the World*, (Translation, 1923)
R. E. Hume, *The World's Living Religions*, 1924
S. H. Kellogg, *A Handbook of Comparative Religion*, 1908
E. A. Marshall, *Christianity and the Non-Christian Religions Compared*, 1910
R. K. Douglas, *Confucianism and Taoism*, 1911
A. LeRoy, *The Religion of the Primitives*, 1922
D. A. Stewart, *The Place of Christianity Among the Great Religions of the World*, 1920
M. Monier-Williams, *Hinduism*, 1911
H. H. Underwood, *The Religions of Eastern Asia*, 1910
W. Tisdall, *Christianity and Other Faiths; Comparative Religion*, 1909
Charles S. Braden, *Modern Tendencies in World Religions*, MacMillan, 1933; *Varieties of American Religion*, Willett Clark and Co., 1936
Albert E. Hayden, *Modern Trends in World Religions*, Chicago, 1934
George A. Barton, *The Religions of the World*, Chicago, 1929.

Psychology of Religion

E. D. Starbuck, *Psychology of Religion*, Scribners, 1900; *The Psychology of Religious Experience*, Scribners, 1911
Stratton, *The Psychology of the Religious Life*, MacMillan, 1911
J. B. Pratt, *Psychology of Religious Belief*, MacMillan, 1907; *The Religious Consciousness*, MacMillan, 1923
R. H. Thouless, *An Introduction to the Psychology of Religion*, Mac-Millan, 1923
E. S. Waterhouse, *Psychology of Religion*, MacMillan, 1923
W. R. Selbie, *The Psychology of Religion*, Oxford, 1924
G. A. Coe, *Psychology of Religion*, Chicago, 1916
E. R. Uren, *Recent Religious Psychology*, T. & T. Clark
L. W. Grensted, *Psychology and God*, Longmans, 1931; *Religion, Fact or Fancy*
George Barton Cutten, *The Psychological Phenomena of Christianity*, Scribners, 1909

John Wright Buckham, *Religion as Experience*, Abingdon, 1922
W. Boyd Carpenter, *The Witness of Religious Experience*, London, 1916
William James, *Varieties of Religious Experience*, New York, 1902
Harold Begbie, *Twice Born Men*, New York, 1909
S. V. Norborg, *Varieties of Christian Experience*, Augsburg, 1937
D. Yellowless, *Psychology's Defense of the Faith*, SCM
C. H. Valentine, *Modern Psychology and the Validity of Religious Experience*
W. R. Inge, *Christian Mysticism; Faith and Its Psychology*
E. Underhill, *Mysticism*, London, 1912
W. M. Horton, *A Psychological Approach to Theology*, Harpers, 1931
Frederich Heiler, *Prayer*, Oxford, 1932
Georg Wobbermin, *The Nature of Religion*, Crowell, 1933
H. N. and R. W. Wieman, *Normative Psychology of Religion*, Crowell, 1935
William Ernest Hocking, *Human Nature and Its Remaking*, Yale, 1923
Dewar and Hudson, *Psychology for Religious Workers*
Waterhouse, *Psychology and Religion*, Richard Smith
L. Weatherhead, *Psychology in the Service of the Soul*, MacMillan
Karl L. Stolz, *The Psychology of Religious Living*, Cokesbury, 1937
Francis L. Strickland, *Psychology of Religious Experience*, Abingdon, 1924
Elmer T. Clark, *The Psychology of Religious Awakening*, MacMillan, 1929
Edmund S. Conklin, *The Psychology of Religious Adjustment*, MacMillan, 1929
J. Cyril Flower, *An Approach to the Psychology of Religion*, New York, 1927
Carroll C. Pratt, *The Logic of Modern Psychology*, MacMillan, 1939
Barbour, *Sin and the New Psychology*
G. Steven, *The Psychology of the Christian Soul*, New York, 1911
F. R. Barry, *Christianity and Psychology*, New York, 1923
H. S. Elliott, *The Bearing of Psychology on Religion*, New York, 1927
W. E. Hocking, *Human Nature and Its Remaking*, New Haven, 1918
T. W. Pym, *Psychology and the Christian Life*, London, 1921
Charles Conant Josey, *The Psychology of Religion*, MacMillan, 1927
Carl G. Jung, *Psychology and Religion*, New Haven, 1938
Rudolf Allers, *The Psychology of Character*, MacMillan, 1931
Frank S. Hickman, *Introduction to the Psychology of Religion*, Abingdon, 1926

Philosophy of Religion

D. Mial Edwards, *The Philosophy of Religion*, Doran
William Adams Brown, *The Essence of Christianity*, Scribners, 1908
A. Sabbatier, *Outlines of a Philosophy of Religion*, New York, 1927
Edward Caird, *The Evolution of Religion*, Glasgow
G. B. Foster, *The Finality of the Christian Religion*, Chicago, 1906
Harald Hoffding, *The Philosophy of Religion*, MacMillan, 1901, 1906
John Caird, *Introduction to the Philosophy of Religion*, Glasgow, 1880
George Galloway, *The Principles of Religious Development*, 1909
E. S. Waterhouse, *The Philosophy of Religious Experience*, London, 1923
Otto Pfleiderer, *The Philosophy of Religion on the Basis of History*, London, 1888
F. Von Hugel, *Essays and Addresses on the Philosophy of Religion*
A. M. Fairbairn, *Studies in the Philosophy of Religion and History*, London
James Martineau, *A Study of Religion*

Albert C. Knudson, *The Validity of Religious Experience*, Abingdon, 1937
Wieman and Meland, *American Philosophies of Religion*, Chicago, 1936
W. K. Wright, *A Student's Philosophy of Religion*, MacMillan, 1922, 1935
E. A. Burtt, *Types of Religious Philosophy*, Harper Brothers, 1939
W. G. de Burgh, *Towards a Religious Philosophy*, London, 1937
E. S. Brightman, *A Philosophy of Religion*, New York, 1940
Buttrick, *Christian Fact and Modern Doubt*, Scribners
A. T. Ormond, *The Philosophy of Religion*, 1922
E. E. Richardson, *The Philosophy of Religion*, 1920
John Morrison Moore, *Theories of Religious Experience*, Round Table Press, 1939
John Baillie, *The Interpretation of Religion*, Scribners, 1928
Vergilius Ferm, *First Chapters in Religious Philosophy*, Round Table Press, 1937
Rudolf Otto, *The Idea of the Holy*, Oxford, 1926
D. Elton Trueblood, *The Trustworthiness of Religious Experience*, Allen and Unwin, 1939
Emil Carl Wilm, *Studies in Philosophy and Theology*, Abingdon, 1922
D. C. Macintosh, *The Reasonableness of Christianity*, Scribners, 1926
G. T. Ladd, *Philosophy of Religion*, 1905
Emil Brunner, *The Philosophy of Religion*, Scribners, 1937

Fundamentals of the Christian Religion

J. A. W. Haas, *The Unity of Faith and Knowledge*, New York, 1926
F. L. Patton, *Fundamental Christianity*, London, 1926
L. T. Townsend, *Credo*, 1869
F. Hamilton, *The Basis of the Christian Faith*, New York, 1927
W. H. Turton, *The Truth of Christianity*, London, 1919
E. H. Johnson, *Christian Agnosticism*, Philadelphia, 1907
L. F. Stearns, *The Evidence of Christian Experience*, New York, 1890, 1916
P. H. Buehring, *Modernism, a Pagan Movement in the Christian Church*, Columbus, 1928
J. G. Machen, *Christianity and Liberalism*, New York, 1923
W. P. King, *Behaviorism, A Battle Line*, Nashville, 1930; *Humanism, Another Battle Line*, Nashville, 1931
B. F. Cocker, *Christianity and Greek Philosophy*, New York, 1870; *Lectures on the Truth of the Christian Religion*, Detroit, 1873
H. Cremer, *Reply to Harnack on the Essence of Christianity*, (Translation by Pick), New York, 1903
W. P. Paterson, *The Rule of Faith*, Hodder and Stoughton, New York & London, 1912

REVELATION AND INSPIRATION

A. B. Bruce, *The Chief End of Revelation*, London, 1887
C. M. Mead, *Supernatural Revelation*, New York, 1889
George P. Fisher, *The Nature and Method of Revelation*, New York, 1890
Edwin Lewis, *A Philosophy of the Christian Revelation*, Harper Brothers, 1940
W. R. Matthews, *The Idea of Revelation*
J. Oman, *Vision and Authority*
Samuel Harris, *The Self-Revelation of God*, New York, 1892
W. T. Conner, *Revelation and God*, Broadman Press, 1936
E. F. Scott, *The New Testament Idea of Revelation*

B. H. Streeter, *The God Who Speaks*, MacMillan, 1936
Baillie and Martin, (Editors) *Revelation*
Karl Barth, *The Doctrine of the Word of God*
D. C. Macintosh, *The Problem of Religious Knowledge*
W. P. Montague, *The Ways of Knowing*
William Adams Brown, *Pathways to Certainty*
C. H. Dodd, *The Authority of the Bible*
John Elof Boodin, *Truth and Reality*, MacMillan, 1911
Etienne Gilson, *Reason and Revelation in the Middle Ages*, Scribners, 1938
H. Wheeler Robinson, *Redemption and Revelation*, Harper Brothers, 1942
B. B. Warfield, *Revelation and Inspiration*, 1927
B. H. Carroll, *Inspiration of the Bible*, 1933
W. E. Vine, *The Divine Inspiration of the Bible*, 1923
R. A. Torrey, *Is the Bible the Unerrant Word of God?* 1922
W. A. Erickson, *Inspiration, History, Theory and Facts*, 1928
J. C. Ryle, *Is All Scripture Inspired?*
W. B. Riley, *Inspiration or Evolution*, 1923
W. G. Scroggie, *Is the Bible the Word of God?* 1922
A. B. Bruce, *The Chief End of Revelation*, London, 1881, 1887
J. H. A. Ebrard, *Revelation: Its Nature and Record*, Edinburgh, 1884
W. E. Gladstone, *The Impregnable Rock of Holy Scripture*, Philadelphia, 1891
William Sanday, *The Oracles of God*, London, 1891
J. R. Illingworth, *Reason and Revelation*, London, 1902
H. Rogers, *The Superhuman Origin of the Bible*, London, 1884
S. J. Andrews, *God's Revelation of Himself to Men*, New York, 1901
C. A. Auberlein, *The Divine Revelation: An Essay in Defense of the Faith*
Henderson, *The Bible a Revelation from God*, Edinburgh, 1910
F. Bettex, *The Bible the Word of God*, Cincinnati, 1904; *The Word of Truth* (Translated by A. Bard), Burlington, Iowa, 1914
James Orr, *Revelation and Inspiration*, New York, 1910
A. T. Pierson, *The Inspired Word*, 1888
J. A. O. Stubb, *Verbal Inspiration*, 1913
R. S. MacArthur, *The Old Book and the Old Faith*, 1900
Cave, *The Inspiration of the Old Testament Inductively Considered*, 1888
G. D. Barry, *The Inspiration and Authority of Holy Scriptures*, 1919
A. W. Pink, *The Divine Inspiration of the Bible*, 1917
L. T. Townsend, *Bible Inspiration*
W. E. Atwell, *The Pauline Theory of Inspiration*, London, 1878
C. Wordsworth, *On the Inspiration of Holy Scripture*, London, 1867
E. Elliot, *Inspiration of the Holy Scriptures*, Edinburgh, 1877
F. L. Patton, *The Inspiration of the Scriptures*, Philadelphia, 1869
William Lee, *The Inspiration of Holy Scriptures*, New York, 1866
J. M. Gibson, *Inspiration and Authority of Holy Scripture*, London, 1908
R. F. Horton, *Inspiration of the Bible*, London, 1906
J. Urquhart, *The Inspiration and Accuracy of the Holy Scripture*, New York, 1904

THE CANON

The Bibliography for this section properly belongs to the Department of Biblical Introduction, and consequently only a few of the older and better known works are cited.

W. H. Green, *General Introduction to the Old Testament*, 1898

Wescott, *A General Survey of the History of the Canon of the New Testament during the first Four Centuries*, London, 1855

J. H. Raven, *Old Testament Introduction, General and Special*

T. Zahn, *Introduction to the New Testament*, 1917

Henry M. Harman, *Introduction to the Study of the Holy Scriptures*, New York, 1878

Marcus Dods, *Introduction to the New Testament*, London, 1909

Alexander Souter, *The Text and Canon of the New Testament*, Scribners, 1913

Wescott, *History of the English Bible*, MacMillan, 1916

H. W. Hoare, *The Evolution of the English Bible*, New York, 1901

E. C. Bissell, *Historic Origin of the Bible*, New York, 1878

James Orr, *The Problem of the Old Testament*, New York, 1906

T. Whitelaw, *The Old Testament Problem*

K. T. Kiel, *Historico-Critical Introduction to the Old Testament*

R. S. Foster, *The Supernatural Book*, New York, 1890

W. C. Proctor, *The Authenticity and Authority of the Old Testament*, 1926

Apologetics

For the Older Works on Apologetics, see Notes, Volume 1, p. 207; for the Later Works on General Apologetics, I, pp. 210, 211; for the Mosaic Authorship of the Pentateuch, I, pp. 208, 209; for a partial list of works on Archaeology, I, p. 208. Mention should also be made of the following helpful books:

G. F. Owen, *From Abraham to Allenby*

J. A. Huffman, *Voices from Rocks and Dust Heaps of Bible Lands*, 1923; *Biblical Confirmations from Archaeology*, 1931

A. W. Ahl, *Bible Studies in the Light of Recent Research*, 1930

G. L. Robinson, *The Sarcophagus of an Ancient Civilization*, 1930

V. L. Trumper, *The Mirror of Egypt in the Old Testament*, 1934

Leander S. Keyser, *The Problem of Origins*, 1926; *A Reasonable Faith*, 1933; *System of Christian Evidences* (last edition), 1935

H. Rimmer, *Voices from the Silent Centuries*, 1934

W. W. Prescott, *The Spade and the Bible*, 1933

E. J. Banks, *The Bible and the Spade*, 1913

G. H. Scherer, *The Eastern Color of the Bible*, 1931

M. G. Kyle, *Explorations in Sodom*, 1928; *Excavating Kirkjeth-Sepher's Ten Cities*, 1934

W. Evans, *His Unchanging World*, 1933

W. T. Pilter, *The Pentateuch: A Historical Record*, 1928

J. S. Griffith, *The Exodus in the Light of Archaeology*, 1923

W. Arndt, *Does the Bible Contradict Itself?* 1926

PART II. THE DOCTRINE OF THE FATHER
Theism

Robert Flint, *Antitheistic Theories*, Edinburgh, 1889; *Theism*, Edinburgh, 1890; *Agnosticism*, Edinburgh, 1909

George P. Fisher, *The Grounds of Theistic and Christian Belief*, New York, 1903

Charles Carroll Everett, *Theism and the Christian Faith*, MacMillan, 1909

W. L. Walker, *Christian Theism and a Spiritual Monism*, T. & T. Clark, 1906

Borden Parker Bowne, *Theism,* American Book Co., 1902
Walter Marshall Horton, *Theism and the Scientific Spirit,* Harpers, 1933
Leander S. Keyser, *A System of National Theism,* 1917
G. D. Hicks, *Philosophical Bases of Theism,* MacMillan, 1937
Samuel Harris, *The Philosophical Basis of Theism,* Scribners, 1883
Davidson, *Theism as Grounded in Human Nature*
Iverach, *Theism in the Light of Present Science and Philosophy*
Kelly, *Rational Necessity of Theism,* 1909
Reuterdahl, *Scientific Theism versus Materialism,* 1920
Balfour, *Theism and Humanism*
Tigert, *Theism: A Survey of the Paths that Lead to God*
R. S. Foster, *Theism,* Hunt & Eaton, 1889
James Ward, *Naturalism and Agnosticism* (2 volumes), London, 1906;
    The Realm of Ends, Cambridge, 1911
J. Lewis Diman, *The Theistic Argument,* Boston, 1882
Robert A. Thompson, *Christian Theism,* New York, 1855
Forsyth, *The Justification of God,* 1917
Valentine, *Natural Theology*

The Existence and Nature of God

William Newton Clark, *The Christian Doctrine of God,* Scribners, 1909
Albert C. Knudson, *The Doctrine of God,* Abingdon, 1930
Clarence A. Beckwith, *The Idea of God,* MacMillan, 1924
A. S. Pringle-Pattison, *The Idea of God in the Light of Recent Philosophy,* Oxford, 1917
A. E. Garvie, *The Christian Doctrine of the Godhead: The Christian Belief in God,* Harpers, 1932
Micou, *Basic Ideas in Religion*
Edgar Sheffield Brightman, *The Problem of God,* Abingdon, 1930; *Personality and Religion,* Abingdon, 1934
James Orr,*The Christian View of God and the World,* Scribners, 1908
W. E. Adeny, *The Christian Conception of God,* Revell, 1912
A. Gratry, *Guide to the Knowledge of God,* Boston, 1892
Illingworth, *Divine Immanence,* MacMillan, 1898
Robert J. Breckenridge, *The Knowledge of God Subjectively Considered,* New York, 1859
Heim, *God Transcendent,* Scribners, 1936
A. C. McGiffert, *The God of the Early Christians,* Scribners, 1924
W. E. Hocking, *The Meaning of God in Human Experience,* Yale University Press, 1912
J. Baillie, *Our Knowledge of God,* Scribners, 1939
Joseph Fort Newton, *My Idea of God,* Boston, 1926
Samuel Harris, *The Self-Revelation of God,* Scribners, 1889
William Temple, *Nature, Man and God,* MacMillan, 1935
Maness, *Evidences of Divine Being,* 1935
W. R. Matthews, *The Purpose of God,* Scribners, 1936; *God in Christian Thought and Experience,* Scribners
Albert Taylor Bledsoe, *A Theodicy,* 1854
E. W. Lyman, *The Experience of God in Modern Life,* New York, 1922
C. C. J. Webb, *God and Personality,* New York, 1918
B. H. Streeter, *Reality,* New York, 1926
Borden Parker Bowne, *Personalism,* Boston and New York, 1908
Albert C. Knudson, *The Philosophy of Personalism,* 1927
J. H. Snowden, *The Personality of God,* New York, 1920

William Temple, *Christ's Revelation of God*, London, 1925

J. E. Davey, *Our Faith in God through Jesus Christ*, New York, 1922

R. M. Vaughan, *The Significance of Personality*, New York, 1930

Robert Tyler Flewelling, *Personalism and the Problems of Philosophy*, New York, 1915; *Creative Personality*, MacMillan, 1926

J. R. Illingworth, *Personality, Human and Divine*, London and New York, 1894

J. B. Pratt, *Personal Realism*, MacMillan, 1937

J. R. Illingworth, *Divine Immanence*, London and New York, 1898; *Divine Transcendence*, London, 1911

H. R. Mackintosh, *The Divine Initiative*, London, 1921

F. J. McConnell, *The Christlike God*, New York, 1927

J. M. Wilson, *Christ's Thought of God*, London, 1920

Gwatkin, *The Knowledge of God*, Edinburgh, 1906

D. E. Trueblood, *The Knowledge of God*, Harper Brothers, 1939

Rees Griffiths, *God in Idea and Experience*

Charles A. Bennett, *the Dilemma of Religious Knowledge*, Yale, 1931

Karl Barth, *The Knowledge of God and the Service of God*, Scribners, 1939

C. Hartshorne, *Man's Vision of God and the Logic of Theism*, Chicago, 1941

D. C. Macintosh, *The Problem of Religious Knowledge*, Harper Brothers, 1940

John Elof Boodin, *Truth and Reality*, MacMillan, 1911

A. C. Garnett, *Reality and Value*, Yale, 1937

E. Gilson, *God and Philosophy*, Yale, 1941

P. E. Dove, *The Logic of the Christian Faith*, Edinburgh, 1856

Asa Mahan, *The Science of Natural Theology*, Boston, 1867

Georg Wobbermin, *Christian Belief in God*, 1918

Josiah Royce, *The Conception of God*, MacMillan, 1902

W. E. Hocking, *The Meaning of God in Human Experience*, New Haven, 1912

J. Iverach, *Is God Knowable?* London, 1874

L. D. McCabe, *Divine Nescience and Future Contingencies*, New York, 1882

J. Fiske, *The Idea of God as Affected by Modern Knowledge*, Boston and New York, 1886

R. L. Swain, *What and Where Is God*, New York, 1921

W. J. Moulton, *The Certainty of God*, New York

W. F. Tillett, *The Paths that Lead to God*, New York, 1924

William Adams Brown, *Pathways to Certainty*, New York, 1930

Rufus M. Jones, *Pathways to the Reality of God*, New York, 1931

L. F. Gruber, *The Theory of a Finite and Developing Deity Examined*, 1918

S. Mathews, *The Growth of the Idea of God*, New York, 1931

John Wright Buckham, *The Humanity of God*, Harper Brothers, 1928; *Christianity and Personality*, New York, 1936

E. H. Reeman, *Do We Need a New Idea of God?* Philadelphia, 1917

J. E. Turner, *The Revelation of Deity*, New York, 1931

R. S. Candlish, *The Fatherhood of God*, Edinburgh

Crawford, *The Fatherhood of God*, Edinburgh

C. H. H. Wright, *The Fatherhood of God and Its Relation to the Person and Work of Christ*, Edinburgh

Scott-Lidgett, *The Fatherhood of God*, T. & T. Clark

Samuel Clarke, *The Being and Attributes of God*
Gordon W. Allport, *Personality*, Henry Holt and Co., 1937
C. C. J. Webb, *God and Personality*, Macmillan, 1919; *Religion and Theism*, Scribners, 1934

THE TRINITY

J. R. Illingworth, *The Doctrine of the Trinity Apologetically Considered*, London, 1907
G. S. Faber, *The Apostolicity of Trinitarianism* (2 volumes), London, 1832
E. H. Bickersteth, *The Rock of Ages*, New York, 1861
R. N. Davies, *Doctrine of the Trinity*, Cincinnati, 1891
P. H. Streenstra, *The Being of God as Unity and Trinity*, New York, 1891
L. L. Paine, *Evolution of Trinitarianism*, Houghton Mifflin, 1902
Pease, *Philosophy of Trinitarian Doctrine*, Putnams, 1875
L. G. Mylne, *The Holy Trinity*, London, 1916
S. B. McKinney, *Revelation of the Trinity*, London, 1906
A. F. W. Ingram, *The Love of the Trinity*, New York, 1908
Samuel Clarke, *Scripture Doctrine of the Trinity*
William S. Bishop, *The Development of the Trinitarian Doctrine in the Nicene and Athanasian Creeds*, New York, 1910
E. Burton, *Testimonials of the Ante-Nicene Fathers to the Doctrine of the Trinity, and the Divinity of the Holy Ghost*, London, 1831

COSMOLOGY

A. S. Eddington, *The Nature of the Physical World; The Philosophy of the Physical Sciences; Science and the Unseen World*, MacMillan, 1929
J. Needham, *Science, Religion and Reality*
F. Leslie Cross, *Religion and the Reign of Science*, New York, 1930
George Allen Dinsmore, *Religious Certitude in the Age of Science*, Chapel Hill, 1924
J. H. Jeans, *The New Background of Science; The Mysterious Universe*, MacMillan
G. M. Price, *Plain Facts about Evolution, Geology and the Bible*, 1911; *New Light on the Doctrine of Creation*, 1917; *Back to the Bible*, 1920; *The New Geology*, 1923; *The Phantom of Organic Evolution*, 1924; *The Predicament of Evolution*, 1926; *Evolutionary Geology and the New Catastrophism*, 1926; *A History of Some Scientific Blunders*, 1930; *Modern Discoveries which Help Us to Believe*, 1931
A. Fairhurt, *Organic Evolution Considered*, 1911; *Theistic Evolution*, 1919
W. K. Azbill, *Science and Faith*, 1914
T. Graebner, *Evolution: An Investigation and a Criticism*, 1921, 1926
W. H. Johnson, *The Christian Faith Under Modern Searchlights*, Revell, 1916
A. L. Gridley, *The First Chapter of Genesis as the Foundation of Science and Religion*, 1913
G. F. Wright, *The Ice Age in North America and Its Bearing on the Antiquity of Man; Scientific Confirmations of Old Testament History*, 1906; *Origin and Antiquity of Man*, 1912
L. T. Townsend, *Evolution and Creation*
F. Bettex, *The Six Days of Creation in the Light of Modern Science*
L. M. Davies, *The Bible and Modern Science*, 1925
Baker and Nichol, *Creation Not Evolution*, 1926
C. F. Dunham, *Christianity in a World of Science*, 1928
G. Bartoli, *The Biblical Story of Creation*, 1926

S. J. Bole, *The Modern Triangle, Evolution, Philosophy and Criticism,* 1926
H. W. Clark, *Back to Creationism,* 1929
A. H. Finn, *The Creation, Fall and Deluge,* 1923
J. W. Gibbs, *Evolution and Christianity,* 1930
L. S. Keyser, *The Problems of Origins,* 1926
T. H. Nelson, *The Mosaic Law in the Light of Modern Science,* 1926
B. C. Nelson, *The Deluge Story in Stone,* 1931
A. R. Short, *The Bible and Modern Research*
J. H. Morrison, *Christian Faith and the Science of Today,* Cokesbury Press
G. B. Nimrod, *Science, Christ and the Bible,* 1929
J. L. May (Editor), *God and the Universe; The Christian Position,* 1932
J. F. Kiskaddon, *Scientific Support of Christian Doctrines,* 1934
W. B. Dawson, *The Bible Confirmed by Science,* 1932
A. N. Whitehead, *Science and the Modern World; Religion in the Making,* New York, 1926
J. A. Thompson, *The System of Animate Nature,* 1920; *Science and Religion,* New York, 1925
C. L. Morgan, *Life, Mind and Spirit,* New York, 1926
J. S. Haldane, *Mechanism, Life and Personality,* New York, 1904
J. Y. Dimpson, *The Spiritual Interpretation of Nature; Nature, Cosmic, Human and Divine*
L. F. Gruber, *Creation ex Nihilo,* Boston, 1918
W. H. C. Thomas, *Evolution and the Supernatural,* Philadelphia
B. G. O'Toole, *The Case Against Evolution,* New York, 1929
H. H. Lane, *Evolution and Christian Faith,* Princeton, 1923
E. Dennert, *At the Death-bed of Darwinism,* Burlington, Iowa, 1926
Philip Mauro, *Evolution at the Bar,* New York, 1922
A. Patterson, *The Other Side of Evolution,* Chicago, 1903
A. C. Zerbe, *Christianity and False Evolutionism,* Cleveland, 1925
H. C. Morton, *The Bankruptcy of Evolution,* London and New York

Older Works

Hugh Miller, *The Testimony of the Rocks,* Boston, 1870
Gerald Molloy, *Geology and Revelation,* New York, 1870
John Phin, *The Chemical History of the Six Days of Creation,* New York, 1870
A. T. Richie, *The Creation,* London, 1882
B. F. Cocker, *The Theistic Conception of the World,* New York, 1875
John Pye Smith, *Geology and Scripture,* New York, 1840
Henry Calderwood, *The Relation of Science and Religion,* New York, 1881
George Warrington, *The Mosaic Account of Creation,* New York, 1875
George Wight, *Geology and Genesis,* London, 1857
Alexander Winchell, *Reconstruction of Science and Religion,* New York, 1877
Joseph H. Wythe, *The Agreement of Science and Revelation,* Philadelphia, 1872
James Martineau, *Modern Materialism and Its Relations to Theology and Religion, New York,* 1877
Tayler Lewis, *The Bible and Science,* 1856; *The Six days of Creation or the Scriptural Cosmogony,* 1879
John Henry Kurtz, *The Bible and Astronomy, or an Exposition of the Biblical Cosmology and Its Relations to Natural Science,* Philadelphia, 1861

T. Landon Bruntin, *The Bible and Science*, London, 1881

J. W. Dawson, *Archai: or Studies of the Cosmogony and Natural History of the Hebrew Scriptures*, Montreal, 1860; *Nature and the Bible*, New York, 1875

William Fraser, *Blending Lights, or Relations of Natural Science, Archaeology and History to the Bible*, New York, 1874

James H. Chapin, *The Creation and the Early Development of Society*, New York, 1880

Providence

A. B. Bruce, *The Providential Order of the World*, New York, 1897; *The Moral Order of the World*, New York, 1899

W. F. Tillett, *Providence, Prayer and Power*, Nashville, 1926

O. Dewey, *The Problem of Human Destiny*, or *The End of Providence in the World and Man*, New York, 1866

R. Anderson, *The Silence of God*, Edinburgh

M. J. Savage, *Life's Dark Problems*, New York and London, 1905

Rudolph Otto, *Naturalism and Religion*, (English translation), New York, 1907

ANTHROPOLOGY

For the best theological discussions of this subject, see the standard works on Dogmatics or Systematic Theology. The following supplementary list is drawn largely from the older works on science in relation to the Bible. The newer works on science are listed under the subject of Cosmology.

John Laidlaw, *The Bible Doctrine of Man*, T. & T. Clark, 1879, 1911

H. W. Robinson, *The Christian Doctrine of Man*, Edinburgh, 1911

G. F. Wright, *Origin and Antiquity of Man*, 1912

R. L. Swain, *What and Why Is Man?* New York, 1925

John Laird, *The Idea of the Soul*, New York, 1927

J. B. Heard, *The Tripartite Nature of Man*, T. & T. Clark

Franz Delitzsch, *A System of Biblical Psychology*, Edinburgh, 1867

J. F. Beck, *Outlines of Biblical Psychology*, T. & T. Clark

Alexander Winchell, *Pre-Adamites*, or a *Demonstration of the Existence of Man Before Adam*, Chicago and London, 1880

Joseph P. Thompson, *Man in Genesis and Geology*, New York, 1870

George Rawlinson, *The Origin of Nations*, New York, 1878

R. S. Poole, *The Genesis of the Earth and of Man*, London, 1860

Dominick M'Causland, *Adam and the Adamites*, London, 1968

Quatrefages, *The Human Species*

Charles L. Brace, *The Races of the Old World*, New York, 1863

John Harris, *Man Primeval*, Boston, 1870; *The Pre-Adamite Earth*, Boston, 1857

F. Lenormant, *The Beginnings of History*, New York, 1882

J. L. Cabell, *The Testimony of Modern Science to the Unity of Mankind*, New York, 1860

D. MacDonald, *The Creation and the Fall*, Edinburgh

James D. Dana, *Manual of Geology*, 1875 (Special reference to the unity and antiquity of the race)

St. George Mivart, *The Genesis of Species*, London, 1871

HAMARTIOLOGY

Julius Muller, *The Christian Doctrine of Sin* (2 volumes), Edinburgh, 1877

F. R. Tennant, *The Sources of the Doctrine of the Fall and Original Sin*, Cambridge, 1903; *The Origin and Propagation of Sin*, Cambridge, 1908; *The Concept of Sin*, Cambridge, 1912

W. E. Orchard, *Modern Theories of Sin*, Boston, 1910

J. S. Candlish, *The Bible Doctrine of Sin*, Edinburgh

J. Tulloch, *The Christian Doctrine of Sin*, New York, 1876

H. R. Mackintosh, *Christianity and Sin*, New York, 1914

H. H. Horne, *Free Will and Human Responsibility*, New York, 1912

King, *Origin of Evil*

R. Tsanoff, *The Nature of Evil*

H. Lovett, *Thoughts on the Causes of Evil, Physical and Moral*, London, 1810

E. J. Bicknell, *The Christian Doctrine of Sin and Original Sin*, London, 1923

Ernest Naville, *The Problem of Evil*, New York, 1872

James Orr, *God's Image in Man and Its Defacement*, New York, 1906

John Young, *Evil not from God*, New York, 1858

Richard S. Taylor, *A Right Conception of Sin*, Kansas City, 1939

Boardman, *The Scriptural Doctrine of Original Sin*

Flower, *Adam's Disobedience and Its Results*

Taylor, *The Scripture Doctrine of Original Sin*

Glover, *A Short Treatise on Original Sin*

John Wesley, *Sermon XIII, On Sin in Believers; Sermon XIV, Repentance of Believers*, (Harrison, Wesleyan Standards, Vol. I)

George P. Fisher, *Discussions in History and Theology*, Scribners, 1880 (The Augustinian and the Federal Doctrines of Original Sin)

Wiggers, *Augustinianism and Pelagianism*

Jonathan Edwards, *Works* (II, part iv), *Original Sin*

Samuel Hopkins, *Doctrine of the Two Covenants*

Jeremy Taylor, *On Original Sin*

Landis, *Original Sin and Gratuitous Imputation*

Straffen, *Sin as Set Forth in the Scriptures*

Wallace, *Representative Responsibility*

N. P. Williams, *The Ideas of the Fall and Original Sin*, Longmans Green, 1929 (Liberal)

PART III. THE DOCTRINE OF THE SON
CHRISTOLOGY

J. A. Dorner, *History and Development of the Doctrine of the Person of Christ*, Edinburgh, 1878

J. J. Van Oosterzee, *The Image of Christ as Presented in Scripture*, London, 1874

W. F. Gess, *The Scripture Doctrine of the Person of Christ*, Andover, 1870

J. A. Reubelt, *The Scriptural Doctrine of the Person of Christ*, Andover, 1870

H. R. Mackintosh, *The Doctrine of the Person of Christ*, New York, 1912

A. M. Fairbairn, *Studies in the Life of Christ*, 1880; *The Place of Christ in Modern Theology*, Hodder & Stoughton, 1907

H. P. Liddon, *The Divinity of Our Lord and Saviour Jesus Christ*, London, 1867

A. B. Bruce, *The Miraculous Element in the Gospels*, 1886; *The Providential Order of the World*, 1897; *The Parabolic Teaching of Jesus; The Humiliation of Christ*, Hodder & Stoughton; *The Moral Order of the World*, Scribners, 1899; *Apologetics*, New York, 1901

Carl Ullman, *The Sinlessness of Jesus an Evidence for Christianity*, Edinburgh, 1858. Later Edition, 1870

R. S. Franks, *History of the Doctrine of the Work of Christ*, Hodder & Stoughton

S. Cave, *The Doctrine of the Work of Christ; The Doctrine of the Person of Christ*, New York, 1925

P. T. Forsyth, *The Cruciality of the Cross*, 1908; *The Person and Place of Jesus Christ*, Duckworth, 1909

Herbert M. Relton, *A Study in Christology*, London, 1922, 1923

Otto Pfleiderer, *Early Christian Conception of Christ*, Bethany Press, 1911

A. T. Robertson, *The Divinity of Christ in the Gospel of John*, 1916

Frank Coulin, *The Son of Man: Discourses on the Humanity of Jesus Christ*, Philadelphia, 1869

John Pye Smith, *The Scripture Testimony to the Messiah* (2 volumes), Edinburgh, 1868

Frederick C. Conybeare, *The Historical Christ*, Chicago, 1914

A. E. J. Rawlinson, *The New Testament Doctrine of Christ*, London, 1926

Charles H. Robinson, *Studies in the Character of Christ*, London, 1900

W. E. Vine, *Christ's Eternal Sonship*, 1934

E. D. La Touche, *The Person of Christ in Modern Thought*, London, 1912

John Wright Buckham, *Christ and the Eternal Order*, Pilgrim Press, 1906

J. Warshauer, *The Historical Life of Christ*, New York, 1926

L. W. Grensted, *The Person of Christ*

W. Norman Pittenger, *Christ and the Christian Faith*, New York, 1941

D. W. Forrest, *The Christ of History and Experience*, Edinburgh, 1899

Edward Mott, *The Christ of the Eternities*, Portland, 1936

P. C. Simpson, *The Fact of Christ*, Revell, 1900

Arthur C. Headlam, *Jesus Christ in History and Faith*

C. E. Raven, *Jesus and the Gospel of Love*

Good, *The Jesus of Our Fathers*

Pope, *The Person of Christ*, London

B. F. Wescott, *Christus Consummator*, Macmillan

Drown, *The Creative Christ*

Adamson, *The Mind in Christ*, T. & T. Clark

J. A. Findlay, *Jesus Human and Divine*

J. A. Huffman, *Old Testament Messages of the Christ*, 1909

Edward H. Bickersteth, *The Rock of Ages*, New York, 1861

C. Gore, *Belief in Christ*, New York, 1922

Edwin Lewis, *Jesus and the Human Quest*

William Temple, *Christ the Truth*, Macmillan, 1924

William Sanday, *Christologies, Ancient and Modern*

E. H. Merrell, *The Person of Christ*

S. W. Pratt, *The Deity of Christ According to the Gospel of John*, 1907

H. S. Coffin, *The Portraits of Christ in the New Testament*, New York, 1926

T. R. Glover, *Jesus in the Experience of Men*

A. T. Case, *As Modern Writers See Jesus*, Boston, 1927

G. E. Merrill, *The Reasonable Christ*, 1893

C. L. Brace, *Gesta Christi*, 1910

F. Bettex, *What Think Ye of Christ?* 1920

418 CHRISTIAN THEOLOGY

Lily Dougall and Cyril W. Emmet, *The Lord of Thought*, Doran, 1923
Shirley Jackson Case, *The Historicity of Jesus*, Chicago, 1912, 1928
C. C. McCown, *The Promise of His Coming*, MacMillan, 1921
C. W. Gilkey, *Jesus and Our Generation*, Chicago, 1925
R. F. Horton, *The Mystical Quest of Christ*
A. Schweitzer, *The Quest of the Historical Jesus*
V. G. Simkovitch, *Towards the Understanding of Jesus*, New York, 1923
J. A. Robertson, *The Spiritual Pilgrimage of Jesus*, Boston, 1921
Halford E. Lucock, *Jesus and the American Mind*, Abingdon, 1930
B. B. Warfield, *The Lord of Glory*, 1907
J. E. Whittaker, *A Biblical Defense of the Divinity of Christ*, 1909
E. Burton, *Testimonials of the Ante-Nicene Fathers to the Divinity of Christ*, London, 1829

The Life of Christ

Alfred Edersheim, *Life and Times of Jesus the Messiah* (2 volumes), Longmans Green, 1898
Bernhard Weiss, *The Life of Christ* (3 volumes)
Theodor Keim, *The History of Jesus of Nazareth* (3 volumes)
F. W. Farrar, *The Life of Christ* (2 volumes); *The Life of Lives*
W. R. Nicoll, *The Incarnate Saviour: A Life of Jesus Christ*
G. Aulen, *Christus Victor*, MacMillan, 1931
A. M. Rihbany, *The Syrian Christ*, Boston, 1916
J. Middleton Murray, *Jesus the Man of Genius*, New York, 1926
C. F. Kent, *The Life and Teachings of Jesus*
Fred F. Kramer, *Jesus the Light of the World*
James Moffatt (Editor), *Everyman's Life of Jesus*
H. F. Rall, *The Life of Jesus*
D. L. Sharp, *Christ and His Time*
David Smith, *Our Lord's Earthly Life*
Philip Volmer, *The Modern Student's Life of Christ*
L. M. Sweet, *The Birth and Infancy of Jesus Christ*
J. J. Taylor, *My Lord Christ*
A. M. Stewart, *The Infancy and Youth of Jesus*
Jacob Boss, *The Unique Aloofness of Jesus*
W. H. Bennett, *The Life of Christ According to St. Mark*
Burton and Matthews, *The Life of Christ*
Charles R. Erdman, *The Lord We Love: Devotional Studies in the Life of Christ*
W. M. Clow, *The Five Portraits of Jesus*
W. J. Dawson, *The Man Christ Jesus*
A. E. Garvie, *Studies in the Inner Life of Jesus*
A. G. Paisley, *The Emotional Life of Jesus*
D. G. Browne, *Christ and His Age*
Samuel G. Craig, *Jesus as He Was and Is*
Henry Ward Beecher, *The Life of Jesus the Christ*
Hall Caine, *Life of Christ*
Ecce Homo, *A Survey of the Life and Work of Christ*
C. J. Ellicott, *Historical Lectures on the Life of Our Lord Jesus Christ*
William Hanna, *Life of Christ*
Robert Keable, *The Great Galilean*
R. H. Walker, *Jesus and Our Pressing Problems*
G. O. Griffith, *St. Paul's Life of Christ*
J. V. Bartlet, *The Lord of Life*

B. W. Bacon, *The Story of Jesus*, New York, 1927
Shirley Jackson Case, *Jesus, a New Biography*, Chicago, 1927
W. Sanday, *Outlines of the Life of Christ*, T. & T. Clark, 1906; *Life of Christ in Recent Research*, Oxford, 1907
G. Papini, *Life of Christ*, Appleton, 1921, New York, 1923
R. J. Campbell, *The Life of Christ*, Appleton, 1921
Baab, *Jesus Christ Our Lord*, Abingdon, 1937
August Neander, *Life of Jesus Christ*, Harper Brothers, 1850
J. de Q. Donehoo, *Apocryphal and Legendary Life of Christ*, MacMillan, 1903
S. Townsend Weaver, *The Biblical Life of Jesus Christ*, Philadelphia. 1911
James Stalker, *Life of Christ*, Revell, 1880
George Matheson, *Studies in the Portrait of Christ*, Hodder & Stoughton. 1900
A. Klausner, *Jesus of Nazareth*, New York, 1925 (Jewish Interpretation)
E. F. Scott, *The Kingdom and the Messiah*, Edinburgh, 1911
C. A. Scott, *Dominus Noster*, Cambridge, 1918

The Virgin Birth

James Orr, *The Virgin Birth of Christ*, New York, 1909
R. J. Knowling, *Our Lord's Virgin Birth and the Criticism of Today*, 1907
T. J. Thoburn, *A Critical Examination of the Evidences for the Doctrine of the Virgin Birth*, 1908
A. C. A. Hall, *The Virgin Mother*, New York, 1894
J. G. Machen, *The Virgin Birth of Christ*, New York, 1930
L. M. Sweet, *The Birth and Infancy of Jesus Christ*, 1907
G. H. Box, *The Virgin Birth of Jesus*, Milwaukee, 1916
G. W. McPherson, *The Modern Mind and the Virgin Birth*, 1923
J. A. Faulkner, *The Miraculous Birth of Our Lord*
William B. Ullathorne, *The Immaculate Conception*, 1904
J. B. Champion, *The Virgin's Son*, 1924
R. J. Cooke, *Did Paul Know of the Virgin Birth?* 1926
W. Evans, *Why I Believe in the Virgin Birth of Christ*, 1924
A. T. Robertson, *The Mother of Jesus: Her Problems and Her Glory*, 1925
J. M. Gray, *Why We Believe in the Virgin Birth of Christ*
F. W. Pitt, *New Light on the Virgin Birth*

The Incarnation

Robert J. Wilberforce, *The Doctrine of the Incarnation of our Lord Jesus Christ*
E. H. Gifford, *The Incarnation*, New York, 1897
T. C. Edwards, *The God-Man*, Hodder & Stoughton
Franzelin, *De Verbo Incarnato*, Rome
Ottley, *The Doctrine of the Incarnation*, Methuen
Athanasius, *On the Incarnation*, English Translation by Robertson, London
Charles Gore, *The Incarnation of the Son of God*, New York, 1900
H. C. Powell, London, 1896, *The Principle of the Incarnation*, London, 1896

THE ATONEMENT

John Miley, *The Atonement in Christ*, New York, 1879
L. W. Grensted, *A Short History of the Doctrine of the Atonement*
A. A. Hodge, *The Atonement*, Philadelphia, 1867

R. S. Candlish, *The Atonement: Its Efficacy and Extent*, Edinburgh, 1867

Albert Barnes, *The Atonement in Its Relation to Law and Moral Government*, Philadelphia, 1859

Horace Bushnell, *The Vicarious Sacrifice* (2 volumes), New York, 1891

D. W. Simon, *The Redemption of Man*, Edinburgh, 1899; *Reconciliation Through Incarnation*, Edinburgh, 1898

Anselm, *Cur Deus Homo*, English Translation by Deane, Chicago, 1903

H. N. Oxenham, *The Catholic Doctrine of Atonement*, London, 1865

T. V. Tymns, *The Christian Idea of Atonement*, London, 1904

R. C. Moberly, *Atonement and Personality*, New York, 1901

A. Sabbatier, *The Doctrine of the Atonement and Its Historical Evolution*, English Translation, New York, 1904

James Denney, *The Death of Christ*, New York, 1903; *The Atonement and the Modern Mind*, London, 1903; *The Christian Doctrine of Reconciliation*, New York, 1918

G. B. Stevens, *The Christian Doctrine of Salvation*, 1905

Rashdall, *The Idea of Atonement in Christian Theology*, MacMillan, 1920

J. K. Mozley, *The Doctrine of the Atonement*, Scribners, 1916

F. D. Maurice, *The Doctrine of Sacrifice Deduced from the Scriptures*, 1854

John M. Campbell, *The Nature of the Atonement*, London, 1873

Thomas J. Crawford, *The Doctrine of the Holy Scripture Respecting the Atonement*, 1875

R. W. Dale, *The Atonement*, New York, 1876

William Symington, *The Atonement and Intercession of Jesus Christ*, New York, 1849

Howard Malcom, *The Extent and Efficacy of the Atonement*, Philadelphia, 1870

G. Smeaton, *The Doctrine of the Atonement as Taught by Christ Himself*, Edinburgh, 1868

Ralph Wardlaw, *Discourses on the Nature and Extent of the Atonement*, Glasgow, 1844

William Magee, *Scripture Doctrine of Atonement and Sacrifice*, New York, 1839

Charles Beecher, *Redeemer and Redeemed*, Boston, 1864

J. S. Lidgett, *The Spiritual Principle of the Atonement*, London, 1901

Ritschl, *The Scripture Doctrine of Justification and Reconciliation*, Clark

Robert Mackintosh, *Historic Theories of the Atonement*, New York, 1920

Grotius, *De Satisfactione* (Editions from 1617-1730), English Translation by Foster, Andover

S. Cave, *The Scripture Doctrine of Sacrifice*, T. & T. Clark

H. R. Mackintosh, *The Christian Experience of Forgiveness*

G. W. Richards, *Christian Ways of Salvation*

H. S. Coffin, *Social Aspects of the Cross*, New York, 1911

J. S. Whale, *The Christian Answer to the Problem of Evil*, 1936

E. W. Johnson, *Suffering, Punishment and Atonement*, 1919

H. Wheeler Robinson, *Suffering: Human and Divine*, MacMillan, 1939

A. S. Peake, *The Problem of Suffering in the Old Testament*, 1904

M. C. D'Arcy, *The Pain of this World and the Providence of God*, 1936

J. K. Mozley, *The Impassibility of God*, 1926

R. C. Moberly, *Sorrow, Sin and Beauty*, 1903

James Hinton, *The Mystery of Pain*, 1866

B. R. Brasnett, *The Suffering of the Impassible God*, 1928

Leighton Pullen, *The Atonement*, London, 1913

Lonsdale Ragg, *Aspects of the Atonement*, London, 1904
P. L. Snowden, *The Atonement and Ourselves*, London, 1919
F. R. M. Hitchcock, *The Atonement and Modern Thought*, London, 1911
George C. Foley, *Anselm's Theory of the Atonement*, New York, 1909
James Denney, *The Christian Doctrine of Reconciliation*
Albert C. Knudson, *The Doctrine of Redemption*, Abingdon, 1933

PART IV. THE DOCTRINE OF THE HOLY SPIRIT
PERSON AND WORK OF THE HOLY SPIRIT

James Buchanan, *On the Office and Work of the Holy Spirit*, Edinburgh, 1856
James B. Walker, *The Doctrine of the Holy Spirit*, Cincinnati, 1880
Julius Charles Hare, *The Mission of the Comforter*, London, 1876
W. T. Davison, *The Indwelling Spirit*, Hodder & Stoughton, 1911
John Goodwin, *Pleroma to Pneumatikon; or Being Filled with the Spirit*, 1670, 1867
William Arthur, *Tongue of Fire*, 1856
Downer, *The Mission and Administration of the Holy Spirit*, 1909
Abraham Kuyper, *The Work of the Holy Spirit*, Funk & Wagnalls, 1908
A. B. Simpson, *The Holy Spirit or Power from on High* (2 volumes), New York, 1895
B. H. Streeter, *The Spirit*, MacMillan, 1919
H. Wheeler Robinson, *The Christian Experience of the Holy Spirit*, Harper, 1928
Selby, *The Holy Spirit and Christian Privilege*, 1894
Welldon, *The Revelation of the Holy Spirit*, 1902
John W. Goodwin, *The Living Flame*, Nazarene
Samuel Chadwick, *The Way to Pentecost*, Revell
T. Rees, *The Holy Spirit in Thought and Experience*
Evelyn Underhill, *The Life of the Spirit and the Life of Today*
Charles A. Anderson-Scott, *Fellowship with the Spirit*
Walker, *The Spirit and the Incarnation*, 1899
Irving Wood, *The Spirit of God in Biblical Literature*, 1904
G. Smeaton, *Doctrine of the Holy Spirit*, 1882
T. K. Doty, *The Twofold Gift of the Holy Ghost*
L. R. Dunn, *The Mission of the Spirit*, New York, 1871
S. L. Brengle, *When the Holy Ghost Is Come*, New York, 1914
William McDonald, *Another Comforter*, Boston, 1890
Denio, *The Supreme Leader*, Boston, 1910
W. P. Dickson, *St. Paul' s Use of the Terms Flesh and Spirit*, 1883
Dougan Clark, *The Offices of the Holy Spirit*, Philadelphia, 1878
W. H. Hutchings, *The Person and Work of the Holy Ghost*, Longmans Green, 1897
Basil, *De Spiritu Sancto*, English Translation by Lewis, London
J. S. Candlish, *The Work of the Holy Spirit*, T. & T. Clark
Manning, *Internal Mission of the Holy Ghost*, London
Wheldon, *The Holy Spirit*, Macmillan
Humphrey, *His Divine Majesty*, London
Owen, *The Doctrine of the Holy Spirit*, T. & T. Clark, 1684, 1826
Joseph Parker, *The Paraclete*, New York, 1876
Heber, *Bampton Lectures on the Personality and Office of the Comforter*, 1846
Raymond Calkins, *The Holy Spirit*, Abingdon, 1930

A. C. A. Hall, *The Work of the Holy Spirit*, Milwaukee, 1907

J. D. Folsom, *The Holy Spirit Our Helper*, New York, 1907

G. F. Holden, *The Holy Ghost the Comforter*, New York, 1908

F. C. Porter, *The Spirit of God and the Word of God in Modern Theology*, New York, 1908

J. H. B. Masterman, *I Believe in the Holy Ghost*, London, 1907

A. J. Gordon, *The Ministry of the Spirit*, New York, 1894

Kildahl, *Misconceptions of the Word and Work of the Holy Spirit*, Minn., 1927

Henry B. Swete, *The Holy Spirit in the Ancient Church*, London, 1912; *The Holy Spirit in the New Testament*, London, 1909

W. H. Griffith Thomas, *The Holy Spirit of God*, London, 1913

C. E. Raven, *The Creator Spirit*

R. A. Torrey, *The Person and Work of the Holy Spirit*, New York, 1910

C. I. Schofield, *Plain Papers on the Holy Spirit*, New York and London, 1899

E. W. Winstanley, *The Spirit in the New Testament*, New York, 1908

Julius Charles Hare, *The Mission of the Comforter*, Boston, 1854

J. Robson, *The Holy Spirit, the Paraclete*, Aberdeen, 1893

L. B. Crane, *The Teachings of Jesus Concerning the Holy Spirit*, New York, 1906

Goodwin, *The Work of the Holy Ghost in Our Salvation*, Edinburgh, 1863

I. Wood, *The Spirit of God in Biblical Literature*, 1904

J. P. Coyle, *The Holy Spirit in Literature and Life*, Boston, 1855

Jonathan Goforth, *By My Spirit*, London and Edinburgh

Older Works on the Holy Spirit

(Cited by Kuyper, *The Work of the Holy Spirit*)

John Owen, *Works* (Richard Baynes, 1826), Contains three treatises on the Holy Spirit published in 1674, 1682 and 1693. Still unsurpassed.

Johannes Ernest Gerhard, *On the Person of the Holy Spirit*, Jena, 1660

T. Hackspann, *Dissertation on the Holy Spirit*, Jena, 1655

J. F. Buddeuss, *On the Godhead of the Holy Spirit*, Jena, 1727

Fr. Deutsch, *On the Personality of the Holy Spirit*, Leipsic, 1711

David Rungius, *Proof of the Eternity and Eternal Godhead of the Holy Spirit*, *Wittenberg*, 1599

Seb. Nieman, *On the Holy Spirit*, Jena, 1656

J. G. Dorsche, *On the Person of the Holy Spirit*, Konigsberg, 1690

J. C. Pfeiffer, *On the Godhead of the Holy Spirit*, Jena, 1740

G. F. Gude, *On the Martyrs as Witnesses for the Godhead of the Holy Spirit*, Leipsic, 1741

J. C. Danhauer, *On the Procession of the Holy Spirit from the Father and from the Son*, Strasburg, 1663

Separate Treatises

Anton, *The Holy Spirit Indispensable*

Carsov, *On the Holy Spirit in Conviction*

Wensdorf, *On the Holy Spirit as a Teacher*

Boerner, *The Anointing of the Holy Spirit*

Neuman, *The Anointing Which Teaches All Things*

Fries, *The Office of the Holy Spirit in General*

Weiss, *The Holy Spirit Bringing into Remembrance*

Foertsch, *On the Holy Spirit's Leading of the Children of God*
Hoepfner, *On the Intercession of the Holy Spirit*
Meen, *On the Adoration of the Holy Spirit*
Henning and Crusius, *On the Earnest of the Holy Spirit*
Beltheim, Arnold, Gunther, Wendler and Dumerick, *On the Groaning of the Holy Spirit*

Dutch Theologians

Sam. Maresius, *Theological Treatise on the Personality and Godhead of the Holy spirit*
Jac. Fruytier, *The Ancient Doctrine Concerning God and the Holy Spirit, True, Proven and Divine*

THE PRELIMINARY STATES OF GRACE

The best treatment of the Preliminary States of Grace, as also the subjects of Justification and Regeneration, will be found in the standard works on Systematic Theology. Representing the earlier, or what is sometimes known as modified Arminianism, are the following: Watson, *Institutes;* Wakefield, *Christian Theology;* Summers, *Systematic Theology;* Pope, *Compendium of Christian Theology;* and Ralston, *Elements of Divinity.* The last named work contains an excellent discussion of the Calvinistic and Arminian positions. As representative of the so-called later Arminianism, Raymond, *Systematic Theology;* Miley, *Systematic Theology;* Whedon, *Commentaries,* and A. M. Hills, *Fundamental Christian Theology.* In the Calvinistic theology, Dr. W. G. T. Shedd represents the realistic position, and Dr. Charles Hodge, the Federal or Representative position. Among the older works on both the Calvinistic and Arminian positions, may be mentioned the following:

John Wesley, *Works*, Volume VI, *On Predestination*
James Arminius, *Writings*, Volume III
John Fletcher, *Checks to Antinomianism*, Volumes I-II
J. B. Mozley, *Augustinian Doctrine of Predestination*, 1855
George Tomline, *A Refutation of Calvinism*, London, 1811
John Calvin, *Institutes*, Book III, Chapters xxi-xxiv
Richard Watson, *Theological Institutes*, Part II, Chapters xxv-xxviii
W. Fisk, *The Calvinistic Controversy*, New York, 1837
Randolph S. Foster, *Objections to Calvinism*, Cincinnati, 1848 (many editions)
Edward Copleston, *Enquiry into the Doctrines of Necessity and Predestination*, London, 1821
John Forbes, *Predestination and Free Will Reconciled, or Calvinism and Arminianism United in the Westminster Confession*, 1878
Jonathan Edwards, *An Essay on the Freedom of the Will*, 1754; also, *A Divine and Supernatural Light Imparted to the Soul by the Spirit of God*, 1734 (A sermon noted for its spiritual philosophy)
Albert Taylor Bledsoe, *An Examination of Edwards on the Will;* Philadelphia, 1845; *A Theodicy, or Vindication of Divine Glory*, New York, 1853
Asa Mahan, *System of Intelectual Philosophy*, New York, 1845; *Election and the Influence of the Holy Spirit*, 1851
Daniel D. Whedon, *Freedom of the Will*, 1864
Martin Luther, *Bondage of the Will*
Thomas C. Upham, *Treatise on the Will*, 1850

Henry Philip Tappan, *A Review of Edwards on the Will*, New York, 1839; *Doctrine of the Will Determined by an Appeal to Consciousness*, 1840; *Doctrine of the Will Applied to Moral Agency and Responsibility*, 1841 (Single volume, Glasgow, 1857)

CHRISTIAN RIGHTEOUSNESS

Here again, the best treatment of the subject will be found in the standard works on theology. The clearest and most specific treatment is found in the earlier treatises.

John Wesley, *Sermons*, V, VI, and XX. (Harrison, *Wesleyan Standards*, Volume I)

Richard Watson, *Theological Institutes*, II, Chapter xxiii

John Calvin, *Institutes*, III, xi-xviii

John Owen, *Works*, Volume V, *The Doctrine of Justification*

Faber, *The Primitive Doctrine of Justification*

Jonathan Edwards (the younger), *On the Necessity of the Atonement, and Its Consistency with Free Grace in Forgiveness*, Three addresses, 1875, which form the basis of the "Edwardean Theory" of the Atonement, generally accepted by the "New England School."

Albrecht Ritschl, *The Christian Doctrine of Justification and Reconciliation*, (Translated by Mackintosh and Macaulay) (Second Edition, 1902)

Charles Abel Heurtley, *Justification*, 1845 (Bampton Lectures)

John Davenant, *A Treatise on Justification* (2 volumes), London, 1844-1846

M. Loy, *The Doctrine of Justification*, Columbus, Ohio, 1869, 1882

James Buchanan, *The Doctrine of Justification*, Edinburgh, 1867

John H. Newman, *Lectures on the Doctrine of Justification*, London, 1874

R. N. Davies, *A Treatise on Justification*, Cincinnati, 1878

Julius Charles Hare, *Scriptural Doctrine of Justification*

Martin Luther, *On Galatians*

S. M. Merrill, *Aspects of Christian Experience*, Chapters iv-vii

H. R. Mackintosh, *The Christian Experience of Forgiveness* (previously mentioned)

G. W. Richards. *Christian Ways of Salvation*, New York, 1923

John Witherspoon, *Essay on Justification*, 1756 (Considered one of the ablest Calvinistic expositions of the doctrine)

G. Cross, *Christian Salvation*, Chicago, 1925

CHRISTIAN SONSHIP

Outside of the standard works on theology, the literature of Christian Sonship or Regeneration is not extensive.

John Wesley, *Sermons*, XVIII and XIX (Harrison, *Wesleyan Standards*, Volume I)

John Fletcher, *Discourse on the New Birth*

Stephen Charnock, *On Regeneration*, (Complete works in Nichol's Series of Standard Divines, 5 volumes, Edinburgh, 1864)

Faber, *Primitive Doctrine of Regeneration*

John Howe, *On Regeneration* (Sermons xxxviii-xlix) *Complete Works* (2 volumes), London, 1724; New York, 1809

Austin Phelps, *The New Birth*, Boston, 1867

John Witherspoon, *Treatise on Regeneration*, 1764

Calvin, *Institutes*, III, i-ii

Jonathan Edwards, *On Spiritual Light* (mentioned in connection with Prevenient Grace)
S. M. Merrill, *Aspects of Christian Experience* (Chapter X)
Witsius, *Covenants*, III, vi
Archbishop Leighton, *On Regeneration*
N. H. Marshall, *Conversion or the New Birth*, London, 1909
G. H. Gerberding, *New Testament Conversions*, Philadelphia, 1889

The Witness of the Spirit

John Wesley, *Sermons*, X, XI, and XII (Harrison, *Wesleyan Standards*, volume I)
R. N. Davies, *A Treatise on Justification*, 1878 (Lecture x)
S. M. Merrill, *Aspects of Christian Experience* (Chapter x)
Walton, *Witness of the Spirit*
Young, *The Witness of the Spirit*, 1882

Modern Related Works

H. Begbie, *Twice-Born Men*, New York, London and Edinburgh, 1909 (previously cited)
H. E. Monroe, *Twice-Born Men in America*, 1914
G. Jackson, *The Fact of Conversion*, London, 1908

CHRISTIAN PERFECTION OR ENTIRE SANCTIFICATION

There is a wide variety of literature on this subject, but in general it has been written and published with the dominant thought of propagating the doctrine and the experience. For this reason, the simple first principles of the doctrine have been presented in an evangelistic manner, and consequently there is not a great amount of scholarly and investigative literature on the subject. The following works may be considered representative:

John Wesley, *Plain Account of Christian Perfection;* Sermon XVII, *The Circumcision of the Heart;* Sermon XL, *Christian Perfection;* and Sermon XLIII, *The Scripture Way of Salvation*
Jesse T. Peck, *The Central Idea of Christianity*, Boston, 1857
R. S. Foster, *Christian Purity*
W. F. Mallalieu, *The Fulness of the Blessing*, Jennings & Pye, 1903
Dr. P. F. Bresee, *Sermons*, Nazarene Publishing House, 1903
Dr. Dougan Clark, *Theology of Holiness*, Boston, 1893; *Offices of the Holy Spirit*, 1878
William MacDonald, *Scriptural Way of Holiness*, 1887; *New Testament Standard of Piety*, New York, 1860, 1871
J. A. Wood, *Purity and Maturity*, 1876, Boston, 1899; *Perfect Love*, 1880, Boston and Chicago, 1907; *Christian Perfection as Taught by John Wesley*, MacDonald and Gill, 1885
Dr. Adam Clarke, *Christian Theology*, London, 1835
R. T. Williams, *Sanctification*, Kansas City, 1928
J. W. Goodwin, *The Living Flame*, Kansas City
C. W. Ruth, *Entire Sanctification*, Chicago, 1903; *The Second Crisis in Christian Experience*, Chicago, 1912
Dr. W. B. Godbey, *The Incarnation of the Holy Ghost*, Louisville; *Bible Theology*, Cincinnati, 1911
W. Jones, M.D., *The Doctrine of Entire Sanctification*, National Association, 1885

Asbury Lowrey, *Possibilities of Grace*, New York, 1888
Dr. A. M. Hills, *Holiness and Power*
Joseph H. Smith, *Pauline Perfection*, Chicago, 1913
Daniel Steele, *Love Enthroned*, New York, 1875, 1902, 1908
Sheridan Baker, *Hidden Manna*, Boston, 1888; *The New Name*, 1890; *Living Waters*
Commissioner Brengle, *When the Holy Ghost Is Come*, Salvation Army, N. Y., 1914
Harry E. Jessop, *Foundation of Doctrine*, Chicago, 1938
Beverly Carradine, *The Old Man*, Louisville, 1896; *The Better Way*, Cincinnati, 1896
Isaac M. See, *The Rest of Faith*, New York, 1871
Mark Guy Pearse, *Christian's Secret of Holiness*, Boston, 1886; *Thoughts on Holiness*, 1884
Benjamin T. Roberts, *Holiness Teachings*, North Chili, N. Y., 1893
S. H. Platt, *Christian Holiness* (Philosophy, Theory and Experience), 1882
Asa Mahan, *The Baptism of the Holy Ghost*, George Hughes & Co., 1870
Dr. C. J. Fowler, *Christian Unity*, Chicago, 1907
Dr. E. P. Ellyson, *Bible Holiness*, Kansas City, 1938
S. A. Keen, *Pentecostal Papers*, Cincinnati, 1895
E. T. Curnick, *A Catechism on Christian Perfection*, Boston, 1885
E. A. Hazen, *Salvation to the Uttermost*, Lansing, 1892
Chadwick, *The Way to Pentecost*, Revell
A. Sims, *Bible Salvation*, 1886
W. E. Shephard, *Holiness Typology*, San Francisco, 1896
G. D. Watson, *White Robes*, Cincinnati, 1883; *The Heavenly Life*
J. A. Kring, *The Conquest of Canaan*, Kansas City, 1930
J. G. Morrison, *Our Lost Estate*, Kansas City
Campbell, *Witnesses to Holiness*
Brockett, *Scriptural Freedom from Sin*, Kansas City, 1941

CHRISTIAN ETHICS

In addition to the references cited in the body of the text, the following books dealing with both Christian and theoretical ethics will be found valuable:

William Burton Pope, *Compendium of Christian Theology*, III, pp. 148-258
Thomas N. Ralston, *Elements of Divinity*, Part III, pp. 733-857
C. F. Paulus, *The Christian Life*, New York and Cincinnati, 1892
H. H. Scullard, *The Ethics of the Gospel and the Ethics of Nature*, London, 1827
W. R. Inge, *Christian Ethics and Modern Problems*, London, 1932
C. Gore, *Christian Moral Principles*, London, 1932
W. E. H. Lecky, *History of European Morals from Augustine to Charlemagne*, London, 1897
P. Gardner, *Evolution in Christian Ethics*, London, 1918
W. H. V. Reade, *The Moral System in Dante's Inferno*, Oxford, 1909
A. H. Gilbert, *Dante's Conception of Justice*, Durham, N. C., 1925
R. Roedder, *Savonarola, A Study of Conscience*, New York, 1930
G. Harkness, *John Calvin, the Man and His Ethics*, New York, 1931
F. K. Chaplin, *The Effects of the Reformation on the Ideals of Life and Conduct*, Cambridge, 1927
J. R. Illingworth, *Christian Character*, London, 1904

W. R. Sorley, *Ethics of Naturalism*, Edinburgh, 1904; *Moral Life and Moral Worth*, Cambridge, 1911; *Moral Values and the Idea of God*, Cambridge, 1918
K. E. Kirk, *The Christian Doctrine of the Summum Bonum*, London, 1931
H. E. Rashdall, *Theory of Good and Evil*, Oxford, 1907
P. Mayers, *History as Past Ethics*, Boston, 1913
J. Rickaby, *Aquinas Ethicus* (2 volumes), London, 1896
W. K. L. Clarke, *The Ascetic Works of St. Basil*, London, 1925
Bernard of Clairveaux, *The Twelve Degrees of Humility and Pride* (Translated by B. R. V. Mills), London, 1929
T. K. Abbott, *Kant's Critique of Practical Reason and Other Works on The Theory of Ethics*, London, 1909
T. H. Green, *Prolegomena to Ethics*, Oxford, 1883, 1906
F. H. Bradley, *Ethical Studies*, Oxford, 1876, 1927
R. H. Murray, *Erasmus and Luther*, London, 1920
F. H. Dudden, *The Life and Times of Ambrose*, Oxford, 1935
Augustine, *Confessions* (Everyman's Edition), London, 1907; *City of God*, F. W. Bussell, London, 1913
Tertullian, *Apologia* (Translated by W. Reeve), London, 1926
A. Slater, *Manual of Moral Theology* (2 volumes), Burns and Oates
F. J. Hall and F. H. Hallock, *Moral Theology*, Longmans Green & Company
K. E. Kirk, *Some Principles of Moral Theology; Conscience and Its Problems*, Longmans Green & Co.

Older Works

William Whewell, *The Elements of Morality* (2 volumes), New York, 1845
Francis Wayland, *The Elements of Moral science* (77th edition), Boston, 1865
Mark Hopkins, *The Law of Love and Love as a Law*, New York, 1875
Henry Calderwood, *Handbook of Moral Philosophy*, London, 1881
D. S. Gregory, *Christian Ethics*, Philadelphia, 1875
Joseph Haven, *Moral Philosophy*, Boston, 1860
Ralph Wardlaw, *Christian Ethics*, London, 1833
J. L. Davies, *Theology and Morality*, London, 1873
H. Winslow, *Moral Philosophy*, New York, 1866
Samuel Spalding, *The Philosophy of Christian Morals*, London, 1843
J. Skinner, *Synopsis of Moral and Ascetic Theology*, Kegan Paul
Archibald Alexander, *Outlines of Moral Science*, New York, 1870
T. R. Birks, *Supernatural Revelation, or the First Principles of Moral Theology*, London, 1879
J. Bascom, *Ethics of the Science of Duty*, New York, 1879
G. C. A. Harless, *System of Christian Ethics*, Edinburgh, 1868
Chr. F. Schmid, *General Principles of Christian Ethics*, Philadelphia, 1872
J. Seth, *A Study of Ethical Principles*, London, 1894
J. S. Mackenzie, *A Manual of Ethics*, London, 1893
Noah Porter, *The Elements of Moral Science*, Scribners, 1885; *Kant's Ethics*, Chicago, 1885
Immanuel Kant, *The Metaphysics of Ethics* (Translated by J. W. Temple), Edinburgh, 1869
John Foster, *Lectures on Christian Morals*, Nashville, 1855
E. G. Robinson, *Principles and Practice of Morality*, Boston, 1888
James Martineau, *Types of Ethical Theory* (2 volumes), Oxford, 1886
Borden Parker Bowne, *The Principles of Ethics*, Harpers, 1892

W. T. Davison, *The Christian Conscience*, London, 1888

Alexander Baine, *Mental and Moral Science*, London, 1868

Marriage and Divorce

Oscar D. Watkins, *Holy Matrimony*, New York, 1895

Herbert M. Luckok, *The History of Marriage, Jewish and Christian*, London, 1895

Hugh Davey Evans, *A Treatise on the Christian Doctrine of Marriage*, New York, 1870

Alvah Hovey, *The Scriptural Law of Divorce*, Boston, 1866

George Walter Fiske, *The Christian Family*, Abingdon, 1929

Flora M. Thurston, *A Bibliography of Family Relationships*, New York, 1932

Annie I. Dyer, *Guide to the Literature of Home and Family Life*, Philadelphia, 1924

Regina Wescott, Wieman, *The Modern Family and the Church*, Harpers, 1937 (Contains an extensive bibliography)

Modern Social Reform

H. Martin, *Christian Social Reformers of the Nineteenth Century*, London, 1927

W. Cunningham, *Christianity and Economic Science*, London, 1914

W. E. Orchard, *Christianity and World Problems*, London

J. A. Hobson, *God and Mammon: The Relation of Religion and Economics*, New York, 1931

A. D. Lindsay, *Christianity and Economics*, London, 1933

E. Troeltsch, *Protestantism and Progress*, London, 1912

R. H. Tawney, *Religion and the Rise of Capitalism*, London, 1925

A. T. Cadoux, *Jesus and Civil Government*, London, 1923

C. J. Cadoux, *The Early Church and the World*, Edinburgh, 1925

M. Weber, *The Protestant Ethics and the Spirit of Capitalism*, New York, 1930

F. E. Johnson, *Economics and the Good Life*, New York, 1934.

THE CHURCH

Some of the best material on the organization, ministry, worship and sacraments of the Church will be found in the treatises on systematic theology. The following list includes a number of miscellaneous works also, together with a few of the treatises on special subjects.

Thomas O. Summers, *Systematic Theology*, Volume II, Book VII, pp. 215-494

William Burton Pope, *Compendium of Christian Theology*, Volume III, pp. 259-364

A. H. Strong, *Systematic Theology*, Volume III, Part VII, pp. 887-980

Samuel Wakefield, *Christian Theology*, Book VI, pp. 538-596

A. M. Hills, *Fundamental Christian Theology*, Volume II, pp. 282-336

The Sacraments

George D. Armstrong, *The Sacraments of the New Testament*, New York, 1880

W. R. Gordon, *The Church of God and Her Sacraments*, New York, 1870

Richard Whately, *The Scripture Doctrine Concerning the Sacraments*, London, 1857

John S. Stone, *The Christian Sacraments*, New York, 1866
Richard Watson, *The Sacraments* (From the Institutes), New York, 1893
C. P. Krauth, *The Person of Our Lord and His Sacramental Presence*, (Lutheran), 1867

Special Treatises on Baptism

Bishop S. M. Merrill, *Christian Baptism*, New York, 1876
J. W. Etter, *The Doctrine of Christian Baptism*, Dayton, 1888
William Wall, *History of Infant Baptism*, London, 1872
Leonard Woods, *Lectures on Infant Baptism*, Andover, 1829
James Chrystal, *History of the Modes of Christian Baptism*, Philadelphia, 1851
W. Elwin, *The Ministry of Baptism* (Historical), London, 1889
Alexander Carson, *Baptism in Its Mode and Subjects*, American Baptist, 1845, 1860
C. P. Krauth, *Baptism: The Doctrine Set Forth in the Holy Scriptures and Taught in the Evangelical Lutheran Church*, 1866; *Infant Baptism and Infant Salvation in the Calvinistic System*. (A review of Dr. Hodge's Systematic Theology), Philadelphia, 1874
Edward Beecher, *Import and Modes of Baptism*, New York, 1849
Edward Bickersteth, *A Treatise on Baptism*, Philadelphia, 1841
J. A. Whittaker, *Baptism*, 1893
R. W. Dale, *Classic Baptism*, 1867; *Johannic Baptism*, 1870; *Judaic Baptism*, 1873; *Christic and Patristic Baptism*, 1874; Rutter, Philadelphia
F. G. Hibbard, *Christian Baptism*, New York, 1853
William Hodges, *Baptism Tested by Scripture and History*, New York 1874
D. B. Ford, *Studies on the Baptismal Question*, Boston, 1879
C. Taylor, *Apostolic Baptism*, New York, 1844, 1869
H. Herbert Hawes, *Baptism Mode-Studies*, Warden, 1887

Church Polity

George T. Ladd, *Principles of Church Polity*, New York, 1882
Samuel Davidson, *Ecclesiastical Polity of the New Testament*, Bohn, 1850
Albert Barnes, *Episcopacy Tested by Scripture* (A review of the work by Bishop Onderdonk), *Essays and Reviews*, Volume I, New York, 1855
W. Walker, *The Creeds and Platforms of Congregationalism*, 1893
W. J. McGlothlin, *Baptist Confessions of Faith*, 1911
Charles Hodge, *The Church and Its Polity*, New York, 1879
E. Hatch, *The Organization of the Early Christian Churches*, London, 1881
R. W. Dale, *Manual of Congregational Principles*
G. A. Jacob, *The Ecclesiastical Polity of the New Testament*
W. Jones Seabury, *An Introduction to the Study of Ecclesiastical Polity*, New York, 1894
C. C. Stewart, *The Scriptural Form of Church Government*, New York, 1872
William Pierce, *The Ecclesiastical Principles and Polity of the Wesleyan Methodists*, London, 1873
William H. Perrine, *Principles of Church Government with Special Application to the Polity of Episcopal Methodism*, New York, 1888
Robert Emory, *History of the Discipline of the Methodist Episcopal Church*, 1864
Francis Wayland, *Notes on the Principles and Practices of Baptist Churches*, Sheldon, 1857

Ralph Wardlaw, *Congregational Independency*, London, 1848
C. W. Shields, *The Historic Episcopate*, Scribners, 1894
Thomas B. Neely, *The Evolution of Episcopacy and Organic Methodism*, New York, 1888

Church History

The field of church history is extensive and properly belongs to another department in the study of religion. Only a few of the more important works, therefore, are included in the following bibliography.

J. L. Mosheim, *Ecclesiastical History* (4 volumes), Translated by Maclaine
George P. Fisher, *History of the Christian Church*, Scribners, 1887
J. F. Hurst, *Short History of the Christian Church*, Harpers, 1893
J. H. Kurtz, *Church History* (3 volumes), New York, 1890
Philip Schaff, *History of the Apostolic Church*, New York, 1853; *History of the Christian Church* (7 volumes), Scribners, 1892; *American Church History* (12 volumes), Christian Literature Company, N. Y., 1893
H. H. Milman, *History of Latin Christianity* (8 volumes), New York, 1871
Gibbon, *History of the Decline and Fall of the Roman Empire* (6 volumes), Boston, 1850
John Fulton, (Editor), *Ten Epochs of Church History* (10 volumes), Scribners, 1911
Williston Walker, *History of the Christian Church*, Scribners, 1924
Leopold von Ranke, *History of the Popes* (3 volumes), New York, 1901
F. W. Farrar, *Early Days of Christianity*, New York, 1882
C. D. Eldridge, *Christianity's Contribution to Civilization*, Cokesbury, 1928
William Warren Sweet, *Story of Religion in America*, Harpers, 1930, 1939
G. L. Hunt, *Outline of the History of Christian Literature*, MacMillan, 1926
K. S. Latourette, *A History of the Expansion of Christianity* (4 volumes), Scribners, 1941
A. Harnack, *The Mission and Expansion of Christianity*
Hans Lietzmann, *The Beginnings of the Christian Church*
Moffatt, *The First Five Centuries*
Abel Stevens, *History of Methodism* (3 volumes), New York and London, 1858, 1878
L. Tyerman, *The Life and Times of the Rev. John Wesley* (3 volumes), Harpers, 1872
T. M. Lindsay, *History of the Reformation*, (2 volumes), 1911
J. Mackinnon, *Luther and the Reformation* (4 volumes); *Calvin and the Reformation*, 1936
M. W. Patterson, *A History of the Church of England*, 1912
Rufus M. Jones, *The Later Period of Quakerism*, MacMillan (2 volumes), 1921
Workman and Eays, *A New History of Methodism*, (2 volumes), 1909
J. W. C. Wand, *A History of the Modern Church*, 1929
S. Bulgakov, *The Orthodox Church*, 1935
A. Neander, *General History of the Christian Religion and Church*, Edinburgh, 1851-1855. New Edition (6 volumes), Boston, 1859

Miscellaneous

T. M. Lindsay, *The Church and the Ministry in the Early Centuries*, 1924
C. G. Coulton, *Five Centuries of Religion* (3 volumes), 1923
B. H. Streeter, *The Primitive Church*, London, 1929
W. P. Paterson, *The Rule of Faith*, Hodder & Stoughton, 1912

William Adams Brown, *The Essence of Christianity*, New York, 1902; *The Church Catholic and Protestant*, Scribners, 1935; *Church and State in America*, 1936

H. Cotterill, *The Genesis of the Church*, Edinburgh, 1872

J. J. McElhinney, *The Doctrine of the Church*, Philadelphia, 1871

C. C. Richardson, *The Church Through the Centuries*, Scribners, 1938

N. Ehrenstrom, *Christian Faith and the Modern State*, 1937

H. R. Mackintosh, *The Originality of the Christian Message*, New York, 1920

Ernest F. Scott, *The Nature of the Early Church*, Scribners, 1941

C. A. Scott, *The Church, Its Worship and Sacraments*, London, 1927

W. S. Sperry, *Reality in Worship*, New York, 1925

T. R. Glover, *The Nature and Purpose of a Christian Society*, New York, 1922

A. B. Macdonald, *Christian Worship in the Primitive Church*

Philip Carrington, *A Primitive Christian Catechism*

C. E. Raven, *The Gospel and the Church*

ESCHATOLOGY

S. D. F. Salmond, *The Christian Doctrine of Immortality*, Edinburgh, 1901

J. H. Snowden, *The Christian Belief in Immortality*, 1925

E. Abbott, *The Literature of the Doctrine of a Future Life*, New York, 1874

S. Lee, *Eschatology*, Boston, 1858

N. West, *Studies in Eschatology*, New York, 1889

L. A. Muirhead, *The Eschatology of Jesus*, London, 1906

William Newton Clarke, *Immortality*, Yale, 1920

Charles E. Jefferson, *Why We May Believe in Life After Death*

A. S. Pringle-Pattison, *The Idea of Immortality*, Oxford, 1922

J. A. Spencer, *Five Last Things*, New York, 1887

G. T. Cooperrider, *The Last Things, Death and the Future Life*, Columbus, Ohio, 1911

James H. Hyslop, *Science and the Future Life*, Boston, 1905

R. E. Hutton, *The Soul in the Unseen World*, London, 1902; *The Life Beyond*, Milwaukee, 1916

E. E. Holmes, *Immortality*, 1908

Joseph Agar Beet, *The Last Things*, London, 1905

Ernest von Dobschutz, *The Eschatology of the Gospels*, London, 1910

William Adams Brown, *The Christian Hope*, New York, 1912; *The Creative Experience*, 1923

B. H. Streeter (and others), *Immortality*, MacMillan, 1917

J. Y. Simpson, *Man and the Attainment of Immortality*

F. W. H. Myers, *Human Personality and Its Survival of Bodily Death*, London, 1913

J. Strong, *The Doctrine of a Future Life*, New York, 1891

W. Smyth, *Dorner on the Future State*, New York, 1883

R. H. Charles, *A Critical History of the Doctrine of a Future Life in Israel, in Judaism and in Christianity*, London, 1899

S. Davidson, *Doctrine of Last Things*, London, 1882

Alger, *Critical History of the Future Life*, Boston, 1880

J. Marchant, *Immortality* (A symposium), New York, 1924

H. R. Mackintosh, *Immortality and the Future*, 1917

M. C. Peters, *After Death What?* 1908

D. P. Halsey, *The Evidence for Immortality*, 1931
P. Cabot, *The Sense of Immortality*, 1924

Ingersoll Lectures

The following titles are selected from the Ingersoll Lectures on Immortality, published by the Cambridge University Press:
George A. Gordon, *Immortality and the New Theology*, 1896
Benjamin Ide Wheeler, *Dionysius and Immortality*, 1898
Josiah Royce, *The Conception of Immortality*, 1899
John Fiske, *Life Everlasting*, 1900
Samuel M. Crowthers, *The Endless Life*, 1905
Charles F. Dole, *The Hope of Immortality*, 1907
George A. Reisner, *Egyptian Conception of Immortality*, 1911
Clifford Herschel Moore, *Pagan Idea of Immortality*, 1918
William Wallace Ferm, *Immortality and Theism*, 1921
Kirsopp Lake, *Immortality and the Modern Mind*, 1922
Philip S. Cabot, *The Sense of Immortality*, 1924
Edgar S. Brightman, *Immortality in Post-Kantian Idealism*, 1925

Older Works

Howe, *The Redeemer's Dominion Over the Invisible World*
N. L. Rice, *On Immortality*, Philadelphia, 1871
Isaac Taylor, *Physical Theory of Another Life*, 1858
Cremer, *Beyond the Grave*
Whately, *A View of Scripture Revelation Concerning a Future State*, 1873
Perowne, *On Immortality*
Bishop D. W. Clark, *Man All Immortal*, Methodist Book Concern, 1864
H. Mattison, *The Immortality of the Soul*, 1864
Thomas A. Goodwin, *The Mode of Man's Immortality*, New York, 1874
John Fiske, *The Destiny of Man*, Boston, 1884
Luther A. Fox, *Evidence of a Future Life*, Philadelphia, 1874

The Intermediate State

T. Huidekoper, *The Belief of the First Three Centuries Concerning Christ's Mission to the Underworld*, New York, 1876
George Bartle, *Scriptural Doctrine of Hades*, Philadelphia, 1870
J. Fyfe, *The Hereafter: Sheol, Hades, and Hell*, Edinburgh, 1889
S. H. Kellogg, *From Death to Resurrection*, New York, 1885
H. M. Lucock, *The Intermediate State Between Death and Judgment*, London, 1879
G. S. Barrett, *The Intermediate State and the Last Things*, London, 1896
A. Williamson, *The Intermediate State*, London, 1891
Watts, *Souls Between Death and the Resurrection*
Charles H. Strong, *In Paradise: or the State of the Faithful Dead*, New York, 1893
E. H. Plumptre, *The Spirits in Prison*, London, 1884
Alford, *State of the Blessed Dead*
Bush, *The Intermediate State*
Townsend, *The Intermediate World*
C. T. Wood, *Death and Beyond*
Wightman, *The Undying Soul and the Intermediate State*
V. U. Maywahlen, *The Intermediate State*, London, 1856

THE SECOND ADVENT

The following bibliography includes the older sources from which most of the recent writers have drawn their material. The various positions are represented: *pre*-millennialism, *post-millennialism*, and *nil* or *a*-millennialism.

Edward Bickersteth, *The Divine Warning to the Church at This Time*, 1849; *The Glory of the Church; The Guide to the Prophecies; The Restoration of the Jews*, (See Works, London, 1853)

Joseph Mẹde, *Clavis Apocalyptica*, Cambrige, 1627 (English translation by R. More, *The Key of the Revelation*, London, 1643)

Thomas Burnett, *Sacred Theory of the Earth*, London, 1681

Joseph Perry, *The Glory of Christ's Visible Kingdom in this World*, Northampton, 1721

Nathaniel Homes, *The Resurrection Revealed, or The Dawning of the Day Star*, London, 1835, 1866

Henry Alford, *Advent Sermons* (Four on the State of the Blessed Dead, and four on the Coming of the Bridegroom), London, 1863

Increase Mather, *Glorious Kingdom of Jesus Christ on Earth now Approaching*, Boston, 1770

Carson, *The Personal Reign of Christ During the Millennium Proved to Be Impossible*, London, 1873

Richard Baxter, *The Glorious Kingdom of God*, London, 1691

Cummings, *Apocalyptic Sketches*, London, 1849; *Great Tribulation*, 1859; *Great Preparation*, 1861

Frere, *Lectures on the Prophecies Relative to the Last Times*, London, 1849

Joseph A. Seiss, *The Last Times and the Great Consummation*, Philadelphia, 1878; *Lectures on the Apocalypse*, New York, 1865, 1901

George Duffield, *Dissertations on the Prophecies Relative to the Second Coming of Christ*, New York, 1842; *Millenarianism Defended*, New York, 1843

J. S. Russell, *The Parousia*, London, 1887

William Burgh, *Lectures on the Second Advent*, London, 1845

Joseph Berg, *The Second Advent of Christ, Not Premillennial*, Philadelphia, 1859

Samuel Lee, *Eschatology, or the Scripture Doctrine of the Coming of Our Lord*, Boston, 1858

John Durant, *Christ's Appearance the Second Time for the Salvation of Believers*, 1653, Reprint, London, 1829

E. B. Elliott, *Horae Apocalyptica* (4 volumes), 1862

Brooks, *Elements of Prophetical Interpretation*

A. A. Bonar, *Redemption Drawing Nigh, Edinburgh*, 1874

H. Bonar, *Coming and Kingdom*, London, 1849

T. R. Birks, *The Four Prophetic Empires and the Kingdom of the Messiah*, 1845; *Outlines of Unfulfilled Prophecy*, 1854; *Plain Papers on Prophetic and Other Subjects*

Fraser, *Key to the Prophecies*, 1795

Capel Molyneux, *The World to Come*, 1853

McNeille, *Lectures on the Jews*
Samuel Hopkins, *A Treatise on the Millennium*, Edinburgh, 1806
Waldegrave, *New Testament Millenarianism*, (Bampton Lecture), London, 1855
Urwick, *Second Advent of Christ*, Dublin, 1839
J. H. Alstead, *The Beloved City, or The Saints on Earth a Thousand Years*, (By William Burton, London, 1643)
G. Bush, *Treatise on the Millennium*
W. Kelly, *Lectures on the Second Coming*, London, 1866
J. C. Rankin, *The Coming of the Lord*, New York, 1885
Israel P. Warren, *The Parousia*, London, 1887
David Brown, *Christ's Second Coming*, Edinburgh, 1849
Bishop S. M. Merrill, *The Second Coming of Christ*, New York, 1879
Joseph Burchell, *The Midnight Cry*, 1849
James H. Brookes, *"Maranatha" or, The Lord Cometh*, St. Louis, 1878
Nathaniel West, *John Wesley and Premillennialism*, Cincinnati, 1894
Daniel T. Taylor, *The Reign of Christ on Earth*, Boston, 1882
Henry Varley, *Christ's Coming Kingdom*, 1893
T. H. Salmon, *Waiting the Coming One*, London
A. B. Simpson, *The Coming One*, New York, 1912
A. Sims, *Behold He Cometh*, 1900; *Deepening Shadows and Coming Glories*, Toronto, 1905
W. C. Stevens, *Mysteries of the Kingdom*, Nyack, 1904
I. M. Haldemann, *Why I Preach the Second Coming*, Revell, 1919
James Edson White, *The Coming King*, Pacific Press, 1898
Jesse Forrest Silver, *The Lord's Return*, Revell, 1914
L. L. Pickett, *The Blessed Hope of His Glorious Appearing*, Louisville, 1901; *The Renewed Earth*, Louisville, 1903
W. E. Blackstone, *Jesus Is Coming*, Revell, 1908
Charles Feinberg, *Premillennialism or Amillennialism*, Zondervan, 1936
The Duke of Manchester, *The Finished Mystery*
Woods, *The Last Things*
J. A. Bengel, *Exposition of the Apocalypse*, 1740 (Translated by John Robertson, London, 1751); *Ordo Temporum*, 1741
Symon Patrick, *The Appearing of Jesus Christ*, London, 1863
David N. Lord, *The Coming and Reign of Christ*, New York, 1858

THE RESURRECTION

C. K. Staudt, *The Idea of the Resurrection in the Ante-Nicene Period*, Chicago, 1910
W. F. Whitehouse, *The Redemption of the Body*, London, 1895
George Bush, *Anastasis, or the Doctrine of the Resurrection of the Body*, New York, 1845
B. F. Westcott, *The Gospel of the Resurrection*, London, 1869
J. Maynard, *The Resurrection of the Dead*, London, 1897
C. S. Gerhard, *Death and the Resurrection*, Philadelphia, 1895
William Hanna, *The Resurrection of the Dead*, Edinburgh, 1872
J. Hall, *How Are the Dead Raised Up and with What Body Do They Come?* Hartford, 1875
J. Hughes-Games, *On the Nature of the Resurrection Body*, London, 1898
W. Milligan, *The Resurrection of the Dead*, Edinburgh, 1894
E. Huntingford, *The Resurrection of the Body*, London, 1897

J. G. Bjorklund, *Death and the Resurrection from the Point of View of the Cell Theory*, Chicago, 1910
William Hanna, *The Resurrection of the Dead*, Edinburgh, 1872
Kingsley, *The Resurrection of the Dead*
Mattison, *The Resurrection of the Dead*
Balfour, *Central Truths and Side Issues*, Edinburgh, 1895
Drew, *Identity and General Resurrection of the Human Body*, London, 1822
Goulburn, *The Doctrine of the Resurrection of the Same Body as Taught in the Holy Scripture*, London, 1850
Landis, *On the Resurrection*
Brown, *The Resurrection of Life*
Cochran, *The Resurrection of the Dead*
Cook, *The Doctrine of the Resurrection*
D. A. Dryden, *The Resurrection of the Dead*, Cincinnati, 1872

THE FINAL CONSUMMATION

Reference must again be made to the standard works on Systematic Theology for the best treatment of this subject. Special treatises on Future Rewards and Punishments are given below.

Future Punishment

J. B. Reimensnyder, *Doom Eternal. The Bible and the Church Doctrine of Eternal Punishment*, Philadelphia, 1880
Alvah Hovey, *The State of the Impenitent Dead*, 1859
Jackson, *The Doctrine of Retribution*, 1875
F. W. Farrar, *Eternal Hope*, 1878; *Mercy and Judgment: Last Words on Eschatology*, 1881
Cochrane, *Future Punishment*
G. P. Fisher, *Discussions in History and Theology*, Scribners, 1880. Chapter on The History of the Doctrine of Future Punishment
Row, *Future Retribution in the Light of Reason and Revelation*, London
McDonald, *The Annihilation of the Wicked Scripturally Considered*
Pusey, *Everlasting Punishment* (Historical)
Mead, *The Soul and Hereafter*
W. G. T. Shedd, *The Doctrine of Endless Punishment*, 1886
Anderson, *Future Destiny*
Vernon, *Probation and Punishment*
Goulborn, *Everlasting Punishment*
Lewis, *Ground and Nature of Punishment*
Bartlett, *Life and Death Eternal*
Hopkins, *Future State*
Newton, *The Final State*
Stuart, *Exegetical Essays* (Cf. Sheol and Aion)
Bishop S. M. Merrill, *The New Testament Idea of Hell*, Cincinnati, 1878
L. T. Townsend, *Lost Forever*, Boston, 1874

Heaven

H. Harbaugh, *Heaven*, Philadelphia, 1861; *The Heavenly Home*, 1853; *The*
S. Fallows, *The Home Beyond*, Chicago, 1884
Thomas Hamilton, *Beyond the Stars, or Heaven, Its Inhabitants, Occupations and Life*, Scribners, 1889

H. Harbaugh, *Heaven*, Philadelphia, 1861; *The Heavenly Home*, 1853; *The Heavenly Recognition*, 1865

Archibald McCullagh, *Beyond the Stars, or Human Life in Heaven*, New York, 1887

R. W. Clark, *Heaven and Its Scriptural Emblems*, Philadelphia, 1856

G. Z. Gray, *The Scriptural Doctrine of Recognition in the World to Come*, New York, 1886

J. M. Killen, *Our Companions in Glory*, New York, 1862

J. A. Hodge, *Recognition After Death*, New York, 1889

R. Winterbotham, *The Kingdom of Heaven and Hereafter*, New York, 1898

I. C. Craddock, *The Heaven of the Bible*, Philadelphia, 1897

GENERAL INDEX

A Posteriori arguments for the existence of God, I, 238

A Priori arguments for the existence of God, I, 235

Abelard, I, 418; Theory of Atonement, II, 237, 241

Absolute, God as Absolute Reality, I, 255; Origin of the Absolute, I, 257; Modern Concepts of the Absolute, I, 261; Absolute and the Idea of God, I, 273; Absolute Attributes, I, 329

Acceptilatio, II, 252, 294

Acquittal (See Justification)

Adam, II, 12, 13, 20, 58, 104, 132

Adiaphoristic Controversy, II, 77

Adikia, II, 82, 84, 85

Administrative Functions of the Ministry, III, 134

Adonai, I, 247, 248, 249

Adoptianism, II, 164, 168

Adoption, II, 428-431; Definition, 428; Relation to Justification and Regeneration, 428; Benefits of Adoption, 429; Evidences of Adoption, 431

Adoration, III, 151; of the Host, III, 197

Adventist Theory of the Millennium, III, 281

Adversary, II, 77

Aeon, Creation, I, 468; Ethical and Spiritual realms, I, 469; Shedd's Statement, III, 371

Aerius, III, 234

Aesthetics, III, 51

Agassiz, II, 8, 23; III, 326

Agnosticism, I, 261, 262

Aix-la-Chapelle, Synod of, I, 418; Adoptianism condemned, II, 165

Albertus Magnus, II, 201

Albigenses, III, 271

Alcuin, I, 72

Akers, III, 145

Alexander, I, 412; III, 24

Alexander of Hales, Theory of Justification, II, 239; Sacrament in one kind, III, 197

Alexandrians, II, 159

Alexandrian School, II, 161

Alford, Dean, Kenosis, II, 200; Continuous Theory of Revelation, III, 273

Allen, A. V. G. Continuity of Christian Thought, I, 57

Allegorical Method, I, 58

Alleine, Joseph, III, 273

Alogi, I, 411

Alstead, John, III, 273

Ambrose, Canonical Books, I, 199; Realistic Mode of Sin, II, 109; Descensus, II, 201; De Officiis Ministrorum, III, 15; Eucharist, III, 196; Hades, III, 227; Purgatory, III, 241

Amphilochius, Canon, I, 186, 195

Amyraldus, School of Saumur, I, 86

American Theologians, I, 86

Anabaptist, Controversy, I, 77; Chiliasm, III, 272

Analysis of Apostles' Creed, I, 41; Nicene Creed, I, 44

Analytical Method, I, 56

Anaximander, I, 257

Anaximenes, I, 257

Andover School of Theology, II, 264, 265; Principles, II, 266

Andrae, I, 89

Angel, of the Covenant, I, 403; of Jehovah, I, 401, 402; of the Lord, I, 401

Angels, Scriptural Teaching, I, 473; Angels and Spirits, I, 473; Nature and Attributes of Angels, I, 473; Martensen's position, I, 474; Ministry of Angels, I, 476; Good and Evil Angels, I, 476; Doctrine of Satan, I, 477

Anger, unholy, III, 70, 72

Annihilationism, III, 359, 360; Wakefield's Refutation, III, 362

Annunciation, II, 308

Anointing with the Spirit, II, 324

Anomia, II, 82, 85

Anselm, Atonement, I, 237; Traducianism, II, 104; Descensus, II, 201; Theory of Atonement, II, 201, 235, 236, 237, 238, 241, 242

Anthropological method, I, 56

Anthropology, Division of Theology, I, 24; II, 7-50; Origin of Man, II, 9; Constituent Elements of Human Nature, II, 15; Unity of the Race, II, 20; Antiquity of the Race, II, 22; Image of God in

437

Important Distinction between Purity and Maturity, II, 506
Imputation, Theory of Immediate Imputation, II, 114; Mediate Imputation, II, 117; Controversy, II, 390; Obedience of Christ, II, 396–400; Imputation of Faith, II, 400
Inability of Man, II, 353
Inaugural Signs at Pentecost, II, 312–314
Incarnation, II, 178ff; Incarnation and the Trinity, II, 181; A Permanent Condescension, II, 182; Redemptive Work, II, 185; Incarnation and the Holy Spirit, II, 307
Individual Ethics, III, 47–67; Sanctity of the Body, III, 47; Intellectual, Emotional, Moral and Aesthetic Powers, III, 51; Intellectual Vices, III, 55; Springs of Power, III, 56; Vices connected with the Will, III, 59; Development of the Spiritual Life, III, 61
Indulgences, II, 240
Infallibility, papal, I, 82
Infant Baptism, III, 184–189; History, III, 186; Objections, III, 187; Connected with the Abrahamic Covenant, III, 187
Infinite, Definition of God, I, 218, 333; God as Infinite Efficiency, I, 279; Idea of God as Finite, I, 281; God of infinite power, wisdom and goodness, I, 333
Infinity, Attribute of God, I, 333
Infirmity, II, 140; Distinguished from Sin, II, 507
Innate, term applied to the primary knowledge of God, I, 214
Inge, W. R., I, 111, 282
Ingram, I, 210
Inherited Depravity, II, 98
Inspiration of the Scriptures, I, 166–184; Definitions, I, 166; Inspiration and Revelation, I, 167; Possibility of Inspiration, I, 170; Necessity of Inspiration, I, 171; Theories of Inspiration, I, 172–175; Proofs of Inspiration, I, 176–180; Value of Inspiration, I, 181; Sources of Inspiration, I, 181; Organs of Inspiration, I, 182; Scriptures Divinely Inspired, I, 183
Institutions of Christianity, III, 79–96; Marriage and the Family, III, 79; Divorce, III, 84, 85; Duties of Husbands and Wives, III, 87; Parents and Children, III, 92; Masters and Servants, III, 95; The

State, III, 96; Obedience Due Civil Magistrates, III, 98; Political Ethics, III, 99
Institution of Sacrifice, II, 220; Baptism, III, 161; Lord's Supper, III, 190
Intellectual Vices, III, 55
Interactio, I, 424
Intercession of Christ, II, 214, 299
Intercommunio, I, 424
Interexistentia, I, 424
Intermediate Community, III, 105
Intermediate Place, III, 234
Intermediate State, III, 224–242; Terms used, III, 225; Development of the Doctrine, III, 226; Patristic Doctrine, III, 226; Soul Sleeping, III, 228; Roman Catholic Doctrine, III, 229; Protestant Doctrine, III, 232
Introduction, Biblical, I, 23, 24
Intuition, Origin of Idea of God, I, 224
Intuition Theory of Inspiration, I, 174
Invisibility, a Note of the Church, III, 114
Ionians, I, 257,
Irenaeus, I, 65, 168, 197, 332, 408, 409, 414, 443, 457; II, 201, 232, 233, 349, 449; III, 148, 194, 266, 337
Isagogics, I, 23, 24
Isidore, II, 348
Irving, Edwards, II, 261, 262, 263

Jacobi, I, 90
Jahweh, I, 244
James, William, I, 111, 277, 283
Jamnia, Council of, I, 192
Jastrow, Morris, I, 101
Jehovah, I, 244
Jerome, I, 186; II, 348; III, 269, 337
Jesus (See Christ; Christology)
Jewish Sabbath, III, 146, 148
John of Antioch, II, 160, 162
John the Baptist, I, 160; II, 145
Judge, Person of the Judge, III, 342
Judicial Theory of the Atonement, II, 242, 244
Judgment, Final, III, 338–354; Particular and General, III, 340; Person of the Judge, III, 342; Development of the Doctrine, III, 344; Principles of Judgment, III, 345; Purpose of the General Judgment, III, 348; Wakefield on the General Judgment, III, 350; Circumstances attending the General Judgment, III, 351

Monologium, I, 73
Monophysitism, II, 163
Monothelitism, II, 163
Montanism, III, 268
Montanists, III, 15, 267
Montanus, III, 270
Moral Argument, I, 239
Moral Attributes of God, I, 365-393
Moral Influence Theories of the
 Atonement, II, 259-266; Socinian
 Theories, II, 259; Mystical The-
 ories, II, 261; Bushnell's Theory,
 II, 263; New Theology, II, 264
Moral Image of God in Man, II, 37
Moravians, I, 111; II, 458
More, Henry, I, 238, 457
Morgan, G. Campbell, I, 468
Morris, III, 124
Mortimer, I, 98
Mosaic Cosmogony, I, 455
Mosheim, II, 450; III, 22, 123, 267
Mozley, I, 61
Muller (or Mueller) Julius, I, 95,
 379, 484; II, 18, 27, 72, 195, 198
Muller (or Mueller) Max, I, 102,
 228
Mulleron, Julius, III, 326
Mullins, E. Y., I, 211; II, 380; III, 218
Muratorian Canon, I, 194
Murray, I, 277
Musaeus, I, 84
Mutability, note of the Church, III,
 112
Mysteries, III, 155, 194
Mystery, used in connection with
 the sacrament, III, 155
Mystical Theory of the Atonement,
 II, 262
Mysticism, I, 111; II, 451

Names and Titles of Our Lord, II,
 215, 216
Naturalistic Evolution, I, 262
Nature, as a source of Theology,
 I, 51, 52; Revelation, I, 126; Na-
 ture and the Personal Spirit, I,
 300; Nature of Primitive Holi-
 ness, II, 39; Nature of Holiness
 in Adam, II, 44; Essential Ele-
 ments, II, 47
National Association for the Pro-
 motion of Holiness, II, 455
Naville, Ernest, I, 208
Nazarene, Church of, (See Manual,
 Church of the Nazarene)
Neander, I, 197
Nease, Dr. Floyd W., II, 504
Nease, Dr. Orval J., III, 8
Nebiim, I, 188

Necessitarian Theories of Sin, II,
 67
Nelson, I, 257
Neo-Hegelians, I, 111, 114, 295
Neo-Platonism, I, 256, 260, 279,
 283, 286, 385
Nepos, III, 269
Nescience, I, 355
Nestorianism, I, 68; II, 159, 162, 163,
 184
Nestorians, II, 161
Nestorius, II, 159, 162
Nevin, II, 359
Newman, Bishop, II, 492
New School, II, 114, 123, 129
New England Theology, II, 252,
 264
New Theology, II, 264, 265
Newton, Sir Isaac, III, 273
Niceae, First Ecumenical Council,
 I, 42, 68; Second Council, I, 69
Nicholson, III, 229
Nicene Creed, Text, I, 42, 43; An-
 alysis, I, 44; Nicene Christology,
 II, 156
Niebuhr, III, 24
Nihilian Heresy, II, 166
Nilus, III, 196
Nitzsch, Carl, I, 93, 97, 322, 328, 429,
 477, 484; III, 265
Noesgen, I, 211
Noetus, I, 410, 411, 412
Nominal Trinitarianism, I, 410, 411
Nominalist, Roscelinus, I, 418; Abel-
 ard, I, 418
Notes of the Church, III, 111ff;
 Unity and Diversity, III, 112;
 Holiness and Imperfection, III,
 112; Catholic and Local, III, 113;
 Apostolic and Confessional, III,
 116
Novatian, I, 412; III, 125

Obduracy, III, 56
Obedience of Christ, II, 147, 154
Oberlin School of Theology, II, 456
Oedipus, I, 109
Oehler, II, 365
Oetinger, I, 91; II, 197
Offices, Church, III, 129
Offices of Christ, II, 210
Offices of the Holy Spirit, II, 315-
 322
Old School of Theology, I, 98
Olevianus, I, 76
Olshausen, Herman, II, 445
Omnipotence, 349
Omnipresence, I, 345
Ontological Argument, I, 236

SCRIPTURE INDEX

Compiled by David L. Mesarosh

OLD TESTAMENT

NEW TESTAMENT